The Future of

THE AMERICAN JEW

BY

MORDECAI M. KAPLAN

1967

RECONSTRUCTIONIST PRESS

NEW YORK

TO MY CHILDREN

Judith
Hadassah
Naomi
Selma

"I shall not die, but live, and declare the works of the Lord."   Psalms 118, 17

———

"The dogmas of the quiet past are inadequate to the stormy present. The occasion is piled high with difficulty, and we must rise to the occasion. As our case is new, so we must think anew and act anew. We must disenthrall ourselves, and then we shall save our country."

Abraham Lincoln

———

"Once we know the thing that we desire to be, the things that we must do will follow of themselves."   Archibald MacLeish

CONTENTS

PAGE

PREFACE — xv

PART I

THE RESURRECTION OF A PEOPLE

CHAPTER ONE

"CAN THESE BONES LIVE?" — 3

1. The inner crisis (p. 3)—2. The courage to face facts (p. 8)—3. The modern challenge to Jewish life (p. 16)—4. The first attempts at meeting the challenge (p. 22)—5. Faith in latent potentialities (p. 26)—6. The wisdom to build for the future (p. 30).

CHAPTER TWO

RECONSTRUCTION—A PROGRAM — 34

1. The need of reconstruction (p. 34)—2. Eretz Yisrael (p. 37)—3. Jewish community organization in the Diaspora (p. 38)—4. Jewish education (p. 40)—5. Jewish religion (p. 44)—6. Cultural creativity (p. 50)—7. Ethics (p. 53).

CHAPTER THREE

THE STATUS OF THE JEWS — 58

1. The status of Jewry an enigma (p. 58)—2. The meaning of Jewish peoplehood (p. 63)—3. The three levels of Jewish peoplehood (p. 66)—4. The struggle for the freedom to be Jews (p. 72)—5. The case against anti-Semitism (p. 76)—6. Freedom that is genuine (p. 79).

CHAPTER FOUR

THE SIGNIFICANCE OF BEING A PEOPLE — 82

1. The sense of peoplehood (p. 82)—2. Peoplehood as a living process (p. 87)—3. A people viewed ethically (p. 89).

CHAPTER FIVE

LIVING IN TWO CIVILIZATIONS — 94

1. Why the Jew cannot do without Judaism (p. 94)—2. The Jew's task to live in two civilizations (p. 96)—3. Living in two civilizations calls for a redefinition of religion (p. 99).

CHAPTER SIX

COMMUNITY—THE SOCIAL STRUCTURE OF AMERICAN-JEWISH LIFE   106

1. *Why Jews need community (p. 106)*—2. *What should be the social structure of American Jewry? (p. 114)*—3. *The principles and aims of Jewish community in America (p. 118).*

CHAPTER SEVEN

THE ROLE OF ERETZ YISRAEL IN THE LIFE OF DIASPORA JEWRY   123

1. *The new role of Eretz Yisrael (p. 123)*—2. *No Jewish homeland without Judaism in the Diaspora (p. 128)*—3. *Eretz Yisrael: its achievements (p. 130)*—4. *Eretz Yisrael: its shortcomings (p. 136).*

CHAPTER EIGHT

THE KEY TO INTERGROUP GOOD-WILL   143

1. *The needed reconstruction in group ethics (p. 143)*—2. *Group equality to be basis of all religious ethical systems (p. 147)*—3. *The ethical relation of religions to one another (p. 149)*—4. *The equality of religions (p. 150)*—5. *Religio-ethical reeducation to begin with our own group (p. 154).*

PART II

THE NEXT STAGE IN JEWISH RELIGION

CHAPTER NINE

NEEDED: A NEW UNDERSTANDING OF JEWISH RELIGION   161

1. *The relation of Jewish religion to Judaism (p. 162)*—2. *The problem of religion ignored in contemporary Jewish life (p. 164)*—3. *The study of religion in need of cultivation (p. 166)*—4. *Reason not to be flouted (p. 168).*

Contents

CHAPTER TEN

THE BELIEF IN GOD 171

1. *Meaning of the belief in God (p. 171)*—2. *The idea of God as index of the idea of salvation (p. 174)*—3. *The modern conception of salvation or human destiny (p. 178)*—4. *The relation of the soterical God-idea to worship (p. 180)*—5. *The soterical God-idea in education p. (185).*

CHAPTER ELEVEN

THE NEXT STAGE IN RELIGION 188

1. *Why a new stage? (p. 188)*—2. *Faith in human nature as the basis of spiritual life (p. 190)*—3. *Spiritual religion vs. humanism (p. 193)*—4. *What changes in attitude will spiritual religion effect? (p. 195).*

CHAPTER TWELVE

THE JEWISH RELIGION OF TOMORROW 199

1. *The changing conception of God in Jewish religion (p. 199)*—2. *The changing conception of salvation in Jewish religion (p. 203)* —3. *What makes Jewish religion Jewish? (p. 207).*

CHAPTER THIRTEEN

THE CHOSEN PEOPLE IDEA AN ANACHRONISM 211

1. *What the choice of Israel meant in the past (p. 212)*—2. *The effort to reinterpret the election of Israel (p. 214)*—3. *What is wrong with the reinterpretations (p. 215)*—4. *Divine election inconsistent with evolutionary conception of religion (p. 219)*—5. *The mission idea and religious imperialism (p. 221)*—6. *The doctrine of election not necessary for Jewish survival (p. 223)*—7. *Belief in election of Israel a source of maladjustment (p. 225)*—8. *Vocation a valid substitute for the doctrine of election (p. 228).*

CHAPTER FOURTEEN

RELIGIOUS DOUBTS AND THE PROBLEM OF EVIL 231

1. *Defeatist vs. creative doubts (p. 231)*—2. *The problem of evil in the world and how to meet it (p. 234)*—3. *The problem of moral evil and how to meet it (p. 238).*

PAGE

CHAPTER FIFTEEN

BASIC VALUES IN JEWISH RELIGION   244

1. SPIRITUAL SELECTION   246

1. *The call of God vs. the call of the wild (p. 246)—2. The modern resurgence of the law of natural selection (p. 250)—3. The real issue before mankind: shall it be natural or spiritual selection? (p. 254).*

2. FAITH   256

1. *The urgent need for religious faith (p. 256)—2. Religious faith a function of the will to live (p. 259).*

3. HOPE   266

1. *The kind of future pre-modern man hoped for (p. 266)—2. The kind of future modern man hopes for (p. 270).*

4. HUMILITY   274

1. *Being Godlike vs. playing the god (p. 274)—2. Why man thinks himself a god (p. 277)—3. How men play the god nowadays (p. 279)—4. Imitatio Dei (p. 281).*

5. INNER FREEDOM   283

1. *"The unreconciled heart" (p. 285)—2. The challenging mind (p. 289)—3. The fearless and cooperative will (p. 291).*

6. PATIENCE   295

1. *Utopianism and disillusionment (p. 295)—2. Meliorism a way out (p. 298)—3. Resolutely and unhurriedly (p. 301).*

7. THANKFULNESS   303

1. *Thankfulness essential to morale (p. 303)—2. Being sensitive to the good in our daily circumstances (p. 306)—3. Being appreciative of life-enhancing opportunities (p. 308)—4. Gratitude for personal and social achievement (p. 309)—5. When thankfulness is religious (p. 311).*

8. JUSTICE   313

1. *Faith in human equality as part of faith in God (p. 315)*—2.
Principle of equality encounters social inertia (p. 319)—3. *Equality as a religious ideal (p. 324)*.

9. LOVE   328

1. *The main function of religion (p. 328)*—2. *The meaning of redemptive love (p. 330)*—3. *Why redemptive love is divine (p. 334)*
—4. *Compassion and loving-kindness as prerequisites to redemptive love (p. 336)*.

PART III

TOWARD A NEW PATTERN FOR JEWISH LIFE

CHAPTER SIXTEEN

THE GOOD AND THE BEAUTIFUL IN
JEWISH LIFE   343

Ethics—1. *The Torah tradition a perennial stimulation to the
good life (p. 343)*—2. *The tradition indispensable to the quest for
the good life (p. 345)*—3. *What is a "good Jew"? (p. 347)*.
Art—1. *Jewish life in need of aesthetic self-expression (p. 350)*
—2. *What is needed to evoke Jewish art? (p. 354)*.

CHAPTER SEVENTEEN

ZIONISM—A RECONSTRUCTION OF THE
JEWISH WAY OF LIFE   359

1. *Democracy as expressed in the evolution of the Zionist aims
(p. 360)*—2. *Democracy as evidenced in Zionist measures (p. 361)*
—3. *Democracy as practiced in Zionist undertakings (p. 367)*.

CHAPTER EIGHTEEN

CONTINUITY AND CHANGE IN THE JEWISH
TRADITION   372

1. *Change in attitude toward the past (p. 372)*—2. *The historical
approach to Jewish tradition (p. 375)*—3. *How to bridge the gap
between past and present (p. 377)*—4. *What is to be gained by reinterpreting the past? (p. 379)*—5. *Torah to include amendment
as well as reinterpretation (p. 381)*.

PAGE

CHAPTER NINETEEN

THE PROBLEM OF JEWISH LAW   387

1. *The place of law in pre-modern Jewish life (p. 388)—2. Jewish life meaningless without Jewish law (p. 389)—3. Jewish law for Diaspora Jewry (p. 393)—4. Is democracy feasible in the area of ritual observance? (p. 398).*

CHAPTER TWENTY

THE STATUS OF THE WOMAN IN JEWISH
LAW   402

1. *The status of the woman in ancient times (p. 402)—2. The status of the woman in traditional Jewish law (p. 405)—3. The struggle in Eretz Yisrael over the status of woman (p. 409)—4. The need to amend the Jewish law (p. 410).*

CHAPTER TWENTY-ONE

TOWARD A GUIDE FOR JEWISH RITUAL
USAGE   413

1. *The need for a point of view on Jewish usage (p. 413)—2. Toward a reconstruction of Jewish ritual usage (p. 416)—3. Principles of evaluation (p. 420).*

CHAPTER TWENTY-TWO

THE AIM OF AMERICAN-JEWISH
EDUCATION   429

1. *The pre-modern aim of Jewish education (p. 430)—2. Why the pre-modern aim is irrelevant (p. 432)—3. The negation of Jewish life in the Diaspora (p. 433)—4. The need of a two-fold norm for Jewish life (p. 435)—5. Educational aim in terms of tradition and social structure (p. 438)—6. The failure to adjust aim to new needs (p. 440)—7. The requisite adjustments in aim (p. 442).*

CHAPTER TWENTY-THREE

A NEW EDUCATIONAL APPROACH TO THE
BIBLE   447

1. *Changes in the purpose of teaching the Bible (p. 447)—2. The different versions of the Bible (p. 452)—3. The aims of Bible teaching in our day (p. 456).*

CHAPTER TWENTY-FOUR

HOW TO VITALIZE ADULT JEWISH STUDY   469

1. *Study to be motivated by need of Jewish orientation (p. 469)*
—2. *How to do our own thinking (p. 471)*—3. *To see relation
of past to present (p. 473)*—4. *To participate in Jewish life (p.
474)*—5. *The application of Jewish values (p. 476).*

CHAPTER TWENTY-FIVE

JUDAISM'S CONTRIBUTION TO EDUCATION
FOR DEMOCRACY   480

1. WORLD BETTERMENT THE AIM   481

1. *What's wrong with education in the democracies? (p. 481)*—
2. *Education in the art of living, the theme of Abot (p. 485)*—3.
Education for world citizenship and betterment (p. 488)—4. *The
education that democracy needs (p. 491).*

2. THE EDUCATIONAL PROCESS   493

1. *Education as religious experience (p. 494)*—2. *Education a
parental responsibility (p. 496)*—3. *Education for freedom (p. 498).*

3. EDUCATION FOR GENUINE DEMOCRACY   501

1. *Democracy vs. mass tyranny the main issue in education (p. 501)*
—2. *Jewish education against mass tyranny (p. 504).*

4. THE PROBLEM OF CHURCH AND STATE IN DEMO-
CRATIC EDUCATION   509

1. *The problem stated (p. 509)*—2. *Religions as programs for living and as organizations of power (p. 512)*—3. *Religions secularized
and nationhood religionized (p. 516)*—4. *The function of historic
religions in the modern world (p. 518).*

CHAPTER TWENTY-SIX

A UNIVERSITY OF JUDAISM   523

1. *The problem of Jewish leadership (p. 523)*—2. *The key persons
in Jewish life (p. 524)*—3. *The affirmations of a University of*

Contents

PAGE

Judaism (p. 527)—4. The educational pattern of the University of Judaism (p. 530).

EPILOGUE   536

NOTES   541

INDEX   557

In a recent article on the Jews of Palestine Arthur Koestler [1] takes occasion to offer advice to the Jews of the Diaspora. "I am in favor," he writes, "of Jews becoming assimilated with and absorbed by the countries in which they live. I think it is high time to liquidate this anachronism of a separate community all over the world, which cannot be defined either as a separate race or nation or religious sect, and whose insistence on remaining in one way apart has led to an unparalleled chain of massacres, persecutions and expulsions for fifteen hundred years."

That advice is entirely uncalled for, as far as orthodox Jews are concerned. For them the Jewish people possesses, in its Torah, the key to salvation, both in this world and in the world to come. They still believe with every fibre of their being that the Pentateuch was dictated by God to Moses. They take for granted that the Rabbinic interpretation of the Mosaic code is divinely sanctioned and, therefore, eternally binding. To Jews, who, believe thus, the career of the Jewish people is central in God's providential scheme for mankind. Even to suggest that such a people is an anachronism and has outlived its usefulness is sheer nonsense. No sacrifice can be too great, no suffering too unbearable for the sake of belonging to such a people.

However, what Koestler has to say about Diaspora Jewry does apply with searching and challenging penetration to those Jews whose faith in Israel's traditions has been shaken. Their number is undoubtedly on the increase. Not being able to subscribe to the traditional assumptions concerning the transcendental role of the Jewish people either as pivotal to the history of mankind, or as the sole bearer of the means to salvation, they cannot reconcile themselves to the anomalous character of the Jews as a corporate entity. Not knowing exactly what it is that unites all Jews and sets them apart from the rest of the world, they are always in a state of painful perplexity and inner conflict. They can see no vital purpose to a tradition which is remembered mainly for the blood and tears of those who lived by it in the past. They are wearied by the multitude of competing and overlapping organizations and by the lack of over-all organization and authoritative guidance. They cannot endure the boredom of having to live in a cultural vacuum. They are depressed by the unrelieved gloom which the dark clouds of fear and insecurity cast over Jewish life. No wonder so many of them try to escape it altogether.

Assuming all this to be true, and even granting that Jewish life *as at present constituted* seems to many Jews to be an anachronism, are we to conclude that the only solution is, as Koestler suggests, for Jews to become "assimilated with and absorbed by the countries in which they live"?

In the first place, that solution is by no means as easy as it sounds. He fails to realize that the fate of Diaspora Jewry as "a separate community dispersed all over the world" is not in its own hands. Its very destiny which, at least in part, is determined for it by others, seems to be that of having to live, even against the will of many of its outstanding men and women. Even Koestler, in his novel, *Thieves in the Night*, recognizes that there is a certain inevitability to Jewish survival. The half-Jew Joseph, though completely gentilized, is rebuffed by Lily, because to her he is still a Jew.

Whence that inevitability?

We are a people from whose tradition two great world societies—Christendom and the Moslem world—derive their faith in themselves as God's chosen vessels of salvation, and as destined to inherit the earth. Fingering a missal, Pope Pius XI, in 1936, said: "Notice that Abraham is called our Patriarch, our ancestor; spiritually, we are all Semites."

To justify their faith, Christian and Moslem alike found it necessary to maintain that the Jews had forfeited the gift of salvation and to consign them to eternal damnation. They resorted to theological dialectics to prove that God had rejected the Jewish people, and engaged in studied efforts to render the condition of the Jews so wretched that there could be no doubt of their accursedness. That, rather than "the insistence on remaining in one way apart," accounts for the "unparalleled chain of massacres, persecutions, and expulsions."

Such sustained and concentrated attention on the Jewish people for centuries could not fail to render it an ineradicable obsession of the Gentile consciousness. Even though all Jews were to agree with Koestler and act upon his advice, it would take a long time for them to accomplish their purpose. For even if they desired to be thoroughly digested by Gentile society, they would have to submit to a quota system. The process of complete assimilation could not be consummated in fewer than four or five generations. So long as one Jew were known to be alive, all persons with the least trace of Jewish blood in their veins would, at the slightest provocation, be regarded as having the Jewish taint.

Secondly, there is a far more feasible and creative method of liquidating the anachronism, which contemporary Jewish life presents to many of our people, than for them to become "assimilated with and absorbed by the countries" in which they live. Such a method is that of putting new life into the Jewish people itself and rendering it once again an instrument of salvation to *all* who belong to it.

The salvation which the Jewish people can and should help its men and women attain consists in the progressive perfection of the human personality and in the establishment of a free, just and cooperative social order. To become an instrument of that kind of salvation, the Jewish people has to undergo nothing less than a complete reconstruction in its social structure, in its traditional outlook and way of life, and in the scope of its creative activity.

How shall we do all this? What name should be given to the kind of society we are henceforth to constitute? How retrieve and reinterpret our tradition, in the light of modern knowledge and the modern world's outlook? How rebuild the social structure so that the Jew will feel at home, at least among his own? What shall we do to render Jewish living beautiful and enjoyable through self-expression in ritual and art? When we have found the right answers to these questions, there will be much to live for. And no matter what the nations may do to us, our resolution will continue: to *live as normally and with as much dignity as is possible on this planet.* If we succeed, we shall be numbered among the enlightened and progressive forces which are at present engaged in the bitter struggle against the most stupid and fatal of all anachronisms, man's violence and aggression against his fellowman.

This book attempts to answer all of the foregoing questions. In doing that it carries forward the argument begun in *Judaism as a Civilization.*[2] The thesis presented there gave rise to the Reconstructionist Movement. That Movement is intended to reawaken in our people the corporate will to live and *to function as a source of human good.* Whenever in the past the Jews' will to live was challenged, it developed new strength and regenerative power. Likewise, the very dangers which at present threaten Jewish life, both from within and without, are reenforcing in the minds of many of us the invincible resolve that the Jewish people go on living. The future of our people in the Diaspora depends less upon outward circumstances than it does upon the will of the Jews themselves. What Herzl said about the future of Eretz Yisrael is equally true of Diaspora Jewry: "If you will it, it is no mere legend."

The basic premise of the Reconstructionist Movement is that Judaism is not merely a religion but a religious civilization. Accordingly, the decisive factor in the present inner crisis of Jewish life is the Jews' necessity to live in two civilizations. These are Judaism and Americanism in this country, or Judaism and some other modern civilization elsewhere. No doubt, many difficult implications in this assumption are still in need of resolution, but they are, by no means, unresolvable.

With the foregoing principles in mind, the sponsors of the Reconstructionist Movement have formulated a two-fold program for American Jewish life: one, over-all or plenary; the other, special or sectional.

The Over-all Program. This is intended to embrace all Jews, regardless of affiliation or rationale, to whom the renaissance of the Jewish people is a matter of deep concern. It aims to arouse our people to the need of (a) replenishing the substance of Jewish living, and (b) reorganizing the social structure of Jewry.

Our stock of cultural, ethical and spiritual values needs replenishing. That stock has run so low that now we are in dire need of evolving a new manifold of those values to render Jewish life significant, interesting, and beautiful. This has to be done without involving ourselves in controversial issues. We need to create new organs of Jewish public opinion that will serve as an incentive to the articulation and functioning of high ethical ideals. We must so replenish our resources of mind and spirit as to render living in two civilizations a means to their mutual enrichment.

No less important than the foregoing is the reorganization of the social structure of our people as a corporate entity. We accept the ultimate integration of Diaspora Jews into the body politic of the Gentile nations. We must, however, take care that the process is consummated in keeping with the spirit of democracy and not with that of totalitarianism. Such integration, therefore, must preclude neither the rehabilitation of Eretz Yisrael nor the establishment of organic communities in the Diaspora. Both are indispensable to the Jewish renaissance.

The Special or Sectional Program. There is a large and growing number of earnest men and women who, despite their eagerness to foster their Jewish heritage, do not find any of the current interpretations of it as intellectually or emotionally satisfactory. Their predicament is due, for the most part, to an inability to harmonize the Jewish tradition and way of life with the two main trends of Western civilization, namely, humanist naturalism and democratic nationalism. What they seek is re-education or re-orientation in the basic ideas of life. The special or sectional program of the Reconstructionist Movement is intended to provide them with guidance into a consistently scientific, though nonetheless religious, reconstruction of our past, and to help them achieve an edifying concept of religion which takes into account all that has been learned about it from the sciences of human nature and history.

Seeing as they do in democracy not merely a particular type of government but an ethical way of life, such men and women reject the authoritarian assumption that any code of laws which has come down from the past is capable only of interpretation and not of amendment. In the Diaspora, Jewish law—within the limits of state jurisdiction and in the spirit of democratic law-making—must come to life again. This would constitute for them a legitimate synthesis of Western democracy with Jewish tradition.

In social ills, suggested remedies generally lag behind diagnosis. Why expect the ills of Jewish life to be an exception? Therefore, patience will be required of those who read this book. Some of its descriptive parts may irritate, while its prescriptive parts may seem inadequate and disappointing. I doubt whether any critic could be more alive to these faults than the author himself, who apologizes for the forbidding length his book has attained. Some of my friends have advised me to publish each of the three parts separately. Had I acquiesced, my chief aim would have been defeated. Instead of portraying Judaism and the problems it presents to us as part of a living, indivisible totality, I should have contributed to its further fragmentation. To divide Judaism is to help its enemies conquer it.

About one third of the contents of the book is based on material which has appeared in print in the form of articles in magazines, or in symposia in book form. The magazines are: *The Reconstructionist*, published by The Reconstructionist Foundation, Inc., *Commentary*, by The American Jewish Committee, *Jewish Education*, by The National Council for Jewish Education, and *The Jewish Frontier*, by The League for Labor Palestine. The symposia in book form are: *Education for Democracy*, published by Teachers College, Columbia University, *Foundations of Democracy*, edited by F. Ernest Johnson and published by The Institute for Religious and Social Studies, and *The Foundations of Jewish Education in America* (in Hebrew), published by the Teachers Institute of the Jewish Theological Seminary of America. To all those publishers I wish to express my thanks for permission to revise and incorporate those of my articles which appeared in their publications.

Chapter XXI entitled "Toward a Guide for Jewish Ritual Usage" is a revised form of the introduction to a summary report prepared by

Rabbi A. Elihu Michelson of a special conference of the Editorial
Board of *The Reconstructionist,* in which I took part. That report
appeared as a series of articles in that magazine Vol. VI, Nos. 13-16.

I gratefully acknowledge my indebtedness to Rabbis Eugene Kohn,
Ira Eisenstein and Jack J. Cohen for having facilitated the publication
of this book by helping me with their research, criticisms and cooperation in elaborating some of the ideas in it. I also wish to thank Professor
Louis Finkelstein and Professor Irving Fineman for having read the
manuscript and having pointed out many rough places in it, which I
have tried to smooth out as a result of their suggestions.

And special thanks to my wife who patiently typed and retyped,
times without number, my much-corrected script, and whose sound
judgment often reminded me that I expected my book to be read and
understood.

M.M.K.

February, 1947

PART I

THE RESURRECTION OF A PEOPLE

CHAPTER ONE

"CAN THESE BONES LIVE?"

1

THE INNER CRISIS

Neither sub-human nor super-human beings are troubled by inner conflict. That is a distinctly human trait. Man is forever being pulled in opposite directions by his longings and desires. This condition becomes abnormal, however, when the tension reaches a breaking point. The strain of the modern Jew's inner life is nearing that point. Jews who have moved into the orbit of Gentile society are at odds with themselves to a far greater degree than non-Jews. Every American Jew who knows that Jews are not desired and whom that knowledge deeply hurts is agitated by conflicting emotions. Outwardly he may seem calm, but inwardly he is worried. He is a divided being, a Hamlet forever soliloquizing—to be or not to be a Jew.

That is true of at least two million of the five million Jews in the United States. Of the other three, one million are too young to realize what goes on about them, and the other two million either play possum or do not care what happens. The Jews who do not care transfer their inner tension to whatever Jewish activity they engage in. Whatever institution, organization, club, trade union, fraternal order or even congregation that includes them in its membership is, through them, rendered uncertain whether to be Jewish to the hilt or only to the point of a needle.

Ultimately, this inner conflict will be resolved in favor of whichever tendency will prove to be the stronger. In the meantime, American Jews may be divided into two groups: those in whom the urge "to be Jews" has the upper hand, and those in whom the urge "not to be Jews" has the upper hand. We shall call the former "affirmative Jews" and the latter "marginal Jews."

Affirmative Jews are those who, despite being troubled by the ill-will of neighbors and the difficulties created thereby, accept their fate without demur. Most of them are identified with the synagogue and all that it represents; it is their principal link with the Jewish people. If they are Orthodox, they adhere to the traditional belief that God manifested, through miracle and self-revelation, His special concern in their ancestors. If they are non-Orthodox, they regard the ethical and

3

spiritual truths underlying the ancient traditions as inherently worth fostering.

There are affirmative Jews, also, among those who have become detached from the synagogue. They find in the creative possibilities of Jewish life sufficient reason for wishing to maintain it. On the basis of what Jews have been able to achieve as individuals in modern times in all fields of human endeavor—economic, social and cultural—they are convinced that, if Jews were permitted to live in peace, they would contribute to civilization more than their share as a people among peoples.

Marginal Jews regard Judaism as a liability and a misfortune. Since they cannot advocate its forcible suppression, they would like to devise for it some kind of euthanasia or death-kiss. "If only Jews were not so stubborn, and permitted themselves to be quietly and blissfully absorbed by the rest of mankind!" they reason. "That would put an end once and for all to the Jewish problem which bedevils the world and upsets everybody's peace of mind."

They are known as Jews, least by what they themselves are or do, more by the company they keep, and most by their antecedents. Some belong to temples; their membership, however, is motivated not by religious convictions but by loyalty to the memory of parents, or by the desire to conform to social expectation. As a rule, to which there are few exceptions, these Jews are abysmally ignorant of the Jewish past and of its cultural treasures. They may be highly literate otherwise, but as Jews they are not even embarrassed at being illiterate. Everything connected with Judaism is for them an exotic orientalism which is entirely out of place in, and out of step with, the occidental way of life.

These marginal Jews are keenly aware that in the minds of non-Jews they occupy a niche apart, reserved for those who are not fully accepted socially and spiritually by the majority population. They know that they are expected by the general community to respond to Jewish appeals for relief. They cannot afford to ignore those appeals, for fear that turning the Jewish poor over to civic relief agencies might cause anti-Semitic outcries. The Y. M. C. A.'s maintain their social and recreational facilities for the sake of strengthening Christianity. Naturally they expect Jews to provide similar facilities for their own young people. Who, if not Jews, should take care of Jewish delinquents? And where shall Jews, who become physicians, find hospitals to admit them on their staffs? These marginal Jews are thus forced against their will to build Jewish settlement houses, centers and Jewish hospitals, and to establish Jewish child-caring agencies. *These modern un-walled ghettos are as much of Gentile make as the ancient ghettos. But the ancient ones had soul; the modern ghettos are spiritless.*

Then, of course, there is the problem of meeting the far-flung menace of anti-Semitism. That is a problem which usually obsesses the mind of the marginal Jew. However true and valuable in itself any Jewish endeavor may be, it must be suppressed if it places the Jews in the limelight of attention. If one of their own number is appointed to high office in the Government, they become jittery and try to influence him to resign. They can see nothing Jewish except from the standpoint of its effect on anti-Semitism.

Most of these marginal Jews are ever ready to come to the assistance of needy fellow-Jews. Although violently opposed to fostering Jewish solidarity and fellowship for its own sake, they sympathize with the lot of the individual Jew whom they regard as handicapped by his Judaism, especially if he is the victim of anti-Semite brutality. They can be counted on to respond to the various overseas appeals. They are willing even to include Eretz Yisrael as a possible haven of refuge for the Jewish victims of persecution, provided it does not awaken any deeper sentiments than those of philanthropy. They can be counted on, also, to do their utmost to obstruct a movement like Zionism.

It is not surprising to find both affirmative and marginal Jews supporting the same Jewish institutions, and cooperating in the same Jewish activities. On the face of it, a fact of this kind should be greeted with approval. What could be better than to have Jews of two diametrically opposed tendencies actually cooperating in socially important undertakings? Jews who otherwise would suffer want or illness are certainly better off, by virtue of the fact that those who are in a position to help them are willing to ignore their own differences.

Yet, it is questionable whether, in the long run, more good than harm will result from this artificial coalition of tendencies as irreconcilable as the ebb and the flow tides. That some should expect to advance Jewish life through like activities that others use as a means of weaning Jews away from Judaism cannot but lead to unwholesome inner conflict. Marginal Jews combat anti-Semitism because it does not let them become one hundred percent Gentile! Affirmative Jews combat it because it does not let them live as Jews! Thus anti-Semitism in itself exerts an ambiguous role in Jewish life, routing some Jews out of Judaism and driving others back into it, thereby robbing Jewish life of focus and persistence.

The fact that these marginal Jews are not only active but are leaders in various Jewish organizations, institutions and agencies indicates that they belong either to the limited number of the very rich, or of the top executives who direct the work of collecting and distributing of Jewish funds. The middle-income group includes both types of Jews about equally. What is surprising is that there are vast numbers of marginal Jews even among those in the lower economic brackets, especially among wage earners. Undoubtedly, this is due to the influence of socialism.

A very serious inner challenge to Jewish survival emanates from those who see in socialism, whether of the communist or democratic type, the only worthwhile "cause" with which all who are oppressed or exploited should identify themselves. Those who hold this view are either personally involved in the struggle of the laboring classes for economic security and a decent standard of living, or keenly sensitive to the insecurity of those who are involved. They maintain that Jews ought to forget their tradition and their will to live as a people, and make common cause with all non-Jews in the advancement of socialism. Convinced that socialism will put an end to all poverty, internal strife and international wars, they would have it replace the hopes and strivings which hitherto have formed part of Jewish religion and nationhood. Jewish culture should be secularized and used as an instrument of winning the Jewish masses for socialism. They do not wish it to be fostered as a means to Jewish survival. Views such as these can lead to but one conclusion, namely, the Jew should give up his historic individuality and merge with the general population; so long as he cherishes such individuality he is diverted from giving himself wholeheartedly to the cause of socialism, thus playing into the hands of the reactionaries, whether religious or national.

The socialism for the sake of which Jews are asked to give up their Jewish loyalty is far from having reached the bandwagon stage. In fact, it is doubtful whether it will reach that stage in this country within the lifetime of those who are now in their youth. To be a socialist is not to take the path of least resistance. Indeed, it often means the risk of becoming a marked man. The Jew who abandons Judaism for the sake of socialism exchanges adherence to a passive minority for adherence to a fighting minority. He is not prompted by selfish motives; neither is he motivated wholly by the desire to escape Jewish life.

It would be futile to attempt to meet this particularly serious challenge to Jewish survival by pitting the teachings of Judaism against those of socialism. There is no point in engaging in dialectics. Karl Marx himself once said he was not a Marxist. The issue is not which has the truer world outlook or the better system of conduct. Theoretically, there is no conflict whatever between Judaism and socialism, in their bearing on economic and social justice. It is in the way socialism functions that it undermines Judaism. Socialism appeals to the working masses as well as to the idealistically-minded among our people because it calls for action and is not contented to remain a way of speaking. It is, therefore, jealous of any loyalty or allegiance other than to itself. Those Jews who heed its call are no less eager than the well-to-do elements to play down all specifically Jewish interests. It is no wonder, then, that, in all questions where the issue is clearly drawn between being for or against Jewish unity and survival, the radical socialist group generally sides with the marginal Jews of the upper bourgeois class.

In recent years, however, there has been considerable searching of the heart among the socialist groups. Not all have remained insensitive to the actual development of socialism in the Old World during the last few decades. Before the outbreak of the first World War, when socialism had a chance of placing the international interests of the working classes above their national allegiance, it yielded to the latter, thereby demonstrating the superior strength of nationalism. In the Soviet Union, to be sure, anti-Semitism is outlawed, but so, also, is active participation in the re-establishment of a Jewish homeland in Eretz Yisrael. As part of the anti-religious attitude of the Soviet regime, Russian Jews are not permitted to foster the historic spirit of organic unity with the rest of world Jewry.

During the interim between the two wars, nationalism became so powerful that it prostituted socialism and compelled it to serve the cruel avarice of nations which were determined to conquer and enslave the world. And now, after World War II, when socialism has had a sweeping victory in England, it has proved beyond a shadow of a doubt that it can be as fanatically nationalist, and as indifferent to the fate of the oppressed of other peoples, as the most greedy capitalist society. The Eretz Yisrael effort should have been welcomed by the Laborite Government, as likely to bring social and economic progress and a higher standard of living to a part of the world where feudalism is still in the saddle. Instead, that Government has proved to be more deceitful and vicious than all preceding Governments, in its dealings with the situation in Eretz Yisrael.

These demonstrations of socialism in action have disillusioned many Jewish socialists; they have been compelled to wonder whether they, too, would be included in the socialist utopia, were it to come about in America. Although their faith in socialism may not be entirely shaken, their conviction that Jews are wrong in fostering their own group individuality has certainly been shaken. Their bitter opposition to Jewish religion and peoplehood has subsided. In some quarters there is even marked interest in Zionism, whereas in others there has been a return to religion and religious observances. These yearnings for a return to Judaism are inchoate, but they are strong enough to create a condition of inner conflict in a large and important sector of American Jewry.

2

THE COURAGE TO FACE THE FACTS

If we Jews had our patron saints, the priest-prophet Ezekiel would be the patron saint of those of us who are vitally concerned in the outcome of the present crisis in Jewish life. It is he to whom we should turn for inspiration and guidance in this apocalyptic age.

In the ancient Jewish colony, formed in Babylon during the sixth century B.C.E. by the captives who had been brought from Eretz Yisrael, Ezekiel found himself in the midst of a spiritual wasteland, comparable to our own American-Jewish scene. Some of the Jews were so cowed and overawed by the might of their conquerors and the prestige of their conquerors' religion that they renounced their own God; they gave as an excuse the utter hopelessness of their people.[1] Other Jews adhered to outworn religious doctrines,[2] enjoyed listening to Ezekiel's preachments, without any intention of acting on them,[3] and blithely ignored the responsibilities to which their new surroundings gave rise.

Although Ezekiel realized that both of these trends were bound to prove fatal to the life of his people, he was hopeful that they would be checked before it would be too late. His confidence in Israel's future was so great that it took on the form of his well-known vision of Israel's resurrection.[4] We should learn from him to refrain from self-delusion concerning the critical character of our present situation and from resignation to the inevitability of a tragic outcome.

Since Jewish life nowadays is either smothered by the deadweight of smug complacency or paralyzed by fright and despair, it is essential that we Jews catch something of that spirit with which Ezekiel sought to imbue the Jews of his generation: *courage in the face of disheartening apathy and spiritual decline, faith in the recuperative and regenerative powers of our people, and wisdom and patience in planning and building for the future.*

It is natural to try to conceal from ourselves what we do not wish to believe. But let us not deceive ourselves. The Prophet Jeremiah excoriated the misleaders of his day who kept on saying, "All's well," when all was far from well.[5] Ezekiel described such people as daubing flimsy walls with whitewash.[6] By resenting the disclosure of the critical state of affairs in Jewish life, we put ourselves in one class with those of whom the Prophet said in the name of God: "They shall have no place in the council of my people, nor be enrolled in the register of the Household of Israel." [7] In the long run, more good is apt to come from being worried by the disintegration which is proceeding beneath the surface of Jewish life than from being contented with its superficial semblance of health.

American-Jewish life seethes with activity. Federations, welfare funds, community chests, United Jewish Appeals, hospitals, orphan asylums, homes for the aged, fraternal orders, public relations agencies, and above all Zionism, make quite a clatter. What permanent significance, if any, do they have? Are all these efforts with their vast expenditure of energy part of the *advance* or of the *retreat* of our inner forces? An army that is beating a hasty retreat presents a picture of the most intensive activity—transporting the wounded, eluding the enemy and saving as much of its material as possible. Nevertheless, all that bustle is no indication of headway. From the standpoint of Israel's future, we have ample reason to believe that, by and large, the contribution of the vast network of Jewish public agencies toward keeping alive or awakening in our young the desire to carry on as Jews, if not altogether negative, is certainly negligible.

Some may regard as irrelevant, if not unfair, the very expectation that these philanthropic and social activities should help to perpetuate Jewish life. Is not the actual good they do in the immediate present their justification? We must remember, however, that these activities constitute a burden which the Jew has to carry alone. Every people has a right to exact sacrifices of the energy, time and resources of those who belong to it. These are expected as a means of helping a people to live. A share in its future is the necessary and legitimate reward to which the individual looks forward; otherwise the sacrifice is a gratuitous and meaningless burden. Rebuilding the ruins of shattered European Jewry and rendering Eretz Yisrael secure as a Jewish homeland—the two largest undertakings of American Jews—are projects which will require two or three generations for their consummation. If Jews lose faith in the future of their people, they will lose interest even in the physical salvaging of its human wreckage.

The amazing fact is that *most of our spiritual leaders carry on routine duties as though nothing cataclysmic has happened to Jewish life.* They are like the famous old lady of the London *blitz* whose house had been so thoroughly bombed that all that remained was a jagged frontage in a flattened street. That did not seem to change her routine in the least. Every morning she would turn up as usual to scrub the doorstep. Likewise, most of our rabbis, educators and scholars carry on their daily chores as if the House of Israel were almost intact. They have done little, if anything, to counteract the tendency to identify Jewish loyalty with "dollar Judaism," the Judaism that begins and ends with philanthropy. They have been derelict in their duty to educate the laity to a realization that *to be a Jew today means nothing less than to aid in the rebuilding of the House and in the reconstituting of the Household of Israel.*

Although there is no way of measuring the amount of idealism that governs people in the different social strata, the impression that the poor are less egoistic and more self-sacrificing than the well-to-do is not without warrant. Nevertheless, the character of a people is generally determined by the standards adopted by its wealthy and near-wealthy, influential classes. The underprivileged classes are inclined generally to imitate the vices of the upper social strata. We may, therefore, regard the interests and the standards of the more prosperous among our people as an index of the direction in which our people as a whole is moving.

Jews of the middle-class—those engaged in business and the professions—are, for the most part too preoccupied with their vocations and too absorbed in the trivialities of their avocations, in the movies, golfing, card-playing and similar diversions, to give much thought to their responsibilities and opportunities as Jews. When the High Holidays come around they rent seats in established or provisional synagogues. The important occasions in life like *Bar Mitzvah*, confirmation, a wedding or a funeral are marked by some religious ceremony. But once the ceremony is over, those occasions begin to border on vulgarity, for lack of spiritual refinement. Some sporadic ritual observances together with the mourners' *Kaddish* and *Yahrzeit* constitute the sum of the average Jew's experience with religion. Neither the ideational nor the emotional phases of religion have any interest for him. These are supposed to be part of the rabbi's function. In fact, many Jews look upon the rabbi as the person who is "paid to be a Jew."

It is difficult to conceive that, in such a milieu, children can grow up with any moral enthusiasm or spiritual yearning. Now and then a child of finer soul texture, or more delicate sensitivity, is found in that kind of environment. The father may be a successful physician who knows only two activities in life: attending to his patients during office and hospital hours, and playing cards or golf during his leisure time. He expects his son to be a physician like himself so that, when the day comes for him to retire, he can turn his practice over to his son. But the son happens to be interested in music and would like to make that his career. He meets and falls in love with a Catholic girl who is a singer. Music is their common, spiritual bond. He comes to share not only the girl's musical interest but, also, her religious faith. He cannot renounce his love of the Catholic girl for the sake of his parents, and cannot understand why he should not join the church which promises to fill his spiritual void with a soul-saving religion.

Situations like this one are becoming more and more numerous. Apart from whatever idealism our worldly successful Jews may manifest in their vocations and family relations, they cherish no high ambitions as Jews. Whatever emotions or ideas they have about Judaism have been borrowed or acquired at random. The modern Jew has been aptly described as "Jacob without the ladder."

Instead of teaching their children from the cradle that "The Torah is the best of all goods," marginal Jewish parents frequently withhold from their children as long as they can the fact that they are Jews. When, one day, the child learns from epithets hurled at him by his classmates, that they regard him as a Jew, and he asks his parents whether he really is one, the hesitant, stammering manner in which the truth is told immediately links in the child's mind the term "Jew" with inferiority, shame and guilt. Jews change their names and affect not only the manners, but also the vices, of their Gentile neighbors, in order to obliterate every trace of Jewish origin. Even when the reluctance of Gentile society to include them in its social life forces them to associate with one another, they avoid all reference to Judaism, and imitate as closely as possible the behavior that characterizes similar non-Jewish circles. Exclusively Jewish fraternities and clubs have been known to celebrate Christmas, on the pretext that it is an American national holiday, while scrupulously avoiding the observance of any holiday of the Jewish calendar.

The modern Jew who lacks faith in the value of Judaism tends to hate himself because, in spite of everything, he detects traits inculcated in him by early Jewish conditioning; to hate his parents because he holds them responsible for his having been born a Jew; to hate his fellow-Jews because their very existence makes it hard for him to be accepted by Gentile society as one of their own; to hate his Gentile neighbors because they identify him with his despised people. He is at peace neither with himself nor with his world. Being thus at logger-heads with his whole environment, he is an utter stranger to that realm of inner serenity in which the religious soul finds refuge from the tur-moil of life's storms. Not having made his peace with the world, he cannot experience the peace of God.

The ominous truth about present-day Jewish life is that the desire to escape it is deepening and spreading. It is taking possession of the entire conscious and sub-conscious life of many Jews in every stratum of Jewish society. We cannot afford to be finicky about noting the flimsiness of the whitewashed wall, because if we persist in hiding the truth from ourselves, nothing will be done about it. If unchecked much longer, the tendency to escapism will develop into a stampede, during which Jews are as likely as not to step over the bodies of prostrate brethren.

One would expect the two main institutions dedicated to the perpetuation of Judaism—the school and the synagogue—to reckon frankly and realistically with the precarious state of Jewish life. Instead, they continue to daub the trembling walls with whitewash. They avert their faces from basic causes of the difficulties that they are encounter-ing, even resenting their exposure. The mechanics of organization and of educational techniques provide the desired illusion that all is well. They shy away from attempts to go to the root of what is undermining Jewish morale.

This false optimism nullifies the good that might come from the many forms of educational endeavor. In some of the large cities there are bureaus of Jewish education headed by able administrators, but their energies are dissipated in devising methods for educational aims in which parents and public have no interest whatever. The traditional aims have become obsolete and those adopted by the educators gen-erally have no bearing on either the character or the welfare of the child.

Parents themselves have evolved a spurious aim of their own: that the child attain sufficient knowledge to go through the *Bar Mitzvah* or confirmation ceremony. All else is extraneous and superfluous. So the overwhelming majority of Jewish young grow up not only in crass ignorance of Judaism, but in possession of all the inner tensions that constitute psychological insecurity. These reveal themselves in resistance on the part of Jewish college students to a Jewish activity such as the establishment of a Hillel Foundation on the college campus. The very fact that we Jews are not shocked by such resistance is itself an inauspicious omen.

If we should take the trouble to discover the basic reason for the unwillingness of parents to give their children a Jewish education, we would realize that we are not living in a world where the old kind of exhortation can work. We cannot start a car by saying "Giddap." Our Jewish life is as unlike the life of our grandparents as the automobile is unlike the buggy. Therefore, we should not expect Jewish life to operate on the basis of wants which they felt, but which we do not feel. Neither are elaborate educational machinery and literature helpful to a solution of the basic problem. That is the problem of how to motivate parents and children to regard education in Judaism in the way our ancestors regarded the Torah, as "our life and the length of our days."

Florence Nightingale is said to have revolutionized hospital methods by insisting that whatever else hospitals may do they should at least not spread disease. We need someone who would do something similar for our Jewish educational institutions, from the most elementary to the most advanced, so that, whatever else they do, they should at least not spread the feeling that Jewish knowledge has no relevance to present-day needs.

Some time ago there was a marked increase in the number of congregational schools at the expense of the Talmud Torah schools, which had been supported by memberships organized for the purpose. Some rabbis were so short-sighted as to gloat over what they called a swing from secularism to religion. What that change actually means, however, is that instead of children giving to Jewish studies at least ten to twelve hours each week, they now give at most two to four hours; and that, instead of being regarded as a communal responsibility, Jewish education has become a private affair. Especially vociferous are those who are optimistic over recent gains in Jewish parochial schools. The truth is that these gains affect at best only one percent of the Jewish population of this country. The most constructive educational effort in American-Jewish life thus far has been the establishment of courses for adults. So far, however, those courses have shown no sign of conquering the general aversion of our young people for Jewish subject matter or for Jewish cultural interests.

The present condition of the synagogue is as little encouraging as is that of the school. The synagogue, through its worship and instruction, was throughout the ages a spiritual fortress for our people. It fostered the unity of Israel through the use of Hebrew and the uniformity of its prayer ritual, and it kept the Jewish spirit alive by interpreting the contemporary needs and problems in the light of Jewish tradition. In pre-modern days the synagogue was able to carry out these functions successfully, because it was aided by the prevailing universal attitude toward religion. Everybody took it for granted that the very act of worship exercised supernatural potency. Everybody had implicit faith in the authority of the past. This religious attitude still prevails in Orthodox synagogues. They are, undoubtedly, a force for Jewish survival, but the kind of Judaism that survives there is intellectually so asphyxiating, and spiritually so bewildering that most Jews, who have grown up under it, have run away from it.

On the other hand, the non-Orthodox synagogues, instead of wrestling with the problem of what should replace the anachronistic supernaturalism and unquestioning acceptance of the authority of the past, are preoccupied with all kinds of schemes to render the services attractive. They have almost forgotten their principal function. In permitting the gradual elimination of Hebrew from the prayers, they are contributing to the dejudaizing influences of the environment. In failing to reinterpret the basic values of Jewish religion in terms of the modern universe of discourse, they are as great a force for the secularization of Jewish life as are the avowedly secular institutions.

Some years ago a questionnaire was sent to the Reform congregations to find out their attitude toward the use of Hebrew in the religious services, and the overwhelming majority replied that they wanted even less Hebrew than was still in use.[8] The Conservative synagogues, too, are gradually finding Hebrew an obstacle in the conduct of the services. The growing ignorance of the Bible and Rabbinics renders irrelevant the function of preaching as a means of interpreting the tradition. People come to synagogue not to worship but to hear the sermon or a lecture. After a while they discover that Town Hall or University extension lectures offer a greater variety of subjects and speakers, or that they can spend the time to better advantage by staying at home to listen to the radio or to read a book. A few outstanding orators whose great gifts afford aesthetic pleasure will always draw large, but transient, audiences. In the smaller towns, where the range of entertainment is limited, religious services are occasionally well attended, especially if there is an out-of-town speaker. In any event, one has to be extremely unrealistic to maintain that the worship and the instruction in the present-day synagogues are in themselves sufficiently potent to counteract the disintegration of Jewish life.

That disintegration is both psychological and social.

Psychologically, it makes itself felt in the sense of inferiority, self-contempt and self-hate, which is undermining the morale of our people, especially of the young. The average Jew stoops mentally and spiritually under a great weight of anxiety and insecurity. Finding oneself hampered at every step, because one is a Jew, tends to destroy one's moral stamina. On the other hand, the environment of Medieval Europe, no less hostile or vicious toward the Jew than is ours, did not evoke today's bitter self-pity and self-disparagement. In the long struggle of the Jewish people for existence, the attitude of the individual Jew was the decisive factor. The spirit of the Jew was not ruffled by the slightest doubt or questioning as to the high privilege of being a Jew, however great a price in suffering and persecution he had to pay.

Socially, disintegration is working its way into Jewish life through the rapidly increasing rate of intermarriage between Jews and non-Jews. As soon as Jews are allowed to mingle freely with non-Jews, even though unaccepted as equals among those at the top of the social scale, intermarriage begins to increase. If we are at all familiar with what has been happening to the Jewish population in Western Europe during the last century, we cannot but conclude that American Jewry, like that of the west-European countries is inevitably bound to be progressively decimated by the growing number of intermarriages. With the present spiritual and structural chaos in Jewish life, it is impossible to halt the devastating effect of these intermarriages.

What is particularly discouraging about the crisis resulting from intermarriage is that even responsible Jewish leaders treat it like the weather. They talk about it, but never dream of doing anything constructive. They lament the spread of intermarriage, and indulge in exhortations and appeals against it, in the name of all that Jews are supposed to hold dear. But they might as well try to get the rivers to flow back to their sources as to expect such an approach to the problem of intermarriage to have any effect.

The marked deterioration in the loyalty of the individual Jew toward his people and its heritage makes the problem of Jewish survival an extremely difficult one. It is not the type of problem that can be solved by "muddling through." It calls for the kind of thinking and planning in which the least self-delusion or faulty judgment is bound to prove fatal. We must, therefore, begin with a sober appraisal of what is wrong with us. That is the first step in the moral realism to be learned from our great teachers, the Prophets.

3

THE MODERN CHALLENGE TO JEWISH LIFE

Does the spiritual weakness of modern Jewry mean that Jewish men and women of today lack the sensitivity, the intelligence and the strength of character of their forefathers? Hardly. The long roster of talented and gifted Jews who have made a name for themselves in every sphere of human endeavor refutes such an assumption. Since the mental and physical endowments of the modern Jew are not inferior to those of his ancestors, the malady and the cause of his maladjustment should be traceable to the world in which he finds himself.

This maladjustment first made itself felt during the last two decades of the eighteenth century, when Jews began to be emancipated from the status of alienage, and were admitted into the general body politic. This coincided with the era of Enlightenment, when human intelligence sought to free itself, on a large scale, from the domination of traditional dogma. The granting of civic rights to the Jews was largely a result of the overthrow of the medieval synthesis of feudalism and other-worldliness. The desire to improve human life on this earth spread far beyond the circles of the intellectual élite, and the response to it proved so exciting and so absorbing that men lost interest in what might be their fate in the hereafter. The American and French Revolutions were inspired largely by the hope of establishing a social order that was to be based on this new conception of life's purpose.

The achievement of such a social order called for a program of political reforms, whereby the disfranchised masses would come into possession of rights to which they were entitled, and of which they had been deprived by the nobility and the clergy. Despite deeply rooted prejudices against the Jews, it was impossible within reason to refuse to free them from the disabilities to which they had been subjected for centuries.

The first Jews to welcome and to benefit from this change in status were those who were well-to-do and whose administrative abilities brought them into close contact with the rising class of industrialists and financiers, particularly in France, Holland and Germany. These Jews saw no longer any need for cherishing the traditional hopes for the coming of the Messiah; emancipation was enough of a Messiah to them. This was the light in which they wished fellow-Jews to see the civic rights that were being grudgingly granted them in Western and Central Europe. Those rights put an end to their state of exile and enabled them to become part of the great nations that had a place in the sun. In addition, they opened unrestricted economic opportunities and granted unlimited freedom of cultural enjoyment and personal self-expression. What more could Jews expect?

Had the liberal democratic movement been carried to its logical conclusion, or had any serious attempt been made to translate the ideal of "liberty, equality and fraternity" into political and economic law, the long awaited millennium might actually have come about. It is difficult to envisage what the Jews would then have done. Some might have resettled in Eretz Yisrael, some might have found a way of living as Jews in their native countries, while others might have become absorbed by the rest of the population. But mankind has yet to acquire the knowledge and the will to make of this world what it should be.

The liberalism of the eighteenth and nineteenth centuries turned out to be mere wishful thinking, without the determination to live up to the great hopes it had raised in men's hearts. As the Jews were the first to sense the promise of a better world, they were also the first to experience the disillusionment, as soon as that promise was broken. *Early in the nineteenth century, medieval Jew-hatred showed signs of being transformed into modern anti-Semitism, which is a secularized form of the theological rationale for persecuting Jews.* The Jews are generally the first victims of economic dislocation in the countries which have granted them citizenship. Their specific cultural needs are not only disregarded, but treated as an obstacle to complete fusion with the cultural life of the majority population. Socially, they remain outsiders.

The equivocal attitude of the Western world toward the Jews during the last century-and-a-half has so confused their minds that they have been unable to formulate a clear and consistent policy of self-adjustment. Their instability and insecurity have been greater than those of any other people, and they have responded in all kinds of ways to the inconsistent treatment which has been accorded them. Some took the promises of Western liberalism at face value, while others have seen the growing signs of danger too clearly to be deluded by the comparative calm. The result is that the Jews are an enigma to themselves and to the rest of the world. The nations are too deeply engrossed in their own ambitions to bother about resolving in a just fashion the perplexities which they have created for the Jews. Not even the fact that, in the clashing of their ambitions, one third of the Jewish people has been most cruelly done to death has struck the least spark of remorse in their hearts of flint.

Modern nationalism, which released the Jews from the status of alienage, and modern naturalism which made sensible the modern version of nationalism are ambivalent in their effect on the future of the Jewish people. Had these movements been allowed to function in the interest of a better world for all mankind, had they not been utilized chiefly for purposes of international rivalry and war, they would, undoubtedly, have made it possible for Jewish life to thrive and contribute its share to world betterment. Having become associated with greed and lust for domination, these modern movements menace our existence as individuals and as a people. Despite this menace, however, we have to live with them. *That is our dilemma. The only way to resolve it is to discover the elements of hope and progress that still inhere in them and to plan our future on the assumption that God's redeeming power will ultimately purge them of their evil tendencies.*

Nationalism today is, undoubtedly, the most strongly entrenched human institution. In its normal and legitimate form, it calls upon all citizens of the state to subordinate to the common good of the nation whatever differences divide them. It expects them to treat differences of race, class, education, economic status, religious affiliation, as inconsequential alongside the interests which affect that nation as a whole. Its purpose is to weld all citizens of a country into a strong, prosperous, homogeneous unity. Even this legitimate demand renders it difficult for an historic minority in a modern nation to retain its corporate being. *Yet actual experience has proved that national homogeneity, unless qualified by cultural and religious heterogeneity, degenerates into totalitarian enslavement of the individual, and becomes a standing threat to universal peace.* Centralization renders the state efficient, but it also tends to make of it a juggernaut. The only way to keep the state human is to have it decentralized along cultural and spiritual lines. Men's eyes will ultimately be opened to these truths. In the meantime, however, we shall need great courage and wisdom to withstand the assimilative pressure of the overpowering environmental forces.

Thus far even the legitimate nationalism of the Western states has been undermining the sense of unity which Jews were able to maintain throughout the past, despite their dispersion. That sense of unity enabled each local Jewish community to constitute for its members a self-sustaining cell, in which the Jew was able to live out his life fully as a social and spiritual being. When Jews, however, accepted citizenship, they threw in their lot with that of the Gentile nations. Some of them began to think that they no longer needed association with a Jewish community or *Kahal*, which had formerly been as indispensable to them as the very air they breathed. In addition, they assumed that they could dispense with the hope for the return of all Jews to Eretz Yisrael, since an end had come not only to their sufferings in exile, but to the very state of exile. The assumption was that Jews would henceforth feel at home wherever they lived.

Nationalism, however, has also developed unhealthy and sinister aspects. Albert Schweitzer,[9] one of the most saintly Christians in the modern world, rightly defines this development as "an ignoble patriotism, exaggerated till it has lost all meaning; it bears the same relation to the noble and healthy kind as the fixed idea of an imbecile does to normal conviction."

Nationalism, in its malignant form, confronts us Jews as anti-Semitism. Anti-Semitism is the Jew-hatred which derives its main rationale not from Christian religion, as was the case with Jew-hatred in pre-modern times, but from modern nationalism. Christian religion, or whatever survives of it, may still serve as the initial impulse to anti-Semitism, but what gives it added momentum is the imputation that the Jew interferes with the normal development of national life. He is accused of acting as a catalytic agent that precipitates the evil tendencies, the selfish interests and corrupting disloyalties in the nation, while his own identity remains intact. To render these accusations credible, anti-Semitism has secularized the myth of the Wandering Jew, and has given it the form of the Conquering Jew, who always schemes to enslave the Gentile world.

Both the expectations of legitimate nationalism and the libels spread by malignant nationalism present a type of problem with which the

Jewish people throughout its long career has never had occasion to grapple. Jews were either let alone or ordered to renounce their Judaism. Never were they expected to subordinate their Judaism, or to render it quiescent and invisible. On the other hand, they were never given a chance to play an integral role in the national life of their neighbors, and, therefore, could never have been charged with corrupting it, much less with seeking to dominate it. Here then, in legitimate nationalism, is a new type of challenge. How shall we American Jews meet it?

Naturalism, too, has its legitimate and malignant forms. In its normal or legitimate form, it stresses the need of reckoning with the newly-acquired knowledge of the physical world and of human nature, and of revising all traditional views and assumptions. Naturalism is bent upon having man rely more upon such experience as he himself can verify rather than upon the authority of the past. The historic sciences to which it has given rise have destroyed traditional beliefs concerning origins, whether of the world, of man or of any of his basic institutions. Naturalism has expanded man's knowledge of the universe and has given him control of the forces of nature. We cannot afford to ignore its call upon us to revise some of the most sacrosanct traditions, if we wish our personal lives to be integrated and free of inner conflict. But how to do it without imperiling the very existence of Judaism is a grave and complicated problem.

Naturalism reached the Jews toward the end of the eighteenth century and has been playing havoc with their tradition ever since. That tradition provided the rationale which encouraged Jews to remain loyal to Judaism under the most trying circumstances. It stressed the miraculous character of Israel's origin and early history. It pictured the glory and the bliss of the future for which Israel was destined. No one had ever questioned the literal truth of the miracles which were assumed to have been enacted in behalf of Israel in Egypt, in the Wilderness, and in Canaan. No doubt ever troubled the mind of the Jew concerning the coming of a Messiah who would gather all Israel from the four corners of the earth and lead the Israelites in triumph to their ancient land. The certainty that life in the world-to-come awaited all who were of Israel rendered the Jew immune to the temptation to renounce his people and his God. Out of all these hopes and dreams the Jew was rudely awakened by the dawning light of the new matter-of-fact knowledge of the physical world, of living creatures and of man's spiritual evolution.

Naturalism, however, like nationalism, has two forms. Its sinister, malignant form is known as "scientism." As scientism, it challenges not merely specific traditions concerning matters of fact but, also, the fundamental verities of the human spirit. It treats all ethical and spiritual values as either defense-mechanisms, rationalizations or wish-fantasies. It makes unwarranted claims for itself. The naturalism which reduces all that differentiates man from the subhuman to illusion, and all life and mind and spirit to the operation of mechanical cause and effect is bound to end up in the denial of all moral objectivity and spiritual sanctity. Man's life and society's history are reduced to "processes of the transformation of energy, subject to the law of energistic mechanics and especially to the laws of least effort and realization of maximum energy." [10] Even in the field of human relations, scientism studies and measures the fears and hopes and loves of people for the purpose of manipulating them, as though human beings were pieces on a chessboard. It removes the last restraints ot human decency, and transforms social conflict into a reign of terror, in which the first victims are sure to be the Jews.

There can be no truer description of the moral devastation which this degenerate form of naturalism is wreaking in our day than the following by Pitirim Sorokin: [11] "Stripping man of his divine charisma and grace, sensate mentality, ethics and law has reduced him to a mere electron-proton complex or reflex mechanism devoid of any sanctity or end-value. 'Liberating' him from 'the superstitions' of the categorical imperatives, they have taken from him an invisible armour that unconditionally protected him, his dignity, his sanctity and his inviolability. Divested of this armour, he finds himself but a plaything in the hands of the most fortuitous forces. If he is useful for this or that, he may be treated decently and cared for as we care for a useful animal. If he is 'harmful' he can be 'liquidated' as we exterminate harmful snakes. No guilt, no crime, no valid reason, is needed for such a liquidation. The very existence of a man or a group as an unintentional obstacle is enough to eliminate them."

As matters stand today, unfortunately, the general education given in the schools is powerless to stem the dehumanizing influence of this malignant type of naturalism. Our schools and colleges seldom take the trouble to stress the difference between legitimate naturalism and sinister scientism. To make matters worse, our Jewish young people are also subjected to this very devaluation of all human values. Thus not only do they become cheap in the eyes of the non-Jews, but they become cheap in their own estimation. This cannot but have a shattering effect on their moral stamina. They grow up to be of infirm and fumbling character, ready to make the mean concessions which our present-day world forever demands.

4

THE FIRST ATTEMPTS AT MEETING THE CHALLENGE

The first Jewish answer to the challenge of modern *nationalism* was given by the so-called Sanhedrin, or Assembly of Jewish Notables, convened by Napoleon, in 1806. As a condition to the granting of civil rights to the Jews, that Assembly was expected to renounce Jewish nationhood. It virtually acquiesced in this condition, declaring that henceforth the Jews of each country constituted a religious community which was to have nothing in common with Jewish communities of other countries except certain religious beliefs and practices, and which was not to engage in any common enterprise with those communities. Although there was an element of duress in the acceptance of that status by the Napoleonic Sanhedrin, its acceptance was approved by many Jews even outside France, and later formed the basis of that effort at Jewish reconstruction which came to be known as *Reform Judaism*. At various conferences, particularly in Germany during the middle of the nineteenth century, participated in mainly by the Reform rabbinate, this renunciation of Jewish nationhood was hailed with approval.[12] This approval was part of the effort to purge Judaism of all its particularist elements which, from the viewpoint of universal religion, were deemed irrelevant. *The Pittsburgh Platform*, which for a long time served as the authoritative statement of the Reform movement in America, was formulated in 1885 by a similar assembly of Reform rabbis in America, and expressed the same denationalized conception of Judaism.[13]

The Reform movement has also reckoned with the challenge of *naturalism*. It accepted naturalism's rejection of miracle. It was thus under the necessity of finding a new rationale for adherence to the Jewish faith, since it could not accept as valid the supernaturalist version of the revelation of the Torah. It found this rationale in the theory of the "mission". Jewish religion, it contended, was superior to every other religion in being the purest form of ethical monotheism. Hence it was the mission of the Jews to attest to the world the truth of this religion. Some of the leaders of Reform, notably Kaufmann Kohler, went so far as to assume a special aptitude for religion inherent in the Jewish race.[14]

The Reform formula was actually an unavoidable response to a situation that prevailed in Western Europe during the decades before 1870. Nevertheless, it proved inadequate. Although the renunciation of Jewish nationhood was accepted by a considerable number of Jews, affirmation of a Jewish mission did not prove a sufficient motivating force to stem the tide of escapism and assimilation.

Early Reform proved no more successful in the way it met the challenge of modern naturalism than in the way it met the challenge of modern nationalism. The mission idea was intended to render the justification of Jewish survival independent of the super-naturalism which had permeated the Jewish tradition. It was based on an idealistic interpretation of history. According to that interpretation, the Jews, as a race, possessed a unique gift for religion, a gift to which they owed their intuitive apprehension of the unity of God and the brotherhood of mankind.

These claims in behalf of the Jews did not contradict the laws of nature, but they had no basis in fact. They implied generalizations about human beings, Jews and non-Jews, which could be disproved by the most casual study of the facts. Furthermore, they held up standards which were so far beyond the capacity of the average Jew to live up to that they tended to degenerate into a form of pious wishing. In the traditional version of Judaism, there was nothing incompatible between the concept of God as revealing Himself to Israel and Israel's rebelling against Him. The entire pattern of traditional thinking allowed for Israel's failure to live up to God's expectation. But the modern idealistic version of the Jews as the bearers of a sacred mission to the rest of the world either has to square with the realities of Jewish life or be dismissed as self-delusion.

Thus classical Reform proved unable to counteract the growing tendency of Jews to regard Judaism as a liability without redeeming compensations. The inadequacy of the classical formula of Reform became increasingly apparent even to rabbis who were trained and educated under Reform auspices. *The Pittsburgh Platform* adopted by the Central Conference of American Rabbis in 1885 has been largely repudiated by the rabbinical adherents of the movement. In the *Guiding Principles* adopted by that same Conference in Columbus in 1937,[15] the peoplehood of Israel is avowed, and the importance of many so-called particularistic elements of Jewish life is recognized. The concept of peoplehood is evidently intended to repudiate the Napoleonic Sandhedrin's disavowal of the oneness and indivisibility of world Jewry.

Renunciation of Jewish nationhood did not gain for the Jews in any country complete economic and social equality with the rest of the population. The rational idealism of the Enlightenment, which had sponsored the emancipation of the Jews, was succeeded by a romantic nationalism which grew progressively reactionary and chauvinistic, and which sought to thrust the Jews back into the ghetto. Jews became aware that, no matter how eagerly they sought to merge with the general population, they would continue to be considered outsiders and interlopers. This became more evident in Central and Western Europe as the nineteenth century drew to a close. In Eastern Europe, where the majority of the Jews then resided, and where the medieval status of the Jews as aliens continued until the end of World War I, all prospects of improvement in the lot of the Jews, as a result of their modernization, had been shattered. It was then that Jews began to realize that they must find some new way of emancipating themselves from the centuries-old state of bondage, and become once again a normal people, free from oppression and discrimination. This led to political Zionism, which saw only one solution to the Jewish problem: to reconstitute the Jews as a nation in their own historic home, where they could have their own government and develop their own civilization, as of right and not merely on sufferance.

But, like the early Reform movement, Zionism was conditioned by the European setting in which it arose. The nationalism of the European nations was becoming so totalitarian that it left little possibility of a future for Judaism in Europe. The entire emphasis of Zionism, therefore, has been on the development of the Jewish national home in Eretz Yisrael. Zionism has been able to deal, at most only sporadically, with the problem of permanent Jewish group life in those countries of the Diaspora where Judaism could survive.

Whatever the inherent merit of the Zionist solution for those who will or can go to Eretz Yisrael, it is no solution for the five million Jews in the United States, the only strong surviving remnant of our people, and without a satisfactory solution of the problem presented by modern nationalism, the status of American Jewry remains ambiguous. Such ambiguity is bound to undermine our children's happiness and peace of mind. In fact, every day that is allowed to pass without effort on our part to come to terms with so urgent and vital a problem as their Jewish status *vis-à-vis* the majority population adds to their inner tension and anxiety. The cliché that Jews constitute a religious community, allegedly united by some common beliefs concerning God and salvation, is flagrantly untrue. We contribute to our children's self-hate and self-contempt by failing to find the appropriate name for that which identifies them as Jews no less than by failing to render Jewish life intrinsically deserving of their loyalty.

Both classical Reform and modern Zionism represent two deliberate attempts to reconstruct Jewish life. Thus far both classical Reform, from the Jewish standpoint, and modern Zionism, from the American standpoint, have proved inadequate in meeting the problem of Judaism, as it presents itself to American Jews.

A third reconstructionist movement, known as Yiddishism or Diaspora nationalism came to the fore among east-European Jews during the first and second decades of this century. We shall have occasion to discuss that movement more fully as part of the general problem of what is henceforth to be the status of world Jewry. At this point, however, where our main concern is with American Jewry, there is no reason for discussing it. It is so out of gear with the American environment that to promulgate it for American Jewry would be quixotic.

Neither can Neo-Orthodoxy come in for consideration at this point. As its name indicates, the very notion of reconstructing either the traditional religion or the traditional status of the Jews is repugnant to it. To Neo-Orthodoxy, the cure for the ills of inner Jewish life is to be found entirely in the return to the traditional world-outlook and the traditional regimen of religious observances. Those who see in the beneficent aspects of modern naturalism and modern nationalism potentialities with which Judaism must come to terms regard such a cure as certain to intensify those ills.

Conservative Judaism, on the other hand, does recognize change in the beliefs and practices of Judaism as an historical fact. Such change, having taken place at a stage of human development, when the authority of tradition was paramount, necessarily insinuated itself quite unconsciously. Only as we look back over the long past of Judaism do we discern in it the process of evolution. It is this kind of evolution which Conservatism has raised to a norm. Accordingly, it yields only to change which has come to stay, but it does not initiate change. This accounts for the curious fact that, although it professes the willingness to reckon with the needs of contemporary Jewish life, it has not, of its own accord, sanctioned a single one of its departures from traditional

Judaism. Only after they were introduced by some more enterprising trend in Jewish life, or had managed to become irrevocable, did Conservatism finally accept them.

5

FAITH IN LATENT POTENTIALITIES

Merely to know, however, what is wrong with us may lead to defeatism. Surely no one was more soul-sick over the sins and misfortunes of our people than the Prophets, yet they were never driven to passive resignation. Their grief over the seemingly hopeless condition of Israel did not paralyze their will. They discerned the social and spiritual rottenness which was eating away at the life of their people. Yet they kept on pleading with the Jews to repent, and never lost hope that ultimately their words would be effective. In the familiar vision of the valley, Ezekiel is shown the depths of despair to which his people had sunk: "These bones are the Household of Israel. Behold they keep on saying, 'Our bones are dried up, and our hope is lost; we are clean cut off.' " [16] Yet God tells him to prophesy and to say to the Household of Israel, "Behold I am opening your graves and will raise you out of your graves, O my people, and I will bring you into the land of Israel." [17]

It is tempting to conclude from the decadence of the inner life of our people in the Diaspora that Israel is spiritually as dead as the dry bones which Ezekiel beheld. Outstanding Jewish thinkers in our day, like Jacob Klatzkin [18] and Ezekiel Kaufman,[19] have long pronounced the doom of Diaspora Judaism. It may well be said of them that "their chief activity is their despair." With apparently irresistible logic, which is borne out by the centrifugal tendencies in Jewish life, they dismiss as sheer folly the belief that it is possible for the Jewish people to survive anywhere except in a Jewish territory, where Jews constitute the majority.

The acquisition of some territory where Jewish life would not have to accommodate itself to other civilizations is admittedly no longer optional. Ever since that turning point in our career as a people which has fated us to integrate our lot with that of other nations, a Jewish land has become the *sine qua non* of the continuance of Jewish life. In the middle of the nineteenth century that truth dawned on the Jewish consciousness with the force of a divine revelation. Its impact is driving Jews back to Eretz Yisrael, and they are becoming ever more insistent that their historic and moral claim to Eretz Yisrael be recognized in deed as it has been in word. But the very assertion of that claim and the willingness to back it up with toil, sweat and tears pre-suppose a type of corporate consciousness that is not subject to the ordinary laws of nationhood, and that demands outlets for self-expression in addition to a national home.

What will become of the Jews in the Diaspora? Some look forward to the future of Jewish life in the Diaspora as a matter of course. Others are convinced that all Jewish life outside Eretz Yisrael is bound to disappear. The truth is that *the future of our people in the Diaspora is unpredictable.* Who can foretell whether our people will strive persistently and intensively enough to enable Jewish life to take root here and elsewhere? The trouble with most of us is that, when evaluating the present condition of Diaspora Judaism, we either minimize or exaggerate the forces of disintegration. Both of these tendencies lead to inaction, one because of blind faith, the other because of blind despair. The case of the modern Jew is largely analogous to that of the neurotic whose will is stymied by inner conflict. What Otto Rank [20] said of the neurotic, therefore, may be applied to the modern Jew: "Only insight into that which he is potentially . . . can form the foundation of a dynamic therapy."

If the Jewish people were *entirely* subject to the social laws which have operated in the case of other peoples, it would have disappeared long ago. Generally, when a people is uprooted from its native soil, it loses the feeling of historical identity. The Jews have proved the exception to that rule. They have exhibited an unparalleled capacity to live in dispersion, united by common historic consciousness, aims and ideals. They have nullified what seems to be an iron law in the life of peoples, that a people can survive only so long as it has a government, or state, of its own. Those who negate the possibility of Jewish survival outside of Eretz Yisrael assume that the Jewish people can no longer escape that law. Yet the only denominator that kept the Jewish people alive throughout the centuries, since the destruction of its Second Commonwealth, was its religion which was an effective substitute for the state, in that it was uniformly binding upon all Jews, and was mediated through authoritative leaders who were in a position to enforce sanctions. If that kind of religion is no longer conceivable as a cohesive force, then the Jewish people can survive only where it can once again exist as a commonwealth, and where the factors of propinquity come into play.

That reasoning is undoubtedly plausible. But both the situation in which Diaspora Jewry finds itself and the momentum of Jewish life render it inapplicable to the realities of our present day problem. First, the situation—from the standpoints of environment and the mass of Jewry—precludes writing off the five million American Jews. Secondly, *the supernormal ability displayed by Jews to reconstruct their social structure to fit the requirements imposed by new surroundings, and their capacity to reinterpret their ideals to conform to the needs accentuated by the new ideas and new problems, are such as to render possible the emergency of new ideological and social forces to keep the Jewish people alive in the Diaspora.*

Thrice in its career our people underwent complete reconstruction of its social structure and thought-pattern without suffering a break in its life-continuity. As we read the Biblical account of Israel's beginnings, the transition from the nomadic stage to the agricultural seems easy and natural. Yet a careful study of that transition reveals the unique power of reconstruction that marked our people from its very beginning. That nomadic tribes should take possession of an inhabited territory and become a nation was nothing unusual in ancient times. But for a nation not only to maintain a continuity with its early nomadic stage, but also to derive from that nomadic stage the initial impulse to its highest strivings, is contrary to all precedent.

The Jewish people did not act according to sociological specifications when its First Commonwealth was destroyed, its Temple burned down and its leading families were carried off to strange lands. While some Jews obeyed the natural urge to national liquidation, both Jeremiah [21] and Ezekiel taught their people in Babylon to maintain the continuity of Jewish life. They reinterpreted some deeply rooted ideas about national sin and responsibility; they indicated new opportunities and new tasks as a spur to national continuity. Ezekiel even drew up new plans for a reconstructed Jewish commonwealth.[22] And when the Second Commonwealth did finally emerge, the changed social structure of the Jewish people—with its inner life reorganized around the Torah of Moses—did not prevent it from knowing itself as the same people whose ancestors had been slaves in Egypt.

The Jewish people refused a second time to liquidate itself, when the Second Commonwealth was destroyed and all seemed lost. Rabban Johanan ben Zakkai and the Sages of Yabneh prevented the Jewish people from meeting the usual fate of dissolution. They evinced once again the Jewish capacity for national reconstruction. From being a nation with a central state, the Jews became a nationality with a common code of law and a common religio-cultural life.

About the same time the general world-outlook was being transformed into one which placed life's center of gravity in a supernatural hereafter. It was then that the entire religious outlook of the Jewish people took on one hue. Notwithstanding all those changes, Jews did not experience in the least the sense of having broken with the past. Jews in Persia, Spain, Italy, Germany and France were linked together by a common consciousness. Every Jew regarded himself as though he personally had gone forth from Egypt with Israel in the Exodus. Thus the twice repeated conversion of the urge to national suicide into a self-transformation and reconstruction, so as to be able to go on living, proves that our people was able to negotiate the dangerous whirlpool of sudden and rapid change in habitat and mode of life.

There is, of course, one important distinction between the task of reconstruction in days of old and that task in our day. Then it was carried out under the impact of a will that was identified as divine. It was not merely because Jeremiah, or Ezekiel, or R. Johanan ben Zakkai wanted the Jewish people to survive, that it was able to effect the needed reconstruction. Those great leaders and teachers were certain that God, who guided the destinies of nations, was using them as His instruments to rescue Israel from impending doom. This confidence gave them power to effect the miracle of national resurrection.

Nowadays, however, it would be presumptuous for any one person to treat as a divine imperative the call to arouse our people from its fatal lethargy, and to invoke the spirit to enter once again its lifeless body. Taken individually, we are too sophisticated and too self-critical to lay claim to experiencing any divine imperative. But a number of Jews, laboring under the same compelling urge to find for our people a way out of its present crisis, might well interpret that urge as a call from God. Alcuin's famous aphorism, "the voice of the people is the voice of God," has all too often proved to be false. Nevertheless, there are times when it is true, especially when the voice of the people is one that pleads for elementary justice and the right to live. What more than that is the plea for Jewish survival? Indeed the only kind of reconstruction which will set Israel again on the path of salvation will be that which will be felt as a high consecration and as a profound religious experience. It is, therefore, essential that those Jews who cannot make peace with the decadence of Judaism should not each sigh in solitariness.

There still are Jews who refuse to stifle their awareness of belonging to an ancient, ageless, never-dying people that has inscribed itself indelibly on the consciousness of mankind through a collection of writings known as the Bible. Those Jews wish to remain Jews and to bring up their children as Jews. They are the survivalists, the affirmative Jews. Despite all handicaps, they feel that to be Jews entitles them to a place in history, a place that confers meaning and solemnity upon their lives. They have a share in the mystery of the universe. Whatever be their theology, or lack of it, if that is the way they feel about being Jews, they should find one another and achieve that community of spirit which will beget the confidence and wisdom necessary to effect the needed reconstruction of Jewish life.

6

THE WISDOM TO BUILD FOR THE FUTURE

The very term *reconstruction* is associated with efforts of populations to resume life after some great cataclysm like an earthquake, war, revolution, famine or pestilence. The changes in the world that are responsible for the Jew's present crisis have been nothing less than cataclysmic. Realization of this fact in its full import would give the Jew an insight into the nature of his predicament and of the overwhelming factors that have transformed his self-confidence and defiance of a hostile world into self-questioning and self-contempt. Such insight is essential, if the Jew is to master the forces that threaten to destroy him, and if he is to use them for the rebuilding of his life.

So long as all the world lived by a philosophy that placed life's center of gravity in a supernatural hereafter, the Jew had every reason to believe that being a Jew was an enviable privilege, a guaranty of life eternal. He had no difficulty in meeting the challenge of either Christendom or Islam, each of which has tried in vain to prove that the Jews forfeited the means to salvation by stubbornly clinging to the Torah and refusing to recognize any subsequent revelation of God's will. The Church and Islam practically justified the Jew's loyalty to Judaism by the very fact of their persecuting his people.

All of this, however, became meaningless when men began to identify salvation with this-worldly self-fulfillment or realization, and to seek it in the opportunities for power, achievement, enjoyment or creativity offered in the natural life of the world. The inalienable right to life, liberty and the pursuit of happiness is the political form of the new conception of salvation, and the modern state arose with the avowed purpose of helping the citizen to attain it. During the first stages of this development, which took place in the century following the French Revolution, the Jews were led to believe that the millennium was at hand. There were new worlds to explore and to exploit, and those in control of the economic situation saw no special need for keeping out anyone who possessed the spirit of enterprise. This was sufficient to raise the hope of the Jews in Central and Western Europe that they would at last be integrated into the body politic.

When, however, in 1806, Napoleon I made it clear that to become part of the body politic, the Jewish people would have to surrender its international unity and become merely a religious sect, fragmented among the various nations to which its members belonged, the representative Jews of the time who composed the French Sanhedrin showed that they, too, had become thoroughly secularized. Allowing considerations of this-worldly salvation to sway them, they submitted to Napoleon's demand and set the standard for the Jewish Reform movement. If that process of integration had been permitted to go on unhampered, it would have led to the complete assimilation of Western Jewry.

About 1870, however, a new trend in European political life set in. Hunger for this-worldly salvation had been whetted. But the national states, which had led men to believe that they would find in them all that they needed to achieve salvation, were unable to keep their promise. The rich were growing richer and the poor less resigned to poverty. The masses were becoming restive. It became necessary to divert their attention from the true cause of their misery. Thus arose a new type of Jew-hatred known as anti-Semitism. Anti-Semitism has since tried to prevent the Jew from becoming so much like the non-Jew that he would be able to claim an equal share in the economy of the land. It has applied itself to the task of pushing Jews back into the ghetto and reducing them once more to the status of pariahs. So Jews have lost all taste for other-worldly salvation and have become avid of this-worldly salvation, with their chances of securing the latter far fewer than those of their non-Jew fellow citizens.

The outcome of the present crisis in Judaism depends, in the last analysis, upon the way the Jew will interpret this-worldly salvation. If it will mean to him personal success in achieving power and pleasure, he will see in anti-Semitism merely an obstacle to such complete identification with the non-Jewish majority as to enable him to join them on even terms in the scramble for success. He will even try to elude the scrutiny of the anti-Semites by changing his name and appearance, and to pass off as a Gentile. He may for a time think himself on the road to this-worldly salvation, only to be disillusioned sooner or later.

Although the traditional notion of this world as an antechamber to the world-to-come [23] is no longer tenable, the Jew should not hastily conclude that the only alternative is to eat, drink and make merry, or to join the reckless race for worldly success. There is a permanent truth in the other-worldly conception of salvation which mankind in general, and the Jew in particular, cannot afford to discard. That truth is that *we must not regard anything as a means of self-fulfillment unless it enables us to add our mite toward rendering this-worldly life more livable for the generations to come.*

This principle must color all of our strivings toward this-worldly salvation, if such salvation is to signify the attainment of virtue and well-being in community and not to degenerate into a sensualist's dream of endless self-indulgence, or into an overlord's complex of unlimited power. The handicap under which the Jew labors on account of anti-Semitism is not merely his own personal problem; it is part of the struggle of the Jewish people and of all minority groups for the right to live.

If we wish to know what, basically, has gone wrong with us Jews, we must resort to a realistic understanding of the revolution that has taken place in the entire world-outlook of mankind. But if we desire to know what is to set us right again, we must resort to the moral realism of the Prophets. They taught us to put faith in God and in the ultimate triumph of His will. We can do nothing better than to adopt that faith as the basis of what must constitute for us this-worldly salvation. This means that *there is no other moral choice for us Jews than to strive with all our might for the establishment of a just social order which will render democratic, benign nationalism safe for the creative survival of the Jewish people.*

To make this choice, however, we have to be fully convinced of the intrinsic value of Jewish survival. We have to see in Jewish life high creative possibilities. We have to find Judaism capable of eliciting the best that is in us. To meet this vital requirement, Judaism must come to possess the kind of social structure which will be organically related to the high purposes of a religious civilization. Moreover, it must have its entire ideology transposed into the key of thought which is relevant to the problems that agitate us today. We have to evaluate our inherited institutions, and, if we discover any elements in them that have become

obsolete or irrelevant, we should unhesitatingly deal with them as we
would with the withered branches of a tree.

The willing ability to reappraise from time to time our spiritual
heritage in terms of ever-increasing knowledge and experience must
henceforth become part of Jewish life. However, the sloughing off of
the old should be only incidental to the creation of the new. Whether
we shall have a future or not depends upon our capacity to elicit new
energy and to discover new resources.

The ultimate hope of American Jewry rests with those whose being
is rooted in Jewish life, and who cannot contemplate the disintegration
of Judaism without a deep sense of frustration. If they are to avert a
tragic anti-climax to the life of their people, they should seek out one
another and together discipline themselves into a community of mind
and heart, animated by the sole purpose of creative Jewish survival.
They should constitute themselves as a kind of religio-cultural fellowship or order, with chapters both within and without the existing organizations and institutions, simultaneously resisting any tendency to
become identified as an additional sect or denomination. In that way
they can act as a ferment within the inert and apathetic mass of our
people. They should seek to enlist, in the service of Jewish life, whatever
creative talent is to be found among us.

Upon Jews of this sensitive and spiritual type devolves the responsibility of preventing American Jewry from deteriorating into a meaningless human detritus, superfluous to itself and to the rest of the world.
They have the opportunity to make Judaism a beneficent influence in
American civilization, by becoming a potent factor for the advancement
of genuine democracy. Theirs is the obligation to function in our day
as part of Israel's faithful remnant; to aid in bringing about the much
needed psychic and moral reconstruction in our day, which the Prophet
Ezekiel [24] urged upon his contemporaries, when he pleaded:

"Make you a new heart and a new spirit, for why shall ye die, O
House of Israel?"

CHAPTER TWO

RECONSTRUCTION—A PROGRAM

1

THE NEED OF RECONSTRUCTION

When we accepted the citizenship of the countries in which we Jews live, we covenanted ourselves to become an integral part of the general population, and to assume the same civic responsibilities as our non-Jewish fellow citizens. Culturally and spiritually as well as politically, our aim is to be part and parcel of the non-Jewish life about us. We no longer have our own vernacular; we are no longer governed by Jewish law in secular matters; we are no longer educated in exclusively Jewish schools. *Yet we need not give up either our continuity with the Jewish past or our unity with the rest of contemporary Israel.* We can maintain both, provided we can devise a method of integrating them into our effort to live up to the highest ideals of citizenship.

Most of the methods that have been proposed consist of attempts to fit Judaism into the religious denominational pattern. A religious denomination is a group united by a common world-outlook and by a way of life which it regards as the most effective, if not the only, means to salvation, and which differentiates that group from all others. Since religion was the most conspicuous and significant element in the life of our people throughout the past, it is assumed to be the one element through which our twofold need for continuity and unity can best be satisfied. Since religious differences are tolerated in the modern state, it is believed that Jews can manage to survive as a religious denomination, even if, in other respects, they are no different from non-Jews.

But what exactly is the Jewish religion?

According to the original version of Reform Judaism, the Jewish religion consists of universal and eternal truths to be derived from our sacred writings. Those truths are not in the category of Jewish laws and distinctive cultural forms, which are purely national in character and, therefore, obsolete, now that Jews are either willing or expected to renounce their nationhood. Neo-Orthodoxy has reacted against Reform's abandonment of all that was distinctively Jewish. It has sought to conserve intact, under the aegis of religion, all of the traditional institutions, the customs, the rituals and the moral legislation of Judaism. But, in order to do so, it has had to adopt a religious dogmatism

34

and authoritarianism that can not reckon adequately with social and intellectual change. Conservatism has sought a compromise between Reform and Neo-Orthodoxy, but so far has succeeded neither in formulating a definitive ideology of its own nor in developing a specific code of observance.

In addition, many Jews find it difficult to subscribe to any of the religionist formulations of Judaism. None is compatible with their world-outlook. They contend that religion is no longer an essential element of Jewish life. In the interests of political freedom and equality, it has been found necessary to separate church and state, and to relegate religion to the individual conscience. The position taken by the Jewish secularists is that if Jews expect to find a place in the modern world, they, too, should remove the problem of religion from their public agenda. They would have the Jews reconstituted into a modern nation like every other nation.

How this secularist proposal can help the American Jew solve his inner problem is, indeed, difficult to see. As a matter of fact, it is only another way of saying that Jews cannot remain Jews, unless they are willing to resume life in a land of their own, on a basis similar to that of every other nation. If there were countries where the experiment of allowing a large measure of cultural and political autonomy could be tried again, it might be possible to have a secularist Jewish life. It is doubtful, however, whether such an experiment would be tried again, since the first one has proved to be unsuccessful. The secularist solution is thus not a solution. Rather is it a way of accepting the dissolution of Jewry in the Diaspora.

If we are to interweave our own historic way of life with the life which we must share with our neighbors, we have to rethink our beliefs, reorganize our institutions and develop new means of self-expression as Jews. Since our problem is to keep alive that which differentiates us Jews as a group from the rest of the world, it is of the utmost importance to have a definition that corresponds with fact. It is certainly not true to fact that religion, or a particular set of beliefs about God, with practices related to these beliefs, is all that distinguishes the Jews as a group from non-Jews. *If Judaism is to mean that which unites Jews into an identifiable and distinct group, then it is a religious civilization. As such, Judaism is the ensemble of the following organically interrelated elements of culture: a feeling of belonging to a historic and indivisible people, rootage in a common land, a continuing history, a living lan-*

guage and literature, and common mores, laws and arts, with religion as the integrating and soul-giving factor of all those elements.

The peoplehood, the culture and the religion of the Jews are one and inseparable. Their mutual relationship may be compared to that which exists among the three dimensions of physical body. They correspond to the three concepts referred to in the popular dictum: *Israel, the Torah and the Holy One, blessed be He, are one.*[1] In this statement, "Israel" represents peoplehood; "Torah," or Israel's way of life, represents culture; and "The Holy One" represents religion. The purpose in pronouncing them one is to stress the fact that none of the three terms can even be understood except in relation to the other two. Jewish religion, Jewish peoplehood and Jewish culture are all aspects of the same reality, and each is meaningless apart from its relation to the totality of Jewish life.

In the light of that conception of Judaism and of the contemporary inner and outer challenge to Jewish life, the problem we have on our hands reduces itself to the following questions:

In the first place, what has to be done, socially and culturally, to enable the present generation of Jews to feel its oneness with all the preceding generations of the Jewish people?

Secondly, how shall we reinterpret our tradition, so that it can be rendered compatible with a reasonable conception of naturalism and an ethical conception of nationalism?

Thirdly, how can we make room in Judaism for diversity of world outlook and religious practice, and have as the test of Jewish loyalty mainly the sincere desire to have Jewish life survive, grow and exert a salutary influence on human life in general?

The reconstruction of Jewish life and thought will thus have to consist in the pursuit of the following objectives:

1. The rebuilding of Eretz Yisrael as the creative center of Judaism.

2. The creation of an adequate social structure for democratic Jewish communal life in the Diaspora.

3. The redirection of Jewish education to conform with the conception of Judaism as a religious civilization.

4. The revitalization of Jewish religion.

5. The stimulation of Jewish cultural creativity in literature and the arts.

6. The participation of Jewry in social movements that seek ampler freedom, stricter justice and better cooperation among men and nations.

2

ERETZ YISRAEL

For the culture and religion of Judaism to survive and flourish anywhere in the Diaspora, they must have rootage in the life of a thriving Jewry in Eretz Yisrael. Under the most favorable circumstances, it is impossible for an ethnic minority to retain its civilization indefinitely, without continual replenishment from some self-sustaining fountain of cultural creativity. As we Jews are constituted today, with our widely divergent interests and beliefs, a Jewish Commonwealth in Eretz Yisrael has become indispensable to us, individually and as an indivisible people. What the Crown is to England, that Eretz Yisrael is to the Jewish people—a symbol both of continuity and unity.

What Eretz Yisrael has come to mean to us Jews can, perhaps, best be conveyed by a recent description of several hundred displaced Jews, huddled together on a rotting ship in the sweltering sun of Haifa Bay. They were seeking entrance into Eretz Yisrael. The reporter found "thin, ill, hollow-faced men and women from every trade and profession living in the most degraded and debased of human conditions." Nevertheless, the musicians and theatrical artists managed to give concerts and entertainments every night, so remarkable was the morale of those on board. When any one of them would be asked how they were able to withstand their trials, their answer always was, "But look we can already see Eretz Yisrael. We are only a half mile away." [2] The plight of those displaced Jews may be regarded as symbolic both of the situation in which the Jewish people as a whole finds itself today and of the extent to which it depends upon Eretz Yisrael for whatever morale it possesses.

If the life in Eretz Yisrael is to fulfill the highest aspirations of Jews everywhere, it must be built on foundations of social, political and economic justice. Eretz Yisrael must be protected from the exploitation which is a concomitant of a competitive economic system, and the *halutzim* (pioneers) must be encouraged in their efforts to base Jewish economy on cooperative labor.

Eretz Yisrael must again become the cultural and spiritual center of Jewry, which looks to it for the *renascence* not only of Hebrew language, literature and art, but also of Jewish religion and law. Jewish religion in Eretz Yisrael should be freed from the authoritarian control of the Orthodox rabbinate, and made responsive to the vital needs of an intellectually alert, democratic, and progressive modern community.

The development of Jewish legal institutions, which was arrested in the Diaspora from the time that Jewish communities lost their civic autonomy, will have to be resumed in Eretz Yisrael. Out of these institutions there will emerge a code of Jewish conduct and practice applicable, also, to life in the Diaspora.

3

JEWISH COMMUNITY ORGANIZATION IN THE DIASPORA

To enable Judaism to function as a civilization in the Diaspora, Jews will have to avail themselves of their democratic right to organize for the pursuit of their common interests. The religious divisions among Jews and the progressive loss of communal autonomy since the beginning of the nineteenth century have left Jewry without any organizational structure to reflect even the degree of community of interest that still unites it. No form of human life can be whole or healthy except in an environment that strives for wholeness. We often speak of a Jewish community, but what goes by that name is only a congeries of organizations and agencies, not one of which includes all Jews or represents all Jewish interests. Most Jews belong to some association that has a vestige of Jewish life. They belong to Jewish burial societies, if to no other. Their affiliation with any Jewish group is largely a matter of accident, and the particular function which that group performs often represents for its members all that there is to Judaism. The conception of Judaism as a religious civilization, however, demands that Jewish life be viewed *as a whole,* and that every partial expression of it be evaluated according to what it can contribute to the totality of Jewish life. That totality, on the other hand, must justify itself by its ability to enrich the life of every group and each individual within Jewry.

From this point of view, not all Jewish associations and institutions can be of equal importance. Most of them are important, and some are indispensable, to a wholesome Jewish life. Some are of relatively little value. Others, like Jewish partisan political clubs, are mischievous. Every Jew must, therefore, learn to evaluate these organizations in accordance with a definitely constructive philosophy of Jewish life, and affiliate with those that offer him the best opportunity for service to Judaism, in accordance with his own individual needs and opportunities.

The nearest approach at present to communal organization is the Jewish community council. These councils are as yet young and inexperienced, and have to overcome many handicaps, before they can function adequately as instruments of Jewish civilization. Nevertheless, they represent great potentialities for the reconstruction of Jewish life, and we should do all in our power to help them establish themselves and develop to the point, where they will be able to outgrow their present limitations.

As yet these councils are hampered by the evil effects of that very anarchy in Jewish life which they are making a valiant attempt to reduce. Their constituent organizations are still too suspicious of one another, and guard their own autonomy too jealously to delegate to the council the necessary authority for important activities. Moreover, they are too unacquainted with the vital needs of Jews and with the spiritual resources of the Jewish heritage to collaborate vigorously and effectively in those communal activities which would make the individual Jew feel that it is worth his while to be a Jew and a member of a Jewish community. It is, therefore, incumbent upon those who have the future of Judaism at heart to guide the Jewish institutions with which they are affiliated in ways that will make those institutions more intelligently cooperative for the enrichment of Jewish life. The principle to be persistently championed is: *Maximum collaboration among different organizations for the purposes that they have in common, without imposing restrictions on purposes that they do not share.*

On the basis of this principle, community councils, representing every legitimate Jewish group in a given locality, can be organized and operated to advantage. They can conduct or direct all activities on the value of which there is a general consensus among constituent organizations. It should also be the function of the community council to facilitate collaboration among those of its constituent bodies that have interests or functions in common. Thus, all congregations with similar ideologies, whether Orthodox, Conservative, or Reform, should be urged not merely to be formally associated but to consolidate and promote their common interests.

Similarly other functional groups—educational, cultural, recreational and philanthropic—should be encouraged to cooperate with one another in every way possible. This deliberate stressing of *common* rather than *competing* interests, combined with respect for differences of point of view, has the inevitable effect of strengthening the Jewish corporate spirit. It can in time overcome the prejudices, institutional rivalry and contentiousness that at present deter our so-called Jewish communities from serving the purpose of a true community. That purpose is to make the collective experience of the group and its accumulated cultural resources contribute to the self-fulfillment of every one of its members.

Causes like Zionism, the protection of Jewish rights, the care of refugees, overseas relief, and the promotion of Jewish research and higher education demand organization on a nationwide scale. But such organizations must no longer be permitted to work independently of one another, and at cross purposes with the various local institutions. They must be united in a body consisting of democratically elected representatives of two kinds of organization—(1) of local Jewish community council, and (2) of national organizations representing intercommunal causes.

Such an organization of Jewry would give it, for the first time since the abolition of the ghetto and the autonomous Jewish *kehillot*,³ a structural form that would enable Judaism to function vigorously as a religious civilization. It would make adherence to Judaism mean participation in a collective effort to achieve economic security, political freedom, physical health, cultural self-expression, ethical character, religious orientation—all of which contribute to human self-fulfillment.

4

JEWISH EDUCATION

Important as is this task of reorganization, it is not enough. Structure is not life. A living organism is more than an organization. It has an awareness of self; it has needs and desires, memories and anticipations; it recognizes values. Civilizations perpetuate themselves by transmitting to each generation their acquired culture and ideals, in ways that inspire in the individual the sentiments of loyalty and self-identification with the collective personality of the group. This process is what we mean by education. *To conceive of Judaism as the civilization of the Jewish people involves the recognition of Jewish education as both a personal and a communal function of paramount importance.*

Education, in this sense, is not only the conscious effort of the group to equip each succeeding generation with the requisite knowledge, and to imbue it with the requisite loyalty to carry on the civilization on which the group depends for its survival. It, also, includes all those unconscious influences making for loyalty which come from the whole visible and tangible environment created by the group. Long before the child's schooling begins, he is subject to these environmental influences in the home; and long after he may have severed his connection with all efforts of the community to provide formal education for him, he is still subject to the influence of the cultural milieu in which he finds himself.

One of the major difficulties of preserving Judaism in the Diaspora arises from the fact that it is difficult for Jews as a minority group to create, in the environment in which they spend the greater part of their working day, visible tokens of Jewish civilization. But this difficulty can in large measure be compensated for, if the home environment is made Jewishly educative. The home environment is under our control, and the technique of utilizing it for the preservation and enhancement of Jewish life is one that has been admirably developed in Jewish tradition.

The influence of the home environment on the entire personality is out of all proportion to the amount of time spent in it. For in the home, the struggle of power between individuals is minimal, and the communion of love and mutual helpfulness maximal. In the home, therefore, we are susceptible to influences that demand the subordination of selfish, individualistic interests to the higher values of civilization. That is why our tradition has invested the home with the symbols of Jewish religion that proclaim the personal and social values experienced by the Jewish people: the *mezuzah*,[4] the Sabbath candles, the Hanukkah *menorah*,[5] the *kiddush*[6] cup, and other ceremonial objects. These give at once a distinctive character to the home, which makes its occupants aware that they are Jews. Such sacred objects associate Judaism with the holiness or supreme worth of life.

The same is true of religious observance in the home: the observance of Sabbaths and festive days, the religious celebration of events in personal life—*Berit Milah*,[7] *Bar Mitzvah*[8] and *Bat Mitzvah*,[9] the dedication of a home, the rites associated with mourning. New religious rites for significant events not provided for by tradition, such as marriage anniversaries, the naming of a daughter, and similar occasions, might well be added, for we should never look upon traditional ritual as final and complete. Conformity with Jewish dietary regulations may well be included among the influences making for a visible Jewish environment in the home. Such regulations possess value as religious folkways which express the desire of our people to sanctify life, by associating every detail of their daily regimen, down to the preparation of the food we eat, with the idea of serving God.

But ritual easily lapses into perfunctory formalism. The Judaism of the home cannot, therefore, be adequately expressed, if limited to traditional and ritualistic forms. There are needed other visible tokens of Judaism associated with the creative aspects, particularly of modern Jewish life. Bookshelves should contain Jewish books, and magazine racks, Jewish periodicals. Jewish pictures should grace the walls, and Jewish art objects adorn the rooms. Jewish music should resound from whatever musical instruments are used, and Jewish songs should be sung in the home on every appropriate occasion.

In these ways, as well as by the precept and example of parents, *the Jewish home should serve as the primary educational instrument for preserving Jewish civilization.* It will protect Judaism not merely against influences that are destructive of social values generally, but no less against the disintegrating tendencies to which all minority cultures are exposed. In conceiving the home not merely as a means of perpetuating the physical life of the people, but of perpetuating and enriching its spiritual culture, it becomes an influence for the sanctity of family ties, the purity and stability of marriage, parental responsibility and filial loyalty. A Jewish home that does not function in this way is not only not Jewish; it is not a home.

Thus Jewish education, like charity, begins at home; but it must not end there. *If the role of the Jewish community is to help every Jew attain self-fulfillment, it can do so only by providing for him at every stage of his development the knowledge and insight he may need to solve the major problems that confront him as a Jew in his personal life.* For this the home is not enough. Nor can we depend on the influences of environment without specific direction and guidance.

Every civilization has found it necessary to perpetuate its culture through the medium of the school. Particularly is this true of Judaism which has made of *talmud torah,* the study of our sacred literature, a religious obligation. That obligation it conceived not as limited to childhood, but as in force throughout life. The ideal of *talmud torah* has broken down in our day and must be reinstated. We cannot permit Jewish knowledge to become a specialty intended only for rabbis and professional scholars. We cannot tolerate a condition in which Jews can confess, without shame, ignorance of the most elementary facts about our Jewish heritage. We cannot submit to a condition in which the crassest ignorance of Jewish values is no bar even to Jewish communal leadership. It is there particularly that Goethe's saying applies: "Nothing is more dangerous than *active* ignorance."

A way should be found to make it a matter of conscience for every Jew to devote some portion of his time to self-education in Torah, and to seek for his children the best Jewish education available. But education in Torah must be conceived in more comprehensive terms than it was conceived in the past. Torah must be understood to mean any branch or product of Jewish culture, from the dawn of Jewish history to the works of contemporary writers and artists. No Jew who values Judaism can be exempt from the pursuit of *talmud torah*. As long as he identifies himself as a Jew, he has the opportunity and the obligation of deepening his understanding of Judaism and his penetration into its values and needs. This is no child's play. Hence *Jewish education must be primarily adult education.* Only adult Jews who are educated in Judaism are capable of educating children in Judaism whether through the school or the home.

Where Jewish education can employ the medium of the Hebrew language it should do so. There is no more potent influence for self-identification with a people than the use of its language. Those adults who have acquired a knowledge of the Hebrew language, or are in a position to acquire it, should make it a point to read Hebrew books and periodicals. Hebrew literature is today rich enough in all branches of culture to afford intellectual and esthetic pleasure, as well as religious edification, to any cultured Jew.

But ignorance of Hebrew need not today, as it did once, prove a complete bar to the study of Torah, as we have defined it. An extensive Jewish literature exists in the English language. In addition to works by Jews and on Jewish themes written originally in English, there are English translations of almost all of the great Jewish classics—the Bible, the Talmud, the Midrashim and post-Rabbinic writings. The reading and studying of this literature can usually be pursued to best advantage in association with others equally interested. Study groups facilitate discussion and a creative exchange of ideas and experiences.

While it is necessary to stress the duty of every Jew to educate himself and his children in Judaism, the individual by himself cannot accomplish much in this direction, without the cooperative ability of an organized Jewish community. Even separate institutions, such as synagogues, schools, community centers and other organizations, can accomplish little when working by themselves. Particularly in the education of the child, tasks of supervision, teachers' training, text-book preparation, and many other directive and administrative tasks demand that Jewish education be thought of as a community project. With due regard to the ideological differences among existing Jewish groups, these must not be permitted to interfere with collaboration in all those aspects of the educational process in which they are not involved. Jewish schools of each community should collaborate through a central bureau to the maximum extent that is consistent with the purposes and principles of the several institutions.

The insistence that Jewish education be regarded not merely as a personal but as a communal responsibility arises not only from considerations of efficiency and expediency. It is based on the inherent relationship of education to communal life. Education is the process by which the Jewish community preserves its identity and achieves the purpose of its existence, which is, to have the collective experience of the group enrich the personality of the individual. *Where Jewish education is neglected, the whole content of Judaism is reduced merely to an awareness of anti-Semitism. Judaism ceases then to be a civilization, and becomes a complex.*

Though we should seek the maximum of communal responsibility for Jewish education and urge the organized collaboration of all Jewish educational agencies, we cannot attach equal value to all their different endeavors. We should guide the efforts of Jewish educational institutions of the adoption of programs that are consistent with the conception of Judaism as a religious civilization, the civilization of the Jewish people. We should utilize the Jewish cultural tradition for helping the individual Jew to live happily as a Jew, and to contribute to the welfare of the Jewish and American communities and of mankind in general. The content of such an education will inevitably include the Hebrew language, Jewish history, Jewish literature, Jewish current events, Jewish music, and Jewish art. Above all, it must stress that aspect of Jewish civilization which expressed the Jew's conception of his place in the world, his relation to the Jewish people and its relation to the rest of humanity. In short, education in Jewish religion is to be not merely instruction in beliefs and ritual practices. Its aim is to develop a sincere faith in the holiness of life and a sense of responsibility for enabling the Jewish people to make its contribution to the achievement of the good life.

5

JEWISH RELIGION

The traditional version of Jewish religion is adequate only for the rapidly dwindling number of traditionally minded Jews. Almost all Jews who have come under the influence of the modern world-outlook find that version of Jewish religion not only unrelated to the needs of contemporary life, but incapable of being fitted into the thought patterns of a modern minded person.

Hitherto, Jews, both among the rabbinate and among the laity, confronted with the challenge of historical science and philosophic outlook, have managed to work out for themselves some kind of reinterpretation, whereby they transpose the traditional religious values into the modern idiom. But there is a wide gap, in all that pertains to Jewish religion, between the thinking of our scholars and men of learning and the actual information imparted in the classroom and the pulpit. That gap must be bridged.

The need for reconstructing the religious phase of Jewish life arises from the effect which the growing knowledge of the part played by religion in the life of mankind has had on the traditional ideas concerning the origin and function of religion. As a consequence of the historical and comparative approach to all cultural phenomena, which is part of modern naturalism, religion can no longer be regarded either as a supernatural revelation vouchsafed to an individual or a people, or as a philosophical doctrine in the mind of an individual, and by him communicated to his fellows. How we are to view religion will be discussed at length in the second part of the book. Among the conclusions there arrived at is the one that religion is the product of a people's life, the soul of its civilization. It is not merely a parenthesis; life can *not* be spiritually, or in any other way, complete without it. It is the effort to discover what makes life worthwhile, and to bring living into conformity with those laws on which the achievement of a worthwhile life depends.

Faith in God means faith that there is an unfailing Power at work in the universe. In the striving for self-fulfillment, man can count on that Power to aid him, provided he conforms with the conditions, inherent in the nature of the universe. Those conditions are conceived variously, in accordance with the particular stage of cultural development. Since all civilizations depend on the willingness of their adherents to cooperate in the pursuit of ends considered to be life-enhancing, they cannot dispense with religion. Even when they avow atheism, their atheism rests on certain unproved assumptions which they consider contributory to self-fulfillment of the group. The loyalty that they expect is essentially a religious loyalty, although they will not admit it, for it assumes the inherent and supreme value, or holiness, of their own civilization.

The religious element in a people's civilization is objectified in those institutions, places, historic events, popular heroes and all other objects of popular reverence to which superlative importance, or sanctity, is ascribed. *These sancta, the attitude toward life that they imply and the specific observances that they inspire, together constitute the religion of a people.* In Jewish civilization, such *sancta* are, among others, the Torah, the synagogue, Sabbaths and holy days, the Hebrew language, Moses and the Patriarchs, the Prophets, the Sages. American civilization also has its *sancta:* Washington and Lincoln, the Constitution, the Declaration of Independence, Thanksgiving Day, the Fourth of July and other national holidays, the Stars and Stripes. They, and what they imply, represent American religion. The American Jew sees no contradiction in reverencing both constellations of *sancta*. No civilization can exist without *sancta*, without a religion; and no religion can originate or continue to operate, except as an element of a people's civilization.

Since, then, every civilization has religious *sancta*, what do we mean when we speak of Judaism as a religious civilization? We affirm the truth that the Jewish people, under the leadership of its Lawgivers, Prophets and Sages, considered the chief function of its collective life to be the fostering of its *sancta*. It sought *consciously* to make its collective experience yield meaning for the enrichment of the life of the individual Jew. That is how the entire life of the Jew came, in time, to be invested with *mitzvot* (divine commands), designed to impress on him the moral and spiritual values which had emerged from the process of Jewish living. The *berakot* (benedictions), which precede the performance of these *mitzvot*, imply that those *mitzvot* are intended to sanctify, that is to confer worth on, Jewish life.

Without this religious emphasis, it is inconceivable that Judaism could have survived in the Diaspora until the present time, or that it will survive in the future. When a people lives on its own soil, its civilization perpetuates itself with a minimum of conscious purpose. Not being challenged by any competing civilization, its adherents take its *sancta* for granted, and think of them only occasionally, while they devote most of their energies to the pursuit of secular, individualistic and materialistic interests. But when our people was exiled and its state destroyed, the only way in which Judaism could survive at all was by stressing its *sancta*, and emphasizing their value for the individual as well as for the group.

This was true during the Middle Ages, when Jewish communities were autonomous and Jews were excluded from Gentile society. It is even more obviously true in our day when, in democratic countries, Jews live simultaneously in two civilizations.* Under such conditions, Jews have no motive for retaining a connection with the Jewish people, unless they derive from that connection values which they cannot find elsewhere. Moreover, these values must be relevant not only to life in an exclusively Jewish environment, but to life in the two civilizations in which the Jew lives. Now, *of all Jewish values, the most universal are those that make the Jew feel he has a place in human society, and that help him to understand what he must do to fulfill his destiny as an individual, as a Jew and as a member of the human race.* Those are the religious values of Judaism. Without them, the Jew is uprooted, socially impotent and unhappy; he becomes a drifter.

But these values cannot be realized if we abstract Jewish religion from the rest of Jewish civilization, and treat it as if it consisted merely in a particular conception of God, one that differs from the conception held by other religions. The difference between Jewish religion and all others does not consist so much in the uniqueness of its conception of God, as in the uniqueness of its *sancta*. Loyalty to Judaism need, therefore, involve no pretensions to religious superiority. Jewish religion differs from the other religions not in being *unlike* them, for they too, have *sancta* that help them to salvation or self-fulfillment, but in being *other*, in having *sancta* that are the products of Jewish historic experience and not of the historic experience of other branches of human society. *We are faithful to Jewish religion, not because we have chosen it as the best of all religions, but because it is ours, the only religion we have, an inseparable part of our collective personality as a people. If some of us find that religion unacceptable in the form in which it has come down from the past, there is nothing but inertia to stop us from making it acceptable.*

Jewish religion can have no meaning apart from the Jewish people and the totality of its spiritual heritage. We ought not therefore speak of *Jewish religion* and *Judaism* as if they were synonymous terms. *Judaism* refers to the whole of Jewish civilization, just as *Hellenism* refers to the whole of *Hellenic* civilization and *Americanism* to the whole of *American* civilization. *Jewish religion,* on the other hand, signifies those beliefs and practices centering in the idea of God, with which the Jewish people assesses the values of its civilization, and seeks to implement them. It thus interpenetrates all elements of Jewish civiliza-

* See below p. 94 ff.

tion or Judaism, as a man's personal ideal affects all of his conscious behavior. That does not mean that religion accounts for the full significance of those elements, or that they are to be derived from it alone.

Jewish religion is that aspect of Jewish civilization which gives it purpose, direction and a definite orientation to the life of nature and of mankind. To this end, Jewish religion utilizes all the other aspects of Jewish civilization, which constitute, so to speak, the bodily organs of Judaism. These must include: (a) the heritage of Jewish tradition, (b) contemporary efforts to insure Jewish survival, such as the upbuilding of Eretz Yisrael and the organization of Jewry on a local, national and international scale, and (c) all Jewish cultural interests, including Hebrew and Yiddish languages and literature, folk ways, ethical standards and esthetic forms. Apart from this body of Jewish civilization, Jewish religion cannot function. Apart from Jewish religion, these various perceptible functions of Judaism would lack coordination and wholesome direction; Jewish life would become increasingly morbid and frustrated, lacking in self-assurance, steadfast purpose and that inner peace which comes from whole-souled dedication to a worthwhile cause.

In the light of this analysis of the place of religion in Judaism, the indifference to religion on the part of so many modern Jews becomes understandable. In part, that indifference is due to the fact that Jewish religion is identified in the minds of most Jews with a particular traditional doctrine to which they find it intellectually impossible to subscribe, rather than with the whole process by which a living civilization evolves its *sancta*. In part, it is due to that social disorganization to which attention was called when community organization was discussed. Religion is a function of community life; therefore, it thrives or languishes equally with all other aspects of Jewish civilization, in proportion as that life is vigorous or feeble.

This gives us a clue to what can and should be done to revitalize Jewish religion. In the first place, it has to be emancipated from bondage to dogmatism. This bondage inheres in the fear that any departure from the specific doctrines that were taught as religion in the past undermines religion itself. But this fear is seen to be groundless when we regard Jewish religion as a function of Jewish civilization. A living civilization is, of necessity, a changing civilization, but in changing itself it does not lose its identity any more than does an individual in passing from childhood to maturity. The same principle applies to the religious aspect of a civilization.

To make revitalization possible, the *sancta* of religion must be reinterpreted in each generation so that their meanings are relevant to the needs of that generation. *Tradition must not be a source of authority*, imposing restrictions on the creativity of later generations, *but a source of wisdom and morale awakening new creative powers.* When *sancta* have become meaningless, they cease, in the nature of the case, to be *sancta*. But this need not trouble us so long as a people lives and creates, for then it produces new *sancta*. To keep religion vital, religious thought must be free. It is a sad commentary on the present intellectual level of religious thought that the *free thinker* continues to be identified in the popular mind with an atheist. Voltaire describes two Athenians conversing about Socrates, and one saying to the other; "That is the atheist who says there is only one God."

Freedom of religious thought will, of course, emancipate religion from all association with magic and supernaturalism. *Jewish religion should discountenance the use of ritual for the purpose of influencing the course of events in other ways than by its influence on the mind and heart of the worshiper.* Nor should any ritual that is morally or esthetically offensive be retained merely because, in an earlier stage of Israel's culture, it was legally enjoined. We should frankly accept the conclusion to which all modern and enlightened people have come, that the realm of law—that is, of standardized behavior enforced by social penalties—must not extend to matters of ritual.*

Stated affirmatively, Jewish worship should be directed to influencing the worshipers to bring their lives into harmony with God as the Power that creates and determines the conditions by which man in general, and the Jewish people in particular, can achieve an abundant and harmonious life. All that is not intellectually and emotionally attuned to this purpose should be eliminated. But that is not enough. We must encourage the writing of new devotional literature, prayers, meditations, and hymns that express the religious experiences of our generation. Traditional forms should be retained, wherever these have something of positive value to contribute to the services, but they should be supplemented by additional material relevant to the interests, needs, problems and ideals of our day.

What has been said of worship is no less true of every other religious activity of the synagogue and the home. In all the emphasis should be on universal values. The distinctiveness of Jewish religion must not appear in any difference of aim between it and other ethical religions.

* See below, p. 394.

That distinctiveness must consist solely in the fact that Jewish religion assumes special responsibility for the Jewish sector of the front in the battle against evil and, accordingly, uses the resources which are available in Jewish tradition for the discharge of its responsibility.

The foregoing views on Jewish religion are not set forth with the expectation that all Jews would subscribe to them. They are intended mainly for those Jews who do not find the prevailing versions of Jewish religion acceptable. This raises the question of how to deal with the multiplicity of conflicting ideas in the matter of religion. The diversity of religious belief and practice which prevails among us is usually treated as if it were a calamity, or at best a necessary evil to which we must resign ourselves. And yet no modern, democratic civilization, which insists on freedom of conscience, is conceivable without diversity in men's attitude toward religion. *If Judaism is henceforth to be based on the principle of democracy, it should accept religious diversity as a normal expression of human life.*

To be sure, our people will have to undergo considerable re-education in their ideas about religion, if they are to understand how it is possible for several versions of Jewish religion to coexist within the frame of Jewish civilization. We shall have to live with the fact that the kind of religious approach that appeals to the rational type of mind does not appeal to the romantic type of mind, and vice versa. Temperament, cultural background and other factors condition our personal choices. Therefore, we cannot expect all Jews to think alike in their religion. We should respect convictions honestly held and sincerely lived up to. We dare not suppress the free expression of religious beliefs or doubts, or segregate ourselves from those who differ from us in matters of religion. *The recognition of the right to be different is compatible with unity; it removes factional rancor and makes possible cooperation for common purposes.* Such cooperation in turn widens and deepens the area of like-mindedness, and prevents religious diversity from developing into conflict or schism.

6

CULTURAL CREATIVITY

Emphasis on religion should not be interpreted as minimizing the importance of the so-called secular aspects of Jewish culture. Whatever enriches Jewish life can only help to re-enforce Jewish religion. Among the activities that enrich Jewish life, the arts must occupy an important place. Even in the ghetto, art was never completely lacking, although the scope of artistic expression was limited; the arts did not receive the attention that a modern civilization would accord them. In the reconstruction of Jewish life, we should make up this defect. We cannot afford to have the individual Jew find *all* his esthetic experiences outside the sphere of Jewish civilization. It was precisely the frustration of their esthetic interests by the limitation of their Jewish environment that led Heinrich Heine and many of his generation to abandon Judaism altogether. That situation must not be repeated.

It need not be. As long as Jews react emotionally to the conditions of their life as Jews, there exist the potentialities of a Jewish art, since art arises from the effort to make emotional experience permanently significant. This is true whether the medium be literature, music, drama, the dance, or any of the graphic or plastic arts. Jewish art can express the experiences of Jewish life in a way that lifts that life above the commonplace, the sordid and the drab. The magic of the arts can renew the radiance of Jewish life.

What consciousness is to an individual, culture is to a people. A people's culture finds expression in history, literature and art. The only way in which a member of a people can share its collective consciousness is by learning its history, reading its literature and fostering its art. The Jewish people has possessed all these means ever since it became aware of itself as a people. But though it possessed them to an intense degree, the range was limited. The last century-and-a-half has witnessed a remarkable widening of the range of Jewish culture. This began with the writing of Jewish history in the modern spirit. Although much progress has been made in historical scholarship, little has been made in translating that scholarship into youth and adult education. The same is true of literature. During the last century-and-a-half there has been a vast output of literature, modern in form and content, which reflects the spirit of the Jewish people, and which can take its place alongside the best in other national cultures. This literature is written mainly in Hebrew and Yiddish, but much of it also in the dominant languages of the Occident. Once again what is needed is to select and organize from that vast wealth enough to constitute a cluster of Jewish literary values as part of modern culture.

As for the arts, we are only at the very beginning in the process of creating a modern Jewish art. We have highly talented Jews in all the fields of art, in music, drama, dance, painting, sculpture and architecture, but most of our people still lack the understanding that, unless all these arts begin to function in Jewish life, there can be no Jewish life in the Diaspora. If Jews are to continue living as Jews despite anti-Semitism, it is imperative to have Judaism spell deep joy for the harassed millions of our people in Western lands. That joy can be derived from nothing so much as from the flowering of the creative arts. These are the means of conveying the wide range of emotions that seethe in the hearts of Jews.

We should, therefore, be interested in giving an artistic form to every aspect of Jewish life. Jewish worship should be esthetically developed; its symbols, rites and music made beautiful and stirring. It should be elaborated with a view to making it not merely sensuously pleasing, but appropriately expressive of the religious values it is designed to impress on us.

The architecture of synagogues, school buildings, and other Jewish institutions should not merely express good taste according to accepted standards and conventional canons; it should express the meaning and purpose of these institutions and the spiritual motives, in response to which they have come into being. If Jewish artists were commissioned to solve some of these artistic problems arising out of Jewish communal life, we should soon have the beginnings of a Jewish art in America, and Jewish artists would find scope for their talents within, as well as without, the area of Jewish life.

A conscious effort should be made to encourage appreciation of Jewish art in Jewish schools, community centers, youth organizations and cultural groups of all kinds. The development of Jewish art is frequently inhibited by an awareness of its present stunted condition. Institutions hesitate to exhibit Jewish art because they do not feel that it can compete favorably with the art of other groups which have a long artistic tradition behind them. They sometimes profess fear that in stressing Jewish art, the artistic taste of Jews would be fed on inferior products. This fear is groundless; Jews are not limited to the enjoyment of Jewish art only. If it is true that Jewish art is at present inferior, this should constitute a challenge not only to the Jewish artists, but also to the Jewish public to stimulate Jewish artistic creativity. Not every painter can be a Raphael or a Rembrandt; but when many lovers of beauty apply themselves to painting and are encouraged by having their works exhibited and critically evaluated, the chances of producing a Raphael or a Rembrandt are enhanced.

A considerable quantity of significant Jewish art has been produced of which even the Jewish public, with sadly few exceptions, knows nothing. This must be brought to its attention. Moreover, the failure to appreciate a work of Jewish art does not always result from its lack of artistic merit. As often as not, it results from the public's unfamiliarity with the Jewish values that the artist is trying to express. No valid art criticism is possible without an understanding of what it is the artist is trying to communicate through his art. If the patrons and directors of Jewish institutions were more imbued with Jewish culture, they would often see merit in Jewish artistic products that now leave them unmoved. The development, for example, of Jewish music in Palestine is proceeding apace, yet a noted writer there has occasion to complain that so little of this flowering of Jewish music is known in America.[10] It is heartening, indeed, to learn that a change for the better is beginning to be noted in the field of Jewish music. "Jewish music," we are told in a critical survey of recent achievements in that field, "has come to play an increasingly important role in our institutional life. Under the impact of the tragic world events, creative artists who were formerly indifferent to their ethnic roots have revealed a more positive acceptance of their Jewishness, and have grown more aware of the need for a spiritual self-identification with the Jewish cultural tradition." [11]

7

ETHICS

Conscious community interest in the promotion of art is something new in Jewish life; not so, Jewish concern for the improvement of human relations. From time immemorial this has been a major interest of Jewish civilization. The conception of the fatherhood of God, which plays so important a part in Jewish religion, was based on the Jewish perception of the essential brotherhood of man, on the insight that a community of interest binds together the entire human race, and that this community of interest must transcend all differences.

The realization of the ideal unity of the human race cannot be effected by imposing one uniform standard of conduct upon all men. Implied in the concept of brotherhood is the sort of unity that prevails among brothers in a happy family in which all members help one another to achieve, each his own purposes. It is unity of cooperation made possible by mutual understanding and sympathy. That is the social ideal of Judaism, its vision of the Kingdom of God, after which it would pattern human society.

This means that Judaism must strive for the establishment of a social order that satisfies simultaneously two contradictory requirements: the maximum of human cooperation and the maximum of personal liberty. The two most imperious impulses in the human being, sex and power, are not to be suppressed or denied, but humanized and spiritualized. The task of ethics is to get men and women to be self-commanding. To this end, *Judaism must seek an equitable distribution not merely of the material goods needed for human living, but also of responsibility and power in the control of human affairs.* Jews must learn to defy the blackmail of anti-Semitic reactionaries and have the courage to commit themselves to social idealism. *In its religion and its ethics, Judaism dare not content itself with easy edification; it must engage in daring moral adventure.*

All Jewish institutions, and particularly Jewish religious institutions, must endeavor to sensitize the Jew to those social evils that impede the realization of a better world. They should render him allergic to violence, corruption, exploitation of every kind. True, none of these evils affects Jews exclusively, and none can be remedied by the exclusive action of Jews. Nevertheless, Jews have special reason for dedicating themselves to the elimination of these evils. Wherever there is social injustice or international, interreligious, interracial or interclass conflict, the distribution of the Jews as a small minority among a large Gentile population jeopardizes their safety. Unlike powerful nations that live in compact masses on their own land and exercise political sovereignty over it, dispersed Jewry cannot possibly find security so long as inhumanity is anywhere in power. *Only when a just social order prevails throughout the world, can the Jewish people find peace, and Jewish civilization thrive.*

The Jewish community in the modern world cannot, therefore, content itself with merely trying to govern justly the relations between Jews and their fellow-Jews, as it was able to do when Jews were segregated in ghettos. The Jewish community in our day should organize the participation of Jews, in cooperation with other communities, in the struggle against poverty, disease, ignorance, oppression and war.

But to qualify for participation in this struggle, Jewry must set its own house in order. *The Jewish community is not free from the evils that beset society in general, and must accept full responsibility for carrying on the fight against them on its own sector of humanity's front.*

The fact that these evils are not limited to us Jews does not exempt us from this responsibility. If conditions of urban life are corrupting the purity and stability of the Jewish home, it is small comfort that the homes of others are similarly affected. We must take measures to remedy the situation. If crime and vice exist among Jews, we must combat them, and not console ourselves with statistics to show that the incidence of such crime and vice is less among Jews than among others. If corrupt Jewish politicians prostitute the synagogue and other Jewish communal agencies to serve their personal ambitions, we must eliminate the abuse, and not apologize for it by blaming it on general political conditions. If money can buy positions of leadership in the Jewish community and interfere with the freedom of the pulpit, the freedom of Jewish education and the freedom of the Jewish masses to advance their interests and welfare as they see fit, then the Jewish community must shoulder the blame, until it has abolished these evils.

At present, we Jews are content to abide by the ethical standard of the majority population. What that standard is has recently been stated in one of America's most serious periodicals: "By the time people have reached fifty, they have fallen into two groups—the great group that hasn't made as much money as it hoped and is bitter about it, and the smaller group that has been financially successful and whose members can't understand why they are unhappy at home, or fight with their business partners, or have no conversation except damning all reformers. All that both groups really ask for is a modicum of good food, enough liquor and tobacco, a sports interest, and a reasonable amount of fornication." [12] None of the higher interests of human life, religion, patriotism, social justice, or international peace is ever given more than lip service. All of them are swept away by the periodic manias for reckless spending and money-making that grip the land.

If we wish to foster Jewish group solidarity, we must live up to a higher ethical standard than the average. No other justification for our remaining an identifiable minority will avail. We have, of course, the great moral axioms like the Ten Commandments, the ethical teachings of the Holiness Code, the inspired admonitions of the Prophets and moral maxims of the Sages. These are trumpet calls to the good life. But what today constitutes the good life must be set forth as specific guidance in the vast maze of conflicting interests and duties and loyalties. Even more important, however, than a series of Jewish ethical codes for the manifold of complex situations would it be to have the Jewish social agencies function as instruments of a wholesome moral atmosphere and public opinion which would banish moral turpitude from Jewish life. By these and other means must we Jews demonstrate that to us religion which takes refuge in "ideals" and fails to make action square with aspiration is not only humbug but sacrilege.

We should do our utmost to keep bright the honor of the Jewish community. We should in all institutions with which we are affiliated protest against any attempt to confer positions of responsibility and dignity upon disreputable men. Lavish gifts for communal purposes must not be regarded as justifying the appointment of the donors to positions of importance, unless they are morally, intellectually and Jewishly qualified for them. Rather should such gifts by unworthy persons be regarded as "the hire of prostitution" which must not be brought into the House of the Lord.

All this implies the development of public sentiment in behalf of moral responsibility and of high ethical standards in all Jewish communal activities and relationships. We should interest ourselves in establishing decent standards for employees of Jewish institutions and decent standards of security in the tenure of their positions. We should insist on scrupulous adherence on the part of institutions to oral and written agreements. Disputes and conflicts of interests between persons and between individuals and the community should be settled by fair methods of adjudication or arbitration, conducted by Jewish communal agencies, rather than by the courts. That would save the good name of Jewry from being tarnished by the reputation that we are a litigious people.

We must endeavor to ban unfair methods of competition between rival institutions and between rival candidates for positions in the service of Jewish communal agencies, religious, educational and philanthropic. We should not be deterred from exposing evil conditions in Jewish life by fear of scandal, when the evils cannot be removed without exposure. It is important to avoid the defamation of Jewry, but it is even more important to prevent *hillul hashem*, the desecration of the name of God, which results from the cynical disregard of ethical values and from condoning social corruption.

Only a Judaism calculated to bring out all that is best in human nature, and to guide us Jews in applying that best to all our human interests, can command sufficient loyalty to insure its survival and advancement. America is a cultural melting pot. Cultural differences that do not contribute to the realization of universal human values are bound to vanish. It is generally recognized that all men need to be rooted in a religious tradition, and that it is to the various historic religions, older than America itself, that the American nation looks for the strengthening of its own morale. It looks to Judaism, and rightly so, to accomplish this for its Jewish citizens. *That expectation is an unequalled opportunity for us Jews not only to retain our group life in this country, but also to achieve a religious orientation that might prove of great value to the religiously starved mankind of our day.* This is the unique chance which the God of history has given us; let us not fumble it.

CHAPTER THREE

THE STATUS OF THE JEWS

1

THE STATUS OF JEWRY AN ENIGMA

Jews are today without a recognized group status. They are almost
an international conglomerate of descendants of what was once the
Jewish nation. That alone is enough to render them an enigma to
themselves and to the rest of the world. On the one hand, in their
eagerness to become part of the majority population, they are determined to abandon all that remains of their former status as a nation
in exile. On the other hand, under the impact of traditional loyalty,
they seek comfort in some form of collective life, be it congregation,
fraternal order or *Landsmanschaft*.

This lack of group status accounts for the lack of a philosophy and
program of Jewish life. Impelled by contradictory drives, Jews are forever frustrating one another's purposes and even their own. Out of
these frustrations proceeds a profound sense of impotence and futility,
of inferiority and self-hatred. Many Jews see no sense in continuing
to belong to a nondescript group, for such a group, far from conferring
dignity, stigmatizes those associated with it, as somehow incapable of
attaining full human status.

The entire mentality of the Jew is deeply, even if unconsciously,
affected by his loss of status. This may be seen from a keen observation
by a Jewish writer concerning the change that has recently come over
Jewish humor. In the east-European ghetto, prior to its break-up, the
Jew knew enough about the great doings in the outer world to realize,
by contrast, his own wretched lot. "For Sholom Aleichem," says Robert
S. Warshow,[1] "the Jewish joke meant: 'I have to live like a miserable
wretch, and I *am* miserable, but the joke is that I am also a king among
men—a Jew. This means: considering the circumstances, I have not
done badly.'" "In America," he adds, "the Jewish joke means: I make
believe I am a gentleman, but the joke is, I am just a miserable Jew,
and this means: The attempt was a bad idea, and it is too late to do
anything about it."

The ominous fact about our American Jewish life is that it exists
for the most part only by dint of momentum derived from old-world
Jewry. That momentum is petering out on account of the centrifugal

58

forces called forth by the environment. The main reason American Jewry has not developed its own momentum is that it lacks that imponderable but most influential factor: status. At present, whatever promise Jewish life in this country possesses is of the old-world type, which has not yet cast off the shell of isolation and segregation. The few areas in metropolitan cities, however, where that type of Judaism has been transplanted, do not spell the whole of America. Even in those areas one may detect the beginnings of far-reaching changes. All of which totals up to the fact that, at present, the process of disintegration of American-Jewish life is proceeding in geometrical ratio, while the process of integration is proceeding at best in arithmetical ratio. Nothing less than tapping some new reservoir of courage, of incentive and of energy for living as Jews will reverse this pace.

The only such reservoir, of which most of our spiritual leaders seem to be aware, is Jewish knowledge and more Jewish knowledge. They put their entire trust in the power of Jewish education. Where else, indeed, is one to get the inspiration to live as a Jew if not from the tradition of his people? As an abstract proposition, its logic is impeccable. If only parents could be persuaded to give their children an adequate Jewish training, and adolescents be induced to learn the history, literature and thought which have gone into the making of Judaism, the future of Jewry would be assured.

But that "if" is unfordable and impassable. It obstructs the path to our goal. Why do rabbis and educators who continually come up against that "if" keep on bombarding it with endless exhortation and denunciation? Why do they not try instead to hew a path by means of skillful social engineering? Is not the basic principle in all education that it must be motivated? One seldom studies just for the sake of studying. *The understanding and appreciation of a social heritage must be motivated by the desire to share the life of the people whose heritage it is.* A prerequisite is the existence of a people which lives and can make itself felt as an influence that enriches one's life. Here is the weakest link in all our efforts to upbuild American Jewish life. *We try to awaken in the young the desire to share the life of the Jewish people, but we do virtually nothing to make sure that there is any such life for them to share.*

We dare not underestimate the primacy of Jewish knowledge, when coping with the problem of how to bolster up the morale of the Jew. But we must not look to knowledge as a panacea, as the Hebraist does to a knowledge of Hebrew, the Yiddishist to that of

Yiddish, the Talmudist to that of Talmud, and the educator to that of Jewish history. We must not assume that a knowledge of Judaism can compensate for the lack of the impact on one's consciousness of a living, functioning people. Knowledge as such does not make one a Jew; a palpitating sense of kinship with Jewish men and women and children, the very thought of whom awakens the we-feeling is essential. Without this we-feeling each one of us is like a grain of sand, and you can't tie knots with ropes of sand.

The interplay of living social forces between the Jewish people and the individual Jew is the matrix of Judaism. Without this there can be no Judaism. The reason Judaism has not yet struck root in American soil is that we have forgotten to make the identity and reality of the Jewish people as unmistakable to our children as is the identity and reality of the Russian, the English or the French people. We should not be surprised if, after telling them all about the great moral and spiritual achievements of the Jewish people, they face us, in the manner of the child in the story of *The Emperor's Clothes*, with the question: "But where is the Jewish people?" What they see and hear is only a medley of Jewish organizations, societies, congregations, clubs and committees. They have not the least experience, as far as their being Jews is concerned, of that security-affording, authority-exerting, soul-stirring corporate entity which goes by the name of "people." All that the term "Jew" means for them is a man *without* a people, without an identity, a nameless being, a shadow among shadows.

The trouble is that we are not even sensitive to the need of making provision for the functioning of world Jewry as a living corporate entity, and of American Jewry as a part of that entity. We are still living on the capital of habits and attitudes which represent the accumulation of centuries, during which our ancestors were socially a self-governing, and culturally, a self-sustaining people. That the Jewish people was fragmented, dispersed and had no central government did not weaken in the least the overpowering feeling of the one life that coursed through all its parts. The individual Jew welcomed the invisible compulsions which radiated from that life into his daily routine. They were conducive to his welfare in this world and to his bliss in the hereafter. His awareness of the Jewish people as a constant presence gave to Judaism the character of a pervasive, inescapable atmosphere. No code of law, however meticulously elaborated, could by itself have accomplished that result.

From that manner of life, to which we Jews had become accustomed by centuries of the most severe testing, we were suddenly catapulted into surroundings so strange and conditions so different from any we had known in our three thousand year career that we cannot be blamed for having lost our bearings. There is nothing in our entire history prior to the end of the eighteenth century that affords any precedent by which we might be guided. Throughout the past, whenever Jews lived, they were regarded as a nation apart. They had no qualms about accepting this estimate of them, though it meant to be treated as aliens, and to be subject to the handicaps that went with alienage. It is true that there have been periods, both in Moslem and Christian countries, when Jews were free from persecution. They then availed themselves of that freedom by sharing and contributing to the culture of their neighbors. But there is little we can learn from those periods as to how to order our lives as Jews now. Throughout those years Jews lived as a state within a state; now we live as an integral part of the state.

During the last one hundred and fifty years, since the problem of Jewish emancipation has been to the fore, there have been only two definite proposals as to what shall be the status of the Jews in the modern Diaspora: the Reform proposal which confirmed the formula arrived at by the Paris Sanhedrin in 1806, and the proposal adopted at Versailles for minority nationalities, which confirmed the philosophy of Diaspora autonomy.*

The Reform proposal is the type of Jewish self-adjustment favored by the wealthier and most influential Jewish element in this country. The basic principle of that adjustment is that, with the acceptance of civic rights, Jews renounced every claim to unity other than a common history and a common religion. All cultural values or civilizational traits not having a specifically religious character should be eliminated, since they no longer serve a worthwhile purpose; in fact, they serve only to render the Jew unnecessarily, and the Gentile annoyingly, conscious of the Jew as distinctly "different." Consequently, the only legitimate status for Jews should be that of a number of independent religious communities, whose only bonds of unity are the memory of a common ancestry and a number of religious beliefs and practices.

The import of that status becomes apparent when we resort to the analogy of an army in its relation to the individual soldier. Though he is no longer a soldier when the army disbands, he remains an ex-soldier or a veteran. It is usual for soldiers, who trained and fought together, to continue their mutual association and to organize them-

* See below p. 68.

selves into veteran organizations. The purposes for which they usually organize are to keep alive the associations and camaraderie built up in the army, to help and protect one another against exploitation and to exert a salutary influence on the nation, as a result of a common war experience. Thus we understand the status proposed by Reform for Jews who wish to remain Jews, and who, therefore, cannot dispense altogether with some form of social structure. Like the soldier, the Jew is the product of a once functioning corporate entity. As there can be no soldier without an army, there can be no Jew without a Jewish people. In pre-Emancipation days, the Jews were like soldiers with the army still intact. The Emancipation made it necessary for the Jewish people to disband. The desire, however, to continue as Jews, in some capacity at least, has made it necessary to organize themselves voluntarily as veteran-Jews, so to speak, into a veteran organization. They, too, unite for mutual association, for self-help and for exerting a salutary influence on society. From the standpoint of classical Reform, our present organizational hodge-podge, flanked by a number of congregations, constitutes a sufficient vestige of the historic Jewish people to remind us of our Jewish mission.

That the veteran type of Jewish social structure has not worked to the satisfaction even of the majority of the Reform rabbis is evidenced by the fact that they have found it necessary to restore the principle of Jewish peoplehood.[2] The reason is not far to seek. If we are to carry out the analogy of a disbanded army, then we must remember that the only kind of army to which we can compare the case of the Jews is an *enemy* army that was captive before it was disbanded. Even when the army is a nation's own and has been victorious, a veteran organization is something of a nuisance. But in the case of a captive army, it is doubtful whether reorganization into a veteran group would even be tolerated.

The truth is that the analogy of an army applies only insofar as the individual Jew is a Jew by virtue of the existence of the Jewish people, just as the soldier is such only by virtue of the existence of an army. But a people is not like an army; it cannot be disbanded at will. After fifty years of trying to live with the idea that the Jews have disbanded as a people, the Reform movement has had to give up the attempt. That should be proof enough that there cannot be Judaism either as a religion or as a civilization, without the continued existence of the Jewish people as an international corporate entity.

One either ceases to be a Jew altogether, or has to accept the fact of membership in a living, continuing organism—the Jewish people. If we are to be free to be Jews, we have to be accepted on those terms. Those are the terms of what religion means to us. The mass of evidence from our tradition and history, in support of the indissoluble relationship in Judaism between religion and peoplehood, is overwhelming. Suffice it to recall the rallying cry which summons Israel to hear that its God is one,[3] or to refer to the frequently repeated statement in the Bible which urges the Jews to be a people to their God as a prerequisite to God's being God to them.[4] No truly democratic society that avows the freedom of religion can have any excuse for hampering the Jew in living his life on the only terms possible to him, namely, as a member of an indivisible Jewish people.

2

THE MEANING OF JEWISH PEOPLEHOOD

"A people" is not an abstract category; it is, like the term "personality," a concrete and identifiable phenomenon. Like all such phenomena, it can be recognized by means of its effects rather than defined. What essentially distinguishes a people from any other societal group, and what alone constitutes the common characteristic of groups designated as peoples, is their own identification of themselves as such. An individual is a person, when and because he knows himself as such; a group is a people, when and because it knows itself as such.

Thus, the first implication of the foregoing conception of peoplehood is that it is ethnic consciousness which makes a group into a people. Ethnic consciousness is not some mysterious entity that hovers over a people. It is the experience which every individual has, when he senses or becomes aware of the existence of the people he belongs to as an indivisible corporate entity. That experience expresses itself as consciousness of kind, like-mindedness, or "we-feeling." The Jews throughout the Middle Ages, and down to modern times, constituted a people despite their dispersion, because they identified with Jewish peoplehood all that was summed up in the term "Jew."

This leads directly to the second implication of our definition of peoplehood which is that the concept of people is not fixed, but varies with circumstances. Its content depends on what actually, in any particular era, happens to be the recognized basis of homogeneity. Thus, in the ancient kingdoms of Israel and Judah, peoplehood consisted mainly of land, government and cult; in the Babylonian Exile, of race and religion; in the Second Commonwealth, of land, law, religion and custom; in the Middle Ages, of religion, law and community life. But in all these epochs, whatever constituted the basis of homogeneity was felt to constitute the *peoplehood* of the Jews. Their ethnic consciousness persisted and maintained the identity of Jewish peoplehood, notwithstanding the variation in the nature of the Jewish homogeneity.

With the advent of Emancipation and Enlightenment came the need to reconstitute and redefine the oneness and indivisibility of the Jewish people. Their advent has brought about the following radical changes in Jewish life: the various local Jewries now form an integral part of various nations; Jewish culture has given way to the cultures of those nations; the Jewish civil law has been abandoned. Jews no longer are unanimous in identifying what it is that renders them a distinct group.

Those who seek to identify Jewish oneness and indivisibility with religion are themselves divided as to how that religion should be maintained and taught. The neo-Orthodox identify Jewish religion with belief in the supernatural revelation of the Torah and its immutable authority. The Reformists identify Jewish religion with belief in ethical monotheism and the mission of the Jewish people to spread it, but regard the traditional religious observances as subject to modification and in need of revision. Those of the center group try to mediate between these two views without advancing a distinct philosophy of their own. Thus, at the very time when our religious leaders seek to identify the Jewish homogeneity with religion, Jewish religion itself has become heterogeneous.

Moreover, the attempt to identify the "we-feeling" of Jews exclusively with religion as conventionally understood, in order to give status to the Jewish group, is useless for two reasons: (1) it would rule out the majority of Jews and leave them without status, and (2) it would not improve their condition either materially or spiritually.

It would leave the majority of Jews without status, because the majority of Jews today do not identify their Jewishness with any positive religious convictions. This applies not only to the very considerable number of Jews who are avowed secularists. Legion is the number of Jews who profess adherence to Jewish religion and retain some measure of affiliation with the synagogue, but neither subscribe to a Jewish creed, whether in the Reform or Orthodox version, nor submit to the discipline of Jewish religious practice. If pressed by questioning, they will admit that they are Jews by virtue of indefinable sentiment rather than of affirmative religious conviction. Religion alone can, therefore, not suffice to confer group status on them, since it plays but a minor role in their Jewish consciousness.

Furthermore, by regarding themselves as a religious sect, pure and simple, Jews will in no way be better off either materially or spiritually. Wherever anti-Semitism is rife, being only a religious sect will not improve their chances of having their civic rights honored, since anti-Semitism attacks Jews on racial rather than on religious grounds. Nor would the status of a religious denomination aid Jews in finding a secure place in the economic order, since it is not as adherents of a particular religion that they are discriminated against. Where there is such discrimination, a Gentile atheist will find employment more easily than the most religious Jew.

Finally, the limitation of the Jewish consciousness to religion exclusively does not promise even the perpetuation and development of Jewish religion. Jewish religion has always represented the conscious effort of the Jewish people to make its collective life contribute to the salvation of the individual and of society. It loses meaning, therefore, when divorced from secular interests. That is why, though Reform Judaism speaks of a Jewish mission, it has no missionaries and no program for converting the world. That, also, is why Orthodox Judaism, although it insists on the divine authority of the Jewish codes, has not been able to prevent their violation even by most of its own professed adherents. Such observance is conditioned by economic and cultural factors about which the denominational theory of Judaism can have nothing to say. That also explains why Conservative Judaism has not been able, throughout the hundred years of its existence, to arrive at a definite program of action.

If Jews are to reconstruct their lives as individuals and as members of a distinct society, they have to convert their present sense of oneness (which is constituted almost exclusively of an awareness of common danger and common suffering) into a sense of peoplehood and into an imperative to keep the corporate entity of the Jewish people one and indivisible. The sense of peoplehood would help to rally the resources of Jewry for improving the lot of the Jew materially and spiritually. Materially, the status of peoplehood would contribute to the political security and freedom of the Jews and to their economic stability and prosperity; spiritually, it would revive their cultural creativity, enable them to play an original rather than an imitative role in human civilization and make their collective experience an aid to personal happiness and social welfare for themselves and their fellowmen.

3

THE THREE LEVELS OF JEWISH PEOPLEHOOD

How is the status of Jewish peoplehood to be realized? The answer is that, in the world as it is constituted today, it has to be realized on three levels. These levels differ from one another, but are not necessarily mutually exclusive. It is important for us to reckon with all of them, and to understand the limitations within which they are appropriate to the Jewish situation.

1. *The first or basic level of Jewish peoplehood would have to take the form of commonwealth status.* Such status implies the occupation of a definite territory and self-government, both of which requirements will have to be met in Eretz Yisrael. A Jewish homeland in which either requirement is lacking is a self-contradiction. Territorial rights are autonomous rights to buy and sell land. Self-government means control of immigration and emigration and of imports and exports, in addition to internal police power and the power of taxation. *The Jewish Commonwealth in Eretz Yisrael need not and should not be a sovereign nation.* For that matter, the very survival of humanity now calls for the surrender, by every nation, of part of its sovereignty. The Jewish Commonwealth in particular should avoid becoming involved in international intrigue.

If it were not for the fact that the term "nation" has become inextricably associated with state sovereignty and exclusive political allegiance, it would have been the most fitting term for the status of Eretz Yisrael Jewry. That term is writ large over our entire tradition. It expresses the high degree of self-awareness as a societal unit attained by our ancestors. But it then carried with it a specific connotation which is, in a sense, the antithesis of that which it carries with it today. In Jewish tradition, a nation was thought of primarily as an organization of religion and culture. The matter of power, particularly in relation to other nations, was entirely secondary. That is the sense in which we Jews called ourselves a nation. "Israel is a nation only by virtue of its Torah," is the way R. Saadyah [5] sums up Jewish nationhood. Nowadays, however, the term "nation" connotes first and foremost an organization of power, in a combative sense. Religion is altogether precluded, and culture or civilization is decidedly secondary.

There was a time, and that not so long ago, when it seemed that the aggressive tendencies of the German-inspired nationalism would be eliminated, and that nationhood would be purged of its malignant traits. The League of Nations was expected to bring about a wholesome and ethical conception of nationhood. Had that state of mind continued, we should not have hesitated to speak of the Jewish nucleus in Eretz Yisrael as a nation. Instead, the nations have grown more insistent upon their sovereign rights, and more jealous than ever of any trans-national claims upon the loyalty of the individual citizen. The recent World War has intensified, rather than weakened, the national tendencies to self-assertion and aggression. For the Jews to continue to use the term "nation" with regard even to Eretz Yisrael Jewry is to expose themselves to misunderstanding and vile slander.

For those reasons it is not advisable to apply the term "nation" to the autonomous Jewish community in Eretz Yisrael. That community should rather be designated "Commonwealth." Eretz Yisrael should be known as the homeland of the Jewish people. We should not like Eretz Yisrael Jewry to serve as an occasion for charging Diaspora Jewry with double political allegiance.

Four States of the United States are officially designated "Commonwealth." They are Massachusetts, Pennsylvania, Virginia and Kentucky. As commonwealths, these States indicate that they wish to be identified with particular communities rather than with particular territories. It is evident that the loyalties and interests which bind the citizens of these States to their respective commonwealths are not binding upon citizens of the other States. Nevertheless, they and the citizens of the other States are members of the one American nation. Likewise, Jews of the Jewish Commonwealth in Eretz Yisrael would be bound by loyalties and interests which are not binding upon the rest of world Jewry. Nevertheless, they and the Jews of the Diaspora would be members of the Jewish people, held together by common religio-cultural loyalties and interests. The Jews in the Diaspora, however, would owe political allegiance solely to their respective countries.

It is clear that the establishment of a Jewish homeland definitely relates itself to the problem of improving Jewish life materially and spiritually. Materially, it would mean that all Jews who are concentrated as the majority group in a land of their own, under Jewish self-governing institutions, would derive from their life as a people the same benefits that the nationals who constitute the majority groups in other nations derive from theirs. Economically, they would have access to natural resources, would not be subject to anti-Jewish economic discrimination, and would be aided by their government in achieving that indispensable economic cooperation which makes for national and individual prosperity. Spiritually, they would benefit by the opportunity of utilizing Hebrew as a vernacular for all purposes and freely fostering the *sancta* of Jewish civilization, thus preserving the spiritual values of the Jewish past which are treasured in our historic culture.

Their economic diversification, based on their possession of the land, would also make for cultural diversity and a freer, richer and more deeply rooted Jewish culture. Their religion and ethical idealism would have a chance to express themselves not only in ritual and a few limited areas of social life such as the home, the synagogue and Jewish philanthropy, but in all human relations. Jews would be aware of Jewish life as work, aspiration and creative achievement. To be a Jew would mean to belong to a people with a history and a still unfulfilled destiny which can be made as beautiful and holy as the Jews are able to make it, when they are not at the mercy of a dominant non-Jewish majority.

This level of Jewish peoplehood, however, provides these opportunities only for those Jews who would live in the Jewish homeland. Since, then, the benefits of Jewish commonwealth status would be reserved only for Jews who migrate to Eretz Yisrael, and since even these benefits would not be fully realized, until Eretz Yisrael Jewry is a majority and Jewish claims to Eretz Yisrael are recognized and adequately guaranteed, the status of Diaspora Jewry would still remain as ambiguous as ever. We must think, therefore, in terms not only of Eretz Yisrael Jewry but of Jewry as a whole, and formulate other levels of the status of peoplehood, in addition to the one of commonwealth.

2. *The second level takes the form of the social structure of Diaspora Jewry advocated by the late Simon Dubnow.*[6] Dubnow tried to fit Jewish group life into a pattern of cultural pluralism, such as was envisaged by the minority rights clauses of the treaties after the first World War. According to that conception, the Jews, although continuing to reside in the lands of the Diaspora, are to constitute a distinct politico-cultural community with proportionate representation in the government, with their own communal institutions and system of education, primarily in the Yiddish vernacular. This view of the nature of the Jewish homogeneity resembles the Reform-religious view, with respect to accepting the dispersion as final, but differs from it funda-

mentally in stressing the secular rather than the religious aspects of Jewish culture, and in favoring Jewish communal organization to promote the secular interests of Jews. Polish Jewry after the first World War was organized on this basis. The Jews, while sharing in the general nationhood of the Poles, to the extent of being bound by Polish law and participating in Polish government, accepted Jewish nationhood not as an alternative to Polish nationhood but as an additional political, communal and cultural factor. This status received government recognition for a time.

It is at once apparent that this interpretation of Jewish status is a program designed to promote the material and spiritual interests of Jews in countries where minority groups would be granted certain political group rights. The representatives of the Jewish minority in the Polish Sejm looked after the defense of Jewish rights and the economic interests of the Jews affected by proposed legislation. There arose an imposing network of educational and cultural institutions of every description. Most of them were conducted in Yiddish, and the rest in Hebrew. They were supported by taxes allocated by the Government to the Jewish community. The community also made adequate provision to Jews for all sorts of social and religious services.

However, although this status made it possible for the Jews in the Diaspora to feel perfectly at home in their native countries, it would not assure their group survival were they to have no commonwealth status in Eretz Yisrael. In the first place, it does not assure to the Jews access to the soil and its natural resources. Hence, it cannot adequately protect the economic interests of the Jews. It still leaves the Jews a political minority. Though, by forming coalitions with other minorities, their minority representation affords them some protection against encroachment on their rights, that protection ceases to function when the majority pits one minority against another.

Finally, this arrangement, although to no small extent stimulating to Jewish cultural activity, does not reckon adequately with the tendency of the less patronized minority culture to be absorbed by the larger and wealthier culture. An author prefers to write for a large reading public rather than for a small one; a musician prefers performing for many rather than few listeners. The minority culture tends to become a mere novel accent or dialect of the majority culture rather than an equal cultural partner. It is significant that in Poland, Yiddish (basically a European language) was the cultural vehicle identified with Jewish peoplehood, while in Eretz Yisrael it has come to be

Hebrew. It is even more significant that in the Soviet Union, where Yiddish is recognized in some districts as the official language, it is largely being abandoned by the Jews themselves in favor of the Russian tongue.

It must also be evident that for Jewish peoplehood to function in the manner advocated by Dubnow, during the first decades of this century, as a political and cultural community with minority representation in the state, the majority group would have to sanction such a status. That sanction has been accorded only where there have been a number of minority nationalities with clearly marked cultural traits. In the Western democracies, however, no such *modus vivendi* would be welcomed either by Jews or Gentiles.

3. *The third level would fit the status of Jewish peoplehood into such a pattern of political monism combined with religio-cultural pluralism as exists in the United States.* In this country, there are no minority groups which are, or desire to be, represented in the state as national-cultural groups. All citizens share as individuals in the cultural, economic and political life of the nation. With their personal liberties adequately protected by law and custom, they feel no need for separate political representation based on cultural differentiations. Nevertheless, *the very recognition of personal rights has resulted in the development of voluntary communal and religio-cultural institutions. This makes religio-cultural pluralism compatible with political monism.*

This religio-cultural pluralism is not one that divides the population into disparate and mutually exclusive groups. All share in the common American culture, but each is free to develop additional cultural interests based on family tradition, religious affiliation, ethnic origin, race or any other natural factor. As long as the interests of such groups are not antagonistic to those of the nation as a whole, they are accepted as legitimate. In such a pattern the Jews would constitute a religio-cultural group with a commonwealth nucleus in Eretz Yisrael.

This involves the formulation of a new societal concept. Its acceptance depends first and foremost upon the Jews themselves. This is undoubtedly the most difficult step to be taken, if they are to achieve that self-renewal which is to give them a new lease on life. But once the Jews determine to regard themselves as a people with a homeland, the rest of the world will in time come to accept them at their own self-valuation. All that is necessary is for the Jews to be convinced that there is nothing, in this new concept of a Diaspora people with a commonwealth nucleus, that can reasonably be regarded as incompatible with whole-hearted loyalty and devotion to the United States or to any other nation. As a religio-cultural group the Jews have common interests for the furtherance of which they associate themselves in communal organizations to maintain educational, social, philanthropic and religious institutions.

It must be obvious, however, that even if Jewish community organization were developed far more efficiently than it is, Judaism could not maintain itself in the United States without a Jewish Commonwealth in Eretz Yisrael. For here, even more than formerly in Poland and Russia, the pull of the majority culture generates a strong centrifugal force, and has to be counterbalanced by the centripetal force provided by American Jewish participation in the renascence of Jewish life in Eretz Yisrael. The Jewish Commonwealth in Eretz Yisrael has to constitute the nucleus of the Jewish people throughout the world. *The nuclear function of the Jewish Commonwealth in Eretz Yisrael vis-à-vis the rest of the Jewish people would not be to exercise authority, either politically or religiously. It would be to exercise only such cultural and spiritual influence as the values which it would evolve would exert of their own accord.*

The status of the Jews throughout the world as one and indivisible people would have to be recognized as a social concept that carries with it both rights and duties: rights implying freedom to foster a degree of group individuality and duties implying the responsibility of translating that individuality into concrete social institutions.

The status of peoplehood, translated into organic community organization, can prove effective in contributing to the material and spiritual advancement of Jews. Materially, it can encourage collaboration by combating the effects of economic discrimination and by aiding Jews to find an economic foothold. It can stimulate participation in establishing in Eretz Yisrael a commonwealth to which any Jew who is maladjusted to the conditions of life in a non-Jewish environment may come and find himself in friendly and hospitable surroundings. Spiritually, it would contribute to the Jew's self-respect by making him feel that he is a part of a great historic people with a present and a future, as well as a past.

An American Jewish community, which would be animated by the status of Jewish peoplehood, would foster Jewish educational and cultural activities designed to make the collective experience of Jewish living in past and present a means for personal and social self-fulfillment. It would encourage Jewish community collaboration with other liberal elements in the American population for realizing in American life the highest ideals which Jews have learned from their own history and religion. It would lift Jewish religion above the dogmatic and ritualistic formalism into which it tends to degenerate, when divorced from the secular interests of Jewish life, and make it again a source of inspiration and morale in our heroic struggle for self-emancipation and self-realization.

These, then, are the conclusions to which our analysis of the Jewish problem has led us. The Jews are in need of status; they cannot continue indefinitely in the anomalous situation in which they have found themselves ever since the Emancipation. The status required by Jews cannot be that of a religious denomination, since the homogeneity of Jewish religion has been destroyed by the Enlightenment, and since the denominational status does nothing to solve those material and spiritual problems, awareness of which is the whole content of Jewish homogeneity in the present day. *The status most appropriate is that of peoplehood, based on the principle that any group with a "we-feeling," consciousness of kind, or homogeneity, has a right to make the most of that consciousness for the salvation of its members.* The only qualification to this right is that it must seek the salvation, self-realization or the maximum fulfillment of *all* their interests, in ways that do not interfere with the salvation of members of any other group.

Such peoplehood is religious, for the essence of religion is the human quest for salvation. Therefore, it has all the advantages, and none of the disadvantages, of denominational status which an earlier generation sought as the solution of the Jewish problem. It is in the main stream of the spiritual tradition of our people, and can avail itself of the resources of Jewish religious tradition. This religious conception of peoplehood saves religion itself from sterile dogmatism and formalism. The religion, which seeks to make of peoplehood a way of salvation for the individual and society, is the only kind of religion that can make the world safe for democracy.

4

THE STRUGGLE FOR THE FREEDOM TO BE JEWS

The clarification of our status as a people is certain to give the only proper meaning to our struggle against anti-Semitism. Once we know we are a people, we cannot view the hostility of which we are victims as injuring us only as individuals, that is, as merely depriving us personally of the means to life, growth and happiness. It would then not occur to us to combat social discrimination, because it prevents us from being absorbed by the general population. Our struggle against anti-Semitism, if waged in defense of the right of the Jewish people to a place in the sun and of our freedom to be Jews, becomes a struggle in behalf of the most oppressed, the most hounded of all peoples, and therefore in behalf of all peoples and persons who suffer a like fate.

To have the courage to fight anti-Semitism in that spirit—the courage that our present defense organizations would do well to acquire —we have to know the whole truth about the Jewish Emancipation.

We live in a part of the world where society professes the ideals of democratic nationalism. Those are the ideals which were enunciated during the last quarter of the eighteenth century and consecrated by the American and the French Revolutions. They promised to usher in an era of universal freedom, justice and peace. Under their aegis, the Western nations threw off the yoke of feudalism and actually gave signs of desiring to render life on earth more livable and worthwhile for all men. As part of the "New Deal" of those days Jews were emancipated from the status of helots and were promised their freedom. While the idea of the Emancipation was still new, it seemed to many Jews that they had at last come to the end of their wanderings.

This is quite comprehensible, for, throughout the Middle Ages (which for the Jews of Eastern Europe lasted virtually until a generation ago) the Jews had lived under intolerable conditions. They had been isolated within a narrow territorial confine called "the Pale", or were forced into walled-off parts of cities called ghettos. As individuals, the Jews had no political status and, as a community, they were subject and tributary to the sovereign power. They were everywhere aliens and exiles, living on the sufferance of the rulers who tolerated them, only to the extent that they found it expedient to do so. When inexpedient, they were expelled. Their economic life was subject to all sorts of disabilities, and they were the objects of legislation designed to degrade and impose on them the stigma of inferiority. Little wonder, then, that they hailed the abolition of these medieval disabilities and their admission to citizenship in the lands of their residence as an act of emancipation. In a sense, it was that.

Yet the emancipation of the Jews, supposed to have been effected by incorporating them into the body politic of the nations of the West, was not what it had at first seemed to be. It had to be purchased at a price, and was granted only conditionally and with reservations. In some countries, the terms were made quite explicit; in others, they were tacitly assumed. Everywhere the purchase-price of emancipation was the surrender of Jewish social and cultural autonomy. Everywhere it was expected of Jews that they renounce their identity as a distinct people. If they were permitted to retain a certain measure of religious distinctivness, it was on the commonly accepted theory that religion was a mere matter of opinion, a private concern of the individual. Yet there were many in the seats of authority who questioned the right of Jews to retain even their religious distinctiveness. Some of them frankly demanded conversion to Christianity as a condition of social equality.

It is not generally known that the Jewish masses were at first suspicious of the Emancipation, and reluctant to accept it.[7] They clung with almost fanatical tenacity to customs that distinguished them from the Gentiles, even when those customs were not prescribed by Jewish law. They sensed that the Emancipation would lead to the dissolution of the Jewish people. Mainly the wealthy Jews were eager to become part of the Gentile World. They were the ones to whom the Gentile leaders turned for assurance that the Jews would accept the conditions implied in the Emancipation. Theirs was the dominant influence in the "Sanhedrin" which Napoleon summoned for the express purpose of having the Jews renounce their group autonomy. The same was true whenever the state negotiated with the Jews. The Jewish masses had no alternative but to accept the Emancipation, on the terms imposed by influential members of the Jewish community. The latter, probably in good faith, were convinced that their own interests coincided with those of the Jews generally.

The freeing of a people from any kind of bondage, when accompanied by reservations requiring the people to come to an end as a corporate entity, can hardly be called "emancipation". A more correct term would be "liquidation". The Gentile advocates of Jewish emancipation were not concerned with enabling Jews to pursue freely their Jewish interests. They were motivated by the desire to make it possible for the general population to absorb the Jews. To those Gentiles who had become skeptical of their own religious tradition, the Emancipation meant that Jews were thenceforth free to become Gentiles, or *goyim*, without having to become Christians. The orthodox adherents of Christianity, however, expected that Jews, upon being emancipated, would seek admission to the Church. They assumed that oppression had embittered the Jews against Christianity. With oppression removed, they saw no reason why Jews should persist in their obstinacy and refuse to accept Christianity. Hardly anyone thought of recognizing the Jews' right to live as a people, with interests and loyalties of their own.

The Jewish emancipation, thus accompanied by unspoken reservations and expectations, left the Jews jittery with regard to their status and with an obsessive fear of forfeiting the individual rights that had been granted them. Their status has since been nothing less than an enigma. They are free to be like their neighbors, but not free to differ from them; free to imitate but not to originate; free to conform but not to dissent. Ahad Ha-Am [8] coined the classic phrase to describe this status. He called it *avdut betok herut*, bondage in freedom. In the democratic countries, the fear of arson, massacre and expulsion has been eliminated from Jewish life. But *Jews have developed a new fear, the fear of living and acting openly and collectively as Jews.* Many of them believe that the only way Jews can stay alive is to play dead.

Thus in our day a new type of Jew has come into being—the Jew who is so fearful of disappointing the Gentiles' expectation of the eventual dissolution of Jewry, that he deems it a duty to hasten that dissolution. He tries to bring his influence to bear—backed with large funds—against all activities that tend to strengthen Jewish solidarity and to perpetuate Jewish life. He hopes thus to weaken the Jewish will to live, and thereby to remove what he regards as the main cause for the persistence of anti-Semitism.

What escapist Jews fail to realize is that neither discouragement nor suppression of Jewish life or activity will appease anti-Semites. Anti-Semites resent the efforts of Jews to merge with the rest of the population, no less than they resent their desire to remain a distinct group. They regard assimilation of the Jews as pollution of the Gentiles, as *Rassenschande*. No anti-defamation leagues, Committees or Congresses to combat anti-Semitism will succeed in counteracting the anti-Semitic libel which charges the Jews with conspiring to dominate mankind. The very fact that Jews organize to fight anti-Semitism is used as evidence of such conspiracy. The anti-Semites who always have the upper hand when they assail Jews know that they are masters, even though the Jews who cherish the illusion of having been truly emancipated are not aware that they are still slaves.

5

THE CASE AGAINST ANTI-SEMITISM

In making out our case against anti-Semitism, we must recognize that anti-Semitism is of two kinds, secular and Christian. The secular anti-Semites hold us responsible for having given Christianity to the world; the Christian anti-Semites blame us for refusing to become Christians.

Secular anti-Semitism is a menace not only to the Jewish people but to the peace of the world. Anti-Jewish prejudice has been so deeply inculcated in the minds of most Western peoples that it can easily be played upon by any unscrupulous rabble-rouser for any sinister purpose whatsoever. The use that Hitler made of anti-Semitism, in his attempt to enslave the world, was only the culmination of a systematic campaign of hate that began in Germany in the first decade of the nineteenth century. The collapse of Nazism has not prevented the spread of anti-Jewish agitation. America is not immune against infection by the anti-Semitic virus.

After the first World War, the lawlessness of the Ku Klux Klan was not unlike that of the Nazi party in its early days. In 1921 Woodrow Wilson, William Howard Taft, Cardinal O'Connell and 115 prominent Americans signed a proclamation which expressed their awareness of the danger of anti-Semitism to America. "The anti-Semitic publications," they declared, "are introducing into our national and political life a new dangerous spirit, one that is wholly at variance with our tradition and ideals and subversive of our system of government." Similar considerations led the British National Council for Civil Liberties, at a conference representing 273 organizations with more than one million members, which was held in April 1943, to adopt a resolution asking the British government to introduce legislation that would outlaw anti-Semitism.

That and similar efforts in this country to crystallize the decent sentiment of mankind into law should be resumed. The weak-kneed liberals, who obstruct the outlawing of anti-Semitism, on the ground that legal measures which limit the freedom of expression are subject to abuse, are contributing to the suppression of all freedom. For anti-Semitism is a front for the reactionary forces which are bent upon destroying democracy and the elementary rights of human beings. When there is a serious desire to suppress an evil, there is always a way of bringing legal sanctions to bear on it. The trial of the war criminals was said to be illegal, because there had been no precedent by which to distinguish aggressive from defensive war. Yet, with the determination once and for all to have aggressive war outlawed, a way was found to set up a precedent and to convict the arch-criminals among the Nazis. Given the determination to suppress deliberate incitement to maltreat Jews, a way could be found to outlaw anti-Semitism.

We Jews must give ourselves no rest and demand that anti-Semitic agitation be made illegal throughout the world. In view of the use made of anti-Semitism as a means of mobilizing the forces of hate and aggression, which must ultimately lead to international and world war, it comes well within the category of those questions which affect the peace of the world. "The menace of war," wrote James T. Shotwell,[9] "cannot be removed from human affairs so long as life and liberty are imperiled by arbitrary power." Woodrow Wilson is said to have pointed to Article XI of the Covenant of the League of Nations as his favorite Article, and to have added: "This Article says that any and every question that affects the peace of the world is everybody's business, and that it is the friendly right of any nation to bring before the League any problem that is likely to disturb the peace of the world, or the good understanding between nations, upon which future peace depends— whether the problem concerns the nation that rings the alarm bell, or whether it is merely a matter of general concern." [10] Anti-Semitism unquestionably falls within that category. It is, therefore, everybody's business and not only that of the Jews.

The case against Christian anti-Semitism is no less in need of being brought to the court of public opinion. The Christian Church, from its very inception, sought to justify its repudiation of Judaism by vilifying the teachings of Judaism and branding the Jews as deicides. The role of the Jewish people in history, according to orthodox Christian tradition, has been that of anti-Christ. "And ever since," an authoritative text-book on church history informs its readers, "the Jews have wandered about; a people without a flag, a country, a priest, an altar or a sacrifice, a living testimony that indeed the vengeance (sic!) of God fell upon them and their children." [11] Copies of the New Testament distributed among the armed forces of the United States during the recent World War contained a note which described the Jewish people as "the Synagogue of Satan." It is true that in response to protests against that note, it was deleted from subsequent editions, but its original insertion was no accident. It was not furtively introduced by some Jew-baiter; it expressed a traditional interpretation of the New Testament passage to which it referred.

It is unfortunately true that in the Christian religious tradition the Jews are assumed to be the accursed of God. There is no use evading the fact, or prevaricating about it. There is only one way to deal with it; it must cease to be a fact. That judgment on the Jews must be expunged from the Christian tradition. No fair-minded Christian can reconcile such vilification of an entire people with a religion which claims to be based on love. The treatment we Jews are still receiving at the hands of the Church is perhaps best expressed in the saying: "It is all very well to dissemble your love, but why did you kick me downstairs?"

Conrad Henry Moehlman,[12] a leading Christian theologian, in his book, *The Christian Jewish Tragedy*, aims to persuade his fellow-Christians to disavow the great injustice the Christian tradition has inflicted on Judaism. He marshals convincing evidence to prove that the anti-Jewish tendencies of the Christian tradition are in conflict with the main teachings of Christianity. "This study," he says, "has added another count to the indictment against Christianity, namely, its failure adequately to confess its sin with reference to Israel. Fortunately, individual Christians are beginning to recognize the duty of repentance toward Israel." In a statement signed by thirty Protestant leaders and quoted in that book, it is said: "We deplore the long record of wrongs from which the Jewish people have suffered in the past, often from the hands of those who have professed the Christian faith, and who have yet been guilty of acts utterly alien to Christian teaching and spirit. We declare our disavowal of anti-Semitism in every form and our purpose to remove by every available means its causes and manifestations, in order that we may share with our fellow citizens of Jewish heritage every political, educational, commercial, social and religious opportunity." This indeed should be regarded as a call to the conscience of the American people.

American Christians, who are shocked at the recollection of the anti-Semitic excesses of the Nazis, owe it to themselves to take stock of the teachings of their respective churches, to reinterpret their Scriptures and to revise their rituals, to the end that the adoration of Jesus shall not imply condemnation of the Jews, or of Judaism, for denying his divinity. Unless they come to realize that Jews can find salvation through their Torah, as readily as Christians can find it through their worship of Jesus, they will continue to breed anti-Jewish prejudice and be responsible for abetting anti-Semitism.

Are we making an excessive demand on the churches? We admit that we are calling for a drastic revision of traditional attitudes, in the interest of democracy, peace, and good will. We cannot ask that of Christians, unless we ourselves make analogous demands of our own people. We must not try to remove the mote from our neighbor's eye and ignore the beam in our own. The traditional Jewish belief in Israel as God's Chosen People is objectionable from the viewpoint that all religions are equally near "to all who call upon Him in truth." We must, accordingly, advocate the elimination from our own liturgy of all references to the doctrine of Israel as the Chosen People. Just as we are confident that Jewish religion will be purified and strengthened by that modification of its doctrine and ritual, so we believe sincerely that the Christian churches have nothing to lose, and much to gain, by a corresponding revision of their doctrine and ritual. In this way they would rid themselves of the burden of guilt for the murderous hatred against the Jews throughout the ages, which they have inculcated, directly and indirectly.

6

FREEDOM THAT IS GENUINE

The only wise and honorable course for us to pursue at the present time is to demand that the Jewish emancipation be made real and complete. We are entitled to the right not merely to live as human beings, but to live as Jews. We seek not merely to be treated as loyal American citizens, but to be so treated without having to surrender our right to be loyal Jews. We must feel free to strive for the realization of the hopes which we cherish in common with Jews throughout the world. We have to meet the challenge of anti-Semitism frankly and firmly, since nothing less than our extinction would silence its ravings. We must insist on the right of American Jewry openly and publicly to function as a corporate entity in any capacity which is legitimate, from the standpoint of American law and institutions. We must definitely repudiate the policy of *avdut betok herut,* of bondage in freedom. We must inaugurate a campaign of self-emancipation by boldly demanding protection against anti-Semitism, as we would against any form of brigandage, not only for Jews of Europe and Eretz Yisrael, but also for the Jews of our own United States and other democratic countries.

That protection must not depend, either implicitly or explicitly, upon our willingness to give up group identity. We should be granted freedom to be Jews, as of right, and not merely on sufferance.

To be sure, that right already exists and is implied in the best tradition of American democracy. But since anti-Semitism is abroad in the land, that right will have to be made explicit in order to afford the Jews the security to which they are entitled. If that right is to have any meaning, it should be translated into legislation that would effectively ban anti-Semitism. Freedom of speech should not be abused to the extent of condoning the incitement of hatred and violence against Jews, or any other minority. Discrimination against Jews, which makes it difficult for them to live without denying or concealing their Judaism, should be forbidden by law.

The emancipation of Jewry from those conditions that render Jewish life unstable and insecure is a right which we shall never achieve, unless we act in the spirit of self-emancipation. *World Jewry should unite as a people, and apply to the United Nations Assembly for recognition of its claim to peoplehood. A bill of individual rights is not enough.* What is needed is a bill to legitimatize Jewish association and cooperation for all purposes that would secure for the Jew freedom of worship and freedom from fear.

Such an application to the United Nations presupposes, of course, a change in the Charter of United Nations. At present only sovereign states are accepted as members. Under that ruling, the newly created shadow-state of Iraq is recognized as a member. Its population is less than one million, most of whom are ignorant fellaheen, exploited by an ancient feudal order, which itself is dominated by British interests. That Iraq should be represented in the Council of the Nations, while we Jews who play a role in the world's affairs, not only as individuals but as a group, should not have their corporate existence recognized, is an unconscionable wrong.

To permit the lack of precedent or legal formulas to stand in the way of our being granted status and admitted to membership in the United Nations is absurd. When the League of Nations was established and it became necessary to prevent small struggling peoples and states from becoming colonies of insatiable empires, a new legal instrument known as the *Mandate* was devised. By that token, the new concept "peoplehood" can now be given legal recognition, if the nations can be persuaded, as a matter of elementary justice, that they owe it to Jews to free them from the fear of anti-Semitism. Such recognition would dry out the roots of that poisonous weed that has spread throughout every country on the globe. *When we have summoned up enough courage and unity to knock at the door of the United Nations for admission as a people, we shall have taken the first step toward our self-emancipation.*

In sum: Our emancipation will not be complete until we are free of the fear of being Jews. That means we must assert our right to status as a people, throughout the world, and as a religio-cultural community in the United States. We need that status for our salvation. We are entitled to it, as free American citizens.

CHAPTER FOUR

THE SIGNIFICANCE OF BEING A PEOPLE

1

THE SENSE OF PEOPLEHOOD

An awareness of peoplehood, or ethnic consciousness, plays as important a role in the lives of human beings as does the awareness of one's ego, of one's family, and of one's community. The question is, does the sense of peoplehood make for the best interests of the individual in whom it inheres, and of the group which is its object? The answer calls for an examination of the conditions under which the sense of peoplehood functions.

The sense of peoplehood is the awareness which an individual has of being a member of a group that is known, both by its own members and by outsiders, as a people. Neither those within nor those without, as a rule, give much thought to the question of what makes the group into a people. Those within are satisfied with the "we-feeling"—which they have with regard to all who belong to their people. That "we-feeling" is more inclusive than the "we-feeling" of family, clan or tribe, and yet definitely excludes others who have a like feeling about their own people. Everyone yearns to be a member of some people, and deems it a catastrophe to have no people to which to belong.

Why is it a catastrophe? Because, as human beings, there are two states or conditions we cannot do without. We cannot do without being needed, and without something of which we are proud. This is why we need this we-feeling to embrace a group inclusive enough in time and space, inclusive of a sufficient number of generations to render certain that our being desired or needed is not ephemeral and that all of us, no matter how commonplace, can recall some person, event or achievement we can be proud of. To be sure, one's own family might be of a kind which could provide these two conditions. But it would have to be a very exceptional family, one with an ancient pedigree, and with many a hero and great achievement to its credit. Very few people are that lucky. The average person requires a whole chain of families to be linked together into a social unit, for him to satisfy these essential needs. This is the psychological aspect of peoplehood as a humanizing force in the life of the average individual. If he lacks it, he feels rootless and nameless. The American-Jew is in the awkward position of having, as it were, but half his personality fulfilled—the American half. As for the Jewish half, that is in a chaotic state because it misses both being needed and having something of which to be proud. As an American, he rejoices in his we-feeling; as a Jew, he often feels trapped.

In the past, no attempt was made to distinguish, except quantitatively, between the we-feeling of ethnic consciousness and the we-feeling of family consciousness. Both were regarded as due to blood kinship. What is actually the difference between the we-feeling which expresses itself as ethnic consciousness from the we-feeling which expresses itself in other types of collective consciousness? The difference should be sought mainly in the factors that contribute to ethnic consciousness. Moreover, it should be one which would account for all kinds of ethnic groups both ancient and modern.

Ethnic consciousness, or the sense of peoplehood, functions through the medium of a living civilization, which is an organic ensemble of the following cultural elements having their rootage in a specific territory, a common tradition, a common language and literature, history, laws, customs and folkways, with religion as the integrating and soul-giving factor of those elements. To this ensemble must be added an active leadership which is concerned with translating that tradition into a means of serving the essential needs of all who are identified with the people. The foremost among those are: being wanted and having something to be proud of.

An ethnic consciousness is thus coextensive with a unit of civilization. An ethnic consciousness is a group soul, the body of which is the particular civilization through which it functions. Both the consciousness and its body, or vehicle, are distinctively human creations. They exist as two aspects of a manifold of specific living realities known as peoples. Neither ethnic consciousness nor civilization exists merely in the abstract. Each exists as a particular process, associated with concrete realities. Each is certainly as real a unit of life as is any individual human being, to say the least. Actually, in that they can outlive many generations of human beings, they are of infinitely greater worth, and the essence of the greatest worth which those who live by them attain. It is normally expected of the individual to prove his worth by sacrificing his life, in order that his civilization may live. According to Milton, "as good almost kill a man as kill a good book." By what standard then shall we measure the unnecessary death of a civilization? Nothing more tragic can happen than for a people and its civilization to disintegrate and die. To be in any way responsible for this tragedy is to be guilty of snuffing out life in its most human and sacred form.

These considerations should help us see each of the various elements of a civilization in a new light—as the highest manifestation of human life struggling to live. Among the earliest evidences of recognition of language as an element of ethnic consciousness and as a mark of people-hood is the story of the Tower of Babel.[1] It is also implied in the term "tongues" as a synonym for peoples, as in the following: "The time cometh, that I will gather all nations and tongues." [2] Why differences of language should mark off one people from another is quite under-standable. Those who speak the same language are in a position to be of one mind and to cooperate. A common language is, therefore, conducive to the we-feeling, whereas when we hear a different language, we become aware of the group-otherness of those who speak it.

Different language groups arose through no premeditated purpose. Peoples which had their beginning in language differences were thus the product of unconscious forces which came into play, with the changing fortunes of war and peace. The formation and dissolution of peoples originally went on without deliberately planned purpose, until the advent of Alexander the Great. It was not unusual, even before his time, for populations to be violently transplanted from one country to another. But that was only for the purpose of preventing rebellion against the authority of a conquering state, and not to bring about a new ethnic consciousness. Alexander, however, was the first leader to conceive the idea of getting all mankind to adopt the language and culture of his own people and thus become one in we-feeling. He was thus the first to tamper with the process of the making and remaking of peoples.

That the variety of languages is the primary factor in the division of mankind into peoples is of utmost significance. It implies that people-hood and ethnic consciousness are not the product of any hereditary tendency or instinct, but of historical circumstances. The outcome of those circumstances constitutes the social heritage which is transmit-ted from generation to generation. *Peoplehood does not originate in the hereditary instincts like those which make for the family. The very fact that it is not inherited biologically makes it a distinctively human value which has to justify itself by the good that it does.* But before pro-ceeding with its justification, we must know more about its various factors and manifestations in human history.

The language, which gives a people its sense of unity, brings in its train a whole complex of elements that go into the making of people-hood. It brings into play the remembrance of past heroes and events of history, the customs to which every member of the people is expected to conform, laws which regulate conflicts of interests and help to maintain the peace, and folkways which include characteristic forms of esthetic self-expression. Besides enabling a people to carry on social intercourse, a common language is thus a vehicle for factors which give content and meaning to that social intercourse.

Just as language enlarges the scope of social relationships in space beyond the confines of family, so it enlarges that scope in time beyond one's contemporaries. It functions as a medium of narratives and myths concerning heroes and events that are a source of pride to all who belong to one's people. These narratives and myths serve as a bond of unity that is stronger than present interests. The very fact that they have come down from the past proves their ability to endure as a uniting influence. Whether contemporary heroes and events will give rise to such narratives is a question which only the future can answer. *By helping the individual to transcend the immediacy of the group life which he shares, the traditions concerning past heroes and events make it possible for him to contemplate the group as a whole, as existing indefinitely and surviving the individuals of whom it is constituted.*

This conception of one's people has undoubtedly been attended by all sorts of fanciful notions. But the fact remains that it brings into the foreground of consciousness the people as a whole in a manner which no amount of involvement only in the contemporary interests common to the people could possibly achieve. There can be no ethnic consciousness without some kind of history, or outstanding past events and heroes. These events and heroes serve as points of reference in the social intercourse made possible by a common language.

Among primitive peoples, the initiation ceremonies of adolescents were the occasion for communicating to them, in dramatic and highly emotionalized fashion, those deeds of the ancestors whereby the people of which they became conscious members had won its place in the world. This initiation was conceived as conferring a second birth, that is, birth into a super-personal life. Not only did it cause the reborn individual to feel that the range of his own experiences had enlarged. It included henceforth experiences which gave him, as it were, a share in the power and the greatness of his ancestors. The sense of personal enhancement which resulted from this self-identification with the past of his people naturally acted as an incentive to deeds on his own part, worthy of such a past. Thus was gratified the need of every individual to have something to be proud of.

Mere awareness of one's people is not sufficient. The people must be felt as a living presence in the course of one's daily routine, if ethnic consciousness is to be more than an occasional flareup of pride in past achievements of one's people. The people must exert a constant pressure on the individual. It does that through its customs and laws; hence their part in keeping alive the ethnic consciousness. It is their very essence to interfere with the self-fulfillment of the impulses, and to set up, even at best, enough of inner conflict to arouse consciousness of a not-self that prohibits and commands, that rewards obedience and punishes disobedience—in brief, that cares for the individual.

This not-self is not merely the person or persons in authority. Whatever authority, or power to compel obedience, such persons possess does not derive from their own will, but from the fact that they are regarded as embodying and expressing the will of the people. That will is neither purely arbitrary nor bent upon subordinating the impulses of the individual, as an end in itself. No matter how unreasonable those customs and laws seem to an outsider, to those within the people itself they express the will to cooperation in the interests of the general good. And just because they tend to call forth a degree of inner conflict in the individual, they help to bring into relief the aspect of cooperation as an active and ever present bond among those who constitute the people.

The sense of peoplehood, or the ethnic consciousness, is further augmented by a whole series of folkways, folk symbols and memorials which belong to a different category from that of laws and customs. Unlike the latter, which are in the main inhibitive, or attended by fear of punishment, when not conformed to, folkways and folk symbols are affirmative and spontaneous expressions of ethnic life. They afford the individual the opportunity to give expression to large reserves of surplus energy, for which he has no outlet in his routine activities. Temples, public worship, processions, dramatic performances, dances, music and song, statues and pyramids have always been associated in some way with the life of the people. This aspect of peoplehood is the one that calls forth the most pleasurable experiences in the life of the individual. To those who possess an extra portion of energy and talent, folkways and folk symbols become a means of creative self-expression which evokes high regard and admiration from one's fellows. To those who are not so gifted, they provide occasions for passive enjoyment. Consequently, they are more instrumental, perhaps, than any of the other elements of ethnic life in endearing the people to the individual.

The foregoing are the elements of the culture, civilization or tradition which constitute the content of the ethnic consciousness or we-feeling of a people. It should be evident from their very nature that they presuppose the possession of a common land. When we define the essence of a tree, for example, we distinguish between its constituent elements, such as the roots, stem, leaves, and its indispensable conditions of existence, such as earth, air and sunshine. Likewise the sense of peoplehood implies language, history, customs, as constituting its very being. But a land is not part of its being; it is the indispensable condition of that being. A common language, like Esperanto, may possibly arise among people who live in different parts of the world, but who certainly do not possess a common history. If a people that is dispersed possesses a common history, that is because its ancestors occupied at one time a particular territory upon which that history was enacted. If not the acquisition of the land, certainly the need of defending it against invaders, and the fortunes attendant upon the struggles waged in its behalf, are the main subject-matter of a people's history. Likewise, every part of the land, in which those struggles were waged and later memorialized in song and story, gives actuality to the people as a living entity which cannot survive complete dissociation from that land.

2

PEOPLEHOOD AS A LIVING PROCESS

What has thus far been said about the elements which constitute the ethnic culture does not account for the living process of peoplehood. There are dead cultures or civilizations. What renders them alive is an indigenous leadership which actively relates the culture or civilization to the present day interests and problems of the people, to their education, to their economic needs, to their inner and outer conflicts and to their diversions. This leadership has been historically of two types: (1) the political type which is expert in dealing with factors of a visible and tangible character; (2) the ecclesiastical type which is expert in dealing with factors and forces of an invisible and intangible type. Those acts of peace and war, in which there is a visible relation between means and ends, come under the control of the type of leadership designated as political. This leadership, viewed collectively and as a going affair, is the state. That phase, however, of those same arts of peace and war, in which there is no *visible* or natural relationship between means and ends, is controlled by the type of leadership known as the church or ecclesia.

The variety of the factors and forces with which the ecclesiastical type of leadership has occasion to deal is of incomparably far wider range than that of the political type. There is intrinsically little difference between the kind of physical force employed by the rulers who constitute the state in a primitive people and that employed by a modern state. It is otherwise with the church or ecclesia. There is a universe apart between totem, tabu and magic, on the one hand, and cosmic divinity and personal ethics, on the other. Though threats may figure in the means of control employed by ecclesiastics, as in those employed by the political rulers, the element of persuasion is always present. In time, persuasion comes to be virtually the sole method employed by ecclesiastics. This is evident when we realize that the state always remains a compulsory institution, whereas the church or ecclesia ultimately evolves as a voluntary institution.

While among all peoples these two types of leadership have always existed—since human beings naturally distinguish between the visible and invisible factors of life—not all peoples have followed the same pattern. With most peoples, the political leadership predominates as a department of state and subordinates the ecclesiastical leadership. In fewer instances the reverse is the case. In ancient Greece and ancient Rome as well as in the Byzantine Empire the church was a department of the state. It virtually is that in modern Protestant countries, where the Lutheran or Episcopalian Church is the established church. The same was true in Japan, before the end of World War II. This was also the case with Israel, during the period of the First Temple. During the era of the Second Temple, except for the period beginning with Herod and to a large extent even then, the priesthood was the ruling power. The Pharisees inaugurated a movement to democratize the ecclesiastical leadership and to take it out of the hands of the priesthood. With the destruction of the Second Temple, their purpose was achieved, and throughout Jewish life thereafter the democratic form of ecclesiastical leadership predominated, though there has always existed alongside it a kind of quasi-political leadership. The latter has had to be fragmented, because the Jews were exiled from their land, and each community had to have its own local quasi-political leadership.

The foregoing analysis should throw light on the question of what type of group the Jews were before the Emancipation. Then they constituted a people. They knew themselves and were known by the rest of the world as such. The question is whether the leadership of the Jewish people was predominantly of the ecclesiastical type or of the political type. To that the only answer can be that they were, on the whole, a people governed by a democratic ecclesia.

By the same token, *the Christian Church, to the extent that it still is visible, is a people.* This becomes clear, when we note some of the historical facts concerning the Church. When Rome fell in 473, the situation was such as to make it necessary for the Church to assume the leadership and to use the state as an instrument of its will. As the barbarian peoples coalesced gradually into distinct peoples, with state leadership of their own, a protracted struggle developed between the Catholic Church and the incipient states as to which should have the upper hand. This is known as the Guelph-Ghibelline struggle. The real meaning of these events is that, when the barbarians conquered Rome and began to evolve the elements of a common culture based on that of ancient Rome, the Catholic Church wished to make of them one people with the ecclesia as the source of authority. That plan failed. But while the whole of Europe divided itself into different peoples, Christendom continued to live on as an international people, with the ecclesiastical ruler as its head.

Historical circumstances have thus brought it about that in the Western civilizations, the individual is a member of two peoples at the same time, the people he calls his nation and the people he calls his church. Not in all cases have the two coalesced. Only in those countries where the church is established, or where a concordat regulates the relations of state and church, is there something of a coalescence between the two civilizations or peoples within each civilization.

3

A PEOPLE VIEWED ETHICALLY

When the Jews became citizens of the several countries that granted them civic rights, they took over the prevailing anomalous condition of belonging simultaneously to two peoples. It was entirely unjust on the part of the nations to expect the Jews to liquidate their own peoplehood, while permitting their own citizens to belong to two peoples, one identified with the state and the other identified with the church. It was more so to expect the Jews, after renouncing their own

Jewish peoplehood, to accept Christianity because it happened to be the religion of the majority. Not for this had the Jews been martyred for eighteen centuries.

The fact is that the sense of peoplehood carries with it the definite moral duty of being loyal to the people into which one is born. Ethics has generally approved the preferential treatment of members of one's family, a principle that applies also to one's people. In seeing a people as merely an extension of the family, the ancients supplied the unity, which was the product of cultural and spiritual factors, with the strength that comes from an awareness of kinship. *It is generally taken for granted that, other things being equal, a person owes the members of his own people more interest, cooperation and love than members of a different people.* Cosmopolitanism is more likely to be an alibi for not doing one's duty to one's own people than the acceptance of the duty to help other peoples in addition to one's own.

Ethnic loyalty becomes a source of trouble only when it is conceived so narrowly as to rule out all loyalties that transcend the limits of one's own people. It is then that every other people is considered a competitor for the world's goods and a potential enemy, and every measure that calls for cooperation with them a menace to one's own people. Such is the national isolationism which still dominates men's minds. Even moral and religious endeavors, to say nothing of economic movements or pacifist activities, that stress the obligation of reckoning with general human welfare, are still looked upon with suspicion.

The ethnic isolationism just described would go further and insist that the individual must regard his own people as not only unique but as superior to all other peoples, and as fulfilling the destiny of human life more adequately than any other. The individual must believe that his own people, divinely chosen, enjoys a greater share of the divine spirit than any other. He must consider its language as the most beautiful, its laws as the most sacred, its history as the most purposeful, its morals as the most just and its folkways as the most humanizing. "My people can do no wrong," must be the motto for each of its members. Whatever adventures it enters upon to extend its dominion or to impose its will on others are to be viewed as a manifestation of its superior energy and will, and as a means of bringing other peoples within the orbit of its bliss. It is not hard to recognize in all this the type of nationalism promulgated by Chauvin, and for a time adopted as a policy of state by Germany, Italy and Japan.

Mankind has come to a point, however, where to exact of the indi-

vidual this worshipful attitude toward his people is to expect him to be immoral. The very idea that any race or people should claim to constitute a higher order of humanity than any other has come to be viewed with disgust and apprehension. What then shall we make of our tradition in which that idea unmistakenly plays an important part? The Jewish tradition expects the Jew to regard his people as divinely chosen and its Torah or civilization the most perfect, with only those who are proselyted and accept its authority as eligible for the life of bliss in the hereafter. To be sure, there are stray passages in Rabbinic literature which sound a universal note. It is true that R. Judah Hallevi [3] teaches that "those who become Jews do not take equal rank with born Israelites, who are specially privileged to attain prophecy." Yet we have in Maimonides [4] an authority who maintains that all human beings are equally eligible to eternal life. But in the main, the Jewish tradition undoubtedly reflects the spirit of ethnic isolationism which was the universal norm in pre-modern times.

There is nothing else that we can do about this traditional attitude except henceforth to disavow it as clearly and as emphatically as we can. This implies, of course, that we cannot afford to treat our tradition as fixed and final. It is always in the making. In the past, its growth was not recognized. Henceforth, it must be not only recognized but directed. It must respond to the increased knowledge and understanding of human life. With the world constituted as it was in the past, with all peoples regarding one another as mortal enemies engaged in a deadly struggle for existence, with each knowing very little of the inner life of the other, faith in the inherent supremacy of one's people seemed to have been necessary for giving an ethnic group a chance to survive. Neither Plato nor Aristotle, despite extraordinary moral insight and intellectual grasp, achieved the idea of universalism. The very idea of a developing Jewish tradition is but part of the more general idea that man's moral conceptions continue to develop. What was perfectly moral in the past may be deemed immoral today.

It is only fair to recall the extenuating circumstances which account for the emphasis in our tradition on the election of Israel. The struggle for existence, waged by the Jewish people since the destruction of the Second Temple, called for a far greater measure of inner reenforcement than that waged by other peoples. Only an extraordinary faith in its own worth and destiny could have armed it against a cruelly hostile world bent upon its destruction. The great Prophets who arose during the era of the First Commonwealth were far from such narrow ethnic loyalty. They had no scruples about castigating Israel with the most bitter denunciation and biting sarcasm. It is noteworthy that they were later taken to task for this by the Sages who lived after the destruction of the Second Commonwealth,[5] by which time the Jews needed all possible encouragement to remain loyal to their own people.

A far more pressing and tragic problem than that of breaking with the traditional assumption that a person belongs exclusively to the people into which he is born, and one with which we are confronted daily is: Has a person who is born a Jew the moral right to withdraw from the Jewish people? Is assimilation or the complete transfer of allegiance from Jewish to a non-Jewish people ethical?

There was a time when the transfer of a person's allegiance from one people to another was unequivocally regarded as unworthy of any decent human being. The modern change in attitude is a typical illustration of change in social standards. There is one important exception to this change, even nowadays. When the people to which one belongs is under attack, to try to escape one's responsibilities to it, by joining another people, is regarded as treasonable.

These considerations indicate, in the first place, why it is wrong for Jews to avail themselves of the modern tolerant attitude toward withdrawal from one's ethnic allegiance. The Jews are today, perhaps, more than ever in the position of a people under attack. The Jewish people will continue to be on the defensive, so long as not all nations have politically emancipated the Jews, and so long as even those which have granted them civil rights do not accept them as economic and social equals. Although the Soviet Union admits Jews to full equality, it does not permit them to have any active relationship with Jews of other lands. The existence of the Jewish people is menaced so long as it has no commonwealth of its own in Eretz Yisrael. Under these circumstances it cannot be moral for a Jew to abandon his people, an act commonly characterized as cowardice, opportunism or treason, depending upon the spirit in which it is carried out.

If the Jewish people is to have a just claim on the allegiance of those born into it, it must possess a leadership that helps them to make the best use of their lives. It must provide the individual Jew with the leadership which makes a serious effort to utilize the Jewish tradition, culture or civilization as a factor in helping or inspiring him to cope with the actual difficulties he encounters as a Jew.

Until the end of the eighteenth century the rabbinate constituted an adequate leadership, and was able to keep the Jewish nation alive.

Since then, however, new adjustments have had to be made, intellectual, social, political; a new type of leadership has become necessary.

The Historical School of Jewish thought helped to formulate a modern presentation of the Jewish past, stimulated by the desire to advance Jewish emancipation. The fact that the "science of Jewish learning" was related to present needs entitles its creators to be accounted as Jewish leaders who helped to vitalize the Jewish tradition, by showing its implications for our day. Their epigones, however, have lost themselves in arid wastes and dry-as-dust scholarship which offers an escape from more vital problems of Jewish life.

Zionism has supplied leadership of another type, one that deals with the visible realities of mass migration, homeland and a place in the sun. Had it not been for the spiritual leadership of the founders of Jewish learning and for the practical leadership of the founders of Zionism, there would no longer have been a modern Jewish people. Unless their work is continued with renewed energy and vision, the assimilationists will have a good excuse for cutting loose from the Jewish people.

The main task confronting Jewish leadership today is to redefine the meaning of peoplehood and ethnic consciousness, in terms that will not only render tenable, but will invest with new purpose and dignity, the status of the Jews who are dispersed among the various peoples of the world. We need a leadership that can point the way to a concept of Jewish peoplehood that would make our status creative of new social and spiritual values as well as compatible with unquestioned loyalty to the non Jewish people with which our lot is cast.

This task involves a spiritual insight into the potentialities for good that inhere in peoplehood, and the practical wisdom to translate these into a way of life not only for Jews, but also for the rest of the world. The Jewish people, through its history and religion, stimulated the ethnic self-consciousness of the Christian and Moslem peoples. That influence, unfortunately, is being viciously distorted into a force for evil. That the Jewish people, through its present struggle for existence, should help to eliminate the dross of collective selfishness and sacred egoism from modern nationalism, and render it essentially a means of social creativity and individual betterment would, indeed, be a vindication of the divine right of peoples to retain their individuality.

CHAPTER FIVE

LIVING IN TWO CIVILIZATIONS

1

WHY THE JEW CANNOT DO WITHOUT JUDAISM

As a matter of principle, we may be convinced of the legitimacy of Jewish peoplehood in a democratic society. Nevertheless, we may find it difficult to fit such a status into the actual frame of American life and democracy. Jewish peoplehood finds expression in a tradition, in a way of life, in milieu and in specific sights and sounds. If Judaism is to be more than a memory of ancient glory, or more than a way of speaking, it must consist of things that are visible, audible and tangible. The sum of all that is recognizable as belonging to Judaism makes of it a civilization.

A civilization, as modern nationalism might define it, is looking and acting like others. But *as a humanizing process, a civilization is the cumulative heritage of knowledge, experience and attitudes acquired by the successive generations of a people in its striving to achieve salvation.* That heritage links the generations together into a continuing unity. It consists of a variety of elements; memories of the people's past and hopes concerning its future; a particular language and literature; specific laws, morals, customs and folkways; evaluations of life and an assortment of art forms. Various items are chosen from each of these elements and are made the object of special regard and reverence; they are treated as sacred. Taken in their entirety those items constitute the religion, or the religious aspect of the civilization.

To grasp, however, the essence of a civilization, we must do more than recognize the organic unity of all of its elements. We must learn to appreciate its inter-related functions which have one basic purpose, namely, that all who live by that civilization should feel the need of one another. Only in that way can they get the most out of life and give their maximum to it. The precept "Thou shalt love thy neighbor as thyself" [1] is not some fantastic aspiration, too good to be practicable. It is nothing more than an elementary requirement that those who belong to the same civilization shall want and welcome one another, and not regard one another as rivals and as a thorn in each other's side. By the same token, the precept "Thou shalt love the Lord thy God" [2] means experiencing a need for and welcoming God. It means so to accept life that for its sake we are prepared to be and do our utmost and even willing to bear the worst that may befall us. Whenever we say "Blessed art Thou, O Lord our God" we, in effect, welcome God on those terms. This is what makes Judaism a religious civilization.

Accordingly, our answer to the challenge of modern nationalism should be: We Jews depend upon Judaism and the fellowship of the Jewish people for that feeling of being needed and welcomed, without which we can neither live a normal healthy life, nor possess the essential ingredients that go into the making of worthy character and personality. We need Judaism to help us maintain our human dignity and achieve our salvation. Almost ten percent of the American people declare themselves anti-Semites,[3] and harbor the criminally insane sentiment of wishing to destroy us. Twice that number are ready to join them upon the flimsiest provocation. In the country as a whole, Jews at best are tolerated, but neither desired nor welcomed. Our best friends will forgive us our being Jews, but can seldom forget it. This is presently true of all democracies.

In a modern replica of Voltaire's *Candide* called *All for the Best* by Bentz Plagemann[4] the principal character, a navy doctor, David Forster, sums up the "excruciatingly broadminded" attitude of the average liberal American toward Jews in the following: "I flatter myself that I am broadminded. I do not go out of my way to make friends with Jews, but I do not avoid them. . . . They weren't in my fraternity at Martin Towers. It seemed the only sensible way to avoid discrimination."

In *Earth Could Be Fair*, Pierre Van Paassen[5] describes a Jew in the person of David Dalmaden. David Dalmaden, who was fully aware of what it meant to be a Jew even under the best of circumstances, said, "The farmers speak of their country, their laws, their market, their religion. It all hangs together like pearls on the same string from one end of the country to the other, and from ancient times onward into eternity. Even the cows and the horses and the sheep and the chickens are an integral and inseparable part of the whole, and all of them, men and beasts, live in self-evident happiness. But I feel as if I am not a part, as if I do not belong. I am an outsider."

All of these facts combine to justify us in strengthening our own Jewish civilization, not for the purpose of making our way to where we are unwelcome, or for segregating ourselves from those who are ready to accept us, but to find in one another that acceptance and welcome which for a long time to come we shall not find among our non-Jewish neighbors.

The fact that our non-Jewish neighbors are not glad to receive us should not make us resentful or bitter. They belong, after all, to a part of the human race that has been indoctrinated for over two thousand years with a vicious hatred toward our people. They have had it drilled into them that we are the incarnation of evil. We should not expect them to overcome in the course of one or two generations the effects of such persistent propaganda of hate. In the meantime, however, we and our children and our children's children are entitled to our share of happiness, for which being needed and welcomed is an indispensable prerequisite. Eretz Yisrael Jews need and welcome their fellow-Jews. That is the way we Jews in the United States should feel toward one another. We need that feeling of comradeship, if we are to be integrated, self-respecting and fearless human beings. Surely the United States can benefit but little from citizens who live broken, self-hating and fear-ridden lives.

2

THE JEW'S TASK TO LIVE IN TWO CIVILIZATIONS

Judaism cannot long survive here, unless we are convinced that corporate Jewish life can fit into the pattern of American democratic nationalism. Such a conviction must square with a tenable philosophy of American life. According to that philosophy, the United States has a right to expect the individual citizen to identify himself completely with her vital interests, and to participate unreservedly in all of her legitimate strivings. The individual is permitted to have interests and to engage in activities which are confined to a limited group within the American population, and which that group shares with nationals of other countries, as long as those interests and activities do not interfere with those of other Americans. This is the meaning of that individual freedom which is the essence of democracy. All genuine democracy recognizes the right of individuals and of groups to be different. The recognition of the Jews' right to be different affords them the opportunity to develop the differential factors in Jewish life, in any way that is not detrimental to the equal and similar rights of other groups and individuals, or to the general welfare. This is tantamount to saying that the American Jew should find it possible to live in two civilizations simultaneously, the American and the Jewish.

Let those who doubt the possibility of living in two civilizations be reminded that this is exactly what every Christian American is trying to do. By the same token that Judaism is a civilization, Christianity also is a civilization.* This, in effect, is the meaning of the remark made recently by a well-known Christian theologian who said: "We are Christians in spite of speculation." [6] He implied that Christianity was not a matter of abstract thought but of collective life. It is highly instructive to learn that, among Christians, the question, "What is Christianity?" is no less perennial than is the question, "What is Judaism?" among Jews. The reason is that each is more than a religion.[7]

Christianity also consists of a tradition, a way of life and customs that are visibly, tangibly and audibly Christian. Catholicism is a highly intensive civilization; Protestantism is an attenuated civilization and a torso of the former. In either case, Christianity happens to have its roots in the same land as Judaism, though it has branched out all over the world. Every land in which it is at home is its homeland. To the Christian American, the Jordan is just as familiar as the Mississippi. He would deem it vulgar to assert that Jesus means less to him than George Washington.

The Jewish judge who, some time ago, wrote that, to the American Jew, Jefferson and Lincoln were more important than Abraham and Moses,[8] spoke only in his own name, and merely proclaimed that he was less of a Jew than most Christians are Christian. For American citizens to live in two civilizations may not be compatible with American jingoism, but it is unquestionably compatible with the American dream. It was the recrudescence of jingoism, among other things, that moved Thomas Wolfe,[9] one of the profoundest interpreters of the American spirit in recent times, to write the following in his posthumous novel, You Can't Go Home Again: "I believe that we are lost here in America, but I believe we shall be found. . . . I think the true discovery of America is before us. I think the true fulfillment of our spirit, of our people, of our mighty and immortal land is yet to come. I think the true discovery of our democracy is still before us." Nothing seems more incongruous than that Jews, who claim that they are Jews in religion only, should make it a specialty to forget the American dream and act the jingo.

The extent to which Jews are fearful of being as frankly Jewish as the Christians are Christian is never so flagrant as when our Government takes a census of its population. That census reflects the extent

* See above p. 89.

to which Americans accept the fact of living in two civilizations. Those who accept it without any reservations show no reluctance in having their church affiliations registered. Jews have been so intimidated by the hostility against them that they are afraid to avail themselves of the rights claimed by other citizens. Their leaders squirm at having the census taker register them as Jews.

It so happens that, in this country, every group in whose life some form of religion either has played, or still plays, a dominant role, is a minority group. Of all such groups, the one which seems to be least afraid, ashamed or confused, and has no difficulty in recognizing who belongs to it and who does not, is the Roman Catholic. This fact comes out in the remarkable definiteness and exactitude of the statistics which give the number of its communicants and the annual increase in their members. The Protestant groups are not able to report similarly reliable statistics about themselves. But the most unreliable and unprocurable are the statistics concerning Jews. The main reason, of course, is that Jews do not know what makes them Jews. For fear of being misunderstood, they dare not use the traditional term "nation." For fear of being discriminated against they avoid the term "race." For lack of a category that properly describes them, they answer to the term "religion" merely because they know no other. But, paradoxically, most of them are not affiliated with any Jewish religious body. They do not actually know what differentiates them from their fellow-Americans.

Consequently when our Government asks for statistics about Jews, no responsible Jewish agency is prepared to submit reliable figures. In certain Jewish circles which engage in protective self-discoloration, underestimating the number of Jews in various communities has become quite an art. The whole matter of Jewish statistics in this country has become the private property of a well-meaning statistician and the few people whom he has succeeded in interesting in his project. Very few of us are aware of the predicament which the absence of an authoritative source of demographic information about us creates for certain Government personnel.

The political pattern to which it is important to have our status as a group conform must be the one that is likely to remain permanent in this country. It would, therefore, be illusory to plan a status based on the hope or expectation that the political pattern of this country will be modified to permit cultural pluralism. Foreign national cultures can, at best, be but a passing phase in the life of the first two or three generations of immigrant populations. *The only kinds of groups likely to remain permanent within the political pattern of this country are those that have religious significance for their adherents.*[10] The Jewish people must have as much religious significance for the American Jew as the Church has for the individual Christian. It would then be as entitled to a place in the frame of American life as is the Church. For a corporate entity to have religious significance, it need not be of a transcendental or supernatural character. There are many ways in which a group can have religious significance for the individual.

American democracy recognizes two distinct types of church groups, visible and invisible, corresponding with a distinction in Christendom itself. The Catholic Church is the outstanding visible Church, possessing visible and tangible manifestations of its international solidarity. Its milieu, its buildings, its personnel, its discipline, its great art, music and sculpture—these are the concrete embodiments of its collective spirit. In large measure, this is true, also, of the Episcopal Church. The other denominations tend to fade into invisibility. That is the main cause of their gradual deterioration. *Because visibility and tangibility are essential to keep any group spirit alive, we Jews should strive to achieve a community status which is analogous to that of the Catholic Church.*

Nothing in this suggestion, however, should be taken to imply anything like the authoritarian or totalitarian character of group organization typical of that Church. On the contrary, the organization of a Jewish community must parallel internally the most genuine type of democracy in the American political pattern, and allow for diversity in matters of religious belief and practice. But as a group that forms part of world Jewry, American Jews should interpret their solidarity as a religio-cultural one, entirely parallel to that of the Catholic Church.

3

LIVING IN TWO CIVILIZATIONS CALLS FOR A REDEFINITION OF RELIGION

It may be asked: How can a community, which permits diversity of religious belief and practice, claim religious status? What would entitle us Jews to be designated as a religio-cultural instead of merely a cultural group? The answer is to be found in a proper understanding of what we mean by "religion." If, for example, we were to accept the popular notion of religion, and maintain that for a group to be called "religious" it must lay claim to having originated with some supernatural event or person, we would have to exclude from the category of "religious" eighty-three per cent of the rabbinate who, according to a recent study, no longer believe in the supernatural origin of the Jewish people.[11] The only way in which it is possible to determine whether we are entitled to designate our communal status "religious" is to ascertain whether that status will fulfill the function that is generally meant by religion.

The function of a religion is to enable those who live by it to achieve salvation, or life abundant. If the indivisible peoplehood of the Jews is as indispensable a means to the salvation of the Jew, as the Church is to that of the Christian, it serves a religious function. Since the Jewish community is the medium through which that peoplehood would enable the Jew to achieve his salvation, it is entitled to all the privileges and immunities that the modern democratic state confers upon all religious bodies. To be sure, salvation would not consist, as it did in the past for all Jews, in a feeling of confidence in the coming of a personal Messiah, who would gather all Jews back to Eretz Yisrael, and in eternal bliss to be enjoyed by each Jew in the hereafter. It would consist rather in the cultivation of basic values like faith, patience, inner freedom, humility, thankfulness, justice and love which enable a man to be and do his best, and to bear uncomplainingly the worst that may befall him.* A religio-cultural community that can help its members achieve that kind of salvation is invaluable to a democratic state, whose strength consists in a citizenry of self-reliant and self-respecting men and women.

What seems to trouble some people, when the idea of living in two civilizations is suggested to them, is that it would necessitate splitting our personalities, and giving, as it were, one half to each civilization. This mechanical notion is as groundless as imagining that we cannot be as proficient in two languages as we can be in one. The very contrary is the case. They who know English only, do not even know English. Those whose life horizon is limited to their one native civilization do not know even that one as well as they should, if they are to be citizens of the world. Moreover, they cannot elicit from it all the good that is latent in it.

The vicissitudes of history have brought it about that the average human being has to draw upon two civilizations to obtain all those

* See Chapter XV.

values which he requires for his self-realization as a human being. It
is a need to which Christians are no less subject than Jews. A way of
life that is exclusively American could nowadays be lived only by the
American Indian. When the Europeans brought Christianity to this
country, they brought a civilization which they have since been synthesizing with those elements of American national life that are the
products of the new American physical environment and of the historical events that have created the American people. This business
of living in two civilizations may call for new powers of mind and heart,
and to that extent may mark an advance in man's development. In
music, too, harmony was unknown five hundred years ago, a fact cited
to prove that, as the human race matures, it discovers latent powers in
itself, the existence of which it did not at first suspect.

One may question the extent to which Protestantism may be regarded as a civilization, since it has broken with the visible Church,
and has given up the distinctive Latin culture of the Roman Catholic
Church. No such question, however, can arise with regard to Catholicism which is, beyond all doubt, an affirmative and aggressive type
of civilization. Yet no one would suggest that being an American
Catholic means living on two different planes, or being a Catholic
part of the time and an American the rest of the time. Nor may the
right of Catholics to live their Catholic civilization simultaneously with
the American be questioned, without impugning the fundamentals
of American democracy.

It is true that an authoritarian and supernaturalistic Catholicism,
carried to its traditional and logical conclusion, does place the Catholic
citizen in an anomalous position. Such a conclusion implies that he
must regard non-Catholic American people as living in sin, because
its Government does not defer to the authority of the Vatican. The
Church, however, is too wise to insist upon translating that implication into practice. That would be incompatible with whole-hearted
allegiance to the American Government. On the other hand, it is part
of American democracy to accept the actual *modus vivendi* by which
the Church abides, and to recognize the right of its adherents to foster
Catholic civilization without let or hindrance.

It is a well-known fact that the Puritans endeavored to establish in
America a way of life based on Biblical law. One does not regard the
Puritan spirit on that account as segregationist and as alien to the
American pattern of life. Why then should the efforts of Jews to live
by Biblical law, as embodied in Jewish civilization, be an evidence of

segregationism? If it is legitimate for the Irish to parade on St. Patrick's day, in glorification of the patron saint of a non-American nation, why would it be less legitimate for Jews to carry the *Sefer Torah* [12] in procession through the streets on *Simhat Torah?* [13] On Palm Sunday, the streets are thronged with Christians bearing palm branches, but on *Sukkot*,[14] Jews, if they must carry a *lulav* [15] through the streets usually wrap it in paper to conceal its identity, because they assume that any flaunting of a distinctively Jewish culture trait will expose them to the charge of ghettoism. Why is it American to go about on All-Saints Eve in masquerade, and an exotic practice to do the same on *Purim?* Why should Jews consider it a good American practice for Christians to display Christmas trees and sing Christmas carols in public, while feeling too inhibited to display the *Hanukkah* lights publicly and to sing Hebrew hymns in the streets?

In the Diaspora, Jews are bound to identify themselves spiritually as well as culturally with the nations among which they live. *Judaism, to evoke American Jews' loyalty, must be not only compatible with their loyalty to America but also corroborative of it.* In the cultural melting pot of American life, no cultural variants have any chance of surviving unless they can make good the claim of transcending in significance the groups that foster them. This means that the cultural variants have to be of a religious character and function, for only thus can their significance be universal. Only thus can they give to each individual who lives by them that which enables him to order his life so as to achieve his self-fulfillment as a human being. Whatever values American life itself begets are at present lacking in that religious character and function. This is why it looks to the religious cultures, which its various historic groups have brought with them, to give the individual citizen the moral stamina and sense of responsibility which are indispensable to national survival and health. Judaism looks to the religio-cultural heritage which Jews have brought with them to accomplish this for its Jewish citizens. *That expectation is a challenge to us Jews not only to retain our group life in this country, but also to achieve a religious orientation that might prove of great value to the religiously starved mankind of our day.*

Judaism, or the religious civilization of the Jewish people, in its present effort to arrive at a *modus vivendi* in the midst of other civilizations has the opportunity of making an important contribution to the recognition of a far-reaching social principle, namely, that *any civilization which has no aggressive purpose or "mission" has an in-*

trinsic right to live either by itself, or in symbiosis with any other civilization.

The commonwealth status which the Jewish people seeks to achieve in Eretz Yisrael is the expression of the desire on the part of the Jewish civilization to live by itself. As a civilization, it is the product of a particular land, and, so long as it survives, it is entitled to live in that land. Having been driven out by *force majeure* did not deprive it of that right. The argument that the modern Italians have a claim on Britain or France analogous to that of the Jews on Eretz Yisrael is the height of absurdity. The Italian civilization has no roots in either country, whereas the Jewish civilization is inconceivable without Eretz Yisrael.

Moreover, *a civilization has a right to live cooperatively with another civilization in any one country so long as it has no intentions of competing with the latter, much less dominating it.* Such cooperative living may be interpreted in terms of group equality, as in countries where minorities as such are granted political rights, or in terms of individual equality, as in the United States. In the latter case, the individual has only one set of religious values to live by.

What would happen, if the civilization that is still without definitive religious values were to evolve them? Would not one who lives in the two civilizations be expected to live by the two sets of religious values? The only possible answer is an affirmative one. For just as the two civilizations are hyphenated in the individual who lives in both of them simultaneously, so would the two sets of religious values have to be hyphenated in him. Religious hyphenism would, therefore, have to be recognized as legitimate. Nothing better could happen to human life, for that would enable religion to function as a unifying instead of as a divisive influence.[16]

Before religion, however, can so function, the various historical and organized religions would have to renounce their exaggerated pretensions to being the sole possessors of the key to human salvation. Each would have to acknowledge that the others are equally apprised of ways of salvation for their own adherents, that each, in its *particular* way, seeks to embody ideals which are of *universal* validity, but which can best be realized for each group in relation to the cultural traits and social institutions resulting from its own collective experience. Just as there can be no peace among nations as long as each insists on absolute sovereignty, so there can be no peace among religions as long as each insists on being in exclusive possession of absolute or revealed truth.

The undertaking to live in two civilizations simultaneously is, to be sure, a new experiment in the art of living. But for us Jews to try out better ways of human living should be nothing new. It may be that we have in us the kind of stuff which, having remained unconsumed in the iron furnace of Egypt, cannot be liquefied in any of the modern national melting pots. Being loyal to two civilizations is as ethical as being loyal to father and mother. "The serving of two masters," said Harry Wolfson,[17] "is not a moral anomaly, unless, as in the original adage, one of the masters be satanic."

Sometimes nature, instead of waiting for chance to bring new species into existence has the same living creature undergo changes in structure and function. The slowly crawling caterpillar, for example, is transformed into the winged butterfly. In such creatures, life seems to be too impatient of evolution's slow course. Driven by some overpowering creative urge, life leaps far ahead of the stage in which it happens to be. The result is a new type of being that emerges from one continuing life. This process is known as metamorphosis.

We would do well to read the meaning of human development in the light of this extraordinary phenomenon in nature. Physically, man is subject to the slow process of evolution which has to be measured with the yardstick of geological eons. But mentally and spiritually, man finds natural evolution too slow. His irresistible urge to be more than what he is may be regarded as a yearning to achieve metamorphosis into a higher order of being. It has somehow fallen to our lot as a people to herald and incarnate this principle of human metamorphosis. With our messianic ideal, we Jews have awakened in the human heart that discontent which is the forerunner of a regenerated humanity. If we can reinterpret our messianism as future-mindedness, then, by all means, let us retain it. Some one well said: "Perhaps, unless we can learn to think of ourselves as we might be a hundred thousand years hence, we shall destroy each other one hundred months hence. Perhaps only the Utopians can help us survive." [18]

From the standpoint of this interpretation of human history and of Israel's place in the world, the circumstances which have made it necessary for Jews to live in two civilizations are part of the metamorphosis which the human race is undergoing at the present time. This necessity is a challenge to the Jewish people. It compels the Jewish people to reconstitute itself into a different kind of people from that which it was in the past. It must assume a new incarnation.

In order to survive as a corporate entity, Jews must now transform themselves into a newly differentiated type of society, partly as a commonwealth developing in its own historic landscape, and partly as a people which can integrate itself with other nations in other lands, without losing its own individuality. In the present world order, with its unlimited national sovereignties, this may sound utopian. That world order, however, is doomed. Humanity cannot survive under it. The same developments that point to a warless world point to the new type of people which the Jews must now become or perish. The will of the Jewish people to live has thus become one with the will of mankind to live and to overcome the forces that threaten to destroy it.

According to our Sages the verse in Psalms which reads "This shall be written for the last generation,"[19] refers to a people that is moribund. "But," they add, "the concluding words of that same verse, 'And a people which shall be created shall praise the Lord,' imply that the Holy One, blessed be He, will transform that people into a new being."[20]

CHAPTER SIX

COMMUNITY—THE SOCIAL STRUCTURE
OF AMERICAN-JEWISH LIFE

1

WHY JEWS NEED COMMUNITY

Throughout the past, wherever a number of Jews lived within reach of one another, they formed a self-governing community. Each Jew was answerable to his community to a greater degree than is the citizen of a modern state to his government. The only way he could escape such responsibility was by joining the dominant faith. But the very thought of such an escape would never occur to anyone, unless he wanted to settle some grudge against his own people, or he was so ambitious of a great career that he could not but find life among them too cramping.

The self-government which Jews exercised was not granted them as a privilege. It was not even a matter of voluntary choice. It was forced on them by the exclusionist attitude of those among whom they lived, and who refused to incorporate into their own body politic. To this autonomy, perhaps more than to aught else, Jews owe their survival as a people. It rendered the Jew dependent upon his people for everything he deemed important to his life. It enabled Judaism to function not merely as a kind of avocational interest for most Jews, or as a highly specialized interest of the few, but as the guiding and controlling influence of the every-day existence of all Jews.

Moreover, in those days *the Jew needed the social heritage of his people for his basic literacy and culture.* In Christian countries, all education, elementary as well as advanced, was completely Christian in character. Jews were not permitted to avail themselves of whatever educational opportunities then existed. How else could Jews then become civilized human beings, if not by making use of their own cultural heritage? Some knowledge of Judaism was indispensable then to every Jew. It was not optional, as it is today.

In addition, then as now, human beings believed that there was more to life than their humdrum existence. Let us call that more, "salvation." It was then universally assumed that the only way to achieve salvation was to live in accordance with some supernaturally revealed laws or teachings. The Jews regarded those laws or teachings,

106

which for them constituted "Torah," as in need not only of being obeyed, but also of being studied. Where was one to get the knowledge of Torah, if not from the recognized authorities or teachers known as rabbis? Is it any wonder that formerly no Jew thought it possible to live apart from other Jews? *The sense of mutual dependence was thus the sustaining force of organized community among Jews everywhere.*

All this has changed. With the granting of civic rights to the Jews, their feeling of mutual dependence has waned. The main reason is that they are not only permitted, but expected, to derive their basic literacy and culture from the social heritage of the majority population. This has removed the principal cohesive factor of Jewish togetherness. From the standpoint of Jewish survival, that is a cataclysm. Yet most Jewish leaders, whether lay or religious, act as though the structure of Jewish life may have been somewhat shaken, but not as though it were in danger of collapsing. Either they are unconcerned about the future of the Jewish people, or they fail to realize that *the inevitable consequence of the generally accepted version of democratic nationalism is to render Judaism superfluous to the Jew.*

The only way to assure a future to Judaism is to enrich its content and intrinsic worth and to evolve a conception of democratic nationalism which would permit religious civilizations to exist within its frame. But we cannot be so sanguine as to expect both of these developments to eventuate within less than a generation. In the meantime, therefore, we have to avail ourselves of the still surviving residue of the past tendencies on the part of the Jews to pool their common interests. That, together with the genuine need of Jews for one another, because of the failure of democratic nationalism to live up to its promise of economic and social equality, will have now to constitute the motivating factor for rebuilding the social structure of American Jewish life.

Jews are still regarded as an alien group in the United States. Many individual Jews, to be sure, have risen to high positions of eminence and power, but the average Jew labors under a severe handicap, by reason of his being a Jew. The antagonism to the Jew and the resistance to his efforts to become economically and socially integrated is the result of centuries of indoctrination in bogey notions about Jews and Judaism. Anti-Semitism is the mental sepsis of Gentile society. If that society were in a state of health, it would manage to overcome the poison. But unfortunately it is nowadays more sick than ever. This is why that poison has become so virulently active of late. The struggle against anti-Semitism, which Jews have to wage as part of their self-emancipation, is a long drawn-out one, and should not be expected to end victoriously, without its first being taken over by the non-Jews.

The bearing which all this has on us Jews is that we have to look to our own efforts to satisfy fully our normal social needs. No man is self-sufficient. Particularly in the complex civilization of the Western world, with its minute division of labor, no one is prepared to maintain himself without the cooperation of others. Throughout childhood, the individual is, of course, dependent on his parents, but not solely. He relies also on the community to provide him with schooling, proper hygienic conditions and security against violence. And when he matures, even though he, in turn, is responsible for his family, he is, nevertheless, still dependent on the community as represented in the agencies of government, economic organization, and associations of all sorts.

In the modern world, the Jew receives few of these benefits from the Jewish community. He does not have the experience of being taken care of by that community, as his fathers had before the Emancipation. If he is poor, he may receive some assistance from Jewish philanthropic institutions, but even that function is gradually being assumed by the state. Most Jews today look to the general community to help them meet their basic physical needs. But here they suffer disappointment. The attitude of the general community toward the Jew is ambivalent. To a certain point the community helps him live, and reckons with his dependence upon it; beyond that it lets him down. He is a kind of civic step-child, not a stranger, yet not fully recognized as an equal. In times of prosperity, or emergency, when labor is in demand, he will be given a job; but as soon as there is a labor surplus, he is among the first to find himself unwanted.

This treatment of the Jew is not always due to malice. It is not always discrimination *against* the Jew, but is largely a necessary consequence of discrimination by Gentile employers in *favor of* persons who are tied to them by the bonds of a common tradition and kinship. Usually, however, the fact of discrimination leads to the attempt to justify it by anti-Semitic rationalizations. The presence of Jews in any occupation in excess of their proportion to the general population is resented, and leads to a demand for a *numerus clausus*. It is no secret that Jews have been studiedly kept out of some of the most important industries. What is true of employment is equally true of higher educational opportunities. Every young Jew finds that the odds are very much against him. When the time comes for him to train himself for some vocation or professional career, the first consideration is the difficulty he will, no doubt, encounter in getting a job. With no organized group to help him find his place in the economic order, he has the sense of insecurity bred into his very bones. Only those of exceptional character and strength of will can overcome the tendency to self-centered individualism and moral cynicism to which such a sense of insecurity must give rise.

It is obvious that Jews can do little, if anything, to induce the general community to care for them as fully as it does for non-Jews. But Jews can, if they take thought, so reorganize their communal life that the individual Jew may realize that "in this unanimously non-caring world," at least his own *Jewish* community cares for him. Both the ends and the means of that concern on the part of the Jewish community are bound to be different from those of the community of the past. It will be a concern not that the Jew shall have the opportunity of attaining bliss in the hereafter, through conformity to an allegedly revealed Law, but that he shall be able in his lifetime to earn a livelihood, enjoy health, and find opportunity for the exercise of his powers in the pursuit of legitimate human interests.

As to the means, it must be clear that the Jewish community cannot—as before the Emancipation—exercise full legal jurisdiction over the Jew or assume exclusive responsibility for his education. The Jew cannot retreat to the ghetto, no matter how much more at home the pre-Emancipation Jew was in his ghetto than the modern Jew is in his wider world. It is unreasonable to ask Jews to forego the advantages of their participation in the benefits accorded them by the general community, particularly since that community cannot exempt Jews from their obligation toward it, without undermining the whole structure of democratic society. *For Jews in the Diaspora, adherence to the Jewish community cannot be an alternative to adherence to the general community; it must be an addition.*

The Jewish community can be so organized that it can help the Jew overcome those political, social and economic disadvantages from which he suffers, by reason of his being identified with a minority group. It should make the individual Jew feel that he is an object of solicitous care to his fellow-Jews, no matter how indifferent the rest of the world may be to his basic interests. To feel that we are needed and cared for, even though that care may not solve every one of our problems for us, is enough to sweeten even adversity. Parents cannot protect their children from all ills, but they can help them endure those ills, by extending to them the moral support of their anxious love. A community can do the same for its members. It can offer them warmth and reassurance. "Children have a right to warm affection from their parents; it gives them a happy outlook upon the world, and is essential to healthy psychological development," wrote Bertrand Russell.[1] Likewise, the individual Jew depends upon communal affection for a wholesome outlook upon the world and a normal psychological development.

Strange as it may seem, ever since the ghetto walls were officially razed, and the solidarity of the Jewish community life has been undermined, little, if any, thought has been given to the problem of retrieving Jewish communal solidarity. This may be due to various fears and misapprehensions. In the first place, Jews are afraid that, if they became too active in caring for their own, they would segregate themselves from the general community. That might lead to the reestablishment of the ghetto. There is, however, no basis whatever for such fear. Jews can be segregated, or the ghetto reinstated only as a result of a fascist revolution that would destroy the American form of government. But as long as the present form of government will continue, Jews will necessarily be permitted to share in the basic advantages of civic life, such as police and fire protection, health and education. This sharing of elemental interests precludes segregation. So long as Jews will be permitted to enjoy even the limited economic equality that is granted them at present, they must of necessity continue to be integrated in the general community. Nothing less than a fascist revolution of the kind that brought on the Second World War would deprive Jews of their elementary rights and build a dividing wall between Jews and Gentiles.

Secondly, it is claimed that, if Jews were to build a strong community of their own they would play into the hands of the anti-Semites who maintain that the Jews are united in a conspiracy to dominate the rest of the world. By this time, it should have become evident that the policy of appeasing the anti-Semites makes as little sense as the late Neville Chamberlain's policy of appeasing the Nazis. As far as the anti-Semites are concerned, we are damned if we do, and we are damned if we don't. Nothing short of our extinction will suit them. It is folly, therefore, even to take note of their ravings against us.

Finally, few Jews, even among those who are loyal to their people and their tradition, realize the vital connection between Judaism and the social structure of Jewish life. To most Jews anything that has to do with organization smacks of the secular or profane. It is at best an instrument which is serviceable as long as it raises no questions. But as soon as it exposes us to the charge of trying to segregate ourselves from the civic community, it ought to be dispensed with. This dualism between the spirit and the body of Jewish life has to be unlearned. *Without an enduring social structure, such as only a well-organized community can provide, being a Jew is like trying to live as a disembodied soul.*

The main reason, however, for the failure to come to grips with the problem of Jewish communal solidarity is, no doubt, the fact that it is not possible, as it was in the past, to build the community around the synagogue. It is, therefore, necessary to evolve a new conception of communal cohesion. This is by no means easy, especially for those Jews who are identified with the synagogue, and who believe that it is the only logical instrument of cohesiveness among Jews. Most of us are loath to have our striving to survive as an identifiable group regarded as arbitrary or unreasonable. We are, indeed, eager for it to be recognized as a normal means to the attainment of our salvation. Since the synagogue is dedicated to the task of reminding us where our true salvation lies, it should naturally serve as the rallying point of the Jewish community.

But the ineluctable fact is that, in the very process of expounding the meaning of salvation and indicating the means to its attainment, the synagogue has become a divisive instead of a uniting influence. The Reform movement was the first to introduce drastic changes in Jewish belief and practice. This has made it necessary for those who conform strictly to tradition to label themselves as Orthodox. Others again prefer a middle course, between strict conformity to tradition and what seems to be like a complete break with it—although the Reformists themselves would deny it to be such. Each religious group develops its own organizations, institutions, commitments and loyalties, and tends to concentrate on itself the interest that should be given to Jewish life as a whole.

It is thus unavoidable that the synagogue should fragmentize Jewry into sects and denominations. As matters stand at present, these sects and denominations find it difficult to overcome their mutual antagonisms, even when common action is most urgent. If any action for the common good is taken, as on occasions it must be, it is outside, and in spite of, the various synagogue groupings.

That dilemma is pointed out here not with the intention of deprecating, or deploring, the numerous divisions that exist in the religious life of our people. On the contrary, if we want freedom of thought, then we must expect differences in religious belief and practice. This is the *novum* in contemporary Jewish life. *The more earnestly and persistently we endeavor to clarify our own religious views, and the more we try to stabilize our religious practice, the more certain are we to sharpen the theological differences among ourselves.* If we are prepared to accept this outcome as inevitable, we should at least prevent it from so fragmentizing us as to place us beyond all possibility of feeling and acting as one people.

The synagogue can no longer be the all inclusive community that it was in the past. Both the necessarily limiting character of its specific version of Judaism, and the urge to satisfy needs of a non-religious character, have given rise to a whole network of Jewish organizations. The fraternal order B'nai B'rith, for instance, was formed more than one-hundred years ago because Jews, who were beginning to divide themselves along religious lines, felt the need of some means of fraternal association.[2] Then came the many *Landsmanschaften*. Later, the various philanthropic societies were established to maintain hospitals, orphan asylums and homes for the aged, and to provide relief for the needy. Still later, these were combined into federations and welfare funds. When the Zionist movement came on the scene, it gave rise to different groupings: the Zionist Organization of America, Mizrachi, Hadassah and Labor Zionists. The menace of anti-Semitism led to the formation of the American Jewish Committee and the American Jewish Congress. These organizations and their activities, which are concerned with the secular needs of Jews, consume almost all of the available time and energies of the public-spirited and socially-minded among us.

It is futile to bewail this multiplicity of societies, agencies and organizations outside the synagogue, and to plead that all of them become an integral part of it. One might as well try to get the chicken back into the egg. The law of the division of labor is the law of human society, in the spiritual no less than in other domains of human activity. It would be entirely impracticable to draw the synagogue into the maelstrom of Jewish public activities. Federation drives and United Jewish Appeal campaigns during the first years of their activity would turn to the synagogue for their initial support, and even depend on it for the bulk of their collections. Experience, however, soon convinced the workers that far better results could be achieved were the campaigns organized along trade lines. Each of the prospective givers would then know the financial rating of the others, and the contributions would have some reasonable relation to their giving ability.

The main issue now is not what kind of Judaism we would like to have in this country, but whether we shall have any kind of Judaism at all. Those who are affiliated with the synagogue are expected to be most concerned that Judaism shall have a future. They should, therefore, look beyond the synagogue for ways and means of maintaining unbroken the organic character of Jewish life in the face of the overwhelming assimilative power of the environment. *It is the duty of the synagogue—be it Orthodox, Conservative or Reform—to arrive at a formula for Jewish life, which shall satisfy the just demands of the modern state, and which shall make differentiation along religious and functional lines safe for Jewish survival and growth.*

The only formula compatible with our continuing to function as a corporate entity is that of the *"Jews as an indivisible people"* with *"Judaism as a religious civilization."* This formula is not intended to be the slogan of any particular group or party in Jewish life. The moment it becomes that, it defeats its purpose of providing a basis for Jewish unity. The term "civilization" is intended to stress that Judaism may be conceived variously. As a civilization, Judaism should be recognized as having room for various religious and non-religious interpretations. As far as the conception of "Judaism as a religious civilization" is concerned, the Orthodox, the Conservative and the Reform group may well unite on it. The Conservatives have virtually adopted it; Orthodox Jews are using it, without having formally adopted it, and the Reform group took a definite step toward adopting it, when in Columbus, Ohio, in 1937, they replaced their Platform with a new set of "Guiding Principles," among which they included Jewish peoplehood and the importance of Eretz Yisrael for Judaism.[3]

The formula of Judaism as a religious civilization is not meant to add another stave, or to mark the splitting of any existing stave, so to speak, in the cask of Jewish living, but to serve as a hoop for the many staves that at present have nothing to bind them. The adoption of that formula, and the conception of Judaism implied in it should commit all synagogue groups to the obligation of transcending their own objectives, in the interest of Jewish unity and solidarity.

2

The basic unit of Jewish life cannot be any one agency. The entire aggregate of congregations, social service agencies, Zionist organizations, defense and fraternal bodies, and educational institutions, should be integrated into an organic or indivisible community. That is the only structure or agency qualified to translate the conception of the Jews as an indivisible people, and of Judaism as a religious civilization, into a living reality. It would be organic, in that *all* matters of Jewish interest would in some way deeply affect the lives of all who desire to remain Jews. The social intelligence of the Jew would be as all-inclusive and as far-reaching as the limits not only of the particular institution or cause he is identified with, but of the entire Jewish people the world over.

In an organic community, all purposes for which Jews unite would converge upon the one purpose of Jewish survival and growth. *In such a community, the structural pattern would be determined by regional propinquity rather than by interest in particular objectives.* This means that all Jewish bodies—all congregations, public-relations organizations, social service agencies, educational institutions within any region or district—would have to collaborate for the express purpose of eliciting fresh energies and tapping new resources for living as Jews and finding Jewish life rewarding.

The spirit in which most of the public-relations and social service activities are presently conducted is far from calculated to render them a means to the survival and growth of the Jewish people. If they can be said to have any objective in common, it is to forestall the spread of anti-Semitism by preventing Jews from falling a burden on the general community. Ironically, however, helping the individual Jew may be entirely compatible with gradual disappearance of the Jewish people.

It is unfortunate that most of those who are closely associated with Jewish social activities think that it is not only possible but necessary to carry them on, without bothering about Jewish mass survival. This assumption is both theoretically fallacious and, in the long run, also bound to prove a source of inefficiency. In the spring of 1946, two agencies, doing family counselling service merged into what is now known as the "Jewish Family Service." The new agency is expected to minister to about twelve thousand families, comprising some thirty-seven thousand individuals. The budget will amount to approximately one million dollars. Among the problems to be brought before the counsellors will undoubtedly be many involving religious conflicts between husband and wife, parents and children, intermarriage, the kind of education to be given to children, and problems of a similar character. With the sources and the control of the funds supplied to the agency and the type of personnel engaged by it, the advice that will be given is not likely to make for the perpetuation of Judaism. Unless this agency is dominated by the purpose of conserving Judaism, it will become a strong factor for liquidating it.

As a rule, the larger part of the financial support and lay leadership of the secular agencies, Zionism excepted, comes from those who would like to use those very organizations as agencies for merging Jews with the general population. Their very desire to exercise leadership is often prompted more by the expectation of finding favor with the Gentiles than with the Jews, a favor often translated into political office. They are in this respect akin to the first of the Rothschilds, of whom it was said that he preferred to be the Jew of the Kings than the King of the Jews. Even the professional leaders of those agencies are, as a rule, far from zealous for Jewish survival. Efficiency in fund-raising and fund-spending is with them a matter of technique, and their interest in increasing it is that of the usual job-holder.

But if American Jewry will aim to achieve organic community, all this will have to undergo change. This is the crux of our entire problem. It reduces itself to discovering Jews of influence and leadership ability, and placing them at the helm of Jewish affairs. This is a tall order. It calls for the overhauling of our educational approach to Judaism, from our elementary school system to our institutions of higher learning. *Should we hope for Judaism to survive in America without the adoption of such revolutionary measures, we are either professional tinkerers or believers in magic.*

At present all secular agencies and organizations take the position that they represent the non-religious interests of Jews, that they should not be expected to collaborate with congregations any more than, in the general community, the state is expected to collaborate with the church. This is a false analogy. If the parallel with the general community were carried to its logical conclusion, our so-called Jewish secular organizations ought to affect the life of the individual Jew as deeply as does the state. They ought to intensify the group spirit of the Jew, as the state intensifies the group spirit of the citizen. This they are far from doing at present. Therefore they cannot justify their neutral attitude by assuming that their activities parallel those of the state.

Organic Jewish community, by giving all Jews a purpose to live for as Jews, would be inherently self-perpetuating. In the first place, it could count on being served in a voluntary and professional capacity by men and women who are capable of enhancing its effectiveness. It would inspire a deep and satisfying security in those who would make communal service their life-calling. Even from a material standpoint, a vitally functioning community is likely to be in a better position to assure permanence of tenure, even if not a high income, than an aggregate of independent organizations. There is a saying of our Sages to the effect that a community can never be said to be poor.[4] That implies that a community somehow finds the resources essential to its survival. While this may not always be the case, it is, nevertheless, true that when we work for an integrated community, we have the feeling that we are laboring for something that has a future to it in that such a community attempts to answer intrinsic human requirements that are part of a person's normal life.

Symptomatic of the precariousness of Jewish life, for want of communal solidarity, is the dire inadequacy of our spiritual leadership. The only reason that the large masses of our people are without the benefit of rabbinic services of men qualified, from the American as well as the Jewish standpoint, is that we are organized for group survival to less than ten percent of our capacity. In the field of Jewish education, the situation is even worse. The recent war, by taking most of the available men into the armed forces almost demoralized our entire religious school system. But even before the war, the Jewish schools were becoming increasingly understaffed due to the lack of an organic community to assure permanent tenure to qualified teachers. Our ancient Sages can hardly be accused of having been materialistic in their outlook. They strongly deprecated using the Torah as a means to a livelihood.[5] Yet, they stated that, if people have nothing to live on, they will not engage in the study or teaching of Torah.[6]

Of no less importance is the long overdue flowering of creativity in the domain of new Jewish cultural values, where the arts reign supreme. This is the area in which it should be possible to render Jewish life visibly, audibly and tangibly beautiful and fascinating. For the development of that area we need the best that the most gifted of our sons and daughters can contribute.

The average American Jew cannot be expected to foster distinctively Jewish interests, while he is engaged in his daily workaday routine. Being a Jew should, undoubtedly, act as an incentive to the highest ethical standards in business, industry and agriculture. But ethical standards are universal and do not afford the opportunity for that expression of cultural individuality which is essential to the normal life of a people. Outside Eretz Yisrael, it is mainly during the leisure hours that one can express himself as a Jew, either culturally or religiously. While that fact, no doubt, narrows the scope of Judaism, it does not prevent it from playing an important role in a person's life. With the progressive mechanization of the daily routine, with the increase of labor-saving devices, and, consequently, with the problem of banishing boredom becoming ever more acute, *the creative use of leisure is coming to be the main problem in the art of living.* If people knew what to do with themselves of an evening, without having to resort to card playing or any of the commercialized methods of time-killing, the whole of human life would take a more hopeful turn.

For Jews to experience their Jewishness as other than burdensome, they must be given reason and opportunity to associate Jewish living with gladness and recreative enjoyment. The Jewish calendar formerly provided the Jew with occasions for relaxation from his daily labors and anxieties, for festivity, song, gladness and mirth. Nowadays, we Jews need more than ever fresh energy for living as Jews. All of us, whether naive or sophisticated, rich or poor, young or old, could acquire such energy through those pleasures of the mind which come by way of the eye, the ear and the imagination.

We need writers to weave for us tales of fact and fancy. We need poets to translate into unforgettable word-pictures and rhythmic utterances the whole range of Jewish experience. We need musicians to explore the possibilities of the entire gamut of musical forms from the folk-song to liturgical and symphonic music. We need dramatists to compose for the stage, scenario and radio themes that treat of Israel's struggle with God and man, and of the sublime and the ridiculous in the life of the common Jew. We need painters to portray on canvas and on the walls of Jewish public buildings memorable scenes and characteristic episodes from the Jewish past and present. We need architects to design buildings which house activities, religious, social and cultural, so that those buildings shall possess character and beauty; and we need sculptors to create a Jewish statuary in harmony with that architecture. We would then be able to have our amateur choral, orchestral dramatic, dance and art groups. Through these groups the large masses of our people would discover what an inexhaustible source of esthetic and creative joy Jewish life can be. *We can be sure of a Jewish future only when Jewish art is so developed as to reconcile the Jew to his lot in life.*

But nothing of all this can come about without the backing and encouragement of the combined forces inherent in American Jewry as represented in an organic community. Here and there a musician may be fortunate in having some Jewish Maecenas enable him to devote his time to the creation of religious music; or he may himself be in a position financially to give a portion of his talent for a symphony on some Jewish theme; or he may be willing to struggle in obscurity so that he might enrich his people with artistic values. But the overwhelming number of our gifted artists and musicians have done nothing to redeem us from our esthetic poverty. *For the abundant and continuous supply of creative talent that could produce a vast variety of Jewish esthetic expression we must have a responsible community, interested in the purpose of breathing a new spirit into the Jewish people, a community that is organized for and around the purpose of transforming Judaism for each and every Jew from a burden to a privilege.*

3

THE PRINCIPLES AND AIMS OF JEWISH
COMMUNITY IN AMERICA

It is neither necessary nor possible to do more than indicate certain principles which have to be followed in the formation of an organic community. The first principle is that *all who definitely desire to see Jewish life fostered, regardless of how they conceive the form or content of that life, should be eligible for membership.* The first step in the self-discipline which the pronounced survivalists among us must take is to cooperate with all who prefer to remain Jews, on any terms whatsoever. No one but a fanatical believer in his own particular brand of Jewish survivalism would withhold membership in the Jewish community from those who conceive of Jewish survival differently from the way he does. One has to be blind to the complexity of our inner problem to claim to have found the only true solution, and to refuse to cooperate with any one who disagrees.

We must have faith in the capacity of the Jewish people to determine for themselves the character of Jewish life. Indeed, not only must no Jew be excluded from the Jewish community for his opinions and beliefs, but the community must provide in its administration for a proper and proportionate representation of every Jewish trend. Each such trend should be given a chance to organize its own adherents and to pursue its own program, so long as it recognizes the right of Jews of other schools of thought to do likewise.

Secondly, if the Jewish community is to be a means of having the individual Jew experience the reality and vitality of the Jewish people, it follows that those institutions and agencies whose main function is to foster Jewish consciousness should occupy a position of primacy. Accordingly, *the synagogues, the communal centers and the institutions of elementary education and higher learning should constitute the nucleus in the organizational pattern.* How to get the various Jewish denominations to operate harmoniously within the communal frame is by no means as insuperable a problem as we have been wont to think. In many large cities, Jewish educational bureaus manage to serve diverse types of Jewish educational institutions, from the most secular to the most Orthodox. This proves that it is possible for widely differing groups to find a common ground. By the same token, it should be possible to establish in each community a synagogue and center bureau that would perform a similar function for the spiritual and cultural needs of the adults.

Thirdly, the multiplicity of organizations and their tendency to perpetuate themselves and to retain their independence might seem to preclude their integration into a united community. The experience, however, with the existing federations and welfare funds throughout this country, which have succeeded in bringing together for common action the most diverse institutions and agencies, shows that the difficulties in the way of their committing themselves to a positive program for Jewish life are not insuperable. Moreover, if we follow the principle that it is always best to avail ourselves of existing forces and agencies instead of liquidating them and beginning *de novo*, there would be no occasion for any of them to feel aggrieved. Being the spontaneous expression of the will to organized effort, they are the medium through which the conservation and growth of Jewish life could best be furthered. *All organizations and agencies at present engaged in specific tasks should, therefore, continue what they are doing, but they should*

be required, in addition, to be represented in local community councils.
All organizations and agencies that are national in scope should have
representation in, and give an accounting to, all the local community
councils of those localities where they have branches. The community
council should in each case be a reviewing, coordinating and initiating
body, from the standpoint of the all-dominant purpose of giving the
Jew the courage, and providing him with the resources, to live as a Jew.

In a number of cities, Jewish community councils have already been
formed; in others they are in the process of formation. At present, they
virtually have no definite purpose, except that of exploring, or perhaps
even generating, the sentiment for Jewish unity. Given the affirmative
purpose of strengthening the morale of the Jew, we would have in
the community councils the groundwork of an overall national Jewish
community. An overall council, which would constitute the executive
committee of that community would be representative of all areas of
opinion, and have first-hand acquaintance with local problems. It could,
therefore, well be trusted not to treat perfunctorily its task of reviewing
and coordinating the activities of the different sections of our people,
and initiating needed lines of action.

Many technical problems are bound to arise. How shall we deal,
for example, with large Jewish populations in metropolitan centers, or
with sparse Jewish populations in rural areas? Such problems are by
no means insoluble. In metropolitan centers, a maximum, like twenty
or twenty-five thousand, might be entitled to a local community council. In the case of rural areas, on the other hand, a population minimum
and a geographic maximum might be combined to form a unit that
would be entitled to a community council. These and similar details
could be worked out by those who are expert in matters of this kind.

In a word, Jewish communal life should be organized on the following principles:

1. The inclusion of all who desire to continue as Jews.

2. The primacy of the religious and educational institutions in the
communal structure.

3. Democratic representation of all legitimate Jewish organizations
in the administration of the community.

What can be done by an organic Jewish community to help American Jews achieve self-fulfillment both as Americans and as Jews? The
potentialities of such a community cannot be fully envisaged, so long

as it is merely a dream. But they would become increasingly apparent, as steps are taken to translate the dream into reality. In the meantime, certain important objectives deserve to be set up as immediate aims. They are the following:

1. To maintain a complete register and vital statistics, and to establish bureaus for gathering information concerning all matters of importance to contemporary Jewish life.

2. To activate the high ethical standards transmitted in the Jewish tradition, by the formulation of specific codes and sanctions for various social and economic relationships.

3. To foster Jewish educational, cultural and religious activities.

4. To coordinate all efforts in behalf of the health and social welfare of Jews and the relief of poverty and suffering among them.

5. To help Jews to meet economic difficulties due to discrimination, by both Gentiles and Jews, and to defend Jewish rights against encroachment and Jewish honor against defamation.

6. To organize the collaboration of the Jewish community with other groups in civic movements for the promotion of the common welfare.

7. To advance the cause for the rebuilding of Eretz Yisrael and to collaborate with world Jewry in all matters affecting the general welfare of Jews.

When envisaging the problem of Jewish community in the United States, we must recognize that a basic prerequisite to the proper approach to the problem is the conviction that world Jewry constitutes an indivisible people which is a living, continuing organism, and that it is legitimate for Jews in a democratic society to be part of that organism.

It is essential to accept for American Jewry the status of a religio-cultural group analogous to that of the Roman Catholic Church, minus its authoritarianism.

The social structure of American Jewry must be that of an organic community.

Finally, the principles to be followed in establishing a community, and the aims to be pursued by it, must grow out of its organic character.

When such an organic community is in active operation, Jews will cease to experience that vacuousness in their lives which comes from being a mere amorphous and nameless aggregate.

To envisage thus the problem of Jewish communal life in America is to see it as parallel in magnitude and significance with the problem of reclaiming Eretz Yisrael as a Jewish homeland. In the words of our Sages, "When the Jews form a united band, make ready for the redemption." [7]

CHAPTER SEVEN

THE ROLE OF ERETZ YISRAEL IN THE LIFE OF DIASPORA JEWRY

1

THE NEW ROLE OF ERETZ YISRAEL

Zionism is definitely a modern Jewish movement. There is nothing quite like it in any earlier period of Jewish history. Generally we date the origin of Zionism, either from the calling of the First Zionist Congress in 1897, or from the beginnings of the Hovevē Zion movement in Russia during the 1880's. Yet it has often been said that Zionism is, in a sense, as old as the Jewish people, or, at least as old as the Diaspora. Since Eretz Yisrael was taken from the Jews, they have dreamed of, and prayed for, its restoration, and at times attempted to effect that restoration by supernatural means. Eretz Yisrael has always had a place in the Jewish scheme of salvation, or in the Jewish conception of what it is that makes life worth living as a Jew.

From the time that the Jewish people suffered defeat in its struggle against Rome, or, more correctly, from the time such defeat appeared inevitable and the conditions of Jewish life in Eretz Yisrael began to be more and more intolerable, Jews commenced looking forward to a miraculous redemption at the hands of a divinely ordained Messiah. Then not only would Israel be restored to freedom and prosperity, but the Jewish way of life, as prescribed in the Torah, would be recognized universally as the true way of life, revealed by the Creator to His Chosen People. All the nations would acknowledge the God of Israel; all Jews would be brought back to Eretz Yisrael, and God's Kingdom of righteousness and peace, under the Messiah, would be established throughout the earth. All Jews who had died before that time would be resurrected in Eretz Yisrael to eternal life. Wherever they might be buried, their bones would be transported miraculously to Eretz Yisrael for the resurrection. Then would the great Day of Judgment take place. The unrepentant wicked would be destroyed, and the righteous would be inscribed for eternal life, since death would be abolished.

The exact nature of the messianic era and its relation to the world-to-come were variously described. Two features, however, remained constant: First, Eretz Yisrael, and no other country, would be the scene of the deliverance of Israel and of the redemption of mankind, through

123

the acknowledgment of Israel's God and Israel's Torah. Secondly, until the coming of the Messiah, the Jewish people would remain exiled from Eretz Yisrael to atone for its sins. By loyal obedience to the Torah, Jews could speed the restoration of their people to Eretz Yisrael, and win for themselves a posthumous share in that restoration. *Thus through the Middle Ages,* which for the Jews lasted until the late decades of the eighteenth or even the beginning of the nineteenth century, *the ideal concerning Eretz Yisrael belonged to the thought-world of miracles.*

Modern Zionism enabled Eretz Yisrael to figure once more in Jewish life as an instrument of salvation. It is part of the present day tendency to transpose the concept of salvation from the key of miracle to the key of human initiative. This, however, does not mean that Zionism must be a secular movement. On the contrary, for those who see in Zionism a necessary corollary of Judaism as a religious civilization, Zionism is fundamentally a religious effort without which other religious efforts on the part of Jews lack meaning or relevance.

If, however, the reestablishment of a Jewish commonwealth in Eretz Yisrael is to be regarded as indispensable to our salvation, we must give thought to the kind of society we would have flourish there. So long as the restoration to Eretz Yisrael was a dream which God was to fulfill for us, we could be as dreamily extravagant as we wished. But when imagination is harnessed to reality, we must make sure that our desires are not beyond the bounds of possible attainment and that they do not fall short of meeting vital needs. It goes without saying that possibility of attainment must mean possibility of *ethical* attainment; we cannot build our hopes of salvation on injustice to others.

This implies, in the first place, that we must definitely disavow the notion, held by our people until modern times, of a completely comprehensive *kibbutz galuyot*, the in-gathering of all the Jews in the Diaspora. We cannot aim at bringing all Jews back to Eretz Yisrael. Not only is Eretz Yisrael incapable of absorbing the entire Jewish people, but millions of Jews have thrown in their lot with the nations of which they form a part, and have no desire to be uprooted from their present homes. However, Eretz Yisrael must be kept open as a haven of immigration for all Jews who are not able to feel at home in the lands where they now reside. In the language of Robert Frost, "Home is the place, where, when you have to go there, they have to take you in."

The achievement of this objective requires that Jews be permitted ultimately to constitute the majority population within a specified territory as belonging to the Jewish Commonwealth. Within that territory, Jews must possess sufficient political independence to exercise cultural and religious autonomy. They must be able to embody their ideals of social justice and cooperation in legal and economic institutions of their own. They must be free to speak their own language, to make it the language in which to worship, as they please, and to observe without interference the religious holidays of their own calendar and all other religious practices that have meaning for them.

But the foregoing objectives of Zionism do not and need not require the sort of irresponsible and obsolete national sovereignty that modern nations claim for themselves. This doctrine of "absolute national sovereignty," with its assumption that the interests of one's own nation must always override those of other nations, is responsible for the international anarchy of the modern world, and is liable to bring about a catastrophe that will destroy the very foundations of human civilization.

Zionist aspirations for Eretz Yisrael are compatible with the inclusion of Eretz Yisrael in a larger and more comprehensive political body, whether it be an Arab Federation, the British Empire (assuming that Eretz Yisrael has dominion status) or the United Nations, provided, of course, that Jews retain the authority to regulate their own affairs. Relief from exclusive responsibility for military defense and foreign policy should be welcome, as long as the freedom and security of the country are adequately protected.

It is inevitable for the autonomous social and cultural life of Eretz Yisrael to articulate itself through new creations in Hebrew literature, Jewish art and Jewish music. These will be accepted as authentic expressions of the Jewish spirit and enrich Jewish life everywhere. Without Eretz Yisrael, Jewish culture tends to be limited to the confines of a Jewish cult, or to archaeological scholarship. With Eretz Yisrael, Judaism becomes a great historic movement with a present and a future as well as a past.

Moreover, by serving as the focal point of Jewish interests, Eretz Yisrael imbues the scattered remnants of the Jewish people with a sense of unity and creates an international Jewish public for the gifted Jewish writer, artist or musician. Such encouragement of aesthetic expression is far more potent than that provided by the local Jewish community of Eretz Yisrael. In this respect, the Diaspora becomes an impetus for fostering cultural life in Eretz Yisrael, no less than Eretz Yisrael is for fostering Jewish cultural milieu in the Diaspora.

Eretz Yisrael reborn is indispensable, also, to Jewish religion in the Diaspora. If we conceive of God as the Power that makes for life as holy or supremely worthwhile, there can be no denying that, in the project of establishing a wholesome Jewish life in Eretz Yisrael, we Jews can experience the reality of God. Eretz Yisrael has again become holy soil for us, because it is associated not only with ancient heroes and martyrs of our people but, also, with contemporaries who have made equally notable contributions to human welfare and equally great sacrifices for their people and their God. If the vision of an ideal social life to be achieved by God in the days of the Messiah made it worthwhile for our ancestors to carry on even to the point of martyrdom, the purposeful effort of our people to live a worthy, hence a godly, life in Eretz Yisrael, has made it worthwhile for modern Jews to carry on despite the almost universal undercurrent of ill-will and hostility.

The foregoing purposes encounter difficult obstacles that render them impossible of immediate achievement. Neither Great Britain nor the Arabs are prepared to grant us the rights that we claim. Together they have succeeded in making of Eretz Yisrael "one of the unhappiest and unholiest lands on earth." Nonetheless, we shall never, as long as there is the breath of life in us, renounce our tie to the land of our fathers, to which the God of history has united us forever. On many points, we shall have to yield temporarily to *force majeure*. But as we yield, whether in the matter of immigration, land sales, boundaries or what not, we shall register our protest and seek by all legitimate means in our power the removal of these limitations. We will see to it that no matter what our adversaries do to us, they shall not break our will to live as a people.

Above all, it is imperative that the Jew be on guard against the arrogance with which the empire-builders of the Western world are wont to regard the peoples and cultures of conquered nations. We must cultivate the goodwill of all who have a legitimate interest in Eretz Yisrael, even though opposed to our objectives. We must seek a maximum of cooperation with the Arabs. Such cooperation cannot, perhaps, be fruitfully and presently pursued in the political field, because the vested interests of today's political and religious leaders of the Arab people render them hostile to our legitimate demands. Nevertheless, we shall seek economic, social and cultural collaboration with Arabs, wherever this is possible. Inasmuch as such collaboration need not proceed through the political leaders of the Arabs, there are abundant opportunities for it. Consideration not merely for the economic interests but, also, for the personal and racial sensibilities of the Arab people must characterize Jewish relations with them. Every effort should be made to cultivate mutual appreciation of Jewish and Arab cultural values, and to make clear the purpose and aims of the Jews in Eretz Yisrael, and the basis of their claim to the land. This is no less important than explaining our objectives to the Western nations.

What, indeed, is the basis of the Jewish claim to Eretz Yisrael? The existence of anti-Semitism, the mere fact that the nations do not want us emphasizes our need for it, but is hardly sufficient to establish a claim to it. *Our claim to Eretz Yisrael rests on our historic connection with it, a connection formally recognized by the League of Nations and by the United States in the mandate for Palestine.* It was our life in Eretz Yisrael that first gave us that we-feeling, or awareness of kind, which makes us a distinct and recognizable society.

We are identified as Jews, that is, as descendants of the former inhabitants of Eretz Yisrael. No other people, not even native Palestinian Arabs, are so identified with Eretz Yisrael. The Arabs of Eretz Yisrael are, after all, in their own consciousness, regardless of what anthropologists may have to say of their racial origin, identified in language, religion and culture with Arabia, not with Eretz Yisrael. Moreover, we are Jews not only because as a people we have our roots there but, also, because it has been the matrix of our religion, and has been included in the goal of our salvation.

The fact that Eretz Yisrael has stamped itself on the collective consciousness of the Jewish people is important not only as establishing the right of those Jews who are homeless to find a haven in Eretz Yisrael; it is no less important as implying the right and the obligation of Jews, who do not choose to live in Eretz Yisrael, to aid in making it a center of their Jewish religious civilization. The only way in which we can hope to carry out our objectives with regard to Eretz Yisrael is through the cooperation of world Jewry. All Jews, therefore, should participate in the project of advancing Jewish civilization in Eretz Yisrael.

2

NO JEWISH HOMELAND WITHOUT JUDAISM IN THE DIASPORA

Jews in the Diaspora will continue to owe exclusive political allegiance to the countries in which they reside. The tie that binds Diaspora Jewry to Eretz Yisrael is a cultural and religious one. Culture and socio-economic life are so closely interrelated that it is difficult for Diaspora Jewry to create new Jewish cultural values, since there is no possibility in the Diaspora of an autonomous Jewish social and economic life.

American Judaism is needed, and will long continue to be needed, as a force to inspire and motivate our participation in the establishment of a Jewish commonwealth. The role of American Jewry in relation to Eretz Yisrael is similar to the role of the American home front in relation to the battlefront during the recent World War. Were it not for the backing of the home front, or for the fact that America proved to be the "arsenal of democracy," the most clever strategy and the most arduous valor on the battle line would have been of no avail. Similarly, *American Jewry will for a long time have to give moral, political and economic support to the Eretz Yisrael enterprise, which is the deciding factor in Israel's struggle for survival in the modern world.* Should the morale of the American Jewish front deteriorate, should American Jewry grow listless and disheartened, or should it lose faith in the significance of its struggle for existence, after the manner of our faint-hearted escapists and assimilationists, what would become of a Jewish Eretz Yisrael? Would the little *yishuv* alone be able to withstand British imperialism, Arab intransigence and ubiquitous anti-Semitism? What it has already achieved with the aid and support of world Jewry is miracle enough, but to expect it to perform similar miracles in the future, without such aid, is to ask the impossible. We dare not let our homefront crumble, and thus betray those who are fighting our battle and holding the line on its most crucial sector, Eretz Yisrael.

An attitude of distrust toward the possibility of maintaining Jewish life in the United States, is, moreover, unfair to our country. Our duties as citizens are not fully discharged by rendering obedience to its laws, or even by participating patriotically in its defense in time of war. We have a part in the social, economic and cultural life of America, and, unless we give to the common welfare of the American people the best that is in our power to give, we are not doing our full duty to our country. But as Jews, the very best we have to give is to be found in Judaism, the distillation of centuries of Jewish spiritual experience. As convinced Jews and loyal Americans, we should seek to incorporate in American life the universal values of Judaism, and to utilize the particular *sancta* * of Jewish religion as an inspiration for preserving these universal values. To fail to do so would mean to deprive Judaism of universal significance and to render Jewish religion a mere tribalism that has no relevance to life beyond the separate interests of the Jewish group. The attitude of Jewish isolationists or the *sholelē hatefuzah*, (negators of the Diaspora) which would keep American Jewry with its loins perpetually girt for a hasty departure for Eretz Yisrael is not likely to inspire our neighbors with confidence in the Jew, or with respect for Judaism.

Those of our young people who possess the abilities that are needed now in Eretz Yisrael to build there a productive economy for the rising Jewish Commonwealth, an economy based on the socialized exploitation of natural resources instead of on the exploitation of the weak by the strong, should by all means be encouraged to go to Eretz Yisrael. The colonizing and constructive effort in Eretz Yisrael should enlist those of our youth who possess the kind of pioneer spirit essential to nation-building. Our Jewish young men and women ought to be made to feel that their going to Eretz Yisrael to serve their own people would be as legitimate and noble an adventure as for other Americans to serve the various peoples in the Far East in a missionary or cultural capacity. But students who plan to go to Eretz Yisrael, with the expectation of engaging in some white-collar profession, would not render any specially needed service there, and only deprive American Jewish life of some needed service they might render here. We American Jews need desperately every available person who has the ability to transmute the cultural and religious values of our tradition into a living creative force.

We Jews who have come to this country bore the gifts of a great historic tradition. To tell us that Judaism can have no future here is to tell us that these gifts are worthless and that, as a group, we can only be cultural parasites. Whatever the future holds in store for us is a matter of speculation, but that there are today five million Jews in the United States is not speculation but a fact that carries with it inescapable responsibilities. We Jews have the same need as have all other Americans of belonging to a community where we are wanted

* See pp. 46 ff.; 178 ff.

and welcomed, and where we can derive the moral and spiritual values that give meaning and dignity to human life. We naturally look to the Jewish community to give us a faith to live by and to live for. Whatever deprives us of faith in the possibility of Jewish life in America not only dejudaizes millions of our people; it demoralizes and degrades us.

The problem of how to make Jewish life a source of self-fulfillment to the American Jew is one of great complexity. Nothing less than whole-hearted and whole-minded concentration on that problem will result in a satisfactory solution. It is natural, therefore, to find excuses for evading the problem altogether, and few excuses seem as plausible as hopelessness about Diaspora Judaism. When Zionism first appeared on the scene, it came as a challenge to those who evaded the urgent task of self-emancipation by projecting the redemption of our people into the distant messianic future. Likewise, those who despair of Jewish survival in the Diaspora, by maintaining that only in Eretz Yisrael can Judaism survive, evade the urgent task of rendering Judaism viable in America. Long distance building of Eretz Yisrael is no less important than building it on the spot, but it cannot serve as a substitute for living a Jewish life here. *Until Jews realize that the Jewish problem in the Diaspora and the Jewish problem in Eretz Yisrael are one, they are running away from reality and defeating their own purpose.* Only as we assume the responsibility for having Judaism live wherever Jews are allowed to live are we likely to succeed in any of our Jewish undertakings.

There can be no question that in the Diaspora we Jews lack the spirit of dedication that goes with our people's renascence in Eretz Yisrael. We are without the magic power that comes with the spoken and creative Hebrew word. We are far from the land where the Jewish spirit is being reborn. But given the will, the intelligence and the devotion, it is feasible so to relive and to re-embody, within the frame of a democratic American civilization, the vital and thrilling experience of our people in Eretz Yisrael that, in the long run, we might achieve in our way as great and lasting a contribution to human values as they are achieving in theirs.

3

ERETZ YISRAEL: ITS ACHIEVEMENTS

By affirming that it is feasible for Jews to maintain permanently their group individuality in the Diaspora, we assume that Eretz Yisrael will serve increasingly as a reservoir of new Jewish life and self-expression. On what do we base such an assumption?

In the first place, *Eretz Yisrael has begun to give us Jews new history that is not cause for lamentation, but an epic of creation.* What is happening in Eretz Yisrael is not merely a sum of chance vicissitudes, but a series of events which go toward the making of Jewish history and which point to the emergence of a new social order. For the first time in centuries, Jewish history has been more than that of literature and persecution. It is the history of social achievements and of changes effected in a barren environment which consisted for the most part of denuded hills, swampy lowlands, and dunes upon dunes of sand. What the Jews have accomplished in Eretz Yisrael is, from the standpoint of human capacity, tantamount to *creatio ex nihilo.* They have constructed cities and villages; they have organized farming, industry, health, culture and entertainment—all in a relatively short time, despite the most heart-breaking odds. They have paid a higher price than has any other people for every square foot of ground they own and cultivate. They have waged a continual struggle against a hostile native population and against the most obstructive and provocative efforts of the very Government that had pledged itself to "facilitate the establishment of a Jewish national home in Palestine."

The events in Eretz Yisrael, during the last fifty years, have given to the Jewish people a long roster of heroes, leaders and builders, who outshine the Ehuds, the Jephthahs and the Samsons of the days of the Judges. In the midst of guerrilla warfare carried on by Arab terrorists, during the years immediately preceding the recent World War, the Jews succeeded in laying the foundations of fifty new settlements. When, in the fall of 1946, the British Government was concentrating all its energies on the destruction of Zionism, the Jews succeeded in laying the foundations of seventeen new settlements, in the Negev, in one day. They have evinced a power of endurance and courage that is a challenge to world Jewry. Their story should be related and interpreted in every Jewish pulpit and in every Jewish classroom; it should become part of the Jewish consciousness of every Jew throughout the world. *Only Eretz Yisrael can give the Jews a common historical consciousness through history in the making.* The civilization that has only a history that is made and closed is a dead civilization. A living civilization needs a history that is living, dynamic and uplifting. Eretz Yisrael provides that in remarkable measure.

This could never have been the case, had there not been the Zionism of Pinsker, Herzl and Nordau. Ahad Ha-Am's program for Eretz Yisrael,[1] lacking the essential elements of large scale immigration and international recognition, could not have developed Eretz Yisrael into a history-making center of Jewish life. Ahad Ha-Am had the correct intuition, when he envisaged Eretz Yisrael as a focal and integrating center of Jewish revival throughout the world, but he erred in his conception of the way that goal was to be attained. He put his faith in a hand-picked selection of highly qualified persons who, of their own volition, would choose to migrate to Eretz Yisrael in order to recreate there the Jewish civilization. However, history is not made in this way. It is made by the driving forces of necessity, plus a degree of preparedness for utilizing them for higher ends. This is the truth in political Zionism and, by virtue of this truth, Eretz Yisrael is contributing what is basic to any living civilization—living history.

A second contribution of Eretz Yisrael toward the revival of Jewish life is the modernization of the Hebrew language and its conversion into a living vernacular. Human consciousness, whether individual or collective, cannot exist without the medium of language. A common language is indispensable to an awareness of ethnic unity. With the integration of the Jewries of the different countries into different bodies politic, the danger was imminent that the Jewish people would disintegrate into different tribes, as it were, which would soon lose touch with each other. Neither religious truths held in common nor their historical background could keep alive indefinitely the indivisibility of the Jewish people. Even a people's memories are bound to fade, unless reinforced by living experience. The day-to-day events in Eretz Yisrael become such living experience, when they become part of the collective mind through the medium of a common language. Eretz Yisrael has made of the Hebrew language such a medium for all Jews, and is daily perfecting it into an instrument for articulating a range of experience that is as wide and colorful as any of the most advanced cultures of our day.

This remarkable development of the Hebrew language has not come about spontaneously. It is the outcome of strenuous efforts long carried on by zealots who dedicated themselves to the task of enabling Hebrew to strike root in Eretz Yisrael. Their determination yielded to no difficulties and obstacles, and their task was accomplished in a spirit of self-sacrifice. The pioneer teachers, who came with the BILU [2] movement, in the eighties of the last century, undertook to transform Hebrew into the daily vernacular of the new Jewish settlements, by making it the language of instruction in the schools. Their efforts bore fruit. This was evident, when in 1919, the directors of the newly established Hebrew Technicum in Haifa insisted on the use of German as the medium of instruction in that institution. All the teachers in Eretz Yisrael were adamantly opposed to this move, and they were supported by the entire new *Yishuv* (community). Their final victory decided not merely the question whether Hebrew should again be a living language, but, by far more important, whether Jews throughout the world should continue to have an homogeneous Jewish consciousness. This victory was consolidated by hard-working laborers in the fields and in the shops. By their idealism and self-sacrifice in making Hebrew the medium of work and conversation they have contributed to the Hebrew renaissance no less than the intellectual workers.

This accomplishment is put to a severe test whenever there is a large influx of refugees. These refugees bring with them deeply rooted habits of thought and expression that would undoubtedly displace the Hebrew language, if it had not taken firm hold on the minds of the first two generations of settlers. In former times, Jewish refugees from persecution always brought with them the language of their persecutors, and conserved it with religious zeal. That was the case with the German dialect that the Jews, fleeing from Germany, brought to Poland, and with the Spanish Ladino, brought from Spain by Jews fleeing to the Levant. That each wave of immigrants to Eretz Yisrael adjusted itself to the use of Hebrew indicates that Hebrew has made Eretz Yisrael into a melting pot of the various Jewries represented therein, and that it functions now as a powerful factor for collective Jewish consciousness.

It is imperative for those American Jews who envisage no future for Judaism other than that of a civilization to apply themselves to the task of making familiarity with the Hebrew language a *sine qua non* of Jewish life. *A Hebrewless Judaism is a Judaism in which the immediate awareness of Jewish peoplehood is lacking,* despite all that one may do for the upbuilding of Eretz Yisrael. A knowledge of Hebrew somehow carries with it a sense of a seldom violated commitment to a Jewish future. It is to be regretted that so little is being done in this country to introduce the teaching of Hebrew in secondary schools and colleges where, if the Jews really asked for it, there would be no difficulty in securing its academic recognition. If Eretz Yisrael cannot influence the Judaism of the Diaspora to the extent of having it remain a Hebrew Judaism, then all the talk of having Eretz Yisrael function as the spiritual center for the Jews throughout the world is mere rhetoric. *No Jew who regards the unity of Israel as basic to Judaism, and Eretz Yisrael as basic to the regeneration of that unity, can afford to go through life without at least some knowledge of Hebrew.*

It may be that what is needed, to give to modern Hebrew that impulse which would enable it to transcend the boundaries of Eretz Yisrael, is literature with a more universal appeal than it has been possible thus far for the Jewry of Eretz Yisrael to produce. That must take time. It cannot be commanded or forced. Meanwhile, despite the comparatively large output of native prose and poetry, it is a fact that the young people even in Eretz Yisrael find it necessary to turn to translations of the best in other literatures for the satisfaction of their hunger for ideas of universal import. It is doubtful whether Eretz Yisrael will be able to produce a great literature before all elements of the Jewish civilization come to full flower there. Which elements have not yet even begun to sprout will be indicated presently.

There is a third contribution which Eretz Yisrael is making toward the revival of Jewish life. That is the emergence of what may be termed Jewish civic religion as distinguished from personal religion. Practices, which formerly were part of the religious regimen of the individual, and which were observed in the legalistic spirit demanded by Jewish tradition, have dropped their individual aspect, have been shorn of the traditional legalism, and are continued as civic religion. This is especially true of Sabbaths and festivals. While, in the cities, these are observed by many in the traditional manner, in most of the settlements and villages they have assumed the character of civic religion. Those days are now associated with a freedom and spontaneity which render them occasions for wholesome physical and spiritual recreation.

It will not be long before that folk spirit will become articulate. The Sabbath day is not just a day of rest even for those who do not observe it in the traditional spirit. Here and there an attempt is made to signalize it by some improvised forms of song, study and discussion, which are evocative of deeper sentiments than mere cessation of work could yield. The radio programs, which give appropriate readings and songs for every Sabbath and festival, utilize most of the religious content associated with those days, in the form of folk expression. The Passover festival is gradually acquiring a deepened significance and a more characteristically Jewish type of celebration, as is evidenced by the issuance of numerous *Haggadot*,[3] some of which contain material that deserves to become part of general usage. Even *Shavuot*[4] and *Sukkot*[5] are beginning to acquire an interpretation other than that of nature festivals. A most interesting religious folkway is that which was introduced some years ago, namely, the practice of having everyone in Eretz Yisrael read daily the same two chapters from the Bible. This practice has caught the imagination even of those furthest removed from the traditional attitude toward the Bible. There are many other minor religious folkways, like the one of adorning the table with flowers on Sabbaths and festivals, which are part of Jewish life in Eretz Yisrael, and which are bound to exercise upon it a fine esthetic influence.

Jews in the Diaspora would do well to grasp the full significance of transforming ritual observances, which have been subject to legalistic scruples, into folkways which belong to the category of civic religion. They might derive from that transformation a highly important regulative principle, which might help to solve the general problem of ritual observances. Some will, undoubtedly, dismiss this new approach to those observances as evidence of the secularism for which the new Jewish life in Eretz Yisrael is all too frequently condemned. This, however, is no way to deal with the complexities of the human spirit. Calling "secular" anything that does not happen to coincide with one's preconceived notions about religion does not make for greater regard for religion. Actually, there may be more genuine spirituality and yearning after God in so-called secularist tendencies than in the legalistic type of religiosity. For the very sake of religion that is truly spiritual, it is essential to arrive at criteria that would be more reliable than those provided by the traditional labels. That presupposes a reconsideration of the entire problem of religion.

In the meantime, we should study carefully this emergence of Jewish civic religion in Eretz Yisrael. The very concept of civic religion affords possibilities of revitalizing many a ritual observance that cannot possibly be resuscitated, as long as it is associated with a legalistic rationale and punctiliousness. It may be that such civic forms do not speak in the conventional accents of individual religion. Nevertheless, if we have any genuinely religious yearnings, they will find in these forms a natural outlet for their expression. That is a lesson taught by the history of all religions, and is confirmed by the experience of the new *yishuv* in Eretz Yisrael. *The real problem is, how to elicit from Jewish life that spirit of personal religion which would be in line of continuity with the highest manifestations of personal religion in our past.* This is a problem for Eretz Yisrael no less than for the Diaspora.

4

ERETZ YISRAEL JEWRY: ITS SHORTCOMINGS

The foregoing account is not intended to place the stamp of approval upon all the events and personalities that form part of the history which Eretz Yisrael is making. On the contrary, that history is full of very serious blunders and even tragic mistakes. The White Paper of 1939 is the penalty Jews are paying for having mishandled the problem of their relations with the Arabs, and for their having ignored the need of educating the English officials in Eretz Yisrael to an understanding of the Mandate. Jews should have realized that they have to live with the Arabs, and should not have attempted to build a Jewish economy by discouraging employment of Arabs. They should have tried to develop a single high-level economy in which exploitation of both Arab and Jewish labor would have been precluded. No effort or ingenuity should have been spared in devising ways and means of effecting a *modus vivendi* that would have been satisfactory to all who have a legitimate interest in the land. Neither is it possible to approve of the extremes to which the spirit of partisanship and of divisiveness has been allowed to be carried among the Jews themselves.

Perhaps even more serious than these practical blunders is the fact that, out of all that has been done for and in Eretz Yisrael during the last fifty years, no religious awakening has come to the Jewish people. Although the men and the women of the pioneer settlements evince a deep spiritual metamorphosis, that metamorphosis has not become religiously articulate. What is even more regrettable is that the Zionist movement as a whole has not taken on the character of a religious reconstruction and revival for entire world Jewry. The *Mizrachi* movement is not a religious revival, nor can it possibly embrace the whole of Jewry with its wide range of religious divergence. It is merely an attempt on the part of Orthodox Jews, who refuse to reckon with the challenge of the modern approach to reality, to transplant their orthodoxy intact to Eretz Yisrael.

Perhaps, we should not expect people, who are as tense and harassed as are the Jews in Eretz Yisrael, to grapple with the religious complexities of our day. Perhaps the Zionist leaders, who have had to arouse the Jews to look to Eretz Yisrael as their homeland, ought not to be blamed for not including in their agenda the problem of religion. Any endeavor to make of Zionism not merely a political, but also a vitally religious, movement might have wrecked it. The reason such endeavor would have been dangerous is that the Jews are unprepared for a sudden religious revival. The shattering impact of modernism upon the Jewish people has been concentrated into a few decades, whereas in the case of the non-Jewish world that impact was spread over as many centuries. In the dazed state in which the Jewish people still finds itself as a result of that shock, it is in no condition to achieve that unity of purpose which is essential for a religious upsurge. For that to happen, Jews must first be sure of what they want, and have some prospect of attaining it.

There is another side, however, to this question. What the Jews in Eretz Yisrael actually did was to circumvent the problem of religion. It is similar to what they did with the city of Jerusalem. The old city including the Temple area, the very place concerning which Jews have been praying, "Build Yerushalayim the holy city speedily in our days," has had to be by-passed, as it were, in the process of rebuilding Jewish life in Eretz Yisrael. Neither the Jews nor the non-Jews are ready, and probably will not be for a long time, to rebuild the old city on modern lines. Instead, the Jews have built up what is known as the town-planning section around the old city. It resembles any newly built section of a Western town. It lacks that unique character which one naturally expects of a city that is actually identified with the ancient city of Jerusalem. This method of going around a difficulty instead of through it, so well symbolized by Ibsen in *Peer Gynt*, may perhaps do when a physical matter, like city building, is involved. But it is not the best method of dealing with the life of a people. Jews cannot afford to by-pass religious traditions while building their new life in a region entirely removed from the one in which their old life had its being. A way must be found to revise and reinterpret those traditions as well as to develop new religious values.

The modern-minded Jews in Eretz Yisrael probably do not miss a feeling of continuity with the old religious traditions, and may feel no need for accentuating the religious *motif* in the civilization which they are doing so much to reconstruct. But for Jewry in the Diaspora that lack of continuity and absence of motivation which might be clearly identified as religious constitute a serious handicap. Thinking non-Jews cannot understand why Jews should insist on adding another civilization to the many which have bedlamized the world with their claims and pretensions. *Not Judaism as a civilization, but Judaism as a religious civilization, with the God-idea clearly proclaimed in public worship, and activated in a way of life, is what the world expects the Jews to foster.* This does not imply the acceptance of a uniform theology. On the contrary, the fact that there is room for diversity in the intellectual comprehension of a living God-idea must become an accepted principle. But there are definite pragmatic implications to the God-idea, which all who designate themselves as Jews should be ready to accept and carry out in practice. These implications will have to be clearly articulated and formally recognized as animating the Jewish consciousness.

A second and no less serious defect in the present form of Jewish life in Eretz Yisrael, from the standpoint of Judaism as a civilization, is its failure to realize the urgency of the need for a modern Jewish code of civil law and judicial machinery. It is amazing that, considering the high intelligence of the leaders who have been fostering the *renascence* of Jewish civilization, the one indispensable element to a civilization, namely, a commonly recognized civil code, should never have been named as an objective in all their efforts. A central state may be important for getting a nation to act collectively as one body, but it is not indispensable for the fostering of a common mind and spirit among the members of a nation. But where there is no central state, a common civil code is the only means of keeping the sense of peoplehood alive. It is possible for a people to exist without a central state. This the Jews have proved by living as a people for twenty-five hundred years. But they were able to live as a people, because they had a common civil law.

When the Jews began to build anew their life as a people in Eretz Yisrael, the first problem that ought to have occupied their leaders, should have been the formulation of a modern Jewish code. To be sure, there would have arisen violent conflict. But such conflict would have been finally resolved. However, the "Peer Gynt" method was again employed. Resort was had to evasion which permits the old narrow rickety path of tradition to serve those who care to travel by it, and builds a newly planned detour for those who seek something better. The rabbinate, which is recognized by the Government, applies the old Talmudic law to all judicial matters which come within its jurisdiction. In addition, there are three types of law courts: the civil courts of the General Zionists, known as *ha-mishpat ha-shalom ha-ivri,* the workers' courts, and the English courts. The English courts administer a civil law which is half-English and half-Turkish, the Turkish part being a survival from the old Turkish regime. The Jews who have become somewhat modernized keep away from the rabbinic courts. Very few of the middle-class Jews resort to the newly constituted Jewish courts. The tendency to ignore any kind of Jewish law has reached a point where litigation, involving even ritual matters, is brought to the English courts.

One often hears the complaint voiced against young couples in the collectives, who live as husband and wife without the sanction of a religious marriage ritual. This complaint implies that the omission of such sanction is a moral offense. This is not an altogether true appraisal. Marriage from the standpoint of Jewish law, is not a religious sacrament, as with the Church; it is a civil contract. That Jewish young couples should not find it necessary to have their marriage officially validated by some one representing Jewish law means either that they deliberately flout Jewish law, or that it does not exist for them. Actually the latter is the fact. With four different codes claiming authority, none is likely to elicit much respect from the general community.

Another anomaly that exists in Eretz Yisrael, from the standpoint of law, is the recognition on the part of the mandatory of two standards in the matter of polygamy. The Ashkenazic community must abide by the decree of Rabbenu Gershom against polygamy. The Sephardic community is exempt from that decree. When the Mormons wanted Utah to be admitted into the Union, they had to renounce the right to polygamy, although it was part of their religion. Such renunciation was regarded as an essential to the unity of the American nation. This was true even in the case of a nation that could well afford a wide range of diversity in its domestic laws, because of the strong central government that it possesses and the numerous common interests that hold together the different groups and individuals. Yet, in the case of a small fragmentized people like the Jews, no thought is given to the need of establishing at least enough homogeneity in its domestic law to preclude polygamy.

The failure to achieve a homogeneous civil code, like the failure to bring about a religious revival, may be ascribed to the fear of internal dissension. If Jews attempted to disestablish the rabbinic civil code and insisted upon having it replaced by a modern code, they would so provoke the fanaticism of the traditionalist Jews that it might lead to civil war. A similar situation existed in Turkey after the first World War. There the old Moslem law was replaced by a modern law code which was based upon that of Switzerland. That, however, was possible in Turkey, because Turkey had a central state which could enforce its will. But Jews in Eretz Yisrael have no such central state. So far they have resorted to voluntarism as a method of cooperation. Voluntarism has proved eminently successful, in that the Jews of the *Yishuv* have actually created many instruments of social control, which are otherwise the creations only of established governments, but they have done this because there was no one else to do it for them. Which goes to show how important it is for the Commonwealth in Eretz Yisrael to become self-governing, if Judaism is to find expression in modern law.

With how much more dignity and courage Jews everywhere would be able to justify their loyalty to Judaism, if principles like those contained in the Zionist Pittsburgh Platform of 1918 had attained the status of Jewish civil law! In that Platform, emphasis was placed upon political and civil equality, irrespective of race, sex or faith, of all the inhabitants of the land. It enunciated the principle of ownership and control, by the whole people of the land, of all natural resources and of all public utilities. It stated furthermore that "All land, owned or controlled by the whole people, should be leased on such conditions as will insure the fullest opportunity for development and continuity of possession," and that "the cooperative principle should be applied so far as feasible in the organization of all agricultural, industrial, commercial, and financial undertakings." Not until Eretz Yisrael can evolve a Jewish civil code in the spirit of principles like these will it be in a position to build the type of Jewish commonwealth which is worthy of serving as the nucleus of Jewish life throughout the world.

Having failed thus far to evolve vital religion and a homogeneous civil code, Jewish life in Eretz Yisrael could not but fail to work out a homogeneous system of Jewish education. There are at present three separate systems of education, the General Zionist, the Workers' and the *Mizrachi*. The *Mizrachi* is out and out traditionalist, perpetuating all the inner conflicts and maladjustments that go nowadays with making the past the authoritative guide, instead of merely the inspiration, of the present. The workers' education is based on a synthesis of the Marxist philosophy of life with modern nationalism, both of which have shown themselves in need of considerable qualification, if they are to be rid of their malignant potentials. The General Zionist schools evade the need of correlating education with contemporary problems both ideological and social. The emphasis in all the three types of education is practically altogether on what differentiates one group from another rather than on what they have in common. Three distinct nations could not be more different from one another in outlook and in general approach to human affairs. Whatever group consciousness Jewish young people at present possess is mainly a result of the common Hebrew language and of such common experience as arises mainly from Arab hostility and British sabotage, which help to accentuate their common desire to build up the country.

Such national consciousness, however, is amenable to jingoism, subject to all kinds of mass hysterias, and devoid of all capacity for self-criticism and of all striving to be governed by reason and justice. It is true that young people by the thousands are daily risking their lives to bring to Eretz Yisrael the homeless Jews of Europe; but one misses in them an awareness of a Jewry that is destined to remain dispersed throughout the world, and that must somehow find a way of maintaining its unity and vitality, despite the mighty forces of disintegration. The only idea Eretz Yisrael Jews have of American Jewry is that it is a sort of milch cow to be milked for funds as long as possible and, with that over, to be left to its own fate.

All these shortcomings are due mainly to the fact that Jews as a people have not given enough of their resources, their thought and their energy to the upbuilding of Eretz Yisrael. The reason for their niggardliness is that they have not been properly taught how to face the future or how to organize and direct their collective endeavors. They are, therefore, unable to appreciate the spiritual revolution that the upbuilding of Eretz Yisrael should have spelled in their lives. Most of those who are in Eretz Yisrael have gone there because they could not go elsewhere, and most of those who support the Eretz Yisrael undertaking do so mainly in a spirit of help to the needy and the suffering. The Jewish will to live as a people has not yet been fully aroused. Only a complete transformation of our traditional habits of mind and ways of life will bring about its awakening.

Without Eretz Yisrael, there would be no motive for reconstructing Jewish life anywhere. Jewish life would lack that basic content which only Eretz Yisrael can supply—a living history which only the struggle to take root in a land can create, a collective consciousness which only a living language can beget, and common folkways which only the sharing of common practical concerns can evolve. *But without a planned program of reconstruction of Jewish life in the Diaspora, Eretz*

Yisrael will lack the stimulus to recreate the elements of religion, law and education in the Jewish civilization. As the upbuilding of Eretz Yisrael is necessary to the reconstruction of Jewish life in the Diaspora, so is the reconstruction of Jewish life in the Diaspora necessary to the rehabilitation of Eretz Yisrael.

CHAPTER EIGHT

THE KEY TO INTERGROUP GOOD-WILL

1

THE NEEDED RECONSTRUCTION IN GROUP ETHICS

It is the fate of all of us who profess any of the historic religions to live in two civilizations, in the ancient civilization of our religion and in the civilization of our country. The ultimate test of our right and ability to do so will be our success in fostering good-will toward our neighbors and eliciting their good-will toward us. To succeed, we have to draw not only on our own traditions but also on the best that the human spirit, throughout the ages, has enunciated concerning human relations. But even that is not enough, because there never has been as much occasion, as there is now, to sense the basic unity of mankind, or as much likelihood for any group conflict to implicate the world. For that reason we shall have to widen the range even of the noblest ideals in the religious ethics of the past, and devise new means of translating them into our daily conduct.

The very desire to achieve intergroup good-will is a modern progressive manifestation. Such good-will implies much more than mutual tolerance among groups. It calls for the extension of the principle of equality from individuals to groups. This means that *every cultural or religious group should be permitted to function as the milieu in which the individual's rights to life, liberty and the pursuit of happiness may be realized.* Its history, its culture, its way of life and its social forms should be allowed to serve as a means of self-fulfillment and salvation to all who so wish. This freedom should be shared equally by all groups. Any interference with this freedom of weaker groups by a dominant group should be regarded and treated as a moral violation fraught with danger to the welfare of society, and as a sin against God.

To accept this principle of equality, historical civilizations and religions would have to reconstruct not only their own traditions, but hurdle some very difficult obstacles that inhere in the very nature of the human being. But what is the function of civilizations and religions, if not to bring our impulses under control, and to transform those inherited human traits which work evil? This means, of course, overcoming the inertia of vicious tendencies that have attained a high degree of sanctity and social approval.

143

The factors that contribute to mutual misunderstanding and ill-will among groups are too well known to require detailed description. Persons interested in promoting intergroup good-will are apt to minimize the difficulty, by assuming that good-will is natural to the individual, and that all ill-will between groups is an artificial product of indoctrination. The truth, however, is that group hostilities have deep roots in human nature and in human history. The consciousness of kind, which is part of our natural endowment, involves a certain dislike for the unlike. That dislike, under certain circumstances, tends to develop into a violent xenophobia. The circumstances that develop this antagonism are those that involve competition between the vital interests of the groups; the more intense the competition the more bitter the antagonism. The antagonisms generated by the natural causes mentioned are perpetuated in the culture of the group. Blood-feuds are handed down from generation to generation, and stories of hostile acts breed further hostilities.

The recognition of the factors making for ill-will between groups enables us to understand why the lofty ethical teachings that abound in all the great traditions have so far been impotent to check strife and warfare between different peoples. The truth is that none of the historical religions is free from the taint of group egotism that inevitably leads to unjust treatment of other groups. An examination of the sacred scriptures and other authoritative writings of the three historical religions reveals a spirit of hostility, persecution and warfare against dissident groups. To be sure, religion early taught—and often very effectively—the love of one's neighbor, but the idea of one's neighbor has always been limited to the members of one's own people, or to adherents of one's faith. In the case of one's own, that commandment has at least been honored in the breach. But in the case of those who are not of one's own, it has not been honored in any fashion whatever.

In all primitive societies it was taken for granted that the gods were interested only in the salvation of the group that worshipped them. Although ethical relations between the members of the group were insisted upon, no such obligation existed toward those of another group. Marauding, pillage and aggressive war were regarded as legitimate and, when deemed necessary, as meritorious. Before expeditions of this character were undertaken, the gods of the group were invariably invoked for aid.

When, as a consequence of trade, war and conquest, groups tended to coalesce, there arose a new conception of humanity. In the Alexandrian empire and, to an even greater degree, in the Roman empire, cultural intercourse between the various races and nationalities within the empire gave rise to Stoicism with its emphasis on a cosmopolitan social order. But cosmopolitanism does not necessitate the recognition of cultural groups as equally entitled to be the source of salvation or self-fulfillment to their individual members. In fact, it is entirely compatible with contempt for cultural differences as too unimportant for insistent preservation. Such an attitude has proved at no time to be a bridge for intergroup understanding and good-will. It may undermine faith in one's own culture, but it does not necessarily breed respect for the culture of any other group.

With the spread of Christianity and Mohammedanism, a new situation arose. The various native cultures were permitted to retain their individuality, provided they submitted to being recast in accordance with the pattern of the beliefs and practices of those religions. The platform on which those religions are based, and which derived from Judaism, was that all human beings were equally the object of God's care and providence. But since each religion looked upon its own institutions as the only revealed and authoritative method of salvation, and could not imagine that any other way of life could be as good as its own, it expected eventually to be accepted by all of mankind. That has remained the traditional doctrine of the historical religions to this day. These religions possess advanced codes of ethics that stress the dignity of the human personality and the equality of men in God's sight, insofar as their own adherents are concerned. But they look upon all "infidels" as not coming within the scope of God's grace, except potentially through conversion and membership in the fellowship of the true faith; hence "infidels" are inferior and not entitled to consideration as equals.

Beginning with Zoroastrianism, persecution of those who do not accept one's own religion, or at least discrimination against them, has been part and parcel of the authoritative religious teaching of all the great historical faiths. From *The Origin and Development of the Moral Ideas* by Westermarck[1] we learn that Zoroastrianism restricted the giving of charity to its own followers, on the ground that to help the unbeliever was to strengthen the dominion of Evil; that Mohammedans are forbidden to give to non-Moslems the alms required by their law; that the principle of the Church was "Regard every believer as your brother," thus limiting the conception of brotherhood only to believers; that in the 17th century the Scotch clergy taught that food or shelter must on no occasion be given to a starving man, unless his opinions were orthodox. Only Jewish law enjoins the giving of charity even to those of other faiths.[2] Even that law, however, does not contemplate the equality of religions; its traditional form insists that Israel is the Chosen People and Jewish religion the one true religion.

The nearest approach to a recognition of the duty of a uniform ethical standard in the treatment of strangers as well as natives is to be found in those sixty or more passages in the Old Testament, which enjoin just and fair treatment of the *ger*, a term usually rendered as "stranger." But when we examine that term in its textual and historical context, we discover that it is only by widening its significance that those passages can be made to contribute to better intergroup relations. The term *ger*, does not mean *foreigner*, for which the Hebrew language has another term, *nokri*; it means, rather, a sojourner or *resident alien*. What the original status of the *ger* actually was is somewhat obscure. One plausible theory has it that the *gerim* were the original Canaanite people who, after conquest by the Hebrew tribes, were reduced to a sort of serfdom. At any rate, their status must originally have been a subordinate and depressed one. The Pentateuchal legislation which insisted that there be "one law for you and for the *ger* who sojourns with you"[3] represents an endeavor to emancipate the *ger* and assimilate him into the Jewish community. This accounts for the fact that, in the Hebrew language of the post-Biblical era the term *ger* is used to designate a proselyte, since conversion to Judaism meant a complete acceptance of the Jewish way of life and admission into the Jewish community.

However, in traditional Jewish religion, as in the other faiths, acceptance of membership in the Jewish community was a condition prerequisite to being considered the equal of every other Jew. Only as Jews come to reinterpret Biblical laws concerning the *ger*, as indicative of a tendency to extend the ethical bond to individuals beyond the Jewish community, can Jewish religion prove adequate to the ethical imperative of intergroup good-will. Needless to say, the adherents of other religions are likewise confronted with the task of reinterpreting their own traditions in the same spirit.

2

GROUP EQUALITY TO BE BASIS OF ALL
RELIGIOUS ETHICAL SYSTEMS

From the foregoing facts it is apparent that the historical religions operate with a tradition that is incongruous with the ethical demands of the modern world for intergroup understanding and good-will, on the basis of democratic equality. The universe of discourse common to all these religious traditions is based on the following postulate, which is entirely reasonable, especially as it lends itself to rational interpretation: *Since man did not create himself, but is part of creation as a whole, the knowledge of what he needs in order to achieve salvation must come from his Creator, or God. Such knowledge, in whatever way communicated to man, constitutes divine revelation.*

But the universal truth of that postulate is qualified in the traditional religions by the following three contentions which are barriers to intergroup good-will: (1) There can be only one true method of salvation for all human beings, regardless of their group affiliations. (2) The individual is the primary unit of human life and, therefore, the primary object of the divine method of salvation. (3) Salvation is not achievable in this world but in the hereafter, where immortality and bliss are free from all social bonds.

In keeping with these assumptions, the existence of distinct groups has been regarded as at best an irrelevance, and at worst an interference with the process of salvation. The Kingdom of God has been conceived as homogeneous, with all people destined to believe and practice one religion. To such an extent were group loyalties conceived as an impediment to full loyalty of the individual to God that, in the Christian tradition, even the family relationship was regarded a necessary evil rather than an inherent good. The same is true of the state, which was regarded as the secular arm of the church to maintain a degree of law and order in an unregenerate human society, but not as itself capable of serving as an instrument of divine salvation.

In order to attain the objective of intergroup understanding and good-will, it is by all means necessary to retain the initial and fundamental postulate of the historical religions, insofar as it concerns the ultimate divine sanction of ethics. Even those assumptions which have hitherto barred the way to intergroup good-will need not be wholly discarded. What is necessary is to extract the two fundamental ethical truths which are contained in them: (1) the affirmation of the worth of the individual, and (2) the recognition that the field of operation for salvation as a goal must extend beyond one's own life.

The religious perception of the sacredness of the individual personality, i.e. of the importance of the individual as an end in himself and not merely as a means to another, is the only adequate rationale for democratic equality; it is the only safeguard against the tyranny of both mobs and state. Furthermore, the religious recognition that the field of operation for salvation must extend beyond the individual life-span is the only safeguard against the feeling of ultimate frustration which inheres in the knowledge of our own mortality.

These two values (the worth of the individual and the faith in a salvation that looks to a posthumous future for its realization) must be combined with our present realization that the human being is not a self-contained atom, but is the product of the biological, historical and social forces that operate in the group to which he belongs. One's personality is a product of a self-generating life principle, on the one hand, and, on the other, of the social environment and heritage supplied by the group. What has been said of words in relation to their context is true of human beings in relation to their communities; they "are not pebbles in juxtaposition; they have only a communal existence; the meaning of each interpenetrates the others."

It follows that, implicated in the process of salvation, are the two elements of individuality and sociality. This means that, *if salvation is to be the lot of all human beings, we must reckon with the existence of different cultural groups as not only legitimate, but as potentially an indispensable factor of salvation.* The sacredness of the person can mean nothing, if we have to abstract from that person all loyalties derived from his connection with his group. If we are to respect the worth of the human being, we cannot demand that he renounce the values he has experienced in his relation to his group. Moreover, ideals which transcend our individual life-span and which seek fulfillment in the future that we project for our posterity are the heritage of the group, and depend on the continued existence of the group for their fulfillment. Hence to deny the group the right of self-perpetuation is to cut off the salvation of the individual. The group personality is, in a sense, more important and more entitled to be the concern of religious ethics than the individual personality, just because the ambivalent character of the group is even more pronounced than that of the individual. Indispensable as the group is as a means of enabling the individual to transcend his blind impulses and selfish interests, all too often it not only reenforces those impulses and those interests but also justifies and sanctifies them.

Teachers of religion should therefore realize that it is their duty deliberately to include all cultural and religious groups within the scope of religious ethics and to foster sensitivity to the wide range of moral possibilities that inhere in any cultural group. We respect the worth and dignity of an individual not on the basis of what he is actually, but on the basis of his potentialities. The same should be true of the group. The notion that the individual is the object of salvation must henceforth be supplemented by the notion that groups are likewise objects of salvation.

3

THE ETHICAL RELATION OF RELIGIONS
TO ONE ANOTHER

In order to grasp how religions can transcend the barriers to intergroup good-will which the religious communions have themselves erected, we must seek to understand what all religions have in common and what trait of human nature is reflected in all the various religions.

Fortunately the historic religions accept the belief in the unity of God. This belief carries with it implications insufficiently realized; if fully understood, these religions could transcend the present limitations of their respective traditions. Peace and good-will between religions as between nations is possible, without any surrender of integrity, if the religions thoroughly acquiesce in and implement two doctrines, which they have been teaching in one form or another. These doctrines are summed up in two verses quoted by Jesus [4] from the Pentateuch as containing the essence of true religion: "Thou shalt love the Lord thy God with all thy heart, with all thy soul and with all thy might," [5] and "Thou shalt love thy neighbor as thyself." [6] Buddha preached, "My neighbor is myself."

The historic religions agree that men should love and worship God, as the source of their salvation. They also agree that men should live together in brotherhood as a condition of meriting God's salvation. But in order to understand how these ideals can be made to function as a bridge to better intergroup relations, we must take such terms as the *love of God* and *salvation* out of their traditional context in the particular theological terminology of our own religion, and translate them into the idiom of our common naturalistic universe of discourse. This we can do by applying the principle of equivalence. A term used in the traditional, theological universe of discourse may be regarded as the equivalent of a term used in the modern naturalistic universe of discourse, if the concepts they denote serve an identical function, and have similar pragmatic consequences, that is, if they result in the like inner attitudes and outer conduct.

The inner attitude which comes with the conviction of salvation is that of having achieved the goal of human life, the utmost fulfilment of human nature. The outer conduct to which the hope of salvation leads is the effort to realize those aspects of distinctively human nature, that transcend the instincts and impulses which man shares with the lower orders of animal life, and that represent the desirable goals of his future evolution. What differentiates man from other orders of creation is that, in him alone, the will to live functions as a will to make the most of life, to use to the utmost all the potentialities of his being. It is the will for life ampler and more harmonious than any he has ever known. *In human nature the will to live becomes the will to salvation.* Since this implies man's participation in a cosmic process that transcends his own knowledge to grasp it and power to control it, he feels his dependence on a Power beyond himself that leads to salvation; to that power he gives the name God. To love God must, therefore, mean to do our utmost to achieve salvation, to transcend the limits of one's natural endowment, to abjure all brutality and cruelty, and to become thoroughly human or humane.

Thus it follows that to love God, we must also love our neighbor. Our will to salvation is bound to be frustrated unless we act in such a manner as to enable our neighbor to live a thoroughly human and humane life. If we cause him to be afraid of us, if we threaten his security or challenge his human dignity, we hinder the Creative Power that is seeking the abundant and good life for men, and we render life insecure for ourselves as well as for others; we are at war with God.

4

THE EQUALITY OF RELIGIONS

If religions, therefore, take seriously their avowed obligation to love God and one's fellow man, they have the duty to curb their own natural tendency to use antagonism to other groups as a means of enhancing their own importance in the eyes of their adherents. The historical religions are organized efforts of men to help one another achieve salvation by utilizing to this end those elements of their common culture which the spirit of the group recognizes as contributing to the supreme worth or holiness of life. These elements or *sancta*,* however, derive their sanctity for the group from its own unique historic experience. It is not to be expected that they should have equal value for members of other religions, which similarly utilize their own *sancta* to achieve salvation.

The recognition of this truth implies the essential equality of all ethical religions. To be sure, some religious traditions may teach truths that others have not yet learned, but there is nothing to prevent these others from appropriating such truths and implementing them through their own *sancta*. Viewed in this light, the differences between religions become like differences between human personalities within the same religious communion. These vary, too, in the degree in which they may embody certain virtues, but we regard them as equal before God, in that they are equally responsible for carrying out His will and equally eligible to salvation, when they do so. In the same way *religious differences do not imply religious inequality, and the assumption that our own religion is superior to all others is no more legitimate than to pretend that we ourselves as individuals are superior to other individuals, or have a superior claim to God's grace.*

When we understand the natural and historic factors that have produced group antagonism, it is not difficult to realize that the pretensions of religious groups to being the chosen of God, or the only vehicle of His salvation for mankind, are a product of those factors. In primitive cultures, people commonly believe that their God is exclusively interested in their own group. He is virtually a member of their community, partaking of the food they offer him in their sacrifices, and committed to helping them both in their peaceful and warlike pursuits. Strangers fall entirely outside of their world and have no claim upon their God. Their love of their God, as the patron spirit of the tribe, carries with it a love for the other members of their community which is under their God's protection, but does not go beyond that. On the contrary, whenever they plan a raid on a neighboring tribe they invoke all the *sancta* of their tribal religion to give them success in their undertaking and are convinced that their acts of slaughter, pillage and rape are pleasing to the deity and an expression of their love for him.

On a higher cultural level, religious groups begin to comprehend

* For further elucidation of the concept of *sancta* see above p. 46 and below p. 178.

the organic unity of the human race. Their God emerges from the status of a mere tribal or national deity into cosmic proportions. It becomes impossible, temporarily at least, for believers to imagine that all the rest of humanity besides themselves is ineligible to salvation; that God, whom they now hail as the Creator of the universe, has no interest in other fellow-mortals.

But how can the rest of mankind avail itself of God's grace and achieve a life of fulfilment, i.e. of true salvation? At this point the natural and historical factors breeding inequality again assert themselves. It is in the people's own culture, and more especially in those elements of its culture that it has come to revere as sacred—its sacred oracles, laws, rituals, holy days, etc.—that the people experiences the sense of communion with God and the assurance of divine salvation. The similar *sancta* of other peoples are meaningless, and so it regards them with contempt. It cannot imagine that those alien practices can possibly serve as a way of salvation for alien peoples. So it concludes again that it is in a special relationship to God, that it is God's Chosen People, that its religion is destined to become the one and only religion as it already is the only "true" religion.

The people then proceeds to extend its boundaries by annexing souls, either through persuasion or, if need be, by force, since to impose its *sancta* upon others is in their ultimate interest. Both Christianity and Islam were largely spread by the sword. Judaism, which was at that stage of its development also a proselytizing religion, imposed its faith and law on the conquered Idumeans, but that was its only venture in forcibly spreading its creed, because soon thereafter it lost its own independence and, consequently, the opportunity for propagating the faith by force. The missionizing religions consider themselves universal. Their religious attitude, however, is not a genuine universalism but is rather a form of sublimated imperialism. Just as empires resulted from the imposition of the civilization of one group on many alien peoples, so religions that laid claim to universality, or catholicity, imposed the *sancta* of their own group cultures on the converts, as a condition pre-requisite to their salvation and true communion with God.

There is no gainsaying that the missionizing religions have rendered a service to mankind. So did the secular empires, and in a very similar way. The latter widened the political, the former the spiritual horizons of men; the one broke down the isolationism of the national cultures, and in doing so implanted the concept of a social order which would one day include all of mankind, and the other broke down the exclusiveness of the ancient religious societies and gave men a vision of the universal Kingdom of God. But neither the one nor the other could become universal, because neither reckoned with the principle of human equality.

For men to be equal before God, they must have an equal right to have their group sancta *respected, so long as these are used for their own salvation, without interfering with other groups.* All proselytizing activity involves disrespect for the *sancta* of the group proselytized. It has always been fruitful of discord. The hatred of the Jews, and later of the Christians, by pagan Rome was a consequence of the missionizing activities of Judaism and early Christianity. The Boxer Rebellion in China is further evidence. It is not the advocacy of new ideas or values that is resented. Ideas or values are common currency among different cultures. The Greek pagan philosophers were studied by Moslems, Jews and Christians in the Middle Ages, and incorporated in the theological writings of all three religions. What is resented is the effort to supplant the *sancta* of the community in which one was born by the *sancta* of a foreign community.

In our present-day world, the coexistence of rival imperialisms each with the goal of universal conquest is unthinkable. If mankind is united on anything, it is one in its resolve that any future scheme of world conquest such as was cherished by the Axis powers must be nipped in the bud.

We know that imperialist wars are wrong, and may well destroy all human civilization and, perhaps, the human race. We seek, therefore, to create a world authority to check aggression and enforce for all nations a policy of "live and let live." Mankind looks largely to religion to motivate this endeavor to unite nations on the principle that each has an equal right to live. But our organized religions themselves are still "imperialistic." None of them has so far made any move to abandon its historic claim to being the sole possessor of the key to salvation. Each religion still refuses to recognize the right of the others to perpetuate themselves.

These pretensions they must now be asked to abjure. They must be asked, also, to motivate the achievement of a truly universal Kingdom of God, by utilizing their own *sancta*, not to inculcate superiority in the minds of their adherents but rather to preach the equality of all religions and the need of cooperation of all in guaranteeing to each full opportunities of its own self-development. If each religion would interpret the principle of loving one's neighbor to mean at least overcoming the inborn malice that impels men to hate the adherents of religions other than their own, it would strengthen its own position and help to bring about an unprecedented revival of interest in religion as a whole. The truth is that all established religions are today in a bad way. They have to prove their worth anew. To do that they must demonstrate their power to lessen the tension between nations, races, cultures and classes. Unless they will play an important role in ushering in the one world which has become indispensable to mankind, they will be reduced to a state of obsolescence.

5

RELIGIO-ETHICAL REEDUCATION TO BEGIN WITH OUR OWN GROUP

It is not enough, however, to transform the theoretic aspect of religious ethics, if it is to serve as a bridge for intergroup understanding and good-will. Change in theory must be accompanied by the adoption of practical measures.

The first step in our religio-ethical reeducation must be to follow the principle of removing the beam from our own eye before trying to remove the mote from the eye of our neighbor. Our own religious groups should henceforth pursue a new direction in their relations to one another. All derogatory allusions to dissenting faiths must be eliminated from religious texts, including rituals, prayers and literature of instruction and edification. But even that is not enough. More affirmative action is necessary. Every religious communion should develop rituals, prayers and teachings which would have for their specific aim the overcoming of the natural and the acquired tendencies toward group antagonism. Moreover, the use of this liturgical and educational material should come to occupy an important part in religious practice.

Secondly, steps should be taken to convene a World Parliament of Religions, similar to the one that was convened at the World Fair held in Chicago in 1892. The purpose of such a parliament should be to translate, into the language of religious ethics, the principle of intergroup understanding and good-will which the United Nations should seek to implement politically. *As the United Nations should call for the surrender of absoluteness in national sovereignties so should the World Parliament of Religions call for the renunciation by every religious communion of any claim to exclusive possession of salvation.*

In addition to these direct methods that religions can apply in the endeavor to put group relations on a solidly ethical basis, there is another method of tremendous importance. In order to develop a conscience with regard to group relations, ethical ideals of justice and equality among groups must be translated into terms of law to be enforced by appropriate legal sanctions. The fomenting of hatred toward any group, or the practice of discrimination against the members of any group on the ground of race, color, or creed must be banned by law and made subject to legal penalties. This development of law should be a project not merely of the state, but of all religious communions that mean to take their ethical function seriously.

This raises two questions. The spiritual question is: Do we not destroy the spiritual spontaneity of an ethical principle when we freeze it into a legal statute, with an accompanying element of forcible sanctions? The political question is: Do not efforts to ban hate propaganda contravene the personal rights guaranteed by the Constitution of the United States?

Our answer to the spiritual question, is that spontaneity is desirable only when it operates within the law; otherwise it is pure licentiousness and anarchy. There is no right to do wrong, and to restrain people from wrong-doing cannot be regarded as an infringement of freedom of conscience or any other human right. Surely the field of spontaneous activity is not narrowed, but enlarged, by any social action which enables all men to live in dignity and security and to enjoy equality of opportunity. Experience with the arts emphasizes this thought. Spontaneity and originality are of the very essence of artistic creation, yet all art that is worthy of the name implies a recognition of esthetic principles of design which, to be sure, conform with the taste of the artist, but which are not merely the reflection of individual whim or caprice. As long as political law conforms with moral law, it is itself an expression of the best in human nature and a stimulus to spontaneous goodness.

Furthermore, law which grows out of an ethical postulate is the device by which human beings help one another to do what they know to be right. The element of compulsion is like that exercised by the ringing of an alarm-clock; it compels a man to wake up, no matter how inclined he may be to sleep, but it was his own will that set the alarm for that very purpose. Woodrow Wilson said of the draft law that it expressed the will of a "nation volunteering." If the preponderant majority of the people had felt no moral compulsion to rally to the defense of the country, the draft law would have been utterly ineffective. Yet it is equally true that, without conscription, it would have been impossible to recruit an adequate army. The natural tendency to spare oneself and to consider the consequences of one's enlistment to one's immediate relatives, plus resentment at the thought that others were playing safe, would have outweighed considerations of patriotism and devotion to democracy and international justice. The draft law, by insuring equality of right and of responsibility, actually carried out the moral purpose of the individual American, as it could not have been carried out without such compulsion; it did indeed, represent "a nation volunteering" for military service.

Our answer to the political question is that mutual help through legislation is needed, whenever what we know to be right is resisted by instinctive and historical forces of great strength. This would be true, even on the assumption that everybody at least willed to do what is right. The truth, however, is that there are many people who do not even wish this, and who upset the most devoutly sought purposes of those who do. An outstanding example is provided by men's yearning for international peace. There can be no doubt that most people would desire that the nations settle amicably any disputes that may exist among them. But there is no way of halting the aggression of governments that are motivated by national selfishness, except by means of international law which would be backed by effective sanctions. This was forcibly stated in Bernard Baruch's proposals to the United Nations Commission on Atomic Energy. "Previous failures to achieve peace," he stated, "have been recorded in trying the method of simple renunciation, unsupported by effective guarantees of security and armament limitation. . . . The peoples want a program, not composed merely of pious thoughts, but of enforceable sanctions . . . an international law with teeth in it."

The legal banning of attempts to stir up hatred against a group on racial, religious or cultural grounds is further supported by what Justice Roberts of the U. S. Supreme Court had to say in the case of *Cantwell vs. Connecticut*, involving the Witnesses of Jehovah who had been convicted for trying to play phonograph records which denounced the Catholic Church. Although the conviction had to be over-ruled for technical reasons, he did not oppose on principle prohibiting by law the spreading of ill-will against groups. "There are limits," he said, "to the exercise of these liberties. The danger in these times from the coercive activities of those who, in the delusion of racial or religious conceit, would incite violence and breaches of the peace, in order to deprive others of their rights to the exercise of their liberties, is emphasized by events familiar to all."

In the case of *Murdock vs. Pennsylvania* (another "Jehovah Witnesses" case) Justice Jackson, also of the U. S. Supreme Court, stated in a dissenting opinion that any religious group is within its rights, when opposing and criticizing any other denomination. "These rights," he added, "are, and should be held to be, as extensive as any orderly society can tolerate in religious disputation. The real question is where do their rights end and the rights of others begin. A common sense test as to whether the court has struck a proper balance of these rights is to ask, 'what the effect would be, if the right given to these Witnesses should be exercised by all sects and denominations.' " The fact is that these rights to spread hatred against groups are at present given to all sects and denominations, and to some extent exercised by them.

In the meantime, it should be part of religious ethics to ally itself with existing law, both Federal and State, as a means of activating the conscience of people with regard to group relations. There are laws on the statute books that at present are a dead letter simply because most of us are not even aware of their existence. There has been a penal law on the statute books of New York State for over sixty years, which declares as guilty of a misdemeanor punishable by fine, "a person who excludes a citizen of this state, by reason of race, color, creed, or previous condition of servitude, from any public employment or from the equal enjoyment of any accommodation, facility or privilege furnished by innkeepers or common carriers, or by owners, managers or lessees of theatres or other places of amusement, or by teachers and officers of common schools and public institutions of learning, or by cemetery associations; or denies or aids or incites another to deny to any person because of race, creed or color, public employment or the full enjoyment of any of the accommodations, advantages, facilities and privileges of any hotel, inn, tavern, restaurant, public conveyance on land or water, theatre or other place of public resort or amusement." A law of this kind as well as the Fair Employment Practices Committee (FEPC) Act passed not long ago in New York State and in the State of New Jersey should not merely remain on the law books, but serve as texts for sermons from the pulpits, and as subject matter for instruction in religious schools, and be made the basis of the kind of religious ethics which we need as a bridge for intergroup understanding and good-will.

The Federal FEPC, instituted in 1941 as a war measure, was

terminated in 1946 largely as a result of the filibuster led by Senator Bilbo of Mississippi. It is to be hoped that, before long, the American people will demand a peacetime bill which will guarantee to every American the right to work, regardless of race, color, or religious affiliation.

In sum: *The ethics of group relations must be clearly articulated in terms of group equality. It must assume the right of religions other than our own to permanent existence. Religious pluralism will have to be recognized as legitimate, not only by the state but also by the various religious communions themselves. The principle of group equality must be translated into legal enactments prohibiting the propagation of racial and religious hatred, and removing all unjust discrimination in the treatment of members of religious and racial minorities. Only in this way will the highest teachings of the Prophets of all faiths be realized.*

PART II

THE NEXT STAGE IN JEWISH RELIGION

CHAPTER NINE

NEEDED: A NEW UNDERSTANDING OF JEWISH RELIGION

"Some modern Jews," writes Prof. E. R. Goodenough,[1] of Yale University, "who are intensely loyal to conservative Judaism confess that they do not know whether they believe in God or not, and one prominent rabbi who spoke for a school of modern Jews told me that no belief, not even a belief in God, was required of a Jew." On the other hand, the late Rabbi Hyman G. Enelow,[2] in discussing "What Do Jews Believe?" wrote as follows: "The Jew has always felt the existence of God as a basic truth of life. . . . This then is our first belief. Without it Judaism is impossible. Without it one may be . . . Jewish in racial or social relations—but one is not a Jew in the true historic sense of the term."

The foregoing quotations indicate that there exists not only among laymen, but even among rabbis, sharp disagreement concerning the place of religion in Jewish life. It is actually true that there are rabbis who "do not know whether they believe in God or not." One wonders what they are doing in the Jewish pulpit. The answer is that they probably believe in the Jewish people, and they try to serve it in ways that have nothing to do with theology. If they use the name of God, it is merely out of deference to social convention. If you were to ask them how they reconcile their lack of religious convictions with their vocation, they would not be at a loss for texts to justify their anomalous attitude. For is it not often stated that God, Torah and Israel are one? [3] Hence it makes no difference which aspect of this Jewish trinity one emphasizes. And did not the Sages actually say that God would not have minded the Jews' "forsaking Him," if they had only kept the Torah? [4] Those rabbis forget, however, the rest of the passage which reads, "for the light in the Torah would ultimately lead them back to God."

On the other hand, if such rabbis are wrong in regarding the belief in God as unessential, did Rabbi Enelow in the above quotation state the case correctly for its indispensability? He was unquestionably right in maintaining that a Jew who does not believe in God is not a Jew "in the true historic sense of the term." But what he unquestionably implied was that the belief in God was more essential to being a Jew than participation in the give and take of Jewish life. In keeping with the theory of the strictly orthodox Reformists, he minimized, by implication, the "social relations" of the Jew. He would probably have taken exception to the teaching of Maimonides, that a Jew who separates himself from the Jewish community, even though he commit no transgression, forfeits his salvation.[5]

The trouble with most Jews, including many contemporary rabbis, is that they are unable to see Judaism steadily and as a whole. Some find the distinguishing trait of the Jew in what they term his racial, social or national heredity. Others insist upon regarding the religion, which has differentiated the Jews from the rest of the world, as essentially that which entitles one to be regarded as a Jew. Neither view is correct. In this instance, actual usage is the best guide. To the average Gentile, any person who has the least connection with the Jewish people, past or present, is a Jew. If, on the other hand, we would like to set up a norm as to what constitutes a good Jew, we should give preference to one who lives a full Jewish life. To be a *good* Jew, one has to be a Jew socially, culturally and religiously. To be a Jew, religiously, means to believe in God. *Without religion, the energies of Jewish life are bound to be those of fear; with it, those of hope.*

1

THE RELATION OF JEWISH RELIGION TO JUDAISM

If we learn to view Judaism as a living, organic process, we are bound to conclude: first, that Jewish religion is neither synonymous nor coextensive with the whole of Judaism; and, secondly, that Jewish religion cannot function without the other elements which constitute Judaism; thirdly, that Judaism cannot be whole or normal without Jewish religion.

In common parlance, Judaism is a synonym for Jewish religion. The result is that people have developed a blind spot for the thousand and one realities in Jewish living which could not very well be classed as religion, and which nevertheless are indispensable to being a Jew. Note, for example, how the late Kaufmann Kohler struggled with the term Judaism. "It is very difficult," he admitted,[6] "to give an exact definition of Judaism because of its peculiarly complex character. . . . Religion and race form an inseparable whole in Judaism. . . . The Jewish people stand in the same relation to Judaism as the body to the soul." Under the unfortunate term "race" and the appropriate term "people," Kohler endeavors to account for the whole complex of so-called secular realities which give Judaism "body."

What Kohler referred to as "race" is essentially kinship, which is based upon consanguinity, and which is reenforced by the actual process of living together. The feeling of kinship among Jews is both the cause and the effect of their common civilization. It is this which has given rise to the belief that the Jews constitute a racial group.

In any event, it is evident that even Kohler realized that the term Judaism must have a connotation beyond the term *Jewish religion.* The fact, however, is that "Judaism" must include much more even than race or sense of kinship. It must be coextensive with all those social, cultural and religious values which the Jewish people, with its long history and rich experience, has evolved.

The only way to avoid getting tangled up in one's traces, when speaking of Judaism, is really to regard it as coextensive with the entire civilization of the Jewish people. As such, it consists of all those elements which go into the making of a civilization, namely, rootage in a common land, use of a common language, possession of a common history, and loyalty to a common tradition consisting of laws, mores, folkways, and art.

It is necessary, however, to reckon specifically with the particular elements in Judaism, or Jewish civilization, which have a direct bearing upon the belief in God. There may have been no past occasion for classifying those elements under the special category of religion. In fact, there is really no word for religion in the entire Biblical and Rabbinical literature. Even in medieval philosophical literature there is no exact equivalent for the concept *religion.* The Hebrew word *dat,* which occurs frequently in Jewish theological writings of the Middle Ages, is wrongly translated by the word religion; it really means law. As applied to the Torah, the word *dat* is used to designate it divine law, or *lex divina,* in contrast with man-made law.[7]

Now, the changes in social and political thinking of the Western nations, leading to such reforms as the separation of church and state and to the emancipation of the Jews, have rendered the concept *religion* indispensable. Likewise, in Jewish life we have to employ the term "Jewish religion," for which the modern Hebrew term is *ha-emunah ha-yisreëlit,* to denote that aspect of Judaism, or the Jewish civilization, which is related to the belief or faith in God. That aspect embraces the various teachings concerning God, the universe and man, and the ritual practices which help to foster our awareness of God. The sum of these teachings and ritual practices is not a random conglomerate. It is animated and unified by the one dominant function of helping the Jew to achieve his destiny as a human being.

Today's discourse demands that the distinction between Judaism and Jewish religion should not imply that either Judaism minus Jewish religion, or Jewish religion detached from the other elements of Judaism, can function normally. Jewish religion tends to become moribund as soon as it is isolated from the context of Jewish civilization or from Judaism as a whole. The classic Reform method of eliminating from Judaism whatever is not directly connected with the belief in God is doomed. Jews who have no concern for the fate of Jewry as a whole, to whom Eretz Yisrael has no meaning whatever in its relation to the destiny of the Jewish people, who regard Hebrew as an ancient exotic tongue, or who cannot conceive of Jewish communal organization as having any other value or function than that of collecting funds for the needy, sooner or later lose all interest in the Synagogue and in what it represents. A study of the descendants of the founders of Reform congregations of two generations ago reveals how few of them profess Jewish religion, or have anything to do with Jewish life.

The reverse, however, is no less true, namely, that without Jewish religion we cannot expect Jewish life in the Diaspora to retain its hold on the Jews. *Jewish religion is nothing less than the soul of Judaism, or of Jewish civilization.* Because of the Jewish concept of God and the various practices connected with it, the contents of Jewish living are meaningful; thus the Jews have been able to interpret their experiences, hopes and sufferings in a way that has enhanced their lives and that has given them courage to face stoically a hostile world.

2

THE PROBLEM OF RELIGION IGNORED IN
CONTEMPORARY JEWISH LIFE

Jews who still believe wholeheartedly that the Jewish religion, as it has come down from the past, is infallible, and that it is therefore the most potent instrument of salvation, can be depended on to maintain Jewish civilization, whether they call it by that name or not. To hold that belief, however, they have to believe literally in the story of the divine revelation to Israel, as recorded in the book of Exodus. They have to believe that a supernatural event took place on Mount Sinai, when the Israelites heard an articulate voice from on high uttering some or all of the Ten Commandments, and that the Pentateuch in its entirety was dictated by God to Moses, together with oral interpretations of its contents.[8]

The moment, however, that belief is questioned, even if it is not entirely renounced, the conviction that the Jews have the truest religion becomes soulless. There are those who force themselves to believe in the supernatural origin of the Torah because they are afraid that, without that belief, they would have no reason for remaining Jews, or bringing up their children as Jews. This lukewarm belief is of such low moral value that it cannot function as an instrument of salvation. It is opportunism that soon degenerates into self-delusion. Deluding others is the next downward step. No people can long survive make-believe.

The only kind of Jewish religion, acceptable to Jews who find it impossible to regard the Torah as of supernatural origin, is one which deliberately endeavors to conform to the highest dictates of reason and conscience. It is hardly necessary to labor the point that the Jewish religion, in the form in which it has come down from the past, is not adequate from that standpoint. That is the fault of the present generation which has done very little, if anything, to render it adequate for the new and far larger horizons within which Jewish life must henceforth move. It is none too soon (before long it will be too late) to undertake the too oft-deferred task of rendering Jewish religion convincing and so capable of eliciting the best in the Jew that for its sake Jews will find it worthwhile to foster Jewish social institutions, the upbuilding of Eretz Yisrael, and the creation of new Jewish values.

One does not have to resort to statistics of synagogue attendance to prove that those who have not been affected by religious doubts and questionings constitute a small and dwindling minority. It is lamentable that, in the higher levels of cultural and intellectual achievement, one can seldom, if ever, see evidence of loyalty to Jewish religion, to say nothing of enthusiasm for it. The late Henri Bergson, the outstanding Jewish thinker in our generation, who perhaps has done more than any one else to revitalize religious speculation, has contributed to the revival of Catholicism. In one of the important universities in this country, it is a Jew who has helped to medievalize higher education by having it reorganized around Neo-Thomist theology. The oft-repeated statement that the Jewish mind has become so totally secularized as to be repelled by religion is entirely without foundation.

It is true, however, that *little encouragement is given in present-day organized Jewish life to the consideration of either the problem of religion in general or of Jewish religion in particular.* There must be something fundamentally wrong either with our people or with its spiritual leaders, when Jewish theological writings like those of Solomon Formstecher,[9] Solomon L. Steinheim,[10] Samuel Hirsch,[11] Hermann Cohen,[12] Martin Buber [13] and Franz Rosenzweig [14] can be permitted to gather dust that is never disturbed. Even if what they had to say were not entirely tenable, it should have engaged the minds of their contemporaries, and by now should have been superseded by what is credible.

Modern Jewish men and women of sensitive soul find Jewish life to be so arid in religious thought and inspiration that they deem it necessary to turn elsewhere to satisfy their religious cravings. The Jewish pulpit, which should have been the chief source of instruction dealing with the belief in God in terms of our current world outlook, at best confines itself to appeals for relief funds and the support of various Jewish undertakings, and at worst merely saves the congregants the trouble of reading newspaper editorials, magazine articles and bestsellers. Discussions of the specific problems of religion, such as the conception of God, human nature and destiny, the existence of evil, and the difference between false and true religion, are almost tabu.

3

THE STUDY OF RELIGION IN NEED OF CULTIVATION

The remedy lies in cultivating in our people a taste for, and an interest in, the study of religion as an integral element of human culture. It is of the utmost importance to break down the notion that religion is a specialized experience or something that can remain outside the vast fabric of practical life—like the "Religion Exhibit" at the World's Fair in 1939 which was tucked away in a little building among the mammoth structures containing industrial and government exhibits.

The light thrown on the evolution of religion in the various ethnological studies, the wide gamut of psychological aspects of religion which extends far beyond what William James dealt with in his *Varieties of Religious Experience*, the relation of religion to the development of the life of nations and their civilizations—all these sources of information concerning the way religion functions and develops should be drawn upon.

Jews need to be made to realize that the aspect of human life, in which their ancestors made the most significant contribution, is one that is rich in cultural and ethical content. *True religion cannot be caught; it has to be taught.* There is, to be sure, the pedagogic problem of making the subject-matter interesting, but that does not exempt the rabbis from the duty of specializing in the study of religion and in the art of teaching it. This is nowadays the main justification for their calling.

The chief purpose of the study of religion should be not merely to spread information concerning the way religion functioned in the past, or among the different peoples of the world, valuable as such information is. That makes for religious literacy only and it should not serve as a substitute for religious experience. It is a means to a more ethical as well as more genuine religious experience. Both the genuineness and the ethical character of that experience will be reflected in the conception of the salvation which is set up as the goal of human life, and in the conduct to which that conception gives rise.

To that end, it is necessary to stimulate an interest in the study of such problems as are dealt with in religious philosophy and in theology. This may sound formidable and frightening to the average layman. There was, no doubt, a time when the mere suggestion that the average young person would have to study geometry and algebra sounded ludicrous. The standard of intellectual life has risen, and these studies are now accepted as a matter of course. The like must happen to questions pertaining to the meaning of human life, which are dealt with in religious philosophy and in theology. Communism has introduced young people into the intricacies of metaphysics. There is no reason why Judaism should not acquaint the Jew with such ideas as are necessary to clarify the meaning and purpose of his existence.

Religious philosophy approaches the idea of God independently of any tradition, and seeks to determine the objective truth, as far as it is possible to achieve it with regard to God and His relation to man and the world. It does not recognize any authority other than that of the thinking and experiencing human mind. In theology, the problem is how to interpret or reinterpret a particular religious tradition, in the light of objective truth ascertained in religious philosophy. *We can have, therefore, Jewish, Christian or Mohammedan theology, but there can not be Jewish religious philosophy, any more than there can be Jewish mathematics.*

On the other hand, religious philosophy itself must be based on the results of a descriptive study of religion. Hence the function of religious philosophy may be said to consist in developing a conception of God and of His relation to man and the universe, which would not only be based on actual experience, both individual and collective, with the belief in God but which would also harmonize with the rest of human experience both historical and scientific. Those who have an interest in fostering a particular civilization will succeed best, if they undertake to vitalize the religious tradition of that civilization by means of the objective truths ascertained through a study of religious philosophy. If the Jewish civilization is to be justified in its claim of providing the Jew with true religion, it must show active zeal in fostering both religious philosophy and Jewish theology.

4

REASON NOT TO BE FLOUTED

One of the main weaknesses in most of the religious-philosophical and theological systems formulated by the spiritual leaders of nineteenth century German Jewry was the tendency to accept from contemporary German philosophers the romantic rationalizations of the political and social status quo as genuine expressions of reason. The truth is that Fichte, Jacobi, Schelling, Schlegel and Hegel invoked reason mainly to combat French revolutionary influence which was identified with rationalism and enlightenment.

Eighteenth century rationalism, which the German philosophers did their utmost to vilify, whatever its failings may have been, had at least the merit of awakening new hope for a better day for mankind. This is something that cannot be said of the ponderous systems of speculative idealism and romanticism which the renowned German thinkers constructed.

Unfortunately, rationalism was cut short by the spirit of reaction that raised irrationalism to a place of primacy as a method of arriving at truth. The eclipse of reason contributed to the deepening of religious obscurantism among intellectuals, and to the rise of bigoted and chauvinistic nationalism on a large scale among the masses. It is no wonder, therefore, that most of the Jewish theology which was produced under the influence of German thought has proved quite sterile.

There are specific criteria of truth which should guide us in our study of religious philosophy, besides those which we must necessarily derive from the objective facts to be found in the descriptive study of religion. One is that *a conception of God must be true not merely as an idea but as religion*. This means that it must have a bearing upon the *whole* of human life, and make for the enhancement of every phase of it. This implies that religious philosophy, to be normative, must take into account the emotional, the intellectual and the volitional aspects of human nature. It must establish, therefore, norms of truth in the fields of mysticism, metaphysics and ethics.

These norms cannot be reliable, unless they support and supplement one another. The recent tendency in certain theological circles to make a virtue of inconsistency should be resisted. If we are not to lose ourselves in the obscurities of word-worship, we have to rely upon inner consistency as an indispensable brake on our uncontrolled imaginings. If a norm in one field of religious philosophy is permitted to contradict a norm in one of the other fields, the mind becomes involved in inner conflict. When people accept such inner conflict resignedly, they help to create a state of society in which conflicting social ideals and institutions are the order of the day.

Human nature normally prefers inner harmony, and cannot accept psychic or social conflicts without experiencing a feeling of defeat and frustration. Religion should help the individual to achieve personal integration while assisting society to collective integration. Both are indispensable to salvation. *Religion should not, in its philosophy, permit a double standard of truth, such as most medieval theologians regarded as inevitable.*

No assumption could have been more destructive of true spirituality than the admission of different standards of truth. Such an admission is at bottom a confession of disbelief in truth as absolute. "The beginning of all spiritual life," says Albert Schweitzer, "is courageous faith in truth and open confession of it." [15] *Religious philosophies which disavow the oneness of truth inevitably lead to spiritual nihilism.*

A second criterion of a true conception of God is that it shall be both enlightening and liberating. The anonymous Prophet whose words are included in the second part of Isaiah defined Israel's mission as being "to open the eyes of the blind and to set free those who are in bonds." [16] Enlightenment and liberation are thus named as the means by which the true kind of religion may be distinguished from religion that is false and misleading.

This sentiment is partly reiterated in the New Testament, where

Jesus is said to have characterized the truth as making men free.[17] The Old Testament, however, goes further. It names not only liberation as a sign of true religion, but also enlightenment. In other words, any mystical, metaphysical or ethical idea about God, which fails to establish new and fruitful connections and meanings among the things we already know and have experienced to some extent, cannot be true.

If the conception of God does not help to liberate the human being from the various thraldoms to which he is ever subject, it cannot be true. There is the thraldom of superstition, and of the fear it engenders. There is the thraldom of wrong beliefs, like those which assume that fate or blind mechanism is the fundamental law of life. There is the thraldom which the strong impose upon the weak. It is the very function of the conception of God to redeem man from all these forms of bondage, and to set men free. *Any teaching about God which fails to make man free cannot be true religion.*

To be both enlightening and liberating, religion must be based on faith in reason, and resort under all circumstances to the rational conclusions of empirical experience. This does not imply that reason is infallible and omniscient. Nor does it mean that there is no room in religion for faith, intuition, or mystic experience. With the human mind inherently incapable of ever actually sounding the nethermost depths of reality, it is impossible for man to wait with the process of living until he has achieved absolute certainty. But even when we recognize that reason as such cannot fully guide us, and learn that there are moments when somehow we find our way in life by non-rational methods, we dare not stray off into by-paths of the mind without the special authorization which only reason is entitled to grant. Human reason, if not perverted by extraneous considerations, can be relied on to be honest and modest enough to recognize its own limitations. *Only reason itself can know what its limitations are, and it alone has the right to determine what they are.*

With this principle in mind, our task is to rethink the problem of religion in general, and reinterpret our Jewish religious tradition in the light of conclusions thus reached. We have come to a pass when to foster religious philosophy and Jewish theology is as essential to Jewish survival as are the rebuilding of Eretz Yisrael, the organization of communal life, and the development of Jewish culture. If those activities are to have meaning for the modern-minded Jew, only Jewish religion that is integral to, and consistent with, the modern universe of discourse can supply it.

CHAPTER TEN

THE BELIEF IN GOD

1

MEANING OF THE BELIEF IN GOD

The objective study of religion the world over has proved beyond a doubt that the belief in God originated neither in speculative reasoning nor in any supernatural revelation. *Gods have to be believed in before they can be beheld, imagined or proved to exist.* Had this fact been recognized centuries ago, thinkers would have been spared an immense amount of mental effort to prove the existence of God. All that effort apparently was in vain, since unbelievers seldom become believers as a result of logical arguments.

To find the root of men's belief in God we have to note how man's will to live progresses from blind instinct to highly articulate purpose. In all living beings that will to live manifests itself in various hungers or drives for sustenance, shelter, a mate, migration, etc. Man, however, possesses the mental capacities which enable him to be aware of ends and means, of whole and part, of self and not-self. Thus he has come to think in general and abstract terms. This heightened awareness augments his chances for life, and brings to the fore of his consciousness his entire struggle for existence.

By the same token that man becomes aware of himself as a person engaged in a struggle against dangers and difficulties, he also becomes cognizant of the help of a Power or powers to conquer obstacles. That awareness finds expression in ideas. What is most distinctive about himself as a person is termed "soul," and what is most distinctive about the Power or powers upon whom he depends is termed "God." The correlation between ideas concerning soul and those concerning God explains why, with the changes in our conception of human personality, we necessarily change our conception of God. As men, for example, learn to think of the soul as independent of the body, they learn also to conceive an over-soul, or super-ego, or God as independent of visible reality.

In time, man's capacity to generalize, which is itself a manifestation of the will to live, led him to conceive of God as a universal God. This is the correlative of man's will to live in its most generalized form, in the same way as the individual deities or divine beings are the correlatives of his specific hungers or wants.

Simultaneous with progress from the notion of "gods" to that of "God," and from specific independent urges to the whole of the will to live there has been an advance from *haphazard* attempts to *consciously directed* efforts to satisfy that will. Man becomes progressively aware of his goal, and of having to choose between more and less desirable objectives and between right and wrong methods of attainment. Thus emerges gradually an awareness of a generalized will not merely to live, but to live abundantly, that is with a maximum fullness. The philosophers designate such an objective as the ultimate good, or happiness. The theologians call it salvation. Thus, simultaneously with awareness of the generalized will to the ultimate good, to happiness, or to salvation, arises awareness of the generalized idea of God.

Both the will to live and the belief in God are phases of one vital process. The belief in God is not logically inferred from the will to live. It is the psychic manifestation of the will to live. We may state, therefore, that *belief in God is belief in the existence of a Power conducive to salvation which is the fulfillment of human destiny.* We must remember, however, that the grounds for that belief are not derived from speculative reason, but directly from man's actual strivings for maximum life or salvation. The inference from the striving for happiness or salvation to the existence of God is not a logical, but a soterical inference (Gr. soterios=saving). The biological will to live implies the existence of conditions that are propitious to life. The will to live abundantly and to achieve one's human destiny, likewise implies the existence of conditions that favor abundant life, or salvation. The taking for granted that such conditions exist is the basis of the religious conception of God. The religious conception of God is thus not the conception of a first cause, or of an ordering principle in the universe, but of a Power predisposing man to his ultimate human good, salvation or self-fulfillment.

Religion is thus man's conscious quest for salvation or the achievement of his human destiny. The quest itself, apart from its objective, is emotionally rewarding, in that it enables one to experience the whole of the life process as having permanent worth or holiness. To believe that life is worthwhile implies that life as a whole has purpose, and that the universe is so conditioned as to fulfill that purpose. Purpose is here used not in the sense of some end capable of being grasped by the human mind, but as the antithesis of blind chance or accident. It is a synonym for meaning. When we see a radio, we are sure it has purpose or meaning, though we are completely ignorant of how it works, or of the principles which underlie its functioning. Analogous is the religious person's feeling about the universe. He is sure it is not a chance happening. He is even certain that, if all men will cooperate with the inherent nature of that universe, they will achieve salvation. It is this conviction that constitutes belief in God.

In human beings the will to live is not merely, as in lower organisms, an instinctive effort to perpetuate the individual organism and the life of the species. The peculiar mental endowment of human beings enables them to envisage alternative possibilities for life and to choose a particular way of life that indicates or promises more abundant and harmonious living. In other words, for human beings the will to live becomes the will to salvation, to the achievement of the good life. Such salvation, or such life, spells fulfillment both for the individual and society.

Humanity is not a monolith. It is divided into various peoples which by reason of kinship, proximity, common traditions and experiences develop a common way of life or civilization. No human being experiences the worth of life apart from his relation to a particular civilization. That is why, though the quest for salvation is common to all mankind, the particular values that constitute one's salvation and the particular method by which one seeks it, are determined by the civilization of the people to which one belongs. This accounts for the existence of the various religions of mankind. *Every religion is an aspect of a particular civilization. It is that aspect of a civilization which aims to render it worthwhile, both for the group as a whole and for each individual in it.*

To experience life as worthwhile means to have faith in its power to overcome the evils that threaten to frustrate it—disease, poverty, strife, cruelty and death. That faith presumes that life, as we know it, by no means represents its totality. Indeed, what we behold is merely the agitated surface of the boundless deep of Being, whence will in time emerge that potential good which will transform the face of human existence. To base one's life on such confidence is to activate that potential good. The existence of that potential good is what man affirms not merely in thought, but in will, every time he looks to a superhuman Power for the fulfillment of his human aims. On this he builds his faith that his ideals are not will-o'-the-wisps, but a divine light illuminating the path to fulfillment. Every religion is thus a complex of values, of beliefs and of practices which center in the idea of God. *Whatever a civilization values highly it views as, in some measure, a manifestation of God in human life.*

Thus the laws that any civilizational group regards as reflecting its fundamental purpose as a group are considered a revelation of God. The classic literature in which its ideals are articulated becomes sacred scripture. The very language in which they are written becomes a holy tongue. The great teachers and leaders that exemplify the ideals of the group are viewed as holy men, men of God, prophets or saints. The events in the early history of the group, that have left their impress on all its subsequent development, tend to be celebrated in commemorative holy days. The symbols, which evoke a sense of spiritual identification with the group, become hallowed objects to be treated with reverence. Places associated with important historic events or important functions of the group life become *holy* places, where people feel the presence of God. All these *sancta* or holy objects, in their relation to one another and to the civilization in which they are hallowed, constitute a religion.

We sometimes speak of "organized religion," as if the different religions were so many organizations designed to give effect to different religious philosophies, or ways of thinking about God. That is a mistake. In one religion, people have often very different conceptions of God based on variations of temperament, education, and environmental influences. Moreover, at diverse stages in their development, civilizations maintain sundry notions about the nature of the universe, and hence about the way God governs the universe. The truth is that *what differentiates the various religions is their existential otherness, i.e., their organic relation to particular civilizations. But all religions are similar insofar as each is that aspect of a civilization which accentuates the values inherent in that civilization and attempts to embody them in human conduct.*

2

THE IDEA OF GOD AS INDEX OF THE IDEA OF SALVATION

The foregoing description of the way in which man has come upon the belief in God furnishes the best clue as to the role which that belief is bound to play in enabling man to make the best use of his life.

*Progress in the truth and spirituality of the conception of the Power
that brings about salvation reflects the progress in the understanding
of what actually constitutes salvation.*

No less important, however, than the progress in the understanding
of the true nature of salvation is the discovery of the actual conditions
that are essential to salvation. It is, indeed, conceivable that we might
have a correct understanding of what is most desirable, and therefore
worthy of being regarded as salvation. Yet, due to the failure to reckon
with the operation of cause and effect, we might come to regard as
conditions essential to such salvation, actions, sentiments, attitudes
which have no inherent relation to that goal. *The nearer we get to
knowing the actual conditions essential to genuine salvation, the truer
is bound to be our conception of God.*

With these facts in mind, we may distinguish the following three
main stages thus far in the development of man's notion of salvation.

In the earliest stage of human development, salvation is conceived
as the fulfillment of the elemental physical hungers, namely, those for
food, mating, shelter, and security. During that stage of human life
the sense of individual personality, as distinct from the common life
of the group, is still inchoate. Hence, the fulfillment even of physical
needs is conceived in terms of the tribe, clan or nation rather than in
terms of the individual.

It is as difficult for us to relive, even imaginatively, that naive stage
of human development, as it is for an adult to relive the experiences
of his childhood. When the Torah said: "If you will walk in My
statutes, I shall give you rain in due season," [1] it did not occur to
those, to whom those words were first addressed, to ask whether the
promise of reward and the threat of punishment referred to them individually, or to their people as a whole. But when the Prophet Amos,[2]
tells his people that not only each city, but each field, will be dealt
with individually in the apportionment of rain, he expresses the first
intimation that the individual would be considered apart from the
group in the bestowal of good, or salvation, in accordance with his
deserts. Ezekiel,[3] two centuries later, still had to labor the point of
individual responsibility and retribution.

The second stage in the development of the conception of God,
from the standpoint of the quest for salvation, arises after that quest
has been fully individualized. Then the individual first discovers that
his notion of God does not square with what he expects of God. When,
due to the uprooting of nations, multitudes of human beings suffer

displacement in their mode of life, and are thrown upon their own individual resources in their struggle for existence, they become more acutely aware of what happens to them personally. They then hope to see in their personal fortunes such a working out of the law of retribution as they had been taught in their tradition to expect.[4] When they are disappointed, they do not conclude that the law of retribution is an illusion. Instead, they arrive at some new assumption of the way that law operates. According to that assumption, this world is, as a rule, negated as the possible *locus* of the *full* operation of the law of retribution.

That fact, together with the growing sensitiveness to the prevalence of all kinds of evil and suffering in this world, contributes to the conclusion that this world is not such as God had intended it to be when He created it. He allows it to exist only for a time, but will ultimately replace it with a better world, in which all the inequities of this world will be righted. There, man will attain eternal life of bliss, which is his salvation.

An important variation of this development is the one which took place among the Greek philosophers. In Athens, especially, there emerged that type of self-aware individual personality which is the unique contribution of Western civilization. Its uniqueness consists in treating the intellectual faculties of man as his differentia from the subhuman. Consequently, salvation or self-fulfillment came to be regarded as the perfection of the intellect, which is the most distinctive element in the human being.

The Greek thinkers assumed that the intellect functioned best when least implicated in the desires and needs of the body. Hence, only after death, when the intellect leads an unhampered existence, can it achieve its maximum power. To be worthy of such achievement, it should be cultivated during this life while it is still chained to the body. Thus, also, in Greek philosophy, salvation was conceived as possible only in another world, namely, that of spiritual bodiless immortality.

A third stage in the development of the idea of God set in when, discovering that it was within his power to change the living conditions in this world, man began to realize that it was not necessary for him to postpone the attainment of salvation to an order of existence different from that of this world. He soon became convinced that he might change *this* world in conformity with his heart's desire. Ever since the European Renaissance, this new conception of salvation has been revolutionizing human life and its values. But far from constituting a definite guide to conduct and to a uniform or universally acceptable idea of God, this most recent development in the conception of salvation has thrown mankind into confusion—so many and so conflicting are the interpretations, and so varied the applications of this new conception of salvation.[5]

The belief in the possibility of mundane salvation is only the inarticulate major premise in the reasoning of the modern man, and does not by itself indicate what practical conclusion is to be drawn from it. The practical outcome depends upon the somewhat less articulate minor premise. This becomes evident when we compare the two opposite types of conclusions regarding salvation that have been derived from the same major premise.

At one extreme, we have the philosophy of life which has culminated in fascism. The minor premise in that philosophy is the assumption that the highest good is the attainment of power over others. It is impossible, however, to permit human beings individually to engage in a scramble for power. That would lead to anarchy and social chaos. It is, therefore, necessary that power should be sought by men collectively. This is the meaning of modern nationalism. The nation gives each individual, no matter how limited in physical and mental capacity, an opportunity to satisfy his natural hunger for power by merging his individuality with that of his nation. *Fascism teaches that a man's nation should be his god, and patriotism his religion. Since struggle is the law of life, he must see in his nation's struggle for existence and power against competing nations the highest opportunity for giving expression to what is the best in him, to courage, heroism and self-sacrifice.*

At the other extreme of this mundane conception of salvation is a minor premise, for which, let us hope, democracy will come to be a suitable name. This minor premise also accepts the principle that salvation consists in the maximum achievement of power through the medium or process of social interaction. But it associates an entirely different meaning with the two important terms in this principle, "power" and "social interaction," from that which fascism associates with them. The power which it considers worthy of achieving is not that of domination, but of creation. Moreover, the social interaction through which the individual seeks self-fulfillment, should include the whole of mankind. *A nation has a legitimate claim upon the loyalty and devotion of those who belong to it, but not at the expense of the peace and welfare of mankind as a whole.*

This type of mundane salvation presupposes a social order in which the transcendence of racial, creedal or national differences is regarded not only as legitimate, but as the norm of all social institutions. That is a social order in which security is compatible with freedom, cooperation with individuality. The test of its success is the liberation and enlightenment of the spirit. That is the very mission which a great Prophet assigned to Israel as the servant of YHWH.[6] God as the Power that makes for mundane salvation of this type necessarily is the God of mankind.

3

THE MODERN CONCEPTION OF SALVATION
OR HUMAN DESTINY

The second factor in the growth of the God-idea is extension in the knowledge of the conditions necessary to the achievement of salvation. During the first two stages of the development of the idea of salvation, especially during the first, many actions, beliefs and attitudes are prescribed as essential to salvation, on the basis of primitive notions of nature, man and environment. These pertain to objects, persons, writings, events, days, or other items, which are regarded as having extraordinary power to help man attain whatever he needs for his well-being and happiness. The word for such extraordinary power is "holiness." Some actual or imaginary experience, usually the latter, might have been the source of the assumption that they possessed such power. Possession of extraordinary power or holiness meant to the ancients being a divinity or being divine. As their ability to think and to abstract grew, the power assumed to be residing within these objects, persons and other items of vital importance was personified and viewed as functioning through them. Those items thus came to be regarded as media through which the gods manifested their power or holiness. As such, they became *sancta*. To reckon with the holiness which was assumed to inhere in these *sancta* was regarded as a prerequisite to the attainment of the ultimate good or salvation.

Later a change came over religion, due to the altered conception of salvation, which thereafter was regarded as attainable only in life after death. What happened to the *sancta* of the first stage or to those items of holiness which had to be reckoned with as a means of obtaining rain, conquering enemies, enjoying prosperity? Were other *sancta* discovered as in need of being reckoned with, and therefore as constituting the conditions of other-worldly salvation? Not at all. What actually happened was that the original *sancta*, or the conditions of salvation as conceived in the first stage of religion, were given meanings which fitted them into the other-worldly pattern of thought. They were thus able to continue as means of salvation, though it was a different kind of salvation of which they then came to be the means.

Now that we are in the third stage of religion, we conceive salvation and the conditions essential to its achievement in terms of this-worldly life, whether our own or that of generations to come. We can no longer rely upon tradition alone to give us adequate guidance concerning the conditions of salvation. We have come to depend upon observation and experiment. We realize, for example, that, in order to develop in people the kind of character which shall enable them to make the most of life, both for their own good and the good of society, they must be put in possession of certain economic, cultural and social minima. Such are the conditions which have an intrinsic and natural connection with the kind of ultimate good or salvation which the modern person hopes to achieve.

On the assumption that God is the Power predisposing mankind to salvation and that He operates through the conditions which are essential to salvation, we should select from among the present day social and cultural interests those which aim at salvation as understood nowadays, and base our religion upon them. Why continue practices that aimed at salvation as understood in ancient times?

The answer is that, as Jews, we feel impelled to maintain the continuity and growth of the Jewish people. There can be no ultimate good or salvation for us, either as individuals or as a group, unless we are permitted to express ourselves creatively as Jews. The conditions essential to our salvation must therefore *include* those which enable us to experience continuity with the Jewish past, as well as make possible a Jewish future. That continuity cannot be maintained without actually reliving the ancient experience of the will to live abundantly. There is no other possible way of reliving that experience than by giving the ancient Jewish *sancta* a new lease on life, which can be done by reinterpretation. Those elements in the traditional *sancta* which can still be proved to have an intrinsic connection with ultimate good or salvation, as we now conceive it, should be singled out and treated as social and mental requirements without which salvation is for us impossible.

Thus, for example, freedom or liberation from all manner of bondage, is the central theme in the celebration of the Passover festival. By observing that festival, the Jew remembers freedom as an indispensable condition of salvation, conceived in terms that are objective, this-worldly and, simultaneously, spiritual and ethical. On the basis of this reinterpretation, God comes to be believed in as the Power that brings about freedom and redemption from bondage. All institutions, laws and tendencies that help to free men should, therefore, be treated as *sancta*, or as media which reveal God's will and holiness. An identical process of interpretation might be applied to the other festivals and holidays, to the Sabbath, and various *mitzvot*.

That kind of interpretation calls for an analysis of the beliefs and purposes which were associated with the traditional *sancta*, and for a selection from among those beliefs and purposes of those that have some relevance to our actual needs. Our traditional *sancta* should henceforth serve as symbols of such present ideals as the combination of security and freedom, of cooperation and personal freedom. Those ideals articulated through the traditional *sancta* of Judaism would be given cosmic sweep. They would acquire the emotional impetus necessary to help us surmount all barriers to our self-realization.

4

THE RELATION OF THE SOTERICAL GOD-IDEA TO
WORSHIP

We have in this soterical approach (so-called because it sees all religion from the viewpoint of salvation) to the belief in God something that is much more realistic and satisfying than ever could be any approach based on speculative reasoning. From the philosophic standpoint, once the existence of God is logically assumed or demonstrated, the interest centers in the attempt to define His nature and His attributes. According to medieval theology which sought to reconcile the Jewish religious tradition with Platonic-Aristotelian philosophy, God could not be known at all, except insofar as He revealed Himself through His works. Even from those works all we could learn was not what He was in Himself, but what He was to mean to us, i.e. only His attributes, such as infinite power, wisdom, justice and mercy.

The intrinsically religious or soterical approach to the belief in God, however, does not have to make use of the concept of divine attributes, which at best is very vague. Strictly speaking, the attributes do not really tell us anything of the nature of God; rather do they tell us what it is not. This is not surprising. We cannot know the ultimate nature even of the things we see, feel or touch. How, then, dare we expect to know what God is? The very nature of the human mind is such that all it can know about anything is the way that thing functions; even that knowledge is arrived at only after long searching and experimentation. *All we can know about God is what happens to human life when men believe in God, and how much improvement in their mode of life and thought is reflected in their belief concerning God.*

As we explore the nature of man and of the world for the purpose of discovering the conditions that are essential to our salvation, we begin to comprehend as much of the nature and power of God as is humanly possible for all practical purposes. More than that is either like the poet's appreciation of the sunrise or like the dream of one who is asleep.

Many are of the opinion that once people discover that the conditions which are essential to salvation are those which exist in the natural world of body and mind, they cease to believe in God. That, however, does not necessarily follow. In the first place, religion even in its primitive stage never exempted man from the need of exerting his own mental or physical effort, if he wanted to achieve what he regarded as his ultimate good. This means that *man always figured as a collaborator with God in the process of salvation.* The perennial emphasis in all religion upon man's possession of a will free to choose between obeying and disobeying God carried with it the implication that man could not achieve the goal of salvation, unless he exerted his own will in that direction. Hence, *the fact that man can manipulate the conditions which are essential to mundane salvation may well go together with regarding the effectiveness of those conditions in helping man to live the life abundant as a revelation of God.*

No amount of ability to control the conditions that make for life abundant should blind one to the fact that their effectiveness as a means to salvation is due to the operation of forces and tendencies which inhere in the cosmos. It is evident that no deliberately formulated plan of salvation can fail to stress the importance of seeing life steadily and whole. Part of that plan must, therefore, be the realization that the cosmos as a whole is so constituted as to make for man's salvation, provided man does his share by learning about, and living up to, the requisite conditions. To view the cosmos in this way is to believe in God.

The foregoing discussion should throw light upon two specific problems which concern us in the matter of religion. One is how to justify worship, and the other is how to teach the idea of God to children.

With regard to the justification of worship, it is well to recall the fact that we must learn to distinguish between the *belief* in God and the *conception* of God. The belief in God is the intuitive experience of cosmic Power upon which we depend for our existence and self-fulfillment. It is, therefore, the basic substance of religion and is a constant factor in it. On the other hand, the particular conception of God is a cultural formulation of that belief. It varies with the particular stage of man's intellectual and social development.

Belief in God does not derive from existing cultural or social ideas, but is largely one of their sources. Viewed objectively and as a whole, it is what we experience when all of our hungers are merged, as it were, into the unitary will to live the life abundant, and to achieve the maximum possibilities for good that inhere in life. Such will is the will to salvation. The belief in God is, accordingly, not a *reasoned* faith, but a *willed* faith, in the existence of a Power in the world that furthers man's salvation. This is the faith that reality, the cosmos, or whatever constitutes for us the universe in which we move and have our being, is so constituted that it both urges us on and helps us to achieve our salvation, provided, of course, we learn to know and understand enough about that reality to be able to conform to its demands.

The chief problem confronting the historic religions nowadays is not how to lead people to *believe* in the cosmic Power that sustains human life, whether we designate it "God" or by any other name. It is rather how we shall *conceive* God. The answer must be such as not only to permit, but to necessitate, worship. Otherwise the historic religions would be deprived of their main function, which is to activate the striving for salvation by keeping alive the awareness of God.

The question which it is important for the historical religions to answer is: Does the awareness of God depend upon our conceiving God as a personal being, or may God be conceived in other ways, and yet be the subject of our awareness, or the object of our worship? In strictly philosophical thought, the very notion of a personal being, especially when not associated with a physical body, is paradoxical. Nothing would, therefore, be lost if we substituted for that notion the one of "process," which, at least with the aid of science, most of us find quite understandable. Why, then, not conceive God as process rather than as some kind of identifiable entity?

Such a conception of God is in line with contemporary thinking. Take, for example, the case of fire. Primitive man personified it. Later it came to be regarded as one of the four elements in the universe. Still more recently, it was considered as due to the presence of a distinct substance called "phlogiston." Today it is conceived as the process of oxidation. Surely, it is no less real by reason of its being recognized as a process. So, too, our conception of God. God has been thought of as a kind of magnified human being, or as an ethereal substance. Instead, *we suggest that God be thought of as the cosmic process that makes for man's life abundant or salvation.* As cosmic process, God is more than a physical, chemical, biological, psychological, or even social process. God includes them all, but what is distinctive about the God-process is that it is superfactual and superexperiential. Were one to add "supernatural," the whole point of this approach would be missed, since the term "supernatural" implies miracle or suspension of natural law. On the other hand, it would be correct to say that *the God-process is "trans-natural."*

Thinking of God as process rather than as an entity in no way tends to make Him less real. By like token, we shall have to change our conception of human soul, or personality. If we were committed to the idea that, to be real, the human soul, or personality, must be a distinct entity or identifiable being, apart from the body, we should soon find ourselves with neither soul nor personality. Viewed, however, as that individual process by which the individual human being achieves life abundant or salvation, the soul, or personality, is entirely conceivable as a reality, without having to be thought of as a being or entity. *The soul-process, too, is superfactual, superexperiential and trans-natural.*

Will this new conception of God as a cosmic process prevent our worshiping or praying to Him? That depends on what experiences we choose to identify as indicative of godhood. God as the Power, transcending ourselves, that makes for salvation, also inheres in all the forces of our minds and wills. As such, *God functions not only in our own bodies, but also in our relationships to one another and to the environment in which we live. By becoming aware of those forces and relationships, we induce them to function most efficiently. The purpose of worship and prayer is to produce such awareness.* Identifying prayer with religion-in-act, William James[7] describes it as "the vital act by which the entire mind seeks to save itself by clinging to the principle from which it draws its life."

We might, for example, find ourselves oppressed by doubt concerning the worth of life, or its meaning. If, however, instead of resigning ourselves to that state of mind, we press on in our quest for God, that very quest constitutes in us the working of the Power that makes for salvation. The 73rd Psalm, for example, is a true expression of religious worship, despite that the Psalmist confesses: "I almost slipped, I nearly lost my footing," implying that he had questioned the very reality of Divine Providence. When we sustain a tragic loss, and for the moment are paralyzed by despair, what enables us to get back to life and resume our tasks, if not a Power beyond us that impels us to go on living? It is that same Power that impels us to make the best use of our lives. The need for communing with that Power is part of our very will to live as human beings. That is why human beings will continue to pray and worship, regardless of the mental image or concept, with the aid of which they think of that Power.

The usual retort to this conception of prayer is that it is tantamount to praying to oneself. This fact should not disturb us. If we really mean what we so often glibly state about God's being immanent as well as transcendent, we should accept the logical consequence of that conception of God. Since God is immanent in man, then there must be something in the individual human being which is part of God, in the same way as the light which enters the human eye is part of the sun.

The human self is not a monad, but a duad, consisting of actualized and potential parts. The actualized part is rooted in the body with its biological needs and a complex of habits, attitudes and ideas bound up with those needs. The potential part represents the operation of those universal forces in the environment with which the individual must cooperate to achieve his maximum. That part operates as truth, when, as reason, it elicits from man the knowledge of reality. It operates as goodness, when, as conscience, it elicits love.

Whenever man reasons or consults his conscience, he is engaged in a dialogue. So, also, when he prays. Then that part of him which is the actualized element in him addresses itself to that part which is potential. It is then that one's entire personality is implicated. When one's personality is entire, it necessarily includes something of the divine which transcends it. Franz Rosenzweig put it well when he wrote that "prayer is its own fulfillment; the soul prays for the power to pray."

5

THE SOTERICAL GOD-IDEA IN EDUCATION

Pedagogically, the problem of teaching religion consists of two parts: a) how to transmit to young people the conception of God as the Power that makes for salvation; and b) how to relate the Jewish *sancta*, in their reinterpreted form, to the conditions of life which are essential to salvation, as we now view it.

a. It is interesting to note that, as soon as the Biblical account of God's doings ceased to be a satisfactory means of giving the child an acceptable idea of God, resort was had to pedagogic versions of the two main arguments for the existence of God, the cosmological and the teleological. This attempt in the text-books on religion for children takes the form of descriptions of the beauty and order of nature as evidence of God.

As much as possible should be done in the school to cultivate what may be described as the beginning of a cosmic feeling, an appreciation of the immensity, the sublimity, the beauty and order of nature. Where, if not in the religious school, should the child be given a sense of humility in the presence of the awe-inspiring phenomena of life? How else is he ever to achieve a sense of proportion which is needed to correct the natural egocentrism with which everyone commences life? Nevertheless, something besides all this is necessary to give the child a vivid sense of the reality of God. Once he has it, he will get the full benefit of whatever cosmic feeling we have succeeded in communicating to him. But if he has not learned to find in anything he actually experiences something that points to what we mean by God, his cosmic feeling is likely to dissolve into vague sentimentality.

We must remember, however, that the child, or even the young person, knows too little of life to appreciate the meaning of life abundant or salvation. Just what it denotes can be understood only against a background of failure and frustration in the higher values of life's gamut. That, however, should not deter us from asking whether or not young people experience anything in their own lives which might help them to understand the meaning of salvation?

The answer is perhaps to be found in the awareness of growth, both physical and mental. That awareness may give the child the same sense of striving that the awareness of salvation gives the adult. *There can hardly be a more real and more God-revealing experience in the inner life of a child than that of growth.*

Every child realizes how much bigger and stronger physically, and how more knowing and more able to do things he grows with every year. There are two aspects to growth which the child can understand at a relatively early age; first, that it is not something he can get himself to do at will, that it is something he possesses in common with plants and animals, and that it happens to him as it does to them; secondly, that although growth happens to his body and mind, he can either hinder or help it. *The experience of growth thus offers not merely an analogue to salvation, but can actually be made to constitute salvation to the child.* It conveys in very realistic fashion the polarity of salvation: on the one hand, God, or the Power outside, making for growth, and, on the other, one's self or the Power within, which does its part in meeting the necessary requirements to growth.

b. The solution of the second part of the pedagogic problem—how to relate the Jewish *sancta* in their reinterpreted form to the conditions of life which are essential to salvation as we now understand it—requires a series of transition ideas, which teachers with skill in devising projects will have to render intelligible to children. Once we ourselves know in what we should believe, it becomes merely a matter of pedagogic ingenuity and mechanics to transmit it to the child.

The first transition idea is that the conditions essential to growth or salvation, taken as a whole, constitute civilization. Language, literature, art, and social institutions including folkways, ethics and law, are the conditions which are expected to help the human being to develop his powers of body and mind. They render man human, and are employed by him in his effort to achieve the maximum of what he regards as humanly most worthwhile. They constitute the social heritage which increases with each generation.

Civilization, however, is not one but many, due to the fact that historically each group of human beings develops a different set of civilizational values. Each people has its own civilization, or set of conditions essential to the attainment of the life abundant.

The second transition idea is the following: The Jews evolved a civilization of which they are actually aware as more capable than any other of helping them to achieve salvation. This means that they did not think of their way of life as an artificial device which may or may not prove successful, but as an instrument supplied by God to enable them to attain the ultimate good. They, therefore, called it the Torah of God. As Jews, we have to cultivate the knowledge and practice of that civilization. That is to say, we have to study and practice Torah. *Torah is a guide to those conditions or requirements which have to be met, if we are to get the most out of, and to give the most to, life. Torah, therefore, reveals the Power that makes for salvation.* To feel that way about our own Jewish heritage is to have that religious experience which makes one an affirmative Jew.

The purpose of Jewish education should be not merely to teach literature, but to enable the child to live and think as a Jew. To accomplish that purpose, the child should be made to feel the civilizational character of living as a Jew. He should also be habituated in establishing a mental connection between living as a Jew and being aware of God as the Power that makes for salvation. Both the feeling of Judaism as a civilization, and habituation in a truly religious approach to it are best conveyed through the Bible and the mass of Rabbinic lore based on it. They are the text material to be associated with the regimen of Jewish living.

Let us not confine ourselves, however, to the traditional texts. Let us supplement them with selections from world history and from the normative, or ethical, material produced by our own environment. This material, taken from current life for the purpose of indicating what is meant by conditions essential to the life abundant, or ultimate good, would constitute the further development of Torah, or Jewish civilization. If we adopt this procedure, we shall be doing consciously what, in previous generations, Jews did unconsciously, whenever they reinterpreted and enriched the contents of the Torah tradition by means of teachings, speculations, norms and practices drawn from the dominant civilization and the universe of discourse of their own day.

CHAPTER ELEVEN

THE NEXT STAGE IN RELIGION

1

WHY A NEW STAGE?

If Jewish civilization will emerge alive from its present crisis, it will emerge considerably strengthened. Its principal strength will consist in the new stage of growth that its religion will have undergone. The present stage which is rapidly coming to a close, and which has been based upon an other-worldly outlook, was itself preceded by two early stages. The first stage coincided, on the whole, with the era from Israel's conquest of Canaan to the fall of the First Temple. It may be designated *theophanic,* because the frequent self-manifestation of Deity through visible and audible means was then assumed to be an actual experience on which men could rely for guidance in their everyday conduct and problems. The second stage coincided with the era of the Second Temple, and may be designated *theocratic.* That term implies that the organization of the Jewish Commonwealth was based upon a written Torah, of which God was assumed to be the author, and that its affairs were administered by a priestly clan explicitly designated by God as His chosen servitors.

After having thus passed through three stages, the theophanic, the theocratic and the *other-worldly,* Jewish religion is about to enter upon a fourth stage, which may be designated *spiritual.* It will not be a new religion; it will be a new method of spiritual adjustment. It will be the Jewish embodiment of the spiritual religion which will have to come into being among all civilizations, if civilization as such is to survive at all. *Such spiritual religion will not be the creation of any one thinker; it will be the product and synthesis of the various endeavors by men who have faith in reason, who love truth and who possess the power to see life steadily and whole.*

All civilizations that wish to escape destruction will have to avail themselves of this method of spiritual adjustment. Civilizations will henceforth have to make spiritual life compatible with freedom of conscience as well as of thought. This can come about only as men learn to realize that religion should concern itself less with specific doctrines and prescribed rules, and more with discovering a method of spiritual adjustment which may have universal application.

With universal human experience as its basis, that method should be applied by each civilization to its own particular heritage, situation and problems. Thus will every civilization either reconstruct its traditional religion, or evolve a new religion. The religion of a civilization will be expected to be vitally responsive to actual, and not to imaginary, needs. The Jewish civilization, however, does not have to evolve a new religion. All it needs is to adopt this new method of spiritual adjustment, to transform, revalue and augment its traditional religious values and render them adequate for the era ahead of us.

Spiritual religion is the only method of spiritual adjustment consonant with the modern world-outlook. It alone can satisfy the demand for open-mindedness. It would not only look everywhere for the truth, but also have the courage to subject truth from whatever source, including that concerning which tradition puts forth supernatural claims, to the test of consistency with knowledge. It steers clear of the traditional belief that the principal knowledge of God and His will must be derived from supernatural revelation, as well as of the negative view that religion is nothing but a delusion and misinterpretation of natural phenomena.

Spiritual religion assumes that *the conceptions of God which have hitherto been dominant in the world are tentative ideas by which men, in accordance with their limited experience and intellectual development, have endeavored to express their affirmative attitude toward life, despite all the hardships it may entail and all the frustrations it may bring.* Far from regarding the historic religions as the ultimate in human spiritual attainment, spiritual religion takes for granted that the conception of God is subject to ever progressive approach to the truth in accordance with our widening experience, that the ideals upon which we set our hearts are in continual need of clarification and reinterpretation to meet the changing conditions of human life, and that the duties, both positive and negative cannot remain static without hampering human life.

Man was wont altogether too readily to accept as truth ideas and impressions concerning religious matters, without having had such means, as he possesses at present, of forming correct judgments. Habits, whether of thoughts or of action, are continued long after their usefulness is outlived. This applies especially to ideas and forms of conduct which fall within the category of religion. No stereotypes are so persistent as those of spiritual life. The fear of moral disintegration which might result from breaking with established practices or tabus has been responsible for religion's having become the victim of undue conservatism.

Many a habit of life, which originated because of some mistaken idea of its usefulness or of some accidental association with a useful outcome, has been known to survive in every phase of human life, even the most practical. The persistence of many outgrown political and economic practices may be accounted for in that way. When we find them in religion, their presence is traditionally accounted for on the ground of their having been willed by God, either directly, or indirectly through human authority.

2

FAITH IN HUMAN NATURE AS THE BASIS OF SPIRITUAL LIFE

The two main assumptions which traditional religion regards as basic to man's leading a spiritual life have been, (1) that man has been apprised by some supernatural revelation of what should constitute the highest goal of his life, and of the specific means whereby he may attain that goal, and (2) that such goal lies not in the present world order, but in a world order which God will bring into being, after having destroyed the present world by means of a great cataclysm.

The first of these assumptions derives from the conception of God as distinct from, and transcending, nature, and as changing the course of nature from time to time, while carrying out His purposes with man. This conception of God accounts for man's experience of the divine taking on a theurgic character, and for the acceptance of theophanies as actual outward events. The second assumption derives from the axiom that life in the present world order, being beset by countless evils, can not but be a preparation for life in a world-to-come.

The world outlook implied in pre-modern religion reflected a pessimistic and disparaging view of human nature and the present world. If we seek a first-hand idea of the kind of religion that was universal in pre-modern times, we need only glimpse at any authoritative Catholic document of our own day. As a typical illustration let us take the Encyclical on Education by Pius XI. It gives us an opportunity to renew our acquaintance with the world outlook which takes for granted the belief in supernaturalism and other-worldliness. In referring to modernist educators, the Pope said: "But many of them with, it would seem, too great insistence on the etymological meaning of the word, pretend to draw education out of human nature itself and evolve it by its own unaided powers . . . Hence every form of pedagogic naturalism, which in any way excludes or weakens supernatural Christian formation in the teaching of youth, is false. Every method of education, founded, wholly or in part on the denial or forgetfulness of original sin or grace, and relying on the *sole powers of human nature,* is unsound." [1]

That world outlook exalted God at the expense of man, and the next world at the expense of this one. The characteristic tendency of all traditional religion was to treat human nature as the source of all the ills from which it suffered, and to deny that any of the good by which man was able to rise to greater heights emanated from himself. Such good was always ascribed to a superhuman source. With that estimate of human nature, it was inevitable that, for any habit or any idea to be regarded as valid, it would have to be traced to some divine authority rather than to the intelligent foresight of man. That always implied the intermediacy of magician, priest or prophet who was supposed to act as channel for communicating God's will to man.

In contrast with this disparagement of nature, whether in man or in his environment, as inherently unworthy of God's self-revelation, spiritual religion understands that God reveals Himself continually, if we only take the trouble to identify His presence. Even where God is not consciously felt or identified, He nevertheless functions through those aspects of man's environment and inner life which make for man's security, welfare and spiritual growth. Due to this creative energy within man's impulses and activities, man has not only been aware of the contrast between his world as it is and as it might be, but has found no peace ever since that awareness first dawned upon him.

The historic religions, despite their many intellectual misconceptions, valuational errors and injurious habits, represent the groping efforts of the human soul to catch sight of its destiny and to mould itself in accordance with that vision. But the authoritative formulations, dogmas and creeds fail to give us first-hand experience of God; as a result, our religious behavior tends to become lifeless and mechanical. To identify such first-hand experience and to relate it to the whole range of human conduct which leads man to ever higher levels of being, sentience, appreciation and creativity is henceforth to be the means of keeping religion alive. It is only such religion that can renew or recreate the aims and ideals which express man's nature at its best.

Spiritual religion affirms that it is unnecessary to resort to super-

natural revelation for experiencing the reality of God. Man's experience of God is as real as his experience of his own personality. On the other hand, his knowledge of God has been just as blundering as his knowledge of his own personality. Man is in possession of slightly more knowledge of God today, because he is in possession of slightly more knowledge about himself and the world. Whether the knowledge of God will ever be a dependable guide of human life as, for example, the knowledge of gravitation is at present for purposes of flying, only the future will decide. At present the knowledge of God is only in its incipient stage. Moreover, it is possible to experience the presence or reality of God, without deriving from that experience any helpful guidance in the art of living, just as it is possible to experience the presence of fire, without learning anything about it that might help us derive any benefit from it. Experience must be translated into organized knowledge before it can be relied on as a source of guidance.

Only religious fundamentalists and unimaginative pedants would insist upon limiting the name and conception of God to the God of supernatural revelation. If words were as fixed in their meanings as are mathematical symbols, each generation would have to coin a new vocabulary. Since, with each generation, experience is enriched, the words in which that experience is recorded necessarily acquire new meaning. Nevertheless, we continue using such words as "world," "matter," "atom" and thousands of other terms, although our conceptions of what they denote have been completely revolutionized. This continued use of terms, despite the changes in the ideas which they convey, points to the underlying continuity of all social life and human culture. Hence, we are entirely within our intellectual rights when we insist upon retaining the greater part of ancient religious vocabulary, particularly the term "God." The ancients did not patent their use of that term. The truth is that, *in using the term "God," men of the past and of the present have been trying to express the same fundamental affirmation concerning the basic rightness and the ultimate achievability of men's aim to leave the world better for their having lived in it.*

The reinterpretation of the traditional religious values and concepts is often resisted more vigorously by the enemies of religion than by the reactionaries and fundamentalists.[2] This resistance of the so-called rationalists is motivated by an animus that hardly comports with rationalism. It is difficult to understand why religion should not be accorded the same right of revising and correcting itself as is accorded to science and philosophy. We need only recall the crude guesses that went by the names of science and philosophy in olden times to realize that *it is not the results attained that constitute the identity of an intellectual or spiritual discipline, but its intention.*

It is, indeed, possible for the very purpose of any science or study to undergo a radical change. Such a change is generally registered by an alteration of name, as when astrology became astronomy and alchemy, chemistry. Likewise with religion, the purpose of which has undergone change. That change should be registered by adding the qualifying term spiritual to designate the type of religion which is now emerging. Supernatural religion is the astrology and alchemy stage of religion. Spiritual religion is the astronomy and chemistry stage of religion. Supernatural religion focused its attention on miracles, theophanies and external authority. Spiritual religion focuses its attention on those needs of human nature which the idea of God, as the Power that makes for salvation, stresses as imperative and as capable of being satisfied.

3

SPIRITUAL RELIGION VS. HUMANISM

Although spiritual religion dispenses with supernatural revelation, it is not humanism. It differs from humanism in the assumption that man's cosmos is *en rapport* with the human will to salvation. Lungs imply air; gills, water; hunger, food, and sex-desire, a mate. Likewise the need for self-fulfillment implies that man's environment is so constituted as to enable him to meet that need. But man's environment, though infinitely manifold, is actually one; all parts are organically interrelated. Hence man's specific needs which form part of the overall need for self-fulfillment, or salvation, should be viewed as capable of being met by the one environment which responds to man in an infinite variety of ways. The environment, conceived in this organic fashion, as capable of responding to man's need for making the most out of his life, is a living universe, with God as its soul. *Together with man's specific necessities, there exists also the need of having his life integrated and whole. This latter need finds its response in the conception of a universe, or world that is interrelated and organic. Religion merely goes one step further and stresses the fact that the universe is not only interrelated but also divine, in that it is so constituted as to help man in his striving after salvation.*

The lack of habitable environment, or modification of the physical circumstances in which man is placed, in order that they be conducive to his existence and happiness, is gradually being dealt with less by religious than by empirical behavior. When it is a question of growing crops, for example, men are no longer content with supplementing primitive agriculture with prayer, but they study the best methods of sowing and plowing, the way to deal with various weather conditions, how to irrigate the soil in places where there is not enough rain, and to fertilize it, should it lack the proper chemicals. Likewise, when one's health is impaired, the proper thing to do is not to depend upon prayers in the hope that God will stop the cause of the ailment, but to resort to the medical aid of a physician who is thoroughly expert in the most scientific methods of diagnosis and therapy. Spiritual religion itself would decry as superstitious and harmful any attempt to substitute religious ideas or activities for scientific experience, viz. the experience based upon the natural working of the elements involved in any situation that has to be improved.

But, in addition, spiritual religion would indicate wherein the empirical and scientific approach is not enough. *Neither the remedy of an evil nor the solution of a problem can dispense with that all-inclusive view of reality which it is the main purpose of true religion to uncover for our inner eye.* The most trivial act that a human being does is lifted out of its triviality by being treated as part of a larger world-setting. Whenever that happens, the specific act or situation comes to have a religious significance. Even if for a time we seem to get along without this larger view of life, in the long run we pay dearly for this spiritual blindness.

All that is true even on the assumption that our preoccupation with empirical means has brought us temporary success. But all too often our best laid plans miscarry, and our most expert devices end in failure. The best scientific methods of agriculture may be rendered futile by an unseasonable drought, and the most skillful precautions of medicine may be nullified by some oversight. Most human beings learn to bear loss, suffering and death of their nearest and dearest without becoming bitter, cynical or despondent. This is because *man's will is borne on the swelling tide of that life-force for which there can be no truer or more fitting name than God.* Nor can most men dispense with religion even when their personal needs are met or hopes fulfilled. The sense of gratitude and of joy which wells up in their hearts implies an inherent rightness in the very nature of things. The awareness that there is at least something that is right with the world is bound to express itself in terms and ways that are definitely religious.

Man has to go through a similar process of re-education with regard to the place of religion in the domain of social betterment. There, too, it is a case of unlearning the wrong uses, and learning the right uses, of religion. Men no longer seek deliverance from crime, oppression, exploitation and war by means of fasting and prayer. Remedies based upon an empirical knowledge of the remediable causes of the ills of society are displacing the theurgic means employed by religion in the past. Exhorting people to give heed to divine ordinances and threatening them with divine wrath, if they will persist in their disobedience, would accomplish very little nowadays. When oppression and exploitation become rife, the political and economic institutions which permit these evils to exist are destroyed, and their place is taken by institutions which are expected to raise human choices and conflicts to a level higher than that of bare animal existence. This is the principle of modern social reform. The question of which method is most likely to achieve the best results, whether revolutionary or evolutionary, can be answered only by empirical experience.

Nevertheless, empirical experience alone cannot account for all that takes place when men strive for, or succeed in, the improvement of the physical environment or the betterment of society. Behind empirical experience is man's intelligence. With its aid, man discovers the uniformities of nature both in his environment and in himself. The knowledge of these uniformities enables him to acquire mastery over the forces of nature and society. In the past, such mastery was regarded with dread and as the source of impiety and rebellion against God. The exercise of intelligence, or the expression of new thought and new ideas was therefore discouraged, unless it bore the imprimatur of divine revelation.

4

WHAT CHANGES IN ATTITUDE WILL SPIRITUAL RELIGION EFFECT?

All this is to be changed with the advent of spiritual religion. The joy of discovering new relationships in the universe, the thrill of dispelling illusions, generates a much more wholesome attitude toward life than the humble submission to authority. Human thought *qua* thought has risen to the dignity of imposing upon itself not only logical re-

straints, but also ethical requirements, in order that it be better qualified to serve the cause of truth. Traditional religion, at its best, has
always feared human intelligence, not because of any vested interest in
ignorance, or because it was being displaced by the self-reliant mind.
It was afraid that intelligence would be arrogant, destructive and love-
less. That very fear helped to create the fact, not the inherent nature
of intelligence.

*Intelligence as such is neutral. Whether it should release the feel-
ings of humanity and love, or those of envy and greed, depends upon
what religion expects it to do.* The very idea that intelligence is dangerous makes it dangerous, because that very thought corrupts its nature
and converts it into folly and wickedness. The most important contribution which spiritual religion can make to human life is to identify
intelligence with the self-manifestation of God in man. Spiritual religion will thus teach man to seek his self-fulfillment through the
augmentation of his powers, which intelligence has made possible. Intelligence, so conceived, cannot but banish all uses of science for
destructive ends. Then it will be known as intelligence only in that it
helps man to re-create the world to his heart's desire, and to re-fashion
his heart's desire in accord with the will of God as the Power that leads
to salvation. Otherwise it will be known as the cleverness of insanity.

The purpose of rendering human life more livable, by having the
world become more clement and all men more cooperative, cannot be
abolished. It keeps on asserting itself, notwithstanding our sins and
follies. That purpose is none other than that which religion has always
tried to attain. The aim of finding the world predominantly so constituted that man shall have no reason to regard himself as an alien in it,
or his life as a meaningless flicker between two infinite darknesses,
never can grow obsolete. How among all the confusion and bitter
hatreds and rivalries of men, this aim can be made the conscious objective of all our strivings, is the problem which spiritual religion must
try to solve. Only when even the most humble human being has a
chance to bring to fruition all the good of which he is capable, can man
be said to have achieved the goal of his existence. That is, therefore,
the test by which we shall evaluate all human endeavor.

Spiritual religion will not permit the individual to rest content with
the civilization of his own people, or of his own church, as the world
within which he is to find his self-fulfillment. This is contrary to the
assumption of all historic religions which claim exclusive possession
of the means of salvation. Thanks to that claim, the individual would

always look upon those, who did not belong to his people or church, as of a lower order of human beings. All this will have to give way before the new need which has arisen in the world to have all mankind become one brotherhood. That eventuality alone stands between mankind and annihilation, so potent are the instruments of destruction which the human intelligence has forged. Civilization literally totters on the edge of the abyss. It may well be that the fissure of the atom and the release of its energy is part of the divine dialectic, or self-corrective process, by which man will ultimately be brought to his senses. In any event, spiritual religion which seeks to widen the horizon of man's human sympathies is no mere refinement of the feelings which only those, who are endowed with a more than usual delicate sensitiveness, should be expected to develop.

The whole point about spiritual religion is missed, if it is not understood as a response to what has become a matter of life and death with the whole human race. If the issue of one world or none is to be met realistically, every people, church and civilization must henceforth foster the kind of religion which will enable the individual to discover in every human being of whatever race or creed or nation a kinsman whose wellbeing and salvation are bound up with his own. *The barriers which have prevented the religions of the different civilizations from learning from one another, for fear of losing their individual character, will have to be broken down. Henceforth, the only rivalry in which religions shall dare to indulge should be that which has to do with the extent to which they can abolish all class, race and national conflicts.*

Spiritual religion is based on the belief that it is possible to achieve salvation without commitment to any theurgic or creedal conception of the nature of God, but not without taking for granted that the universe is divine and, therefore, so constituted as to be *en rapport* with the highest needs of human nature. Those who believe with all their being that the world is fundamentally divine are adequately conditioned to lead a spiritual life, whatever their conception be of the world, or of what it is about the world that renders it divine. The very striving for salvation postulates God, but does not imply any specific theory concerning God's relation to the world, or the manner of his self-manifestation in human life.

How the divine character of the world is compatible with the existence of evil depends upon the knowledge, experience and temperament of those who attempt to resolve the apparent contradiction. But no explanation shall be regarded as authoritative and indispensable to the leading of a spiritual life. This optional character of religious theory, as contrasted with the obligation to translate religion into ethical practice, is not entirely new. The great spiritual leaders of mankind have always stressed the difference that religion should make in the way people live in their relations to one another, and not in the way they think of, or picture, God. That, however, does not mean that a religion is exempt from the task of stimulating its adherents to achieve a vivid and practical conception of God—vivid in apprehension, and practical in being related to the most significant experience.

When we think at all about the world and arrive at conclusions that justify our right to feel at home in it, or that warrant our striving after perfection and self-fulfillment, those conclusions constitute a conception of God. This does not preclude our being cognizant of the mystery of existence. On the contrary, *no religious experience is genuine without elements of awe and mystery, provided they do not lead to occultism or supernaturalism.* No religious experience is possible without an overwhelming awareness of reality as baffling man's power of comprehension.

According to Emile Durkheim,[3] the main content of religious experience stems from the impact of society upon the individual. According to Rudolph Otto,[4] religious experience is the response to the impact of a transcendent presence upon the human mind. Actually, these two ways of viewing religious experience supplement each other. Due to society's impact on the individual, religion finds expression in rules of conduct. At first those rules deal predominantly with ritual and tabus, and only to a limited degree with human relationships. In time, the tendency arises to reverse the emphasis. Due to the impact of a transcendent presence, religion stresses the awareness of that presence as an end in itself; it would have us see in communion with God the ultimate of human self-fulfillment. This is, indeed, the purpose of worship, religious symbols, ceremonies and all other activities and disciplines, which are intended to foster an awareness of God. In the type of spiritual religion in which the whole of human nature will come to expression, both society and the cosmos will be experienced as the source of man's salvation.

CHAPTER TWELVE

THE JEWISH RELIGION OF TOMORROW

Religion is articulate on two levels which normally correspond to each other: the level of doctrine about God, or the origin, nature and purpose of the universe and the fullness thereof, and the level of doctrine about salvation, or what constitutes man's ultimate good and how to attain it.

1

THE CHANGING CONCEPTION OF GOD IN
JEWISH RELIGION

In the form in which Jewish religion has come down to us, to believe in God meant to believe, (1) that God appeared to the Patriarchs, to Moses and the Prophets in the manner described in the Torah, (2) that He gave proof of the authenticity of His revelation by the miracles that He performed, as recorded in the Bible, and (3) that He dictated the text of the Torah to Moses in order that this Law might be an infallible guide to Israel, to which nothing might be added and from which nothing might be subtracted. From the standpoint of that tradition, you are not a religious Jew, if you deny any of these three facts, even if you believe that there is a God who created the world, who governs human life and with whom we should commune in worship.

It must be plain that these three credos can hardly be accepted today by those who apply the same strict intellectual standards to religion that they do to other phases of human life. Even in the Middle Ages, Jewish philosophers were troubled by the fact that the Biblical accounts of God's self-revelation were inconsistent with a truly spiritual conception of God. In the Bible, God is represented as walking in the Garden of Eden,[1] as appearing in human form before Abraham's tent,[2] as talking to Moses "face to face," [3] or, as covering Moses' eyes but permitting Moses to see His back after He had passed by.[4] Though the medieval philosophers managed to reinterpret the Biblical passages so as to reconcile them with a spiritual conception of God, to their own satisfaction, their method of reconciling these contradictions are not convincing to us today. The great masses of our people, at any rate, continued to conceive of God in crudely anthropomorphic form.

The use of miracle as a means of validating divine intervention is common to all ancient religions. It is understood now that miracles are merely the attempt of people in a pre-scientific age to interpret extraordinary events or phenomena of nature. In the light of their knowledge then, such an interpretation was reasonable enough. In those days, men's imagination ran away with them. They were given to projecting their own thoughts and feelings into everything about them, whether animate or inanimate. They saw a purposive relationship between occurrences which had only an accidental connection. They had almost no understanding of the natural working of the human mind. They had no way of distinguishing between objective and wishful thinking. That is why they regarded the power to perform miracles as indispensable evidence of the Power that helped them achieve their salvation. That is why they would interpret, in terms of miracle, events that favored the fulfillment of their desire to live life at its best and in full, and would feel that God had proved His claim to worship by the performance of miraculous acts.

The modern man's attitude is best voiced by what George Meredith once wrote: "There is no impiety excelling the desire for miracles; there is no folly equal to the belief in them." If modern man is to believe in God, he must have more convincing reasons than the record of miracles to satisfy him. Were he to accept the occurrence of miracles as validating belief in God, he would have to consider such occurrence as validating other religions no less than his own. That in itself, would be a departure from all traditional conclusions.

The traditional belief that God revealed the entire text of the Torah to Moses helped to substantiate and to validate for our ancestors their faith in God. That belief, however, has been refuted by a mass of evidence accumulated by modern Bible scholars. The theories which these scholars have advanced concerning the authorship and background of the Torah may be all wrong. But that the Torah is a human document of composite origin, and that many authors living in different times had a hand in the writing of it, some of them having lived long after the time of Moses, is no longer a matter of doubt. That disposes of the existence of the Torah as a proof of the existence of God.

That modern Jews, however, cannot conceive of God in the same way as their fathers did does not mean that they can dispense with the belief in God. Our conception of all things changes, with the growth of our experience and knowledge. In this age of electricity, our conception of lightning is very different from the conception of it held in all ancient mythologies which viewed it as a weapon of the gods.

Nevertheless, lightning is as much a fact as it ever was. Similarly, the reality of God is as true as ever, despite the dissipation of the thick clouds of miracle with which tradition enveloped it.

The reality of God will haunt man so long as man is impelled by an irresistible drive to achieve the fullest measure, and the most satisfying kind, of life. That drive cannot be accounted for exclusively in terms of the individual, for it often takes the form of self-sacrifice. Once in a while some of us are aware of an inner compulsion to seek the good, to seek that which could make human life tremendously worth-while. During those luminous moments when human yearning reveals an all-comprehending superhuman love, when difficulties, dangers or temptations fail to break us, we sense an increase in the strength of our spirit. We then cannot help feeling as though the whole universe triumphed with us. That is the way we feel the presence of God.

Man is made of the same elements as the rest of nature. He is not responsible for his own growth and the forming and cooperative functioning of his own organs, the beating of his own heart, the chemistry of his own blood, on which his whole life depends. His very ego is not born with him, but is evidence of a Power, incomprehensible to him, that has created him as a responsible agent for organizing and directing all his own bodily activities. And at every step in life, he appropriates external matter to his own ends, for food, shelter, clothing without his reason being able to give him any appropriate answer to the question why his partaking of food, for example, should be able to sustain his conscious life. His life is never wholly his own, nor his salvation his own achievement. Not on himself, but on a Power not himself that makes for salvation, he must rely to make life worth living. To the modern Jew, therefore, belief in God should henceforth mean belief in the Power that makes for salvation.

Belief in God thus comes to mean belief in a Power that helps us face suffering and death. When we are aware that we are not isolated units of life struggling against odds, but part of a cosmic lifestream of which we are, as it were, temporary eddies, we cannot lose ourselves in self-pity over our own hard lot. We then see in suffering a challenge to seek a remedy from the ills that cause suffering, or show by our fortitude and courage how suffering, bravely borne, can make life easier and better for those who love us, and enrich life with the blessings of sympathy, kindness and consideration. We then lose our fear of death, for we know that death does not defeat the purposes which give meaning and value to our lives. For all those purposes are related to God, the Power that makes for salvation, and will continue, after we are gone, to render human life increasingly worth-while. We thus become immortal, not in the sense that we go on living for ever as individuals, but in the sense that we add to the sum of eternal life, which triumphs over death, and does not go down to defeat, when our own life is ended.

So to believe in God is to be sure of the distinction between good and evil. We then know the difference between conscience and the fear of what others may think of us or do to us, if we do not behave in the way they should like. We then recognize in the urge to decency an inherent sense of responsibility, by which we share in the creative activity of God. Every experience of success in overcoming the misery of cowardice, envy, hate and greed is an experience of God. Faith in God is faith in the possibility of such achievements, without which we inevitably sink into moral defeatism. That is why religious belief, in the sense of faith in the Power that makes for salvation, is indispensable to modern man no less than it was to his forefathers, as reenforcement for ethical living.

So to believe in God is to be confident that we can create out of the present social chaos, with its national, racial, religious and class antagonisms, its intolerance, oppression and warfare, an ordered society of human beings—the Kingdom of God. We know that all the miseries of our day are due to the failure to achieve such an order, and that we cannot desist from the effort to achieve it, under penalty of losing all the fruits of human civilization. That very knowledge is the beginning of the wisdom which leads to an awareness of God as the Power striving to redeem us. His striving is in our yearning for a better and happier world, and reveals itself to our consciousness as a command to persevere in the creation of such a world, and a prophecy that such a world will ultimately come into being.

We, in our day, no less than our fathers in theirs, have need to believe that God is omnipotent. *Belief in God must mean for us, even though we no longer believe in miracles, that nothing is too difficult for God, that whatever ought to be can and will be.* But we conceive of God's omnipotence differently. We cannot believe that even God can, in a moment and by a single act, cause all wickedness to vanish like smoke. God is omnipotent from the standpoint of eternity, viewed either as timelessness or as infinite time, but He is not omnipotent, from the standpoint of any particular moment. Only through the cooperation of the entire universe could all evils be remedied. That would involve the elimination of all chance and accident, which is as unthinkable as the elimination of all darkness. Thus without expecting God to eliminate the element of chance, which is the source of evil, we must look to Him to help us in our effort to make life worth living.

This then represents the meaning that modern Jewish religion should give to belief in God. Such an understanding of what it means to believe in God would enable religion to function for us as it did for our fathers. It would enable us to transcend suffering and the fear of death, overcome weakness and temptation, and persevere in the establishment of a Divine Kingdom of justice, peace, and brotherly love.

2

THE CHANGING CONCEPTION OF SALVATION IN JEWISH RELIGION

To enable Jewish religion to meet the needs of modern men and women, we must achieve an acceptable conception of salvation, as a prerequisite to an acceptable conception of God.

Traditionally, salvation was conceived as blissful life in the hereafter. From of old, men were keenly aware of the disparity between human life as they felt it ought to be lived and human life as they experienced it. They felt that life as experienced was not life as God must have intended it to be. Observing the tendency of things to deteriorate with time, they assumed that, originally, human life had been free of all ills, that it had been like the portrayal of it in the Biblical story of the Garden of Eden, where there was no toil, suffering or shame, and where death itself was not inevitable. Only later did mankind become subject to toil, suffering, shame, remorse, and death. That was because of the depravity inherited from the first ancestors of the race. Yet God wanted man to find life livable and worthwhile. He therefore could not leave him without hope for salvation. God, therefore, as the Power that makes for salvation, revealed to the Patriarchs, Moses, the Prophets and Sages of Israel those precepts and practices "which, if a man do them, he shall live by them." [5]

At first, in those early stages of our culture, when the individual was almost submerged in the nation, this promise of life was conceived in terms of the life of the nation. But as the individual rose to importance as an object of salvation, and as the death of the individual was an ineluctable fact, it was construed as a promise of resurrection after death, or of survival of the soul in a life that was free of all those ills experienced on earth, and that fulfilled all the yearnings which on earth were frustrated.

The means for achieving the bliss of the world to come were the study of the Torah and the observance of the precepts or *mitzvot*. Inasmuch as these were given only to Israel, it followed that only those who adopted the Jewish way of life were God's elect, chosen for salvation. True, the *haside ummot ha-olam*, "the pious of other nations of the world" were also conceded a share in the world to come.[6] Racialism was seldom a part of the Jewish doctrine of salvation. But "the pious of the other nations" was construed to mean those who obeyed the No-ahitic laws of the Bible, or the way of life as laid down in Israel's Torah for the non-Israelite population. Implied in this conception is the recognition of the revelation of the Torah as the exclusive way of salvation, and of Israel as God's Chosen People.[7] There is no implication here that other religions could serve as ways of salvation.

That doctrine of salvation and of the means to its attainment fitted perfectly into the thought pattern that was common to the whole Western world, from the decline of the Roman Empire and the official pagan cults of classic antiquity to the beginning of the modern era. During all that time, men despaired of being able to do anything constructive to remedy any of the universal human ills. In the state of technology that existed before the invention of power-driven machines and of scientific methods of agriculture, scarcity of the necessities of life seemed an inherent condition of human life, and poverty the inevitable lot of the masses of men. In the absence of scientific medicine, there was no way to combat disease, save by an appeal to divine intervention, through penitence and by various acts of religious theurgy or of magic. The essential conditions of life changed so slowly and imperceptibly that men were not aware that any changes had taken place within historic time. They supposed that the world had always been as it then was, and could not conceive of its ever having been different. *In a static world full of ills for which no human remedy could be imagined, salvation could be conceived only in other-worldly terms.*

But even men's projection of their hopes for a future life must be based on their experience of good in this life. Because the Jewish people experienced in their way of life, in life lived under the Torah, a quickening contact with the Power that makes for righteousness, because the Torah organized their life into a pattern in which they found a deep satisfaction of their will to live, they were convinced that it offered the way to salvation. They could conceive of no other civilization, no other way of life as having equal worth. Hence, only their laws were felt to have been divinely revealed by the Power on which man's salvation depended, only their religion was the way of salvation.

That such conclusions were natural to the state of the Western world's culture at that time is evidenced by the facts that the same general conception of salvation as belonging to life after death was also shared by the Christian and Moslem religions, and that they, too, conceived of their own traditions respectively, and the practices these enjoined, as the exclusive way of salvation.

This traditional conception of what constitutes salvation is certainly not a satisfactory definition of what modern men feel must be the goals of human effort, in order to achieve the highest good. Nor are the means on which our fathers relied to achieve their other-worldly salvation adequate for us as means to achieve what for us makes life worthwhile. We today are deeply interested in the problems that confront us in our daily living. We long to improve the conditions under which we have to live. We strive to enable our children to be born in a better world than that with which we are familiar. Neither the rewards nor the punishments in a life after death are any incentive to us in the pursuit of those interests which, while we live, give worth to our lives.

Even most people who believe in the immortality of the soul do not find that belief motivating their behavior. They are moved to act by the satisfaction or dissatisfaction that they find in certain forms of conduct related to their interests in this world. Belief in a future life, that shall compensate us for the ills from which we suffer during our earthly sojourn, more often inhibits than encourages worthwhile activities that are directed to improving the lot of men. *Other-worldly religion glorifies resignation to evil rather than protest against evil.* It has, indeed, brought all religion into disrepute with those who are most sensitive to human suffering.

When we shift the objective of salvation from other-worldly to this-worldly goals, it also becomes clear that the Torah and *mitzvot*, although helpful, if intelligently reinterpreted in the light of modern knowledge and experience, are not, in themselves adequate as means of salvation. The study of the Torah is capable only of suggesting the general direction which solutions of the political, economic, scientific, artistic and other problems ought to take, but not of supplying specific guidance. Nor can the observance of *mitzvot* provide the necessary technique for dealing with those problems. Moreover, no scheme of salvation that is limited to one people can be adequate for modern needs. The world has so shrunk in size by reason of improved methods of travel and communication that nations, even if they have not yet learned to get along with one another, have certainly discovered that they cannot get along without one another. All mankind is today implicated in a single social and economic order. If salvation is to mean overcoming the obstacles to a full and abundant life on earth, it calls for a program that seeks salvation for all men.

What is the best sort of life that men can live, what kind of life satisfies the maximum of human interests and releases the maximum of creative energy, what, in short, shall constitute the goal of human salvation can, of course, never be stated in a final formula. As life progresses we acquire new insights into possibilities of worthwhile experience. But at the present stage of human development, salvation would involve living according to the highest truth that experience has thus far revealed. Some of the most significant of these truths may be stated as follows:

1. For the individual, salvation should henceforth be regarded as consisting in the satisfaction of three primary needs. In the first place there are the physical needs the fulfillment of which constitutes what we mean by health. Men seek food to sustain them, shelter to protect them from the elements, and the gratification of the mating instinct. In the second place, man needs love. He needs to feel that he is in close relationship to other human beings to whom he is important and who are important to him. Finally, man needs creativity. He needs the opportunity to express himself and to give effect to his purpose in work and play. If he lacks any of these conditions, if he suffers illness, loneliness or enforced idleness and inactivity, he experiences frustration.

2. All human beings, regardless of race, nation, or creed are equally entitled to be treated as ends in themselves, and not merely as means to the satisfaction of other people's desires. Any form of slavery, exploitation or oppression is an offense against human dignity and a bar to the attainment of salvation or life harmonious, abundant and creative.

3. As ends in themselves men are entitled to realize their creative potentialities. This means that society must seek to provide men with the economic and cultural opportunities necessary for their maximum self-realization as persons. This is what is meant in the affirmation that men are created equal. They are created with an equal right to whatever opportunities exist in our society for making the most of their native capacities as human beings.

4. The purpose of society should be to enable each individual to

achieve salvation. By organizing opportunities for social communion, intellectual intercourse and collaboration in productive work, society can immeasurably add to the creative power of every individual member. Society must further insure that collaboration is effected by means that are consistent with, and tend to confirm, the principle of human dignity and equality.

3

WHAT MAKES JEWISH RELIGION JEWISH?

Such a conception of salvation is, indeed, universal. There is nothing particularly Jewish about it. The question may therefore be raised: If our conception of salvation is universal, how does Jewish religion differ from universal religion? The answer is that *universal religion consists of conclusions concerning God and salvation which are based on the experience of mankind in general, and which addresses itself to all men without distinction. But Jewish religion is the interpretation of the experience of the Jewish people in the light of the universal conclusions, and the application of these conclusions to present-day Jewish needs.*

In seeking to strengthen our faith in God as the Power that makes for salvation, we find encouragement in recalling the past experiences in which we see evidence of God's power at work in history, helping men to defy death, to resist temptation, and to achieve great works of creative imagination and prophetic insight. As Jews, we naturally revert to the Jewish past and to Jewish cultural achievement as the main source of our religious inspiration. From the days of the Prophets, we have been taught to try to trace the hand of God in history. Our fathers derived courage for meeting life's issues by reading the record of the miracles by which earlier generations had interpreted their experience of God's salvation. We today can read those same records, and, though not accepting at their face value interpretations which the ancient annalists put upon our history, we, in the light of modern knowledge, can read between the lines of the ancient chronicles and also trace evidence of God's manifestation in history, by interpreting the same events in a manner consistent with our scientific and philosophic outlook. To reinterpret the classic cultural heritage of the Jewish past from the viewpoint of our modern this-worldly and universal conception of salvation is one of the main tasks of Jewish religion of the future, as distinct from merely universal religion.

Moreover, as Jews, we have the special obligation of enabling all Jews to obtain salvation. *The fact that we conceive salvation in universal terms does not release us from special obligation to effect that salvation particularly in that segment of humanity which we represent, and over which we have most direct influence and control, namely, the Jewish people.* The regiment of an army that achieves the military object set for it on its own sector of the front is not, thereby, merely seeking its own victory; it is advancing the cause of the army. Jewish religion loses nothing of its universal significance in assuming special responsibility for its own. It should see to it that the Jewish people live as blessed a life as it can create for itself.

Jewish religion should interest itself in the quality of the social, economic and cultural life being established in Eretz Yisrael. It should interest itself in the effort to impart enough Jewish education, guidance and inspiration for helping Jews collectively to meet the problems that face them as Jews, in conformity with the highest standards of ethical idealism. It should encourage Jews to make the spiritual heritage they have received from the past available as a source of inspiration to others who might be interested. It should encourage Jews to appropriate for the enhancement of Jewish life the wisdom they may learn from any source whatever. In a word, it should bring the Jewish people in contact with God as the Power that makes for salvation, to their own advantage and to that of all mankind.

Finally, in order to insure the maximum collaboration of Jews in the quest for salvation, Jewish religion should encourage Jewish ritual and symbolism. To be sure, religious observance must be pursued in a different spirit from that in the past. In the traditional form of Jewish religion, ritual observance was regarded as obligatory because it was enjoined by the Torah, the revealed word of God. Although various meanings were attached to many of these observances, and Jews were enjoined to practice them with *kawwanah*,[8] that is to say with attention concentrated on their meaning, there were others, such as many of the dietary regulations, to which no meaning was attached. In either case observance was mandatory. Whether the rite was meaningful or not and, if meaningful, whether it was observed with or without *kawwanah*, its observance was an act of obedience to God and hence a means to personal, other-worldly salvation.

With our changed conception of salvation and the means to attain it, there is no longer any point to the legalistic approach to religious observance. There is, however, an important value in traditional religious ritual, even from the point of view of the needs of modern Jews. *Jewish religion is Jewish only because of its functioning in and through the Jewish people.* In order that it shall be able so to function, Jews must be kept aware of their identification with the Jewish people. *Ritual and religious symbolism are the main technique for effecting "consciousness of kind" among Jews, or what is commonly called Jewish consciousness.* Just as the American flag causes all Americans to feel themselves united in a common enterprise, though they live as far removed from one another as New York and San Francisco, so such symbols as the *sefer torah,* the *mezuzah,* the *tallit* and all the other concrete objects, and rites of Jewish tradition bind the individual Jews to all other Jews who live, have lived or will live, in the consciousness of belonging to Israel, and participating in a common historic civilization, Judaism.

Naturally, it does not follow from such a conception of the function of ritual observance that all observances handed down by tradition are indispensable, or of equal value. Many former observances, such as the practice of animal sacrifice, for example, have become obsolete. Many others will become obsolete, and new observances will come into being. That is what happens in every live civilization. Once we cease taking a legalistic attitude toward observances and regarding a ritual transgression as a sin against God, we shall be under the necessity of determining new criteria with which to evaluate religious rituals. What shall determine which rites and symbols we shall preserve and which we should discard?

The answer is, to exercise our judgment on the basis of spiritual rather than of legalistic considerations. We should not ask ourselves of any ritual observance under question: "Is it prescribed, and would its neglect be a transgression of a traditional rule?" but rather, "Has it any power to move to religious thought or action of significance?" "Does it, or does it not, help to make Jewish life more worthwhile by its effect on our emotions, or by its power to suggest a significant idea?"

In Jewish life and thought, three main concepts have always been related as a sort of trinity, each implying and illuminating the others— God, Israel, and Torah. They may well serve as touchstones in our application of spiritual criteria to Jewish ritual. If a rite or symbol makes us God-conscious, if it makes us aware of contact with the Power that makes for salvation, then surely it is of value and should be retained. If it makes us Israel-conscious, if by observing it we are the more disposed to seek Jewish associations and to accept Jewish responsibilities, then again, it has a distinct value for Jewish religion. Finally, if it relates to

Torah or religious education, if it stimulates our thinking about life's values, particularly if it helps us appreciate the religious significance of Jewish experience, then again, it is of undeniable value. But a rite that conveys no meaning related to any of these main concepts of Jewish religion deserves to become obsolete, even though it is prescribed in every one of the Jewish codes. And conversely, a religious ritual of value, such for example as that of *Bar Mitzvah*,[9] or of Confirmation, for which no authorization can be found in any code, should be given a place in our religious tradition. Once we free religious ritual from its bondage to legalism, there are great possibilities for enriching Jewish life with new rituals, rituals that draw on all the arts known to man as media for the expression of significant religious ideas.

This completes our program of Jewish religion for the future. Timid souls are wont to fear even a slight departure from tradition, lest such departure lead to the destruction of Judaism. For this reason they try frequently to gloss over those changes in our thinking which challenge ancient beliefs. Paradoxical though it may seem, the only way to preserve the Jewish past as a living tradition is by centering our attention on the present need, and drawing on the past only where it can help us to meet that need. The effect of trying to preserve Jewish religion in its traditional form, without adequately reckoning with modern experience, is to make Jewish religion appear an anachronism in the modern world. That we cannot afford to do.

We must, therefore, base Jewish religion of tomorrow not on what our ancestors have told of their experience with God, but on our own experience with God. When we do that, we shall find that the Jewish past assumes new meaning, that it ceases to be a collection of archaeological relics, and that it becomes again a living tradition. We can best revere our ancestors and continue their unfinished task in their spirit when we look upon ourselves not merely as their descendants glorying in their achievements, but as the ancestors of posterity responsible for achieving something in which our descendants may glory, and which may inspire them to seek and find God in their lives.

CHAPTER THIRTEEN

THE CHOSEN PEOPLE IDEA AN ANACHRONISM

Despite the tendency in certain quarters to consider ideas as mere by-products of the interplay of blind social and economic forces, and to regard reason as a mere rationalization of instinctive passions and desires, we Jews must insist on clear and forthright thought as indispensable. We must strive to overcome the inertia which keeps us chained to a thought-world entirely alien to the modern spirit. There is as much difference between our universe of discourse and that in which our fathers lived before the Emancipation, as between the modern mind-picture of the physical universe and the one which prevailed, until Copernicus proved that the earth moves around the sun. Just as, in ancient times, men thought that the earth was the center of the universe, and that their own homes, being equi-distant on all sides from the horizon, were the center of the earth, so our fathers, in pre-modern times, regarded the drama of human life as exhausting the whole meaning of creation, and the Jewish people as the hero in that drama, with all other nations merely the supporting cast.

The idea of Israel as the Chosen People, must, therefore, be understood as belonging to a thought-world which we no longer inhabit. It fits in with a set of ideas that were congruous and rational enough in their day. But it can no longer help us to understand relations, or to orient ourselves to conditions, as they exist today. The very notion that a people can for all time be the elect of God implies an epic or dramatic conception of history, a history predetermined in form and aim. Nowadays for any people to call itself "chosen" is to be guilty of self-infatuation. It is paradoxical for the Jewish people to be collectively guilty of self-infatuation, when individually so many Jews are guilty of self-hate. The skeptical attitude of the average Jew toward the doctrine of the Chosen People may be sensed in the Yiddish folk-rendering of the classic phrase, "Thou hast chosen us from all peoples." That rendering is "*Vos hostu gevolt hoben fun die Yiden?*"—"What didst Thou want of the Jews?"

1

WHAT THE CHOICE OF ISRAEL MEANT IN THE PAST

The Bible goes out of its way to deflate all delusions of grandeur that the assumption of being God's Chosen People might arouse. "Not because you were greater than any other people," says the Deuteronomist, "did the Lord set his heart on you and choose you—for you were the smallest of all people." [1] Long before him, the Prophet Amos spoke in an even more humbling vein, when he said, "You only have I known of all the families of the earth; therefore will I punish you for all your wrongdoing." [2] We know by now that the assumption of being God's chosen people was at first merely a way of expressing Israel's self-awareness as a distinct and unique people. That mode of expression is common to virtually all primitive and ancient peoples. In the Bible, the assumption of Israel's election merely implies that YHWH, the God whom Israel acknowledged as its god, was so incomparably greater than the gods of the other nations, that the Israelites might well consider themselves fortunate in being His people.

That belief acquired a deeper significance after the Babylonian exile. From that time on, it meant that the Jews were convinced that they alone were in possession of the Torah which contained all that a people needed to live by, in order to achieve wellbeing and perfection. Regarded as having been dictated by God, the Torah conferred upon the people that accepted it the title of "kingdom of priests and a holy nation." [3] Throughout the period of the Second Commonwealth, the accent in the doctrine of election was not on national self-awareness as such, but on being the most privileged of all peoples, by virtue of possessing God's Torah.

This accent was reenforced throughout the Christian centuries, as a result of the moral support it gave the Jews in their struggle for existence. With the destruction of the Jewish State and the forced dispersion of the Jews among the other nations, that struggle became embittered. No less intense than the physical war waged against the Jews was the "war of nerves" which consisted then, as now, of unrelenting defamation. By the time the Christian Church was firmly established and its doctrine fairly crystallized, that slander had acquired a definite pattern which was calculated to make it extremely effective. The pattern consisted in basing it on the very concept of God which the Jews had evolved, and on the very Scriptures which the Jews themselves regarded as the word of God. Their very doctrine of election was used as a weapon against them.

Christianity, both Catholic and Protestant, has gone far beyond Judaism in utilizing the doctrine of election to affirm the divine prerogative of the Church. That doctrine became its very *raison d'etre*. It set itself the task of realigning mankind into the chosen and the damned. The criterion was faith in Jesus, as the Son of God, and as identical with God. The objective was the establishment of a church that was to supersede all human governments. In this process, the Jewish people was singled out as the people which, having at one time been the elect of God, repudiated Him and thereby became a people accursed and damned.

In the face of this ruthless attack on its reputation, there was little else for the Jewish people to do but so to elaborate its traditional claim to superiority as to counter effectively the claim to superiority advanced by the Church. With the interest of Western mankind during the premodern Christian centuries focused on the question of salvation and eligibility for it, all of Jewish thought was cast in the mould of the doctrine of divine election. All of creation was regarded as having come into being for the sake of those who were worthy of being God's chosen. The company of the elect, by reason of their kinship with God, wielded a power not vouchsafed to ordinary mortals. Not only could they vanquish death, but even in this life they exercised, especially in their collective capacity as the divine *ecclesia*, an influence over the very course of nature. Thus did the doctrine of election, to whomever applied or by whomever used, connote two specific ideas: one, that of cosmic centricity; the other, that of mystical or supernatural power.

Both of these ideas became integral to the conception of the Church which regarded itself as the Israel of the New Covenant, and as the heir of the Israel of the Old Covenant. The Church, moreover, viewed itself as a "fellowship with divine gifts," to use the technical phrase of Christian theology. Whether in direct response to the challenge of the Church, or as a spontaneous reaction to claims which began to be voiced by various religious sects during the early centuries of the Christian era, the Jews likewise advanced the claims of cosmic centricity and mystic and supernatural power for their own people, which thenceforth was designated not only "*ummah*," or nation, but also "*kenesset*," or ecclesia, the exact analogue of church.

Throughout the Rabbinic writings, the Israel-centered conception of the cosmos and of human history is the theme of a vast manifold of *aggadic* similes. The following is typical: "The straw, the stubble and the chaff were disputing with one another. Each one said, 'For my sake was the field sown.' Said the wheat, 'Wait until we get to the threshing floor, then we shall know for whose sake the field was sown.' When they arrived at the threshing floor and the owner winnowed the grain, the chaff was scattered in the wind, the straw was left on the ground and the stubble was burned. The wheat, however, was taken carefully and piled up into a heap, and whoever passed by fondled it with admiration. Likewise do all the nations contend among themselves, each claiming, 'The world was created for my sake.' But Israel retorts, 'Wait till the day of reckoning; then we shall know for whom the world was created.' " [4]

Moreover, the Sages ascribed to Israel the possession of supernatural power. According to R. Eliezer ben R. Jose, the Galilean,[5] "God said to the Angel of Death: 'Although I have given you power over every one of My creatures, you can have no power over this nation Israel.' " Time and again we come across statements which stress the apotheosis of Israel. Israel is said to be a people transfigured and deathless, occupying a rank equal to that of angels or "holy princes." [6] This and numerous other statements to the same effect imply that the *ecclesia* of Israel possesses the status of a mystic being which transcends the laws of nature.

2

THE EFFORT TO REINTERPRET THE ELECTION
OF ISRAEL

Emancipation has undermined the status of the Jews as a nation. Enlightenment or rationalism has undermined the status of Jews as a *kenesset* or an *ecclesia.* The traditional basis for the belief that Israel was God's Chosen People was the assumption that the miraculous events recorded in the Torah concerning the Patriarchs and their descendants in Egypt represented factual truth. By far the most significant of these miraculous events was God's self-revelation to Israel on Mount Sinai. It was as unthinkable to question the truth of those events as to question the reality of one's own body. Under those circumstances, Jews could not possibly regard themselves as other than the most privileged of all peoples. Those circumstances, however, no longer obtain with the majority of modern-minded men and women. The modern-minded Jew cannot consider the miraculous events recorded in the Torah and in the rest of the Bible as other than legendary. He, therefore, cannot accept them as evidence of the traditional Jewish doctrine that Israel is God's Chosen People. The attempt to supply other evidence is itself a departure from tradition. Such an attempt might be justified, if at least the new evidence were convincing. But is it convincing?

· Unable to accept literally the traditional version of the doctrine of the chosen people, the religious wing of the early *Maskilim*,[7] the first *Reformers*[8] and the middle group who designated themselves as the *Historical School*[9] reinterpreted that doctrine to mean one or all of the following propositions, which are set forth in Kaufmann Kohler's *Jewish Theology*, as justifying the claim of the Jews to being a chosen people:

1. Jews possess hereditary traits which qualify them to be superior to the rest of the world in the realm of the religious and the ethical.

2. Their ancestors were the first to achieve those religious and ethical conceptions and ideals which will, in the end, become the common possession of mankind and help them to achieve salvation.

3. Jews possess the truest form of the religious and ethical ideals of mankind.

4. Jews are entrusted with the task of communicating those ideals to the rest of the world.

3

WHAT IS WRONG WITH THE REINTERPRETATIONS?

First, the proposition that Jews possess unusual hereditary traits which entitle them to be God's elect is based on a series of unproved generalizations concerning certain qualities as being characteristic only of Jews, and on biological assumptions concerning heredity, which are entirely unwarranted.[10] It is one thing for an ancient sage to express his love for his people by describing them as unique in the possession of the traits of chastity, benevolence, and compassion.[11] But it is quite another thing for a modern person seriously to assert that, because Jewish life has manifested these traits, Jews alone are inherently qualified to grasp and promulgate the truth of religion. We expect a greater regard for objective fact than is evidenced by such sweeping statements about hereditary Jewish traits.

If Jews were to adopt the foregoing reinterpretation of the doctrine of election, they would, by implication, assent to the most pernicious theory of racial heredity yet advanced to justify racial inequality and

the right of a master race to dominate all the rest of mankind. The truth
is that historical circumstances, as well as geographic environment and
social institutions, are greater determinants of national traits than heredity. Moreover, to represent divine election merely as confirming
naturally inherited traits is to identify it virtually with natural selection.
It is but one step from such identification to the identification of God
with the process by which the physically weak are weeded out. We
know all too well from current experience how such a concept of God
is only another name for the apotheosis of the will to power.

Secondly, for Jews to claim sole credit for having given mankind
those religious and ethical concepts which hold out the promise of a
better world smacks of arrogance. The Greek philosophers, the Stoics
in the Roman period, the humanists of the Renaissance, and the rationalists of the 18th century have made highly significant contributions
to spiritual and moral truth. The religious philosophies of the Hindus
antedate all others, and are experiencing a remarkable revival in our
day. Even if Jews were the first to enunciate the great moral and spiritual teachings, it would be immodest of them to boast about it. That
would not make them better or superior to the rest of the world,
in any sense whatever. The first-born has no right to claim that he is
better or more beloved than the other children. Special privileges no
longer attach to primogeniture.

It is said that to express at this late date dislike of what sounds like
pretension is merely to yield to "the conventions of Anglo-Saxon
taste." [12] Since when is humility a virtue prized by the Anglo-Saxon
rather than the Jewish tradition? Our Torah praises Moses for his meek-
ness. It records the prayer of Moses that he be blotted out of God's
book, if only his people might enjoy God's grace.[13] It tells of his refusing to be disturbed by the news that Eldad and Medad were prophe-
sying in the camp and his exclaiming in response, "Would that all the
Lord's people were prophets!" [14] Can we imagine Moses thanking God
that He had not made him like the rest of Israel, but had made him
the chosen vehicle for conveying God's message to his spiritually inferior brethren?

Thirdly, for Jews to maintain that they possess the truest form [15]
of truth would be understandable, if they still believed that the teachings of their religion are immutable and infallible. However, with the
modern dynamic conception of Jewish belief and practice being accepted by those of light and leading among them, the only meaning
such claim can have is that Jews generally have managed to advance

a bit ahead of every new development of spiritual truth. No one, however, who knows how far behind the best thinkers of their day some of our greatest Jewish spiritual leaders have been at times can subscribe to this reinterpretation. Spinoza, who truly did forge ahead of his contemporaries, was excommunicated.

The very assumption of a predetermined and permanent superiority, no matter in what respect, does not lend itself to reinterpretation. Our purpose in reinterpreting traditional values should be to retain and emphasize those elements in them which are compatible with our own highest ethical standards. Among those ethical standards, to which any traditional value must necessarily conform if it is to continue functioning in our lives, is that conception of human worth and individual dignity which regards as immoral any classification of human beings into superior and inferior. This does not mean that we must shut our eyes to the fact that human beings are unequal in their gifts and attainments. What it means is that we should not assume *a priori* that a particular race, group or people is endowed, by nature or by God with any gift which entitles it to regard itself, *ipso facto*, as superior. *By no kind of dialectics is it possible to remove the odium of comparison from any reinterpretation of an idea which makes invidious distinctions between one people and another.*

Finally, the fourth proposition confuses the doctrine of Israel's *election*, as expressed in the overwhelming majority of Biblical allusions which deal with Israel's relation to God, with the doctrine of Israel's *mission* which is the subject of less than a dozen passages in the second part of Isaiah. There is not the slightest implication in the multitude of references to Israel as a Chosen People that it is expected to fulfill the mission of making God known to the nations.

As for the few unmistakable allusions to the mission of Israel, the manner in which the mission is to be discharged has very little in common with what we usually associate with missionary activity, or even with exemplary conduct. The light which Israel is to be unto the nations is portrayed by the Prophet as radiating from Israel's brilliant career as a nation in its own land, dispensing justice and maintaining peace in the name of its God. The establishment of the ideal Kingdom of God in the land of Israel is what the Prophet hoped would lead the rulers of the world and their nations to acknowledge the God of Israel as sovereign.[16]

There are many apologists for the doctrine who cling to the assertion of divine election, but compromise on its implied claims. They even confess to an awareness of the distaste which the assertion of divine election provokes in many modern-minded people. They seem to understand and even to admit that "extolling God for 'not having made us like other peoples' is grating." [17] Nevertheless, they maintain that properly interpreted, the doctrine still remains valid and should not be discarded.

Though the belief expresses a certain national pride, or a sense of national privilege, "it carries with it also a sense of consecration and responsibility." [18] No one can question the fact that the belief of being divinely elect has long been associated in the Jewish mind with consecration and responsibility. However, we cannot ignore the other implications of that belief, especially those which are often sharply stressed, as in the *Alenu* and the *Havdalah* prayers. In the latter, the invidiousness of the distinction between Israel and the nations is emphasized by being compared with the distinction between light and darkness. It is that invidiousness which is highly objectionable, and should be eliminated from our religion.

There are some who argue that the Chosen People idea is not out of harmony with our modern universe of discourse. They reject the supernaturalist version of the revelation of the Torah on which tradition bases belief in the election of the Jewish people. For them that belief rests rather on the evidence of history that at least the Western world is indebted to Israel for its fundamental religious ideas and institutions, as are also those peoples and individuals in the East who have been converted to Christianity or to Mohammedanism. This fact seems to them to indicate that the Jews are committed by their history to the purpose of converting the world to belief in the unity of God, with all the ethical implications of that belief. "Those who today believe in the election of Israel," writes Dr. Bernard J. Bamberger,[19] "are those who regard Judaism as a universal religion, as *the* universal religion, with a message for all men."

Though none would dispute the spiritual indebtedness of the Western world to Israel, the inference from that indebtedness that Israel was chosen by God to be His messenger to mankind is nevertheless a "grating" *non-sequitur*. When a delegation of Chicago ministers visited Abraham Lincoln to urge the abolition of slavery, one of their number told him that it was God's will that he free the slaves. To which Lincoln [20] replied: "If it is, as you say, a message from your Divine Master, is it not odd that the only channel He could send it by was the roundabout route by way of that awful wicked city of Chicago?" The Jewish people may not be awfully wicked, but one may still ask: "If God has a message for all mankind, is it not odd that the only channel through which He could send it should be the roundabout route via Zion?" To say that many of the most significant religious ideas of the Western world are of Jewish origin does not answer that question. For all we know, Lincoln might have gotten some very good suggestions from Chicagoans. But Lincoln rebuked the arrogance which assumed that he himself had less access to divine guidance than the Chicago ministers, and his rebuke was justified. *The assumption by an individual or group that it is the chosen and indispensable vehicle of God's grace to others is arrogance, no matter how euphemistically one phrases the claim to being chosen.*

Moreover, if Israel's having influenced the world religiously in the past proves that the Israelites are God's Chosen People, what inference are we to draw from the fact that Israel is today *not* influencing the religions of other peoples, but rather being influenced by them? Who can read the works of such men as Sholem Asch, and Franz Werfel, to name two of the most distinguished Jewish writers, by way of example, without perceiving the profound influence that Christianity has had on many Jews? Does that prove that the Christian Church has been chosen and Israel rejected? Would we not resent such an inference? It has been well said that "Ideals remain real only when one continues to realize them." If that is true then the doctrine of the Chosen People, whatever validity it may have had in the past, is today utterly unreal.

4

DIVINE ELECTION INCONSISTENT WITH EVOLUTIONARY CONCEPTION OF RELIGION

The apologists for the doctrine of Israel's election do not take the trouble to think through to a conclusion the role of religion in human civilization. Formerly the adherents of all the traditional religions of the Western world maintained that religion was supernaturally revealed truth. That such truth was transmitted only by one's own people was sufficient evidence that only one's own people had been chosen. Since it was assumed that salvation could be achieved only through revealed truth, the possession of that truth imposed the obligation to convey it to others and to induct them into one's own "chosen" community by way of conversion.

But when one abandons the idea of supernatural revelation, what becomes of religion? If religious truth is independent of any historic self-revelation of God to a particular people, then it is no different from scientific truth in being accessible to and attainable by all mankind. Indeed, one of the main criteria of truth is its universal applicability to and conformity with universal reason. No one can take seriously the theory advanced by Kaufmann Kohler and Abraham Geiger that the Jews, as a race, have a particular genius for religion.[21] Certainly, the *capacity for grasping and conveying truth in the realm of religion, as in every other field of human knowledge and experience, varies more among the individuals of any one group than it does between group and group.* The propagation of specific religious truth cannot possibly be the distinctive function of any particular group. Different religions may actually stand for the same truth about God, while, in any one religion religious truth has always to contend with religious error and superstition.

A religion is the organized quest of a people for salvation, for helping those who live by the civilization of that people to achieve their destiny as human beings. In the course of that quest, the people discovers religious truths and abiding values. These truths and values, like all others, are universal. They are not the monopoly of the group that discovers them. They may be discovered by other groups as well. Religions are distinct from one another not so much ideationally as existentially. Each religion represents a particular area of collective life marked out by the *sancta* of the group. These are a definite product of the group's unique historic experience. Such *sancta* are its saints and heroes, its sacred literature, its holy places, its common symbols, its customs and folkways, and all objects and associations which have been hallowed, because of their relation to that people's quest for salvation. There is no more reason for having all the world adopt the *sancta* of one people or church than for all people to wear an identical type of garment. What is important is that the *sancta* of each people or church help to humanize all who belong to it, by implementing those universal values which it should share with all other peoples and churches. *A religion is universal, if its conception of God is one that imposes on its adherents loyalty to a universally valid code of ethics. It is only in that sense that the Jewish religion is universal.*

The role of religion in human life is to humanize men by enabling them to transcend the limits of present human nature. It emphasizes that which differentiates man from the beast; it identifies the divine element in that which man can make out of himself. That differentia is the creative urge manifest in man's will to salvation, in his will to the achievement of the good and full life, to the realization of the holiness of human life. To the extent that any civilization contributes to this end, it is religious. That is what we mean when we speak of Judaism as a religious civilization.

Religion is not one of a number of coordinate elements of human culture, but rather the process which organizes all of them into a pattern. It is what personality is to the individual, and nationalism to the nation. That is why Jewish religion is both particular and universal. It is particular, insofar as it functions within and through Jewish life. It is universal, insofar as it seeks to integrate Jewish life with the universal life of mankind, through the worship of the one God of all men and all peoples.

5

THE MISSION IDEA AND RELIGIOUS IMPERIALISM

The conception of the Jewish mission may be said to have originated in the tension between the belief in the one God of all the world and the belief that God has manifested His purpose with reference to human life only through Israel's Torah. The particularistic notion of Israel's exclusive possession of revealed truth had somehow to be reconciled with the universalistic concept of the unity of God. The reconciliation took the form of a compromise between universalism and particularism. The mission idea is such a compromise. Whether it is a satisfactory one is another question.

Indeed, the assumption that only by accepting one's own religion, or by acknowledging its hegemony, can the world be saved is the religious analogue of what, in the political realm, we condemn as imperialism. There was a time when *imperialism* was an honorific word. The Romans were convinced that, in extending their empire, they were extending not merely Roman civilization but *civilization*. They were very proud of the *Pax Romana*. Britons not so long ago boasted of the civilizing influence of their colonial empire as a great service to humanity, as "the White man's burden" of responsibility for the welfare of the "inferior" or "backward" races. Moreover, the claims that empires have frequently extended the area of human cooperation and peace are not without foundation. Empires represent an intermediate step between national isolationism in which every people regards every other with hatred and suspicion and the long-awaited federation of nations. They are a preparatory stage for that eventual development, when mankind will be recognized as an organic whole, and all its populations as equally concerned in, and equally responsible for, the common welfare.

Similarly, missionizing religion represents an intermediate step between a situation, on the one hand, in which peoples regarded their gods as exclusively interested in them, and regarded themselves as possessing the only way of salvation from which all others were permanently barred, and, on the other hand, the ideal situation in which the implications of the unity of God will be fully realized.

In that ideal situation we shall have, not a cosmopolitan religion of the kind advocated by rationalists who lack appreciation of history, but universal religion—with the "the" omitted—which will be based upon the following principles: (1) all men and all peoples are in need of salvation, or of fulfilling their human destiny; (2) all groups seek salvation in accordance with their own collective experience, and by utilizing their own respective cultures; (3) the ultimate salvation of mankind depends on the recognition that no people can attain complete salvation, until all peoples attain it; and (4) all peoples can attain salvation, only when it is recognized that God is equally accessible to all religious groups, through the proper development and interpretation of their own *sancta*.

An intermediate stage, which may be designated as that of "religious imperialism," is reached when a group, that believes itself the exclusive possessor of a divinely revealed way of life, seeks to impose it on others, whether by force of arms or by propaganda. And just as political imperialism has to its credit the widening of men's political horizons, so may the expansion of God's Kingdom through missionary zeal have to its credit the widening of spiritual horizons. Nevertheless, both are forms of imperialism, and imperialism involves injustice.

When rival imperialisms co-exist, as in the modern world, the inevitable consequence is warfare on a global scale. Religious imperialism has likewise been a source of warfare. Not only Islam, but also Christianity, was spread by the sword. The Thirty Years' War was motivated by the rival imperialistic claims of Protestantism and Catholicism to universal hegemony. Only after Europe had been bled white and the fighting ended in a draw, did the world begin to conceive the need for religious tolerance, the actual achievement of which awaits the future. But even where the missionizing of a people proceeds by peaceable means, it works havoc with human lives. It invades the family and disturbs its unity. It dissolves the integrity of ancient civilizations, by acting as a sort of fifth column for alien groups. There has never been a people that has been missionized, without resenting the implied insult to its own civilization and religion. The Boxer Rebellion in China was largely a protest against foreign missions. The hatred against Jews and Christians in pagan Rome was another manifestation of the ill-will inevitably provoked by missionary activities.

Our apologists would contend that Jewish missionary activity was not comparable to that of Christianity and Islam, because it always relied solely on persuasion, and because it always recognized that "the pious ones of the Gentile nations have a share in the world to come." [22]

But the truth is that even peaceful missionary activities inevitably create ill-will. One cannot help wondering, moreover, whether the peaceable methods of Jewish missionary activities were not mainly the result of Jewish military impotence imposed by Rome rather than of superior religious insight and tolerance. When one believes one's own religion to be the only true religion, it is easy to justify a "holy War" as waged to extend the domain of God's Kingdom and to help redeem mankind. It is historical fact that, at the height of the Hasmonean power, the Jews did actually impose Judaism on the Idumeans by force of arms.

As for the recognition in Jewish tradition that individuals among the Gentiles might attain salvation by conforming to the ethical laws revealed to mankind through Noah, its application did not extend nearly as far as modern Jewish liberals would like to believe. Maimonides, for example, maintained that for a Gentile to conform to the Noahitic laws was not enough. To obtain salvation he must look upon those laws as revealed by God.[23] Since the only evidence of any revelation to Noah is to be found in the Torah of Israel, the achievement of salvation by a Gentile was thus made to depend on his recognizing Israel as the chosen vehicle of divine salvation for mankind.

6

THE DOCTRINE OF ELECTION NOT NECESSARY FOR JEWISH SURVIVAL

The question naturally coming to mind at this point is this: Since the proponents of the various reinterpretations of the doctrine of the Chosen People no longer believe in the factual truth of the Patriarchal stories, or of the miracles and the Sinaitic theophany, why are they at such pains to reinterpret that doctrine? The reason often suggested for their insistence upon retaining the doctrine of Israel's election, namely, that it permeates the whole of Jewish tradition, cannot be true. For, by the same token, they ought to insist on the traditional doctrine of the divine authorship of the Torah. There surely is not a single syllable or letter of the Jewish tradition which is not thoroughly saturated with the idea that the whole of the Pentateuch was dictated by God to Moses. Yet these men have managed to emancipate themselves from that assumption. What then prompts them so to resist any tampering with the doctrine of Israel's election?

The only reasonable motive to which such zeal can be ascribed is not one which derives from the momentum of tradition, but from considerations of Jewish survival. They seem to think that Jews would give up their struggle to live as an indivisible people, unless they were to believe that they are endowed, either individually or as a group, either biologically or culturally, with some moral or spiritual preeminence over the rest of the world.

In reply, be it said that the very attempt to bolster up the Jewish will to live by reasons or assumptions of questionable validity not only defeats its own purpose, but is injurious, from the standpoint of Jewish self-respect. The Jewish will to live cannot be fortified by spurious means. Any claim to moral or spiritual superiority, that is not based on incontrovertible proof, either supernatural or natural, is spurious and unworthy even of ordinary morals, to say nothing of a high spiritual standard.

Judaism can certainly not afford to harbor any doctrine which is in conflict with the ethical basis of democracy. That basis is the intrinsic worth of the individual human soul, a worth which is independent of the people, race or church to which one belongs. This implies that no people, race or church can confer upon its members a higher human status than does any other. Democracy as such calls for the treatment of individuals, despite their marked differences, as equals, from the standpoint of law and of their right to happiness and salvation. Ethical democracy goes one step further and calls for the treatment of all peoples, races and churches as equals in all respects. Indeed, *societies are far more like one another in their characteristics and behavior than are individuals. Hence, discrimination between one people and another is even more irrational and unethical than between one individual and another.*

Continuity of the Jewish consciousness demands that as large a number as possible of traditional Jewish values be retained. This does not mean, however, that all traditional values must necessarily be retained. Some are inherently of such a character as not to be capable of reinterpretation, or of being fitted into the pattern of the present-day outlook on life. Not even the fact that they suffuse the entire tradition, and that their elimination must produce a radically altered tradition, should be sufficient to save them. Take, for example, the traditional beliefs concerning the restoration of the Temple with its sacrificial worship, or concerning the status of Jews in the Diaspora as exiles. These beliefs are an integral part of Jewish tradition. But life is stronger than tradition. The Jewish will to live has managed to survive the desuetude of these beliefs. Why then should we assume that the Jewish will to live would be weakened, if we were to eliminate one more belief which runs counter to the progress of the human spirit at its best?

7

BELIEF IN ELECTION OF ISRAEL A SOURCE OF MALADJUSTMENT

Far from being a factor for Jewish survival, *the doctrine of Israel's election is henceforth bound to be, ideologically, a definite hindrance.* In its traditional form, that doctrine belongs to the same universe of discourse as the one in which God was conceived as a magnified human being, sitting on a great throne in the heavens, surrounded by hosts of angels and demons who were at His beck and call, ready to carry out His will on earth. It belongs to the universe of discourse in which the supernatural miracles, believed to have taken place in the past, were a guarantee of like miracles in the future. In that thought-world, the divine sound of the *shofar* on Sinai was an assurance of the shofar of the Messiah at "the end of days." It is part of a world-outlook in which all human suffering, even the fact of death, was attributed to sin, in which animal sacrifice was accepted as an indispensable means of atoning for sin, and in which a whole people could be conceived as subjected to unceasing torment of body and mind for centuries, because of failure to atone for some anonymous ancestral sin. To get back to that pre-modern universe of discourse is possible for the modern-minded man only in the same sense as it is possible to revisit the scene of one's childhood. People do that sort of thing to satisfy a feeling of nostalgia, but not with a view to finding a permanent home.

If the Jewish people is to have a future, it must so reconstruct its ideology concerning the world and God that it may feel itself perfectly at home in the universe of discourse in which those who are most advanced intellectually, morally and spiritually dwell at present. Their religion is not based on the tradition of miraculous events and theophanies supposed to have taken place in ancient times. It is based rather on the fundamental fact that all normal human beings are endowed with a capacity for striving to achieve their human destiny, provided that, individually and collectively, they coordinate their conduct and their institutions with the conception of God as the Power within and without them that makes for salvation. That conception of religion points to a better world in which Jews, without giving up their historical uniqueness and continuity as a people, want to have a share. *In that better world, the orchestration of human life is not to serve merely as an accompaniment to any one nation or ecclesia playing solo.*

A far nobler motive for Jewish survival than the assertion of a claim to spiritual superiority is the need for a people always to strive to outdo itself, always to keep on growing in moral and spiritual capacity. There can be no better evidence of such growth than the surrender of notions and beliefs that may have served some useful purpose in a people's childhood or youth, but that have become outdated, when that people has attained maturity. Retaining a doctrine like the election of Israel, which is so out of harmony with the modern world-outlook, is bound to produce further maladjustment in the Jew and to stunt the growth of Judaism. This becomes evident, when we consider the actual effect which the continued retention of the doctrine is having on the two predominant types of people, the rational and the romantic.

The rational type of Jew insists on clear and distinct thought in religion. This does not mean that he will not admit into religion anything but that which is scientifically demonstrable, or that he has no feelings, or that he is averse to mysticism. All it means is that in religion as in everything else we must not say what we do not mean. The rational type of Jew knows very well that, in religion, symbols and metaphors are indispensable, and that we cannot always articulate clearly what they imply. But while it is true that we cannot always say what we mean, we definitely should not say what we do not mean. The fact that we have not paid sufficient regard to this simple ethical principle is probably responsible for our having alienated from Judaism some of the most worthwhile men and women.

A striking illustration of the harm done by failing to reckon with the rational type of Jew is what Felix Adler says about himself in his *An Ethical Philosophy of Life.*[24] He there states that, when he was a young man, he was urged to enter the rabbinate, though he held views which he could not openly avow to his congregation. He was told that, by remaining within the Jewish fold he could contrive to have his people accept his views. "Would this be fair to them, or to myself?" he inquires. "Was I to act a lie in order to teach the truth? There was especially one passage in the Sabbath service which brought me to the point of resolution. I mean the words spoken by the officiating minister as he holds up the Pentateuch scrolls, 'And this is the law which Moses set before the People of Israel.' I had lately returned from abroad where I had had a fairly thorough course in biblical exegesis, and had become convinced that the Mosaic religion is, so to speak, a religious mosaic, and that there is hardly a single stone in it which can with certainty be traced to the authorship of Moses. Was I to repeat these words? It was impossible. I was certain that they would stick in my throat. On these grounds, the separation was decided on by me, and became irremediable." Felix Adler was by no means alone in this insistence on absolute sincerity in religion. We shall never know how many of our most brilliant minds have been kept out of the rabbinate, because we have made of intellectual honesty a prohibitive luxury. Their number is undoubtedly legion.

The effect of the retention of the doctrine of election on the romantic type of Jew, though of an entirely different character, is not less detrimental to Jewish survival. The romantic type of Jew deprecates all insistence on taking literally matters of ritual and liturgy. They are not intended, according to him, to convey exact truth, but to arouse the religious emotions. That purpose, he contends, is defeated by all attempts to submit the language of prayer or religious creed to the scrutiny of reason. But why flout reason unnecessarily, when it is possible to evoke an even more profoundly religious emotion which can be shared by everybody, by using language which calls forth no mental resistance? When raising the Scroll of the Torah, is it not better to recite the formula: "This Torah is a tree of life to those who hold fast to it; and of them that uphold it, every one is rendered happy," [25] than to arouse disturbing questions in the minds of an increasing number of people by reciting the traditional formula which alienated Felix Adler from the synagogue? Is it not more in keeping with spiritual religion, when we recite the "Alenu," to thank God for having given us "the Torah of truth and planted eternal life in us," than for not having made us "like the nations of other lands?" One may well suspect the romanticist of being so fond of tradition as to sacrifice his people for its sake.

The romantic policy of "Hands off!" from anything, however obsolete, that is sanctified by tradition is sure to paralyze all spiritual initiative. This is just what has happened with the doctrine of Israel's election. The romantic fondness for it has narcotized, yea lulled the Jew into a state of dangerous somnolence. It has prevented the Jewish mind from applying itself seriously and with all its might to the task of reformulating the place of Israel among the nations. *So long as the Jew takes it for granted that he belongs to a people that is divinely chosen, he can see no need for canvassing the problem of the political and religious status of the Jewish people.* In seeing no such need, Classical Reform and extreme Orthodoxy (Agudaism) display the same romantic type of mentality.

8

VOCATION A VALID SUBSTITUTE FOR THE DOCTRINE OF ELECTION

Jewish survival depends entirely upon our achieving a moral realism which, on the one hand, will wean us away from the futile compensatory mechanism of imagined superiority, and, on the other, will enable us to find the basis for intrinsic worth of Jewish life in the daily round of contemporary living. The only kind of Jewish survival that would constitute a creative adjustment to the world as it is today is one in which the two elements of our tradition would continue to function, namely, Jewish peoplehood and Jewish religion. *But what peoplehood and religion represent today must be stated in different terms from those which were current in the past.*

The essence of Jewish peoplehood can no longer be identified either with political unity or with religious uniformity. Political unity will have to be confined to Jews living in their own homeland. Uniformity will have to be replaced by a fundamentally common spirit. Likewise, the essence of Jewish religion can no longer be made to depend upon the factual truth of the supernatural events which are recorded in the Torah and on the presumable conclusion that they prove the election of Israel. Jewish religion will have to be based on what objective study has shown to be the function of a religion in the life of a people. That function is so to inspire and direct the energies of a people as to help its individual men and women to achieve their destiny as human beings, or to make the best use of their lives.

The place previously occupied in the Jewish consciousness by the doctrine of election will have to be filled by the doctrine of vocation. The whole course of Jewish history has been so dominated by religious motivation that Jews cannot be true to themselves, as a people, without stressing the religious character of Judaism. Jewish religion would have Jewish civilization make for the enhancement not only of Jewish life but of the life of mankind, and thus help to render manifest the cosmic purpose of human life. Jewish religion expects the Jew to live the civilization of his people in a spirit of commitment and dedication. To live thus is to live with a sense of vocation or calling, without involving ourselves in any of the invidious distinctions implied in the doctrine of the election, and yet to fulfill the legitimate spiritual wants which that doctrine sought to satisfy.

It is generally assumed that the idea of "vocation" is a Christian, particularly a Protestant, idea. As a matter of fact, that idea is no less Jewish than it is Christian. Thus we read in the Talmud: [26] "A familiar saying in the mouth of the Sages of Yabneh was this: 'I (who study Torah) am a creature (of God); my work is in the city, his in the field; I rise early to my work, he rises early to his. Just as he cannot excel in my work, so I cannot excel in his.' Perhaps thou wilt say: I do much and he does little (for the Torah). But we have learned, 'He who offers much and he who offers little are equal, provided that each direct his heart to Heaven.' " Judaism should extend the significance of vocation to include nations as well as individuals. *No nation is chosen, or elected, or superior to any other, but every nation should discover its vocation or calling, as a source of religious experience, and as a medium of salvation to those who share its life.*

It has been suggested that for an individual to experience the presence of God in his life as a divine calling, he has to meet the following conditions: He has to be engaged in doing needful work, work that calls into use his best powers and encourages their development, and, finally, that enables him to contribute his share to the welfare of mankind.[27] If Jews wish to feel a sense of vocation, all they need to do is to apply themselves to those tasks which would be most likely to meet for the Jewish people the foregoing three requirements. What they are has been outlined in Chapter II—*Reconstruction—A Program.*

If we Jews would accept that, or some similar program, as our vocation, we would not need to have our morale bolstered up by such a spiritual anachronism as extolling God "for not having made us like the other nations." [28] Instead, we would find our calling as a people so absorbing, so satisfying and so thrilling that we would have every reason in the world to thank God for having manifested His love to us, as He does to all men and nations who have found their true vocation, and for having rendered us worthy to be identified with His great and holy name.

It may be argued that not all vocations are of equal importance to society. The role which the President of the United States has to fill is far more crucial than that of some janitor of a "Five and Ten." It is not belittling either Mr. Jones or his vocation, if we regard the President's task as infinitely more crucial.[29]

Granted. And granted, too, that Israel's role in the history of mankind is also a crucial one. That would still not justify inclusion in the liturgy of prayers praising God for making Israel's role more crucial. What would Americans have said, if, on his accession to office, a President would pray, "I thank Thee, Lord, that Thou hast not made my vocation that of the janitor John Jones, but hast chosen me from among all Americans to lead the nation and mankind to peace?" A truly religious soul never reacts in that way to the fact of his being given a crucially important vocation. He is rather humbled by that fact and disposed to question his own qualifications, accepting as a grave and burdensome responsibility the tasks to which, in loyalty, he feels dedicated.

All these considerations make it clear that, whether we apply rational or pragmatic criteria, the traditional formula concerning Israel's divine election is objectionable. Rationally, it has no place in the realm of discourse from which belief in the supernatural revelation of religious truth has been excluded. Pragmatically, it is objectionable, as barring the way to peace and harmony among religions, and as making for self-righteousness and cant. All the genuine values that once attached themselves to this belief can be maintained by substituting for it the doctrine of "vocation." What more important calling could a people have than to promulgate, by its way of life, the truth of the universal presence of God in all religions, and the universal obligation of every man to use his traditional *sancta* for glorifying not merely his own people or church, but mankind as a whole?

CHAPTER FOURTEEN

RELIGIOUS DOUBTS AND THE PROBLEM OF EVIL

1

DEFEATIST VS. CREATIVE DOUBTS

The attitude of traditional religion towards those who doubt its tenets has been one of unqualified condemnation. Throughout the Middle Ages, the skeptic was damned as a heretic. The tenets of religious faith that were deemed indispensable to man's salvation were conceived as revealed truths, possessing an altogether higher degree of authority than human reason or experience. If some of these tenets seemed absurd in the light of human intelligence, the devoted believer suppressed his doubts by assuming with Tertullian, "*Certum est quia impossibile est.*" (It is certain because it is impossible.) That God saw fit to reveal His word to man meant that human experience and reason were not to be trusted, at least when they contradicted revelation. To such an extent has the notion that doubt is essentially irreligious taken hold on the minds of men that the term *free-thinker,* denoting a man who assumes that he has the right to doubt allegedly revealed truth, has been used almost interchangeably with *atheist.*

In Jewish tradition, too, doubt was frowned on. To doubt a religious tenet was to forfeit salvation. If a man could not subscribe to the belief that the resurrection of the dead is expressly proclaimed in the Torah, he forfeited by his unbelief whatever share he might otherwise have claimed in the world to come.[1]

Nevertheless this assumption that doubt is incompatible with religion may itself be questioned. Charles Francis Potter, a Unitarian clergyman, put the matter cleverly when he said: "If you want a safe religion with all doubts removed, you can easily find it, if you promise not to think. But if you want a live religion, you'll have to go fishing in your own soul and catch it." Our Bible is not lacking in expressions of religious doubt. Skepticism with regard to traditional beliefs is the dominant note in Ecclesiastes and Job, and is expressed in many passages in the Prophets [2] and Psalms.[3] Even more notable is the fact that the Torah pictures Abraham, who is always taken as the exemplar of religious faith, whose faith, tested by ten trials, withstood them all, as nevertheless questioning the justice of God. When God tells Abraham of His plan to destroy Sodom and Gomorrah, Abraham exclaims: "Far be it from Thee to do such a thing, to destroy the righteous with the wicked, that the righteous should fare like the wicked: Far be it from Thee: Shall not the Judge of all the earth deal justly?" [4]

This skepticism of Abraham did not escape the notice of our Sages. The *midrash* compares Abraham with that other great skeptic Job, who expressed the same thought in what would seem to most of us but slightly different language. Job said: "It is all the same. Therefore, say I, 'He destroys the innocent and the wicked.' " [5] The Sages, however, see a subtle distinction between the quality of Abraham's doubt and that of Job's, and this distinction, though subtle is enough, in their opinion, to account for the fact that Abraham was rewarded for his doubt and Job punished for his. Job's doubt, they tell us, was like an unripe fig, Abraham's like a ripe fig; Job's was bitter and unpalatable.[6] If we try to analyze the difference between the two utterances, we note in Job's a hasty acceptance of a negative conclusion, a summary dismissal of the notion of God's justice, and a readiness to commit himself to the consequences of his unbelief. Not so Abraham. His doubt wrings from him an exclamation of horror, but he expresses it interrogatively. He cannot reconcile his belief in the justice of God with the total destruction of the cities of the plain; but he will not commit himself to a denial of God's justice. He knows that, regardless of his doubts, and without denying or concealing them, he will continue to act on the assumption that God is just. His was "a faith that inquires."

This is, indeed, a subtle but significant distinction. The astonishment implied in Abraham's doubt has an intrinsic relation to the sincerity of his faith. Because Abraham believed so firmly in a God of righteousness and justice, because he so completely identified his own purposes with those of God, he was all the more sensitive to every fact that challenged the truth of that faith. A less spiritual character, one less faithful to God, would have rested content with God's having saved Lot and his family from the catastrophe that befell Sodom and Gomorrah, and would have seen in that an evidence of God's discriminating justice in having rescued his kin from destruction, in recognition of his own virtues. He would have smugly assumed that all those who were destroyed had somehow merited their fate.

But the truly religious are never smug. If they are saved from calamity, they do not credit it to their virtue, but are rather grateful to God that, in the words of the traditional *berakah*, "He bestows loving kindness on the unworthy." [7] When others suffer, the truly pious do not ascribe it to the fault of the sufferers, but find themselves doubly tormented, first, by their sympathetic participation in their neighbor's suffering and, secondly, by the wound to their faith in God. Every injustice is, for them, a *hillul hashem*, a derogation, so to speak, of the divine honor. They are, therefore, forever wrestling with God in prayer, pleading with Him to assert His justice, and to wipe out the blot that obscures it for them and for their fellows. *Their very doubt is thus a prayer and an expression of their faith.*

But while they neither conceal nor suppress their doubt, they also never permit it to suppress their faith. They seek no escape from the conflict between things as they are and things as they ought to be, by surrendering to the former. They will make grace of necessity or, to state the situation more accurately, they will never accept as an inevitable necessity any situation that has not their moral approval. They will not yield to the smugness of cynicism any more than to the smugness of self-righteousness. For there is a cynical smugness, such as that which, apparently, the Sage detected in the words of Job. There is an attitude which when it finds its faith challenged says: "*ahat hi*," "It is all the same," it makes no difference whether one does right or wrong. How do we know that there is any Power in the world that makes for righteousness? We may as well assume that *let din velet dayan*, "there is neither judge nor justice in the universe."

It is apparent that, although there is such a thing as a doubt that is destructive of religious values, there is also a doubt that is an inseparable accompaniment of religious faith, and that particularly characterizes the lives of the great creative geniuses of religion. The destructive doubt is one that results in the cynical acceptance of evil as inevitable, in a defeatist attitude to moral issues. But there is also a constructive doubt arising from the eternal refusal of the human spirit to acquiesce in evil. This doubt is capable of becoming a great force for good. To condemn all doubt in others and to suppress all doubt in ourselves is, therefore, not in the best interest of religion, understood as faith in the Power that makes for human salvation, and as the endeavor of men to bring human life under the domination of that Power.

2

THE PROBLEM OF EVIL IN THE WORLD
AND HOW TO MEET IT

But doubt is disturbing. Even when people find that they cannot suppress it, they frequently resort to devious efforts to divert their thoughts from it. They devise elaborate theories for resolving their doubts. They try to prove to themselves that the evils which have given rise to their doubts are not really as evil as they look, or that they are only of a very temporary nature and will ultimately result in good. The whole doctrine of reward and punishment in a life after death is one of these efforts at circumventing doubt, by resolving the contradiction between our faith in a just God and the manifest injustices and wrongs from which good people suffer.[8] The doctrine that, "according to their suffering here, will be their reward hereafter"[9] was clearly designed to soothe the sense of protest against these injustices and wrongs. With the modern world's release from the social defeatism of the Middle Ages, other-worldly religion, as a mode of resolving our doubts about the government of this world, has lost favor. The modern temper is disposed to resent as an opiate the other-worldly religion which makes people complacent of the evils that exist in this world, and that should be abolished. We want religion to effect for us in this world redemption from recognized evils and the achievement of a worthwhile life.

But the psychic mechanism of escape from doubt-producing experiences is very subtle and can avail itself of many other opiates beside that of other-worldly religion. There is a kind of idealistic metaphysics which tries to prove that evil is only evil, from the standpoint of the finite human mind, but that, in the larger perspective of the Absolute, this world is "the best of all possible worlds." To a man of genuine religious faith, such doctrine is meaningless. His faith in God results from his awareness of his own inadequacy, and that of men in general, to achieve their deepest desires without the help of a Power other than themselves, that makes for human salvation. But people, in whom the yearning for human salvation is not as deep and as strong, permit such philosophies to lull to sleep their protest against wrong, by making them resigned to the existence of evil as though it were a mere illusion of the human mind.

We must be extremely wary of any doctrine that makes evils appear "not really" evil, or that assures us that they will be remedied, without our having to assume any responsibility for remedying them. To be sure, the rose-water theologies have lost their vogue, but the mind-habit which produced them still functions. The communist who argues that the proletarian revolution will "inevitably" lead to a classless society and the crumbling of the compulsory state, is using this doctrine to resolve for himself or for others the doubts created by the realities of proletarian dictatorship and the misery caused by the proletarian revolution and its aftermath. Communism is today as much the opiate of the Russian masses as other-worldly religion was in the pre-revolutionary era.

The fascist, who descants on the beauty of war, and on how it brings out the best in men by its demands on courage and self-sacrifice, is trying by his theory of romantic nationalism to still in himself and others the doubts as to the worthwhileness of a life in which great masses of men find themselves insecure and despised, until they wrest a measure of security and a tribute of fear, if not respect, by their organized and aggressive violence. Much of the hatred of the Nazis for the Jews stemmed from their true perception that the religious tradition, which has its source in Judaism, is opposed to such a resolution of the doubts from which the German masses tried to escape through the glorification of militaristic racial nationalism.

But if, on the one hand, we are not to succumb to doubt and permit it to destroy our faith in God, and, on the other, we are neither to suppress nor resolve it, what escape is there from the torment of a divided mind, fearful both of yielding to doubt and of dismissing it? There is an escape which lies open to the religious person, but that escape must come not by a process of thought but by an act of will. That act of will must be directed not to negating the doubt, for that would be suppression, but to reaffirming the faith which the doubt challenges; not to denying the reality of evil, but to admitting the reality of good and to focusing our attention upon it. This is neither to suppress doubt nor to resolve it, but to transcend it.

The question why evil exists is one to which the human mind should never expect to find an answer. It seems to be a necessary condition of life which we accept as part of existence. For, as human beings, we can never really know why anything exists. But *if the existence of evil is part of the mystery of the world that baffles human understanding, the existence of the good is no less a part of that mystery.* We know, as a matter of experience, with a knowledge as positive as any data supplied by the senses, that there are matters that give us deep and immediate satisfaction, that there are times when we feel in the depth of our being that it is good to be alive. There is goodness in the world that flows in on us sometimes, when we least expect it. This, too, is part of the mystery of life and this, too, is real. By focusing on this reality, this possibility of experiencing salvation, we transcend those doubts that are born of human suffering.

This does not mean that we lose sight of the evil in the world. It merely means that we do not permit it to represent for us the essential and ineradicable nature of reality, in whole or in part. We identify the good that we have experienced with that which ought to be, with that we intend, so far as in our power lies, shall be; while the evil becomes identified with what ought not to be and with what we intend, so far as in our power lies, to abolish. The achievement of the good expresses for us, therefore, the direction of our life's current, while the evil appears as an obstruction which resists the current, but cannot stop it.

Since our life is, after all, but part of the life of the world and dependent on that universal life which existed before we were born and continues after our death, and which unites us with all else that is, the current of our life must derive its impetus and general direction from the current of the universal life. Our purpose in intending the good, becomes to us a symbol of a divine purpose that wills the good, and thus our faith in God is reborn. It is reborn in a way that does not overlook evil, but makes us seek to overcome it, and enables us to find peace by making evil less important to us than good. For *this deliberate focusing on the good confers on our contemplation of the good the power of making us will the abolition of the evil, while our refusal to focus attention on the evil deprives it of that fascination which enables it to inhibit our pursuit of the good.*

But this drawing of the focus of our attention from the evil and concentrating it on the good is not the only method by which we are enabled to transcend our doubts. *Another method is to shift the problem of evil from the field of thought to that of action.* Instead of asking ourselves, "How can life be considered good when there is so much evil in it?" let us ask ourselves, "What must I do to make the world better?" Instead of despairing of the goodness of God, because the world is not such as to reflect that goodness, let us accept a responsible share of the task of making the world over so that it does reflect God's goodness.

There is no experience which brings home to us so effectively the reality of God as the zest of living that accompanies all creative achievement. We cannot doubt the power for good in the world, when our own personalities function as part of that power. Particularly when, as a result of our efforts, a condition that threatens us with a feeling of frustration and helplessness is beneficently changed by us, and, like God in the Biblical legend of creation, we look upon the work that we have done and say, "Behold, it is very good," we can no longer doubt the reality of God. Thus, *in the very effort to overcome evil, we find a peace and joy that makes it impossible for us to think of the evil as the last word.* Evil is not overlooked or pronounced as unreal, but neither is it permitted to become a bogey that paralyzes our will to live and to achieve. Rather is it then regarded as a challenge to us to bring out the best that is in us. Nobody who habitually practices the art of transcending the ills of life by accepting them in this spirit ever feels himself God-forsaken, because this very power to transcend the evils of life is the experience of salvation, and implies God. For just as the evil did not exist exclusively within the human mind, so the power to overcome it did not. Man's power to alter an evil condition is merely his ability to draw upon the Power of God in the world for the achievement of his own purpose.

Until comparatively recent times, all manner of pestilences and famines were the order of the day throughout the world, as they still are in India and Indo-China. To render that fact compatible with the conception of a beneficent God, priests and prophets, theologians and philosophers would try to fit it into some divine plan that would make it appear other than evil. This tendency to be content with explaining away the dire visitations that wrought havoc with human life, though still extant, is gradually giving way to the striving to eliminate them altogether. Among the progressive elements of the world's population, intelligence is slowly but surely gaining the upper hand. Careful observation, study, inference and ingenuity have been brought into play. With the aid of the laws of health and disease, of heat and electricity and numerous other forces at work in the body of man and in his physical surroundings, long rampant and dreaded manifestations of nature are being brought under control.

What conclusion shall we draw from the change in man's attitude toward the forces of destruction that blast alike saint and sinner, hero and coward? Shall it be the superficial one that man, self-contained and self-sufficient, has at last solved the riddle of the Sphinx, in discovering that its human head is illusion and that only its tiger's paws are real? That nature is naught but a blind and meaningless conglomerate of untamed forces? On second thought, it would seem that man's powers of observation, intelligence and reason, when they finally burst upon the world, are as unaccountable, and as little due to man's own willing as man's own appearance on the scene. They are as much part and parcel of the universe in its totality as the very brains and hearts of men. Moreover, the physical forces and the natural laws which are employed in preventing the devastations, and in rebuilding the ruins, where prevention has failed, are themselves an integral element of the universe. The lightning-rod is the combined product of both universal mind and universal matter, and as such diverts the lightning from the work of death and destruction. If it had not been a part of nature from the beginning of the world, man could never have devised it.

So it is whenever we accept an existing evil as a challenge to our creative will to remedy it. When we act in that spirit, the world brings out the best in us, and we bring out the best in the world. That is the very essence of religious experience. *God saves man, when man serves God. When we put our wills to the task of improving the world, we find them mysteriously reenforced by natural powers that seem to have been waiting for our action to make such use of them.* Thus we feel ourselves secure and at home in the world. Although evils still exist for us and still loom as hostile to our interests, we feel able to face these foes of ours without being intimidated by them.

3

THE PROBLEM OF MORAL EVIL AND HOW TO MEET IT

This power to transcend evil by focusing on the good, and by transferring the problem from the realm of speculative thought to that of purposive action, applies not only to ills that are external to ourselves, but no less to our own personal shortcomings. The experience of sin is universal. That is why it appeared to the ancients as a hereditary taint, derived from the first parents of the human race.[10] Hence the doubt that inevitably insinuates itself: If there is a good God, how can He have endowed man with so sinful a nature, with such a ready capacity to yield to temptations that work harm to himself and others? Or, conversely, if man is so sinful, how can we believe him to be the creature of a good God? That God should put upon men the responsibility for conformity with moral law, and yet leave them with an inclination toward forms of behavior that are definitely evil, is an unresolved paradox. *Oi li miyozri, oi li miyizri,*[11] "Woe is me by reason of my Creator: and woe is me by reason of my evil inclination!" Thus our Sages give expression to the tragic dilemma that in every generation raises doubts in men's minds as to the reality of a good God.

With regard to moral evil, as with regard to the ills of nature, it is easy to fall into a smug cynicism that denies the very existence of a moral law, that treats morality as a mere human convention, or as an effort of a governing class to impose its will on others. There is also the attempt of men to suppress the doubt, or to resolve it. We suppress the doubt, when we pronounce it wrong to question man's absolute freedom and responsibility for what he makes of his own life. We resolve the doubt, when we try to persuade ourselves that we can find absolution from sin in ways that do not require of us a complete transformation of our characters. But neither suppression nor resolution is the right way to deal with the doubts born of man's experience with sin. The right way, again, is that of transcendence by shifting the focus of our attention from the evil to the good and by transferring the problem from the area of speculation to that of action.

Man is evil by nature. "There is no man on earth so righteous, that he doth good and sinneth not," says Koheleth.[12] That is true, but it is no less true that man is good, and that there is no man on earth who is so consistently wicked in all his relations that he has done no good deed of any kind. It would not be difficult to quote from Midrashic literature passages that insist on this composite and paradoxical aspect of human nature. Man can be more beastly than the beasts, and more angelic than the angels.

Although we must recognize the existence in man of sinister and brutal passions capable of working havoc with human life, we are not encouraged to regard this aspect of human nature as expressive of man's essential nature and indicative of his ultimate destiny. On the contrary, we are encouraged to think of man as created in the image of God. This affirmation is declared [13] to be an even more comprehensive moral principle than, "Thou shalt love thy neighbor as thyself," for it protects us from that smug cynicism which says, "Since I am a contemptible creature myself, I am free to be scornful of others." That is to say, since I have no reason for loving myself and all mankind is merely scum, I need not treat others with consideration.

Perhaps that is why our Sages could not condemn Abraham for protesting against the injustice of God's destruction of Sodom and Gomorrah. Not only did Abraham find it difficult to believe that so many people were wicked enough to merit such a fate, but his pleading with God that the cities be saved for the few righteous that lived there is revelatory of his own religious attitude. He pleads with God to do what he himself was in the habit of doing, to center his attention not on the wickedness of the wicked, regardless of their numbers, but on the righteousness of the righteous. That, perhaps explains why Abraham's doubt did not harden into destructive denial of God. *He did not suppress his doubt nor did he resolve it, but he focused his attention on the good in man, seeing in it a symbol of an infinite capacity for goodness, a reflection of the image of God.*

What is man to do about his sins? In the first place, he must not permit them to lead to self-hate or self-contempt. He must be able to see good in himself. He must believe that he has a soul that reflects something of the goodness that exists in the world. He will find qualities that express what he believes to be the best that is in him. Let him try to make the most of these, and the very effort to do so will divert his mind from his temptations in a way that will make them lose their obsessive power.

Self-confidence is necessary for the enterprise of living. Most of our moral failures are due to a distrust of our capacity for virtue. We all of us have ideals of the man or woman we should like to be. Let us see in the very fact that we project that ideal for ourselves the evidence that it must have some affinity with what we really are. If, in our hearts, we were wholly unlike it, we should not even regard it as ideal. This is the image of God in us. Though it may be obscured by our sins, if we can see it at all, we must come to love it so much that we find satisfaction in removing the moral stains which obscure it. It is only when we focus on the stains, and lose sight of the reflected image that we find it difficult to believe in God and in the power of God to make life worthwhile for us.

Moreover, *to experience the reality of God as the Power that saves us from sin, in a way that does not minimize the fatal reality of sin, we have the further recourse of shifting the problem from the area of speculative thought to that of action.* We have done wrong, and it has worked harm. Nothing that we can say or think can really undo what has been done. The past can never be relived and it always conditions the present and future. Therein lies the inexorable reality of sin. Having failed, however, does not mean that we are failures, for the future lies before us with its infinite possibilities. True, it will be conditioned by the past, but who can tell how many different futures can be built on the same past?

For human beings, to live is to will, and to will means to choose between alternatives, to determine one's future. We learn truth by being disillusioned with falsehood. Our achievements are based on the observed consequences of our failures. *True science is based on the technique of learning by experiment through trial and error; true religion is based on the technique of learning by experience through sin and atonement.* Science would get nowhere, if the scientist abandoned his quest of truth in discouragement because an experiment had failed, or if he permitted himself to brood on man's incapacity to solve the riddle of the universe, and began questioning whether nature has any intelligible laws on which men can rely. To escape from this brooding, he devises new experiments and puts his hypothesis, revised as a result of his demonstrated mistakes, to new test. In a word, he verifies his notion of truth by putting it to the test of action.

Similarly in relation to moral laws. Experience has taught us that certain forms of human behavior work harm to ourselves as individuals, or as human beings sharing in the life of humanity. Such forms of behavior we have good reasons to castigate as sins. They show that our behavior has led us onto a wrong track. In our discouragement, many of us brood over our incapacity for good behavior, instead of trying to find out what bad consequences of our acts make them sinful, and how we may put our conduct on the right track so that it will not lead to wreckage of our abiding purposes. If, instead of thinking of our sin as though it were a taint on our ego, we regard it as a form of bad behavior in our relations to the world about us, a disposition to *wrongdoing* rather than *wrong-being*, we will not brood about what has already been done, but try to learn from our experience *how to do better.*

In this way *we answer the paradox of sin by a sort of paradox of salvation.* We use our experience of sin in order to attain virtue. The Rabbis [14] gloried in this paradox. "The power of *teshuvah*" (that is, turning in the direction of the will to moral achievement) "converts what were wilful sins into virtues." They [15] reinterpret the despairing cry of Job: [16] "Who can bring purity out of impurity? *lo ehad*, no one," by the simple device of reading the last clause interrogatively instead of declaratively. "Who can bring purity out of impurity? Is it not the One, i.e., the one and only God?" When, instead of brooding over our sinfulness and doubting our own worth or despairing of our capacity to improve, we learn from our misbehavior how to manage our lives in the future, we experience that same progress in the quest for goodness that the scientist, in learning by his experiments, experiences in the quest for truth. We experience a restoration not merely of our confidence in ourselves, but of our faith in God.

Just as sin exists not in our own ego, but in our relation to persons, to society and to the life of the universe, so the Power, by which we are able to learn from our sins and make them contribute to the enhancement of life, cannot be confined to our own ego, but must inhere in the universe. The Power that brings purity out of impurity is indeed that Divine Power that is manifest in the healing and improvement of human character. Because the repentant sinner knows this from experience, his faith is of a quality superior even to that of the *zadik gamur*, the untempted, and untested righteous who had never strayed far from the beaten path of respectability.

Suffering and sin are real, and inevitably raise questions in the human mind as to the reality of God, the Power on whom man depends for salvation. To yield to this doubt and to act on the assumption that there is no God and that life is necessarily bitter and futile is dangerous. *It is the spirit of defeatism that brings about defeat.* But it is hardly less dangerous to dismiss these doubts as sinful, and try to suppress them. To suppress them is to stifle man's protest against evil, the protest which is the dynamic power behind religion, and which makes it possible for religion to improve human life. Nor is it much better to attempt to resolve these doubts by making suffering and sin appear more tolerable than they are, or shifting from man to God the burden of responsibility for correcting them. The way to deal constructively with religious doubt is to learn to transcend it, by focusing our attention on the reality of happiness and virtue rather than on that of misery and vice, and by thinking of the problem not in terms of speculative thought but of ethical action. In our effort to improve the world and ourselves, we are bound, if we persevere, to meet with some measure of success, to achieve some degree of salvation. Notwithstanding all the suffering and sin which mar human life, that achievement will suffice to sustain our faith in God, the Power that makes for human salvation.

These, then, are the conclusions to which we are led concerning religious doubts and the problem of evil. They are conclusions, be it remembered, which derive from a premise that is totally different from the one which is assumed in all religious discussion. In all such discussion, it is taken for granted that religion begins with some idea of gods or God. This fallacious assumption that in the beginning is the idea, the *logos*, the word, has by this time been eliminated from the social sciences, but it still persists in the study and discussion of religion. As long as we labor under that assumption, we shall expect religion to give us an intellectually satisfying explanation of the existence of evil. To regard the concept of God as the beginning of religion is as erroneous as to regard the idea of food as the beginning and motivation of all our ado about eating. As with eating so with religion, the motivation is some kind of hunger. On the basis of the various manifestations of religion, it is logical to assume that the particular hunger which gives rise to religion is the all-embracing one for life abundant, or salvation.

That premise inevitably leads to the conclusion that to satisfy hunger for salvation, it is not necessary to have the kind of ultimate solution of the problem of evil for which the intellect craves. How we should react to evil and what we should do about it, from the standpoint of religion as a process of satisfying our need for salvation, is all that is here attempted. If some of us still continue to crave for an intellectually satisfying answer to the problem of evil, we may or may not give heed to the warning of some of mankind's wisest that this is only a false hunger. But if we are determined to disregard their warning, let us at least realize that we are not engaged in a *religious* pursuit, when we insist upon squaring the conception of a just God with all of the misery we encounter in the world. We are then philosophers or metaphysicians, with a boundless intellectual appetite. Religionists have always been satisfied with the modest fare of faith. It has been the purpose of this chapter to point out how truly nourishing to the human spirit that fare can be.

CHAPTER FIFTEEN

BASIC VALUES IN JEWISH RELIGION

Moses Mendelssohn brought discord into the ranks of the Jewish theologians when, in his *Jerusalem*,[1] he argued that Judaism had no dogmas. Until a generation ago that thesis was the great topic of debate among them. Though the debate has subsided, it is still of interest to look into the reason that motivated Mendelssohn to express that thesis, because it indicates that, in him, Jewish religion unquestionably turned a new corner. This is attributable to the fact that Mendelssohn, being both a loyal Jew and an ardent spokesman of the Enlightenment, deemed it necessary to achieve a different synthesis between Jewish tradition and reason from that achieved by the Jewish theologians of the Middle Ages. The main assumptions of the Enlightenment was that not supernatural revelation, but reason, was the medium through which man could learn what he needed to know in order to make the best use of life on earth, and to attain the bliss of immortality in the hereafter.

Since reason was not the exclusive possession of any one group, or society of human beings, all who fostered it and lived by the truths it revealed were qualified for salvation. This principle implied the negation of all orthodox religion which assumed that salvation could be the lot only of those who professed faith in the validity of some supernatural revelation. Mendelssohn, nevertheless, thought it possible to square this principle with Judaism. To do that, he defined Judaism as revealed legislation intended only for the Jewish people.

On the face of it, Mendelssohn's thesis was in conflict with Jewish tradition. Throughout that tradition, beginning with the Bible and ending with the writings of the Jewish theologians of the Middle Ages, belief in the historicity of certain events in the past, and in the inevitability of others in the future, was peremptorily required of the Jew. What Mendelssohn tried to do was to force that tradition into the pattern of his own rationalistic and Deistic conceptions. In doing that, he adopted Spinoza's interpretation of the Torah as revealed legislation, and identified loyalty to Judaism with action rather than with thought.

This forced version of traditional Judaism as not expecting its adherents to subscribe to dogmas was welcomed by those who found themselves unable to subscribe to the Thirteen Principles of Maimonides.[2] Though those principles had never been formally adopted as authoritative, nevertheless they were binding upon anyone who wanted to be accounted a good Jew. Mendelssohn's thesis provided those Jews for whom the traditional creed had become irksome the release they were seeking.

Solomon Schechter was, no doubt, right when he castigated such an apologia for the rejection of the traditional dogmas.[3] To reduce Jewish religion to a series of mechanical observances, and to exempt all thought and inner conviction from its control, was to degrade it. Schechter properly felt that it was important to prove that Jewish religion "regulates not only our actions but also our thoughts."

But the debate remained inconclusive, despite Schechter's recital of evidence proving that Judaism was never devoid of dogma. So the important question is not whether Jewish religion expects its adherents to think as well as to act. It is, rather, what does Jewish religion expect them to think. If the thoughts which the Jewish tradition regarded as essential to being a good Jew had been plausible and inherently felt to be of great moment, no one would have suggested that Judaism merely expected conformity to a prescribed regimen of behavior. The fact is that certain beliefs had come to be regarded as contrary to reasoned experience. To begin with, there were the beliefs in bodily resurrection and in the coming of a personal Messiah. Additional beliefs came later to be seen in a similar light. What was to be done about them? That question has not been dealt with frankly. Instead, the discussion has been made to turn on the abstract question of whether or not the Jewish religion insists on dogmas. The reason for avoiding the reexamination of the specific beliefs and either rejecting, reaffirming or reinterpreting them is that, until recently, it was regarded dangerous to the future of Jewish religion to tamper with its time-honored doctrines.

Enough has been said in previous chapters to indicate which of the traditional dogmas have become either obsolete or irrelevant. Their place cannot be left void. "We usually urge," says Schechter in his essay on the dogmas of Judaism, "that in Judaism religion means life; but we forget that a life without guiding principles and thoughts is a life not worth living." What we need is to ascertain what guiding principles and thoughts we can find in our religious tradition that are compatible with our modern conception of salvation, and that might serve as an incentive to strive for that salvation. These "guiding principles and thoughts" would have to serve as the basic values of Jewish religion for our day. *A value is any attitude or belief which is stressed as of high worth, because of its importance for the impetus which it supplies to the striving for salvation.* The alternative to authoritative dogma which has to be accepted, regardless of reason's approval, is not creedal an-archy. It is rather the acceptance of values which, without offending reason, are capable of satisfying our most distinctively human needs. Those are the needs which belong in the domain of the spirit.

Some of those needs are: awareness of the operation in human life of a higher law than that of natural selection; feeling at home in the world; a sense of security, despite the seeming heartlessness of nature; courage to go on trying, despite repeated frustration and disillusion-ment; accepting our human limitations, without being overwhelmed by sheer bigness and strength; realization that, in man's relation to man, justice and not force must have the final say; acceptance of life, not with resigned bitterness, but with loving gratitude, and above all the love that is itself the manifestation of God as the Power that makes for salvation—these needs are religion's main concern. The religion of any civilization has to counsel, to solace and to guide those who live by that civilization. It has to reckon with their innermost thoughts and feelings. *Jewish religion should articulate, and urge upon us, those values which would impel us to utilize our abilities and opportunities both for our own salvation and for that of our fellowmen.*

These considerations make it necessary to emphasize at least some of the basic values which Jewish religion has always stressed as repre-senting what God expects of us. Those are the values of spiritual selec-tion, faith, hope, patience, humility, inner freedom, thankfulness, justice and love. Conventional religion has worked these terms beyond the limit of their endurance; they are very tired words. Before, however, we judge them as too weary to carry the weight of truths that really matter, let us give them another chance.

1. SPIRITUAL SELECTION

1

THE CALL OF GOD *VS.* THE CALL OF THE WILD

The traditional doctrine of divine election, which must today be rejected, implies the superiority of the individual or group elected over others. The assumption that any people or ecclesia is in exclusive enjoyment of a divinely revealed way of salvation denied to others has been shown to be entirely untenable. The traditional Jewish doctrine of Israel as the "Chosen People" is open to this criticism. So also is the Catholic doctrine of "No salvation outside of the Church," and the orthodox Protestant doctrine that salvation is possible only through Christ.

But even if we reject this implication of superiority, we can still find in the doctrine of divine election an implication which is not only acceptable, but also of utmost cogency in our day. This is the implication that man alone, of all creatures, hears not only nature calling him but also God. As such he is exempt from the law of natural selection, and becomes subject to the law of spiritual selection.

The first clear reference to God's call to men in mass is in the story of the revelation of the Ten Commandments. There the Israelites are promised that, if they would obey God's law, they would be His own treasure. Not knowing of any other people to whom God had made known His law of righteousness, they naturally thought themselves especially singled out for salvation. We, today, who think of God as the God of the entire world, and who know that it is characteristic of all peoples to think in categories of right and wrong, just and unjust, must assume that salvation is attainable by all of mankind. But the significant fact emphasized in the story of the revelation on Mount Sinai is that salvation is conceived as conditional on conformity to a divine law. *Man cannot achieve salvation, his destiny as a human being, or a life experienced as worthwhile, except as he submits his native impulses to the discipline of a law other than his own inclinations or desires. This is the call of God.* In the idiom of the ancients, this is expressed in the formula: "The Lord our God, King of the Universe who hallowed us by His commandments and commanded us."

The significance of this implication of the call of God becomes clearer, if we contrast that call with the call of the wild, as it is discernible in the process of *natural selection.* The term "natural selection" first gained currency through the publication by Charles Darwin in 1859 of his epoch-making book, the full title of which was "On the Origin of Species by Means of Natural Selection, or the Preservation of Favored Races in the Struggle for Life." The term "natural selection" is descriptive of the process by which certain species are able to survive. The term "spiritual selection" may, therefore, be used to describe the process that makes for the survival of human beings. The Ten Commandments, the moral and spiritual laws in action, represent the process that makes for *human* survival and salvation.

The assumption of spiritual selection was, for the ancient world, as all embracing as the principle of natural selection has become in modern thinking. The animals were conceived as subject to the same law of survival as man, though they were not conscious of it. This is clearly implied in Genesis 9:15 which represents God as punishing the beasts for homicide. In fact the deluge was decreed not only because of man's sin, but because "all flesh had corrupted its way." The redemption in the days of the Messiah was conceived as a time when the "lion will eat straw, like the ox," because "they shall not hurt nor destroy on all My holy mountain." [1] The ancients conceived of the moral law as permeating and dominating all of nature. That is what our Sages had in mind when they asserted that the Torah existed even before the creation of the world, and that God had consulted it as an architect consults his plans. [2]

For the Jewish people, in Rabbinic times, the standards of behavior laid down in the Torah represented the divine laws "by which, if a man obey them, he shall live." [3] They were the key to salvation, the condition of survival. The Stoic philosophers, on the other hand, taught that God revealed Himself through man's reason, that reason in action is the process that makes for survival or salvation. As our Sages maintained that all nature was spiritual, so the Stoics maintained that all nature was rational. Both assumed that man must subject his instinctive and impulsive nature to the discipline of a transcendent law, in order to survive and attain self-fulfillment.

Christianity took over from Judaism the principle of spiritual selection. It, too, assumed that conformity to a divinely revealed way of life was a condition of salvation. That assumption, however, combined with a narrow interpretation of divinity, became a means of bolstering up entrenched power and vested interests of a tyrannical character. The concept of divine law was further narrowed by the emphasis on other-wordliness in Church doctrine, and the belief that salvation consisted in survival after death in a different order of existence.

With the movement for Enlightenment, which culminated in the revolutions of the eighteenth and the nineteenth century, the idea of the Stoics was revived. There was a revolt against superstition, priestcraft and authoritarian dogma in religion. Men began to turn to reason for the knowledge of the process that makes for survival and salvation. The American nation was the first to be founded on that principle.

The doctrine that all men are created equal and endowed with inalienable rights to life, liberty and the pursuit of happiness means that the vital interests of society and the individual, which condition their salvation in terms of survival and self-fulfillment, demand that all men be regarded as equally entitled to such salvation.

The slogan of the French Revolution, "Liberty, Equality and Fraternity," similarly pointed to the need for subordinating our native impulses to those reasonable rules of behavior which made for the enhancement of human life for all human beings. Since the authority of reason is inherent in human nature, and derives from the same source as human life itself, it merits to be considered divine. It fits into the pattern of spiritual selection, since it envisages salvation as conditional on conformity with a divine wisdom, and as a direct consequence of such conformity. That selection, however, is not arbitrarily limited to a particular group, but applies to any group or individual that is willing to accept its conditions. Such is the call of God to man.

Whether one thinks of spiritual selection as operating through human reason, or as operating through norms held to be supernaturally revealed, as in the Judeo-Christian tradition, its acceptance is a challenge to innate impulses and desires. It demands that these be tamed and brought under control. The physical appetites for food and sex gratification, the derivative drives for power, acquisition, glory, all the sadistic impulses born of the conflicts into which these interests have led men and their pre-human ancestors before them—all these need to be checked, controlled and brought into a pattern of integrated personality and cooperative society, if the conditions of spiritual selection are to be met.

Our Sages identified these tendencies that needed to be tamed and controlled as the *yezer hara* or evil inclination, and they very significantly equated this evil inclination with Satan and the Angel of Death.[4] For these turbulent and violent passions belong to the powers that threaten to frustrate the divine purpose of salvation, to seduce man from conformity to the way that leads to salvation, and hence to compass man's destruction. The salvation experienced by those who commit themselves to God may be conceived as a deliverance from the power of these satanic tendencies that operate in the human personality and in human society.

Modern psychology has come to recognize in these destructive tendencies an inheritance from our animal ancestry. Among man's animal ancestors, the principle of natural selection operated in such a way that those hereditary strains which were most successful in destroying their enemies survived. Although man's survival becomes more and more dependent on his development of reason and his capacity for cooperation in society, the primitive, the instinctive endowment continues to operate.

The fact that man's bestial heredity is ever ready to rebel against the restraints imposed by reason and morality has always been recognized, but, until recently, it was assumed that it would do so only within the soul of the individual. In our day we have been made to realize that the bestial heredity may be resorted to in organizing entire nations for a world order, in which all moral law and reason are blacked out. *A large sector of the human race is still ready to answer the call of the wild instead of the call of God.*

2

THE MODERN RESURGENCE OF THE LAW
OF NATURAL SELECTION

This new role of man's bestial heredity is one to which many factors have contributed. Only one of these, the intellectual factor, will be touched on at this point. If we trace the intellectual genesis of the ideology that arrogantly and shamelessly acknowledges the revolt against moral law and reason, we shall be better able to understand it and to withstand it.

The first breach in man's intellectual defenses against the insurgence of his savage impulses came with the discovery that man cannot be considered as the sole purpose of creation. *The notion that everything in nature was designed to serve man and contribute to his salvation, which was universal throughout antiquity, received a severe shock with the acceptance of the Copernican astronomy.* That notion was easy of acceptance so long as men thought that the earth was the center of the universe, and that the heavenly luminaries, which revolved about the earth, were designed "for signs and for seasons, for months and for years." [5] It was easy then to people the regions above the firmament with God and His angels, all of them interested in aiding man to achieve salvation. But when it was discovered that the earth was only one of the smaller planets revolving about the sun, and that the sun itself and the whole solar system occupied a relatively small place in the universe, that notion was, if not shattered, at least subject to severe strain.

Then came another shock to the faith that man was the main concern of all nature, and that the moral law was the plan according to which the universe had been created. It came as a consequence of the series of discoveries of physical and mental traits possessed in common by man and beast. The skeptical assertion of Koheleth that "the superiority of man over the beast is naught," [6] an assumption which did not prevent our Sages from assuming the election of man to a totally different destiny as a child of God and object of His solicitous providence, was now vindicated by the cumulative evidence of morphological and functional resemblances between the human and animal organisms. Man seemed to be but one more experiment of nature, and not a unique and semi-divine order of being. If man was an animal, it became easy to justify his yielding to animal impulses, on the ground that it was *human* nature to behave in that manner.

But the greatest encouragement to revolt against the restraints of reason and morality came with the discovery by Darwin of the principle of natural selection. To be sure, Darwin himself drew no such inferences from his epoch-making discovery. He did not proceed from judgments of cause and effect to judgments of value. He applied his theory merely to the explanation of how existing species came into being; he deduced from it no normative principle of how men should behave.

But others who accepted his theory did not exercise the same restraint. Nietzsche, in particular, perceived in the doctrine of natural selection a justification for the vigorous assertion of all those tendencies of human nature which the doctrine of spiritual selection called on man to restrain and control. Salvation, in the sense of survival, was to be sought through the maximum assertion of all those powers that made for the success of men in their competitive struggle with their fellowmen. He denied the validity of the categories of good and evil, and the moral imperatives that the spiritual tradition of mankind had associated with the good. He derived from Darwin's unassuming formula of natural selection the new gospel that mankind needed to liberate it from the yoke of reason and the moral law. His doctrine expounded and elaborated by such men as Heinrich von Treitschke, Houston Chamberlain and Oswald Spengler seeped down to the masses, and served as a convenient rationalization, by which frustrated elements of the population could justify to themselves usurpation of power and savage onslaughts against the decent elements in society.

We have recently witnessed a great nation adopting the doctrine of natural selection as its gospel, in consequence of which it set itself to overrun, enslave and barbarize the world. In its "new order" it undertook to effect just that "transvaluation of values" for which Nietzsche pleaded, and to emulate the "virtues" of the "blond beast," Nietzsche's ideal of the superman.

To realize what the doctrine of natural selection implies, when made normative for human behavior, we have to set it off against the implications of the doctrine of spiritual selection. The doctrine of natural selection challenges the claim of the doctrine of spiritual selection that man is certain to survive and achieve the maximum of life as a human being by taming the beast in him and striving to be Godlike. Instead it would have man take over, for the sake of survival and maximal achievement, the process which presumably makes for survival among the sub-human species.

This means, in the first place, the primacy of instinct, of the irrational impulses as against reason and intelligence. Unbridled ambition, the intoxication of power, frenzied heroics—these are deemed preferable to moderation, common sense, balance. A nation is not to be guided in its policy by any universal ideals or objective truth, but to answer the call of blood and soil. The very existence of objective truth is challenged. Even mathematics is not deemed to have universal validity. For Germans, only German mathematics, whatever that may be, was true. As brilliant a mind as Spengler's hailed with joy the advent of the barbarian in man, who had risen to destroy the rational order: "The age-old barbarism," he wrote, "which for centuries lay bound and hidden under severe discipline of a high culture is again awakening that warlike healthy joy in one's own strength which despises the age of rationalistic thought and literature, that unbroken instinct of a strong race which wishes to live otherwise than under the pressure of a mass of books and bookish ideals." Elsewhere he says, "The more important a civilization is the more it resembles the formation of a noble animal or plant body."

Among a people and in an age in which philosophy abdicated its function of intellectual guidance, and was willing to pay such homage to the brutal and irrational elements of human nature, it is little wonder that there should have emerged as supreme leader such a personality as Hitler. He was the embodiment in action of the philosophy of Nietzsche and Spengler. When he stated his ambition in words, it was a statement of that doctrine in the first person: "I shall eradicate the thousands of years of human domestication. I want to see again in the eyes of youth the gleam of the beast of prey. A youth will grow up before which the world will shrink." By the cunning manipulation of all the diabolic forces at work in modern society, he sought to realize this mad ambition.

A second implication of the doctrine of natural selection which sets it against the doctrine of spiritual selection is that natural selection exalts inequality as a creative principle in human life, whereas the doctrine of spiritual selection sees in the effort to establish equality among men through just laws and the exercise of compassion and kindness an evidence of divine creativity. The ideology of fascism not only accepted as normal and desirable such inequalities as existed among men, but it deliberately conjured up imaginary inequalities for the sake of creating actual inequalities where none existed. It trumped up false theories about strong and weak races, and declared that the former must become master races and the latter slave races. Thus both real and fictitious inequalities were utilized to encourage the German will to domination and to free it from the yoke of the moral law.

In contrast to this attitude toward inequality based on natural selection, consider Rousseau's statement: "It is precisely because the force of circumstances always tends to destroy equality that the force of legislation should tend to maintain it." In contrast to the assumption of the doctrine of natural selection that, because man is descended from the beast, he must seek his salvation by means similar to those by which the sub-human species insured their survival, the doctrine of spiritual selection sees in man's reason and ethical aspirations the evidence of a different destiny from that of the other species and stresses the human differentia. These distinctively human endowments put at man's disposal other means for survival than those available to the beasts, which makes human evolution proceed by a different principle. *What differentiates man from the beast is that his nature not only makes for the survival of the fittest, but aims to make the greatest possible number fit to survive.*

The doctrine of spiritual selection sees in this principle of making the greatest number fit to survive the destined direction of human evolution. Man has, as it were, been selected from among all orders of existence to find survival and self-realization through rational self-control and disinterested love. Man thus transcends the rest of nature in introducing a new method of survival. He, therefore, cannot accept natural inequalities as final, but seeks, in every way that he knows to enable every man to find the maximum of self-realization. That is to say, he acts in this way whenever he is most faithful to his human, in contrast to his sub-human, heritage. He then tries to secure for every human being the right to education, to comfort, to happiness, to the general participation in the fullness and opportunities of life. Such a conception of human nature reaffirms the dignity of man, which can thus have meaning only on the assumption of the equality of all men.

Finally, the doctrine of natural selection glorifies war; the doctrine of spiritual selection exalts peace. Since the struggle for existence is the condition that gives the strong the opportunity to survive through their strength, it was welcomed by the advocates of fascism as necessary to the achievement of the will to dominate. It was regarded as the occasion and opportunity for the display of those martial virtues which alone constituted human excellence. But peace was derided by these neo-pagans as encouraging softness and weakness. Its emphasis on law, on the binding force of covenants, on processes of reconciliation and resolution of conflicting interests were ridiculed as sentimental humanitarianism. When men adopt the law of natural selection as their norm, they inevitably conclude that might creates right. Right is what helps in the struggle for power. A treaty or obligation is valued and kept only as long as it is deemed to be useful. Only thus is it possible to maintain a state of war in which man threatens man, and one people the other people. Then men revert to the primal savagery of wolves, and seek their self-fulfillment in struggle and conquest.

3

THE REAL ISSUE BEFORE MANKIND: SHALL IT BE NATURAL OR SPIRITUAL SELECTION?

The strange fate of communism is most instructive in illustrating the corrupting influence of the doctrine of natural selection, when taken as the norm for human conduct. In its origin, socialism was a movement to carry out more fully the process of spiritual selection. For it sought to carry over into the economic field the egalitarian principles which the Enlightenment had made part of the political theory and practice of democratic nations. The tragic plight of the dispossessed classes led to the quest of a new economic order in which the resources of the earth and the fruits of the collective labor of men would be equitably shared. How could a movement dedicated to such a purpose give rise to the sort of totalitarian, dictatorial regime that characterizes the Soviet Union?

The explanation is to be found in Karl Marx's effort to convince himself that socialism would triumph by putting it on a "scientific" basis. To make it appear scientific and its triumph inevitable, he devised an elaborate theory of class-struggle, which fits into the pattern of the struggle for existence. He attempted to prove that, in this struggle, the advantage eventually would lie with the proletariat, if only they became conscious of their class interests and pressed their advantage ruthlessly, without regard to moral inhibitions. Just as Nietzsche denied any objective validity to the moral law, and conceived it merely as a device of the weak to tame the strong in their own interests, a "slave morality," so Marxism ridicules, as "bourgeois morality," the moral scruples, which might conceivably stand in the way of the proletarian revolution. Just as fascism regarded the national interest, so communism regards the class interest, as the only norm, and repudiates the very concept of universal law equally applicable for all men.

It is impossible to repudiate the authority of universal reason and moral law, without unleashing those sub-human traits inherited from man's animal ancestry, which that law seeks to control. Once these traits are unleashed, there is no telling what mischief they may effect. Reliance on force, combined with the denial of spiritual values, always makes for the domination of the strong over the weak; hence the inherent contradiction in communism. Although differing in origin and in original purpose, fascism and communism come in time to resemble each other very closely because of their common reliance on natural rather than on spiritual selection. Because communism also stresses man's common heritage with the brute, rather than that differentia which impels him to share in the divine process of making the greatest number of human beings fit to survive and to make the most of their lives, it tends before long, to take on all the vices of sinister nationalism.

In the light of the foregoing discussion, the real question at issue is: *Will mankind answer the call of the wild, and reinstate the process of natural selection? Or will it come to answer the call of God, and submit to the process of divine selection?*

As Jews, our situation in the world, and our historic tradition, both commit us to answering the call of God. We are a weak, harassed and persecuted minority. We can survive only in a world in which the processes of spiritual selection will reign supreme. The whole of Jewish experience, both past and present, should therefore lead to an affirmation of the principle of spiritual selection. This thought is implied in a significant *midrash* which sees, in the very persecution to which the Jews were subject, evidence of their being God's chosen. " 'God seeks out the persecuted.' [7] Because Israel was persecuted by the other nations, God elected Israel." [8] For the Jewish people, the suffering imposed on them by the strong and cruel made them realize that their source of salvation must be the spirit that seeks to restrain domination and cruelty and to establish the supremacy of love and peace. They have suffered too much from brute force to worship it; they depend too much on the spirit not to acknowledge that as divine.

Our task as Jews is clear. As a people taught by bitter experience, we must, in teaching and in practice, bear witness to the truth that man's survival depends on his transcending the law of natural selection, and subjecting himself to the law of spiritual selection. Only thus will man succeed in taming his lust for domination and conquest, and in achieving a human society founded on justice and brotherly cooperation. All those who today are the victims of the chaos in human life bred by the process of natural selection are bidden to remember that, for the survival of humanity and of that which makes human life worthwhile, the only law of selection is the one on which all Jewish religion is based. That is the law enunciated by the Prophet Zechariah: [9] "Not by might nor by strength but by My spirit, saith the Lord."

2. FAITH

1

THE URGENT NEED FOR RELIGIOUS FAITH

The crisis in human affairs in our day has led many people to feel a deep need for religious faith. They are profoundly disillusioned with the materialistic outlook on life. Their reliance on the scientific control of natural forces as a solvent of all human ills has turned out to be illusory. Their expectation that out of contending social forces there would evolve a program of universal welfare has proved a will-o'-the-wisp.

Men would like to believe that the horrors and brutalities of the contemporary world are not the forerunners of ultimate doom; that the light of a new day, which will soon dawn, will dispel them as though they were a mere fantasmagoria of some hideous nightmare. Men would welcome a religious interpretation of life, which assured them of the indestructibility of spiritual values. They would welcome an interpretation of life, which assured them that life is worthwhile despite suffering; that there is a real and absolute difference between good and evil, and that it is well to identify oneself with the good, in spite of the apparent success of the wicked, that history, notwithstanding the chaos of our present social life is not meaningless, but is a process of creation out of which will emerge a nobler type of man.

Even though "man's inhumanity to man" has, in our day, assumed such vast proportions that all that men have ever held dear seems imperiled, yet there is something in the spirit of man, some stubborn instinct for life, that cries out against letting the drama of human history end as a senseless farce. That instinct demands not only the survival of the human race, but also the survival of those values by which and for which, men have lived: ideals of truth, righteousness and mercy. But can that instinct be trusted? Do our ideals give us an insight into reality, or are they mere deceptive lures?

There can be no question of the survival value of the religious affirmation of life, if only we can be sure that our confidence is not misplaced. Consider the case of the sensitive modern woman who is afraid to bring children into the world such as it is today, lest, at some future time, they curse the day on which they were born. What frustration of the instinct for life is involved in this attitude! What a denial of the opportunity of achieving the dignity and importance of motherhood, of becoming indispensable to a child born of her love and labor and dependent on her care, protection and guidance! What unnatural abdication of the privilege of achieving that terrestrial immortality through one's posterity that human beings have always desired!

It may be that, by this self-denial, the woman of today is refraining from adding to the number of the innocent victims of violence and injustice. But it is also true that she is thereby helping to turn over the world to the posterity of those very people that have converted it into a shambles, and who glory in reproducing abundantly after their kind a race of ruthless brigands and gangsters. Would not such a woman welcome a religious faith that assured her that she could trust her instinct to bring children into the world, and need not fear that they will deplore having been born of her, because they will find life worthwhile, no matter how much suffering it may entail? Would she not be glad to bring children into the world, if she could feel assured that, even if suffering be their lot, they would still be grateful for the gift of life, would bless her for having made their life possible, and nurtured them, when they were still too young to take care of themselves?

Or consider the situation of the young man who is experiencing difficulties in his quest for a livelihood. He would like to fulfill the normal cycle of human life. In his childhood, he was sheltered in the parental home and was dependent on the care and toil of his parents, and now that he is grown, he would like to establish a home with the woman of his choice, and to assert his manhood in becoming himself the responsible protector and provider of a family. But he has difficulty in getting and keeping his job. He sees others rising to affluence by corrupt, dishonest and unscrupulous behavior. He fears that his dreams of family life may never come true, and, in the meantime, he is tempted into sex adventures that he knows are a shoddy substitute for the love experience to which he looks forward; but he is prone to accept them, nevertheless, as being more easily attainable.

He is beset by doubt on every side. He is told that honesty in business is a code by which the propertied class finds it easier to exploit those that are without possessions, that the only golden rule in business is: "Do others or they'll do you." He is told that to inhibit his sex impulses in the interest of a spiritual ideal is sentimental rubbish, that romantic love is an illusion and that the institution of the family is a relic of a patriarchal age and an anachronism in modern times, and that only fools permit themselves to be inhibited by tabus and social conventions. He cannot yield to these temptations without feeling his life cheapened and degraded. He cannot resist them, without knowing that he is denying himself satisfactions that might be his. He could deprive himself of these immediate satisfactions, if he believed that in every situation there is a right and a wrong, and that in resisting the temptation to do wrong, he is discarding a lesser satisfaction for a greater; that he is thereby achieving something worthwhile. He would like to believe in a moral law which is divine and makes life worthwhile for those who abide by it, whereas none can violate it, without injury to one's deepest interests. The faith in God, as a Power who manifests Himself in a moral law as inviolable in its operation as the law of gravity, would be most acceptable to our youth in the hour of temptation—if only they could be convinced that there is a God who can make resistance to temptation worthwhile.

Consider the demand voiced again and again not only by religious leaders, but by philosophers, scientists, educators, publicists and statesmen for an ideological basis for the democratic way of life, one that would command as much enthusiasm for democracy as fascism and communism seem to have aroused in their adherents. Does it not bear testimony to the need of a religious faith that history has a meaning and that that meaning, rightly read, is a confirmation of the democratic ideal? Can democracy work? Does representative government necessarily involve a debating-club-parliamentarism incapable of decisive action? Does economic freedom necessarily involve insecurity and unemployment? Does freedom of speech necessarily prevent the spiritual unification of the nation by subjecting it to a confusing multiple leadership? Can a system of education be devised that shall do justice to the need for individual independence and creative thinking as well as for voluntary cooperation in behalf of common welfare? Can government be invested with sufficient power to suppress anti-social behavior, and at the same time be trusted not to suppress individual liberty and initiative?

All these are questions that democracy must answer in deeds, not words. But to be able to work out a program that shall provide an affirmative answer to these questions, men must believe that such an answer exists.

2

RELIGIOUS FAITH A FUNCTION OF THE WILL TO LIVE

Faith in God cannot come to us by the mere process of reasoning. All such argument necessarily moves in a circle. Philosophers, who set about proving the existence of God, always believed in God, before they began to think up arguments that proved His existence, so that what concerns us is how they came to believe in God in the first place. It would never have occurred to men to conceive of God, had life run smoothly. But when men were aware of needs, the fulfillment of which was necessary to make life worthwhile, and were aware at the same time that the fulfillment of these needs depended on other factors than their own wills, they were impelled to believe in a Power at work in the universe on which they could depend to satisfy their needs. There is nothing in logic to prove that there must necessarily exist the means of fulfilling human needs. The fact that some men's needs have been satisfied so that they have found life worth living, has given rise to the feeling that the world is governed by a Power that does provide for man whatever is necessary to make life worthwhile for him. *Men must acquire a religious faith, not by being reasoned to about God, but by experiencing God's power in making life worthwhile.*

Men do not learn to see objects by being taught about the power of light; the fact that they can see implies light. Modern man is in the position of a man going blind, or rather, of the whole race of men going blind at the same time; they are not certain whether something is wrong merely with their power of sight, or whether light was only a passing phenomenon, and not an essential aspect of the universe, and they yearn to be convinced that light is real, and that there is a possibility of their seeing again.

The fact, that we cannot prove by reasoning that there is a God need not trouble us at all as invalidating our belief in Him. One of the most important insights of modern thought is the recognition that man cannot learn the nature of things, as attempted formerly by academic and scholastic philosophers, namely, by merely analyzing ideas; that, to learn nature, we must experiment with her; that our understanding of reality is not derived from reason, but from experience. The function of reason is to point out possible inconsistencies in our ideas about things, because consistency is, after all, a criterion of truth and necessary to a correct interpretation of experience. Reason can never take the place of experience. *Men have attained to a profound and satisfying faith in God through experience rather than through reason. But through what sort of experience? That is the question which it is of utmost importance for modern man to answer.*

There are two ways of learning by experience: by that of others, and by our own. What we learn by our own experience is, indeed, more fully integrated into our lives, more completely a part of our very selves than what we learn indirectly through the experience of others. That is what is meant by the saying: "experience is the best teacher." But to learn by trial and error in experimenting with our own lives has its dangers. It is surely the course of wisdom to learn as much as we can from the experience of others. How have men, who stand out in the tradition of mankind as the heroes of faith, come by those convictions of which so many of us are desperately in need? What we learn from them we can then later apply in our own lives, and test by our own experience.

It was doubtless with some such purpose in view that the anonymous Prophet, whose prophecies are recorded in the latter part of the Book of Isaiah, addressed these words to the people of his generation:

> "Hearken to me, ye that follow after righteousness,
>   Ye that seek the Lord;
>   Look unto the rock whence ye were hewn,
>   And the hole of the pit whence ye were digged.
>   Look unto Abraham your father." [1]

Apparently the generation of the so-called Deutero-Isaiah period (the generation on whom devolved the duty of laying the foundations of the new Zion in the face of innumerable obstacles) were also in search of a sustaining faith. They, too, were seeking the Lord. That is, they were seeking a religious faith to validate their "following after righteousness" in the face of discouragement. And the Prophet directs them to Abraham as the exemplar of a sturdy faith. If they were discouraged that they who held to the vision of a righteous world were so few, they were reminded that the promise, to which their faith committed them, originated in the experience of a single individual, their ancestor in flesh and spirit:

"For when he was but one I chose him,
and I blessed him and made him many." [2]

We may well take the Prophet's advice today, and see what the career of Abraham, as interpreted in Jewish tradition, may have to teach us. For Abraham lives in Jewish tradition as the founder of the faith, who "believed in God" and whose belief "was accounted to him as righteousness." At God's behest, he left "his land, his kindred and his father's house," in order to become "in the land that God would show him" the father of a people in whom "all the families of the earth shall be blessed." In his love of God, he committed himself and his posterity "to keep the way of the Lord, by dealing rightly and justly." He persisted in his faith, when it was put to the supreme test by God's bidding him sacrifice "thy son, thine only one, whom thou lovest," the very son through whom God had previously promised to raise up for him a uniquely blessed progeny.

Rabbinic comment on the story of Abraham and the folklore that gathered about his personality particularly delighted in stressing the persistence of Abraham's faith in the face of challenge.[3] The test on Mount Moriah was but the last and most formidable of ten tests by which Abraham's faith was tried, and through which it persisted.

Religious faith, as exemplified in the career of Abraham, is not merely belief in God and the spiritual values on which that belief is based, but it is a belief that is maintained in the face of the most adverse circumstances that entail sacrifice and suffering of the highest degree. Instead of such sacrifice and suffering resulting in loss of faith, it had the very opposite effect. Abraham's faith did not abandon him even under the most trying circumstances; his ability to survive those circumstances, with his faith intact, strengthened that faith, gave to his moral purpose a self-confidence that might otherwise have been lacking, and convinced him that his life was being sustained by a divine power for a blessed end.

Religious faith is a function of the will to live as manifest in man. It is the recognition in us of a vital strength that links us with the inexhaustible life of the universe, with the "life of the worlds," with God. Every victory of the spirit that makes for more abundant life strengthens that spirit, gives it self-confidence and courage. And such victories of the spirit are not necessarily victories which the world recognizes as such. *Whenever we courageously face danger, in the interest of an ideal, we experience within us a triumph of life over death, that bears witness to the reality of God.* Even if we die in the effort, our death is a triumph of life, for it is the vital interest of the race that impels us to persevere in our ideal, and our dying has, by its necessity in the service of life, justified itself to us. Study the lives of the men of faith and vision, and you will find invariably that they are the lives of men who persevered in the pursuit of their ideals undaunted by suffering or danger. Pessimism and cynicism are often found among men who, from the vantage point of a relatively secure and comfortable existence, look fearfully out upon the horrors of life around them, and are obsessed by a sense of impotence. But pessimism and cynicism are seldom to be found among those actively engaged in fighting evil, even though they be fighting in what, so far as the immediate issue is concerned, is a lost cause.

The choice with which modern man is confronted is between two ways of life: the one, that of democracy which is based on belief in the divinity of "righteousness and justice," which the Torah identifies as "way of the Lord;" the other, that of totalitarianism, based on the aggressive will to power, with domination as the supreme expression of the meaning of life. Which of these assumptions is correct cannot be proved by argument. One can make out as good a theoretical case for one as for the other. Our preference, both as Jews and as Americans, is clearly for the democratic way of life. We want to believe in it; we need to believe in it. We are, therefore, grateful for the example of men whose faith persisted through ordeals that again and again challenged its validity.

In the Rabbinic comments on the meaning of Abraham's life, we find (if we know how to read between the lines) the explanation of how persistence in our faith in spite of suffering, temptation and apparent defeat, strengthens our conviction of its truth. To understand these comments, however, we must realize that the problem of faith presented itself to our Sages in a different form than it does to us. They took God for granted. It never occurred to anybody in their generation to doubt the existence of a Power who was able to make human life happy and blessed, if He so willed. Therefore, the challenge to faith took the form of the question: "Why, if there is a just God, do the righteous suffer and the wicked, to all appearances, prosper?" We, on the other hand, start out with human experience. We want to find in that experience ground for faith that there is a God on whom men can depend for making life worthwhile. For us, therefore, the question is: "In the face of the fact that the righteous suffer and the wicked prosper, how can we believe in God, in the reality of a Power in the world other than ourselves, on whom we can depend for the satisfaction of our needs?" To understand the full significance of the Rabbinic comments on the life of Abraham, we must, as it were, transpose them from the key of the ancient mode of thought, which was God-centered, to that of the modern way of thought which is man-centered.

If we bear in mind this difference of viewpoint, we can see that their comments have reference to the psychological realities to which attention has been called. Thus one comment states the problem in the following parable: [4] "If a man has two animals, one strong the other weak will he not, by preference put the yoke on the strong animal?" Another compares God to a potter who does not take the trouble to test earthenware which he knows to be so fragile that a touch will break it, but tests only such of his products as give evidence of strength. A third compares Him to one who prepares flax for spinning. Part of the process is to beat the flax, and although the poorer quality of flax is destroyed by this process, the better quality is improved thereby.

These comments are of course, unsatisfactory as a theodicy which attempts to justify God's treatment of the righteous by putting them to the test of suffering. No theodicy, which assumes that God must use evil means to achieve good ends, can serve its purpose. But transposed in the manner we suggest, each of these explanations has something to tell us, not about God's dealing with men, but about men's experience of God.

In saying that God imposes the yoke on the strong rather than on the weak, the Rabbinic author of the parable attests that *the work of God, i.e. the improvement of the world, is achieved by those who accept the yoke of tribulation and suffering.* The homily of the potter who tests the strong and not the weak pots, implies that *it is a mark of moral weakness and inferiority to yield to discouragement, when perseverance in the defense of our ideals involves sacrifice and danger.* The comparison of the trials of the righteous with the process of beating the flax suggests the further thought that *trials and tribulations not only reveal the strength or weakness of our moral fibre, but, unless we are made of very poor stuff to begin with, actually strengthen our moral fibre.* That access of new strength is the very experience of God's help which confirms our faith in Him. Thus, these ancient Rabbinic homilies, although they fail in their purpose to "justify the ways of God to man," succeed in justifying man's perseverance in the ways of God. They are intended to confirm man's faith that his moral insights are real, that his true interests in life demand his acceptance of moral responsibility, come what may.

That is what can be learned from the experience of all the heroes of the spirit in every age and among every people as to the method of reassuring ourselves that there is a God who will make it worthwhile for us to live. By being *faithful* to Him, by dismissing from our hearts that doubt in the value of our ideals which is the counsel of cowardice, and persevering in our efforts to realize them, we experience such a strengthening of our will to live, such a rallying of our moral forces, such an assertion of our personality, such a resolution of the conflict between impulse and inhibition that our whole nature is transformed and glorified in the process. And whence this new strength, if not from "the fountain of life," from God?

That faith in life which is born of the very travail of the modern world is well summed up in the words expressed by the chief character in Robert Sherwood's play *There Shall Be No Night.* After hearing the news of his son's death and before engaging in the desperate fighting which cost him his own life, he writes a letter to his wife which contains these words: "Erik and the others who give their lives are also giving to mankind a symbol—a little symbol, to be sure, but a clear one—of man's unconquerable aspiration to dignity and freedom in the sight of God."

Such is the lesson of faith that may be learned from the experience of others; to make it really our own, we ourselves must put it to the test of experience. Life today is testing the Jewish people. Will it find us of the same tough fibre that is strengthened by suffering, or are we—to recall the Rabbinic homily—the inferior flax that is destroyed by beating? At no time in its history has our people been subject to more widespread hostility or more cruel torment of body and mind than at the present time. Even our own country has not escaped the infection of anti-Semitism.

Shall we then say: "This is the end?" Shall we bemoan with Heine, "Judaism is not a religion but a misfortune?" Shall we seek to make the best, that is, the safest individual adjustment to our situation, and liquidate Jewish community life, as many, even of our communal leaders, would have us do? Shall we accept the conclusion that the Zionist dream is over? Shall we write our own obituary, as a people, and as an historic religious movement?

Or shall we identify ourselves with the spirit of our father Abraham? Shall we look upon the will to destroy us as a divine test, as an opportunity not only to show our strength, but to acquire strength, by our resistance to evil and assertion of our faith in God? Shall we answer our detractors not with apologetics, not with eulogies of our past achievements that, in effect, are elegies to a dead past, but with a scornful silence, while we go about in the pursuit of our own ideals? Shall we answer the spirit of hate unleashed by anti-Semitism with deeds of courage, as well as with compassionate love for all who are oppressed and hounded? Shall we answer the attempt to destroy Zion, by persisting in its rebuilding? When the Babylonians were at the gates of Jerusalem, and the doom of the nation that the Prophets had long predicted was imminent, Jeremiah bought land in Eretz Yisrael, as a testimony of his faith in Israel's divine title to his land.[5] Shall we not contribute now more than ever to Zionist funds, in similar testimony of our faith in the future of our people?

In the persistence of the *yishuv* of Eretz Yisrael through all the hardships they have had to endure, through all the violence directed against them and all the betrayals to which they have been subject, we have another example of the perseverance in faith that justifies and confirms faith. There is a song in Eretz Yisrael, born of the resistance of anti-Jewish riots, which has a sort of refrain: *af-al-pi-ken velamrot hakol,* "nevertheless and in spite of everything!" That is the spirit of the *yishuv,* that is the spirit of Abraham, that is the spirit of religious faith. If, indeed, we feel that the need of the hour for Israel and for mankind is a firm conviction in the reality of God, and we should like that conviction to be our own, this is what we must do: *we must strive with all our might to realize our ideals, and, whenever we are confronted with seemingly insuperable obstacles to their realization we must say to ourselves: af-al-pi-ken velamrot hakol, "nevertheless and in spite of everything!"* We shall then be surprised and delighted with our own strength, and, whether we succeed or fail in our immediate objectives, we shall not feel that our life has been wasted. We shall know, not inferentially and by persuasion, but at first hand and by experience, that there is a Power that makes for human salvation. We shall know God.

8. HOPE

1

THE KIND OF FUTURE PRE-MODERN MAN HOPED FOR

To find life in the present worth living, men must have faith in a future. The ultimate in human tragedy is not suffering or even death, but hopelessness. This is the true meaning of damnation. Men have been known to suffer all manner of torments and to maintain, through them all, a deep and abiding interest in life, to experience life as worth living. Martyrs, like Akiba and Socrates, have gone to their death with serenity, because they believed that their death was not the final verdict on all they lived for. But it is hell to suffer evils without feeling that there is anything that we can do about them, or without the confidence that they will be abolished.

It is the function of religion to save men from this hell, and Jewish religion did so function. How keenly our Sages appreciated the need of faith in a future to give meaning and worth to the present is beautifully expressed in a *midrash* that comments on the prayer of Jacob at Beth El. We are told in Genesis that Jacob, when fleeing from the wrath of his brother Esau, was accorded a vision of God in a dream, and when he awoke, he set up the stone, on which he had lain, as a pillar and vowed that, if permitted to return in safety, *vehayah adonay li lelohim*, "the Lord shall then be my God." [1] In saying this, our Sages explain, "Jacob gave expression to the key-word by means of which God would in future ages redeem his descendants." [2] All the solace and bliss that would fall to the lot of Israel would be theirs, by virtue of the rallying cry *vehaya*, "it shall come to pass," that is to say, by virtue of faith in the future.

Indeed, *the faith in the future, which characterized the religious heritage of the Jewish people proved the key-principle of salvation not only to them, but to the Western world*, which took over that principle along with other treasures of the Jewish heritage that went into the making of Christianity. By its use, the world was redeemed from the deepening gloom into which it had fallen, and from which the classic paganism of Greece and Rome was inadequate to save it.

In the ancient world, there was little in life, as the majority of men experienced it, to encourage an optimistic view of the possibilities of human living. Poverty, oppression and war were so generally prevalent as to seem inherent in the nature of things. Disease, accidents and death all seemed alike unpreventable and inscrutable manifestations of the will of God. The pessimistic assumption of Koheleth, that "the crooked cannot be made straight" [3] seemed to be borne out both by every day experience and by the records of life, which had been handed down from past ages. In relation to the fundamental ills that beset men, nothing seemed ever to change. The possibility that men could alter the natural conditions of life by scientific study of nature and the application of human ingenuity to technological problems never entered their minds. And that men could take it into their own hands to change the structure of human society was even more remote from their thought. That they could challenge laws which had been presumably handed down to their fathers by God or the gods, and deliberately adopt constitutions for governing themselves according to their own notions, was beyond their wildest imagination. Just as modern man assumes that human life is in constant process of evolutionary change, so the ancient world assumed the opposite, namely, that human life is merely the weary repetition of a changeless cycle, that "what hath been is that which shall be, and there is nothing new under the sun." [4]

Nevertheless, the will to live, which is active in all men in all ages, protests against the notion that life is meaningless, and that suffering has no end. People, therefore, commonly assumed that the ills of human life were not part of God's original intention for mankind. They took it for granted that somehow all the evils to which men are heir must be due to a corruption of mankind, by which men forfeited their divine heritage of happiness. The world of antiquity was almost unanimous in believing in a Golden Age, at the dawn of the human race. For the Jews, this was depicted in the life of Adam and Eve, before their sin. From the Greek world comes the very term "Golden Age," which was followed by the "Silver Age" and the progressively deteriorating ages to the "Iron Age," in which the world then lived.

But here the parallel between the Greek and the ancient Jewish viewpoint ends, and a significant difference must be noted. Among the Greeks, the conviction of the degeneracy of man and nature was unmitigated by any hope for the future. They assumed that, in the end, even the gods, from whom they received whatever measure of good they still enjoyed would be overwhelmed by fate. Not so the Jews. The same zest for living, which convinced them that life could not have been intended by God to contain all the ills that it did contain, led them to trust that, in the future, these ills would be abolished. The same vital logic, which led them to assume that there must have been a Golden Age for mankind in the past, led them to posit a similar Golden Age in the future.

This faith arose among the Jews in the darkest hour of their history, just as Jacob's faith in his future was inspired by a vision that cheered him when he was a lonely wanderer, with nothing to look forward to. It was when the destruction of the Jewish people was impending that the hope of a Messiah, a divinely sent redeemer was born. The longer the Messiah delayed in making his appearance, the more glorious became the blessings that were to be associated with his coming. In time, those blessings came to include not only the liberation of Israel from exile and from subservience to other nations, and the abolition of every yoke of unjust and tyrannical rule, but even the regeneration of nature itself. As originally intended in Eden, where the way to the Tree of Life was not barred until Adam sinned, human life was at last to be freed from the curse of death, to become immortal. Moreover, those of the people who had been loyal to God's Torah during their life would not be prevented by their death from participating in this new Golden Age of the future, but would be resurrected, in order that they might share in it. Thus, the days of the Messiah came to be merged with the idea of a world to come, a miraculous era of redemption to be effected by the will of God.

This vision of the future, however remote, gave our ancestors something to live for in spite of all that they had to suffer. If misfortune entered their life, it did not mean that they were unloved and of no account. It might be an act of punishment, to admonish them, and thus lead them to improve their ways and merit a share in the world to come, "For whom the Lord loveth He chasteneth, even as a father the son in whom he delighteth." [5] If they were oppressed, there was no danger of their oppression leading them to self-contempt or self-hate. *In the light of the more hopeful destiny that awaited them, they could afford to be contemptuous of their oppressors and to declare: "It is better to be of the persecuted than of them that persecute."* [6]

The Torah, obedience to which determined the Jews' claim to the world to come, was the main preoccupation of the Jewish people. Jews studied its teachings to the minutest details, with a view to practicing them. To outsiders the number of regulations to which the Jew thus became subject seems an intolerable burden. But it did not seem so to the Jew, who felt that the Torah was God's instrument of salvation, that "because God desired Israel's justification, he has made the Torah great and mighty." [7] For the Jews, the study of the Torah and the practice of the *mitzvot* made life worth living. "Thy statutes have become my songs, in the house of my sojourn." [8]

In the Western world, faith in the world to come, which was taken over from Judaism, assumed a somewhat different form under the influence of Greek thought. Already toward the end of the pagan era, the increasing discontent and the need for some form of salvation had motivated religious movements among the Greeks. These movements found expression in rituals designed to confer immortality upon men, by assuring their apotheosis, or their merging with some divinity after death. Inasmuch as these religious movements did not have their source in the official religion of the Olympic gods, but were cultivated by private esoteric cults, their objective was the individual salvation of their adherents, not the salvation of mankind. Their task was not to redeem the world, but to redeem men from the world, by promising them bliss in the Elysian fields, after their death.

Greek philosophy, moreover, by identifying matter with that which is subject to change, accident and death, and by regarding form, idea or spirit as changeless and immortal, helped to sharpen the contrast between spirit and body. Under the combined influence of that philosophy and the esoteric cults of the day, Christian thought came to conceive of the world-to-come as identical with the survival of the soul after death in some blissful state of existence, entirely apart from the earthly scene. Jewish medieval philosophers, notably Maimonides, [9] drew similar conclusions from their study of Greek philosophy. But for the Jewish masses, *ha-olam ha-ba* meant, not another world in the sense of a purely spiritual state of being, but a *future era for this world*, miraculously freed from all the ills of our present life. In the enjoyment of that era the righteous, who had died, would share after experiencing bodily resurrection.

It is in the temper of our age to condemn as an opiate such religious faith in a future. Such hope, it is said, promises relief from all the ills flesh is heir to, without our having to give thought as to how they are to be removed, and encourages the resigned acceptance of intolerable evils. That criticism, however, is shallow, in that it never stops to ask what would have been the alternative, if men, in those days, had been deprived of this opiate. For medicinal purposes opiates are often prescribed as necessary anodynes. Without them, the shock of pain might kill the patient.

The alternatives that confronted the world in antiquity and in the Middle Ages were not: Shall men hope in a divine redemption from evil, or redeem themselves from evil? The alternatives were: Shall men hope in a divine redemption from evil, or acquiesce in evil as normal and legitimate? To have chosen the latter alternative would have been to yield to defeatism, to regard the evil as normal. It would not have given more significance and value to social life, and it would have deprived personal life of the significance which the hope of other-worldly salvation gave to it.

The recognition of a divine law governing human salvation, and of a divine love that human beings could court, gave direction, purpose and importance to the lives of men and women. It not only made for their personal well-being and happiness, but also for more amiable and less cruel and brutal social relations than would otherwise have prevailed. And it preserved the ideal of a better life, of a Kingdom of God, for such time as men might, with the aid of subsequently acquired knowledge and skill, be able to utilize that ideal as a pragmatic program.

2

THE KIND OF FUTURE MODERN MAN HOPES FOR

The Renaissance seemed to be the dawn of a new era. Men began to recover confidence in the possibility of human achievement and to become interested in the satisfaction of the natural human impulses directed to this-worldly goals, in the acquisition of wealth, in the enjoyment of comforts and luxuries, in the assertion of ambition, in seeking adventure, in gratifying curiosity, in expressing themselves through the arts. At first the changes in outlook and attitude proceeded slowly, but with the development of a scientific technique for understanding nature and employing its powers for human uses, the tempo of change accelerated, until it reached the giddy pace of our own day. For a time, the awareness that life was not static, that change could and did occur, that man could, through science, change radically the conditions of his life resulted in a great wave of optimism. Men turned then from the hope of other-worldly salvation to faith in a millennial future for mankind on earth, to faith in that "one far off divine event to which the whole creation moved." Men believed that modern technology would be able to produce in abundance all that men needed to make living secure and comfortable, that preventive medicine would conquer disease, that universal education would abolish superstition, and that democratic government would actually bring about liberty, equality and fraternity among men.

The older generation whose youth was spent before the first World War has no difficulty in recalling the hopeful spirit of youth that prevailed in those days, the confidence of men that, with even moderate intelligence, industry and thrift, one could look forward to a reasonably secure and happy life, while the exceptionally gifted looked forward to fame, or fortune, or both. Those were the days when every boy born in the United States was regarded as a potential President. Not even the disillusioning experience of that first World War could suffice to shatter this mood. That War was believed to be Armageddon; its sufferings were thought to be the birth-pangs of the messianic era; it was a war to end war, and to make the world safe for democracy. When the War actually was over, many hailed the League as a fulfillment of Tennyson's optimistic vision of the "Parliament of man, the Federation of the World."

Then came a financial depression, the rise of communism and fascism, a brief era of cynical appeasement and finally a blackout of civilization in Europe that threatened a complete debacle of all that men of good will have hoped and yearned for through the ages. That cycle is being repeated. Great victory followed by an international scramble for power, dishonesty, infiltration, unrest, disillusionment, deflation, depression, and then—will it be war again, and the last war? The youth of today is perhaps the most unhappy, uninformed or misinformed generation of youth that the world has known. It faces grim and bitter prospects, without faith in a supernatural, other-worldly salvation to compensate for the sacrifices and the suffering recently and presently endured, and bitterly disillusioned. In contrast with the former generations who thought of evolution as an inevitable change in the direction of a better world, modern youth looks upon evolution as insuring the survival only of those who are most brutal and unscrupulous in lording it over their fellowmen.

If youth in general faces the future with gloom and trepidation, this is infinitely more true of Jewish youth. The forces that are turning life into a nightmare have seized upon the Jew as the symbol of all that they are determined to destroy. Upon him falls the worst on-slaught of their fury, and the rest of the world is afraid to come to his assistance. When men dreamed millennial dreams of the future of mankind after the first World War, the messianic dream seemed almost to be patterned after its classic expression in Scripture. It was to include the restoration of the Jewish people to its homeland. After the second World War, Jewish refugees were being turned away even from Eretz Yisrael by the very power that was given a mandate to facilitate the establishment of the Jewish national home.

We always seem to be confronted with the alternative of either ac-cepting the present situation as the norm, with its violence, falsehood and hate as the ultimate reality, or we must seek to save ourselves from demoralization by applying the traditional key-principle of salvation, *vehayah*, "it shall come to pass." There is still a future, and in it are concealed unfathomed possibilities for good. We cannot expect that future to come to pass by a miracle of divine intervention. We cannot dispense with the scientific method in the quest of knowledge and truth. The scientific method presupposes uniform and universal laws of nature. But we must not, in spite of the fiasco that mankind has made of its efforts to work out its salvation to the present time, give up the hope that salvation is achievable, if we seek it aright, that the time will yet come when war and the causes of war will be abolished, when there will be no oppressors or oppressed, when the world will not only be safe for democracy, but will be a democracy. We must believe that our desire for such a world is a divine command to achieve it in order to find life worth living. We must realize, too, that the striving to achieve it, if carried on with sincerity and perseverance, is itself part of the achievement.

That is the vision of the future to which we must cling and, in clinging to it, we shall find salvation. It will not spare us suffering, for now, as in the days gone by, "the reward of the righteous belongs to the future," [10] but it will spare us the humiliation of cringing before the power that strikes us down, admitting defeat. He who does not admit defeat remains undefeated. This vision will enable us to face dangers and difficulties without being overwhelmed. Our foe is teaching us the strategy by which we shall learn to circumvent and defeat him. So in-stead of feeling discouraged by our mistakes and misfortunes, let us learn from them and derive new courage from the very fact that we *can* learn from them. As our vision of the future appears more clearly to us, the evil in the world will cease to be an obsession that prevents us from beholding and enjoying the good there is in it.

When we recognize an evil, let us see whether we can do something to correct it. If we can, let us do it. If not, let us defer the correction of that evil until some future time, pressing on, meanwhile, to other goals that are immediately attainable. Our tactics in contending against evil should be those of modern, mobile warfare. When we encounter an obstacle that we cannot surmount, we need not let is stop us; we can bypass it while moving onward in the general direction of our goal, as determined by our ethical ideals.

There is a certain joy in the very battle with the forces of darkness. This zest of combat comes from merging ourselves with the eternal and unconquerable spirit that impels men in all ages to seek the good. We then feel as did the Psalmist [11] when he sang:

> "By Thee do I run upon a troop
> And by my God do I scale a wall."

This is the experience of salvation. It is not so much dependent on our attaining our goal as on our confidence that the goal is worth attaining, and on our wholehearted devotion to attaining it.

In this then we can evaluate the function of religion in the modern world. It is to preserve our morale, by keeping before us the vision of the brotherhood of man as the mundane goal of human effort. The fact that man can conceive that goal means that man can seek ways to realize it. There is no human being who, in his manifold relations to other persons and groups of persons, is not continually being given opportunities to further or obstruct that ideal. *Remote as is the day when it can be reasonably expected, from an objective analysis of conditions, that mankind will achieve a truly fraternal order, that future is nevertheless a key that can unlock the gates of salvation to us today.* For that ideal can give direction, purpose and value to all our acts, just as the hope of heaven, or of a share in the world to come, gave meaning and dignity to the lives of our fathers.

If the function of religion in general is to preserve morale by giving meaning and purpose to life in general, the specific function of Jewish religion is to preserve Jewish morale, by giving meaning and purpose to Jewish life. It must bring salvation to the Jewish people, by holding out the key of a Jewish future. That vision of the Jewish future cannot be something separate and apart from the vision of the future of humanity, for Jews are human beings. But it must be a future that gives such purpose and direction to the organized efforts of the Jewish people that they can bear even the tragic burden which the present imposes on them.

4. HUMILITY

1

BEING GODLIKE VS. PLAYING THE GOD

From time immemorial the problem of sin and suffering has occupied the human mind. Men have felt that human life is not what it ought to be, that it is very different from what God had originally designed for man. Somehow man, in the exercise of his freedom of will, must have taken a wrong step that set him on the wrong track, and frustrated God's benign purpose in creating the world. The ancients naturally ascribed this wrong step to the common ancestor of the human race, the first man. The sin of Adam, as told in the Biblical myth, is not merely *a* sin but the *original sin*, the archetype from which all sin, the source of all human suffering, springs. That sin is symbolically represented by the eating of the fruit of "the tree of the knowledge of good and evil." What made that act of such transcendent importance, so fatal in all its dire consequences, was that eating of this fruit had the effect of making man "like a god, knowing good and evil."

The sin that is symbolized by man's eating the fruit of the tree of the knowledge of good and evil has nothing to do with man's aspiration to imitate God's ways. It implies the very opposite of that aspiration, namely, the attempt of man to *play the part of a god*, to set himself up as a deity, to usurp God's role of law-giver and to become a law unto himself, to make his own desires the standard of his action, to *taste* for himself the *good* and the *evil* without reference to divine sanctions or to any law that says, "Thou shalt," or "Thou shalt not."

"Being like a god" is thus at the opposite pole of being Godlike, which is what the Torah would have man be. "Be you holy, for I the Lord, thy God am holy" [1] is given as the sanction for the observance of our religious precepts. Before creating man, God is represented in the Torah as saying, "Let us make man in our image, according to our likeness." [2] This would seem to imply that man's being Godlike was intended by God, and hence could not possibly be resented by Him. Our Sages, too, gave every encouragement to man's imitating God's ways. The injunction, "Thou shalt love the Lord thy God and cleave unto Him," they interpreted to mean that man was to "cleave to His attributes," to imitate Him; as God is merciful, so man should be merciful; as God is just so man should be just.[3]

If we interpret the symbolism of the Eden story in the light of the foregoing contrast, it immediately becomes clearly intelligible. *The sin, which is the source of all sins, and which may well be held responsible for the whole gamut of preventable human ills, is the abuse of human freedom by the attempt of men to make their own interests and passions the sole determinants of their behavior.* When we consider how mortal men have oppressed and exploited their fellowmen, and have ruthlessly disregarded the feelings, the needs, the very lives of the men and women whose vital powers they appropriated to their own uses as though they had indeed created them, it was not far-fetched to assume that even death came into the world out of the necessity of thwarting this tendency of men to play the god, and to make havoc of the world in doing so.

There are many other passages in the Bible, besides the story of Adam and Eve, that express this same thought. The sin of Nebuchadnezzar, the Babylonian tyrant, is made to figure, in a prophecy ascribed to Isaiah,[4] as this same sin of playing the god:

"And thou saidst in thy heart;
'I will ascend into heaven,
Above the stars of God
Will I exalt my throne:
And I will sit upon the mount of meeting,
In the uttermost parts of the north;
I will ascend above the heights of the clouds;
I will be like the Most High.' "

Ezekiel [5] denounces the ruler of Tyre in the same vein:

"Thus saith the Lord God:
'Because thy heart is lifted up,
And thou hast said, I am a god,
I sit in the seat of God,
In the heart of the seas;
Yet thou art man and not God,
Though thou didst set thy heart as the heart of God—'

Therefore thus saith the Lord God:
'Because thou hast set thy heart
As the heart of God,
Therefore will I bring strangers upon thee,
The terrible of the nations;

Wilt thou yet say before him that slayeth thee:
I am God?
But thou art man and not God,
In the hand of them that defile thee.' "

We might cite passage after passage, in which the Bible represents the assertion of arbitrary power by the proud and strong as a usurpation of the divine authority. The whole story of the exodus from Egypt is dominated by the thought that Pharaoh had to be humiliated and destroyed, because he had set himself up as a rival to God, challenging the divine authority with his supercilious: "Who is the Lord, that I should hearken to his voice to let Israel go?" [6] His doom was included in God's determination to execute judgment "on all the gods of Egypt." [7]

To such an extent did the assertion of arbitrary dictatorial power by any man seem a usurpation of divine prerogative that in Israel the whole institution of monarchy came in time to be suspect. It seemed almost inevitably to involve the self-deification of the king, a common practice among ancient peoples. This religious objection to monarchy is clearly expressed in the Book of Samuel. When Samuel is hurt that the people demand a king to rule over them, instead of being governed by his prophetic counsel, he prays to God and is answered in these words: "Hearken unto the voice of the people in all that they say unto thee; for they have not rejected thee, but they have rejected Me, that I should not be king over them." [8] In other words, monarchical government was regarded as equivalent to repudiation of the kingship of God. [9]

Playing the god and imitating God's ways are based on two radically different conceptions of God. Common to both is the assumption that the essence of godhood is being a source of salvation. But he who plays the god regards himself, his own individual ego, as the source of his salvation, whereas, he who imitates God's ways regards that source as transcending himself.

There exists in all of us a will to power. We have abilities and we like to use them. There is a satisfaction that accompanies every assertion of our will that achieves its object. Life seems to fulfill itself, when we succeed in getting whatever we want, in having our way in the world. Nature has imposed on us the responsibility for maintaining our life against all that opposes it. Self-preservation is the first law of nature. But self-preservation, as it functions in human beings means more than merely resisting from moment to moment whatever dangers happen to arise, or satisfying momentary hungers and wants as we become aware of them. It means seeking the maximum power to meet all future contingencies which our imagination can conjure up. That is why man's will to power can be so ruthless and insatiable. Man is never secure enough, never strong enough. He cannot be content until he is all-powerful, and his egoism becomes a self-deification, an identification of his will to live with the will to dominate his whole environment, both his social and his natural environment. *The abuse of power is said to be the occupational disease of being human.*

2

WHY MAN THINKS HIMSELF A GOD

When we regard the successful assertion of a self-centered will to power as evidence of divinity, as conferring on the individual who thus asserts himself authority to dominate others, we are deifying man. "If there were gods," said Nietzsche, "how could I endure not to be a god?" When we regard our own domination of others for selfish ends as legitimate, we are playing the god. In all ancient civilizations kings tended to be deified, because their will to power so imposed itself on their subjects that these recognized it as legitimate. Lacking similar power themselves, but deeming it supremely desirable, they worshiped it as clear manifestation of the divine, even though it imposed untold hardships upon them. And the tyrant himself could easily believe in his own divinity, for his authority was undisputed, and his power brought him the adoration and worship even of the victims of his lust for power.

In reality, the power that those tyrants possessed did not reside in themselves, as they imagined. That was an illusion largely created by the very worship that was accorded them. It was not the power of the Pharaohs, but the power in the muscles of their innumerable armies of slaves that built the pyramids. But, since a word from the Pharaohs could apparently set these hordes of slaves in motion to achieve the purposes of the Pharaohs, that power seemed to reside in them, and they felt themselves to be gods. It was for them to lay down the law, for their subjects to obey; they themselves had no law to which they felt responsible.

There is deep psychological and sociological insight in the percep-

tion that original *sin, the source of all preventable evils, lies in self-deification, in the assumption that the salvation of the individual can be achieved by self-assertion, without reckoning with a Power, not ourselves, that lays down the conditions of such achievement.* Both the tragedy and the dignity of human life derive from the circumstance that man has to effect, by deliberate conscious choice, a reconciliation of the interests of the individual and of the race which, among the so-called lower animals, is effected by instinct.

To say that self-preservation is the first law of nature is true, but misleading. Every organism tries to maintain its own life, when that does not interfere with maintaining the life of the species. But when it is a question of its own life and that of the species, nature provides animals with instincts that frequently compel them to endanger or even to sacrifice the life of the individual to that of the race. The salmon is a salt-water fish, but it must spawn in fresh water. Before the spawning season it will seek the shallow streams, exhausting itself in leaping up cataracts, in order to be able to reproduce its kind, and the effort often costs it its life. But it does this in obedience to a blind instinct, not to a conscious purpose.

But in man, there is always the awareness of many possible courses of action. Some of these seem to offer greater measure of security for the individual, some for society. But the choice has to be made consciously. Where there is a conflict between the common good and the interests of the individual, the choice has to be made consciously by the individual. That is why it is so easy for him to imagine that all depends on him individually, that his ego is supreme, that he is a god. It is in his power to taste of good and evil; that is why he thinks himself a god.

And yet, if we follow the story of Adam and Eve further, their tasting of good and evil, although it opens their eyes, it does so to a realization of disillusionment, of nakedness and of shame. Playing the god alienates man from God. It is bound to end in downfall and frustration. It is a mistake to assume that, because the human ego has freedom to choose between alternatives, it has absolute and arbitrary freedom. It can choose between alternatives, but it cannot foresee or determine the consequences to itself, or to others, of its own choice. Self-assertion can not lead to self-fulfilment; it can only lead to self-destruction. Our selves are not as completely our own as we commonly imagine.

Modern psychology stresses the fact that we are not born with any true selfhood, but that the attainment of selfhood is part of a process of growth, over the early stages of which we have no more direct control than we have over the growth of our bodies, or the development of our sense organs. What we call our ego, our personality or our self, expresses itself and makes use of all our sense organs, our muscles, the whole organic mechanism of our bodies, but it did not create them or call them into being. Our thoughts, we say, are our own; but are they? We cannot think without words, and words are part of a language, but the language we speak existed before we were born. An infant listening to music that emanates from a radio set, would think of the music as emanating from the radio set. But does it? It must first be "picked up" by the radio set from the ether, and the radio set can only pick up these waves and transmute them into sound by conforming to certain natural laws. The human personality, likewise, appears to initiate action and, in a sense, it does, but it does so by a power that does not reside in itself, and that can be "picked up" only in accordance with laws not of its own creation.

That is why, when we look to the great creative achievements of men, we find that they are not the work of people dominated by the will to power. The great conquerors of history built up concentrations of power, but sooner or later that power was dissipated, with nothing of permanent value to justify the tremendous energy that was spent in accumulating it, not to mention the pain and humiliation that were involved in the process. The Pharaohs in their lifetime were gods who could compel thousands of slaves to build the pyramids, beneath which their bodies moulder (except those that are exhibited in museums). But Moses, who was only a faithful servant of God, and whose body lies in an unknown grave in Moab, was the founder of a civilization that still lives. Modern psychology, too, leads us to be less disposed than we were formerly to worship untrammeled self-assertion. Such megalomania is a manifestation not of the divine, but of an immature personality that has not outgrown the tantrums of the childish refusal to recognize reality.

3

HOW MEN PLAY THE GOD NOWADAYS

It may at first seem that the deification of individual rulers belongs to a state of culture that no longer exists. Even dictators do not lay claim to being gods. But the essential sin involved in such self-deification still exists. Even in so-called democratic countries, there are ruling cliques and classes of men, of whom each claims special prerogatives and authority by reason of his success in imposing his will on others. The general may send thousands of soldiers to their death for no other purpose than to satisfy his ambition to go down in history as a great conqueror. The captain of industry feels that his ability to "handle men" quite justifies his arbitrary hiring and firing men for his own profit. The labor organizer also frequently construes his ability to organize the forces of labor for class warfare, and to make them follow his leadership, as entitling him to use them to promote his personal ambition. These petty monarchs live on the assumption that the power which they wield raises them above obedience to the conventions and decencies of society, and absolves them from accountability to anyone but themselves.

But that is not enough to explain all the mischief that the desire to play the god has worked in modern society. Our very political democracy, the extension of the suffrage, the extension of education and the tendency to conceive of sovereignty as vested not in a person or group of persons, but in the people or the nation conceived as an abstract collective entity, have been exploited as a means of collectivizing, as it were, the desire of men to play the god.

In their individual lives, the weak are prevented from carrying out this desire by the control exercised over them by the strong. Even so they are able to experience this sense of power vicariously, when they belong to a group that can lord it over others. In this way, their very weakness can contribute to their feeling of strength. Their abject submission to the will of the powerful makes it easy for strong usurpers of divine authority to regiment them and use them to promulgate their own ambitious schemes. This makes the man on the street feel that his dictator is his *Fuehrer*, the man who is the executive agent of his own purposes, while the dictator himself can delude himself into believing that he, indeed, is a child of destiny, for he does the scheming and planning on behalf of great masses of men, who would be lost but for his assertion of the national will to power. He is thus able to lead his people into the most sinister adventures. As long as he is successful, he can count on the loyal support of the group at whose head he stands, for in enabling him to play the god, his followers are also vicariously playing the god. *In totalitarian countries, the nation is not a group of human beings who look to God for their salvation; it regards itself as a god, exercising irresponsible power and sovereignty, and its individual units have doffed their humanity to partake of its divinity.*

4

IMITATIO DEI

Playing the god is a form of madness, of irrational megalomania, the tantrums of a child, but a child who toys with bombing planes, tanks, U-boats, and who directs them with the craft and cunning of a mature intelligence. There is only one way by which humanity can be saved from this insanity, i.e., by an about-face from playing the god to being Godlike. Instead of trying to behave as if we possessed the irresponsible power and absolute authority of God, let us learn to think of ourselves as God's creatures, created in His image and fulfilling our lives only by conformity with His creative design. What that design is may be inferred from the attributes which men at their best have ascribed to God and to which they have sought to cleave. The one all-inclusive divine attribute to which our religious tradition would have us cleave is God's love. What this implies is set forth in the concluding section of this chapter.

From the standpoint of our general experience, we are aware that to seek those forms of behavior which add to the value of life both for ourselves and for others means to live in harmony with God as the Power that makes for righteousness. We know that justice, kindness, mutual helpfulness, tolerance of differences are qualities that do make life more livable for ourselves and our neighbors. We know that the achievement of these qualities is a necessary condition to a satisfactory social order, as definitely as we know the most elementary laws of nature. We do not yet know how to apply these principles to solving all the problems of government, of production and distribution, of education and of many other indispensable activities. But, if we want to face life rationally, we must approach these problems with the faith that they can be solved. If we are *faithful*, if we persist in seeking their solution in the light of our best insight into moral law, a solution will be found.

Approaching life in this religious spirit removes from us the temptation either to play the god ourselves, or to contribute to the deification of any other mortal, that is, either to assert a brutal will to power, individually or collectively. It prevents us from using other human beings as mere tools for effecting our own desires, because we see God not only in the most powerful, but even in the most feeble among them.

The mother, who holds an infant in her arms, understands that the tug of that child on her heart strings is certainly one of the things that makes life meaningful and beautiful for her, that it reveals God. She knows that the child's cry for food has the authority of a divine command which she must reverently acknowledge and obey. And yet the child's cry is born of its weakness, not of its strength. Moreover, if she is truly religious, she will view with reverent awe the growth of the child's physical, mental and moral powers, recognizing that neither her will, nor the will of the child's own growing personality can account for that physical growth and spiritual maturing, but only the will of God. She will, therefore, never make the mistake of many a mother and seek to hold on to her gratifying sense of power over her child, to keep her child unduly dependent on her and incapacitate it to meet life's issues confidently and bravely. She will not seek to possess her child. *Possessiveness belongs to the realm of power, not of spirit, to the attempt to play the god, not to* imitatio Dei.

The employer of labor who views life religiously will not feel that his possession of the tools needed by the worker, or even of superior skill and experience in management and executive direction of production, ever justifies him in treating his employees as if they were mere hands, mere cogs in the mechanism of production. He will be aware of their personal needs and their personal dignity and the personal labor that they have invested in the economic enterprise. He will realize that he serves in his capacity and they in theirs. He will ever be ready to meet with their representatives to discuss and to adjust conflicting interests. The will to power will not be suppressed, but it will be, in the spirit of *imitatio Dei*, a will to create and not to destroy, to help and not to hurt, to command the love of men, not their fear.

Moreover the religious spirit of seeking to be Godlike will prevent men from contributing to the deification of others, to the apotheosis of the dictator. Believing himself possessed of a soul created in God's image, of powers that make him a responsible partner in God's creative work of fashioning a better world, a man is not ready to abdicate his responsibility to satisfy the whim of one of nature's spoilt children, whose megalomania is evidence of moral weakness or spiritual immaturity.

The truly religious person is a lover of freedom, because he feels the need to be free from obedience to arbitrary decrees, in order to serve

God, *in order to give himself to the pursuit of those interests that lie at the heart of the human hope for salvation.* He is a patriot, passionately loving his country and seeking its welfare, but he loves it too well to want it to embark on ungodly enterprises of aggression against other nations, or to permit it to stultify itself by a mad self-worship that forgets God, that forgets that no man and no people can find complete salvation, until all men and nations can live together in peace and fraternal cooperation. No national sovereignty can transcend for him the sovereignty of God, no loyalty can be higher than his loyalty to humanity, the Kingdom of God.

The truly religious person is fearless. He feels that his interest in life is not an interest in his own individual ego, but an interest in his relation to life as a whole, the life of God. How he serves God is more important than how he serves his own ego. *He can respect his ego only if it is more than an ego, only if it is a soul, a responsible focus for the creative energy of God in bringing about a better world,* one in which life is more secure, more abundant and more happy. He will not waste his life, but he will gladly spend it. He will love God "with his whole soul," that is, according to Rabbi Akiba's interpretation, he would be willing to sacrifice his very life itself to the love of God.

Men like that do not permit themselves to be shoved around by dictators. A nation of such men would be invincible, yet no other nation would ever have occasion to fear it. *A nation that sought, in all aspects of its national life, to understand and conform to the will of God, of the Power that makes for human salvation, would be the first true democracy that the world has known.*

5. INNER FREEDOM

American Jews have a more crucial stake than any other group in the struggle of democracy against the new barbarism with which mankind is threatened. So long as the rest of the world is in danger of political serfdom and economic slavery, the Jewish people is in danger of annihilation. Its only hope is in the triumph of democracy. *Destiny has placed us Jews on the firing line in defense of freedom.*

The triumph of democracy is the triumph of social order based upon freedom. Any attempt to keep alive in the Jewish people the hope of survival and redemption, associated with the triumph of democracy, must seek to make us aware of the meaning of freedom. We must understand what constitutes freedom, and what we must do to attain it.

Democracy is freedom conceived as a condition of society, or as a quality of social relationships. It is freedom embodied in political forms or institutions—in universal suffrage, parliamentarism, the bill of rights. Those forms are based on two principles. The first of these is the principle of the "government of the people, by the people," which implies that all adult persons are entitled to participate in the government under which they live. The second is the principle of government "for the people," the subordination of the state to the welfare of the people, on the assumption that the state exists for the people, not the people for the state.

But if democracy is to hold its own in the struggle against anti-democratic forces, political freedom must be sustained by an inner freedom, a freedom of the spirit. *Freedom must be conceived not only as a condition of society, but also as a state of mind.* We Jews may not have played a considerable role in the shaping of the political instruments of democracy; but from the time that our fathers identified God as the Power that brought us forth from the "house of bondage," freedom became part of our religious tradition with which we sought to inform our personal habits. The understanding of the close relationship between freedom as a state of mind and freedom as a condition of society is what Jews are in a position to contribute to the struggle for democracy. Such a contribution would be more effective in securing the eventual triumph of democracy than any, however important, that we are now making toward the progress of science or the development of industry. For, in democracy's struggle for survival, the decision will rest upon the extent to which those who fight under its banner will possess inner freedom.

What is this inner freedom, the state of mind or quality of character that is indispensable to the triumph of democracy? *It is the unyielding refusal to recognize the legitimacy of brute force, or to bow before its authority.* This inner freedom determines a person's entire attitude toward the world, toward his fellowman, toward his group, toward his momentary wishes and impulses. It makes his whole life one long protest against all the brute forces that would interpose obstacles to the achievement of his worthiest aims.

These brute forces operate through various media. They operate through the violent phenomena of nature, through storms, floods, earthquakes, famine, pestilence, and cosmic upheavals. They operate no less through human tyrannies, like those of despots, great or small, or like those of organized multitudes, whether mobs or nations, whether savage or highly civilized. Brute force, to defy which is a mark of inner freedom, is as varied in its forms of expression as in the media it employs. It may take the form of blind destructiveness or of planned devastation, of sheer physical strength or of diabolic cunning, of outright violence or of fomented treachery, of undisguised banditry or of smooth-tongued diplomacy.

But whatever medium brute force employs, and in whatever form it expresses itself, to the man who has inner freedom, it is ever an abomination. If he must live with it, he will never leave off resisting it, taming it, seeking to master it. That is how freedom as a state of mind, or quality of character, asserts itself. To resist brute force, to tame it and master it takes all that a man has in him. His entire personality is involved—heart, mind and will. But the initial sign of inner freedom is always "the unreconciled heart."

1

"THE UNRECONCILED HEART"

There is an inveterate tendency in most men which runs counter to this inner freedom. It assumes that the deciding factor in human destiny is not reason, or goodness, or righteousness, but inexorable fate, and it commends resignation and submission to fate as the ultimate wisdom. Fate is, however, but another term for the supremacy of blind, unaccountable forces against which man, with all that distinguishes him as human, struggles in vain. All the ancient religions of mankind conceived their gods as subordinate to fate. Even Ikhnaton, who promulgated monotheism in ancient Egypt, did not deny that the Sun-god whom he worshiped was ruled by fate.

Our ancestors could not get themselves to accept such a view of life. They could not reconcile themselves to the conception of a fate that meant the triumph of brute force over man's will to live and exercise his capacities and powers to the maximum degree. To them God was the Redeemer and Liberator of man, the Power on whom men must rely in their eternal struggle against the blind forces of nature that endanger them and against the irrationalities and brutalities of their own human nature. They could not, therefore, conceive Him as subordinate to brute force, to meaningless and purposeless fate. They could conceive

Him as subordinate only to justice. "Shall not the Judge of all the earth do justice?" [1] asked Abraham, the founder of the faith. His free heart could not reconcile itself to the destruction of the cities of Sodom and Gomorrah, as the working of an inevitable fate with which even God must make peace.

True, one occasionally finds in the Bible characterizations of God in which force seems to play the dominant role, as in Koheleth and Job. In the book of Job, God is represented as overwhelming Job by His power.[2] But these books are exceptional. They contain more of what Jewish religion as a whole deprecates than of what it accepts. Their significance for Jewish religion is as a corrective to certain abuses of faith, rather than as an affirmation of positive religious belief. Their inclusion in the Biblical canon, therefore, does not invalidate the truth of our contention that *Jewish religion maintains the eventual triumph of justice over brute force, as the very essence of faith in God.*

This is a faith of which the modern world is particularly in need. The pagan notion of the dominance of irrational forces and the inevitable frustration of human hopes pervades most of our modern culture. The pessimistic appraisal of life that one finds in the writings of Thomas Hardy and Theodore Dreiser, and in the dramatic works of Henrik Ibsen and Eugene O'Neill, to say nothing of the recent school of writers abroad known as "Existentialist," may serve by way of illustration. All express a defeatist mood, a conviction that each man is inevitably and necessarily a victim of circumstances over which he has no control and from which there is no salvation. They leave us with the impression that man only makes himself ridiculous by trying to measure his puny strength against the overwhelming blind forces of chance that course through the life-stream or the bloodstream.

The average person readily succumbs to this doctrine of the inevitable. He finds in it an excuse for his failure to achieve the good life. He accepts implicitly the half-truths about the dark forces which are assumed to inhabit the subconscious in man, and does not avail himself of the resources of the human spirit that are also dormant in his subconsciousness. He is like a man caught in a blizzard who could keep himself alive by keeping awake and active, but is tempted by fatigue into lying down to sleep, though sleep means certain death.

The man who possesses real inner freedom remains undaunted in his will to live. He will not accept as inevitable the triumph of blind fate over the achievement of his purposes in life. He will not even permit the fear of death to deter him from striving for the things that make life worthwhile, and will find in the assertion of this will to live a method of triumphing over death. His life's purposes are related to values that do not die with his individual death. He sees in the disappointments and frustrations of life merely a new challenge to a Spirit that lives in him, and will live after him, and that is forever transforming human life in conformity with a will to justice and brotherly cooperation. That Spirit he identifies as God. To the service of God he commits himself utterly, and will not permit the fear of any chance or fate to divert him from it, for in this service he sees the whole meaning and value of his life. His "unreconciled heart" tells him that justice must prevail, and that he must never make peace with brute force, whether exerted by nature or by man.

And just as "the unreconciled heart" of the free man refuses to be overwhelmed by the bogey of fate and circumstance, so it refuses to be overwhelmed by mere bigness and size. The average man tends to be overawed by mere mass, even though it serves no special function. In the presence of any massive phenomenon, he feels himself insignificant; it makes him lose confidence in his own worth and in the importance of his purposes and strivings. Abject in the presence of its majesty, he rates his own individuality as nothing, and bows down in servile worship before it. Of the pyramids of Egypt, Thoreau says in *Walden*: "Most of the stone a nation hammers goes toward its tomb only. It buries itself alive. As for the pyramids, there is nothing to wonder at in them so much as the fact that so many men could be degraded enough to spend their life constructing a tomb for some ambitious booby, whom it would have been wiser and manlier to have drowned in the Nile and then given his body to the dogs."

Of a piece with this worship of physical mass is the worship of massed social power, the surrender of the personal judgment of the individual to the passions and prejudices of the mob, whether organized or unorganized. Conforming one's individual behavior to that of the majority may abet the disposition to escape personal responsibility. One's personal inadequacy and impotence may be overcome by ascribing to oneself the manifest power of the multitude with which one identifies oneself. Such self-identification, however, leads to the effacement, not to the fulfillment of self.

In deprecating the worship of vastness in social organization, we are not minimizing the value of large-scale organization. The function for which an organization is needed must determine the scale of the social forces involved. But the mere vastness of the numbers involved is entirely irrelevant to the value of the social function performed. Where this principle is not recognized, and it is assumed that numerical size confers moral authority, there we have, in essence, the substitution of physical power for moral law. It is but another expression of that worship of brute force against which the heart of the free man remains forever unreconciled.

But perhaps the most significant aspect of inner freedom, from the standpoint of "the unreconciled heart," is the refusal to make peace with fraud and violence, regardless of the success to which they lead, or the prestige achieved by means of them. The desire for success is so great in all men, that there is a tendency to admire the successful man and to surround him with flattery and adulation, even though the aims which he succeeded in achieving and the means by which he achieved them are both of them reprehensible. That is why there is nothing that succeeds like success, even where the success is not merited. The man who "wades through slaughter to a throne" is glorified once his throne is secure, and the man who by fraud and chicanery rises to a position of eminence will not lack panegyrists who will disguise even his vices as virtues.

But *the free man will not pay homage to what is not truly admirable.* He will never be a flunky or a sycophant. The attitude of inner freedom in relation to malefactors in power is best exemplified by the Prophets. It was their outstanding trait. No matter how intrenched those in power, whether they were of their own people or of other peoples, the Prophets did not mince words in denouncing their treachery and foretelling their doom. Whether it is Nathan confronting David,[3] or Elijah warning Ahab,[4] or Amos taking Jeroboam II to task,[5] or Isaiah defying the mighty enemies of his day [6]—the same spirit of revolt against the glitter and pride of ruthless might breathes in them all.

The slavery of the spirit, which has taken possession of modern mankind, began to manifest itself in the spell which Napoleon cast over the greater part of the world. His dazzling victories on the battle-field, and the skillful treachery by which he rose to the pinnacle of worldly power have won for him the admiration of multitudes. It requires considerable freedom of the spirit to be able to give that estimate of him given by H. G. Wells, "This dark, little archaic personage, compact, capable, unscrupulous, imitative and neatly vulgar, Napoleon was a reminder of ancient evils, a thing like the bacterium of some pestilence . . . He was an unmitigated scoundrel." [7]

Napoleon was essentially "a glorified gangster." If this judgment had been passed upon Hitler sooner and had been more generally extant, the world might have been spared the cataclysm which has brought it to the brink of ruin. At last men are coming to their senses. They are beginning to realize, in the words of John D. Voelker, that "a dictator is an international brigand and political mobster, heading a gang which gags and seizes control of a nation and a people and operates under a 'front' which may cynically allow itself to be called among other things, a socialistic or communistic state, a monarchy or even a democracy." Our hope for the future lies in those free spirits whose hearts remain forever unreconciled to brute force, no matter to what heights of success and prestige it may lead those who direct it.

2

THE CHALLENGING MIND

"The unreconciled heart" needs, however, to be reinforced in its struggle against brute force by the challenging mind. To be free, men must be able also to understand the impact of irrational forces of another kind than those which inhere in nature. They are the irrational forces which are of man's own making. They derive from the authority of the past, or from the authority of the multitude. Their power over us proceeds from a disposition of the mind to seek the path of least resistance. There is an inertia of the mind that operates similarly to the law of physical inertia, a tendency to persist in ways that we are used to and to fall in with prevalent currents of thought and action, without questioning whither they are leading us. We thus are in constant danger of being enslaved to ancient superstitions, to inherited social prejudices, to conventional lies and to specious rationalizations of the mob mind.

To possess inner freedom, the human mind must be able to rouse itself from this inertia, to challenge or question the inherent value of any purpose, ideal, belief or standard, which we are asked to accept, merely because it has back of it the prestige of a long tradition or the weight of numbers. This does not mean that man can make himself independent of tradition, or need not reckon with the opinion of his fellows. Man is a social being. His progress depends on his being able to utilize the accumulated culture to which innumerable individuals in all the past generations have contributed, and to avail himself of the experience of his contemporaries, particularly of those whose opinions may be more valid than his own, because of better access to the facts on which they are based. But when the pressure of tradition or public opinion imposes itself on the individual to the extent that he feels called upon to abdicate his right to think for himself about anything whatsoever, then tradition or public opinion has become a tyranny. Such abdication of the individual judgment makes for the salvation neither of the individual nor of society. It is a form of slavery which the man who possesses inner freedom will confront with the challenging mind.

The challenging mind sees in enslavement to tradition but another form of enslavement to habit. It is generally recognized that a person may become enslaved by his own habits. Habits are indispensable; habit formation insures the most efficient discharge of necessary functions. But when circumstances make the discharge of this function unnecessary or undesirable, the inability to break away from habit is slavery. The child develops habits of dependence on his parents; if he retains these habits in later life and does not acquire new habits of self-reliance, economic independence and the emotional capacity to form new family ties, he is a slave to them. Similarly a society develops traditional customs, laws, standards and conventions which help it to meet the demands of life and contribute to welfare of all its individual members. But these customs, laws, standards and conventions originated, at the time of their origin, in response to the needs of that society. As long as they seem to function well, it is good that the individual conform to them rather than yield to mere passing whim or egoistic impulse. But when the traditional culture pattern does not contribute to the welfare of the society and its component individuals, the mind must be free to alter and reconstruct the traditional culture pattern, to seek the development of new and better social habits to meet the changed situation.

We must realize that tradition is social habit, habit multiplied a thousandfold through the reinforcement which each individual receives from every other and from the cumulative strength acquired through repetition by each generation. Beliefs, values, institutions become second nature and maintain themselves by their own momentum long after the purposes which they originally served have been outlived.

In the past, both church and state were able to exercise unlimited despotism, by virtue of the power lent them by tradition. *It has become fashionable to ascribe to organized religions the principle of the dignity of the individual. That is not true. The organized traditional religions have always deprecated and frowned down the challenging mind. They* have always treated it as dangerous and in need of suppression. In traditional religious circles, free thought is still regarded as synonymous with irreligion and anarchy.

The flame of intellectual freedom, the freedom of the challenging mind, was kindled in ancient Greece and has burned only intermittently and very dimly most of the time. But, even in Greece, Socrates had to pay the price of martyrdom for his intellectual freedom. Socrates, Plato and Aristotle should be credited with having been the first to foster the inner freedom of the challenging mind. The Stoics managed to keep alive intellectual independence, but the Church extinguished it, and brought on the long night of the Middle Ages, until it was rekindled by the Renaissance and the Enlightenment.

Just as humanity, however, was beginning to enjoy its emancipation from bondage to the past, it commenced to forge for itself the chains of an infinitely worse bondage. It became enslaved to the tyranny of the multitude. With the spread of superficial literacy, the invention of numerous new means of communication, and the acquisition of the power to release at will a flood of printed matter, the art of propaganda was developed as a technique for making men slaves. Propaganda has been employed to regiment the human mind and to make it think and believe whatever those in power want it to think and believe. *Never in the history of mankind was the human being so much in danger of becoming de-individualized and depersonalized.* Totalitarianism means the complete subordination of the individual to the mass. There is but one way in which it can be resisted and ultimately defeated. If the individual is not to be sucked into the vortex of the mass, he must consciously retain his selfhood; he must refuse to accept blindly and unquestioningly purposes imposed from without.

3

THE FEARLESS AND COOPERATIVE WILL

Something more even than the challenging mind and the unreconciled heart is necessary, if human purpose is not to be thwarted by the irrational forces in nature and human society. Both of these together do not suffice to rescue us from being overwhelmed by the demonic forces in the world, unless we can develop sufficient will power to make them effective, unless we translate their dictates into action. If freedom is good, it is because "we know that freedom has given man the best he has ever had." It has given man knowledge, wisdom, love, kindness, growth. But these best things man has ever had to fight for and defend with his life.

If we do not want to forfeit the products of human civilization and culture and to relapse into the dark night of barbarism, we must learn two things: to banish fear and to cooperate with all who detest tyranny and are willing to throw off its yoke. The fearful man suffers not merely from present evil, but from anticipated evil. The mere anticipation of possible defeat leads the fearful person to behave as though he has already been defeated, and prevents him from warding off defeat, although the opportunity for doing so still exists. And when evil comes, fear prevents a man from salvaging as much as he can of his wrecked purposes, envisaging a possible escape from its worst consequences, and turning present defeat into ultimate victory. The banishing of fear is, therefore, indispensable to the achievement of freedom.

But how banish fear? There are many ways and all of them must be used. The first is to remove the main cause of fear, namely, the danger of being deprived of the means to life. There are some who can say with the Psalmist: "God is for me; I am not afraid; what can man do to me." [8] Their faith in God assures them that they will be provided for, either in this life or in another, regardless of what happens. But such faith is rare. Most people find their sense of security dependent on large accumulation of resources for living.

It is unfortunate that, too often, in the very process of accumulation, its purpose is lost. Instead of aiming to achieve the security that makes freedom possible, by banishing fear, we strive to achieve domination over others. But, as soon as the goal of freedom is lost sight of, man tends to become a slave to his own possessions. When he sustains considerable losses, he loses heart. Luxuries become necessities, and the fear of being deprived of them operates as strongly as the original fear of lacking the means to life. In times of economic crisis, it happens not infrequently that men commit suicide, because of the loss of their possessions although, at the time of their death, they are still possessed of more wealth than most persons enjoy in prosperous times.

Important as it is, therefore, in order to banish fear, that we remove the main cause of fear by securing the indispensable means of living, it is no less important to that end that we train ourselves to desire little. There must be something of the ascetic in us, if we do not care to succumb to the enslaving fear of insecurity. Why have so many human beings shown a marked tendency to asceticism, and why have so many actually practiced it? Basically it was the deep desire to be independent of those wants of the body which makes slaves of us. Although asceticism has often been carried to extremes and has assumed forms that were ill adapted to the achievement of this purpose, nevertheless an appreciation of the dangers of ease and self-indulgence and of the need of limiting our material wants is part of the discipline of freedom. The generation that emerged from bondage to the Egyptian Pharaohs had to emancipate itself also from the fleshpots of Egypt and learn to subsist on the manna, the *lehem hakelokel*, "the light bread" of the wilderness,[9] before they attained enough inner freedom to qualify for national life in the Promised Land.

Finally, to banish fear, it is necessary that we discipline ourselves in the soldierly spirit of being prepared for the worst that may befall us as a consequence of defying the onset of tyranny. "The ultimate question," says William Hocking, "which every man has to face and answer for himself is: Will you be a hero or a coward?"[10]

However fearless a will we may possess, we cannot withstand the elemental impact of barbarism, unless we meet it with a degree of strength of our own. That can only be secured through the increasing cooperation of all who value liberty and deem life worthless without it. Here, of course, we come upon the crucial problem of freedom: how to guard our individuality and the capacity to think for ourselves, and yet cooperate with those whose background, upbringing and whole outlook are different from our own. That is an art human beings are slow to learn. Democracy may well be conceived as the process of social experimentation by which men are seeking to learn that art, and to apply step by step the wisdom acquired as a result of this experimentation. That is why *the art of free voluntary cooperation, the ultimate objective of democracy, needs constantly to be cultivated.* But, eventually, it will have to be learned, else mankind is doomed.

And the only way to learn it is to realize that, no matter how human beings may differ, one thing they have in common; they are, at bottom, desirous of being free. To doubt this is to lose faith in man. And, since faith in God is essentially faith in His power to redeem man, to lose faith in the potentialities of human nature is to lose faith in God as well. *The cynicism that surrenders to brute force, as inevitably supreme, is the ultimate atheism.*

It is hardly necessary to expatiate on how these truths concerning the freedom which is a state of mind or quality of character apply to our present salvation as Americans and Jews. The barest indication will suffice.

The new barbarism which recently swept over mankind tried in vain to crush out the spirit of freedom in one country after another. But from "the serpent's root has come forth a basilisk." The new barbarism is still abroad in the world. Hence, above all, let us heed the heart that is unreconciled to brutality. "Above all that is to be heeded," we read in Proverbs, "heed the heart, for from it come the issues of life." [11]

To retain our human dignity and permit our minds to challenge whatever is unnecessary, unreasonable, unkind, and unjust, we must, as Americans and as Jews, bear in mind the following:

In our religious life, we should not associate religion with the surrender of reason, with the blind acceptance of whatever is meaningless. *Reasonableness in our religious beliefs, candor in our religious education, and sincerity in our religious ritual must be deliberately fostered as indispensable to true religion.*

In political life, *we should not deem as justice any harmful law that is imposed, however legal the means by which it may have been formulated and enforced.* Nor must we ever take for granted that might makes right, whether it be the might of a despot or the might of a majority that encroaches on the rights of a minority.

In economic life, *we should emancipate ourselves from the assumption that ownership of property is synonymous with the right to its exclusive control or irresponsible use.*

In social life, *we must free ourselves from the tyranny of the artificialities and arbitrary standards set up by social cliques, from the slavery of having to "keep up with the Joneses" in waste, display and debilitating luxuries.*

In order to cultivate the power of will necessary to defy brute force, we must, as a nation, be strong on land and sea, *strong for the sake of freedom.* We must think less of the much vaunted "American standard of living," and more of the American standard of freedom as the ultimate value of our American way of life. We must be prepared to make untold sacrifices for the sake of the only kind of life that is worthwhile. We must renounce the policy of isolationism which was, in large measure, responsible for having brought on the recent World War, and cooperate with all other nations in the establishment of universal justice and peace.

As Jews, we dare not, in all this melee, give up our faith in God whose first revelation of Himself to our people was as the Power that brought them forth from "the house of bondage." We must retain our individuality by refusing to die, so long as nations that believe in freedom are struggling to live. We must be prepared to sacrifice to the utmost, in order that our people shall live, that they who flee from the fires of persecution shall find a haven of refuge, and that Eretz Yisrael shall be able to play its part in the struggle for human hope and freedom.

We must shake off all the phobias which inhibit us from being true to ourselves and from making the most of our lives as Jews. We must not be afraid of standing shoulder to shoulder, and demanding the rights due us as human beings; the rights of community, cultural individuality and spiritual freedom.

Thus, with hearts unreconciled to the supremacy of brute force, with minds challenging the Frankenstein monsters of man's own making, and insisting on the high worth of the human soul, and with wills that are dauntless and cooperative, insisting on the love of freedom as the potential bond of human brotherhood, we shall help to speed the day when man's inner freedom will assert itself in the creation of a worldwide democratic order of freedom, justice and human welfare.

6. PATIENCE

1

UTOPIANISM AND DISILLUSIONMENT

Important as it is for us to recognize the truth that a genuine democracy requires that inner freedom which will not bow before brute force, we must not imagine that this quality alone will suffice. If we do, we run the danger of eventual disillusionment. The danger lies in our assuming that, by refusing to bow before brute force, we abolish it, and that nothing stands in the way of the fulfillment of our desires. Though we dare not give up hope that the evils, which have their roots in the tyranny of brute force, can be overcome, we dare not give way to impatience. We must not assume that they will yield easily, or that we shall ever achieve a complete and final triumph over brute force in all its manifestations.

If we do not wish to be disappointed in the hopes which our inner freedom engenders, we must learn to expect no speedy realization of them, and to address ourselves with patience and perseverance to removing one by one the impediments to their fulfillment. If we expect immediate and thorough emancipation from all that interferes with human freedom, we are doomed to disappointment, and are likely to be dashed from an excessive optimism to an equally excessive pessimism and defeatism. The ultimate issue of such impatient and extravagant expectations can only be frustration. "Cynicism," it has been well said, "is after all simply idealism gone sour."

Many decry the mood of defeatism that is so prevalent in our day, but few understand that this defeatism is the tremendous price we are paying for the utopianism of the 150 years prior to the First World War. We can still recall the utopian optimism of the pre-war era. The enormously accelerated tempo of progress in the conquest of man's natural environment, and the rapid emancipatory changes in his political and social institutions, seemed to forecast the speedy coming of a millennial era, when poverty and disease would be abolished, when illiteracy, superstition and prejudice would yield to universal education, when all governments would be governments "of the people, for the people, and by the people," and international disputes would be peaceably adjusted by processes of arbitration and adjudication.

It was then the vogue to reject with scorn ancient doctrines that spoke of original sin from which men must be redeemed, or taught that "the imagination of the heart of man is evil from his youth." [1] Men shut their eyes to the evidence of sinister forces at work in their own day, to the ruthlessness of imperialistic conquest, to the callousness of capitalistic exploitation of labor, to the abuse of education, religion and the authority of the state in the interest of a governing class. Their dream of the future was so vivid and so entrancing that they lost sight of the sinister play of brutal forces behind the surface aspect of things. Their dream was enough to convince them not only that "God's in His heaven," but also that "all's right with the world."

Few, indeed, were they who perceived that man had yet a long way to go, before he would be rid of the irrational surges within him, of his capacity for bloody exploits and for studied cruelty and cold sadism. So strong was this feeling of utopian optimism that even the outbreak of the First World War was unable to shatter it. Men were shocked by the war, but they soon found a convenient rationalization to fit it into their pattern of thought. It was heralded as a "war to end war," to mop up the last dregs of human violence, "to make the world safe for democracy."

But when the Treaty of Versailles was being negotiated, it soon became apparent that those sinister aspects of human nature, and those inveterate evils of society which had erupted in the violence of the war, had not been exorcised. The great war was followed by the little peace. Men had expected the treaty to justify the war by ushering in a new era of international cooperation, humanitarian achievement and democratic progress such as the world had never before experienced. But its negotiation and implementation brought out the egoism, chicanery, malice and vindictiveness, the undisguised lust for economic and financial power, which lay at the root of the war itself. Discerning people began to see in the treaty the seed of future wars.

Thus came the great disillusionment. From utopian idealism, men turned to the opposite extreme, to an embittered and pessimistic cynicism. Wilson and his idealistic slogans were discredited. The democracies lost faith in themselves and in their capacity to achieve a democratic world order. The great powers delegated no part of their authority to the League of Nations, and invoked its sanctions only where their own national interests were immediately involved. They withdrew from all social and political responsibility to prevent repetition of world disaster. The United States, which had originally sponsored the ideal of the League, and had professed no other interest in the war settlement than the assurance of a lasting peace, was the first great power to withdraw from responsibility for world peace through collective security. Its isolationism and pacifism contributed to spreading the mood of defeatism.

This defeatism played into the hands of the forces of barbarism, which have since erupted with greater violence. Since the nations had no faith in their own capacity to unite in maintaining a just and democratic world order, and refused to vest power in the very instrument they had jointly devised for this purpose, those powers that felt themselves at a disadvantage, rightly or wrongly, were able to resort to aggression and power politics, confident that no collective international force would be invoked to stop them. Instead of resisting brute force as soon as it emerged, the democratic powers, in their desire to be let alone, had recourse to appeasing the aggressors at the expense of other weaker nations. Thus isolationism begot appeasement. The extent to which the policy of appeasement tended to frustrate the hopes of the democracies and threaten their very existence is a matter of history. Had the democracies not expected the millennium to follow in the wake of the First World War, and had they realized that the removal of the causes of so inveterate an evil required long, patient and persevering effort, they would not have been so quickly disillusioned, so ready to withdraw into isolationism, and so prone to respond with a panicky appeasement to the threat of aggression.

We Jews have much in our tradition that should qualify us to be expert in patience. We have paid dearly for our many false Messiahs, who came in answer to our impatience. As if to inure us to the long and severe testing of our patience that awaited us, we were initiated in it at the very beginning of our career. When our ancestors left Egypt, we are told, God led them by a circuitous route through the wilderness lest, when they encountered an enemy, they return to Egypt and its bondage.[2] Thus they had their first lesson in endurance, without which they did not deserve to be free.

The real testing, however, came much later. It was then that our Sages repeatedly warned our people against yielding to the lure of wishful thinking, only to be bitterly disappointed when their premature hopes would come to naught. Using the language of allegory, our Sages quoted the verse from the Song of Songs: "I adjure you, O maidens of Jerusalem, that you rouse not or awaken love, until it please." [3] This, they explained, means that Israel should not seek any short-cut to the final goal of redemption.[4] "A malediction on those," says R. Samuel bar Nahmani, "who are forever calculating when the redemption will take place," [5] as if the redemption were bound to arrive on schedule.

2

MELIORISM A WAY OUT

How shall we escape from the dilemma of defeatism, on the one hand, and utopianism, on the other? Meliorism seems to offer a way out. It regards perfection not as a stationary goal toward which we are moving, and which we shall one day attain. Perfection is a "flying goal," which determines the direction in which we must advance, but which we never can expect to overtake. Human life is a creative adjustment to the environment. The spirit of man is constantly bringing order out of the chaos without and within him, in order that he may live. He is constantly evolving new meaning in the casual and irrational circumstances of his existence. That new meaning makes it possible for him to direct his own powers and to appropriate the forces of his natural environment for purposes that enhance his life. Nevertheless, chaos, although continually yielding, is inexhaustible, and the play of irrational forces, though continually subject to control, can never be completely subdued.

Religious faith, proceeding from the inherent will to live, is justified in assuming that we can also eventually throw off any tyranny which crushes the body or the spirit, if we apply our best powers of intellect, emotion and will to the task over a long period of time. But experience tells us that other forms of tyranny will emerge, and that every act of emancipation still leaves us laboring under some yoke that remains to be cast off. This does not mean that progress is an illusion, but that it consists of the successive attainment of continually emerging goals, and not of a steady approach to a final goal conceived from the start. Such a view of life, based on meliorism, is the belief that, *though we cannot expect human life or human society ever to be perfect, it can continually improve and the human spirit can continually find fulfillment in an expanding freedom.*

Such a philosophy saves us from the disillusionment that is involved in utopianism. Having no expectation of easy and conclusive victory for freedom, we are not disappointed by the recrudescence of brute force. We are saved thereby from the defeatism that proceeds from this disillusionment, by not accepting existing tyranny as inevitable, and not making peace with brute force. Meliorism has this important implication for the art of living: it teaches us that the choices which we must exercise in life are never between absolute good and absolute evil, but between a greater and lesser good, when it is a question of choosing a good, and a greater and lesser evil, when it is a question of avoiding an evil.

Thus in the momentous decision of war or peace the question is not: Is war good, or is it evil? The mischief done by war, the suffering and cruelty of it are patent to all. No sane person can think of war as an absolute good. The question is: Which is the lesser evil in a particular situation, war or tolerance of wrongs which cannot be righted without war? Neither course is to our liking. If wishing were effective, we should wish that the evils, for the removal of which our fighting seems necessary, did not exist. But wishing is not effective, and the choice that we must take is not between the absolute evil of an arbitrary and utterly irrational resort to violent and aggressive war, on the one hand, and, on the other, a just and enduring peace. Such a choice could be made without a moment's hesitation. Had the choice of war or peace in specific instances been a choice between absolute good and absolute evil, war would have been abolished long ago. Its persistence is due entirely to the fact that men have not discovered effective peaceful methods for averting certain evils that have seemed to them greater than the evils of war, terrible as these are.

If the melioristic rather than the utopian attitude had been adopted by the democratic peoples in the First World War, they would have realized that the war had not been fought in vain, that, even if it did not bring the millennium, it averted the greater evil which a victorious Germany would have inflicted on the world. Unsatisfactory as the Treaty of Versailles and the other post-war treaties proved to be, they afforded a better opportunity for continued effort in behalf of international justice and peace than would have resulted from a victory by Germany.

Nor is it even correct to say that, though the First World War may have averted a greater evil than any to which it gave rise, no positive good came of it. It actually did lead to results which were at least *potentially* beneficent. True these potentialities were not exploited, but they are nevertheless real, and their promise for the future still affords some measure of encouragement. That war led at least to a mass hatred of war, a deflation of the glory with which martial adventures in the past had always been invested, and to a more extensive preoccupation with the problem of abolishing war than the world had ever before known. It led to the growing perception of the need for world unity, even if it did not lead to the discovery of the correct formula by which that unity could be achieved. *The experience even of the First World War justifies the melioristic attitude. Although it disappointed the utopian expectations of those who took literally the slogan "a war to end war," it actually did help to set in motion forces that will one day lead to the abolition of war.*

In the situation in which the United States found itself in consequence of the temporary career of conquest of the Axis powers, in the first two years of the Second World War, public opinion was divided between defeatist pessimism and utopian optimism. The defeatists saw no hope for democracy in resisting aggression, and were disposed to fall in line with the fascist tendencies of the age rather than take any risks of war. The utopian optimists again raised the same extravagant hopes that, by crushing Germany, we would solve the whole problem of democratic living. The former regarded war as an absolute evil and overlooked the evils arising from submission to a tyrannical social order; the latter regarded victory over aggression as an absolute good, and overlooked the need for minimizing the physical and moral dangers of war, and preparing for the removal of the conditions that would lead to a recurrence of aggression.

Under those circumstances, a consciously melioristic attitude would not have assumed that a mere military victory against the menace of the totalitarian powers would assure the establishment of democracy. It would have recognized—and to an extent such recognition actually did prevail—that there were better chances for the achievement of democracy, if Nazism were defeated than if it were victorious. While, therefore, seeking to accomplish this defeat resolutely, such an attitude would have led to the taking of precautions to minimize the evil post-war effects, and would have anticipated the need for those healing processes which have had to be applied since the end of the War. We should then not have expected to establish peace merely by the writing of a peace treaty, even the best kind of a peace treaty. We should then have sought to incorporate in such a treaty provisions that would encourage and facilitate the processes that make for the peace, security and freedom of men everywhere.

3

RESOLUTELY AND UNHURRIEDLY

In the world in which we live today, in the ideologies, institutions and culture patterns of the modern nations, in the prejudices, superstitions, blind impulses and inhibitions of men, there is still too much of chaos, madness and surrender to brute force to justify the hope for the speedy establishment of a secure and harmonious social order in the near future. Above all, it is unreasonable to expect that such an order can be brought about, as a sort of automatic consequence of the triumph of one military force over another. If we would save ourselves from disillusionment and despair, we must not expect that we shall soon have universal disarmament, a perfect adjustment of conflicting economic and political interests, and a sudden conversion to mutual tolerance and good will by nations, races and religions that have been indoctrinated with distrust and hate for one another. The best that we can hope for is a better chance to work for the realization of these social objectives.

But *our recognition of the reality of the chaos and moral and social confusion of our day should not impair our recognition of order, law and love as also operative in the world in which we live, nor destroy*

*our faith that it is the destiny of man to participate in the continual
reduction of chaos to cosmos, of anarchy to law, of discord to harmony.*
Chaos, anarchy, discord will not be abolished. But any true perception
of a desirable social good still points to a goal that marks the direction
of our progress, still is an indication of the possibilities of human
achievement, still bespeaks faith in a God who both sets the goals of
human endeavor and makes possible man's attaining them, still holds
forth the possibility of salvation through an unreserved consecration of
our entire being to our effort to achieve the sort of human life that is
most desirable.

When we take this attitude, every defeat leads not to despair but
to a better understanding of what is required to achieve victory. Not
only scientific experiment, but ordinary human experience, is a method
of learning by trial and error. What we regard as desirable today may
not be achieved tomorrow or the day after. It may not even, in the light
of later experience, seem wholly desirable on the morrow. But our
ideals are not mere will-o'-the-wisps that lead us astray. If we are patient
in our study of the best means of achieving our ends, and apply the
knowledge learned from experience, with perseverance and courage,
we shall arrive at our goal, even though by that time new horizons will
beckon to new goals. *It is not the mere arriving that makes life worth
while, but the journey itself.* Our attaining one goal is a spur to seeking
a newer and higher one. When we realize this, nothing can dismay or
discourage us.

We need not despair of the millennium, however long the struggle
for reaching it. The fact that we can perceive it is an intimation that,
in the long run, it, or something better than it, can be achieved. Our
faith, however, must make us patient. We can reach our ends only by
patient, plodding attention to the means. Mere wishful thinking retards
rather than advances our progress, but fearful thinking and a yielding
to intimidation get us nowhere. *Resolutely and unhurriedly, with alert
caution and patient deliberation must we proceed, if we are to make
progress.* But if we proceed in that spirit, our progress toward a just and
free social order is sure.

It is related in the Talmud that two sages, Rabbi Hiyyah and Rabbi
Halafta were once walking the valley east of the Jordan in the early
morning. As they saw the dawn rise, R. Hiyyah said to R. Halafta:
"Even so shall the deliverance of the world break forth, as it is written,
'Though I sit in darkness, the Lord is a light unto me.' [6] The dawn
comes on slowly and imperceptibly. At first the light is scarcely visible,

then it gathers strength, then it spreads over the entire sky. Even so will the redemption of mankind come, gradually but surely." [7]

In the words of Franz Kafka: [8] "There are two cardinal sins from which all others spring: impatience and laziness. Because of impatience we were driven out of Paradise, because of laziness we cannot return. Perhaps, however, there is only one cardinal sin: impatience. Because of impatience, we were driven out; because of impatience, we cannot return."

7. THANKFULNESS

1

THANKFULNESS ESSENTIAL TO MORALE

We all wish to make the most of our lives. With this in view, we commonly measure our achievements against our desires to see what it is that we lack, and we try to figure out how we can meet the deficit in our happiness. This keeps us discontented with the *status quo*, and serves as a spur to ambition and growth. Society as well as the individual can be stimulated to creative effort, by being kept aware of the discrepancy between present attainment and possibilities of attainment in the future.

And yet there is great danger that our constantly dwelling on the disparity between the real and the ideal, on the deficit in the happiness that we conceive to be due us, may defeat its purpose. Instead of serving as a spur to our ambition, it can very easily issue in a restless discontent and feeling of frustration. If, no matter how much we achieve, the gap between achievement and aspiration remains the same, does not all our striving again resolve itself into "futility and striving after wind?" Thus, the focusing of our minds on that gap may, instead of stimulating us and leading us into creative activity, induce in us a neurasthenic feebleness of will, a blasé world-weariness that finds no savor in life, an extreme debility and loss of vitality.

To avert such a fate and to save life from the stagnation of discouragement as well as from the stagnation of complacency, *it is necessary that, in addition to making ourselves sensitive to what it is that we lack, we cultivate sensitivity to what it is that we have.* Therein lies the significance of religious thanksgiving. This universal religious practice expresses the realization of how important it is for men to appreciate the blessings that have enriched their life, and to see in them evidence of a Power that makes for human salvation. If we are truly appreciative of the good already realized in our lives, we cease to be daunted by our knowledge of the fact that hope will always outrun attainment, because we know that, in the pursuit of our hopes, we shall meet with experiences like those with which we have already met, that will make life worthwhile for us. Seeking new horizons may seem a futile quest, indeed, for no one overtakes the horizon, yet adventurers who have followed its lure testify to the zest of exploration. In every obstacle they overcome, in every hardship they withstand and in every peril from which they escape they find a joy that they cherish in memory for ever.

In a sense, all life is just such a quest of new horizons. If we use the memory with which we are endowed to store the recollection of every experienced good, and the imagination with which we are endowed to conceive of similar experiences in the future, life can never be uninteresting to us. So to view life is to view it religiously. *The essence of religion is the affirmation of the worthwhileness of life. Belief in God is belief in a Power that assures the possibility of experiencing life as worth living. When, therefore, we are gratefully appreciative of the good in life, both the realized good and the hoped for good, we are experiencing the reality of God and communing with Him.*

The ritual of thanksgiving is often, in our day, subject to shallow criticism which can see in it nothing more than the attempt of men to cajole an anthropomorphic deity, by flattering phrases and obsequious gestures, into granting some desired boon, on the principle that "gratitude is the appreciation of favors yet to come." That rites of thanksgiving may often have been observed in this spirit, and are often so observed even in our own day, is doubtless true. But this spirit by no means explains the manifest joy that accompanies such religious rituals.

When the Psalmist says: "It is good to give thanks unto the Lord," [1] he is telling us in very straightforward language that he enjoys expressing his gratitude to God, that he finds it inherently worthwhile and life-enhancing. A Rabbinic dictum states that, in the millennium, all other sacrifices of the Temple ritual will be abolished, but the thank-offering will never be.[2] Since the millennium implied the realization of all Israel's hopes and yearnings, the retention of the ritual of thanksgiving would have no point, if thanksgiving were conceived as a means to an end. But when the salvation of Israel is finally achieved, communion with God can have no other meaning than an eternal thanksgiving, a continual awareness of salvation.

Although the spirit of thanksgiving should be fostered at all times, its importance is most evident in time of crisis. In such times there is no escaping an awareness of evil, an awareness of the forces that menace life and threaten our spirits with frustration. And precisely because we cannot evade them, because we must face the foe that imperils our future, we are in danger of panic. When fear, that is to say, the anticipation of calamity so dominates our minds that no other possibility except our succumbing to it presents itself, then it becomes panic and we are, indeed, lost. But if, at the same time that we face the evil we fear, we also are aware of our resources, if we are inspired with a certain self-confidence and trust in God, based on past achievement, if we feel that, even under great difficulties, life can yield unexpected, thrilling experiences, we do not encounter our problem in a defeatist mood, and our chances of success are immeasurably enhanced. This is why the Jew is enjoined to bless God even when misfortune befalls him.[3]

In our modern life, when the whole structure of our civilization is menaced by sinister forces, it is only too easy to be so hypnotized by their display of violence that we lose faith in those spiritual values which make civilization worth defending, in human freedom and the dignity of the individual soul, and in human solidarity and brotherhood. The serpent before striking its prey fascinates it with terror, so that it cannot even flee. If the evil in the present world engrosses our whole attention, we, too, will fall under its spell, will lose confidence in our power to resist, will forget God and worship Satan. Only as we feel sincerely grateful for all the good that is today being menaced, and as we permit our experience of the good to strengthen our faith in a God who will not abandon us, can we make life worth living for ourselves and for the generations after us. Only then can we walk unafraid through the valley of the shadow of death, because experience has taught us to find comfort in the rod and staff of God's salvation.

If our confidence in the happy possibilities of life is not to desert us in our crises, it is important that we cultivate the spirit of thanksgiving in normal times. Morale is a result of training. Untrained troops rarely show good morale under fire. If the Jewish people was able to survive under conditions to which other nations have succumbed, it must be ascribed, in no small measure, to Judaism's cultivation of the spirit of thanksgiving. The will to live was itself kept alive by a ritual that emphasized appreciation of blessings enjoyed, and still to be enjoyed. The Jew was encouraged to pronounce one hundred benedictions each day.[4] Every detail in the routine of his daily living was accompanied by a benediction. There were benedictions on partaking of different kinds of food and drink, on contemplating inspiring natural phenomena, on hearing glad tidings. Every religious rite was accompanied by a benediction designed to make the Jew aware that it was a privilege to be able to perform it, in that its performance enabled him to experience the sanctity of life. The typical traditional form of Jewish prayer is the *berakah*, the form commencing with the words: "Blessed art Thou, O Lord our God." Even prayers of petition generally conclude with blessing God, as the source from which the hoped-for boon is expected. In this way, our Sages stressed the thought that the prayer signified for them not merely an expression of desire for some concrete good, but of appreciation for their being able to rely on God as the source of good.

If we wish to cultivate that spirit of grateful appreciation by which religion strengthens our morale and enables us to meet the crises of life, we should endeavor to sensitize ourselves to perceiving the good in the daily circumstances of our life, in the opportunities for worthwhile activity that lie open to us, and in our experiences of successful achievement, both personal and social.

2

BEING SENSITIVE TO THE GOOD IN OUR DAILY CIRCUMSTANCES

There is a passage in our daily prayers which thanks God "for Thy miracles which are daily with us, and for Thy marvels and bounties which are manifest at all times, evening, morning and noon." [5] Were it not that repetition, habituation and preoccupation with affairs dulls our capacity of appreciation, we should find in our natural surroundings and in the marvelous adjustment of the human organism to its natural environment such deep gratification that the things we do, and the things that happen to us, would seem to have been created for our express enjoyment. Our waking every morning from the oblivion of sleep would be to us a miracle of resurrection. The light of the sun, enabling us to discern a world of interesting objects that had been obscured by the darkness of night, would be a miracle of creation, a repetition of the creative fiat, "Let there be light." Every breath of fresh air that we inhale, would be God's breathing into us the spirit of life, for by that breath we live. We would understand our forefathers' identifying breath with life, spirit, soul. "Every soul shall praise the Lord," [6] said the

Psalmist. Our Sages interpret that verse to mean that we are to be grateful to God for every breath that we draw.

We should eat our daily bread with a prayer of thanksgiving not only on our lips, but also in our hearts, for the whole process, beyond human comprehension, by which we sustain our powers of body and mind. And so, with all the circumstances of our daily routine, down to the time when, fatigued by the exertions of the day, we surrender ourselves to the sweet oblivion of sleep. For we know that, even in sleep, our needs are being ministered to, that the marvelous chemistry of our organism keeps our heart beating, and our lungs breathing, and our blood circulating. Without the participation of our conscious wills, we are being refreshed and strengthened to start a new day when God, "who slumbereth not nor sleepeth" will again summon our consciousness to active life.

Out of this grateful awareness of how the world in which we live not only sustains our life, but does so in ways that bring us delight and the feeling of well-being, there develops a sense of at-homeness in the universe. The quality of *bitahon*, of confidence in God, of willingness to commit oneself to Him, whatever the vicissitudes of life may have in store, of imperturbable serenity in times of crisis, is largely a product of this ability to see in nature the evidence of an all-pervading friendliness to man. The correspondence between the vital needs of men and the capacity of nature to satisfy those needs engenders the faith that even the unsatisfied needs of men are capable of being satisfied and will be satisfied.

Nature does not then seem something foreign or hostile to man, a medley of blind or even malicious forces. It seems, instead, to be animated by the same spirit that in human nature makes for man's self-realization; it manifests God. The exemplars of trust in God among our fathers were, by no means, ignorant of the fact that not all aspects of nature were friendly, that there were earthquakes, floods, pests and plagues of various description. But these did not seem to them to express the essential character of life, as they experienced it. It did not trouble them that they could not see God in the destructive and cataclysmic aspects of nature, in the earthquake, the tempest and the conflagration. They recognized his "still, small voice" in those orderly processes on which man could depend.

In our modern age, science, by revealing to us the laws behind forces that once seemed arbitrary interferences with human life, has enabled us to turn even those forces to human needs, to make the power manifest in the lightning illumine our homes at night, deliver our messages for us and bring music and entertainment into our homes. If we learned to appreciate the daily miracles by which we live, we, too, would develop a spiritual poise and tranquillity that would save us from the jitters so characteristic of humanity in our era of unheeding and reckless speed. We pass through life so quickly that we do not regale our spirits with its beauties and marvels. We are so eager to go ahead that we lose our way, and get nowhere. If we stopped sometimes to enjoy the landscape, we would see landmarks that could orient us; we would then very much enhance our chances of finding the road to our heart's desire.

3

BEING APPRECIATIVE OF LIFE-ENHANCING OPPORTUNITIES

In addition to accustoming ourselves to see, and gratefully enjoy, the good in the daily circumstances and routines of life, we should habituate ourselves to discovering opportunities for life-enhancing experiences, as they present themselves to us, and taking full advantage of them. We look at people who enjoy certain advantages that we lack, and are vexed that we lack them; meanwhile we possess advantages that we do not utilize. Only when they are threatened, do they become precious to us. We are horrified at the spread of intolerant regimes that do not allow freedom of speech, that do not acknowledge the right of men to tell the truth as they understand it; yet, we who have the freedom to speak truth are content to voice conventional lies, and, when prophets arise among us to proclaim God's truth to us, we seek to silence them with mockery and derision.

We recognize religious persecution as a great evil, and would resent any pressure designed to prevent our communing with our God as we see fit. But, when that pressure is removed, are we grateful for our religious freedom? Do we flock to synagogues and churches to take full advantage of religious freedom?

To be literate was, at one time, the exclusive privilege of a narrow circle of upper class society. Democracy has put literacy within reach of the masses. But how many people make use of their literacy to acquaint themselves with the best thoughts of the greatest minds of all times?

Every one of us has at his command cultural resources for living that can make life intensely interesting, but we lack appreciation to make the effort required for their utilization.

We are fretfully aware of the opportunities we lack, and are kept perpetually unhappy in our endeavors to push our way to the head of the procession, while the opportunities for happiness that we have at hand we let go by default.

The American Jew, who sees what has happened to Jews and Jewish life in Europe, cannot help thanking God for America and its democracy. But most of us have so neglected the cultivation of the spirit of thanksgiving, that our thankfulness is shallow and superficial. It lacks a deep appreciation of what American democracy means, in terms of opportunity for Jewish living. In the great centers of European Jewish population, Jews developed, in the very shadow of anti-Semitism, and despite enforced poverty and restrictions, a communal life abounding in cultural and spiritual values. Hasidism, Haskalah, Zionism, movements that made life interesting and sacred to Jews and distilled sweet and exalting influences from bitter and depressing experiences—all of them originated in those Jewish centers that are now extinct. In comparison with their achievements, what use has American Jewry made of its freedom and opportunities? What great religious, social or cultural movement capable of making life more worth living for Jews, for generations to come, has emanated from American Jewry, to represent its thank-offering to God for the political, economic, and educational opportunities that American democracy affords? In common with most other elements of the American population, we have, until the present crisis, been disposed to take the opportunities of American democracy for granted, and hence have failed to make the most of them.

The cultivation of the spirit of thanksgiving demands of us, therefore, not only an appreciation of those blessings that nature puts at the disposal of man in general, but of the more specific opportunities for worthwhile living that inhere in the particular situation in which we find ourselves, as individuals or as a community.

4

GRATITUDE FOR PERSONAL AND SOCIAL ACHIEVEMENT

There is, however, also a third series of blessings which we must bring into the focus of our consciousness. We should be mindful of the many occasions in our lives, when we have reason to feel that our own efforts, however humble, have borne fruit and have contributed, in however small a way, towards our self-realization; provided, of course, we can do it without feeling stuffy or pompous about it. It is a common practice to celebrate birthdays and anniversaries. We observe them usually with joy, but not with all the joy that they would yield, if we were fully aware of what is implied in such a celebration. For every year that a man lives represents an achievement. To be sure, we live largely by natural processes which are not at all subject to our voluntary control. A grateful awareness of these processes is fruitful of good. But, from the time when, in early childhood, we first began thinking of ourselves as individual human beings, our life has proceeded largely by the efforts we have made to fulfill the desires which arise from our needs. *The Power that sustains our lives, although infinitely transcendent, is also manifest in each directing self that organizes all its activities.* This truth is what the Jewish religious tradition has sought to express in the doctrine of *hashgaha peratit*, individual Providence.

That attitude of thanksgiving should include an appreciative evaluation of all those powers of thought, feeling and will by which we project purposes and achieve them. It is true that we do not achieve all our purposes. But, if we did not achieve most of them, we would not be alive. What is more, every achievement prepares the way for new achievement. This is the basis of all education. It is all a learning by experience. The education of a child is not an achievement of parents or teachers, although they have an important share in it; rather is it an achievement of the child himself, a result of his projecting his wishes and seeking the means for realizing them. The part of parents and teachers is to create such a situation for the child that his experiences will help him to learn what he needs most to learn for his own good and for that of society. Education, therefore, does not cease with schooling. There is no fixed limit to spiritual as there is to physical growth. The celebration of a birthday should be the celebration of a year of achievement. It means that our powers have proved adequate to meet the needs of life during the year that has been completed, and by reason of that year's added experience, are better qualified to meet future needs.

True, not all of our purposes have been realized, but what of it? Our life is not over. All those purposes that we have achieved were once also only purposes. And what if some of our purposes were frustrated so that we cannot hope ever to achieve them. We can even learn by our failures. At any rate life keeps generating new wants and new purposes, and many of them we shall be able to achieve.

Even the certainty of death cannot detract from the significance of our achievement. The fact that our purposes go beyond the sphere of our individual life is due to our being members of society. But society does not die with our death, hence death need not be the frustration of our purposes. Just as the life of the individual is a continuous acquisition of experiences and achievements that can be helpful in meeting new situations, so the life of society is a continuous acquisition of social experience registered in the civilization and culture of mankind, which it can use to advantage.

To be truly thankful for achievement means, therefore, to be thankful not only for one's personal achievement, but for those achievements of men which help us to live and to find life worth living, for the heroism of ancient heroes and martyrs, for the wisdom of ancient sages, for the beauty created by ancient artists, for the beneficent laws and social institutions inherited from the past, for all that is included in the terms "civilization" and "culture." *One might almost define the distinction between a cultured and a vulgar personality, in terms of their relative ability to appreciate past achievement.*

There are thus ample occasions for thanksgiving in every human life. They are to be found in our circumstances, our opportunities and our achievements. All of these can be utilized to cultivate the spirit of thanksgiving. But in what does that spirit itself consist?

5

WHEN THANKFULNESS IS RELIGIOUS

It is, in the first place, a spirit of appreciation without complacency. It is recognized in the Bible as the very opposite of that smugness which accepts as one's due all good fortune that one enjoys, and assumes that prosperity is exclusively one's own achievement and not evidence of the blessings that God has made available for man. In Deuteronomy, Moses cautions the people against just this tendency to assume that they possess virtue and valor, on account of the blessings that they would reap in the Promised Land: "And thou shalt eat and be satisfied, and bless the Lord thy God, for the good land which He hath given thee. Beware lest thou forget the Lord thy God . . . lest, when thou hast eaten and art satisfied, . . . thou say in thy heart: 'My power and the might of my hand hath gotten me this wealth.' " [7]

The Jack Horner attitude of feeling oneself a "good boy" or a good man, because one has managed to pull out a few plums from life's pie is not the spirit of thanksgiving. This applies to nations as well as men. Kipling, the poet *par excellence* of British imperialism, seems to sense the danger when, in his *Recessional*, he warns his countrymen, "Lest we forget." But he is not very clear on what they should remember, for he is too prone himself to credit British superiority. James Russell Lowell in his critique of American imperialism during the Mexican War sees and speaks more clearly. He satirizes the complacency of his compatriots, who feel justified in bullying the Mexicans, because "our nation's bigger'n theirs, an' so its rights air bigger." A Rabbinic *midrash* rebukes the tendency to assume that the fertility of a nation arising from ample rainfall and sunshine is necessarily a mark of divine favor, based on merit. It construes the verse "God saveth man and beast" [8] to mean that sometime man benefits only incidentally, because of God's concern for the needs of the cattle for which he sends rain and sunshine.[9]

The true spirit of religious thanksgiving is always accompanied by humility. Jacob, returning to meet his brother Esau, is gratefully aware of the wealth he has acquired in Mesopotamia, which made it possible for him to appease his brother's anger with gifts, but he does not credit that wealth to his own virtue. "I am unworthy," he says to God in his prayer, "of all the kindness and truth that Thou hast shown to Thy servant, for with only my staff did I cross this Jordan and now I have become two camps." [10] The traditional *berakah*, on escaping from some actual or threatened calamity, thanks God for bestowing "lovingkindness on the unworthy."

There is nothing abject about the humility that accompanies thanksgiving. It is not the tortured humility of the soul, haunted by a sense of sin and self-contempt. *Thanksgiving implies not only the awareness of man's dependence on God, but of God's dependability, of man's being able to feel secure in the possibility of salvation.* It implies the recognition of God, not only in nature and human society, but in our own souls, helping us to organize our purposes so as to make the most of our lives. It makes us feel that God is love. Not being God-forsaken, for the evidence of His bounties is constantly with us, we cannot feel unloved or unwanted in the world.

The feeling of thanksgiving, like all human feelings, craves expression. What is the appropriate form of its expression? One obvious form of expression is the verbal one. Language makes it possible for us to bring to consciousness all the many occasions for being grateful, and to recognize the implications of appreciation and humility that inhere in them.

Language alone is not enough. Our feeling of the dependence of our life on a life that flows through society and the world makes us feel the necessity of union and complete identification with that larger life. This means that we cannot look upon any blessing which we genuinely appreciate and acknowledge to be a manifestation of God, as though it were intended exclusively for us. *Unless we pass on these blessings, using them to enrich the lives of others as well as our own, we cut ourselves off from their divine source and forfeit them.* Our fathers who were sincerely and profoundly grateful to God for the gift of Torah, expressed their gratitude by adherence to the principle that, just as God gave the Torah freely to Israel, so is it the obligation of all who have learned Torah to teach it without remuneration to others. They likewise appreciated Eretz Yisrael as a divine gift, and they expressed their appreciation in the principle that it was not to pass for ever into any private hands. "The land shall not be sold in perpetuity, for the whole earth is mine." [11] The spirit of thanksgiving makes us feel no sense of property in what can be expropriated from others, but only in wealth that we create by our toil, and freely and voluntarily interchange and share with others. For we recognize in the power to labor the divine power of creation, and in the object of labor that personal and social salvation which is the will of God.

It is good, indeed, to give thanks to God in word and action. We cannot have too many expressions of sincere religious gratitude.

8. JUSTICE[1]

The ideal of justice is based on the assumption that human beings are intrinsically equal, notwithstanding their apparent inequality in all possible respects of ability, character and fortune. Justice is the antithesis of discrimination either in favor or against. As discrimination is based on that which either actually or supposedly makes men unequal, so is justice based on the belief that what makes them unequal is either secondary or illusory. *In respect to that in them which is their very essence, all men are equal. This is the standard by which all justice is measured.*

The principle of human equality is not derived from any moral or spiritual experience, but is that which itself makes such experience possible. It stands above all human formulations of justice, and yet is immanent in them all. Unequal treatment, when meted out in compliance with the demand of justice, is no more a negation of equality than are the differences between age and youth, between gifted and average persons. On the contrary, the very purpose of such unequal treatment is to compensate for the inequalities which differentiate human beings. When, under conditions which necessitate food rationing, priority is given to the sick, justice is done. Unequal treatment of that kind is equitable treatment.

But there is unequal treatment that arouses our resentment; this is because the inequality which comes with nature or circumstances is accepted as a norm, or as normal. When a retiring war veteran is unable to get materials for a little three-room house to live in the whole year, while the banker or slot-machine operator is given all he wants for a summer mansion at a beach resort, we have an instance of the type of injustice which results from accepting financial disparity as a proper reason for discrimination. Why is financial disparity a wrong basis of treatment? Because it is a disparity in power. It is the purpose of all laws and institutions, insofar as they are just, not to maintain such disparity, but to ignore it, in the interest of a higher law than that of unconscious nature, the law of human equality, which is the law of God.

The burden of most Prophetic utterances in the Bible is emphasis upon the teaching that God is a God of justice, and that justice is His law. It is to that end that God is represented as having chosen Abraham. "Behold, I have chosen him that he might command his children, and his household after him, to keep the way of the Lord to do righteousness and justice." [2] In all problems involving human relations, there is the natural tendency for injustice to enter through the door of partial treatment. Unfairness or injustice is a violation of the fundamental human equality, and is reprobate, whatever the human relationship in which it manifests itself, whether between judge and litigants, or government and citizens, or parents and children, or teachers and pupils, or employer and employees. In all cases where those at one end of the relationship have more power than those at the other end, there is the danger of freezing that disparity of power into a right or a privilege. To do so is, according to the consistently passionate exhortation of the entire Jewish tradition, to be guilty of *hamas*, violence. *The one thing God does not tolerate in man is violence. The only way, therefore, to avert violence is to reckon with the religio-ethical imperative of human equality, which is the soul of justice.*

1

FAITH IN HUMAN EQUALITY AS PART OF FAITH
IN GOD

In our present mad world, in which all important issues seem to be submitted to the arbitrament of brute force and cunning, it must appear incongruous to talk of equality. To be realistic, we must recognize the overwhelming mass of evidence to the fact that nature not only permits the domination of the weak by the strong, but seems to have endowed man with a will to power that finds its natural expression in the lust for domination, in the assertion of superiority over others. Even those who view with abhorrence all ruthless aggression feel called upon to equip themselves with the weapons that would establish their own superiority over the aggressors. If nature, as we know it, has the last word to say about human destiny, then, indeed, democracy is doomed.

The answer to the attacks on democracy, which is the order of society based on justice or equality, must indeed be a rallying to the defense of democracy. But to effect that, we must understand what we mean by democracy. The lack of a clear understanding of democracy is nowhere so apparent as in relation to the ideal of equality. That this is a part of the democratic ideal hardly needs to be stated. *The Declaration of Independence* affirms as the basis of those democratic rights which Americans have always cherished, that "all men are created equal." In the ideology that inspired the French Revolution, the source of all democratic movements in modern Europe, equality was ranked with liberty and fraternity as an essential social objective.

Nevertheless, in all the vast literature about democracy and about social and ethical problems of the modern world, very little has been written that casts any light on the questions: What do we really mean by the equality we are seeking? What must we do to achieve it? It is significant that, in the voluminous *Encyclopedia of Religion and Ethics*, there is no article under the rubric, *Equality*, although ample space is devoted to subjects of relatively minor import. If one were to look for an article on that subject in that encyclopedia, one would search in vain for it between the two rubrics, *Epistemology* and *Equiprobabilism,* which are deemed important enough to be included.

We cannot deal adequately with the problem of how to conceive of human equality and how to achieve it, unless we understand that its realization depends *not* on the working of natural forces, as these have been observed to operate in the whole past of human and pre-human life, but on the working of a spiritual Power that runs deliberately counter to the natural course of events. In the course of nature, there is among men a perpetual struggle for existence which results in the survival of the fittest, that is, of the physically strongest and mentally most alert. But in human life we find manifestations of a Power that run counter to this natural tendency. That Power aims not at insuring the survival of the "fittest" men, but at so changing the conditions of human life that all men shall be fit to survive. Instead of encouraging the strong and cunning to assert their power at the expense of the weak, God seeks to curb their power to hurt. He seeks to make them feel guilty and ashamed, when they do not help their weaker fellowmen to survive. Though it is entirely *natural* for strong men to use their strength, and for the quick-witted to use their wits to take advantage of their fellowmen and exploit them for selfish ends, it is neither moral nor ethical for them to do so. Morality and ethics belong to the spiritual Power which is creating a new era for man, one in which cooperation, kindness and love will bestow upon all men a chance to survive.

In the history of religion, one sees reflected a conflict that exists in the heart of man himself, the conflict between his natural and his moral nature, between his evil inclination—i.e. his self-assertive will to power—and his good inclination, between his natural depravity, often referred to as original sin, and the redemptive power of God. There is much confusion in the conception of God, owing to the fact that man's natural will to power tends to worship power as manifest in the world of nature, and to identify the assertion of power with God, thus making God out to be the protector of the vested interests of the strong. But *the universal belief in miracle and in divine redemption through miracle, and the traditional emphasis on a supernatural influence intervening in nature for man's salvation, testify to the intuition that nature has not the last word in determining the destiny of man.*

In modern religion, supernaturalism, in the sense of the temporary suspension of natural laws by a personal will capable of imposing itself on nature, is not tenable. We have discovered that, even for the attainment of spiritual goals, men must reckon with natural law as determining the means by which those goals can be attained. But we must still reckon with a trans-natural spiritual Agent, a Creative Power. This spiritual Power which we identify as God, does not abrogate or suspend any of those uniformities of behavior in natural objects by which it is possible for us, within the limitations of our knowledge, to predict the future. Nevertheless God, as the Creator, so influences the operation of natural law as to make it accommodate itself to spiritual aims that involve a reversal of the direction in which nature seems to have been operating. Though nature, therefore, seems to make for inequality among men by permitting only the fittest to survive, the spiritual forces operative in human life tend so to transform the conditions of life that all men shall be fit to survive.

When we trace the history of the ideal of human equality in the Jewish tradition, we note that, from early times, the inequalities of men were assumed to be evidence of the corruption of the world resulting from human sin. The very fact that Genesis ascribes the origin of the whole human race to a single pair of human beings is a protest against the pretensions to hereditary racial superiority of any people over others. Perhaps even more significant are what appear to be Biblical protests against the right of primogeniture. The special privileges of the first-born were based on the "natural" advantages that were his by reason of his priority of birth. Nature seemed to intend him for special privilege. He was the *reshit on*, the product of the unimpaired strength of his parents. Yet, in any number of Biblical stories, the first-born seems to have been deliberately passed over, as not necessarily being the child of destiny. The instance of Jacob's obtaining the birthright and blessing from Esau will at once come to mind. Yet this is only one of many stories of first-born sons who failed to make good. Here are a number of others: Cain, who killed his younger brother Abel only to become a fugitive and a vagabond on the earth; Ishmael, whose blessing was inferior to that of his younger brother Isaac; Reuben who forfeited his birthright; Manasseh, who was passed over in favor of his younger brother Ephraim; Aaron, who was subordinate to his younger brother Moses; Eliab, the first born of Jesse, who was passed over in the choice of a king in favor of the youngest, David, and Amnon, David's oldest son, who nevertheless did not succeed him, because he met an untimely death at the hands of his brother Absalom, while their father yet lived.

But religion, as has already been noted, often wavers between the natural and the spiritual attitude toward social inequalities. The history of the religion of Israel in pre-exilic times is a history of conflict between the deification of nature, as expressed in Baalism, and the deification of a spiritual power that transcends and transforms nature, as expressed in the Yahwism of the Prophets. The former tended to accept social stratification as "natural," and hence divinely ordained; the latter tended to regard it as unethical, and hence ungodly.

Our Sages, many centuries later, tried to reconcile their people to the inequalities of social status. They taught that such inequalities were divinely ordained. Even a supervisor of a well is appointed in heaven,[3] kings govern by "divine right," and "the law of the realm is the law." [4] Every man in his station, whether it be a high one or a low one, was called upon to conform to God's law in conducting his affairs, but he was not to abdicate a hereditary privilege, or to revolt against a heredi-tary status of inferiority. From the Rabbinic point of view, Esau's loss of the birthright was a penalty for disdaining the privileged position to which God had called him.[5]

Such teaching mitigated the suffering caused by social inequalities, but did not help to bring about a democratic society or a just social order. The rich would be disposed by such teaching to be charitable toward the poor, and to feel that their wealth was a trusteeship, impos-ing on them a sense of *noblesse oblige,* but they would, nevertheless, retain a privileged status in society. The poor would have the solace of feeling that their poverty did not mean that they were unloved, that it even had the advantage of enabling them, by their patience under their burdens, to win their share of the world to come more easily than if they were wealthy, for "proportionate to the suffering here will be the reward hereafter." [6] But their religion would not lead them to revolt against their inferior status. Inequality may involve evils, but these evils are part of the general burden of sin that the world carries. That burden could be lifted only by God, and would be lifted for those who conformed to His Law.

Under the influence of such teaching the situation with regard to human equality tended to deteriorate rather than to improve. This is notably true in respect to the position of woman. Although her legal status in Biblical times was perhaps no better than in later times, a reading of the 30th chapter of Proverbs, shows her as occupying a social position of dignity and importance that gave scope to the de-velopment of personality. But in Rabbinic times, although the study of Torah was regarded as the most rewarding spiritual activity, women were looked upon as essentially too light-headed to participate in it.[7] Though great store was set on the observance of religious precepts, there were only three rites that were deemed obligatory on women. Men praised God daily that they were not created women, while women, in pious resignation to God for having assigned them an inferior position were taught to say, "Blessed art Thou, O Lord, our God, King of the Universe, who has created me according to Thy will." The same attitude was taken over by the early Christian Church. Paul, in his Epistle to the Ephesians, tells his followers that just as the Church is subject to Christ, so wives are to be subject to their husbands in every respect.[8]

The Greek philosophical tradition did no better than the Jewish religious tradition in advancing human equality. Neither Plato's Republic nor Aristotle's Politics could conceive of a social order in which men were entitled to equal opportunities. Indeed, Aristotle, basing himself on a naturalistic view of society, justified slavery on the ground that some men are only fit to be human tools.[9] The classic writers assumed that inequality was an ultimate principle in human relations. Greek philosophy and Roman law regarded the purpose of the legal order as being that of preserving the social *status quo*. According to Roscoe Pound,[10] their purpose was "to keep each man in his appointed groove and thus prevent friction with his fellows. Thus in Plato's ideal state every member of the community is to be assigned to the class for which he proves to be best fitted. To Aristotle also, rights, i.e. interests to be protected by law, existed only between those who were free and equal. The law was in the first instance to take account of relations of inequality in which individuals were treated according to their worth . . . The well-known exhortation in which St. Paul calls upon everyone to exert himself to do his duty in the class in which he finds himself, brings out the same idea."

2

PRINCIPLE OF EQUALITY ENCOUNTERS SOCIAL INERTIA

Only with the gradual abolition of feudalism, and the incidence of those social forces that have ushered in the modern era, do we note the beginnings of a serious effort to realize the ideal of equality, and

to transform human society in some degree in compliance with it.
That such effort has so far met with but little success is evident in the
disillusionment of great masses of men with the whole conception of
democracy. This should not be surprising, in view of the fact that
equality means a complete reversal of the course of nature, and that
the naturalistic worship of power is much more deeply rooted in the
past of the human race than the religion of the spirit, which demands
equality. The power of the social inertia that resists any attempt to
break up the stratification of society finds no better illustration than in
the social structure and social attitudes of the English people. In many
respects, England is the most democratic of countries, and has been
a pioneer in the equalization of political power. In some ways, notably
in its political institutions, it is even more democratic than the United
States. Yet the social conditions there which were described by the
French critic and historian Taine as having obtained in 1872, though
much improved, are far from having disappeared entirely.

Taine [11] describes England in 1872 as a country governed by 100,000
families, with incomes of £1000 a year or more and upwards, "in
which the lord provides for the needs of his dependent, and the dependent is proud of his lord." He comments on the "haughty benevolence" of the lords and on the "submissive gratitude of the tenantry."
The change from a feudal to a capitalistic economy changed the com-
position of the upper class, through the inclusion of successful capi-
talists in the ranks of the landed aristocracy, but changed very little
the relations of the classes. The idea of a more or less uniform public
education for all citizens, without distinction of class, gained very slow
headway in England and, to this day, is much further from being
realized there than in the United States. Higher education is generally
deemed the natural prerogative of the "gentlemen," or of the hereditary
upper class. "It seems natural that working-class children should go to
the factory at an age, when the children of the well-to-do are just beginning the serious business of education. Equally natural that different
sections of the community should be distinguished not merely by differences of income, but by different standards of security, of culture, and
even of health. Social injustice survives, not so much because the rich
exploit the poor, as because the poor, in their hearts, admire the rich." [12]

Nevertheless, it is true that the change from the medieval to the
modern world does include putting the ideal of human equality on the
agenda of social action. The first efforts in this direction, which indeed
go back to very early times, represent the insistence on equality before

the law, on not respecting persons in judgment, and on just weights and measures. That much effort to realize the ideal of equality is met with even in Biblical times. But that this equality does little to correct the disparity between the rich and poor becomes immediately apparent, when we try to apply it more concretely. Of what benefit is it to men, who cannot earn their daily bread, that the theft of a loaf of bread by a rich man will be punished with equal severity as the theft of a loaf by a poor man? The very insistence upon equality before the law may thus operate to put the poor at a disadvantage, unless the law itself provides for removing other factors of inequality.

One of the important steps taken in modern times to equalize the opportunities of men was the achievement of political democracy, through the abolition of class-privilege in government and the extension of the ballot to all adult citizens. Abraham Lincoln, in referring to the Declaration of Independence as having given hope to all the world, for all future time, added, "It was that which gave promise that in due time the weight of the world would be lifted from the shoulders of all men, and that all men should have an equal chance." [13] But experience has taught us that the apparently equal power possessed by the citizens in having, each of them, but one vote is more apparent than real, as far as the influence of each on public policy is concerned. Government by ballot is government by public opinion, and public opinion is made by propaganda. Inequalities of wealth, education, and social prestige definitely give to those who already possess more power than is good for them the advantage politically over those who are underprivileged economically and socially.

The fact that the political institutions of democracy, while failing to eliminate poverty and economic crises, have permitted the economic and social inequalities of men to become sharpened, facilitated the rise of fascism and communism. Fascism promised to make good the failure of democracy in the matter of poverty and economic crises. But to do so, it reverted to the glorification of inequality and the worship of power. It hoped by national self-assertion to secure a position of superior status for its own nation over others, and, within the nation it sought to divide the population into more or less fixed castes taking orders from dominant personalities, who, in turn took orders from those above them, until the final arbiter was reached in the person of the dictator.

Communism, on the other hand, entered the arena against democracy with the avowed intent of creating an equality of economic opportunity, based on the collective ownership of all means of production. It did not overlook the natural differences in the capacities of men for physical and mental work, nor the differences in their needs arising from hereditary and environmental conditions, but it gave a definite formulation to what is meant by a classless society. It avowed its goal to be a social order that conformed to the principle, "From every one according to his ability, to every one according to his need." This, whatever one's opinion may be of the way in which communism has operated, is the clearest formulation to date of what equality of opportunity, the equality for which democracy strives, really means.

But, if one looks from the theory of communism to the actual conditions of life in Russia, the country which avows communism as its social creed, it at once becomes apparent that the mere adoption of the creed has not brought about the actual equalization of status which it commends. Men do not give to society according to their ability, but according to the demands made upon them by a governing bureaucracy, under penalty of dire consequences, if they practice "sabotage," i.e. if they do not produce as many bricks as the Pharaoh-commissar demands of them. Nor do they receive according to their needs. The strong, those that can produce more of the commodities that the controlling bureaucracy deems necessary, receive more, and those who can produce less receive less, regardless of their needs.

Communism, perceiving that the mechanization of industry had but enhanced, among the political democracies, the tendency to give power to the possessing classes over the propertyless, has sought to change the situation, through the socialization of the machine. But, putting its faith in power and in the organization of the will to power among the dispossessed rather than in spirit, it has made a god of mechanism, and has reduced the individual to a cog in the social machinery. And, again, those who possess the knowledge and power to direct and control that machinery have become absorbed in the mechanistic process of production, and have neglected the vital processes of satisfying the human demand for personal dignity and voluntary choice in directing one's own destiny. A regimented push-button society is the result, and those who push the buttons have every advantage over those who have to spring to attention when the button is pushed.

If, therefore, we sum up the achievements in the direction of equalizing the opportunities of men, since the rise of modern democracy first put such equalization of opportunity on the agenda, we find them apparently *nil*. In the Victorian era, when men were most hopeful of democracy, Matthew Arnold [14] could write: "A system founded on inequality is against nature and, in the long run, breaks down." In the light of modern experience, it would be difficult to maintain that inequality is against nature. But the breakdown of the capitalistic social order supports Arnold's contention that a system founded on inequality breaks down. Unhappily, modern experience also supports the contention of Lecky [15] to the effect that liberty and equality are irreconcilable enemies, since equality can triumph only at the expense of liberty. For, if men are free, they naturally assert their powers to the utmost and, being of unequal power, they produce social inequalities. Is there, then, no escape from the dilemma that equality demands regimentation, and can be achieved only by regimentation and tyranny, if it can be achieved at all? Must we, in the interest of liberty, abandon our insistence on equality?

The truth is that, in nature, equality and liberty may be contradictory, but in God, they are complementary. From a spiritual standpoint, there can be no liberty, or fraternity, without equality. "When liberty is construed realistically," says R. H. Tawney,[16] "as implying not merely a minimum of civil and political rights, but securities that the economically weak will not be at the mercy of the economically strong . . . a large measure of equality, so far from being inimical to liberty, is essential to it. In conditions which impose cooperative, rather than merely individual effort, liberty is, in fact, equality in action."

When we view in retrospect the whole experience of mankind with the ideal of equality, we find that it divides itself into two eras, and that we today may be standing on the threshold of a third. The first era was one in which human equality was conceived in terms of spiritual equality, but not in terms of social equality. During all of ancient and medieval times, although one finds many expressions of the equality of all men before God and the irrelevance of their status to their inherent worth as spiritual beings, one does not find any program for equalizing human rights. One finds, at best, efforts to mitigate the suffering caused by the inequalities of social status and to penalize what were considered abuses of privilege, as when the master injured his slave, rather than to do away with privilege, or to abolish slavery altogether.

The second era, from the downfall of the feudal system and the emergence of democratic concepts of government down to our own day, has been one in which the equality of men has been conceived in terms of economic rather than spiritual equality. The emphasis has been on equalizing the opportunity of men to secure the goods and services that they need to live a worthwhile life, and this has sometimes been achieved, as in Russia, at the expense of spiritual equality and of the equal opportunity of men to achieve human dignity and a feeling of personal worth.

In the future, we must reckon with equality both as an economic and as a spiritual requisite. As a spiritual requisite, equality implies counteracting the natural impulses in man that make for inequality, and helping all men to survive and achieve their legitimate goals. Equality as an economic requisite means reckoning with the obstinate realities of physical nature and acquiring the techniques by which all men may be equipped to survive in the struggle for existence and to fulfill as much as possible of the promise that inheres in them.

3

EQUALITY AS A RELIGIOUS IDEAL

More concretely, *the ideal of equality when conceived both as spiritual and as economic equality would mean that all human beings are entitled to experience the dignity of selfhood or personality, the moral character of society, and the reality of God.*

To experience the dignity of selfhood means that every individual must be able to feel that the society in which he lives regards him not merely as a means to an end, but recognizes him as an end in himself. He must not be treated as a mere cog in the machinery of production, but must be given as much of freedom of choice, in the way he earns his livelihood, and in the way he spends his leisure, as is consistent with the similar rights of others and the security of all. As long as he contributes to the productive process in accordance with his abilities, whether it be little or much, he is entitled to be treated with respect, and not be made a tool for the compulsory service of others, who take advantage of his dependence on them.

To experience personal equality in this sense, it is not necessary that all people have equal or identical powers or tasks, or that none must be in any way dependent on others. It is right that the skillful surgeon be permitted to operate, and the incompetent forbidden. The fact that I put my life in the surgeon's hands, when I permit him to operate on me, does not make me feel inferior to him, even though I do not possess his powers and am dependent on his skill for my very life. Differences in the circumstances of life or in physical and mental ability of individuals, would not be felt as constituting a serious problem, if every man knew that, under no circumstances would he lack the opportunity to feed, clothe and shelter himself and his dependents by engaging in work of his own choice, to marry and raise a family, without the specter of destitution, and to engage in those physical and mental exercises, and pursue those cultural and recreational interests, that are nearest to his heart.

To experience the moral character of society, we have to be aware that society is neither an organized mob that imposes its will by violence on other social groups or individuals nor a mechanism in which every man's life follows a predetermined pattern, wherein his own choices hardly count for anything. We have to be aware of society as functioning in the spirit of a community. A *community might be defined as that form of social organization in which the welfare of each is the concern of all, and the life of the whole is the concern of each.* In such a society there would still be differences in authority, based on functional divisions. Traffic regulations would still have to be obeyed, and engineers, rather than hucksters, poets or clergymen would direct the building of bridges. But men would, nevertheless, know themselves to be equal, if each one could feel that, under no circumstances would he have to be alone, unwanted, unimportant to his fellow men, insecure and forced to fend for himself, unaided against starvation, disease and all the natural and social ills. Under no circumstances, would he be compelled to join the pack in murdering and pillaging other societies. Under the principle of equality, such a society would have to embrace all the men and nations of the earth.

By being entitled to experience the reality of God, much more is meant than what is known as freedom of religion, though that is, of course, included. God, as the spiritual Power at work in, and upon, nature, as the Power that confers value on life, is experienced whenever we feel life to have meaning or worth. In whatever advances the dignity of the human personality or the moral character of society, there is implied the operation of a spiritual power that is moulding the course of nature.

The individual is not self-sufficient. Apart from his relations to his natural and social environment, his individuality has no meaning. In work, in play, in love, in art, in all that gives meaning to life, his individuality is inconceivable, except in terms of his relation to other persons. If he has within him spiritual powers that make him a creative personality, these are never wholly in him, but in his relation to the world. They merely come to a focus, as it were, in him, but they exist in God. They function as God in man, as a soul or moral personality, and, through them, he experiences himself as being in God.

To experience society as moral similarily implies the dependence of society itself on a spiritual power operative not merely in man, but in the cosmos. What mankind has become, and all that it aspires to become, must be achieved in accordance with the conditions of nature. If, therefore, man must learn from nature itself how to subdue nature, not in the sense of using it for his individual survival but of learning from it how to insure the survival and abundant life of all men, that Power cannot be limited to man but must interpenetrate nature itself and the whole cosmos.

Whenever men experience their dignity as responsible agents of spiritual power, whenever they can envisage society as the Kingdom of God, they realize what it means for the Spirit of the cosmos to emerge out of nature and give it worth and meaning. To realize that is to experience the reality of God. That experience is implicit in whatever is done for the happiness of the individual and the welfare of society. The function of organized religion is to render that experience explicit. By articulating that experience, by encouraging men and communities of men to seek such experience as a conscious purpose, we further the ideal of human equality. On the other hand, by discouraging any honest effort of men to commune with God, the source of life's value for them, we deny them equality of spiritual status. This it is what makes religious freedom so important. It must be conceived as the right of all men to seek to cultivate in themselves, and in such free association as they may choose, the religious experience, the sense of their rapport with all that renders life worthwhile for them as individuals, as members of a particular society or communion, and as human beings sharing in the life of the cosmos.

The claim of any religion, therefore, to be the exclusive custodian of the opportunities of human salvation, to deny validity to the claims of other religions to the experience of the reality of God, or to assume that only through its doctrines and rites can men experience that reality, is vicious, and is a sin against the ideal of equality. The Spirit, which is turning human nature away from the proclivity to seek only the survival of the individual, or of his own limited social group, and is in the process of establishing universal human brotherhood to insure the opportunity of survival to all men, operates within every human being and human society that seeks communion with it. Although some individuals and religious communities may possess more, and others less of this spiritual power, none is totally lacking in it, and none has a monopoly of it.

The contempt of one religious tradition for another, the ready assumption of that other's inadequacy, and the effort at religious hegemony, are evidences of the naturalistic worship of power, and are inconsistent with the worship of the Spirit. Consequently the pragmatic implication of the demand for equality of opportuniy to experience the reality of God is the abandonment of all efforts at trying to win people away from one religious communion to another. *Any ideal that is of universal significance, that belongs not to the worship of Power but of Spirit, is capable of adoption by, and adaptation to, any and all religious traditions.*

This then is what the ideal of equality demands of us: that we seek self-fulfillment by developing our powers for creation and not for destruction or domination; that all men should be encouraged to use their creative powers to the utmost; that, in seeking to advance the interest of our nation, our race, our class, or any other societal unit to which we belong, we insist on their behaving in their collective capacity as moral agencies, on their respecting the personal dignity of their constituent individuals, and on their seeking cooperation with, and not domination of, similar societal groups; that, finally, we recognize the universal right of all men to seek communion with God and the spiritual security of sharing in His omnipresent and eternal life, by reverencing their loyalties to those traditions and institutions through which they have experienced God, and by not permitting the hegemony of any one tradition over others.

Such an ideal of equality or justice involves no denial of the inequalities that exist in nature. It involves no such resolution of those inequalities as that which relegates the functioning of the ideal of equality to some imagined life in another world, and prevents the recognition of the spiritual equality of men before God from functioning in our practical every day human relations. The ideal of equality here enunciated would create on this earth a better, more just way of life than is ours today.

Men may differ from one another in the conditions and circumstances of their lives and even in their respective capacities without being frustrated and unhappy. But we must recognize and acknowledge, in deed as well as in word, their equal right to experience the worthwhileness of life. If only we sought justice sincerely, even though we did not succeed in achieving it fully, this world would be a sufficiently blessed place to live in.

9. LOVE

1

THE MAIN FUNCTION OF RELIGION

The new approach to the problem of religion, developed throughout these pages, not only distinguishes between believing in God and having an intellectual conception of Him. It also emphasizes the primacy of belief in God and treats the conception of God as secondary.[1] *To believe in God is actually to experience the urge to achieve our human destiny, or to attain salvation.* On the other hand, to form an intellectual conception of God is to arrive at some formula of being that would not only account for all that is, but that would also throw light on men's nature and destiny. The hunger for salvation is as real as the hunger for food; it embraces the belief in God, just as the hunger for food embraces the belief that there is something which can satisfy it. *Belief* in God is thus a *datum*, a given fact. The *conception* of God, on the other hand, is like the *explanation* of the hunger for food. The explanation may be true or mistaken, but the datum or fact for which the explanation is given cannot but be genuine, unless the very yearning to achieve one's destiny is itself an illusion. All that one then needs to know about God is how His existence validates the yearning for salvation, and conveys a sense of its being rooted in the ground of reality.

This distinction between the belief in God and the conception of God is not merely a matter of semantics. It is intended to focus attention upon what should be the main function of religion. If the main function of religion were to provide us with a proper conception of God, we would have to assume, with some of the medieval theologians, both Jewish and non-Jewish, that man's salvation or destiny is to be achieved in the domain of the intellect. That would confine salvation to the very few people in the world who have a special gift for highly abstract metaphysical speculation. To be sure, they would have to be free from all moral taint. It would, however, not be their moral purity that would qualify them for salvation, but their extraordinary intellectual power. This would reduce the masses of men to mere adjuncts and background for the elect few, with no hope of ever achieving the goal for which the human being is destined.

Whatever hold this notion of the function of religion may have had on thinkers in the past, including even Maimonides,[2] it is alien to the genius of Jewish religion, and was imported into it by some medieval philosophers and mystics. Traditional Jewish religion, in stressing the functional value of the *belief* in God, centered its interest on having man know what constitutes our true destiny or salvation, and the means that are to be employed in achieving it. From that standpoint, the belief in God, as the Power that makes for salvation, gives validity to man's striving for it, and enables him to persist in this striving despite continual frustration. It becomes essential for man to hold on to the belief in God, for only thus is man kept mindful of the fact that no matter how long his quest for salvation, or how beset it be with hindrances, he will ultimately achieve his goal.

With that as the function of religion, its principal concern is bound to be not the sharpening of the intellect, but the conduct of men toward one another. For it is essentially the way men live together that determines whether they shall achieve life abundant, or reduce life to mere "vanity and striving after wind." The particular ideas, conceptions or notions they hold concerning the metaphysical nature of God then have their value chiefly as a reflection of what they consider to be the nature of man's destiny and the possibilities of his achieving it.

The theologians and religious thinkers, during the past twenty centuries, have tried very hard to have religion function as the source of the truth concerning the metaphysical nature of God, even though they realized that it is impossible for man to attain a knowledge of the ultimate reality of God. They insisted that it was man's function to achieve a knowledge of "the side of God which is possible of comprehension." And when we ask what aspect of God they regarded as possible of comprehension, we are told "it is the consideration that all existing things are due to His influence, and that He is their cause and their maker." [3] Likewise Albo [4] states that "the purpose of the Torah is to teach men intellectual conceptions and true opinions."

Religion, however, as it has actually been lived by the vast majority of human beings, has had little to do with that distortion of its function. For them, the belief in God, together with what it implies concerning the nature and certainty of salvation, has constituted the essence of religion. Jewish tradition goes so far as to impose limits on the extent to which we may speculate concerning the metaphysical nature of God. Interest in anything beyond the actual world of time and space is deprecated as not only irrelevant, but as liable to divert man from the salvation he should strive to achieve. "Ask now of the days past, which were before thee, since the day that God created the earth." [5] Bar Kappara [6] interpreted the verse as meaning: "You may speculate on what happened from the day that days were created, but not on what was before then."

The real purpose of religion is to direct men's attention to the problem of salvation and to the means of its attainment. This is the point in the frequent exhortations both in the Torah and in Rabbinic lore that we be *like* God. In the Torah we are commanded: "Be ye holy, for I, the Lord your God, am holy." [7] "Ye shall walk after the Lord, your God. . . . and cleave unto Him." [8] "Is not God a consuming fire? How then is it conceivable that man should walk after Him?" asks Rabbi Haninah bar Hama.[9] The term "consuming fire," suggested to the ancients that aspect of divinity which God does *not* share with other beings.[10] That aspect could not possibly be emulated by man. The only aspect of the nature of God which might be emulated is that which they assumed was common to God and man. That could be none other than the aspect of love. A well-known rendering of the verse, "This is my God and I will glorify him," [11] sees in it an exhortation to glorify God, by being Godlike in the exercise of His attributes of mercy, grace and long-suffering.[12]

2

THE MEANING OF REDEMPTIVE LOVE

When we consider the divine attributes of mercy, grace and long-suffering in the light of the events which, according to the Torah, provided the occasion for their being revealed to Israel, we find that they add up to the divine quality of forgiveness. For the occasion on which they were made known was the inner crisis in the life of the Israelites in the Wilderness, when they worshiped the Golden Calf. Moses then interceded in their behalf. It was then that he is said to have learned that God was "full of compassion, and gracious, slow to anger and plenteous in true lovingkindness, keeping lovingkindness for thousands, forgiving iniquity, transgression and sin." [13] He learned at the same time, however, that only those who repented of their sins could benefit from the divine attribute of forgiveness, that God "will by no means clear the guilty." He therefore pleaded with God to reverse the process, and manifest His forgiveness, in order to evoke Israel's penitence. That is apparently the meaning of Moses' response to the revelation of God's attributes. "Let the Lord, I pray Thee, go in the midst of us," said Moses, "for it is a stiff-necked people; and pardon our sin and take us for Thine inheritance." God, we are told, yielded also to this second prayer of Moses.[14]

If we interpret psychologically this ancient tale and the use made of it in our tradition, it will be found to imply a number of highly significant religious truths. In the first place, it implies that man's capacity to repent, or to remake himself, is the source of his continuing to believe in the ultimate achievement of his destiny, despite his repeated frustrations. This capacity to repent presupposes forgiveness. Repentance and forgiveness are like the two sides of the same shield. Secondly, the trait of forgiveness is a manifestation of a transcendent Power that makes for the realization of man's destiny. And finally, as part of our striving for salvation, we have to learn to forgive those who have wronged us, for thus we do emulate God.

Reduced to a single basic truth, the foregoing principles amount to the following: In contrast with man's cardinal sin, which consists in playing the god, man's cardinal virtue consists in being Godlike. *To be Godlike is to exercise that redemptive love which expresses itself as forgiveness in such a way as to elicit penitence from the sinner.*

Redemptive love has nothing in common either with erotic love or with possessive love. It not only calls forth the best in others as well as in ourselves, when the love is mutual and no grievance of any kind mars it; it can also break down the wall of evil and wrongdoing that divides men, and re-establish happy and wholesome relations among them. The commandment, "Thou shalt love thy neighbor as thyself," [15] has evidently nothing to do with erotic love, which does not have to be commanded but controlled, nor with possessive love, which can hardly be regarded as love. The only kind of love which does not emerge spontaneously is redemptive love. Though we must assume its presence deep down in our nature at its best, we have to exert our powers of mind and will to bring it forth. That is why it is the subject of divine command.

We are least prone to love our neighbor when he has done us injury, when he has harmed us in our well-being or reputation. The natural course is to allow ourselves to be swept on by the urge of anger, hatred and the desire for revenge. Comes the divine behest and pulls us back. "Thou shalt not take vengeance nor bear any grudge against the children of thy people, but thou shalt love thy neighbor as thyself." [16] Whether we should wait with our forgiveness until he who has wronged us repents, or should extend it before he has repented is a moot question in Jewish tradition. In the Testament of the Twelve Patriarchs, one of the apocryphal writings, we are bidden "If anyone seeketh to do evil unto you, do well unto him and pray for him." [17] This precept is found not only in the unofficial writings. Even in our canonical writings we come across the specific teaching that a man should turn the other cheek to him who has smitten him on the one cheek.[18] But there are no two opinions anywhere in Jewish tradition with regard to retaliation, even where the wrongdoer is in no repentant mood. "They who do not persecute those who persecute them, they who suffer wrong in silence and requite it not, are deemed the friends of God." [19]

It may well be that, from the standpoint of punitive justice, we have the right to give vent to our hatred and to retaliate the wrong done to us, particularly when the wrongdoer shows not the slightest evidence of regret or repentance. Even then we should hold ourselves in check. For every time we give way to hatred, we impair our capacity for love. So much is that capacity an integral part of our nature at its best that, when it is weakened or destroyed, we cannot help but experience frustration. Revenge may be sweet, in that it is the gratification of a hereditary biological impulse which we share with the animal world. But it is not part of the essential humanity in our nature. That essential humanity yearns to express itself in outgoing redemptive love. *When we defeat love by yielding to an impulse which we share with the subhuman, we cannot be happy.*

When it is actually possible to elicit repentance by exercising forgiveness in advance, we are expected to emulate God who forgives in order that men may repent. This is what the story of Moses' intercession seems to teach. Such is the Godlikeness which we are bidden to practice. According to Rabbi Akiba, the fundamental teaching of the Torah is the precept: "Thou shalt love thy neighbor as thyself." [20] According to Ben Azzai, it is the doctrine implied in the verse in Genesis which reads, "This is the book of the generations of Adam. In the day that God created man, in the likeness of God made He him." [21] Rabbi Akiba and Ben Azzai [22] are in reality agreed on the basic idea that to love one's neighbor constitutes being Godlike. They merely differ as to where to place the accent. Rabbi Akiba would place it on loving one's neighbor; Ben Azzai on the need of achieving Godlikeness.

Why forgiveness should be the highest manifestation of redemptive love it is not difficult to understand. Redemptive love is the interest we take in our neighbor, not because of any good to ourselves that we may get out of him. It is awakened by our faith in those possibilities of his nature which, if realized, would enable him to achieve his human destiny. It is not difficult to love our neighbor, if he himself is alive to the meaning of human destiny and self-fulfillment, even though he may rarely summon enough will-power to live up to that meaning. But such must be the redemptive power of our love that it should be able to penetrate to the hidden springs of goodness beneath the hard and re-pellent exterior of man's selfishness, pettiness and moral insensitiveness, and by forgiveness and kindness bring that goodness to the surface.

In modern literature, this truth is embodied in *Les Miserables* by Victor Hugo. The central figure of that story is Jean Valjean, a simple hard-working peasant, who was sentenced to serve in the galleys for five years, for having stolen a loaf of bread to save his sister's child from starvation. His punishment is lengthened to nineteen years because of several attempts to escape. When he is finally freed from prison, he begs in vain, until he is given food and shelter by a saintly Bishop who takes him into his own home. Valjean returns the kindness by stealing the Bishop's silver and escaping. When he is caught, the Bishop saves him, by declaring that he had given him the silver as a free gift. This act of forgiveness awakens the dormant goodness in the heart of Valjean. He throws off the hates and fears drilled into him by his years as a convict, and succeeds in becoming a man highly respected and loved for his generosity and kindness to many an unfortunate.

The universal appeal of this romantic tale is due to the fact that it reflects a basic trait of human nature, one covered by so much that is sordid and cruel that its very existence is often questioned. We deem ourselves realists and worldly-wise when, in a spirit of cynicism, we laugh off the very thought that there is an inherent goodness in man, which can be elicited by the power of redemptive love. We are inclined to pooh-pooh both goodness and love, as the wishful thinking of im-practical visionaries. Yet, they are the only foundation on which we can build the future of mankind. We are bound to fail, if we try to build human life on the assumption of self-interest as the dominant trait in man. That assumption always turns out to be naught but a foundation of sand. Insofar as we believe at all in man's inherent goodness and in the power of love to elicit it, we believe in God as the Power that makes for the realization of human destiny. *Both goodness and love are themselves the principal manifestations of God in human life. It is through them alone that we can experience His reality and worship Him in truth.*

3

WHY REDEMPTIVE LOVE IS DIVINE

Jewish tradition actually identifies redemptive love as divine. In the Prophet Hosea's vivid dramatization of God's relation to Israel as the relation between husband and wife, Israel's toleration of the idolatrous cults and her intrigues with one or the other of the great empires, Assyria or Egypt, are likened to marital infidelity. For these sins, God should cast off Israel. He forgives her, however, because He discerns in her a latent sense of loyalty and fidelity.

Both the bitterness which Israel's infidelity calls forth in the soul of the Prophet, and God's tender love which he envisages as arousing Israel to her true self, are enunciated by him with matchless power and beauty. The Prophet does not spare his people. He castigates them for their moral depravity, for their perjury, murder, highway robbery, adultery, sacred prostitution and the usurpations and assassinations of kings. How much more corrupt need a people be to be considered irredeemably doomed? Yet the Prophet cannot get himself to believe that there is no hope of moral recovery for his people. Identifying himself with God—the God of redemptive love—he utters the heartbreaking cry: "How shall I give thee up, Ephraim? How shall I surrender thee, Israel? How shall I make thee as Admah? How shall I set thee as Zebaim? My heart recoils. All my compassion kindles. I will not execute My fierce anger to ruin Ephraim again, for I am God, not man, the Holy One in the midst of thee." [23] As the God of love, He can see the good even when it is hidden by the thick layer of moral corruption. He therefore does not judge His people merely by what they are, as man would; He takes into account what it is in their power to become, and He wards off their destruction.

This divine quality of confidence in the existence of good beneath outward insensitiveness to higher values, or even beneath manifest evil, is the redemptive love which man must acquire. It does not come spontaneously, as do those desires and tendencies which are part of a long biological heredity. But it is indispensable as a means of enabling man to break through the seemingly interminable round of sin and suffering. We behold evidences, on every hand, of the creative power of the redemptive love which has an unfailing eye for the latent possibilities, for the real self in each of us, which we seldom reveal even to ourselves. Before, however, we are in a position to practice redemptive love in our personal relationships to one another, between parents and children, between teachers and students, between employers and employees, between members of different racial, creedal and national groups, *we must start out with a broad premise of love with regard to the human being as such.*

It is very difficult, after we get our daily fill of news about what goes on in the world, to retain our love for man as man. He seems to us a most disgusting creature. There is no conceivable crime or folly from which he is free. Whatever powers he succeeds in achieving he somehow manages to apply to the worst possible uses. The old saying about nature's being red in tooth and claw is an accurate description of the way human beings feel and act toward one another. Under the veneer of civilization, man is not only a beast, but a foul one at that, using all his cleverness to hide the most dastardly crimes which he would commit, were he not prevented by fear of retaliation. And so we can go on exposing the human being as he is, and, by accumulating reasons for hating man, become misanthropes. In our hate and disgust, we must, if we are consistent, include ourselves. We need only read what modern depth psychology tells us about our dreams, our rationalizations, our slips of the tongue, to realize that our subconscious is a kind of menagerie that harbors all manner of wild beasts.

We are all too prone to fall into this mood of self-hate and self-contempt. It becomes a slough of despair against which we must ever be on our guard. "I said in my haste," declares the Psalmist, "all mankind is a failure." [24] We must take hold of the divine command, "Thou shalt love thy neighbor as thyself," in the same way as one who has fallen into a dangerous swamp, if he is to save himself, has to take hold of a rope that is thrown out to him. We must allow ourselves to be drawn out from the fatal mood of misanthropy by the divine imperative. We must habituate ourselves in that redemptive love for man which knows how to forgive, because it understands man, his antecedents and his limitations, and because it judges him not for the evil he has done but for the good he has it in him to do.

It is at this point that our more recently acquired knowledge of man's slow climb, from beastliness to barbarism, from barbarism to civilization and from civilization-based-on-fear to civilization-based-on-love, can stand us in better stead than the traditional assumption that man came forth perfect from the hand of God, and by his own rebellion forfeited the power of being Godlike. *When we bear in mind the relatively short period during which man has had to transmute himself into the higher being he genuinely wishes to become, we can be more patient with his recalcitrance and seeming incapacity to learn from his own experience.* We then realize that we have no right to expect hungers or tendencies with an ancestry of millions of years to be brought under control by ideals and standards of yesteryear.

This faith in the human being, this right to expect him to rise to greater heights of the spirit, is the way in which we must learn to love the humanity or divinity in ourselves and, by the same token, the humanity or divinity in our neighbor. In fact, it is possible to love our neighbor with a redemptive, and not merely with a narcissistic, love, only in so far as we love God. For God is the Power that makes for man's salvation or the fulfillment of his destiny. To love any one with a redemptive love is to love him to the point of helping him to achieve that destiny. On the other hand, it is impossible for us to love God without loving our neighbor, for without loving our neighbor there is no meaning to salvation or human destiny.

When redemptive love finds expression as creative forgiveness, it has reached its maximum potency. To expect any one to achieve such power at the beginning of his career is like expecting one to begin school at the final grade. Beside a long preparatory training in the acquisition of the proper intellectual background, the highest manifestation of redemptive love presupposes a strenuous self-discipline in two traits that are more elementary—compassion and lovingkindness.

4

COMPASSION AND LOVING-KINDNESS AS
PREREQUISITES TO REDEMPTIVE LOVE

In the Hebrew language, the word for *compassion* is closely related to the word for *womb*. The genius of the Hebrew language seems to have realized that mother-love is the source of all compassion. What is there that a mother will not do for her child? Whenever her child suffers, she suffers with him. She gives her whole strength to serving his needs, without so much as a thought of herself. She sacrifices her ease, her health and, if need be, even life itself that her child may live. That compassion, to be sure, is instinctive. It is a natural response of tender emotion aroused by the helplessness and dependence of the child. Yet it rarely exhausts itself in the care of the infant whose protection and nurture are its immediate biological function. That love is likely to be aroused by other children as well, particularly if they are orphaned and are thus dependent on adults other than their own parents. It is aroused, indeed, by all human beings who are known to suffer physical or mental agony. Rabbi Johanan, commenting on the Proverb, "All the days of the poor are sad," [25] declares the word "poor" refers to the compassionate, for as long as there is suffering anywhere, the compassionate cannot be happy.[26]

The Hebrew writer Jacob Steinberg relates, in one of his inimitable stories about life among village Jews, of the impression made on them, when a certain non-Jew suspected of stealing was being questioned and tortured by the police. His cries were heard outside the village jail and, although he was not one of their community or faith, all the Jews of the village were so moved by his suffering that they too suffered with him.

In a recent account of the harrowing experiences of a few survivors of the Hiroshima tragedy, the writer tells of a pastor who, when he encountered the wounded and bereaved, felt that he must apologize for emerging from the disaster unscathed.[27] We are told that he felt so "overwhelmed by the shame of being unhurt," that he kept saying to them: "Excuse me for having no burden like yours."

Such compassion goes far beyond the mere biological impulse to protect one's own progeny or immediate dependents. It has reached that Godlike quality of loving one's neighbor as oneself. It is part of the love of all that lives; this is equivalent to the love of God. As such, it exemplifies not only the attribute of *rahamim, compassion,* but also the attribute of *hesed, lovingkindness.* Lovingkindness is the disposition not only to enter into the suffering of others but to give relief, comfort and happiness to others. It has its roots in the gregarious impulses of man, in the desire to share, in the feeling that blessings which cannot be shared cannot be enjoyed.

The statement by Rabbi Johanan quoted above, that the compassionate person cannot be happy, because he is sensitive to all the suffering about him is only half the truth. For if his pity issues in remedial action, he can find a deep joy in dispensing relief and helping others out of their misery. It is by giving to life rather than by demanding from life that life yields its abundance, that we live abundantly.

It is inconceivable that anybody, who ever gave himself whole-heartedly, courageously and with utter devotion to a great cause in which he believed, should ever regret his having done so. We cannot imagine that Moses, despite all that he had to suffer with his people and even at the hands of his people, ever hankered for the life of ease, pleasure and security which he might have enjoyed in the palace of Pharaoh. His compassion and lovingkindness impelled him to throw in his lot with his oppressed and enslaved people.

Eugene V. Debs, when told that he had thrown away opportunities for a distinguished personal career by identifying himself with the struggling labor movement, replied that he did not want to rise above his class, he wanted to rise with them. When declared guilty of having violated the espionage law in a speech given at Canton, Ohio, on June 16, 1918, he replied to the court: "Your honor, years ago I recognized my kinship with all living beings and I made up my mind that I was not one bit better than the meanest of earth. I said then, I say now, that while there is a lower class, I am in it; while there is a criminal element, I am of it; while there is a soul in prison, I am not free." [28]

Those who are imbued with compassion and lovingkindness understand and identify themselves not only with those who suffer, but even with the criminal and the sinful, not merely in condemning sin, but in understanding and forgiving the sinner. The discipline of compassion and lovingkindness has reached in them that maximum potency which results in redemptive love.

Such a life cannot be drab and desolate; it is adventuresome and triumphant. Men who live such lives, even though they may not lead their cause to victory, though death may call them before they enter the promised land, envisage their goal from afar, and know that it will be reached and their toil rewarded with achievement. They live lives not of frustration but of self-fulfillment, of salvation. They have perfected those human attributes which, precisely because they are distinctively human and represent man's transcendence of the beast in him are also divine, part of the creative Power at work in the universe that makes for realization of human destiny.

That ideal has always been in the forefront of Israel's religious consciousness. Whoever lacked the qualities of compassion and lovingkindness could not, they said, be considered a true descendant of Israel's Patriarchs. [29] And when our people were most gratefully aware of God as the Power on which their salvation depended, and from which all their blessings flowed, they exclaimed: "Give thanks unto the Lord for He is good, for His lovingkindness endureth forever." [30] Only as our religion can foster these ideals in us can it succeed in fulfilling the function of religion. If it does succeed, it can help to redeem the world by the divine power of redemptive love.

PART III

TOWARD A NEW PATTERN
FOR JEWISH LIFE

CHAPTER SIXTEEN

THE GOOD AND THE BEAUTIFUL
IN JEWISH LIFE

ETHICS

1

THE TORAH TRADITION A PERENNIAL STIMULATION
TO THE GOOD LIFE

In the past, Judaism helped the Jew to live at his best. By making him feel that he was accountable to God for everything he did or failed to do, it gave dignity and worth to his personal life. The belief that the Jew was a member of a Chosen People imbued him with a spirit of *noblesse oblige*. It meant that in the Torah, God had revealed to him through his people a way of life. To know and to obey the Torah was at once the responsibility and privilege of the Jew. It gave him the key to eternal life hereafter; but it did more, it prescribed a way of life for him, an ideal and a discipline; it enabled him to organize his impulses and desires into an harmonious pattern of personality; it adjusted him to his fellow-men; it contributed to justice, cooperation and love. Not only did the Torah bring out his ethical powers, but it also awoke in him the desire to penetrate as deeply as possible into the meaning of the Divine Word. It led to intellectual pursuits which were satisfying in themselves, and rewarding in the respect they elicited from his fellow-Jews.

Can Judaism do as much for the modern Jew? In a world in which the Jew has been singled out as the victim of violence and injustice, life must be utterly meaningless for him, or possessed of sinister purport, unless he can find satisfaction in his very struggle against violence and injustice, and be helped in overcoming these evils in himself, the better to defeat them in the world. Can the Torah tradition of the Jew still aid him to this end? Every emotion experienced by the Jew in the past, from the mirth of Purim to the elegiac mood of Tishēa BeAb, found aesthetic expression in musical modes, art-forms, poetry and ritual. Can Judaism in our day make the tragic experience of Jews in the present time meaningful and edifying to future generations through expression in the arts?

Apparently, most modern Jews have found little inspiration to

343

ethical living, or artistic expression, through adherence to Judaism. The fact that so many Jewish parents are reluctant to give their children a Jewish education would be shocking, indeed, if one were to infer from it that they were indifferent to the character training of their children. The truth is, however, that they are not indifferent, but have lost confidence in the power of Judaism to contribute to the development of indispensable ethical traits, and are disposed to depend on the public schools for such training.

It does not lie within the power of the state to provide all that is needed to bring out the best in a person. In the early years of the child's life this is mainly the task of parents. But whence do parents obtain the ethical principles and attitudes that they, partly deliberately, but even more so, unconsciously, impress on their children? To some extent these are derived from the general cultural environment and from public education through the school, the press, the motion pictures, the radio. But they are also derived from the cultural tradition in which one is born. That cultural tradition is the more influential, because of its association with the warm and friendly atmosphere of home.

The Jew who has broken away from Jewish affiliation and has repudiated the Jewish cultural heritage is deprived of that influence. In this respect he is not in an equal position with the non-Jew because the latter, like the loyal adherent to the Jewish group, has a cultural tradition of his own derived from his particular ancestral strain, whether it be Catholic or one of the many Protestant versions of Christianity, whether it go back to the Pilgrim fathers or the Swedish settlers of the Middle West, or the planter aristocracy of the South or the Negro cabin of a slave ancestry, with the African jungle in the remote background. The expectations of those near and dear to us, who show their love and concern for our welfare, are more effective influences in developing our ethical and social attitudes than the expectations of those who are remote from us, and who are relatively indifferent to our interests. The Jew cannot partake of any of these potent traditional cultures which combine to make the pattern of American life. Unless, therefore, he avail himself of his own Jewish culture, he inevitably lacks one of the strongest influences for bringing out the best in himself.

Moreover, the measure of a person's ethical responsibility varies in accordance with his power to be ethically effective. We must, therefore, develop our ethical powers by exercising them in the more intimate relations of the family first, and thereafter in the community of families with which we feel most at home, because of sharing in a common tradition and common interests. Our loyalty to these intimate ties can serve as basic ethical experience upon which we can draw for the more comprehensive loyalties to nation and humanity. *The Jew who does not adhere to the Jewish people is, therefore, at an ethical disadvantage, through his repudiation of a natural loyalty to an ancestral tradition and to the group that shares it with him.*

We must not assume that it was mere perversity on the part of so many modern Jews that made them cease looking to their tradition for ethical inspiration, and cease applying its norms to guide their behavior and to organize their personal habits and attitudes. At some point and for some reason they must have discovered that that tradition was no longer adequate to guide them, as it had their fathers. If we understand why the tradition that was capable of meeting the ethical demands of our fathers is not resorted to by many of us today, we may be given a clue how to get the Torah tradition of the Jewish people to function in our own spiritual life.

2

THE TRADITION INDISPENSABLE TO THE QUEST FOR THE GOOD LIFE

What led our fathers to throw themselves so wholeheartedly into the study of Torah and to permit it to direct the most minute details of their routine behavior was the conviction that the Torah had been revealed by God and expressed His will. Conformity to it was rewarded, and violation of it was punished by God. Even if one suffered martyrdom for the Torah, what mattered a few hours of agony if it opened the way to eternal bliss in the hereafter?

The modern-minded Jew cannot accept this version of the origin of his sacred Scriptures. He cannot accept the notion that to his people exclusively God revealed the way of eternal salvation. He knows that other religions have similar pretensions and he can see no valid reason why his tradition is, in this respect, more reliable than theirs. Moreover, the cumulative evidence of historical research favors the theory that the Bible, and even the Pentateuch, is of composite origin and shows the handiwork of many human authors who not infrequently contradict one another. The modern Jew finds in the Torah many primitive ordinances for which he sees no earthly use. The irrationality of these ordinances affected our fathers differently. It seemed to them that those laws, unintelligible to men, were dictated by a superhuman intelligence. For most Jews today, however, these laws are merely superstitious tabus, such as are found among most primitive people, and derive from ignorance of natural law. The whole evolutionary outlook on life makes it inconceivable that a law which was promulgated centuries ago can be an adequate guide for conduct in our day.

Despite all these facts, however, the Torah can still function in the life of the Jew to bring out the best in him, if he learn to approach it in the right way. *Though the modern Jew cannot believe that God revealed the Torah to Israel, he cannot deny the historic fact that the Torah revealed God to Israel.* The recognition of the truth that the Torah is a human document gives it a different, not necessarily a less important, significance to the Jew. The content of that document is Israel's quest for God and the discoveries made in that quest. The record of a people's attempt to find meaning and worth in life, to see in it the evidence of a spirit that makes for truth, goodness and beauty, is always significant. Perfect it is not, since the quest for God is endless. But the very imperfections can be valuable, since we learn truth by discovering our errors.

The difference between our fathers' attitude to the Torah and that which we today must take is this: They assumed that the Torah was perfect and its value realized through obedience and conformity with its standards; we should see in it the beginning of an eternal quest which we must continue. *We can discover value in the Torah by utilizing it as a living tradition, a sort of collective memory of valuable experience.* Just as the individual, meditating about important experiences of his life finds in them a measure of guidance and direction, and dwells particularly on those experiences which encourage him and give him hope and confidence, so modern Jews can use the Torah for inspiration and guidance, even though they cannot commit themselves blindly to an acceptance of all its teachings.

If Jews, as a people, were determined to renew their commitment to the quest for the good life, they would find the sacred traditions of their people, even if not regarded as infallible, at least helpful in the formulation of those intellectual, ethical and spiritual ideals which would enhance their personal and social life. They would not necessarily seek agreement on detailed rules of behavior, such as the traditional codes laid down to be observed implicitly, rules predicated on the assumption that every Biblical and traditional ordinance was a divine revelation.

Neither would Jews rest content with the complete lack of group *mores*, which has characterized Jewish life since the Emancipation.

They would attempt to define those standards of ethical conduct and those social amenities to which the Jewish community would have a right to demand that the individual Jew conform. They would develop guiding principles, based on present experience no less than on traditional values, to help us determine the proper line of action, whenever there arises a conflict of duties. They would find means of registering the Jewish public opinion of behavior which merits approval as well as of that which deserves rebuke.

3

WHAT IS A "GOOD JEW"?

There should be some consensus on what essentially constitutes *a good Jew*, one who fulfills what his fellow-Jews expect of him in respect to his ethical and social life. Whether we need a *ritual* code or not is a moot point, but we certainly need an *ethical* code to establish criteria of what is true, good and edifying in human behavior. We must be able in some way to distinguish between the desirable Jew to whom we are proud to point as a member of the Jewish community, and the undesirable Jew, whose conduct belies what we should like to believe are Jewish traits.

An ancient Rabbinic dictum has it that the descendants of Abraham are recognized as being "compassionate, modest and benevolent." [1] The author of that dictum could not have been describing all Jews as he knew them. He was rather defining the criteria by which the "true Jew," the desirable Jew, was to be recognized. It is such criteria, couched however, not in abstract terms, but with reference to clearly recognizable forms of behavior, which we must, through the pursuit of Torah, endeavor to formulate and make effective in our day. This is how Judaism can help us to make the best use of our lives.

Let us take, for example, the criterion of truth. When we look about us, we see the extent to which people, including our fellow-Jews, are faithless to their plighted word, how often they dishonor their promises and fail to meet contractual obligations, we realize that a cynical contempt for truth prevails among us. There can be no greater obstacle to our achieving ethical personality and decent social relations than acquiescence in such forms of behavior. Their eradication should be one of the conscious purposes of Jewish life.

Our fathers took seriously the Biblical injunction, "keep thou far from a false matter" [2] for fear of violating the law of God whose "signet is truth." [3] A man, known to be untrustworthy, was held up to contempt. Does the fact, that we no longer conceive of the Torah as a supernaturally revealed code, detract from the validity of this ideal? The whole weight of human experience testifies to the need for honesty and trustworthiness in human relations, if men are to make the most of their lives. Were Jews in our day devoted to the pursuit of Torah as a quest for truth, they would develop such a public opinion that a man who was guilty of breach of contract, or of repudiation of a sacred pledge, would be ashamed to appear in a Jewish assembly, and certainly would not dream of seeking office in any Jewish institution.

Jews today show a great concern in defending the Jewish name from defamation. Such activity serves a legitimate purpose. But our fathers rose to a higher level of concern when they were afraid that reprehensible conduct on the part of the Jew might cause *hillul ha-shem*, the profanation of God's name.[4] They looked upon scandalous behavior as weakening men's faith in God. More important than any protective measures against the defamation of the Jew would be activity to offset the profanation of the Jewish ideal and the cheapening and vulgarizing of Judaism, and to restore the notion that to be a Jew means to be held to standards of honor and truth.

Similarly, being a Jew should commit one to a specific standard of goodness. A Jewish code of ethical conduct should act as a brake on the insatiable hunger for power. Success in life should not be construed as success in outdoing others. It should be construed rather as success in outdoing oneself, in transcending one's limitations and developing one's creative capacities. The laws of the Torah indicate clearly the effort of our fathers to define and enforce forms of behavior which involve a limitation of the tendency of the strong to exploit the weak, and which apply in concrete terms the ethical norm: "Thou shalt love thy neighbor as thyself." [5] Under the changed conditions of life in which we live, some of those laws may no longer be applicable, but the ideal they express is still valid, and Jewish life must still concern itself with giving effect to that ideal.

In a limited degree, the laws of the state are designed to serve this purpose for the community in general. However, in view of our responsibility for making Jewish life bring out the best in the Jew, we cannot be content with the minimum standards which finally are enacted into law. The laws of a nation represent those minimal requirements which the state is prepared and competent to enforce by the application of its police power. The more sensitive ethical conscience of men is never content to act merely within such legal standards. *Being a Jew should mean belonging to a group which is interested not merely in satisfying the minimum ethical requirements of the law*, but in *living* lifenim mishurat haddin,[6] *on a standard more exacting than the legal requirements*, a standard which may point the way for future legislation, but which will, at all events, reflect the ethical purposes of the membership.

Just as professional groups have found it necessary to formulate codes of professional ethics and to devise sanctions for their enforcement, so should Jews formulate codes of ethical practice in the relations between individuals and institutions within the Jewish group. Principles of social justice, fraternal considerations, and respect for sincere differences of conviction and the right to express them must be implemented in Jewish community relations. There must be an end to vulgar, careerist competition in the professions that serve the Jewish community, and to destructive jurisdictional and factional strife among rival institutions and causes. Norms of communal procedure embodying the highest democratic principles must be formulated and applied, which will safeguard Jewish institutional life from exploitation by the vulgar and arrogant for private or partisan ends. The study of the principles and practices which should be incorporated in such a code of ethical practice for the guidance of Jewish institutions is one form of *Talmud Torah*, which would go far in conferring on the Jew a sense of personal dignity and honor indispensable to making the most of his life.

When the synagogues, schools and other cultural and social agencies of Jewish life conform to such ethical norms, it will be within their power to influence the ethical behavior of Jews in their other relations as well. The problem of developing the highest ethical potentialities of men is largely one of widening the range of their loyalties. Most people are fairly decent toward the members of their own family, to whom they are bound by ties of natural affection and common interest. But the kind and indulgent father may be an oppressive employer and ruthless competitor, and may make it impossible by his behavior for other fathers to provide for the needs of their families. Similarly, institutional, racial, class, national, and other limited loyalties are too often pursued at the expense of loyalty to the larger society of which they are a part. Yet these loyalties, in themselves, are desirable and life-enhancing. The ethical problem is how to utilize loyalty to the narrower group as training for loyalty to the more comprehensive group. Jewish religion, through its commitment to the ideal of a universal Kingdom of God as the goal of human society, has endeavored to make Jewish life contribute to human welfare generally.

There is no reason why these beneficent influences need be lessened by the changed approach toward Torah, indicated previously. New thought must be given to having the ritual of home and synagogue help the individual to discharge his loyalties to the larger units of the nation and all mankind. Nothing which vitally concerns the welfare of the human being can be beyond the scope of that spiritual activity which is the modern continuation of the tradition of *Talmud Torah*.

The threat of reverting to the law of the jungle always hangs over mankind. We must count on the recurrent tendency to deny the validity of all universal ethics and to see in human evolution merely a consequence of the triumph of the strong over the weak and a justification of the doctrine that might makes right. Judaism must, therefore, strengthen in the Jew his devotion to the fundamental ideal of a humanity united by ties of sympathy and understanding, in a common effort to make life worth living for every human being.

The recognition of the fact that there is in nature a perpetual struggle for survival, in which all living organisms are engaged, must not be permitted to deter us from pursuing that ideal. Instead of accepting as ultimate and inevitable the process by which the animal ancestors of man sought survival through the dominance of the strong and the elimination of the weak, we should lay stress, as our tradition has taught us to do, on the differentia between man and the other orders of creation. *Our objective must be so to compensate for the weakness of the weak, and so to direct the strength of the strong, as to render as many human beings as possible fit to survive.* If belonging to the Jewish group will mean adhering to a community which deliberately cultivates these attitudes in its members, such adherence will elicit the best that is in them.

ART

1

JEWISH LIFE IN NEED OF AESTHETIC SELF-EXPRESSION

There is another ideal interest which Judaism must help the Jew to realize, in addition to his desire for truth and goodness, and that is his desire to enjoy and create art. Art may be defined as endowing emotionally charged experience with meaning which transcends that experience. To communicate such meaning, we resort to music, literature, painting, sculpture, drama, dance, and variations and combinations of these media. But whatever the media and whatever the emotions, it is a fundamental need of human nature to wish to communicate what is significant in our emotional reaction to life, and to seek to have our experience of life enlarged and enhanced, by sharing vicariously the reactions of others, as art conveys those reactions to us.

No society has ever existed which did not express itself in art. By reflecting on our experiences in life and selecting the emotions which we seek to communicate and, as it were, immortalize, we discipline our emotions to prevent them from being merely a disturbance to orderly processes of living, and to make them life-enriching. Whether the emotional tone of the expressed reaction be comic or tragic, whether it be a response to the ridiculous or to the sublime, its aesthetic impression helps us to live and to find life worth living.

Our fathers knew the value of giving aesthetic expression to emotional experience. In religious ritual, they emphasized the *hiddur mitzvah*,[7] the embellishment of the *mitzvah*, as the elaboration of ceremonial objects suggests. Traditional modes for the chanting of sacred texts sounded the emotional keynote suggested by the words, or the occasion of their utterance, from the lamentation of *Tishēa BeAb*[8] and the poignant pathos of the *Kol Nidre*[9] chant to the rollicking tunes of *Simhat Torah*[10] or *Purim*.[11] Purim was made not merely the occasion for celebrating an ancient instance of the villain fallen in the pit he had digged for others, but for finding occasion for laughter and mirth in parody and satire of all types. *Tishēa BeAb* lamented not merely the destruction of the Temple by Nebuchadnezzar, but also the whole martyrology of the Jews during the Crusades and other tragic events, as told in the *kinnot*.[12] The tunes without words and the ecstatic dances of the *Hasidim*[13] were other aesthetic expressions of the religious emotions. The structural forms of the synagogues and the emphasis on the *aron*[14] and the *bimah*[15] as architectural features, the adornment of the *paroket*[16] and the mantels and silver decorations of the sacred scrolls, the very form of the characters used by the scribe in writing the text of the Torah and The Five Scrolls—all of these are evidence of appreciation of aesthetic values by our forefathers. The aesthetic character of the home was as distinctively Jewish as that of the synagogue itself. The *mezuzzah*[17] on the doorpost, the Sabbath lamp or candle sticks, the *mizrah*[18] on the wall, the goblets for *kiddush*,[19] the spice-box for *hav-*

dalah,[20] the ponderous volumes with their commentaries and super-commentaries which filled the book-shelves—these and more gave a distinctive form and expressed and evoked a feeling of the sanctity of the Jewish home, by virtue of the emotional associations attached to them.

The arts, to be sure, were all subordinate to, and an outgrowth of, the religious liturgy, as is true of most ancient cultures. In Europe, also, it was only under the aegis of the Church that art flourished until the time of the Renaissance, which was the beginning of modernism. For the Jew, the Middle Ages lasted to the Emancipation in the eighteenth and nineteenth centuries. During the Jewish Middle Ages, ghetto conditions were not conducive to the elaboration of aesthetic techniques. Wealth and security are required to produce architectural works like the medieval cathedrals. Moreover, the puritanism of the religious tradition of the ghetto, its horror of anything which might resemble idolatry, its ascetic insistence on refraining from instrumental music in the synagogue as a sign of mourning for the ruined Temple, the objection to women's singing in public, and many other self-imposed restraints inhibited such technical developments as the mastery of sculpture and painting and the cultivation of polyphonic music.

Nevertheless, with all these limitations, there was, as noted above, a Jewish art in the ghetto, not a sumptuous or luxuriant art, but one that was sincere and moving in its simplicity. *Today we have many Jewish artists, but almost no Jewish art.* Jews, ever since the Emancipation, have thrown themselves enthusiastically into a mastery of artistic techniques, but their work is, for the most part, irrelevant to Jewish life. It does not originate in, or contribute to, the enrichment of that life. It does not express an aesthetic reaction to those experiences which Jews go through, by reason of their being Jews. How shall we account for the almost complete disappearance of Jewish art, precisely at the time when, contact with the artistic traditions of Europe, new opportunities for artistic training, removal of legalistic traditional inhibitions and the general widening of the Jews' cultural horizons, would all seem to favor a Jewish artistic renascence?

The answer certainly cannot be that modern Jewish life is not in need of aesthetic expression. It cannot be that the Jew does not react emotionally to the circumstances of his life. He broods over anti-Semitism; he feels frustrated by anti-Jewish discrimination; he is thrilled by the heroic spirit of *halutzim* [21] and *shomerim* [22] in Eretz Yisrael; he is proud when one of his people is accorded honors; he is annoyed by the follies and foibles of representative Jewish personalities and institutions. But he takes these emotions in the raw; seldom does he seek to sublimate them, by giving to them that artistic expression which would help him to live. This tends to make the Jew emotionally restless and unstable, neurasthenic and hysterical in turn, anything but serene and self-possessed.

In the recent prize-winning novel *Wasteland*, the author, Jo Sinclair,[23] gives a psychiatric description of a Jew who suffered periods of mental depression, as a result of his attempt to escape from his people which he knew only through his unhappy home background. The story is about John Brown, a skilled photographer on a newspaper staff among whom he passed off as a Gentile. As an avocation he would take pictures on his own. What these meant to him as artist and as Jew is set forth in the following, which throws light on our present theme:

"His 'own pictures' as he calls those special photographs he takes," writes the author, "are a strong symbol of his identity, as well as a longing to fulfill his identity. He has made of these pictures a powerful mental and spiritual drive, and at the same time he attempted to close his creative room to his family, his people, his own emotions. Instead of permitting his art to portray his inner self, his freedom, his identity as Jew as well as artist, he attempted to keep his ego under lock and key. . . .

"The fear and doubt which have kept him from any kind of adjustment have muffled his creative powers as well. The pictures are fine, showing great talent, but he does not believe in them. He locks them in a dark place that is known as death. In his mind as well as in the morgue drawer, his creative talent is not alive."

Referring to the fact that he had never photographed members of his own family, the writer adds, "He has tried to keep from these pictures any 'stigma' of family, Jews, self. He has tried to keep these photographs 'untainted,' untouched by the emotions which tortured him. Yet their great talent, their sensitiveness and art lie in the fact that into these pictures have seeped his hunger and shame, his tormented family relationships, his 'name.' The power and beauty of the pictures come from the very things he has tried to bar from them. The pictures, all along, have been a more truthful mirror of his identity than any physical act or gesture on his part. . . .

"His feelings and his pictures must be released at the same time; the two are synonymous in him . . . He will, in this way, bring a free creative ability to the world, achieve his rightful place and identity in that world."

The modern Jew could find a safety valve for his irritations, annoyances and resentments by turning them into ridicule, deriding his contemporary foes as he has continually derided Haman, the archetype of the anti-Semite. How much self-hate and cynical contempt for the cruel and bloodthirsty human race he might be spared, if he could detach himself long enough from his situation to see the irrationalities and incongruities of the social scene in their utter absurdity, and express his feelings in satire or comedy. Laughter is a catharsis of the spirit that rids it of the poison of hate and despair.

If the Jew cannot find relief from unhappy emotions in this manner, if he cannot laugh away his afflictions, and his spirit protests against wrong too strongly to enable him to find amusement in his contemplation, then let the Jew give to his suffering the tragic dignity of the protestations of Job. Or let him find a transcendent value for his afflictions, accepting them as an opportunity to testify to the depth and sincerity of his faith, by finding meaning in his afflictions and articulating it in such poetry as we find in the prophecies of the "suffering servant of the Lord," in the fifty-third chapter of Isaiah, or in the *piyyut* [24] of the Ten Martyrs read in the Yom Kippur service. *Art, which helps to give some meaning to tribulation, no more vindicates it than does theodicy, but it at least renders it creative of some good.* Suffering ceases then to be isolated from the rest of life, and becomes a symptom of a moral evil, to the eradication of which our lives should be dedicated. We feel that we have not endured in vain when our suffering, expressed in glowing words, or glowing colors or tones, can evoke that compassion which will eventually abolish human evil.

2

WHAT IS NEEDED TO EVOKE JEWISH ART?

This only gives greater pertinence to the question: Since the modern Jew is in need of Jewish art, and since there is no dearth of artists who are Jews, why should there be a dearth of Jewish art? It is significant to note that whatever of Jewish art there is in our day has been associated with Zionism and the Jewish national renaissance. In poetry and fiction, the revival of Hebrew literature has produced notable aesthetic expression of modern Jewish reactions to life. In Eretz Yisrael, Jewish music,[25] drama and art, in spite of the economic scarcity and the physical insecurity of life in such a frontier existence, are much in evidence.

This suggests the answer to our problem. It is not the change from medievalism to modernism, which is responsible for the lack of Jewish art in the Diaspora. That should rather have favored the development of the arts, as it did in the Western World generally, by freeing art from control by religious law and tradition, and encouraging each of the arts to explore more fully the possibilities of expression that inhere in its particular medium. Responsible for the lack of Jewish art is the disintegration of Jewry, the severance of the individual from the group, his spiritual isolation from his fellow-Jews which renders artistic communion through common symbols difficult. *It is because of the corrosive doubt as to the value of Jewish life that the Jewish artist has lost confidence in the validity of his own emotional reactions to Jewish experience.* Not identified wholeheartedly with the Jewish community, he is self-conscious and embarrassed in expressing himself as a Jew, and cannot articulate with simplicity and sincerity what he feels about life.

Nor is the problem of Jewish art merely a problem of artistic expression of the artist. *Art is a form of communication as well as of expression, and implies a community of spiritual interests between the artist and his public.* There is a functional relationship between the creativity of the artist and the measure of appreciation of art among his public. If Jews do not read Jewish books, there will be few Jews willing to write Jewish books. If Jews do not like to hang Jewish pictures on their walls, Jewish painters will not express their reaction to Jewish life in painting. If Jews are not interested in Jewish worship, we cannot expect the development of a distinctive synagogue architecture. So long, therefore, as Jews generally do not feel the need of identifying themselves with Jewish community life, no matter how much of artistic genius may exist among Jews, it will not produce Jewish art.

There is an affirmative inference from this negative conclusion, which must not escape us. Although genius of every description is a profound mystery, and we cannot produce geniuses at will, we can, in a measure, enhance the productivity of Jewish genius by fostering appreciation of its product. Cultivating an appreciation for the aesthetic expression of Jewish values should be as much a part of Jewish culture, as cultivating an appreciation for their ethical and social expression. The aesthetic and the ethical ideal are not unrelated, although neither can be wholly derived from the other. The refinement of the emotions, the capacity for recognizing qualitative differences that do not lie on the surface, is of deep ethical significance.

If Judaism is to be enabled to bring out the best in the Jew, the

Jewish community must assume responsibility for stimulating among Jews an understanding and utilization of art and, indirectly, the creativity of the Jewish artist. It must develop in Jewry the habit of expressing its emotional reactions to the circumstances of Jewish life aesthetically. It must foster that reciprocal bond between the artist and his public which will encourage the artist to create, by making him want to communicate his experience as a Jew, and will enable the lay Jew to perceive new values in Jewish experience by the magical power of art.

Recognizing the limitation imposed by the fact that the Jewish public is necessarily much smaller than the general and, therefore, offers the artist less incentive to produce Jewish art than to create art which might have a wider appeal among those who have no interest in Jewish life, the Jewish community ought to seek ways of compensating artists for the sacrifices involved in producing Jewish art. Subventions, prizes, scholarships, special commissions by societies and individuals to Jewish artists for producing Jewish art should be provided.

Every opportunity should be utilized for employing the services of artists to enrich Jewish life and to stimulate the artistic impulse among Jews. Synagogues and other Jewish public buildings should afford occasion for expressing, in their architecture and interior decoration, the functional purpose which they serve in the community. Museums devoted to Jewish art, libraries of Jewish literature, concerts of Jewish music, Jewish theatrical organizations both professional and amateur, Jewish dance groups, could all be encouraged by community and individual sponsorship. The theater is one of the most important moving influences of our time. It does not merely hold up a mirror to contemporary society. It is itself a medium for the moulding of thought and the fostering of attitudes. Jewish theater would provide the creative stimulus which Jewish life is badly in need of. It has well been said, "Literature is one age talking to another; the theater is an age talking to itself."

In Jewish religious ritual and the ritual of Jewish societies, fraternal and humanitarian, we should avail ourselves as much as possible of newly created Jewish art forms. The Jewish home should seek to express its role in Jewish life by the aesthetic display of beautiful ceremonial objects, as of old, and by Jewish pictures and art objects of every sort.

In Jewish education, whether for the child, the adolescent or the adult, familiarity with the artistic expression of Jewish values and appreciation of Jewish art should constitute an important objective. Education must no longer, as in the ghetto, neglect training in self-expression through the arts. The introduction of handicrafts into the curricula of some of the more progressive Hebrew schools is a step in the right direction. So, too, is the cultivation of aesthetic expression by youth groups and adults in some of our Jewish community centers. In the main, however, Jewish institutions have hardly begun to foster aesthetic appreciation or creativity, and they have too seldom realized the importance of utilizing art specifically as an expression of the Jewish reaction to life.

In the era of Emancipation, the lure of European art, the drabness of the ghetto and the undeveloped state of its artistic tradition led many cultured and sensitive Jews to abandon Judaism. In our day, the development of the arts by Jews could make Jewish life entrancing. It could answer the Jew's need for the articulation of those intimate aspects of life which he shares with his own people as well as his need for making his inner life understood by his non-Jewish neighbors.

Art possesses the magic whereby it is able to express the seemingly ineffable and to communicate what is ordinarily regarded as incommunicable. The distinctive and individual, when expressed in artistic form, acquire universal significance. In their art, peoples reveal themselves to each other at their best, and learn to respect and reverence each other. In ancient times, the Bible made other peoples respect the Jew largely by the potency of its written word. Today, however, it no longer can have that effect, because people find it hard to identify the modern Jew as the "people of the Book."

If, however, Jewry produced a modern literature, or art, or music as significant in meaning and as potent to move men as was the Bible, the effect would be of incalculable help for viewing the Jew in a better light than through the thick fog of inherited prejudices. In some of the public schools, the problem of group relations among various national and racial groups is being solved by programs exhibiting the aesthetic creations of the different group cultures. Thus, both directly and by its effect in interpreting the Jew to the non-Jew, the cultivation of the aesthetic expression of Jewish life would enhance the Jew's self-respect and self-possession.

It is thus within the power of the Jews themselves, in democratic countries, to make of Judaism a way of life which would elicit the best of which the Jew is capable. By utilizing Jewish tradition and Jewish community life for the development of ethical standards and aesthetic content, Judaism can give the modern Jew a spiritual culture that would be the equivalent of what the Torah meant for his fathers. It can generate a culture capable of organizing and directing his social conduct and his personal will. It can give him a pattern of living which will yield experiences felt to be intrinsically life-enhancing.

CHAPTER SEVENTEEN

ZIONISM—A RECONSTRUCTION OF
THE JEWISH WAY OF LIFE

In this, the darkest period in the long annals of Jewish history which abounds in tales of woe and tragedy, the Jewish people through its very struggle for existence, is keeping alive the hope of a juster and kinder humanity. Such a contribution to civilization comes mainly from the collective enterprise of the Jewish people in its endeavor to reestablish its national home in Eretz Yisrael. That enterprise holds a significance which far transcends the fortunes of the Jewish people. Insofar as it is interwoven with interests of an international character, it constitutes resistance to those interests everywhere which are selfish and reactionary, and offers aid and comfort to those which are enlightened and progressive. By reason of its problematic future, the Eretz Yisrael project may be designated as still only an experiment in democracy. In that respect, it is no worse off than many other promising movements which have appeared on the horizon. In a sense, all the Occidental peoples are as yet only in the experimental stage of democracy.

In this discussion, democracy is identified with three of its most conspicuous manifestations. They are the following:

(1) All exploitation and oppression of the weak by the strong must be dealt with as morally evil, economically ruinous and politically intolerable. This applies to all human relations both individual and collective.

(2) No exploitation or oppression should be regarded either as part of the divine government of mankind, in the sense of being a means of divine discipline or an expiation for sin, or of being an inherent part of the order of nature which it is futile to try to change.

(3) Democracy cannot exist in a void; it is a quality of nationhood. Under its influence, national solidarity functions as a means of fostering the maximum welfare and collaboration of all who compose the nation, regardless of race, color, or creed. Such welfare and collaboration presuppose unity in diversity and freedom from oppression and exploitation.

1

DEMOCRACY AS EXPRESSED IN THE EVOLUTION OF THE ZIONIST AIMS

To what extent has this concept of democracy played a part in the evolution of the aim to establish a Jewish national home in Eretz Yisrael? *Zionism is not merely the revival of traditional Jewish messianism. It is that messianism, recast into the pattern of modern democratic peoplehood.* Traditional messianism coincided with democracy's aim to eliminate exploitation and oppression from human life. It held out the hope of the establishment of God's kingdom of justice and love, and the prospect of Israel as a nation restored to its ancient land. In that land, Israel would demonstrate the potency of the Divine Kingdom, through the social order which it would maintain there.

Messianism, however, assumed that such a future would come about only through divine intervention of a miraculous nature. There was nothing the Jews could then do other than try to conform to the traditional teachings concerning the proper means to salvation. Included in the traditional teachings was the one which interpreted the exile of the Jews from their national home as a means of expiation for the sins of their fathers and for their own sins, and as a means of discipline to render them worthy of redemption, when the time for it would finally arrive. To take human measures for resuming national life in Eretz Yisrael was traditionally condemned as sinful impatience.[1]

It is this aspect of traditional messianism which Jews have been unlearning during the last century-and-a-half. They put in the place of that messianism the assumption that no exploitation or oppression should be accepted as part of the divine purpose with man, and that it is more in accord with that purpose to throw off the yoke of oppression, and to achieve the freedom to make the most of life in the here and now.

The course of events during the last two decades of the nineteenth century brought into sharp relief the contradiction between the hopes raised by the French Revolution for a free and just society, in which Jews would be treated as human beings on a basis of equality with all their fellow-citizens, and the rise of chauvinistic nationalism, with anti-Semitism as one of the principal means of inculcating it.

It was Theodore Herzl[2] who created the movement known as "political Zionism," and who gave the democratic impulse to the forces that are driving Jews to rebuild their national home in Eretz Yisrael. In his conception of the movement, all of the three main principles of democracy constituted an integral part: (1) the reinterpretation of the messianic ideal from that of passive waiting for a supernatural miracle to the exertion of initiative to throw off the yoke of oppression; (2) the refusal to continue to regard the dispersion of the Jews as a divinely decreed expiation or a form of divine discipline, and (3) the decision to reinstate Jewish nationhood where it might function as a means of securing the maximum welfare and collaboration to all who came within its purview, in keeping with the highest ideals of democracy. *Zionism has properly been defined as "Jewish democracy in action."*

2

DEMOCRACY AS EVIDENCED IN ZIONIST MEASURES

Democracy as an orientation to life in which primacy is accorded to the purpose of combating all forms of exploitation and oppression and of furthering freedom and equality in all human relations among individuals and groups has operated not only in the evolution of the aim to acquire a Jewish national home in Eretz Yisrael; it has operated, also, in the measures which have been taken to prepare the conditions necessary for the achievement of that aim. Those measures have been taken for the most part by Jews, but to a certain extent also by non-Jews.

The Zionist movement was bound to supplant that form of migration to Eretz Yisrael which had existed since the thirteenth century [3] and which drew to Eretz Yisrael men and women who journeyed there in a spirit of religious pilgrimage. They usually remained, devoting their days to prayer and to religious exercises. They were supported by *halukah*, moneys sent by, or collected from Jews all over the world, who considered their contributions not merely as charity, but as keeping alive their connection with Eretz Yisrael. Though probably the most harmless kind of parasitism, *halukah* was, nevertheless, bound to breed unwholesome human relations, from a democratic point of view. To have brought about its virtual elimination is the least intended and least notable of Zionism's contributions, yet it deserves mention.

There was another form of philanthropy in Eretz Yisrael, however, which clashed even more directly with the democratic spirit of Zionism and which had to give way before it. That was the large-scale educational and philanthropic endeavor engaged in by the *Alliance Israélite Universelle* [4] to westernize the Jews in the Levantine countries. The organizers of the *Alliance* expected that such westernization would redeem the Jews in those countries from the squalor and ignorance of their surroundings. Eretz Yisrael was one of those countries.

The principal activity of the *Alliance* was the establishment, in 1870, of a farm school, *Mikveh Israel* near Jaffa. The purpose of that school was to educate some of the younger generation of Jews, whose parents lived on *halukah*, to become farmers. Their training was conducted in French, and in a spirit of loyalty to French institutions. No wonder that many of the trainees in the farm-school later preferred the glamor of the Paris boulevards to toiling on some lonely farm in Eretz Yisrael. Later a similar organization among well-to-do German Jews known as the *Hilfsverein der deutschen Juden* [5] also conducted educational and philanthropic work in Eretz Yisrael. These organizations possibly furthered the imperial interests of their respective countries, but they did not awaken in the Jewish communities a desire for self-determination and self-reliance—the prime requisites to a spirit of democracy. Nothing less than the moral awakening that came with Zionism could have achieved that.

On the other hand, a more deliberate manifestation of democracy is to be noted in the avowed aim of Zionism to have Jews achieve their own redemption as a matter of justice and not of charity, and by means of justifiable demands made in the name of the Jewish masses, and not through political wire-pulling of some individuals who happen to be favorites of, or influential with, the powers that be. In the past, these individuals, known as *shtadlanim*, or intercessors, had to come to the aid of the Jews every time there was trouble brewing. The fate of enslaved Jewish communities would often hang upon the whim of some nobleman or bishop, and upon the willingness of the Jewish intercessor to humor him. This placed the community in the power of the *shtadlan*. Zionism has taught Jews not to entrust their fate to individuals, whether Jews or non-Jews, who might come to exercise arbitrary control, but to have faith in democratic procedure and in the justice of their cause. It ended, once and for all, the authority of self-appointed oligarchs, however beneficently disposed they might be toward their fellow-Jews.

This democratic attitude brought by Zionism to all efforts involved in persuading Jews to settle in Eretz Yisrael, and in creating there the conditions essential to their welfare, derives from Herzl's insistence that Zionism assume political form. That form has rendered Zionism an excellent training ground for the Jews in the art of self-government as a modern people and not merely as an *ecclesia*—something they had had no chance to exercise for over eighteen centuries. Political Zionism is based on the principle that the homeland of the Jewish people must be "publicly recognized and legally secured." So convinced was Herzl of the importance of public or international recognition as a prerequisite to the upbuilding of the Jewish national home that he deprecated the continuance of piecemeal colonization efforts which had been in progress for almost fifteen years, and which had depended for their success upon the lethargy and corruptibility of the Turkish regime rather than upon its formal consent. What Herzl wanted was a charter, which he hoped to obtain from the Sultan, and which he expected to be duly guaranteed by the other European nations. *Herzl was determined to take the fate of the Jewish people out of the hands of any one government, however well disposed, and to entrust it to the conscience of mankind.*

The recognition and security which were to be the basis of political Zionism presupposed willingness on the part of the nations to do two things; (1) to carry on formal transactions with the Jews as a people through their duly authorized representatives, and (2) to concede to the Jews the right to a homeland of their own as a matter of moral and legal justice. Such willingness could not possibly be due to any political pressure, since Jews were in no position to exercise any kind of force. Herzl could have counted upon the public recognition and legal security of a national home for the Jews only on the basis of the inherent justice of his cause. The very fact that his purpose of placing the solution of the Jewish problem on the agenda of international affairs did not materialize before the end of the First World War (which was fought, to some extent at least, in order to make the world safe for democracy) indicates how closely bound up with the spirit of democracy the Zionist project was from its very beginning.

It may be asked: How, with the spread of anti-Semitism, could Herzl expect the governments to act in the spirit of democracy? The answer is that governments often act more justly than do their people. To be sure, in the instance of Zionism, they were unprepared at first to do so. But under favorable circumstances, there could be, as there actually was, a break in the policy of calculating selfishness on the part of governments. Like the Allies' action in organizing the League of Nations itself, the incorporation of the Balfour Declaration in the Mandate for Palestine was no doubt due to a momentary inspiration of justice. Indeed, much of our best hoping and planning for a better world in the future has to depend upon such spurts of genuine justice and good-will.

Political Zionism may, accordingly, be described as the application of democratic methods to the measures to be employed by Jews everywhere in their efforts to prepare a homeland for those who hope to, or must, go there. Its principal instrument is the World Zionist Organization to which belong all Jews who subscribe to the previously mentioned aim of creating "for the Jewish people a home in Eretz Yisrael secured by public law." That aim was formulated at the first Zionist Congress called together by Theodore Herzl in 1897. The World Zionist Organization has no way of enforcing any strict discipline, since its existence is necessarily based on voluntary membership. It represents a wide diversity of opinion in its Congresses and in all of its institutions.

The World Zionist Organization has demonstrated for the first time in the history of the Jewish people the possibility of inducing religiously and socially divergent groups to collaborate. This democracy is all the more evident, in that there are some groups which hold religious and social views both so extremely rightist and so extremely leftist that they refuse to collaborate with the main body of the Jewish people, as represented by the World Zionist Organization. But apart from their nuisance value or disvalue, they serve to emphasize the remarkable democratic achievement manifested in the large area of collaboration among the divergent groups within the World Zionist Organization.

Long before political Zionism came on the scene, an East-European Jew, Herman Schapira, who started in life as a Talmudic scholar and ended as a mathematical genius who taught at Heidelberg, conceived the idea of establishing a fund to purchase land that would forever remain the property of the Jewish people. This, he maintained, would make it possible for the agricultural development in the Jewish homeland to take place in accordance with such ethical ideals as are expressed in the ancient agrarian laws of the Torah and have become the objective of most modern efforts in land reform. Thus both the Torah law of the Jubilee Year which provided that all bought land should revert to the original owners and the influence of Henry George's idea about private land ownership being the main source of economic ills of civilized society are reflected in the strenuous effort made by the Jews to forestall the evils of land speculation and mounting rents, to which a newly developed country is subject. In 1901, at the Fifth Zionist Congress under the leadership of Herzl, the Jewish National Fund (J.N.F.) was finally established. All National Fund land was then declared to be inalienable and capable only of being leased for forty-nine years, after which period the lease could be renewed. The lease to the land could be inherited by the children. No more land was to be leased to any one settler than he was able to cultivate. Most significant of all was the principle laid down that no hired labor should be permitted on National Fund land. The National Fund also acquires land in cities for the use of public buildings and workers' homes.

The manifold methods employed in collecting the Jewish National Fund are of a kind that enable all Jews, even the poorest, to feel that they have a share in it. With contributions ranging from endowments and bequests, which can come only from the well-to-do, to collections from charity boxes, which are kept in the homes of the poorest, and with all manner of devices in between to give every one a chance to contribute to the Jewish National Fund, every Jew can be made to feel that he has a share in the rebuilding of the Land.

Unmistakable evidence of democratic purpose and policy as animating the Zionist movement was evinced in the set of principles which were formulated in 1918 at the Convention of the Zionist Organization of America and were reaffirmed at subsequent conventions. They are the following: "(1) Political and civil equality irrespective of race or sex or faith for all the inhabitants of the land. (2) To insure in the Jewish national home in Eretz Yisrael equality of opportunity, we favor a policy which, with due regard to existing rights, shall tend to establish the ownership of the land and all natural resources and of all public utilities by the whole people. (3) All land owned or controlled by the whole people should be leased on such conditions as will insure the fullest opportunity of development and continuity of possession. (4) The cooperation principle should be applied as far as possible in the organization of all agricultural, industrial, commercial and financial undertakings. (5) The fiscal policy should be framed so as to protect the people from the evils of speculation and from every other form of financial oppression. (6) The system of free public instruction which is to be established should embrace all grades and departments of education."

The most far-reaching effect of Zionism on democratic world tendencies made itself felt at the end of the First World War when, as a result of the idealism which Wilson had injected into the war purposes of the Allies, the atmosphere was electric with hopes that the peace would usher in a new and better world. Those hopes had been stimulated by the determination to remove the principal factor which had brought on the war. That factor was believed to be the domination exercised by the great powers over the small nations and the oppression of minority nationalities by the nations which harbored them. For the first time an attempt was made to give to democracy international scope, by recognizing that nationalities, or historic groups which were conscious of a common destiny, were no less entitled to freedom and equality than individual men and women. How to achieve that in practice, with so many nationalities unable to stand on their own feet, seemed to pose an insoluble problem. The problem of minority nationalities though also far from being simple, at least had some earlier precedents and experience to fall back on. Already in the famous Council of Vienna of 1878, that problem had been dealt with. For peoples, however, which constituted the majority populations in their own territories, but were incapable of self-government, there was as yet no internationally recognized means of assuring them help without endangering their independence. In the democratic fervor which attended the organization of the League of Nations, such a means was evolved. That was the system of mandates. The mandate system which authorized a strong nation to act as guardian of a small and weak people, until that people would attain to political maturity fitting it to become an independent nation, marked a radical break with imperialism. It was expected to put an end to the military domination and exploitation of weaker peoples.

Zionism afforded the League an opportunity to demonstrate its adherence not only to the letter, but also to the spirit, of international democracy. The Jews constituted a people which first had to get to the land of its origin before the mandatory power could exercise its guardianship over it. But so strong and clear a case had been made out for their historic claim to Eretz Yisrael that not one of the fifty-two nations in the League, together with the United States, saw any reason for questioning the justice of having the Jewish people included within the system of mandates. Accordingly, the Balfour Declaration pledging the British Government "to facilitate the establishment of a Jewish national home in Palestine" was duly incorporated in the Mandate for Palestine, and Great Britain was given the mandate over Eretz Yisrael. This act, judged by itself apart from any ulterior motives and mental reservations which may have been entertained by the mandatory power, very definitely constituted a most noteworthy development of democracy both in depth and scope. *If eliciting the good in others is itself a contribution to the good life, then by eliciting from the nations such an avowal of democracy on an international scale, Zionism may be said to have made an important contribution to civilization.*

3

DEMOCRACY AS PRACTICED IN
ZIONIST UNDERTAKINGS

With so much of the spirit of democracy manifest in the evolution of the aim to establish a Jewish national home in Eretz Yisrael and in the measures under way to colonize, it is to be expected that the actual process of Jewish settlement in Eretz Yisrael will translate that spirit into a way of life and embody it in institutional forms. How this expectation is gradually being met in Eretz Yisrael may be inferred from the following:

The first element in the process of Jewish settlement in Eretz Yisrael to be considered, from the standpoint of an experiment in democracy, is the creation of a new economic structure. In contrast with a country like the United States to which the frustration of their hopes for freedom and equality drove the Jews, and where they found a ready economy into which they had to fit themselves, the Jews who turned to Eretz Yisrael to redeem their hopes realized that they were coming to a backward and neglected land. They regarded that very character of the land as an opportunity to demonstrate their ability to resume their national life which had long been in a state of suspended animation. That Eretz Yisrael had been depleted of its natural fertility, and that, except for patches of wretched cultivation, it was a land of denuded hills and swampy pestilential plains, was a challenge to the Jews to provide the agricultural foundation of a new and progressive economy that would be able to harbor a vast population. *The principle that this economy must be a Jewish creation, planned by the intelligence of Jews, and consummated by the treasure, toil and sweat of Jews is the soul and essence of Zionism.* It is the one opportunity Jews have of negating the lie that they can live off the economy produced only by others, being unable to create any of their own.

From the very beginning of the Jewish recolonization of Eretz Yisrael, in 1882, the necessity of an agricultural foundation became apparent. But the early pioneers did not realize the full implication of an agricultural base for the creation of a new economy which would be capable of sustaining a national home. They thought that all that was necessary was to acquire a farm, engage any cheap labor that could be obtained, and exercise efficient management. There were plenty of Arab fellaheen to be had, for no matter how little the Jewish farmer was willing to pay them, it was much more than they could ever hope to earn by working the land for their own landlords. In the relatively short space of fifteen to twenty years, however, the ill effects of this short-sighted policy became visible and served as a warning to the leaders of the Zionist movement against any such private enterprising. The idealism of the first generation of pioneers and their great hopes of rebuilding the national life of their people survived in but a few of the second generation and would have died out with the next.

When political Zionism came along and gave larger vision and significance to the task of building a new economy which would be the Jews' own creation, it saved the first efforts of the early pioneers from being assimilated to the prevailing tendency of native exploitation of the many by the few. The first step political Zionism took was to establish the principle of nationally owned land on which no hired labor of any kind, Jewish or Arab, was to be permitted. Moreover, a policy of encouraging small farms was adopted, thereby ensuring fairer distribution of farm income and better care of the soil. Over two-thirds of the 6,000 Jewish citrus groves are less than five acres each. The second step was to foster the type of collective colonization which, in the opinion of so expert an authority as Walter Clay Lowdermilk, the noted American soil conservationist, may be regarded as "the most successful of modern times." He characterizes the agriculture of the collective as "the most remarkable devotion to the reclamation of land that I have seen in any country in the New or Old World." [6]

Cooperative colonization in Eretz Yisrael has been a direct product of necessity and common sense. The extremely difficult conditions confronting the settlers and their inexperience in agriculture constitute the necessity. Their only assets are youth, social idealism and devotion to Zionism. They are imbued to a profound degree with the teachings of socialism, but not to the point of being doctrinaire about it. The two main considerations have been: (1) ability to produce enough to maintain a high standard of health and culture, and (2) the need of refraining from any form of exploitation either individual or collective. The degree of collectivism in these cooperative settlements varies from the complete absence of any private property and full submission to collective control and discipline to a mixed system of private ownership of the produce with cooperation in many of their activities. Flexibility in type and degree of cooperation gives, on the one hand, free play to diverse human elements and distinctive characteristics and, on the other, makes possible unity of spirit amid a large variety of social and economic forms.

On an even larger scale than in the collectives, which are laying the agricultural foundation of the country, the spirit of democracy is being promoted by the large network of cooperatives of all kinds, such as credit unions and cooperatives in insurance, in home-building, in buying, in marketing, in contracting and in supplying services. The fundamental purpose of these cooperatives is to build up the land without having to resort to the competitive system of capitalism, with all the attendant ills of speculation and crisis. The common earnings of all these cooperatives are shared equally. The significant fact about them is that they are not motivated merely by the desire to achieve greater economies, or to make greater profits through the elimination of jobbery and middlemen. They conduct various social experiments which are necessitated by the urge to build a new national economy. Otherwise such a national economy could not come into being.

Of all manifestations of the democratic spirit in Eretz Yisrael as a whole, the most remarkable is, no doubt, that of the Workers' Federation (Histadrut). It is an over-all organization of all workers in the collectives and cooperatives and of all white collar workers who are unaffiliated with any group; in a word, of all who earn their livelihood either through mental or manual labor. The essential requirement is that they shall live by their own labor and not exploit others. The general structure of the Histadrut is unique and reflects the unique character of the Palestinian experiment in democracy. The purpose of protecting the trade union interests of its members is, though highly important, not the primary one. The primary purpose is to function as the principal land-building agency and thus to pave the way for a workers' community in Eretz Yisrael.

With that ambitious aim in view, the Histadrut engages in a wide range of activities, which no trade union could ever dream of attempting. The following is the list of some of the activities, as summed up by A. Revusky in his book, Jews in Palestine.[7] "It establishes collective farms, supervises their progress and helps to provide them with funds; it organizes the sale of agricultural products and the cooperative purchase of consumers' goods; it conducts cooperatives in transportation and several lines of production; it operates contracting firms in various fields of rural and urban work; it organizes home building groups and maintains a central office to coordinate their activities; it controls a labor bank and local credit unions; it possesses a countrywide health organization with its own clinics, hospitals and sanitaria; it maintains workers' schools and encourages various cultural activities, including lectures, drama, music, etc.; it sponsors sports clubs and, in the case of Arab outbreaks, has actual control of Jewish self-defense; it regulates and organizes labor immigration by creating groups of pioneers (the *halutzim*) in the Diaspora and preparing them for future tasks in Palestine."

This last function of regulating and organizing labor immigration differentiates it from many other trade unions in the world. They have generally advocated the shutting of their countries' gates to all immigration. One can understand the reason for such a policy. Under the capitalistic system, immigration is attended by the lowering of wages and the standard of living. With no such fears, however, present in Eretz Yisrael, due to the dominance of Labor Socialism, the advent of new man-power is counted on to raise the productivity of the country and the standard of living. With the purpose of strengthening the Jewish National Home uppermost in its mind, the Workers' Federation is bound to exert as much effort as possible to avert strikes and to bring about a better understanding between workers and employers. Of particular value is the success it has had in enforcing an equal distribution of work during the periods of economic adversity. The action taken by the Palestine government in creating a Labor Department and engaging in the organization of Arab workers into trade unions, is undoubtedly due to the activities of the *Histadrut*. The fact that the influence of the *Histadrut* reaches out to the neighboring countries makes it perhaps a most important factor for democracy in the near East.

The *Histadrut*, despite its predominant influence in the rebuilding of the Jewish homeland, does not monopolize what is after all the most important development in the life of the growing Jewish community in Eretz Yisrael, from the standpoint of democratic nationalism, that is, the capacity of a heterogeneous population to achieve self-government. We must remember that the majority of the Jewish population in Eretz Yisrael lived, until very recently, under conditions and in a universe of thought virtually medieval. They have been catapulted, as it were, into the modern world where they can no longer expect uniformity of outlook nor unanimity of opinion with regard to what is to be accepted as authoritative. Jews who are emancipated from the medieval ghettos, or pales of settlement, need to become accustomed to having some of their number question the most sacrosanct traditions. Parents have to be able to bear the shock of having their most deeply rooted sentiments challenged by their children. When Jews from all parts of the world began coming to Eretz Yisrael in large numbers, the problem arose whether they would be capable of achieving orderly self-government. Such self-government could no longer be of the theocratic type by which Jews had lived throughout the centuries. Those who were chiefly responsible for the reawakened Jewish life in Eretz Yisrael would hear of no other but the democratic form of self-government.

The first practical moves to inaugurate Jewish autonomy were made in 1920. It took several years of passionate debate for the community to arrive at a common understanding. The most difficult issue that had to be fought out was woman suffrage. In traditional Jewish law, the woman did not have equal status with the man. To grant her political equality in the new Eretz Yisrael was, in the opinion of the traditionalists, a violation of divine law. To be sure, not all of the difficulties in achieving autonomy were due to disagreement among the Jews. The British Administration afforded enough obstructive tactics of its own. The fact, however, that by 1928 the right of the Jewish community to exercise some degree of autonomy was formally recognized is incontrovertible evidence of how speedily and effectively Jews as a people are capable of transforming themselves from an ancient theocracy to a modern democracy.

A small and vociferous group known as *Agudat Yisrael,* which represents extreme and militant orthodoxy, has stayed out of the Jewish community or *Kenesset Yisrael,* but it has been bypassed as a pocket of intransigent resistance to democracy, resistance that will no doubt disintegrate in time. Fortunately, the majority of the Orthodox have refused to take such an intransigent attitude and are cooperating even with the radical elements in the community.

Thus, from whichever angle we view the movement to reestablish a Jewish homeland in Eretz Yisrael, we cannot but see it as a unique experiment in democracy; the circumstances and forces which led to the adoption of that aim, the various measures which are being taken in order to prepare the conditions necessary to attain that aim, and the unparalleled achievements which the prospect of putting an end to the homelessness of the Jewish people has been able to elicit—all these attest to the creative power of democracy. The Jewish reclamation of Eretz Yisrael may rate small in the affairs of mankind, but it is invaluable as a social experiment and as a means of demonstrating the power of democracy to transform social chaos into social order.

CHAPTER EIGHTEEN

CONTINUITY AND CHANGE
IN THE JEWISH TRADITION

1

CHANGE IN ATTITUDE TOWARD THE PAST

For a people to survive, it must face the future with confidence. This does not mean that Jews should have no interest in their people's past, or that each generation must produce out of its own immediate experience, without the benefit of the acquired wisdom of past generations, the faith which enables it to meet the issues of life. It means rather that Jews must not merely remember the past and try to perpetuate it, but that they must use past experience to help them meet present-day problems in a manner which will assure them a future, a future that, in its fulfillment of present needs, shall represent a richer and more abundant life. Jews cannot afford to be those of whom it has been said that "in trying to warm their hands by the ashes of a dead past, they only freeze in the process."

In the past, Israel always knew God as "He who has hallowed us by His precepts," that is to say, who has manifested Himself in those ideals and in that discipline of life by which Jews hoped to attain salvation or life abundant. The various memorials and symbols of the Jewish past were employed to inspire our people with confidence in their future, as the people through whom God would one day assert His rule of righteousness and peace over all the earth.

In the modern attitude of most Jews toward the Jewish past, even of most Jews who are interested in that past, including many great scholars who have contributed important researches into Jewish antiquities, there is little evidence of this motivation. The impulse for preserving our ancient heritage in modern times has been not so much to provide inspiration or wisdom with which to shape the Jewish life of the future as to provide the apologetics with which to justify our survival as a people. Ever since the Emancipation, when the promise of freedom and equality was dangled before the eyes of the Jews, Jewish scholars have engaged in research into the past of their people to justify to themselves and to others its right to survive. The possibility of incorporation into the body politic of the modern nations has made the Jews sensitive, to the point of morbidity, to the opinion of the

372

Gentiles. The persistence of anti-Jewish prejudice has rendered them eager to assure not only others, but themselves, that they were descended from good stock which had contributed much to the development of human civilization. The Jew exhibits his interest in the Bible and other Jewish historic documents in the same spirit that aristocratic families display their family trees, the portraits and armor of their ancestors, and ancient patents of nobility.

Such an interest in the Jewish past cannot effect even that little for the future of the Jewish people which it is calculated to accomplish, the raising of their esteem in the eyes of others and even in their own eyes. That it will not impress the virulent anti-Semite and make him respect Jews goes without saying. The very fact that Jews made important contributions to civilization is what irritates him. That our ancestors have given the Bible to the world is, in his eyes, our supreme offense, for he is contemptuous of the "slave morality" of the Bible.

As for the liberal non-Jew, however, who is not blinded by prejudice, how will the achievements of our glorious past affect his esteem for us? If he is a true liberal nurtured in the democratic tradition, his answer to Jewish pretensions to honor based on the Jewish past would likely take the form of a laconic, "So what?" Democratic liberalism is not impressed by *yihus*, or aristocratic lineage. It insists on judging a man's worth on the basis of his own accomplishments, not on those of his ancestors. Only Jewish achievement in the present, directed to worthwhile goals in the future, can impress the true liberal with our worth. Our pride of ancestry, therefore, betrays a lack of self-assurance, and makes us out a very undignified figure in the eyes of modern liberals.

And how does this attitude toward the past affect our own self-respect? There is in us enough of the true liberal to feel the validity of the contention that our generation ought to justify itself not by the achievements of the past but by its own accomplishments. As heirs of a great spiritual tradition, we are derelict when we fail to cultivate it and to render it productive of values for our day. In view of the paucity of creative achievement in the present, of what good is memory of a great past, if contemplating it leads only to the conclusion expressed by the Rabbis when they said of their forebears: "If they were angels, we are men; if they were men, we are but asses." [1] Pride of ancestry may, for a time, engender in us illusions of grandeur, but sooner or later disillusionment comes, and it is devastating. Thus as Jewish preachers endeavor to impress on congregations the greatness of their spiritual heritage, the Jew who is familiar with present-day realities of Jewish life is disposed to feel depressed by the contrast, and to question the worth to him of that heritage. If we are descended from great creative geniuses in the realm of religion the descent has been steep, indeed.

What makes the situation more tragic is that not only eloquent appeals for loyalty to the Jewish past are ineffectual in making Jewish tradition function now as an influence to help us face the future, but that almost equally ineffectual are the painstaking and devoted labors of gifted and erudite scholars. Lacking creative imagination and spiritual insight to understand the kind of spiritual food Jews need to sustain their courage in modern crises, our scholars do not know how to extract from the past experiences of our people the elixir of a living faith. All scholarship, to have religious significance, must be interpretive. It must not merely accumulate facts but evaluate them. When research is not guided by a deep interest in timely problems and knowledge of present needs, it makes of history, instead of a living tradition, a mere archeological museum, interesting to the archeologist and serviceable, it may be, to the historian with imagination and insight, but not directly useful to people who need aid in living. This is not said in belittlement of the archeologist. His work is not wholly wasted, because it can be appropriated and used by the spiritual leader when he arises. But *spiritual leadership must take a different attitude to the Jewish past from that of the antiquarian scholar or research worker. It has to cause the dead-wood of tradition to blossom anew.*

Why were our fathers able to use the past as it was handed down to them for purposes of living in the present, and why cannot we? The answer is to be found in the fact that the change in man's general outlook on the world, marking the transition from the medieval to the modern world, is far more radical than any which has taken place in Jewish life since traditional Judaism came into being. When, in the course of his studies, Rashi [2] encountered Rabbi Akiba,[3] he could feel that he was confronted by a person very much like himself, who saw the world as he did, who reacted to life in much the same way, who expressed himself in similar terms, who interpreted the world of nature and of society in the light of much the same common stock of knowledge as he did. That is how Rashi felt not only toward the *Tannaim* [4] and *Amoraim* [5] but also toward the Biblical heroes. To be sure, their world was very different from Rashi's, but he was not aware of the difference. For him King David was not a tribal chieftain who mounted to the throne and established an empire, but a pietist and scholar, whose harp aroused him at midnight to commune with his God while the world slept,[6] in other words, an ascetic medieval saint.

By reason of their very lack of historic perspective, our fathers viewed all Jewish history as contemporary. The law of Moses did not mean merely a law which had been given to their forefathers, and which came into their own possession as an heirloom; it was a law given to Moses for *them,* with them in mind, and designed to show them how to live to best advantage, how to achieve salvation. The observances of Jewish ritual were not for them ancient customs, interesting in their quaintness. The symbols of the ritual were no more quaint to them than the Stars and Stripes are quaint to the American of today.

Paradoxically, without understanding wherein our own outlook differs from that of our fathers, we cannot recover that feeling of kinship with them, that understanding of their ideas, ideals and strivings which can make their lives significant to us. We cannot translate their thought into our language, so long as we imagine that we and they speak the same tongue. When we labor under this illusion, their talk seems mere barbaric babbling; but when we recognize the difference in language and try to translate what they have to tell us into our own idiom of thought, we often discover that they are sufficiently like us, and their experiences are sufficiently like our own for them to have something of importance to communicate to us. Traditional symbols then would be significant to us not merely as relics of the past. By reinterpreting their meaning in terms relevant to modern life, we would invest them with new associations and link them to interests which have survived the vicissitudes of time.

2

THE HISTORICAL APPROACH TO JEWISH TRADITION

A tradition is not a static sum of ideas, directives and institutions. It is a people's response to its environment which is ever changing. Those identified with the Historical School in Judaism virtually acted on that principle, in their approach to the Jewish tradition. That school in Judaism represents the first concerted effort to grapple with the problem of having to accept the tradition and to harmonize it with the modern universe of discourse. They availed themselves of one of the dominant concepts in the modern thought-world—that of evolution. They applied it to Jewish tradition in the form in which it had come down to us, in order to prove that despite its own claim, it did not possess that form from the very beginning, but came to possess it only after having gone through a long evolutionary process.

Jewish tradition itself has, of course, been aware that the different situations in which Jews found themselves were bound to give rise to different practices and beliefs. It has, however, consistently maintained that, no matter how different those practices and beliefs were from those which our ancestors lived by in the Wilderness, or during the First Commonwealth, they merely represented an unfolding of the original revelation at Sinai. The Talmudic Sages, during the first centuries of the common era, Maimonides [7] during the Middle Ages and David Hoffman [8] in recent times, stressed the doctrine that the Oral Law was handed down simultaneously with the Written Law at Sinai. The Historical School, however, has replaced the traditional assumption of an unfolding tradition by the dynamic one of "a tradition in the making." The two assumptions are as far apart from each other as are the pre-modern and the modern world. The essential point in "tradition in the making" is that change in environment elicits from the people, in its effort to survive, a new and unprecedented response.

One has only to read the opening paragraphs of Isaac Hirsch Weiss's great work, *Dor Dor V'Doreshav*,[9] to note the effect of the modern historical approach to the Jewish tradition. Citing the claim of that tradition that it originated, in its entirety, with Moses at Sinai, Weiss argues that we cannot rely upon any tradition's testimony concerning itself and maintains that we should study the history of the Jewish tradition just as we do that of any other national tradition. On the principle that a religious belief or practice must be organically related to its background, he points out that the status of Jewish religion, during the entire period prior to the return from the Babylonian exile, was such that it could not have served as a background for the part of the Jewish tradition known as the Oral Law. He, therefore, advances the theory that the traditional belief, according to which the Oral Law was supposed to have been promulgated simultaneously with the Written Law, developed during the bitter contest between Sadducees and Pharisees. The Pharisees, in their eagerness to assure the general acceptance of the Oral Law, claimed for the latter a divine origin identical with that of the Written Law.

The Historical School broke ground, but it failed to proceed with the construction of the building for which the ground had been cleared. It took the first, and inherently the most difficult and radical step, but it seemed to have been frightened by its own daring. Instead of drawing, from the evolutionary approach, conclusions for the future of Judaism, it has confined itself to archeological research. No one can question the value of retrieving as much as possible of the Jewish past. But for the majority of our people who look for guidance to live as Jews in the present, it is necessary to draw out more fully the implications of the historical approach to our tradition, if we hope to harmonize that tradition with the contemporary universe of discourse.

The historical approach implies that the Jewish tradition is a human phenomenon subject to the natural laws of human behavior and to the normal action and reaction between human life and the environment. Those who accept that approach are not at all impressed by that tradition's claim to supernatural origin. They recognize that claim itself as entirely natural and normal, and as being, under the conditions of cultural development which obtained in pre-modern times, a way of expressing awareness of supreme worth and binding authority.

If then the Jewish tradition is a natural phenomenon, the Jewish people, instead of appearing in the light of a passive recipient, has to be reckoned with as its creator, and the tradition itself has to be viewed as both the stimulus and the product of that people's will to live and to render its life worthwhile. As a natural phenomenon, a tradition represents the past stage of that collective life process which we identify as a civilization. It is also a civilization as matter for transmission to the coming generation, or as matter for education. In accepting the Jewish tradition, we are not accepting the ideas, habits, attitudes and institutions as the petrified sediment of a lived past, but as pent up energy which, when released, generates new life. Thus the alternative to regarding Judaism as a specific tradition which consists of supernaturally revealed laws and teachings is to regard Judaism as a civilization which is both the product and the incentive of the will to live as a people.

3

HOW TO BRIDGE THE GAP BETWEEN PAST AND PRESENT

To accept the Jewish tradition, therefore, need no longer mean to subscribe to beliefs and practices which clash with our entire outlook on life. It means to accept the role of living as a member of the Jewish people. It is impossible to fulfill that role without an awareness of that tradition, not merely as an archeological memory, but as a determining influence in our every day life. Since it is impossible to have the tradition function in that way, so long as we know it only in its own terms, it is essential that we come to understand it with the aid supplied by the modern perspective on life.

We have found that the evolutionary approach opens up new possibilities of comprehending the tradition, in terms of natural creative responses to needs, needs which grew out of the will of the Jews to make the most out of their unity or we-feeling, in their struggle to retain it in the face of overwhelming odds. In order, therefore, to fulfill our role as Jews effectively, and in a way that would yield the greatest good to ourselves and to others, it is necessary for us to reinterpret that tradition in the light not only of the evolutionary approach, but of the increasing knowledge of human nature. That knowledge might throw light upon those universal aspects of the Jewish past, which could well serve as a means of integrating our tradition with the best in the thought and striving in the world of today.

We now realize that the miracle-tales in the Bible are merely the record of how events impressed our ancestors who had to interpret those events in accordance with their own thought-world, even as we interpret current events in accordance with ours. When we take that fact into account, it becomes possible for us to understand their psychological reactions to life. Our ancestors are then seen as the same sort of men and women who live in the world today, with capacities for pleasure and pain, joy and sorrow, hope and fear similar to ours. They, too, had to provide food, clothing and shelter for themselves and their families; they had to organize their political life, to defend themselves against enemies, to adjust conflicting interests, and to try to make life secure and abundant. So their problems, too, differed little from ours.

Once we acknowledge that miracle-tales are not records of objective fact but *interpretations* of reality, we find ourselves inhabiting the same world as our ancestors, and their experiences become significant. Their heroism can then thrill us, their idealism inspire us, their wisdom stimulate us. Even their errors can instruct us. In a word, once we free ourselves from the illusions which our fathers cherished with regard to miracles, we can reinterpret the ancient miraculous story in a manner which yields meaning relevant to contemporary living.

The evolutionary approach in general, and the method gleaned from modern human sciences, instead of weakening one's faith as a Jew, can actually strengthen it. The fact that we have to go outside the tradition, if we wish to utilize it as a motivating factor in our life as Jews, is at times singled out for attack and disparagement. As a rule, those who indulge in such disparagement themselves often follow that procedure. They, too, resort to ideas and values taken from the environment to give meaning and validity to the tradition, in their own way. The only difference is that they do not realize to what extent they themselves follow the procedure they vociferously condemn. The truth is that it is no more possible to keep a tradition alive and functioning, without reinterpreting it somehow in terms of contemporary thought and needs, than it is possible to keep ourselves alive without taking in food to restore our bodies.

4

WHAT IS TO BE GAINED BY REINTERPRETING THE PAST?

The affirmations of a tradition are accepted at face value, by those who regard it as inherently reliable and infallible, on the assumption that it is of superhuman origin. Of what value, however, can those affirmations be, if we have to reinterpret them in order to bring them into line with our own world outlook? If all that such interpretation means is making a traditional idea or practice convey what we regard beforehand as true or proper, independently of the tradition, little or nothing would seem to be gained by adopting this roundabout process of being guided by principles derived from one's own reasoning or experiences. The well-known statement of Maimonides about the interpretation of the Biblical account of creation gives point to this question. He maintains that, if reason had led him to believe in the existence of eternal matter, he could readily enough have found warrant for that belief in the Torah.[10] What then would the Torah add to what one could well know without it? If tradition is to serve merely as a sanction for the results of our own reasoning and experience, what actually do we gain from it?

The answer is, that however wrong a tradition may be, from the standpoint of fact, it reveals the collective mind of the people that evolved it. *The Jewish tradition, interpreted from an evolutionary and socio-psychological point of view, enables us to recognize and identify the collective Jewish mind.* This does not mean that we become aware of the existence of some mystic entity which hovers over the Jewish people, independently of the individual men and women who belong to it, and regardless of what happens to them. The collective Jewish mind lives and functions in each Jew, insofar as he interacts with his fellow-Jews, as part of a people that knows itself as such.

By using the Jewish tradition to familiarize ourselves with the Jewish mind, we learn how we should interact with our fellow-Jews, or what we should be and do, in common with them. This is how we become one with the Jewish people. If we could achieve such oneness directly by accepting and living up to the tradition as it came down to us, there would be no need for any further ado. Since, however, we cannot accept the tradition on its face value, we achieve the purpose which the tradition was meant to serve by trying to envisage the mind that evolved it.

That collective mind, being human, could not be fundamentally different from our own. Evidently, in creating that tradition, it was trying to express in the terms of its own world something we, too, feel the need of expressing or becoming aware of. The discovery that some of our deepest needs, the needs of experiencing personal worth and the worthwhileness of life, have actually been motivating influences in the lives of the men and women of the Jewish people, establishes an indissoluble bond between us and the Jewish people and activates those needs in us as they never would be activated otherwise.

Furthermore, a knowledge of the collective Jewish mind, besides helping us discover in a general way that what we are at our best was anticipated by our ancestors, actually helps us identify what constitutes our best. In learning to interpret the Jewish tradition as the creation of the Jewish mind, we learn to interpret our own minds, from the point of view of what in our innermost self we want to become. How one thing leads to the other becomes apparent, when we realize that what a people deems worthy to make part of its tradition is the distillation of what it has come to regard as essential not only to survival, but to the attainment of the maximum good.

It is inevitable that the prerequisite to the attainment of the maximum good should include cooperation with others and subordination of one's egoistic desire to the general good. A tradition reflects a people's conception of salvation. *This is why a tradition is so essential to the normal life of a human being. It not only gives meaning to his life, beyond and above the satisfaction of his bodily and egoistic desires, but it also creates the presumption in the minds of others that he lives purposefully, and that they can count on a large measure of cooperation from him.* Lacking tradition, a person is likely to be a riddle to all except those who know him intimately. They are not apt to find him ever forgetful of self, unless he happens to be a very original person who has worked out a pattern of salvation of his own. Ordinarily it is impossible for any person to arrive at a conception of salvation without some tradition to start him off, or to help him on his way. A conception of salvation implies some idea of the best possible use we may make of our powers and opportunities. To expect a person to arrive at such an idea alone is like expecting him to learn to speak and develop a language by himself.

5

TORAH TO INCLUDE AMENDMENT AS WELL AS REINTERPRETATION

The most difficult obstacle to be overcome in the reinterpretation of the Jewish tradition is no doubt the dogma that the Torah is supernaturally revealed. Our fathers, in accordance with their belief in miracles, accepted as historic fact the account of God's revelation on Mount Sinai. They also drew from that fact the inference that only through obedience to the divine law could either the individual or society achieve this salvation. Any action which disregarded a precept in the Torah was sin, even though human reason might see nothing objectionable in such action.

In the light of modern research into the past and inquiry into religious practices and beliefs of civilizations other than our own, both ancient and modern, that assumption is no longer tenable. We have discovered that among all ancient peoples, the origin of laws and customs was ascribed to divine revelation. That was natural. Not having the benefit of an objective record of the actual human origin of their laws, and recognizing the dependence of the very life of the nation on reverence for its laws, the ancients identified the intent of the laws with the will of God or the gods.

Today, however, we are in a position to perceive that the experience of our people was not unlike that of other peoples, and we are able to explain, with the aid of the human sciences, the origin of legal institutions and to trace most of the features, which are unique in any civilization, to specific conditioning circumstances. It becomes, therefore, too pretentious for us to assume that our Torah is the *only* way of life for *all* peoples. We may recognize its value as the organized effort of our people to realize its highest ideals, and this may make it truly a way of salvation for the Jewish people. No other doctrine and discipline can serve them as well because, as a matter of historic fact, no other doctrine and discipline developed out of the exigencies of their own collective life in response to their own special needs and as an expression of their own collective purpose.

Evaluated in this light, the Torah may still be considered as a divine revelation in the sense that it testifies to the reality of God as the Spirit that promotes righteousness in the world. To assert this is not, however, to affirm what our fathers meant when they spoke of *Torah min hashamayim*. It affirms that the Torah reveals God, not that God revealed the Torah. It assumes that *the process by which the Torah actually came into being is divine, in the sense that it is a manifestation of the will to salvation or life abundant, and that the doctrines and laws of other civilizations, being part of the same process, also are divine*. To be sure, they are divine only to the extent that they actually do express principles which help men to live well; a limitation that applies also to Jewish law.

The modern Jew cannot, therefore, look to the Torah as a source of authority, in the sense that whatever it permits is right and whatever it forbids is wrong. He reverses the process and says: *Whatever is right should be incorporated in our Torah, and whatever is wrong should be eliminated from our Torah*. Inasmuch as no man can know, merely on the basis of personal experience, what is right and wrong in every situation, the traditional standards of right and wrong cherished by our people, and the institutions sanctioned by the Torah as aids to spiritual discipline, can and should be regarded with reverence, and should be observed, wherever experience has not challenged their validity. But we must not cling to the standards of the past, if they work mischief in the present. This is what happens often even to legal institutions which were beneficent in their day, but which have become detrimental to the realization of our highest ideals in the circumstances under which we live. In the era before the Civil War, for example, the Biblical laws designed to mitigate the lot of the slave were cited by advocates of slavery as proving that the Bible regarded slavery itself as legitimate—a perfectly logical inference.

Traditionalists in our day endeavor to minimize the difference between the pre-modern and the modern attitude toward the exclusive revelation of the Torah. They maintain that the Torah is capable of interpretation, and that, where its standards do not seem adequate for modern needs, it is because we have not found the correct interpretation. On that basis, amendment of the Torah is, of course, precluded. They admit that God also may have revealed some saving doctrine to other peoples, and point to our Sages as having declared that Gentiles who obeyed the laws of Noah would be granted a share in the world to come. They admit that we may learn from research and experience important truths as to how we should live, but they insist that any truth which is important for man's salvation must have been anticipated in the Torah.

This sort of apologetic, however, instead of helping the Torah to function as a dynamic tradition really has the effect of removing it from life. We encounter numerous problems for the solution of which we would not even think of referring to our Jewish codes, because we know that those problems did not exist at the time these codes were formulated. How, for example, should the economic arrangements of marriage be affected by the fact that women, in our economic system, are no longer necessarily dependent on men for support? This is a question which we would naturally discuss not on the basis of what authorities had to say in the past, but from the point of view of the need for stability in the relationship between husband and wife, or of the needs of the child, or from similar criteria by which we relate the problem to the personal and social welfare of those involved.

Even the most tradition-minded among Jews today would admit the legitimacy of these considerations; but such people would take one of two courses in dealing with that problem. For lack of what they would regard as adequate authority to make a change, they would insist on retaining, even in our day, the relationship that existed between husband and wife in a society in which the woman had no opportunity for independent life; in that event they would be perpetuating an injustice. Or they might seek in the legalistic literature some precedent which could be so interpreted as in fact to alter the practical application of the law, while permitting it in theory to remain unchanged. This amounts to a confession that they look for guidance to reason and experience, and that only after they have come to their conclusion do they consult the law, and consciously pervert its original meaning in order to make it conform to their ideas.

Those who have recourse to this expedient presume erroneously that they honor the law by continuing the process by which it was developed until now. When the Rabbis in the pre-modern period were confronted with a problem caused by the discrepancy between their ideal of what was right and the standard of the law as interpreted in their day, it did not occur to them that changed conditions required that the law be given a new meaning. They were not aware of what to us is a commonplace, that legal institutions are subject to evolution. What was law in their day, they were sure, had been the law also in the time of Moses. Indeed, according to Raba,[11] the outstanding Amora of the fourth century, Abraham observed the law of *erub-tabshilin*, the legal device to permit the preparation on a holiday of the meal for the following day when the latter happened to be a Sabbath.

In all cases of conflict between tradition and current expectation, the Sages of the Talmud acted on a two-fold assumption that: No law of the Torah could be abrogated or amended, and since the Torah was the revelation of a benign God, any interpretation of the law which worked harm to man must be a misinterpretation.[12] This led them to seek, by a process of casuistic reasoning, an interpretation which would reconcile the letter of the law with what they felt should represent its spirit. When they arrived at such an interpretation, they were honestly convinced that this was what the law had always meant, that they were not making an innovation, but were rediscovering a long forgotten meaning. One cannot say as much for those who nowadays would have recourse to legalistic processes of interpretation to give to the law a meaning which it did not have previously. They are not, in reality, developing the law through interpretation; they are amending the law, under the pretense of interpreting it.

The effect of this process is to relieve the Jewish people today of all responsibility for making Jewish law an effective instrument of social advancement. Jews of necessity are governed by the laws of the lands in which they live. These laws they recognize as useful and as responsive to human need. They recognize, also, that these laws are responsive to human need, since they operate democratically by the consent of the governed and can be, and frequently are, amended by the people. They know that they would not tolerate living under a law which, because of its alleged supernatural origin, could not be subject to any legislative amendment, but only to interpretation by the courts. When, therefore, Jewish law is presented in this light, it appears as a matter of interest only to a few professional scholars. It can no longer continue to function as "the law of Moses and Israel"; it can serve only as a cultural relic of a dead past without functional value for our age.

When one considers how much of thought and life went into the development of Jewish law, it is nothing less than tragic to consign it to the dusty archives of the past. If we treated it frankly, from the standpoint of our modern outlook upon law, if we discarded the notion of its being the way of salvation revealed exclusively to Israel, and acknowledged it as the embodiment of the efforts of our people to make of their civilization a source of salvation to themselves and to the world, it could be reinstated as an important and even indispensable element in our civilization. In Eretz Yisrael, Jews could establish democratic communal agencies to study the law from the point of view of applying what is of value to the actual problems of modern life, of declaring obsolete what ought to be discarded, and of adding to the law whatever the exigencies of life call for. They might devise effective procedures for progressive changes in the law which would make it a democratic agency of social control; they might remove from the category of law all ritualistic practices, which should be left to informal regulation by those intellectually and spiritually qualified to advise on such matters. For the Jews of the Diaspora who in their everyday affairs and dealings are governed by the law of the state of which they are citizens, the legal developments in Eretz Yisrael would develop standards of behavior supplemental to those laid down by the secular law of the lands they live in. Jews might reasonably be expected to conform to those standards which would have behind them the pressure of public opinion, as expressed in democratically organized Jewish communities.

But all this is impossible as long as Jewish law is conceived in the traditional manner which makes it either oppressive or inoperative. Consequently, the refusal of traditionalist Jews to apply modern concepts to Jewish law, and their insistence on operating with the ancient notion that the Torah is a way of salvation revealed by God to Israel alone, prevents it from functioning henceforth as a way of salvation even for Israel.

That traditionalist attitude, moreover, stands in the way of the mutual tolerance and good will between different civilizations on which the salvation of mankind depends. By the same token that Judaism will have to renounce its exclusive claim to salvation, Christianity and Islam will have to renounce theirs. In an era when religious civilizations assumed that they were divinely ordained and destined to dominate the world, it was natural and legitimate for Judaism to do likewise. The scientific approach to the study of civilization has shown, however, the fallacy in all these pretensions. It has, thereby, paved the way for a genuine religious tolerance, based on the fact that each civilization tends to develop the religion that best answers the spiritual needs

of its members. It has taught us to realize that all religions are responsive
to the common needs of human nature, and have some affirmative
contribution to make to the establishment of God's kingdom of justice
and peace. Thus only by a candid acceptance of the modern denial of
exclusive revelation of God to any one people can we, at the same time,
utilize our Torah tradition as a way of salvation for ourselves and as a
contribution to the salvation of mankind.

CHAPTER NINETEEN

THE PROBLEM OF JEWISH LAW

Both Orthodoxy and Reform take, each in its own way, a clearly defined attitude toward traditional Jewish law. Orthodoxy regards that law as supernaturally revealed and unalterable, except through some subsequent revelation. Reform regards it as a product of historical evolution and as having lost its function as a result of the Emancipation. It maintains that Jewish religion in our day requires no legal precepts; ethical principles suffice as guides to Jewish behavior. Conservatism rejects both of these assumptions, though it has not arrived as yet at a definite understanding concerning the place of Jewish law in Jewish religion and Jewish life. Among Conservative Jews, great diversity prevails both in the theory and in the practice of Jewish law.

Thus far the spokesmen of Conservatism have contributed two important principles to the definition of its attitude to Jewish law. The first of these is that the binding character of Jewish law for the Jew does not derive from the belief that it was supernaturally revealed. The law is binding intrinsically, in that it is the expression of the religious spirit of the Jewish people.[1] A Jew who is loyal to his people and its religious aspirations derives from that loyalty sufficient motivation for desiring to strengthen Jewish law as an expression and implementation of Jewish ideals. The mere fact that he regards the law as human and fallible would not interfere with this purpose, any more than an awareness of the inherent limitations of science would weaken a scientist's devotion to his particular scientific interest.

The second contribution of Conservatism to the definition of the attitude which Jews should take to Jewish law is the principle of historical continuity, which was expounded under the term of *positive historical Judaism*, by Zechariah Frankel,[2] a century ago, and under the term *Catholic Israel*, by Solomon Schechter,[3] a half century ago. That principle was intended to guide us in accepting or rejecting any proposed changes in Jewish law. Changes in law, according to that principle, must not be made arbitrarily, to accommodate a local or temporary situation. Only such changes are admissible as can be accepted universally throughout Jewry, and are in harmony with the organic integrity and development of the Jewish people. No more influential spokesmen could be sought for any principle than Frankel and Schechter. They carried out the ancient injunction of raising many

387

disciples.[4] Yet nothing whatever has been done by their disciples to implement that principle. That is the case, undoubtedly, because the principle as such is unworkable. It merely illustrates the definition of "Conservative" as one who does not believe in doing a thing for the first time. It is a compromise between wishing to stand still and being afraid to go forward.

1

THE PLACE OF LAW IN PRE-MODERN JEWISH LIFE

A realization of what we mean by law in general, and how it functions in human life, will help us to cope with the problem of Jewish law. Law which regulates human conduct expresses the collective will of some organized society, and is such only so long as that society exercises sanctions to enforce it. This implies that law exists as one factor in an organic complex, of which the other factors are: an organized society, a collective will, and sanctions. Not having an independent existence apart from one another, any one of these four factors can be defined only in relation to the remaining three. The concept of law has no meaning except in relation to an organized society which enforces its collective will by means of sanctions. *The differences between various systems of law, or between different stages in the development of the same legal system, correspond to differences in the form of social organization, in the conception of the collective will, and in the nature of the sanctions used to enforce it.*

In every one of these factors, a wide range of variation is possible. Thus the form of organization may vary from a closely knit state, as that of ancient Sparta, to a widely dispersed group like the Jews. The conception of the collective will may vary from one which identifies it with the will of God, so that its principles are supposed to be as inherent in the nature of things as any natural law, to a purely secular covenant. The sanctions may range from an elaborate system of rewards and punishments at the hands of authorized agencies to a vaguely conceived form of divine retribution in the hereafter. Corresponding to these variations, the law itself, as the instrument of the collective will, may vary from a definite, fixed code to customs and conventions which register the kind of behavior society expects of the individual.

Until modern times Jewish law functioned organically. The Jews always constituted an organic society. They had a collective will, which they identified with the will of God. The recognition of the societal status of Jewry is evident from the fact that, up to the time of the Emancipation, in such matters as taxation, for example, governments dealt not with Jews as individuals, but as members of the Jewish community. Nor did the civil law of the nations among whom Jews lived apply to the relations between one Jew to another; these were governed entirely by Jewish law. Moreover, the Jew who excluded himself from participation in Jewish community life, could find asylum in no other community, unless he took the drastic step of apostasy.

The interpretation of the collective will expressed in Jewish law was that its mandate was of supernatural origin. This gave to the authority of the law an absolute and infallible character. The law was enforced both by divine and human sanctions. The divine sanction was principally the fear of punishment and the hope of reward in the hereafter. The fact that this sanction was divine added to its efficacy, since, unlike human sanctions, which are dependent on finite powers for their execution, divine sanctions are imposed by an almighty Power. The human sanction, in addition to general approval and disapproval of neighbors, would take the form of the *herem*, or excommunication.

In view of the fact that there was no other community which assumed any responsibility for the welfare of the Jewish individual, the fear of excommunication was tremendously effective. Thus even the irreligious and heretical person, who might not be deterred from nonconformity by the divine sanction of the law, was effectively deterred by the human sanction. Until the Emancipation, therefore, Jewish law, even though the police power of the Jewish community was limited, was enforced by sanctions no less effective in their operation than those of any modern state. That applies to the whole range of Jewish law—civil, marital and ritual. Before the Emancipation, Jewish law was everywhere a functioning reality.

2

JEWISH LIFE MEANINGLESS WITHOUT JEWISH LAW

A cataclysmic change took place, however, with the granting of citizenship to Jews. The first formal recognition of that change was the set of resolutions passed by the Sanhedrin which Napoleon convened in 1806. This was followed by the acceptance of those resolutions by the Brunswick Conference of 1841.[5] These resolutions were in effect a renunciation by the Jewish community of its juridical authority, except in ritual matters and, to a limited extent which involved no conflict with the law of the state, in marital affairs. This undermined the very status of Jewry as a people. To be sure, while governments were so constituted as to make affiliation with the Jewish group or community obligatory, as an alternative to affiliation with the Christian or any other distinctly identifiable group, communal sanctions could still be employed to enforce conformity, at least to a few limited areas of Jewish law. The Jewish community could still define the terms on which the individual would enjoy the benefits of membership in it. The individual Jew, unless he was prepared to join some other religious communion, had to comply with the legal standards on which the community insisted.

But what possibility is there for Jewish law to function in a country such as ours, where church and state are separate, and where the government refuses to interfere in the internal affairs of any religious group? No law can function without sanctions; but sanctions can be applied only by a society from which it is impossible, or extremely disadvantageous, for the individual to withdraw. In American life, Jews and Gentiles do not live in mutually exclusive communities. Theoretically at least, one does not have to become a Christian in order to be accepted in non-Jewish society and to derive the benefits of business, professional and cultural association with Gentiles. It is not even necessary to relinquish membership in the Jewish community. A Jew may at present disregard every one of the distinctively Jewish ordinances, without fear that his right to membership in any important Jewish agency or organization might be challenged. His financial contribution would never be refused on that account. A Jew who has achieved worldly success is welcome in most congregations, regardless of how he came to be successful.

When we see how non-Jewish it is possible for a Jew to be we are inclined to propound the riddle: when is a Jew not a Jew? But to whom shall we turn for the solution of that riddle? There is today no Jewish body which is authorized to answer that question. Ever since the Jewish community abdicated its autonomous jurisdiction over the civil relations of Jews to one another, Jews have lost the status of a people, and their law has lost the status of law. That is one of the reasons why Jewish law has become defunct.

No Jew who experiences in his own being anything of his people's will to live should accept with equanimity this defunct state of Jewish law. He himself should do something, or persuade others to do something about it. But what he should not do is to resort to self-deluding, compensatory reasoning. Such reasoning is indulged in by those who maintain that the validity of a law has no relation whatever to the number of persons who obey it. According to this view, even if all Jews disregarded their traditional code of law, it would remain just as valid as if every Jew obeyed it, since it derives its authority from God and not from man. This does not square with the general assumption that the law exists for man and not man for the law, an assumption implied in the Rabbinic statement: [6] "The Sabbath is delivered to you, and not you are delivered to the Sabbath."

How absurd it is to maintain that even defunct Jewish law can be valid may be seen from the fact that the application of sanctions is assumed as an integral part of the actual laws as enunciated in the written and in the oral Torah. Even the ancients, from whom we have inherited the conception of our law as divine and independent of human authorship, insisted on its functional relationship to the Jewish people as a societal entity. It is true that they speak of the Torah as having existed before creation and as having been consulted by God when He created the world,[7] thus apparently regarding the Torah as prior to the world. Such hyperboles about the Torah are merely part of their tendency to apotheosize it. But when they spoke of Torah as law, they treated it as existing for Israel. The view that Israel existed for the Torah did not gain much favor among them.[8]

The notion of Jewish law as inherently valid, regardless of the extent to which it is ignored by Jews, is not only untrue but harmful. It obscures the urgent need of reconstituting Jewish society in order that Jewish law may be reinstated. But that is not the only hindrance to the reinstatement of Jewish law. The momentum of the past has for a time, and in certain circles, tended to preserve at least some vestigial remains of the habits which the law enjoins. That fact often obscures the fatal disintegration which is undermining Jewish life. Self-deluding optimism, inertia and lack of imagination prevent us from envisaging the full measure of the upheaval that has overtaken Judaism, in consequence of the loss of its juridical autonomy, and from undertaking the task of reconstructing Jewish law, so that it would resume its function in Jewish life. It is high time that we awake to the fact that the Jewish people has been atomized, and that Jewish law has been nullified. If we still believe in the value of Jewish life and in the importance to it of Jewish law, a difficult but imperative task lies ahead of us. We must reconstitute the Jewish people so that it may again express its will through the medium of law.

The Jewish people, in our day, will be reconstituted as a law-making and law-enforcing body, only when a sufficient number of affirmative Jews become convinced that there are need and room in Jewish life for a modern type of democratically instituted law. Such law would have to be supplementary to the law of the land and recognize its authority. In that respect Jewish law would merely be conforming to one of its own long established principles: "The law of the state is law." [9] To be sure, the original application of that legal maxim was limited in scope, whereas now its scope would have to be widened. The reason is that Jews are no longer a "state within a state" but an integral part of the state. This fact would also make it necessary for Jewish law to refrain from interfering with the freedom of economic and social intercourse with the non-Jewish elements of the population. *Whatever Jewish individuality is to be developed in the Diaspora must be the intrinsic product of Jewish creative effort in the domains of religion and culture, and not the result of artificial barriers.*[10]

In rehabilitating Jewish law, it is necessary to take into account the fundamental difference between the opportunities for Jewish living in Eretz Yisrael and those in the Diaspora. In Eretz Yisrael all human relationships, both those of status and of contract, come within the province of Jewish law. In the Diaspora, Jewish law is necessarily limited by the need for conforming to the law of the land and sharing in the economic, political, social and cultural life of the majority population.

In a previous chapter,* the failure of Eretz Yisrael Jewry to evolve a modern constitution and code of law was dealt with. Despite the desire to foster a collective Jewish life and to create agencies that make for a maximum of Jewish consciousness, there is no common system of Jewish civil law for the growing population. Whenever those who belong to the old *Yishuv* or to the Orthodox elements in the new *Yishuv* have any disputes that need adjustment, they apply to the rabbinic courts. These courts are notoriously oblivious to the social ideals and spiritual strivings of modern men, and they have no program for developing the law to meet the complicated conditions of life in our modern industrial age. In view of the present heterogeneous character of the population in Eretz Yisrael and its preoccupation with pressing economic, political and defense problems, it is, perhaps, asking too much of the Jews there to work out a civil code that shall adequately express the aspiration for social and ethical idealism of the modern *Yishuv*, and that shall provide effective means of enforcement.

* Ch. vii, p. 138 ff.

In the democratic countries where Jewish life is free from besetting fear and danger, Jewish scholarship would do well to concentrate at present on the task of evolving a way of living as Jews in our own day. They should study the general process of social reconstruction and the part in it played by law-enactment and law-enforcement for the purpose of formulating a constitution and a code both for Eretz Yisrael and for the Diaspora Jewry.

This suggestion will, undoubtedly, be scouted by those who take the position that law is a natural growth and must be permitted to emerge spontaneously from its native soil. All attempts deliberately to formulate law on a rational basis, whether in constitutions or in codes, are said to be artificial. This is exactly how all the romantic reactionaries among the jurists argued in the early nineteenth century Germany. Their attitude was one of reaction against rationalism that, presumably, was an invention of the French Revolution.

History, however, has demonstrated where such anti-rationalism leads. Nazi Germany, with its flouting of reason and justice and its glorification of the folk spirit in law, has proved to what absurdities and cruelties the assumption that only native law can have validity is liable to lead. Some of the most successful societies, in point of stability and successful combination of freedom with social order, owe their success to so-called artificially formulated constitution and codes of law. Their experience shows that Eretz Yisrael Jewry would do well to call upon Diaspora Jewry to help it in the upbuilding of Jewish law.

3

JEWISH LAW FOR DIASPORA JEWRY

In reconstructing law for Diaspora Jewry, there are but few areas which have to be considered. First is that of domestic relations. That would involve reckoning with the change in the status of the woman from one of inferiority to one of equality. Anyone familiar with traditional Jewish zeal for keeping domestic relations free from all taint of illegality must realize that this much needed change in the status of woman will not come about without systematic and patient re-education of the Jews. But that change is one of the most crucially necessary because of its social and psychological significance.

There are other areas of Jewish life, however, in which either new law will have to be created or old law changed. The entire range of communal activities presents a field for new Jewish law. If our communal agencies and organizations are not to be merely lengthened shadows of the individuals that control them, but are to contribute toward a sense of Jewish unity and peoplehood, they will have to abide by some over-all set of laws and values which would make for mutual coordination and division of labor, and for internal efficiency and justice. These laws and rules should set forth the duties, the authority, the qualifications for office and the conditions of tenure of all Jewish public servants, and establish codes of right relations between different Jewish corporate agencies, and between them and individuals affected by their operation. But most important of all, the machinery of fund raising for various causes should have its basis in, and be subject to the control of, communal law.

A third area is ritual practice. That is at present where most Jews look for guidance. Ritual practices are the concern of every one who wants to be a Jew, in the fullest sense of the term. However much or little either the observance, or the neglect, of these practices may affect our human relationships, they cannot be ignored. They can serve as a source of immediate good in the life of the individual. In their present state, they are either a nuisance, or an occasion for a sense of guilt. To disregard them in any serious effort at reconstructing Jewish life, on the ground that there are more important problems to cope with, is like disregarding the food and sanitary problems of an army, because the main purpose of an army is not to eat and keep healthy, but to fight and win battles. In the chapter "Toward a Guide for Jewish Ritual Usage," * the area of ritual practice will be discussed more specifically.

How can Jewish society be reconstituted to enable Jewish law to function in these areas? We cannot rely on divine sanctions to enforce the law. That God rewards every act of obedience to Jewish law, and punishes every act of disobedience, is a belief that has long become desiccated, even among those who profess it. There are too many who disregard ritual practice with impunity in this world, and have doubts about any posthumous reward or punishment, particularly for ritual transgressions. We cannot invoke the police power of the state to enforce Jewish law, for that is in violation of the principle of religious freedom, as understood in a democracy. The only sanctions we can apply are those which are applied by all voluntary organizations in democratic countries.

The Jewish community as a whole might constitute itself as an

* Page 413 ff.

organized body, for the purpose of satisfying the Jewish needs common to all its members. Being organized on a voluntarist, democratic and quasi-contractual basis, the member of that community will be under implied contract to conform to its rules, and to receive the benefits accorded to all members. The part of the law which needs to be elaborated first is what may be called constitutional law. In traditional Jewish law, this was lacking, because Jewry was not a voluntarist society. The Jew had no other community in which he could live. Furthermore, the "divine right" of the interpreters of the law to demand obedience to what they considered the word of God made democratic sanctions of constitutional government superfluous. But, in our day, the first task must be to define the obligations and privileges of membership in a Jewish community, and to set up the legal basis for the workings of its administrative machinery.

Although it is not intended here to present a blue-print of the constitution of the Jewish community (a project for a constitutional convention), certain suggestions may be made, by way of illustration, of the kind of content that would have to be included in such constitutional law. One of the measures it would have to deal with would be requirements for admission to membership. These might include some sort of token payment of dues, by way of registration, agreement to marry within the faith, or to proselytize the non-Jewish partner to a marriage, agreement to provide for such Jewish instruction as the community may deem necessary, willingness to pay such communal taxes for Jewish purposes as the community may require. In turn, the member may then claim such privileges as permission to worship in any of the community's synagogues, religious education for his children, religious services in celebration of Berith Milah,[11] Bar Mitzvah,[12] marriage, burial in a Jewish cemetery and with Jewish religious rites. All these services would have to be denied to non-members.

Constitutional law would make provision also for instituting a sort of Jewish civil and religious service. It would lay down the qualifications for such public servants as rabbis, cantors, teachers, social-workers, shohetim,[13] mohalim,[14] et cetera. It would also define the scope of their authority, their duties to the community and their rights in respect to emoluments, tenure of office and promotions. It would define the method by which these detailed regulations could be arrived at and promulgated. Constitutional law would also have to define the necessary institutions through which the services of the community would be extended to the individual. It would have to provide for the orderly functioning of those institutions, so as to avoid jurisdictional disputes and needless duplication. It would have to authorize courts for adjusting violations of its rules and arbitrating conflicts for which no law exists. It would, of course, have to define the legitimate methods of taxation for communal purposes. These taxes would be voluntary, in the sense that they could be evaded by one's resigning from the Jewish community, but would be enforceable by the same method that any organization employs in relation to its own members.

An analogy to the way that such Jewish constitutional law could function is provided by the functioning of the Canon Law of the Anglican Church in England. Although it is the "established Church" of England, its laws are not enforced by the police power of the state. There is as much religious freedom in England as in the United States. Nobody has to belong to the Church. It is assumed, however, that the Church has the right to define, in accordance with its own constitution, the obligations of its members in general, and the special obligations of its functionaries. When one becomes a member of the Church, one assumes the obligation of abiding by its rules. The state, therefore, confirms at one and the same time the Church's right to impose Canon Law on its members, and the right of the member to resign from the Church at will, without being subject to penalty other than deprivation of the privilege of such membership.

The only difference between the functioning of the projected Jewish constitutional community and that of the Anglican Church would be that, in the latter, the secular courts are authorized to inquire into the conformity or non-conformity of the individual with the canons of his Church, whereas, in our case, it would be courts established under the Jewish community's constitution that would conduct the inquiry. These same courts would have jurisdiction only in matters which come within the scope of the over-all constitution of the community. In matters which pertain to any one constituent group affiliated with the community, only that group would be in a position to exercise authority or sanctions. This means that in a democratic environment such as ours, Jewish community life would have to be based on the principle of federation, leaving a large measure of autonomy to each congregation, Jewish center or social service agency.

Only after the Jewish community has established a framework of constitutional law, would it be in a position to define substantive Jewish law in the three main areas open to Jewish life in the Diaspora. In these areas, it would have to reckon with the principles of historic continuity and universal applicability. But it will have to reckon with them, from the standpoint of the modern democratic conception of law. Law can no longer be conceived as unilaterally imposed by a transcendent Deity. We cannot, in our day, hold Mount Sinai over the heads of the Jewish people and say: "Accept this Torah, or else. . . ." [15] We must assume that law is the instrument by which human beings, who feel the need of sharing life, define their common purposes, the mutual relations necessary for their achievement and the sanctions to be employed in enforcing the common will.

Since God is the Power that makes for salvation, and since democratic polity is expected to function as an instrument of a people's quest for salvation, *the law in a democratic polity derives its ultimate validity from the extent to which it conforms with the divine will, by actually contributing to the salvation of the individual and of human society generally.* Government which is based not merely upon the consent, but upon the active participation, of the governed is in a position to verify the deepest insight of religion that every human being is created in the image of God. Consequently any law, which reflects the interests of those who are governed, and who, by obeying it, expect salvation, may be regarded as having divine sanction. When a law is not just or good, it frustrates men's quest for salvation, and therefore, may be viewed as running counter to the will of God.

Any conception of legal authority that denies to the individual, unless he happens to be a rabbi learned in the law, a voice in the determination of the law by which he is to be governed, is undemocratic, unjust and intolerable. Modern man who has tasted of life in a democratic society will not submit to a law to which he is expected to be subject, but in the formulation of which he is denied any share. That share need not take the form of direct referendum or plebiscite. Representative government has proved to be far more democratic than government by plebiscite. The right to choose who shall represent him gives every individual the most effective means of expressing his will in the determination of the law.

Democratic law cannot be developed by interpretation alone; it requires legislation also. Wherever possible, resort should be had to interpretation of existing law rather than to legislation of new law. But when a law has become so obsolete that no reasonable interpretation of it can

either remedy some evil or advance some good, it should be superseded
by new law in accordance with the vital needs of the people.

4

IS DEMOCRACY FEASIBLE IN THE AREA OF RITUAL OBSERVANCE?

The attempt to apply the principle of democracy to the area of ritual
practice is without precedent, and beset by many difficulties. We must
expect much fumbling, before we succeed in beating out a path. On the
one hand, as modern-minded men, we cannot conceive of ritual practice as having a theurgic or magical efficacy. At best it can only be a
form of religious self-expression. It is unthinkable to resort to sanctions
to compel conformity with ritual practices that do not honestly express
one's own personal convictions. On the other hand, to treat ritual as if
it were a private affair is to fail to appreciate its very significance. A
salute to the flag would be meaningless, if every one designed his own
flag. Ritual arises from and is directed toward awareness of social unity
and communion. Is there a middle course between, on the one hand,
unjust and futile effort to impose ritual uniformity and, on the other,
complete anarchy, ranging from an excess to the complete abolition of
ritual?

The fact that ritual answers an intrinsic need of human nature leads
us to believe that it ought to be possible to come upon such a course.
Even Jews who are far removed from the traditional way of life are not
averse, on principle, to ritual. They would welcome ritual that is endowed with beauty and significance. However, to try to impose on all
Jews a regimen of uniform religious observance is out of the question. It
should, nevertheless, be possible for like-minded groups to define their
own minimum standards of ritual observance, which they would agree to
accept, and conformity to which would thus be self-imposed.

The *modus vivendi* here envisaged certainly would not result in that
uniformity of Jewish ritual observance which prevailed in the past. But
it would do away with the present amorphous and anarchic character of
Jewish life. It would make Jews realize that to belong to a Jewish religious organization of any kind imposed more important obligations
than merely paying one's dues. It would tend to foster religious self-
expression without which religion is starved from inanition.

In the area of ritual observance, psychological as well as legal or rational considerations play an important role. Many people, who have intellectually broken with traditional beliefs or practices, remain under their emotional spell. Although they may long ago have given up all notions of the theurgic efficacy of ritualistic acts, they continue to harbor some vague fear of transgressing a ritual injunction. Even though the utility of some ritual observance may never have been apparent, its arbitrary character may nevertheless have been regarded as essential, so that any attempt to tamper with it is looked upon as destructive of its efficacy.

To the ancients, it did not seem at all unreasonable that the slightest deviation from the dietary laws, or from the laws of the Sabbath should be fraught with unforeseen dangers in this world or the next. That was, in effect, the argument of R. Judah Hallevi [16] for the meticulous observance of the *mitzvot*; he compared such observance to the need of following punctiliously a chemical formula as a prerequisite to obtaining some wished-for chemical compound. Those who have acquired this attitude concerning ritual observances cannot shake it off easily. They are inhibited by their irrational sentimentality from contributing to a satisfactory solution of the problem which the ritual practices raise in our life as Jews.

The inertia which is largely responsible for the refusal to recognize any other source of validation for ritual practice than the traditional law places us before the following dilemma: On the one hand, the Jews that we have to count on to evolve the kind of ritual practice needed in our day are necessarily those in whose lives ritual observances play a profoundly religious role. Yet, such is their intransigence that no amount of persuasion will get them to cooperate in behalf of a reasonable and vital approach to this problem. On the other hand, the generation that has never experienced the religious serenity of sincere ritual observance balks at the very idea of bothering with it.

Finally, the fear often expressed by those who oppose all tampering with ritual observances is that, if we permit ourselves to depart in the slightest from the traditionally prescribed routine, we are certain to get farther and farther away from it, until our lives are left entirely void of all religious self-expression, so that Jewish religious life is bound to disintegrate. It cannot be denied that, in our present state of anarchy, and with no sanctions or restraints of any kind to hold us back, leaving the matter of ritual observance to the uncontrolled and unguided will of the individual Jew is certain to undermine the little of Jewish life that still remains. Since religious ritual is essentially a social manifestation, anyone who disregards it embarrasses his neighbor who would like to take it seriously.

Notwithstanding all of these psychological factors which militate against revision of the traditional attitude toward law in the area of ritual practice, we must go through with that revision along the lines here suggested, and to be further developed in the chapter on "Toward a Guide for Jewish Ritual Usage." Social sanctions will have to take the place of the supernatural sanctions assumed by tradition. These sanctions will have to function within the ambit of each religious society or congregation, which shall be expected to set up specific standards of ritual practice for its members.

As previously stated, these standards would vary with the ideological differences among Jews. Sincerely Orthodox Jews would, of course, expect members of their group to conform to all the observances prescribed in the traditional codes. They would have no problems of revaluating Jewish observance, for the traditional ritual laws are in harmony with the ideological premises of their thinking. But that is not true of the other religious groups. Having rejected the notion of laws unilaterally imposed by a transcendent personal Deity, which have to be implicitly obeyed, the other groups must accept the logical consequence of their position, and assume responsibility for developing a regimen of ritual practice that meets their spiritual needs. This means that they must formulate for themselves the criteria by which they will discriminate between observances that should be maintained, or, perhaps, that should be created, and observances that ought to become obsolete. What these criteria are to be for those who accept the main principles underlying the religious approach promulgated in these pages is stated in Chapter XXI.

Thus we are led to conclude that Jewish law cannot function except in a society whose collective will it expresses. That collective will must make itself felt not only through prescriptions, but also through sanctions. The renunciation of Jewish legal autonomy has destroyed the organic character of Jewish society and has rendered Jewish law inoperative. To reinstate Jewish law, it is necessary to reestablish Jewish society. The problem takes on one form in Eretz Yisrael, another in Diaspora. In Eretz Yisrael the great need is for a code of civil law to govern all human relationships. In the Diaspora, Jewry must organize voluntary constitutional communities that would regulate Jewish interests, and formulate such laws as would be binding on all Jews. Though ritual regulations cannot be included as part of Jewish constitutional law, they need not be left to individual caprice. Ritual regulations would be observed by members of voluntary associations that would undertake to abide by them.

By such democratic processes Jewish law could again be made to function in Jewish life.

CHAPTER TWENTY

THE STATUS OF THE WOMAN
IN JEWISH LAW

Few aspects of Jewish thought and life illustrate so strikingly the need of reconstructing Jewish law as the traditional status of the Jewish woman. In Jewish tradition, her status is unquestionably that of inferiority to the man. If the Jewish woman is to contribute her share to the regeneration of Jewish life, and if in turn Jewish life is to bring out the powers for good that are in her, this status must be changed. She must attain in Jewish law and practice a position of religious, civic and juridical equality with the man, and this attainment must come about through her own efforts and initiative. Whatever liberal-minded men may do in her behalf is bound to remain but a futile and meaningless gesture. The Jewish woman must demand the equality due her as a right to which she is fully entitled. That right is conceded to her in other civilizations where she is treated as a full-fledged person. There is no reason why the Jewish civilization should persist in treating her in this day and age as though she were an inferior type of human being.[1]

1

THE STATUS OF THE WOMAN IN ANCIENT TIMES

As a prerequisite to her self-emancipation, the *Jewish woman should be on her guard against being misled into believing that all she need do to improve her position is to carry out the spirit of Jewish traditional teaching.* The first step in her struggle for equality is to open her eyes to the truth concerning her position in Jewish life and teaching of the past. She must be made aware that her status, as defined in Jewish tradition, is not only incompatible with enlightened opinion, but also prejudicial to her material and spiritual interests. Too much of what has been said and written about the Jewish woman is apt to act as an opiate, instead of arousing her to an awareness of the disabilities which are imposed upon her by traditional law. Numerous discourses have been delivered and essays written on the glorious role of the Jewish woman in the past, the implication being that, if there is anything wrong with her present condition, it is entirely due to her unwillingness to play an identical role in our day.

It has become a stereotype procedure with Jewish lecturers and writers to cite a number of instances of women whose names figure in our history. We are continually reminded that the Matriarchs were held in almost as high esteem as the Patriarchs, and that Abraham was commanded by God to "attend" to Sarah's voice.[2] The fact is stressed that two books in the Bible are named after women, the one Ruth, progenitor of the great King David, and the other Esther, who saved a large section of Jewry from extermination. Likewise in post-Biblical literature women like Judith, Susanna, and Hannah, the mother of the seven martyred sons, and Queen Salome are shown to have enhanced Jewish life.

Much ado, also, is made of the appreciation accorded to outstanding Jewish women during Talmudic times. Women like Rachel, the wife of R. Akiba, Beruriah, the wife of R. Meir and Imma Shalom, the wife of R. Eliezer, are upheld as great models of virtue, honor, wisdom and self-sacrifice. The Middle Ages likewise are replete with names of Jewish great women who were Talmudic scholars, who delivered addresses in public and who rendered great social service in rescuing the victims of persecution from dire distress. It is further pointed out that not only these women of note contributed to the conservation of Jewish life, but that myriads of nameless Jewish women have displayed unparalleled loyalty and devotion to their people and faith. The fact that Jewish women contributed so materially to the survival of their people, it is argued, necessarily presupposes due appreciation and regard on the part of the men of Israel.

As further evidence of the high place accorded to the Jewish woman in the life of ancient Israel, numerous maxims are quoted, which recommend due deference to her worth and character. In the Torah, the son is commanded to honor and revere his mother.[3] The author of Proverbs urges the son not only to listen to his father's instructions, but also to obey his mother's directions.[4] The Talmud abounds in teachings that advise the husband to love and honor his wife even more than himself.[5] The Rabbis undoubtedly paid woman a high compliment, when they interpreted the statement: "Thus shalt they speak into the house of Jacob, and declare unto the children of Israel" as implying that Moses was to give priority to the women of Israel when telling his people about the meaning of the revelation at Sinai.[6]

All of the foregoing facts and maxims, however, tell only half the story. It is well known that among ancient peoples, both primitive and civilized, the woman was regarded as possessing mystic power which, in some instances, was believed to be witchcraft, in others, the gift of prophecy. That had nothing to do with the actual position which the woman occupied in every-day life. The Christians, who deified Mary, did not allow women to come near the altar.[7] It is, therefore, incorrect to infer from the renown enjoyed by the few exceptional women of Israel that woman was accepted as the equal of man, or that she even enjoyed what we now consider the inalienable rights of a human being. The ancient world was man's world, and the Jews were no different from the rest of mankind in that respect.

The other side of the story of woman's position in the past is reflected in the maxims in disparagement of her that counterbalance those in her favor. In the Biblical account of man's origin, it is man alone who is described as coming from the hand of God, whereas woman had to be formed from man's rib, as an after thought, so to speak, when man failed to find a companion for himself among the other living beings that were made to pass in review before him. Abimelech, the King of Shekem, in his dying moments, could not bear the thought of meeting his death at the hands of a woman; so he ordered his armor bearer to kill him outright.[8] Not much respect is shown to the woman in the *Mishnah* in *Abot*, where the man is warned against engaging in too much conversation with a woman, even with his own wife.[9] Few statements can be so repugnant as the one which associates indecency with the woman's singing.[10] R. Eliezer, the man who had Imma Shalom for a wife, should have known better than to say that the only skill a woman has is to work the distaff.[11] And R. Meir, who had Beruriah for a wife, should have been the last to give us that benediction in the liturgy in which the Jew thanks God that he was not born a woman.[12]

The truth is that the Jewish woman was treated far better than her status would indicate. In this respect, too, the Jews were no different from any other people. Westermarck points out that even among primitive peoples, where the woman is in bondage to her male relations, either to a father, husband, or brother, she is seldom made to experience the logical consequences of her position.[13] The husband, for example, cannot punish or divorce his wife without the consent of the tribe. Husbands, as a rule, are fond of their wives, and wives are loyal and affectionate to their husbands. Among the Guinea Indians, woman is legally held to be the property of man in as literal a sense as is his dog; he may even sell her, if he chooses. Yet, even among them, the woman manages to exercise considerable influence. In general it is true that among savages the married woman, though subject to her husband's authority, often occupies a respected position in the family and the community. All this, however, does not mitigate the evil of inferior status which the woman occupied in ancient society. A happy lot often goes together with a status of subjection. Thousands of slaves in the South of the United States deplored their emancipation. They undoubtedly enjoyed greater security and were accorded much kindlier treatment than have fallen to the lot of the Negro since the Civil War has made him a free man. But, from the standpoint of human values, that can hardly serve as a reason for regarding slavery as ethical.

It is this confusion between lot and status which is responsible for the usual misunderstanding of the well-known chapter in the Book of Proverbs about "the woman of valor." [14] That chapter is mistakenly regarded as placing the woman on a high pedestal. It does nothing of the kind. It is flattery paid by a parasitic husband to the hard-working wife who slaves for him. She works from early dawn to late at night, buys and cultivates her fields, attends to all the needs of her family, dispenses alms and renders service, and all for what? That her husband might have no lack of gain, and spend his time with his cronies in the city gate, where they squat all day in idleness and smoke their narghiles.

2

THE STATUS OF THE WOMAN IN TRADITIONAL JEWISH LAW

Whatever the woman's lot may have been in past Jewish life, *traditional Jewish law undoubtedly treated her as a lower type of human being than man.* In Jewish law, the woman is on the same plane with minors, slaves, and people of unsound mind.[15] Like them she is exempted from all observances which are intended for fixed times,[16] with very few exceptions. She is exempt from such *mitzvot* as *shema*,[17] *tefillin*,[18] *zitzit*,[19] *shofar*,[20] and *sukkah*.[21]. She is not counted in a quorum necessary for public prayer, nor is she considered worthy of being included in the *mezumman* [22] for the recital of the benedictions after a meal. If, as an expression of pious devotion, she should write a Torah scroll, it would be unfit for use in public worship.[23] Together with minors and slaves, women are exempt from the study of the Torah.[24] The father is under no obligation to teach his daughter Torah,[25] nor is the mother expected to teach her son.[26] She is permitted, not commanded, to study Torah, and that permission is extended only to the written, not to the oral Torah.[27] It is a generally accepted principle in Rabbinic literature that the reward for performing a duty, which is optional, is far below that for the performance of a duty which is obligatory.[28] Hence, the woman who does take advantage of the permission to study the written Torah must not expect any too great reward. The father who teaches his daughter Torah is regarded as though he taught her frivolity.[29] Although this last statement was the opinion of R. Eliezer and not that of Ben Azzai, the fact is that it reflects the prevailing attitude of our forebears.

It is not only in matters religious, however, that the woman is made to feel her inequality, but principally in matters juridical. The woman is not qualified to act as witness,[30] to say nothing of her acting as judge.[31] Exception is made in the case of a woman testifying in behalf of another woman whose right to remarry is in question.[32] Maimonides, in quoting that law in his Code,[33] finds it necessary to tell the reader not to be surprised at this concession. The reason her testimony is accepted is that the truth is bound to come out in the end anyhow. Even a slave's testimony would be accepted under those circumstances. Moreover, the woman holds an inferior status in the law of inheritance.[34] The provision made for the sustenance and marrying of daughters at the expense of their father's estate was not derived from the principle of inheritance, but was dictated by the fear of the social consequences of their being left without some means of support.[35]

But it is in the marriage relationship chiefly, where the woman's inferior status is fraught with tragic consequences to her. In traditional Jewish law, the marriage relationship is practically on the same plane as the relationship between master and slave. The man, in marrying the woman, acquires her or gains possession of her.[36] The technical term in Jewish law is *kinyan*. The term *kiddushin* for the marriage act has nothing of the connotation of sacredness about it, all the fine preachments to the contrary notwithstanding. The fact that the husband must perform the threefold marital duties toward his wife in no way raises her status much above that of a menial.[37] This is evident from the law which prescribes that every woman must perform for her husband the five following services: spin and weave, wash his hands and face, pour the wine, prepare the bed, and wait on him.[38] These services are obligatory no matter how much wealth the woman brings to him at marriage. If she refuses, says Maimonides in his Code,[39] she may be compelled by the use of the rod.

"The Sages have commanded," writes Maimonides, "that the husband should love and honor her more than himself, and should not intimidate her unduly. He should speak gently with her; he should not be irascible or cranky. On the other hand, they have also commanded the woman to honor her husband implicitly. She should always stand in awe of him. She should do his bidding and consider him as though he were a prince or a king. She should comply with all his wishes and remove from his presence whatever annoys him." The homiletic statement that a woman's place is in the home, Maimonides formulates into law.[40] According to him, the husband should prevent his wife from being seen too frequently outdoors. About once or twice a month is all that she should be permitted to leave her house. Maimonides declares that it is the husband's duty to be distrustful of the wife's fidelity, though he advises the husband not to carry such attitude too far.[41]

According to Jewish law, whatever the wife earns or happens to find,[42] as well as the income derived from possessions she brings to him at marriage, belongs to her husband.[43] Even what she earns by working overtime belongs to her husband.[44] If she dies during his lifetime, he alone can inherit her.[45] After his marriage, no promise to waive this right is binding upon him.[46]

The woman experiences the worst effects of her status when she can no longer continue to live with her husband. It is then that his mastery asserts itself. He alone has the power of divorce.[47] According to traditional law, he can divorce her arbitrarily without her consent, or refuse to grant her a divorce, no matter how much she would welcome it. The reform instituted by R. Gershom,[48] which necessitates her consent, has not been universally respected, and can be circumvented easily, since the husband can threaten to desert his wife and thus deprive her of the right to remarry. On the other hand, the wife cannot divorce her husband under any circumstances. It is true that there are a number of specified conditions under which the Jewish court may compel the husband to divorce his wife.[49] In the first place, those conditions are far from including the more personal reasons for incompatibility, and secondly, if the husband leaves the jurisdiction of the Jewish court, the woman is left without redress. Unfortunately our spiritual leaders, instead of taking steps to change the ancient law, try to explain it away. "While, in form, the husband executed the divorce," writes Louis M. Epstein,[50] "in essence Talmudic law recognizes the woman's right to divorce her husband, or to be more exact, to institute divorce action. And if her petition is granted, the court forces the husband to issue the bill of divorce." This statement is typical of the kind of apologetics which have all too long led us to evade the issue, instead of attacking it frontally.

Another instance of the ill effects of the woman's inequality is apparent in the case of the childless widow, whose deceased husband is survived by one or more brothers. The childless widow cannot remarry, unless she obtains a release (*Halitzah*) [51] from her husband's brother. This situation can be, and all too often is, exploited by an unscrupulous brother-in-law to extort money. But even where extortion is not resorted to, unfortunate developments may hinder her remarrying, as when, for example, the deceased husband is survived by a brother who is only an infant. Under these circumstances, the woman has to wait thirteen years, until the infant becomes of age to grant a release, before she is permitted to remarry.[52]

The purpose in calling attention to these laws is not to convey the impression that the status of the Jewish woman was worse than that of the woman in any other ancient civilization. The fact is that in many respects it was much better than that of the woman under Roman or Greek civilization. In pre-Christian Germanic law, the man could with impunity sell, give away, lend, and even kill his wife.[53] In Christianity, St. Paul's teaching, that it is the duty of the woman to be subservient to her husband, has been regarded as authoritative.[54] As late as the thirteenth century, we find that, in Germany, the husband was advised to chasten his wife only with a rod, as comported with the dignity of an honorable man. Toward the end of the sixteenth century, the Church was still discussing the question whether the woman was a human being in the full sense of the term.[55]

There can be no question that the Jews possessed a more wholesome sex morality and a more adequate appreciation of the family institution than other peoples. This fact by itself was sufficient to mitigate the evils resulting from the inferior status of the woman. Nothing, however, can be gained by glib attempts to misrepresent what actually was, in the past, the recognized law. "The testimony of Jewish scholars, whose utterances have been so extensively cited," says an apologist,[56] "lend support to the conclusion that woman was not accorded by Jewish law a position essentially inferior to man." This is not true. The very statement by George Foot Moore quoted in proof of this generalization contradicts it. "It is interesting," says Moore, "to note that the tendency of courts and custom has been to protect the woman. The law could not be abrogated, but ways to minimize its ill effects as society changed were adopted." This is different from the statement that her position was not inferior to that of the man.

The important point to remember is that *modern* civilizations are gradually recognizing the need of granting woman complete equality with man. It cannot be long before the woman will enjoy all the rights that go with full-fledged personality. This fact is enough to constitute a challenge to us Jews. *The question we must be prepared to answer is: What will Judaism do to abolish the woman's judicial, civic, and religious disabilities?*

Already during the first decades of the era of Jewish Emancipation the Jewish woman became aware that she was accorded a more dignified status outside Jewish life. This explains why many talented Jewish women not only began to lose interest in Jewish life, but actually turned against it. Women of the type of Henrietta Herz, Dorothy Mendelssohn, and Rachel Levin felt that it was too circumscribed. If we do not want our talented women to follow their example, we must find in Judaism a place for their powers. This cannot come about, unless all taint of inferiority will be removed from the status of the Jewish woman.

3

THE STRUGGLE IN ERETZ YISRAEL OVER THE STATUS OF WOMAN

The first clash with Orthodoxy on the question of woman's status took place in Eretz Yisrael in 1921, when the mandatory power called upon the Jews to organize themselves into the Jewish Community (*Kenesset Yisrael*). That Community is represented by the National Jewish Assembly (*Asefat ha-Nivharim*), the members of which are elected by the people. The question then arose whether the women should be granted the right to vote. In Eretz Yisrael and in Orthodox circles throughout the Diaspora, the question was thereupon debated with a great deal of heat and rancor. Even the somewhat liberal Mizrachi came out against the woman's right to vote. The learned Orthodox opinion was, on the whole, uncompromisingly opposed; only a few ventured the belief that women might vote. Orthodox spokesmen were unanimous that women might not hold office. The basis for this unanimous decision was the Deuteronomic law with reference to the appointment of a king in Israel.[57] Commenting upon that law, the Sages add that only a king may be appointed, not a queen.[58] Maimonides, disregarding the fact that this Tannaitic comment had not been incorporated into the Mishnah, nevertheless included it in his Code, and extended its application to all official appointments.[59]

In spite of Orthodox opposition, however, the women in Eretz Yisrael banded themselves into an organization known as the "Jewish Women's Equal Rights League," which agitated for the right both to vote and to hold office. The Jewish women in Eretz Yisrael are by now well on the way toward attaining civic equality. Even the Mizrachists who fought bitterly against them no longer object to sitting with them in council.

Of even greater significance is the problem with regard to juridical equality of the Jewish woman in Eretz Yisrael. When the mandatory government reorganized the judicial system of Palestine, it accorded to the rabbinic courts exclusive authority over matters of marriage and divorce, maintenance, and probate of wills. In view of the fact that the practice of polygamy has not ceased among Sephardic Oriental Jews, the law of Palestine finds it necessary to recognize both the Ashkenazic and Sephardic interpretations of the traditional status of the woman. The British civil administration, realizing that it would be impossible for those women who have emancipated themselves from the stringency of Jewish tradition to submit all their difficulties to the rabbinic court, asked the "Jewish Women's Equal Rights League" for suggestions. The League, in reply, advised that secular Jewish courts be established which should have the power to decide on issues of inheritance, guardianship, majority, and maintenance, and that it be optional with Jews as to which court one resort, the rabbinical or secular. *What is this compromise, if not an admission that there is no hope of ever getting the traditionalists to adjust Jewish law to the needs of present day life?*

4

THE NEED TO AMEND THE JEWISH LAW

The problem of the status of the Jewish woman is not confined to Eretz Yisrael. In the Diaspora, it is bound up with the entire question of the future development of Judaism. If Judaism were to develop along classical Reform lines, the problem could be regarded as solved. But it would be solved with the same kind of success as that of the surgical operation which, from the surgeon's standpoint, may be entirely successful even though the patient is dead. The problem of the status of the Jewish woman is solved by the Reformists at the price of the disappearance of the last vestige of autonomous Jewish life.

On the other hand, if Judaism is to continue along Orthodox lines, the difficulties in marriage and divorce due to the traditional status of the Jewish woman will remain forever unresolved. Her status would continue to be one of inferiority to that of the husband, and no way would be found to alter that status. Recently those who belong to the left Orthodox wing, known as the Conservative group, began an attempt to solve the problem of the *Agunah* [60] within the limits of the traditional law. So far they have met with nothing but abuse from the Orthodox rabbinate. They have even been threatened with excommunication, if they should dare to put their proposal into effect.

The only hope of a satisfactory solution rests with those who will learn to accept Judaism as a civilization, which means that Judaism must find expression in law, not necessarily in traditional laws. As a civilization, Judaism must, in the first place, express itself through the medium of civic organization, or authoritative communal life. Secondly, it must exercise juridical authority, in that it ought to be in a position to adjudicate in cases of conflicting interests. *Henceforth, however, social justice, rather than immutable precedent, must govern the civic life of Jewry and underlie whatever juridical institutions Judaism can manage to maintain in the Diaspora.*

The basic issue in Jewish life today is: What shall be done with the law? Shall it be defended, or amended? Those who are Orthodox insist upon upholding the traditional law in all its details, despite the radical changes that have rendered many of those details contrary to our notions of social and spiritual welfare. The early Reformists, who abjured Jewish peoplehood, consistently declared the prerogative of administering law in human relationships as outside the scope of modern Judaism. In the face of these two untenable positions, as illustrated by the pressing problem of the civic and juridical status of the Jewish woman in modern Jewish life, it is impossible to build Jewish society on any other lines than those implied in Judaism as a living social process, in which the right to amend traditional law and to legislate anew is accepted as indispensable to the very life of the Jewish people and as the only guarantee of its future.

Henrietta Szold [61] once had occasion to indicate that what had led her to become a Zionist, long before Herzl, was not anti-Semitism but the hope that Eretz Yisrael would restore the Jewish people to normality. "But for me," she added, "normality was the development of the Jewish laws under the circumstances of modern life." She deplored, however, the fact that "the law has not even been touched in the case of women, and Jewish law in the case of women is very retrograde. Take the question of the *Agunah,* who is neither wife nor widow. Our rabbis have not even touched that phase, despite the fact that we have the possibility of a normal development."

Though the traditional status of the Jewish woman compares favorably with that of the woman in other civilizations in the past, it is today a stumbling block. It stands in the way of her contributing her best to her people. It prevents her people from enhancing her life as much as it could. There is no way of reconciling that status with her welfare and highest interests in our day. It is high time for the Jewish women throughout the world to inaugurate a movement that will aim to remove the religious, civic and juridical disabilities which traditional Jewish law imposes on them and that will win for them the status of equality. This change in the status of the Jewish woman is an immediate and urgent need for Eretz Yisrael Jewry. Without such change, Jewry in the Diaspora is bound to grow culturally sterile and spiritually anemic.

According to Rabbinic legend,[62] the Israelite women in Egypt displayed a piety which helped to bring about the redemption of ancient Israel. By demanding an equal share in the responsibility for the social and spiritual well-being of their people, the Jewish women of our day will manifest the piety which will speed the redemption of modern Israel.

CHAPTER TWENTY-ONE

TOWARD A GUIDE FOR JEWISH
RITUAL USAGE

1

THE NEED FOR A POINT OF VIEW ON JEWISH USAGE

Even without exact statistical studies,[1] it is fairly obvious that the practice of religious ceremonials and rituals is rapidly declining among American Jews. Those who wish to ignore the obvious can still point with satisfaction to crowded metropolitan synagogues, to food corporations catering to the demand for *kosher* products, and to young people's organizations dedicated to the observance of the Sabbath. An optimistic appraisal of the status of Jewish observance, however, indicates a refusal to face the simple fact that the overwhelming majority of American Jews have already cast aside such Jewish institutions as daily prayer, *kashrut*, and the Sabbath, which have undeniably played an important part in traditional Jewish religion. The main streets of every Jewish community in America bear testimony to the blatant abandonment of Jewish ritual usage. This rejection is, moreover, characteristic not only of the Jew who has grown to maturity without religious home-training, or under the influence of a Reform temple; it is equally true of that vastly greater number of Jews who are the products of Orthodox homes.

The complete elimination of all Jewish religious rituals would render Jewish survival difficult, if not impossible. In the light of what we know of the past, there is no reason to regard their complete elimination as inevitable. Jewish history records a number of instances in which the masses were won back to Jewish practices after they had neglected them. It is not beyond the realm of possibility that a concerted effort on the part of religious leaders could, in this cataclysmic era in Jewish life, stem the tide of desecration which is sweeping away the sanctities gathered from the long and bitter experiences of the Jewish people.

To deal with the economic, social and ideological factors which account for the breakdown of the traditional way of life, something more is needed than repeated homiletical harangues urging Jews to remain loyal to their heritage. There is little that official rabbinical and synagogical groups can do to remove the almost insurmountable economic and social obstacles which American life places in the path of

413

those who want to continue a maximum observance of the traditional rites. Jewish laymen might, however, have expected from their religious leaders an *ideological* orientation which would enable them to meet the challenge of the American environment. But instead of formulating such a guide, most of our leaders have persisted in demanding devotion to a past which is rapidly becoming more and more nebulous for an increasing number of Jews.

Why should one observe this or that ceremony, and what is its religious or social significance? It is precisely these questions that demand an answer. Any program designed to revive the observance of Jewish rites will have to provide a rationale for such ritual usage. Moreover, such a program will have to indicate along what lines traditional practices may be changed and new practices instituted, without endangering the entire structure of Jewish religious life. Unless a rationale for ritual and a guide for its modification is formulated in the near future, we will lose so much of the momentum of the past as to nullify the possibility of a revival in Jewish religious practice. The possibility of affirmative adjustment recedes with every passing day.

The Attitudes of Reform, Neo-Orthodoxy and Conservatism

We cannot look to Reform for guidance in these problems. The philosophy of Reform, at least in its classic formulation, deliberately rejected many valuable religious usages. The declaration of principles adopted at the memorable Pittsburgh Conference of 1885 retained, in addition to the moral elements of the "Mosaic legislation," only such ceremonies as were both edifying and compatible with modern conditions.[2] Inasmuch as Reform held modern conditions to demand the denationalization of Jewish life, compatibility with those conditions involved the elimination of all ritual usages that had nationalistic or separatistic implications. Reform specifically discarded *kashrut*, took great liberties with the liturgy, relaxed the observance of the Sabbath and holidays, and only mildly discountenanced intermarriage. The entire problem of change cannot be significant for those who consciously set out to alter radically the pattern of Jewish life. In Reform Judaism, as it has functioned until recently, and still functions in most Reform congregations, the Torah is, in effect, reduced to the abstraction of a moral law, and ceases to serve as an all-embracing guide for everyday living. Classical Reform retained, to be sure, some of the traditional ceremonials, but it retained them only as means of symbolizing moral principles in concrete form, or of arousing sentiments of unity among Jews as co-religionists.

More recently many Reform rabbis have accepted Jewish people-hood [3] and have consequently been led to introduce much more of traditional Jewish ritual. Nevertheless, they have not yet, any more than the other religious groups, articulated a satisfying rationale for perpetuating and developing Jewish ritual usage. Unlike the old-line Reformists, the Zionist element within Reform is confronted with the need of formulating principles that should guide Jewish ritual usage.

From the standpoint of Orthodoxy, there is a ready answer to the question: Why retain Jewish ceremonial? Jewish observances must be maintained, because God ordained them. The decline of ritual ob-servance fails to perturb Orthodox thinkers. They argue that, in every generation, some Jews rejected God's law. If the sinners do not turn penitent, and if they eventually sever the last link binding them to Israel and Israel's God, there will still be *she-ar yashuv*, a saving rem-nant.[4] Who says that Israel must be numbered in the millions? God can accomplish His ends, and fulfill the destiny of the Jewish people through a loyal remnant.

From that standpoint, any fundamental change in Jewish usage is precluded, because such usage is part of the immutable divine law given to Israel at Mount Sinai. Every prohibition and every positive injunction is a *mitzvah*, God's direct command to the individual Jew. There is no essential difference, from the Orthodox point of view, be-tween a Biblical commandment, a Talmudic regulation and the last responsum of an authorized contemporary *halakist*.[5] All are Torah and, therefore, not susceptible to abrogation or amendment. In theory, to be sure, new rabbinic decrees, interpretations or suspensions of existing laws are possible, if sanctioned by proper authority. In practice, no Orthodox rabbi or rabbinic group, since the dawn of the modern era, has been willing to assume such authority, nor can we be sanguine about the prospect of a more lenient standard of observance emanating from Orthodox circles.

This rationale for religious usage and this attitude toward change fail to satisfy any one unable to accept the doctrine that the minutiae of the Torah—taking Torah to include the latest formulation of Jewish practice—are of supernatural origin and of eternal transcendent signifi-cance. The non-observance of many who give lip-service to the Ortho-dox creed indicates that their faith no longer actually functions in their lives, since few men would have the boldness consistently to violate what they really believe with perfect faith to be the direct command of God. Orthodoxy's insistence upon the supernatural origin and the immutability of Jewish law is, therefore, objectionable, because of its ideological inacceptability, and because of its practical ineffectiveness. Not only is it unable to stem the tide of disintegration; by its rigidity, it actually contributes to the further dissolution of Judaism.

Conservative Jews, who rebel instinctively against the laxity of Reform Jewish practice and find themselves unable to accept the intransigence of Orthodoxy, have developed another theory to explain their own refusal to relax the rigidity of Jewish ritual observance. In the interest of preserving historical Judaism, it is claimed, we must uphold the entire body of traditional practices. Once we remove the barriers, there is no end to the process of disintegration. No matter what lamentable hardship the law may work upon an individual Jew, he may properly be asked, in the name of loyalty, to sacrifice his own well-being to the welfare of the group.

Like the Orthodox, Conservatives frequently insist that change can be introduced only through authoritative interpretation of the existing codes. There can be no innovation and no abrogation, since it is obviously undesirable that each Jew be a law unto himself, with no guide other than his own whims. The tendency of the great majority of Jews to take the law into their own hands does not alarm such Conservatives any more than it perturbs the Orthodox whose position they rationalize. The Conservative is likely to interpret the law strictly, in order to counterbalance the popular tendency to take liberties with ritual regulations. Conservatism has absolute faith in a Jewish future, and will presumably be prepared to accept the practice of the majority of Jews, once that practice has crystallized and become authoritative, but it will take only a minor part in guiding and channeling the change. Its sole contribution to the molding of a Jewish future is to cling fast to the codes and standards of the past.

2

TOWARD A RECONSTRUCTION OF JEWISH
RITUAL USAGE

It is well to be reminded that, as far as Diaspora Jewry is concerned, neither its survival nor its absorption is a foregone conclusion. The Jewish people will exist only as long as individual men and women desire to live as Jews. Without falling into a fallacy of numbers, we may insist that the greater the proportion of Jews who can be brought to observe Jewish rites, the greater the chances that the Jewish people will survive. Too much reliance has been placed on the questionable proposition that Jews cannot escape their fate, that they must perforce remain Jews because of external pressure. That proposition has afforded a pretext for evading the problem of how the Jewish will to live should express itself in the lives of Jews in the Diaspora.

Both Orthodoxy and Conservatism, insofar as they are logically consistent, make Judaism the exclusive possession of that constantly diminishing minority who are prepared to sacrifice their personal interests for the preservation of Jewish life. The vast multitudes, as they lose the momentum of a Jewish past vividly recollected, cannot be persuaded, in the name of Jewish survival alone, to live under "the yoke of a law," [6] which has become burdensome. An organism fights to live only as long as life yields satisfactions. Our ancestors lived joyously under the law of the Torah, because that life offered them social standing in this world and salvation in the world to come. In our day, too, we can expect Jewish religious practices to be maintained only in the degree that Jews feel their personal lives thereby enriched.

In spite of elements of strength, each of the contemporary formulations of Jewish religion suffers the weakness of its onesidedness. The Conservative emphasis on the importance of Jewish usage as an expression of the collective will of the Jewish people to survive is correct. *But it is wrong to make the existence and continuation of the group the sole end of Jewish observance.* In doing so, Conservatism impairs the religious significance of Jewish group life, and evades the problem of making the law function as an instrument of salvation. Orthodoxy is correct when it asserts that piety involves more than intellectual assent to a body of dogma, that it involves a constant awareness of God's presence in the world of nature and man, an awareness which expresses itself in a religious way of life. But Orthodoxy fails to reckon with the need for an adequate theology that can meet the challenge of modern thought, and with the political, social and economic realities that condition Jewish group survival. Reform leaders were right in their emphasis on the supreme importance of ethical ideals and of reenforcing them by faith in God, articulated in religious symbols and acts of worship, but they erred in renouncing Jewish nationhood, neglecting the group aspect of Jewish living, and failing to recognize the importance of ritual norms and standards to identify the individual Jew with his people by a specific and distinctive way of life.

The only tenable position is that, in the matter of ritual observance as in so many other phases of life, it is necessary to strike a balance between the interests of the group and the interests of the individual. This is implied in the fundamental principle that Judaism is a religious civilization. For a religious civilization is one which not only identifies the individual with his group, but makes the group responsible for the salvation of the individual, for helping him to experience life as supremely worthwhile or holy, and thus to commune with God. *A satisfactory rationale for Jewish usage is one that would recognize in it both a method of group survival and a means to the personal self-fulfillment, or salvation of the individual Jew.* Through it, the individual Jew will know the exhilaration of fully identifying himself with his people and, thereby, saving his own life from dullness, drabness and triviality. Jewish tradition brings to the daily living of the Jew, to his holiday celebration, to the celebration of turning points in his life, a wealth of beautiful and meaningful symbols embodying the *sancta* of his people, expressive of its ideals and native to its culture. These should be retained and developed; for, no creed, no value, no self-identification of the individual with his people is effective, unless it is translated into action of a systematic and habitual nature.

If we accept this rationale of Jewish usage and recognize its dual function of contributing both to Jewish group survival and to the personal self-fulfillment of the individual, we must accept as a corollary the sanctioning by the group of variations in ritual usage. The circumstances of life are so different for different Jews, their economic needs and opportunities, their cultural background, their acquired skills and inherited capacities are so varied that it is unreasonable to expect all of them to find self-fulfillment in the traditional rituals. That was possible only where the Jewish community lived a self-contained life and could make possible for all its members, without undue sacrifice on their part, the observance of all usages which were the norm in Jewish life. It is not possible when, as in democratic countries, the Jew has to live in two civilizations, and find his place in the economic and cultural life of the civic community as well as of the Jewish.

From this point of view, no stigma attaches to those who permit themselves a wide latitude in their departure from traditional norms. It is not appropriate, in dealing with matters of ritual, sanctimoniously to invoke God's pardon for transgressions which are unavoidable, or to refrain from teaching the law, on the basis of the principle that it is better for Jews to err unwittingly than to sin presumptuously. Adherence to tradition is henceforth to be evaluated not solely in terms of group needs, but also in terms of individual satisfactions. It certainly cannot be considered in terms of a supernaturally revealed code. *The vocabulary of "law," "sin," "pardon," is ideologically and pragmatically unjustified as applied to ritual.* Parental and synagogical insistence on observance of the totality of Jewish ritual has resulted in the complete breakdown of traditional usage. We have asked too much and have received nothing.

For those of us who have been trained to think of ceremonial observance as divine commandments, or as part of a self-sufficient mystic "law" which is the essence of historic Judaism, the elasticity of this new approach will, at first, seem unsatisfactory. There is, however, literally no alternative. Modern thought acknowledges the propriety of the concept of "law" only in nature and in human relationships; in the sphere of ritual, of the relationship between man and God, there can be no law. A modern state is separated from any established church, and refuses to legislate on matters of religious practice. In a Jewish commonwealth, religious usages could be embodied into the law of the land, only insofar as they had social repercussions, as, for instance, in matters of Sabbath observance, where it would be necessary to insure the opportunity for such observance to all who desire it, and in marital law, where the social efficacy of the home has to be protected.

But to deny that ritual usage can appropriately be treated as law does not mean that it can be left solely to the whim of the individual. The benefit which the individual hopes to derive from ritual usages is dependent on their power to effect his self-identification with the Jewish group. Consequently, it is important for those who feel the need of such self-identification through ritual to evaluate the heritage of traditional Jewish usages, and to adopt those that are capable of functioning beneficently in their lives. Moreover, since the obsolescence of much traditional usage is inevitable, they would do well to consider the possibility of also introducing new usages that can similarly contribute to self-identification with the Jewish people and to personal self-fulfillment as Jews.

These are the considerations which make desirable the effort to define what, under various circumstances of life, shall be the norm of Jewish practice for those Jews who cannot accept the traditional attitude toward the Jewish codes, who may even find that some observances are obstacles rather than helps to self-fulfillment, but who wish to remain Jews and to make the most of their Judaism. For Jews who are satisfied with the traditional codes and can find complete self-realization in their observance, such a guide would have no message. Nor would it have a message for those Jews who see no good to be gained by identifying themselves with the Jewish people and its religious tradition. All other thinking Jews, however, should either encourage, or engage in, the effort to arrive at a Jewish way of living which will insure both the survival of the Jewish group and the enrichment of their own lives as Jews.

The time when any one authoritative voice might be sufficient sanction for any law, or code of laws, pertaining to ritual practice is long passed. To wait for an authoritative body that would be recognized by the whole or even a considerable part of Jewry, and that would undertake to draw up a guide of ritual practice, is to postpone the solution *sine die*. The only way to extricate Jewish life from its impasse in the matter of ritual observance is for a group of rabbis to whom people look for religious guidance, together with scholars expert not only in the knowledge of ancient texts but also in the understanding of contemporary human needs, to collaborate in the issues here discussed and to draw up the long awaited guide. In time such a guide would become authoritative. All that this discussion attempts to do is to set forth arguments to stimulate both the learned and the laity to action.

3

PRINCIPLES OF EVALUATION

A wide diversity in the practice of religious rites exists among Jews who continue to find a place in their lives for the traditional ceremonials. *Nothing is basically wrong with the existence of variety in ritual usage.* It is even possible that, from the conflict of differing evaluations and practices, new creative forms may emerge which will express the ideals and keep alive the *sancta* of Israel. In course of time, some particular set of ceremonies may gain wide acceptance and displace all others. Or several standards of observance, comparable to the traditional liturgical *minhagim* (local variations of usage), may prevail simultaneously. At present, however, observance of Jewish usage is so much a matter of individual whim, and so arbitrarily determined by accidental circumstances, as to render Jewish religious observance utterly chaotic. In such a chaos, the few vestigial remains of Jewish observance, torn out of their context in a consistent pattern of Jewish living, tend to lose all meaning and value and become mere conventional routines or superstitious practices. This wide and confusing diversity of practice prevails not only as between the various groups in American Israel—Orthodox, Conservative, Reform—but also within the groups. It is difficult to find two Jews, even among those who profess to regard the *Shulhan Aruk* as authoritative, whose evaluations of the multitudinous ritual and ceremonial practices coincide.

Much of this confusion may be attributed to pure ignorance. In the present state of Jewish illiteracy, Jews have to be taught what values Jewish rites can yield them and to discriminate between those of greater and those of lesser significance. That is why there is need for a guide which will not only state what it is desirable that Jews should observe, but specifically why each observance is desirable. It will, moreover, have to state these values in such terms that each individual will be able intelligently to adapt his Jewish behavior to the particular conditions that affect his personal life.

A modern guide, unlike the ancient and medieval codes, should not contain a profusion of prohibitions and injunctions, but a statement of general principles and an illustration of ways in which it is possible for individuals to apply them in their daily living. It must be free from the authoritarian, absolutist approach; it must not show an excessive reverence for precedent or resort to a mechanical application of legal principles, abstracted from the discussions of legal issues in past genera· tions. It must show a sympathetic insight into the actual religious wants of living Jews, and be helpful to them in satisfying those wants to the very best of their ability. The number of Jews honestly desirous of just such guidance is legion. It is to them and them alone that the guide should address itself. If their needs are satisfied, all Jewry will benefit, for it is to them rather than to the dogmatic traditionalists, the opinionated secularists, or the unabashed assimilationists, that we must look for those who will carry the burdens and the glories of Jewish life into the world of tomorrow.

Unity of Purpose, Not Uniformity of Procedure

Uniformity of observance is neither attainable nor desirable. The diversity of the conditions under which different Jews live renders it unattainable, and the need to reckon with the existence of differences in personal taste, aptitudes and interests renders it undesirable. *Unity there must be, unity of essential purpose: the preservation and maintenance of a Jewish group life that shall be experienced by the individual as making his own life as a Jew worthwhile.*

An analysis of this essential purpose reveals it to have two aspects: one concerned primarily with the group, the other with the individual. The group aspect represents *the principle of survival* as opposed to assimilation. Any ritual that evokes in the individual Jew that feeling of oneness with the Jewish people which impels him to live as a Jew, has, by that fact alone, much value for Judaism. The individual aspect represents *the principle of salvation*, or making the most of life, as opposed to the cynicism that is skeptical of all life's values, and wants only to be left alone. Any ritual, therefore, which helps the Jew to find life interesting, meaningful and worth living is clearly possessed of value.

These two aspects reinforce each other. The more the individual Jew tends to identify himself with his people, the easier it becomes for him to rise above all morbid preoccupation with personal cares, and all bondage to self-seeking interests that set him at war with his social environment, and hamper the harmonious flowering of his personality. The more a Jew can find inspiration, joy and life-giving purpose through Jewish usages, the more loyal is he likely to be to the Jewish group and the more ready to make necessary sacrifices in its interest.

Elasticity

Once unity of purpose is assured, diversity of form need no longer be feared or deprecated. When people are given no alternative but to accept in its entirety a body of Jewish usage containing many practices which they are unable or unwilling to perform, their interest in all Jewish usage as well as loyalty to Judaism in general is thereby jeopardized. There is no saying to what degree the widespread indifference to positive Jewish values among modern Jews may not be due to the intransigence of Orthodox and Conservative Jews, who insist that any transgression of traditional usage is sin. As an alternative to this "take it or leave it" policy, the guide should indicate the limits within which, in each area of Jewish ritual usage, the individual can find an opportunity for Jewish self-expression, in accordance with the circumstances of his life and the bent of his personal interests.

The lower limit of this range of choice will represent that minimum of observance without which the traditional usage under discussion cannot be said to function at all. The upper level will represent such a creative adjustment of traditional usage as will yield the highest conceivable value to any considerable number of modern American Jews. Somewhere between these two levels, if not on the highest level, any Jew who wishes to permit Jewish ritual usage to find a place in his life will discover helpful suggestions to guide him in the intelligent selection of those practices by which he can identify himself in spirit with the Jewish people and find his personal self-fulfillment.

From a psychological point of view, there is always the danger that a formulation of minimum standards will tend to invite general acceptance of the avowed minimum as a personal norm. *The guide will, therefore, have to state categorically that, if only the minimum level were generally accepted among Jews, it would fail either to yield the individual any real satisfaction or to insure Jewish survival.* Nevertheless, Jews who feel that they cannot observe more than this minimum should at least cling to that much of Jewish usage, for, without it, there is grave danger that Judaism will cease to have any value for them or their posterity. Even observance of the minimum, while inadequate, will make it easier for a Jew to experience Jewish life as worthwhile.

At the other extreme, there are some Jews who, although they regard Jewish usages as folkways, and are therefore not to be classed with the Orthodox who regard them as divine commandments, find any deviation from the traditional norm insufficient for their self-fulfillment as Jews and contrary to their well-established and deep-seated habits. Their devotion to the Jewish heritage is so intense that they desire to continue all our religious folkways, as though these had all the force of categorical imperatives. In the case of such persons, the formulation of a guide will be of little value, except insofar as it may help them to deal with some of the religious problems of their fellow-Jews. Obviously, *it should not be the aim of the guide to aid in sloughing off traditional practices which have meaning for any individual Jew, but rather to set forth a practical optimum which will be spiritually edifying, ethically significant and possessed of Jewish survival values.*

Stress on Affirmative Jewish Usages Rather Than on Prohibitions

A necessary corollary of the criterion, that Jewish ritual must enable the individual to experience Jewish life as worthwhile, is a reversal of the relative importance which, in the popular mind and in the traditional codes, attaches to prohibitions and affirmative injunctions. From the legalistic viewpoint, the violation of a prohibition is a sin of commission, while the neglect of an affirmative injunction is only a sin of omission, and consequently less reprehensible. But *the moment we get away from the legalistic approach, we treat Jewish observances as religious folkways designed to insure the enhancement of the value of Jewish life, the affirmative injunctions assume the more important role.* For, in the realm of ritual usage, *desisting* from a specific act seldom carries with it the feeling of satisfaction that comes with the actual *performance* of a ceremony. The formidable list of traditional *don'ts* has served to alienate from Jewish religious life a large number of Jews who could not see in what way they, or anybody else, benefited by these prohibitions.

A word of caution against discarding prohibitions is, however, in order. A guide for usage should attempt to preserve, with respect to any practice, the atmosphere—often indescribable in words—with which it has been traditionally surrounded. Frequently the atmosphere that has been part of a traditional custom can be preserved, or revived, only by giving heed to the prohibitions traditionally associated with its observance. The most beautiful *Seder* [7] service would, for most Jews, be irremediably spoiled by a failure to reckon with the prohibition of leavened food on the Passover. Even the individual, who personally finds no value in a prohibition that is widely observed by Jews, should conform to it in public, wherever his failure to conform would be offensive to the religious sensibilities of a large number of Jews.

Both the prohibitions and positive injunctions tend, in the course of time, in consequence of changing circumstances, to become obsolete. If this obsolescence is not to lead to the eventual abolition of all Jewish religious usages, it becomes important that new rituals be introduced, growing out of the needs and experiences of modern Jews, to displace those that have been discarded. These, in accordance with criteria already discussed, should be made as beautiful as possible. In every culture, care is lavished on objects that are hallowed by association with religion, in order to make them aesthetically appealing and meaningful. In seeking to develop affirmative symbolic and ritual usages, the guide should suggest methods by which Jewish literature, music and art can be so utilized in the habitual life of the Jews as to enhance its value.

Other New Criteria for Judging the Relative Importance of Usages

Every attempt to introduce standards or norms of Jewish ritual usage needs to distinguish the more and the less important among them. Even the traditional codes, which assumed that all Jewish ritual regulations were divine commands, found it necessary to distinguish between a *mitzvah kallah* (a light precept), and a *mitzvah hamurah* (a rigorous precept).[8] For reasons previously set forth, we cannot accept these legalistic norms as valid for modern Judaism. The fact that one observance is explicitly or implicitly enjoined in the Pentateuch while another is of Rabbinic origin is no indication as to which is of greater import to Jewish life in our day, although from the traditional point of view the former would be regarded as the more important.[9] The fact that, in the traditional codes which prescribed penalties for infraction of Jewish law, the slighting of one observance was severely, and the other, only mildly, punished gives no clue to their relative importance for Jewish life in our day. *Entirely new criteria must be formulated, and explicitly stated, as guides to the intelligent direction of religious usage for modern Jews.*

A modern hierarchy of ritual values suggests itself, when we classify customs or observances in regard both to their form or method, and their content or purpose. It then becomes apparent that, in the customs of any group, three categories can be distinguished:

(a) There are some customs which commend themselves to us as meaningful and possessed of value both in form and content. An example of such an observance is the public reading of the Torah.

(b) The class of observances, that are arbitrary in form but significant in content, is exemplified by the use of *tefillin* or *mezuzah*. Their significant purpose is to remind the individual Jew of his commitment to fulfill Jewish ideals as implied in the concept of Israel's covenant with God, of which they are symbols. But the specific form of the *tefillin* or *mezuzah* is largely an accident of Jewish cultural history.

(c) The third class of observances, that are arbitrary in form and convey no clear meaning or purpose, is illustrated by some of the Jewish dietary prescriptions, such as those prohibiting the flesh of all animals that have no cloven hoof and do not chew their cud.

It is clear that those observances which are significant both in form and content are the most valuable; those that are significant at least in their content come next in importance; and those that are arbitrary in both respects have relatively the least value.

This relative evaluation does not mean, however, that any one of these categories can be dispensed with as of no value. In any normal civilization, everyone who lives within it partakes of the practice of all three categories of usage. There is no point in making a principle of discarding neckties, on the ground that wearing them serves no particular purpose. On the contrary, the immigrant to America acts quite sensibly, when he starts the process of his Americanization, by adopting the American style of clothing, though it be neither more beautiful nor more comfortable than his native garb. Similarly, the Jew who wishes to participate in the Jewish civilization does well to register that intention by accepting, as far as is possible without detriment to higher values, those conventions that have become associated with a Jewish way of life.

The presumption with regard to Jewish usage should always be in favor of the traditional procedure. If the Jewish group is to maintain its contact with its past, and is to preserve a full body of usages, a large conservatism is needed in dealing with its folkways. These should be surrendered only when either their form or content is objectionable on aesthetic or moral grounds, or when circumstances make their observance a practical impossibility. Even when the full traditional form of an observance is virtually impossible, an attempt ought to be made to preserve it, in modified form, rather than discard it altogether. Even where it is necessary to discard a custom, it is desirable to substitute for it some new practice that would serve the same function as the one discarded.

Reinterpretation of Traditional Symbols and Rites

Since usages, that are significant in form or content, have more value than those that convey no meaning, it is important that the guide specify the meanings that make a rite significant. This is contrary to the tendency of the traditional codes, in which the fact that a precept was held to be divinely ordained afforded sufficient reason for its observance. Indeed, the effort to define the specific significance was deprecated, for fear that people would utilize knowledge of the ideal symbolized to justify abandoning the use of the symbol, as henceforth superfluous. But in our day, when few Jews regard ritual practices as divine commands, the more meaning we can attach to such practices and the more explicit we are in explaining the values to be derived from them, the greater are the chances of preserving them.

The meanings expressed by traditional Jewish symbols and observances must, however, not merely be stated, but stated in terms that are relevant to the needs and interests of living Jews. Explanations of rites and symbols, in the terms in which our fathers explained them, may convey no meaning to Jews of our generation. To say, for example, that the whole complex of rites observed on *Yom Kippur* has for its purpose to effect atonement for our sins means nothing to us as modern Jews, unless the terms *sin* and *atonement* are given new meanings. Only when these are reinterpreted in a way that reckons with modern psychological and ethical insights, and we are made to understand how the observance of the traditional Yom Kippur rites can help us to redirect our own purposes to advantage, to surmount our personal limitations, to escape frustration and achieve self-fulfillment—only then can we, as modern Jews, fully benefit by their observance.

One important value of the use of symbols is that, unlike articles of a creed, they permit new meanings to be read into them, without any resulting conflict or confusion. Creeds are also capable of reinterpretation, but, as long as the original terms of the creed are used, the attempt to give new meanings to them is often resented. Moreover, confused thinking often results from the uncertainty as to whether a word is intended in its original, or in its acquired meaning. But this difficulty is not encountered in the reinterpretation of religious symbols. Consequently, such symbols are invaluable in preserving the continuity of a cultural tradition, even when circumstances result in a radical change in fundamental ideas.

To illustrate the way new meanings may be read into traditional usages, we may consider the reinterpretation of the custom of breaking a glass in the wedding ceremony. This custom, no doubt, originated in ancient superstition. It was thought that the breaking of the glass served as a sort of substitute for any impending disaster which might mar the happiness of the couple. The rite has, however, been reinterpreted in a way that dissociates it completely from any superstition, and gives it genuine significance. It has been construed as a memento of the destruction of Jerusalem, in accordance with the passage in Psalms 137: "If I forget thee, O Jerusalem, let my right hand forget her cunning. . . . If I remember thee not above my chief joy." The fact, that the new meaning has no relation to the original significance of the rite, in no way detracts from its value. But without such reinterpretation, the performance of the rite would be so void of value that nothing would be lost if it became obsolete.

Two criteria must be applied to the reinterpretation of symbolic objects and acts: (a) the new meaning given to the symbol must associate it with an ideal that has social or personal value, and (b) the association of the symbol with the ideal must be appropriate and credible.

To be sure, the attempt to give new meaning to an ancient symbol or rite that would otherwise be meaningless for modern Jews is not always successful, even though it satisfies our criteria. The particular interpretation may or may not appeal to Jews. The effort to reinterpret should, however, be encouraged, since it is preferable that a traditional usage be raised to the level of one that is meaningful in content, if not in form, rather than that it be observed only as a meaningless convention, or cease to be observed altogether.

The foregoing are the principles of evaluation, which the guide must apply to the various areas of Jewish ritual usage. By their aid, it should be possible to satisfy the needs of those Jews who are looking for a ritual expression of their Jewish interests and loyalties, but can find no adequate guidance in existing codes. Such guidance should enable them to find in Jewish traditional usages ways of maintaining their self-identification with the Jewish group, and experiencing spiritual joy and satisfaction in doing so.

CHAPTER TWENTY-TWO

THE AIM OF AMERICAN-JEWISH EDUCATION

"Jews in the United States" wrote a keen observer of American Jewry, "are not very much interested in evaluating American Jewish life. They seem to be satisfied with dollar Judaism. As long as a man contributes to his local Welfare Fund and to Jewish needs abroad, he considers himself a Jew. The wider aspects of Judaism are too broad and too deep for him because of the failure of Jewish education in America. Little has been done by rabbis and educators in this country to enable the average American Jew to understand that philanthropy alone does not constitute Judaism." [1]

This severe indictment of the rabbis and educators is not unwarranted, but to be altogether just it should include the lay leaders. No less responsible for the failure of Jewish education in this country are the boards of trustees of the religious and educational institutions. They have dictated the aims which they wanted the rabbis and educators to achieve. The traditionally-minded laymen have insisted on an Americanized replica of the old-world *heder*, which had been outlived even in the old world. The modern-minded laymen have sought nothing more than a Jewish replica of the Protestant Sunday-school, which even the Protestants consider inadequate. The only choice which the rabbis and educators have had has been either to yield to the wishes of the one or the other group or to exchange their calling for another. There can be no future to American Jewish life, unless both the lay and the educational leaders realize that they have been on the wrong track all these years, and together try to find a way to amend their common failure.

If we want the young of our people to accept the Jewish heritage of culture, religion and ethics and to make the most fruitful use of it, we have to re-think the purpose to be served by our transmitting that heritage to them. Changes in the social environment are reflected in men's ideas of the maximum or highest good worth striving for. Those ideas in turn determine the character and aim of the educative process. The kaleidoscopic changes that have taken place in the life of our people within recent years, have rendered the traditional conception of maximum good inoperative. This could not but weaken the interest of parents in the Jewish education of their children. To ignore this and to proceed with our educational efforts, without being clear in our minds what it is we hope to achieve, is to engage in irrelevancies. This is why American-Jewish education has been functioning in a vacuum. *No amount of improvement in the techniques and the externals of pedagogy can make up for lack of an aim which both teachers and parents must heartily accept as the motive for educating the child.*

1

THE PRE-MODERN AIM OF JEWISH EDUCATION

For our ancestors, the conception of the highest good, whether of the individual or of the group, was no problem. It was clearly defined in the tradition, as set forth in the Sacred Scriptures and in the interpretation given to them by our Sages. That tradition provided them with a complete orientation toward the main elements of human life: toward the universe, man, the vicissitudes of good and evil fortune, the origin of their people and its destiny. It not only gave them a rationale for the state of exile in which their people found themselves and the suffering that attended it; it also held out definite promises of reward, both national and individual, which would more than compensate for all the misery inflicted upon them by their enemies. The belief that God would send a Messiah who would restore Israel to its former glory and win for them the homage of the rest of mankind was sufficient to outweigh the misery of exile in which the Jews found themselves. The certainty that after this world order has come to an end, a new world order would arise, in which the resurrected dead would be given their earned reward or merited punishment, was an answer to all questions concerning the disparity between what men apparently deserved to get out of life and what they actually got.

The attainment of bliss in the hereafter was the Jew's ultimate goal. The heritage which he acquired from his parents, and which he was responsible for transmitting to his children, was the indispensable means to the attainment of that goal. This rendered the teaching of Torah to the young the highest duty of the parent and of the community. The traditional definition of the aim of Jewish education had a tremendous advantage, in that it was in keeping not only with what Jews implicitly believed, but with what was accepted by the very peoples that persecuted them.

Despite their segregation from their Gentile neighbors, the Jews were thrown into frequent contact with them. They could not help noting the basic elements that were common to their own world-outlook and that of their neighbors. *Although Jews, Christians and Mohammedans regarded each other as rivals, and themselves as in exclusive possession of the saving truth, they actually lived in the same universe of thought, and breathed in virtually the same spiritual climate. Under these circumstances, the aim of Jewish education was* EN RAPPORT *with the aim of education as conceived by the rest of mankind.* The Jewish child thus acquired through his education a sense of both moral and spiritual security. Moral security comes from such urge to a life of decency and uprightness as to leave no room for doubting their imperative character. Spiritual security comes from that certainty concerning the meaning of life which leaves no room for questioning its worthwhileness. Both of these sources of security were communicated to the Jewish child with his Jewish training.

In addition to supplying a definite conception of what constituted the ultimate good for both the child and his people, pre-modern Judaism supplied the social structure, in and through which that good was to be realized. To be sure, the structure was that of a nation in exile; but every community, or fragment of that nation, was permeated by a deep sense of unity with the rest of the nation throughout the world. Each community was, therefore, capable of fostering a high standard of civilization. This national unity and indivisibility were fostered by a uniformity in belief and practice, which was enforced by means of social sanctions. There was no ambiguity about the status of each Jewish community, whether large or small. *Vis-à-vis* the general community, it was entirely a group apart and autonomous. The only external obligation, to which the Jews within each community were subject, arose from the contractual relationship between them and the rulers of the majority population. It consisted merely of the payment of taxes and revenues. To the majority population, however, the Jews were aliens and pariahs.

Within that social framework of the Jewish community, the child was destined to live his entire life. It was, therefore, essential for him to acquire that literacy which would enable him to be a respected member of the Jewish community. If he observed the proprieties of that community life, he developed an awareness of being rooted, of belonging, of being cared for. He gained both social security and social status.

Thus the mental, moral and spiritual orientation, on the one hand, and the belonging-feeling, on the other, which the child acquired with whatever education he received, supplied him with the knowledge of how to live, and impelled him to make the most out of life. From these two factors in his upbringing he learned that, by doing the will of God, as defined to him by his heritage, he would earn for himself a share in the world to come. The possibility of achieving salvation through one's own individual merit, apart from the Jewish people and its tradition, was entirely unthinkable. Through these bonds of interest and devotion which united the child to the community, the community in turn had its own life perpetuated. Thus did the education which the community gave the child bring it returns in added chances of survival.

2

WHY THE PRE-MODERN AIM IS IRRELEVANT

For Jews who have moved away from old world habitats and conceptions, all that belongs to the past has little more than an historic interest, from the educational point of view. Likewise, some of the controversies which followed immediately upon the breaking up of those conditions have become irrelevant. By this time, there are whole areas of Jewish life where the fires of controversy which raged first around French rationalism, and later around German historicism, have burned themselves out. All that remains of the traditional beliefs in those areas are smouldering ashes. The loss of those traditional beliefs has resulted in moral and spiritual aimlessness.

No less devastating than the challenge to traditional beliefs has been the anomalous position of our people as a group, ever since we have been granted civic rights. *By accepting civic rights, we Jews did something which no other people has ever attempted. We are eager to be integrated with other nations, yet we refuse to disappear as an identifiable group.* How it is possible to combine two such contradictory purposes is the crucial problem with which we American Jews are grappling. Most of us are convinced that the problem is not insoluble. But as long as that problem remains unsolved, our social status in democratic countries cannot be anything but ambiguous.

The Orthodox among us do not experience any of these difficulties. To them the Jewish heritage is based on supernaturalism and meta-history. As such, it has a sufficient *raison d'être*. Reform, on the other hand, has formulated a modern reinterpretation of the place of the Jewish people in the divine plan for mankind. From the standpoint of modern thought, however, the Reform reinterpretation is scarcely more acceptable than the Orthodox view.

When the Orthodox, in their conception of the universe, stress the centrality of Israel and the suspension of nature's laws at times for the sake of Israel, they do so at least in terms of the universe of discourse in which natural law, in the modern use of that term, was still unknown, and in which all that happened was regarded as emanating from the purposeful will of a personified Deity. When, however, the Reformists reiterate the doctrine of the Chosen People, they, too, stress the centrality of Israel, despite their having given up the belief in the historicity of the miracles recorded in the Bible. This is like continuing to believe in the centrality of the earth in the physical universe, despite admission of the truth of the Newtonian law of gravitation.

The modernist religio-cultural group which has the ambition of combining what is most valid both in modernism and in traditionalism, is, educationally, at a disadvantage. Though it has come nearer than the other groups to seeing Jewish life integrally, and in relation to the contemporary realities, it has so far not succeeded in giving an understandable account of itself. It has not as yet found a rationale for Jewish survival in America. Not having made up its mind concerning what constitutes the maximum good either for the Jewish child or for the Jewish people, it can have no philosophy of American-Jewish education. Basic, therefore, to any consideration of how to bring up our children as Jews in this country is a definite conception of how it is possible for us to retain our group identity, in a modern democratic environment, in the modernism and democracy of which we hope to participate.

3

THE NEGATION OF JEWISH LIFE IN THE DIASPORA [2]

At the present time the most vocal among the educators who subscribe to the religio-cultural conception of Judaism take a negative attitude toward any prospect of a future for Judaism outside Eretz Yisrael. From all that has recently happened to European Jewry they conclude that anti-Semitism is not merely a passing madness; it is a chronic disease of all Western civilization. They maintain, therefore, that it is quixotic to expect the democratic countries to give us Jews the sense of security necessary to the leading of a normal life. Whatever Jewish education is to be given to our children must, accordingly, be based on the acceptance of suffering and exile as our lot in life, from which there is only one escape, and that is migration to Eretz Yisrael. The principal aim of Jewish education, therefore, should consist in fostering in the child a yearning to live in Eretz Yisrael, and, in case that is not feasible, in fostering in him heroic resignation to a life of self-denial and sacrifice, made necessary by the sadistic tendencies of the dominant population toward all minority groups.

The foregoing view of the course of democracy is entirely unacceptable, and the conclusion drawn from such a view for Jewish education is the height of absurdity. If the future in the democratic countries is, indeed, as dark as our pessimists paint it, then they might as well advocate some kind of physical or spiritual suicide for the Jewish people. To assume that, with the democratic countries constitutionally incapable of bringing anti-Semitism under control, it is possible for Jews to achieve freedom and security in Eretz Yisrael is to forget that the world is one, both for good and for evil. Moreover, resigning ourselves to injustice and oppression at the hands of our fellow-men may be the only course of action open to us, but it certainly cannot constitute the highest good upon which to base the purpose of educational endeavor.

It is true that, in the past, Jewish education did train the child to regard himself as belonging to a people in exile, and to be prepared to suffer on that account. But it then laid the chief stress not on the present suffering, but on the future glories that awaited his people and on the ineffable bliss in the world to come, that awaited those who lived in accordance with the will of God, as expressed in the Torah. That prospect more than compensated for all the suffering that his people endured in this world. Does the modern Jewish educator, who insists on having the child realize the full meaning of *galut*, exile, hold out the same naive faith in the advent of the Messiah and in the bliss of the world to come? If not, then he has nothing to offer the child, but a sense of misery in being fated to be born a Jew. Only sheltered and cloistered pedagogues, who seek to avenge themselves upon the young for their own frustrated lives, could devise such a fantastic purpose. No one, with any love of children, and with the real desire to have them grow up to be happy, would want to turn life for them into that kind of nightmare.

Another approach to the question whether it is possible for the Jewish people to retain its identity, under the terms of the Emancipation and the Enlightenment, is to point to the actual disruption of Jewish life which goes on apace, as the result of being integrated into the general population. Some Jewish educators stress that result as an inevitable consequence of the democratic process. These educators, too, consider it misleading to try to persuade Jewish children that it is possible to lead a normal Jewish life in the Diaspora. On the contrary, they claim, it is necessary to make clear to the child that, even under the best of circumstances, Jews cannot possibly retain their group identity outside Eretz Yisrael. They believe that the child should be saved from the illusion that Judaism is being given a fair chance to prove its potency as an influence for good in their lives. When the child grows up, he will then realize that Jewish life is not to be blamed for its shortcomings, its lack of vitality and creativity. *Such Jewish educators assume that, by inculcating in the child a feeling of discontent with the odds against being a Jew in a non-Jewish environment, we can develop in him a passionate yearning for Eretz Yisrael as a national Jewish home.*

This kind of Eretz-Yisrael-centered education in America is bound to have a ruinous effect on the happiness and character of the child. It holds out to him no reason why he should be condemned to lead an abnormal life all his days, since, either by migrating to Eretz Yisrael, or by ignoring Judaism altogether, he might lead a normal life. The assumption that it is inherently impossible for the Jew to feel at home in a non-Jewish environment, which one may reasonably expect in time to be free of anti-Semitism, is a counsel of despair, and *we cannot build an educational system on despair.*

4

THE NEED OF A TWO-FOLD NORM FOR JEWISH LIFE

There is an alternative to either of the two preceding types of approach to the question of survival in a democratic state. Instead of judging the democratic process by the way it has worked hitherto, we should judge it by what it was intended to become. It was intended to become a means of enabling human beings to make the most out of their lives, or to achieve salvation as they view it, provided, of course, they do not interfere with the salvation of their fellows, as the latter view it. Whatever prevents people, as individuals or as a group, from achieving salvation cannot be ascribed to the democratic process. Whatever militates against the salvation of a minority group, which does not aim at aggression or domination, must in the end jeopardize the salvation of the majority population as well.

As Jews, we cannot achieve our salvation, unless the democratic process permits us to retain our identity as an indivisible people. If, therefore, democracy is so interpreted that it prevents us from fostering our religio-cultural tradition and from being true to our destiny as a people, then we are presented with a very strange paradox which we must try to resolve, not only in our own interest as Jews, but also in the interest of a better world for all mankind. Only when we have come to understand this paradox fully, can we be in a position to suggest a possible solution. That solution will have to be the basis of a Jewish educational system in this country.

We can best learn the nature of the paradox which complicates the status and future of Jewish life in democratic countries by asking the question: "How was democracy intended to function in relation to historical groups and religions generally?" This question has not been answered, as most people think, by the separation of church and state. That separation has by no means solved the problem of the relation of religion to the social, economic and political interests. Actually, religion is inextricably bound up with those interests. No religion that hopes to be treated seriously can afford to take a neutral position in any matter pertaining to human welfare, and true welfare is unattainable without the benefits which good religion can confer.

Is, then, the legal separation of church and state a fiction? Not at all. Such separation affirms the very important principle that the democratic state should not monopolize the life of the citizen. It should leave place in his life for ideals and loyalties that transcend the state. The democratic state should undertake to provide for the social security of the citizen, but should not claim to be the sole source of moral and spiritual security. Even if it helps him to some extent to lead a moral and spiritual life, it encourages other agencies—especially historic groups —to make that their principal function.

The significance of this underlying principle of democracy has become apparent of late, by reason of the systematic effort that is made by totalitarian states to prohibit all international affiliations and loyalties. This area in the life of the individual, which the democratic state should leave to each citizen to cultivate in whatever way he chooses, is placed under the control of the church by the majority of Americans. That is the area which we Jews should dedicate to Jewish interests and affiliations. Orthodoxy and Reform would have that area in the life of the individual Jew come within the purview of the synagogue. Modern Jews, however, to whom Judaism is a religious culture, do not regard the synagogue, as now constituted, adequate for the cultivation of that area. Many potentialities of Jewish life would remain forever dormant, if it were not fructified by values emanating from Eretz Yisrael. It is important to bear in mind, however, that *if Judaism is to meet with a loyal response on the part of the individual Jew, it will have to prove its relevance to the whole of his life.* It will have to penetrate into those innermost recesses of the mind and the heart, which no political state can possibly reach, and try to guard them against moral and spiritual deterioration.

When we realize the opportunity which is thus presented to Judaism, we can have no doubts concerning the legitimacy of Jewish corporate life in the American environment. Only a spurious democracy, a democracy which is handicapped by the lag and the inertia of old-time and old-world prejudices, is a menace to Jewish life. Genuine democracy would always give Jewish life free rein. That means that our destiny as Jews is bound up with that of genuine democracy. We cannot do otherwise but put our faith in the democratic ideal, because without at least a partial realization of that ideal, there would be no place anywhere in the world for us Jews, either in the Diaspora or in Eretz Yisrael. *By staking our fortune upon the ultimate establishment of true democracy, we are contributing to that consummation.* By fostering those interests which unite American Jews with the Jews of the rest of the world, we are helping to effect that division of function between the nation and the trans-national group which is indispensable to the life of the democratic state. That division of function is an essential part of the personal freedom which the democratic state was established to foster. Being a Jew in America must, therefore, be regarded as nothing less nor more than a normal expression of the democratic process.

This means that there must henceforth be two standards of normality for Jewish life; one standard for Eretz Yisrael, where Jewish life can be lived out fully as a complete civilization that provides those who live by it with all the elements of life necessary to their self-fulfillment and happiness; and a second standard for democratic countries like the United States, where they must look for economic and social security to American citizenship, which in turn expects them to find their moral and spiritual security elsewhere. That security they can for the present find mainly within their own Jewish people and its tradition. In time,

however, with American democracy having achieved more self-awareness and consistency, it, too, will become for Jews, as well as for the
rest of the population, a source of inner peace.[3]

5

EDUCATIONAL AIM IN TERMS OF TRADITION
AND SOCIAL STRUCTURE

The position advocated in this discussion may be summarized as
follows: There is nothing inherently abnormal in a synthesis of the
democratic process with the maintenance of Jewish group individuality,
though such a synthesis in the Diaspora would undoubtedly constitute
a new development of Jewish life. Secondly, by educating our children
to live as Jews in an American environment, we shall not be imposing
on them an abnormal kind of existence.

But the real question is whether such a synthesis is at all possible.
Jewish group individuality is articulated by means of a tradition which
arose and developed under conditions very different from our own. If
we expect that tradition to help us live as both Jews and Americans,
we must have it speak to us in terms that are relevant to ethical and
spiritual problems of our day. This calls for the following:

In the first place, it is essential to realize that our tradition, as it has
come down to us, belongs to a universe of thought that was radically
different from our own. *We are bound to fail in our effort to revitalize
that tradition, if we yield to the temptation to ignore the wide gap that
divides us from the ancients in the general outlook on life.* We must
become accustomed to the idea of growth in experience and meaning.
The essence of growth is continuity in change. Before we can discover
the permanent elements in tradition, we must be fully aware of the
changes in knowledge of the physical world, in the conception of God,
and in the ethical values which differentiate the modern man's world
from the ancient man's.

Secondly, in order to render the tradition relevant to present day
ethical and spiritual concerns, it is necessary to discover the latent
and permanent ethical and spiritual urges beneath such elements in the
tradition as the miracle story, the obsolete law or the primitive rite. This
calls for research into the historical background of the tradition not
only in Israel, but in the entire universe of thought within the scope of
which Israel came. Upon the results of such research a knowledge of

the human sciences should be brought to bear, in order that we may discover to what extent the Jewish tradition verifies the existence of the higher trends in human nature.

A third step is to relate these verifications of the higher trends in human nature to the social and spiritual problems that are agitating mankind today, the problems pertaining to the meaning of life and death, to the rights and duties of the individual and of society, to the prerogatives of the various loyalties and to the proper utilization of power. *There is need for evolving something that will be in our day the analogue of the Talmud and Midrash in ancient times.*[4] In this development, the ancient Talmud and Midrash should constitute the greater part of the tradition to be reinterpreted and reworked.

Finally, provision must be made for dealing with the many situations that were not provided for by the ancient tradition. No tradition that ceases growing can live. But this step cannot be taken within the tradition itself. The impetus for it must come from a living body which is the carrier of the tradition, and without which no tradition can live. All this research can not, of course, be expected of those who are engaged professionally in elementary education. We must realize, however, that unless this research is carried on to the point where the Jewish traditions can be made to function in our day, there can be no modern kind of Jewish education, no education that can generate in the young of our people the will to live as Jews.

In addition to revitalizing the tradition as a means of synthesizing Jewish life with Americanism, we have to create the kind of social struc ture which would set in motion the newly interpreted and evolved Jewish values. The most inspiring and wholesome teachings are likely to remain a dead letter, unless they become part of the consciousness of a living, functioning community. All efforts at reinterpreting and revaluing our tradition are carried on in a vacuum, so long as we are without an organic Jewish community that possesses the educational machinery to put into circulation the results of those efforts. In the past, for example, though the Torah was regarded as having been given by God to Moses, it would have remained at best esoteric doctrine, had there not been a nation to adopt it as its constitution. It was the social structure of the Jewish people which gave the Torah its potency throughout the centuries.

Before the era of Emancipation, it was impossible for Jews, whether they happened to be few or many, to live without some kind of communal structure to make them aware of their solidarity with the Jewish nation. As soon as Jews, however, were permitted to become part of the body politic of the majority, they lost the urgency for Jewish communal life. The various organizations, including congregations, do not constitute the kind of communal organism which is essential to the functioning of a tradition, any more than scientific and philanthropic societies constitute a nation. *By the same token that we need to reinterpret the Jewish tradition properly, if we want it to live in the modern universe of thought, we need, also, to reorganize the social structure of the Jewish people properly, if we want it to have a place in the frame of modern society.* Judaism cannot function in a vacuum. It has to be geared to a living community. In that community all who wish to be known as Jews should be registered, and expulsion from it should deprive one of the right to use the name Jew. The creation of such organic communities based on the spirit of democratic constitutionalism is the first and most indispensable prerequisite to Jewish survival in the Diaspora.

6

THE FAILURE TO ADJUST AIM TO NEW NEEDS

It is generally assumed that to have a definite conception of education, we ought to have a definite idea of the kind of society for which we want to educate the child, and of the quality of life we hope to see prevail in that society.[5] Neither the Orthodox nor the old-school Reformists experience any difficulty in meeting this requirement. To both these denominations, the Jews constitute a religious group in the conventional sense of the term, and the only quality of life which they regard as desirable for that group is the religious. They should, therefore, have no trouble in arriving at the appropriate kind of Jewish education or training to give the child.

But what of those who subscribe neither to the Orthodox nor to the classical Reform conception of Judaism? The very fact that they, nevertheless, hope for, and believe in, the future of Judaism in this country implies that Judaism means to them the civilization of the Jewish people. This is especially true, for the most part, of those who are engaged professionally in Jewish education, after having undergone a systematic training for that purpose. But, unfortunately, the kind of social status and quality of life that should mark Jewish society, from the standpoint of Judaism as a civilization, have not yet received sufficient recognition to be avowedly translated into educational practice. As a result, the temptation to yield to expediency leads many of our Jewish educators and teachers to evade some of the most basic issues in the transmission of our Jewish heritage, lest they offend their employers. Jewish education can least afford to come under the indictment pronounced by Bertrand Russell against education in general. "Educators in every country except Russia," he said, "tend to be constitutionally timid, and, either by their income or by their snobbery, to be adherents of the rich."[6] By now we know that Russia is no exception either.

The average layman does not have the least conception of what is involved nowadays in the task of transmitting Judaism. All considerations with regard to the need of a complete reorientation in ideas and values and of a thoroughgoing reorganization of educational content are alien to him. For him Judaism can only be what he himself has been taught, or what he has absorbed from his own particular environment. The teachers and educators find themselves helpless, under the pressure which these average laymen bring to bear upon them. Moreover, the precariousness of their positions is such as to preclude their giving sufficient time and thought to the working out of the kind of subject matter that would be relevant to actual needs of children in an American environment. Those needs could never have been experienced in Jewish life of former times. As a result of the temporizing and lack of initiative on the part of the Jewish teaching personnel, the process of Jewish education, where it is still carried on with any degree of intensity, is at present based for the most part on the Orthodox version of Judaism.

The small percentage of children who manage to complete a course of study in a Jewish school is never given to understand that there can be a Judaism which is *not* committed to the traditional view of the supernatural origin of the Torah, the historicity of the miraculous events recorded in the Bible, or the finality of Rabbinic law and of the Maimonidean creed. The teachers who have long outgrown this conception of Judaism nevertheless teach it to their pupils, justifying their action on the ground that they themselves were taught that version of Judaism, yet it did not prevent them from working out their own intellectual and spiritual adjustment as Jews. They claim that their function is merely to transmit the tradition in the form in which it functioned in the past, and to leave it to their pupils to achieve their own orientation when they grow up. Thus, *where conviction ceases, inertia takes over.*

The effect of this attitude on their work and on the children can be nothing but morally and spiritually disastrous. Where the content of education consists chiefly not of objective facts but of ethical and spiritual values, any mental reservation which prevents forthrightness in teaching is bound to have a corroding effect on the character of the pupil. It undermines his integrity and develops in him a contempt for the subject matter. *No amount of technical improvement in the means and methods employed can compensate for the evil wrought by the lack of unreserved sincerity in transmitting a social heritage.* The failure to reckon with this evil is responsible for the futility and sterility of American-Jewish education.

The Jewish pedagogic literature and text material produced in this country do not even betray the awareness that such a problem exists. With the exception of the series of history text books written by Jacob S. Golub,[7] virtually no attempt is made in modern Jewish historical texts to reckon with the difference between fact and fiction in the account of the first thousand years of our history as a people. Few synagogue or communal schools ever make it a point to acquaint the pupil with the fact that the Jewish religion underwent some very radical mutations in the course of its career. As a result, he is totally unprepared for the further changes which Judaism as a whole, and Jewish religion in particular, must undergo in our day, if it is to have a future. Everything that he learns about Judaism seems calculated to give him a distorted conception of its very nature and manner of functioning.

7

THE REQUISITE ADJUSTMENTS IN AIM

Modern Jewish teachers and educators, who no longer subscribe to the traditional or Orthodox version of Judaism—and they are unquestionably in the majority—should dedicate themselves to the task of utilizing the very process of education for the purpose of developing an acceptable version of the Jewish tradition, and of preparing the ground for Jewish communal life. This may seem incompatible with conventional educational procedure. All cultural and social changes are supposed to be effected directly through, and in, adult society. They are supposed to precede and not to follow the educational process. The usual assumption is that the society of today conditions the education of tomorrow, and not the reverse. But we Jews, in our struggle for existence, have had to resort to extraordinary measures. We have a precedent in our past for the use of the educational process to create a new social structure and a relatively new universe of thought. Such was the achievement of the first few generations of teachers known as *Tannaim*,[8] during the first two centuries of the common era.

When the Second Temple was destroyed, our ancestors were virtually without the kind of tradition and without the kind of corporate frame which the new circumstances of exile and dispersion demanded. They were on the verge of national and religious collapse. It was then that the *Tannaim*[8] made use of the educative process to evolve both the necessary tradition and the requisite corporate frame. This they did first with adults who were to function as the spiritual guides; then they brought their teachings down to the level of the child.

Similarly creative effort in Jewish education must be undertaken in our day, if Judaism is not to die out in this country. Such effort calls for abundant energy, far-seeing initiative and willing sacrifice. In modern times the Jewish teacher, particularly in east-European countries, has shown himself equal to the task of moulding the Jewish consciousness in the spirit of the Hebrew renascence. In Eretz Yisrael, the Jewish teacher succeeded in transforming Hebrew into a living vernacular. There is no reason why the Jewish teacher should not be able to cope with the particular task which devolves upon him now to save Diaspora Jewry from disintegration.

In utilizing the educational process as a means of reinterpreting our traditional values, an important role will have to be played by the way we organize the content of instruction into different kinds of subject matter. In contrast with the tendency of Western education to break up the content of a social heritage into different kinds of subject matter, the traditional type of Jewish education retained the Jewish social heritage in the undifferentiated form in which it was lived. When the youngster studied Torah, he studied simultaneously everything that had to do with making him a worthy member of the Jewish community. The Western habits of thought, however, which our children acquire with their non-Jewish education, necessitate similar differentiation of the Jewish educational content into different subjects. This very differentiation necessarily results in new meanings and emphases. That itself is perhaps the most important step in the process of reinterpretation. There are, however, certain lines of differentiation which must be followed, specifically with a view to their effect on that process.

It is essential, for example, to create in the mind of the child an awareness of the several facets of our tradition, and of the fact that each facet represents a distinct pattern of values. Thus, while, in actual life, Jewish religion and Jewish peoplehood are always found together, it is essential to learn to differentiate one from the other in thought. The first effect of such differentiation, in modern times, has been to create at least one new subject in the Jewish curriculum—Jewish history. Jost,[9] Graetz,[10] Weiss [11] and others, in developing new Jewish historical content, have done what the *Tannaim* and *Amoraim* [12] did for their day. These new content values have been translated by the text-book makers and pedagogues into subject matter for the elementary school.

It is also necessary to draw a distinction between the legendary and the historical. The child should be made to realize that our traditional narrative material has two facets to it, legend and history, with legend predominant in the earlier narratives of the Bible, and history in the later narratives. The practice of ignoring that distinction results in the distorted notions which most Jews have of their people's past. By permitting our children to carry away the impression that the stories in the Pentateuch are meant to be taken as history, we plant in their minds seeds of inner conflict for the rest of their lives. "The folklore and myth of a people," says Henry N. Wieman,[13] "convey in aesthetic form the quality of events critically determinant of their history." Not until Jewish education assimilates the truth expressed in that statement, will the early narratives of the Bible exercise their proper influence on the thinking and conduct of the coming generations of Jews.

Another important area to be delineated in the content of Jewish education is that of ethics and religion. While that area constitutes part of the content of tradition, it must be enlarged, organized and developed into distinct subject-matter. What we mean by such central ideas as God, holiness, personality, responsibility, goodness, truth, human destiny and salvation, must henceforth be clearly articulated and recognized as in need of being studied and translated into action.

In utilizing the educational process for evolving the social structure of Jewish life, which normally should have preceded that process, it is advisable to organize projects in what might be called "Jewish civics." That should not be difficult. Many Jewish schools have succeeded in making Eretz Yisrael the theme of instruction and project activity. By the same token, Jewish civics should come to occupy a place in the curriculum, for the purpose of creating in the mind of the child an appreciation for the need of Jewish communal life in America. Projects should be developed entailing the study of all educational and social service institutions, public relations organizations, community councils, as well as the organization and functioning of congregations, and the huge fund-gathering campaigns like those for welfare funds, the Joint

Distribution Committee and the United Jewish Appeal. The purpose of these projects should be to discover the forces at work in all those activities, their accomplishments, their ideologies, their inherent defects, and what would be necessary to integrate them into an organic Jewish community. All this would have to be accompanied by combining the various schools into a kind of youth *Kehillah*, out of which would evolve, in the course of ten to fifteen years, the beginnings of real community life.

No doubt, the most difficult problem, which will have to be met in developing the educational content both for the reinterpretation of traditional Jewish values and the establishment of Jewish social structure, is that presented by the vast variety of conflicting ideas and interests. The only possibility of achieving collaboration at least among the majority of those who profess the desire to see Judaism flourish is to have them accept the principle of diversity in unity not grudgingly, but wholeheartedly. With all that, however, there must be a definite pattern of Jewish living, which should constitute the criterion by which to judge all educational effort. The basic principle of that pattern must be that *Judaism is a religio-ethical civilization, to be fostered by the American Jew to the maximum degree compatible with the legitimate claims which American citizenship has upon him.*

Analyzed into its elements, the foregoing principle implies the following.

(1) As a civilization, Judaism is the sum of all manifestations of the life of the Jewish people whose being is rooted in Eretz Yisrael. It consists, therefore, of a continuing history, a common language and literature, folkways, mores, laws, ethical norms, and in addition, possesses a distinct social structure.

(2) That which makes Judaism a religious civilization is the fact that all its manifestations are permeated by the purpose of having the people so order its life ethically and spiritually that the individual Jew may make the most out of his life. This purpose, which was always implied in what it stressed in the idea of God, should now be made explicit.

(3) In accepting symbiosis with other nations, the Jews must be governed by a twofold standard of normality: one for Eretz Yisrael, the other for the Diaspora. A prerequisite, however, for the achievement of normality in the Diaspora is the normality of Judaism as the majority civilization of Eretz Yisrael.

This is the only tenable conception of the Jewish way of life to be imparted to the American-Jewish child, from the standpoint of those who are modernist in their general world-outlook and religio-culturist in their attitude to Judaism. The principal aim to be kept in mind in the Jewish education of the American-Jewish child, from the standpoint of his maximum self-fulfillment as an American and as a Jew, is, accordingly, to render the Jewish heritage relevant to his moral and spiritual needs, and to qualify him, when he matures, to establish the kind of Jewish communal environment that will provide opportunities for the satisfaction of those needs.

CHAPTER TWENTY-THREE

A NEW EDUCATIONAL APPROACH TO THE BIBLE

1

CHANGES IN THE PURPOSE OF TEACHING THE BIBLE

The first pedagogic reference to the teaching of the Bible is to be found in the Mishnaic treatise of *Abot*.[1] We are told there that the study of the Bible should begin at the age of five and continue to the age of ten. It should then be followed by the study of the Mishnah. We are tempted to see in this pedagogic advice an anticipation of the modern departure from the long standing practice of having the child leave off the study of the Bible, after he has had a year's study of the Pentateuch, to take up the study of the Talmud. When we recall, however, how the Bible was studied at the time that pedagogic principle in *Abot* was formulated, we realize that the author of that principle had a different conception of Bible study from that we have. The Bible text was then given the kind of interpretation which is recorded in the Tannaitic and Amoraic *midrashim*.[2] That interpretation formed the basis of what was known as "oral Torah," or Rabbinic lore. It was regarded as the *authoritative* rendering of the written text. Accordingly, it was not really the Bible, as we know it, that occupied the first five years of a child's training, but a kind of combination of the Bible with Rabbinic lore.

Before the modern era, which we date from the end of the eighteenth century, in countries like Holland and Italy of the sixteenth and seventeenth centuries, where the beginnings of modernism first made themselves felt in the Jewish ghetto, attempts were made to revive the long neglected principle in *Abot* concerning the study of the Bible. Although in those countries the study of the Bible was not as interwoven with the Rabbinic interpretation as it had been throughout the preceding centuries, it still was largely dominated by the spirit of that interpretation.

The first radical break with the traditional method of teaching the Bible took place under the influence of the Enlightenment, toward the end of the eighteenth century. That was the beginning of the *Haskalah*[3] period. Mendelssohn and the *Biurists*[4] then translated the Bible into German, and wrote commentaries on it, with a view to emphasizing the literal meaning of the text. The Enlightenment awakened in the Jews a yearning for aesthetic form, as an end in itself. The national literatures of England, France and Germany were then growing by leaps and bounds. Jews, who became aware of the great literatures of the nations among which they lived, were spurred on to discover in their own traditional culture literature of great beauty and power. This is how they came to center anew their interest in the Bible, and why they wanted to have it taught to the young as literature.

Two additional purposes motivated the teaching of the Bible during that period. One was to have the knowledge of the Bible serve as a stimulus to the recovery of the classic Hebrew, for the new literature which the Jewish *illuminati* hoped to encourage and produce. Another purpose was to transfer the attention of the Jews from the legalistic casuistry, in which the study of the Talmud had become involved, to the broader problems of human conduct and perspective.

These purposes continued to function in the environment of the Jewish *illuminati*, until the advent of Zionism, when a new purpose was enunciated and subordinated all else to itself. With the establishment of the Hebrew Gymnasium in Tel Aviv and the formulation of its curriculum, the study of the Bible was given a position of primacy, on the ground that it was "to serve as a means of enabling the students to visualize what living as a normal people on its own land meant for our ancestors, and to awaken in the young a passionate love for that life and an eager striving to reestablish it as of old." [5] When Ahad Ha-Am visited the Tel Aviv Gymnasium in 1912 he used that purpose, with which he was in hearty accord, as a standard to criticize adversely the instruction that was being given there. He found that the pupils had learned much concerning the background and the personalities of the Bible, but did not know the Bible text itself, because of the numerous meticulous emendations which the teachers, following a German commentary popular at that time, had made in the text. It is doubtful whether we would have had reason to regard the instruction as then given in the Gymnasium entirely adequate, even if the teachers had not been so fond of making emendations, and even if the students had had a more intimate knowledge of the text.

After all, something in the nature of an upheaval happened to the Bible as a result of the modern scientific study of it. To any one acquainted with that study, and with some of its implications and, by now, unquestionable conclusions, the Bible can never be the same Bible that it was to our unsophisticated ancestors. What the Copernican astronomy did to men's ideas of the universe, the modern scientific study of the Bible text has done to the Bible. It has not only opened up new vistas in the understanding of the Bible, but it has scrapped beliefs and assumptions that were considered sacrosanct, beliefs and assumptions concerning God, the origin of man, of the Torah, of Israel and of numerous other central values and beliefs in our life as Jews. It is difficult to comprehend how a teacher, who has never wrestled with the problems created by this Copernican revolution in the conception of the Bible, can be qualified to teach the Bible properly. We might as well imagine one teaching the Ptolemaic conception of the universe to a class in astronomy. Even if some teachers would be able to hold the students' attention, and delight them with the description of the spheres revolving around the earth, that fact would not render their teaching any the less misleading.

It is high time that we ask ourselves again the question: *What is the purpose to be served in teaching the Bible? That purpose must evidently derive from what we believe to be the actual nature of the Bible, and have a bearing on the mental and moral growth of the child.* According to Jewish tradition the Pentateuch was actually dictated by God, and the rest of the Bible inspired by Him in a supernatural manner. All those who formerly taught the Bible actually believed it to be the word of God, in no sense comparable to anything written by man. So long as the Bible was implicitly believed to be a collection of divinely inspired writings, the main purpose in teaching it could only be to impart to the student what God would have him know and do.

The ideal of "Torah for its own sake" sets forth the pedagogic purpose to which the teacher of the Bible was expected to conform in the days of unquestioning faith, as well as the motive that was to impel the pupil in the pursuit of his study of the Bible. That ideal implies that the awareness of God should be regarded as the highest goal which one would wish to attain; all else, like prestige in this world or reward in the hereafter, is either secondary or should be dispelled from the mind. The only way the ideal of "Torah for its own sake" could be maintained in the past was to treat instruction and study themselves as a form of worship.[6] That is actually stressed time and again in Rabbinic writings. This is why the *bet hamidrash*, or house of study, was regarded as far holier than the *bet hakenesset*, or synagogue.[7] The main theme of *Abot* is the study of Torah as a means of salvation in the here and in the hereafter. To be that, the study of Torah had to be carried on with unrelaxing awareness that the Torah articulated God's own will.

We thus see how the traditional conception of the nature of the Bible as supernaturally revealed gave rise to the kind of purpose in teaching the Bible which permeated the entire pattern of the Jews' traditional way of life. To have a pedagogic purpose that is as pervasive as all that is to possess the key to the problem of how to make education relevant to life. We may well ask: Is so all permeating a purpose possible only on the traditional assumption of the Scriptures as supernaturally revealed?

The conception which the *Maskillim*, or Jewish *illuminati*, during the nineteenth century, had of the nature of the Bible did not generate as intensive and all-pervasive a purpose as the one which had dominated the study of Torah throughout the past. That is quite understandable. The purpose of cultivating in the student an aesthetic appreciation of the style and subject-matter of the Bible and a facility in the art of writing Hebrew, free from the corruption of the post-Biblical dialect, could appeal only to a very limited number of students, and influence even their lives only in the area of literary interests. This, also, is true of the modern scientific study of the Bible, in which the interest is primarily of an historic character. Here the purpose is to enlarge the cultural horizon of the student. In that spirit, the teaching of the Bible would be possible even in a public high-school or college. It would be foolish to discourage that kind of instruction, on the ground that it is not only untraditional but completely neutral, from the standpoint of Jewish life. Better by far to have that kind of instruction than none. Thousands of Jewish children, who now remain abysmally ignorant of the Bible, could in that way acquire some knowledge of it.

Nevertheless, as far as our own Jewish schools are concerned, we should not be content with an aesthetic, historical or philological approach to the Bible. We should strive to achieve, on the basis of a scientific conception of the authorship of the Bible, some such purpose as might well compare in scope of influence with the purpose it served when its supernatural origin was taken for granted.

To formulate such a purpose for Biblical instruction was what the Tel Aviv Gymnasium attempted with its very first curriculum. As Ahad Ha-Am put it: "The purpose is not to train merely the intellect but the mind as a whole, in order that it develop in accordance with what we want it to be, and in order that the character of the child take on the stamp of Jewish national individuality, that individuality which is in need of being deliberately cultivated." [8] The knowledge of the Bible was to serve, together with other literary possessions of the Jews, as a means of developing national self-awareness in the child. From the standpoint of pervasive influence, such a purpose can measure up to the traditional one described above.

However, with national self-awareness as its sole purpose, there is the danger that the teaching of the Bible might be utilized to strengthen and deepen Jewish national sentiment as an end in itself, and without any bearing on the entire context of human relationships through which the personality has occasion to function. Moreover, in the Diaspora such emphasis on group self-awareness might be made to appear as nothing more than an attempt to create in the child a discontent and feeling of maladjustment with life outside Eretz Yisrael. For that reason it is important so to redefine the purpose of Biblical instruction that it will embrace the whole life of the Jew and render his Jewish group awareness itself a source of ethical guidance and inspiration in all his other relationships, including those to his non-Jewish environment. To arrive at such a formula for our purpose in teaching the Bible it is necessary to recall the part which the Bible has played in Jewish life throughout the ages.

The Bible has served, throughout the past, essentially as a means of giving continuity to the life of the Jewish people. It has made it possible for one hundred generations of that people to experience a sense of oneness, notwithstanding their wide divergence from one another and their separation in time and space. *Its legends, histories, laws, exhortations, reflections and prayers are motivated by three definite purposes: (1) to arouse in the Jew an awareness of God, (2) to fortify his collective consciousness and (3) to direct him to the proper way of life.*

Just how these purposes are achieved depends upon the spirit of the age, the intellectual climate and the most urgent social and spiritual needs of those who study and interpret the contents of the Bible. What constituted awareness of God in the first stages of Jewish history became largely irrelevant during the later stages, and what was regarded during the later stages as essential for the belief in God was not even suspected in the earlier stages. At the time that the legislation and the Prophetic oracles were first framed, no one could possibly have foreseen the problems with which the Jewish people would have to come to grips in subsequent eras. The ethical principles, exhortations and reflections, when first expressed, referred to a way of life in which none of the complex issues of later times could possibly have been anticipated.

2

THE DIFFERENT VERSIONS OF THE BIBLE

How then has it been possible for all of these various writings in the Bible to arouse and keep alive the awareness of God, to fortify the national consciousness and to serve as a guide to conduct over so many generations, amid all possible climes, and under so wide a range of varying circumstances? The answer is that *the Bible is not merely a text or collection of texts; it is what the interpreter derives from, or reads into, those texts.* The meaning of any passage in the Bible is not what the surface reading of it seems to convey, but what the interpreter reads out of, or into, it. The interpreter himself is not a scientific scholar interested in objective fact. What the scholar finds may at best be the raw material out of which the Bible was formed, but not the Bible itself. The interpreter, on the other hand, is a Jew who has, in common with the rest of his people, the threefold interest of having the Bible give him a keen awareness of God, a deepened consciousness of his people, and a passionate devotion to the right way of life. This is what the Jewish interpreters have always tried to find in the Bible. As a result of their efforts, we Jews are by this time in possession not of one version, but of four different versions of the Bible, and we are on the eve of evolving a fifth version.

The four versions of the Bible are the products, respectively, of the four different kinds of interpretation: *Peshat, Remez, Derush* and *Sōd.* A brief characterization of each type of interpretation will make clear wherein it gave rise to a different version of the Bible.

Peshat means literal interpretation; yet it would be incorrect to say that the ancients were always true to the literal meaning of the text, when they thought they were giving its *Peshat.* It is doubtful e.g. whether most of the statements which speak of God in human terms retained their literal significance, after they were incorporated into the Bible. The verse in Genesis, which speaks of God as having smelled the sweet savor of Noah's sacrifice,[9] or the oft-repeated phrase, "a sweet-smelling offering to the Lord," [10] may be a desiccated remains of an ancient way of speaking. A safe description of *Peshat* might, therefore, be the following: That which constituted the functional meaning of the text, or that meaning of it which formed the basis of action or belief, at the time it came to be part of the Bible.

Derush is not just any kind of interpretation that departs from the original or literal meaning of the text. As one of the four types of

Biblical interpretation, *Derush* refers only to those meanings which the *Tannaim* and *Amoraim* have read into the Bible, and which constitute the content of the *Midrashim* and the groundwork of the *Gemara* in the Talmud. The five years which, according to the *Mishna* in *Abot*, should be devoted to the study of the Scriptures, were to be spent in learning the *Derush* of the Bible. The term *"debē rav"* appended to one of those collections of Rabbinic interpretations betrays the early school environment in which the Bible was taught, in the light of *Derush*.

It is important to mention some of the main Rabbinic doctrines and interests that changed radically the original or literal meaning of the Bible text. The belief in the world to come, as the world in which alone man achieves salvation, transformed such simple statements as those which refer to life, or to long life, as a reward for obedience to God, into promises of reward in the world to come.[11] The dominant Rabbinic interest at that time was to give Biblical sanction to accepted norms, in civil and ritual law. We have, accordingly, the well-known reinterpretation of "eye for eye" as a money fine,[12] and of the threefold repetition of the ordinance forbidding the seething of the kid in its mother's milk, as the basis of all those practices which forbid the mixing of milk and meat diets.[13] When in the former years the child would be taught "Humesh with Rashi," he was introduced at once into the version of the Bible, which is the product of the Rabbinic method of interpretation, known as *Derush*. This was the version of the Bible which bulked largest in the Jewish consciousness, during the eighteen centuries of pre-modern times. The only exception to this was the *Song of Songs*, which will be dealt with in the next category.

A third version of the Bible, which is the least popular, is the product of *Remez*. *Remez* refers to metaphorical or figurative rendering of a text. As a method of interpretation, it is found even in those Rabbinic writings which are generally characterized as *Derush*. The interpretation of the *Song of Songs*, for example, as symbolic of the love that unites God and Israel, though part of Amoraic literature, properly belongs to *Remez*.

Remez refers to that perspective in Judaism which resulted from the impact of philosophic thought, whether Platonic or Aristotelian, on the Jewish tradition. The whole of Philo's exegesis has the effect of giving us an entirely different version of the Bible from that which either *Peshat* or *Derush* yields us. According to this version, the Bible presents, in symbolic form, teachings and values derived from Plato and the Stoics. Ibn Ezra's commentary on the *Song of Songs* and Isaac Arama's commentary *Akedat Yizhak* on the Pentateuch belong to the same genre of exposition as that of Philo. Maimonides and Albo read many philosophical ideas into the Bible, thereby transforming the character of whole sections of it.

The version of the Bible which was the product of the method of interpretation, known as *Remez*, reads like a treatise on subjects like the following: the good and evil inclination, the relation of philosophy to revelation, of human reason to human passion, of the spirit to the body and of the intellect to the feelings. That version includes, also, the discussion of such ethical themes as prudence, courage, humility and temperance. Under its influence Biblical characters, places, and events become embodiments of philosophic problems which are dealt with by Plato and Aristotle. One can understand why this interpretation of the Bible should have antagonized the strict traditionalists. They saw in it a danger to the authoritative or Rabbinic rendering. Abba Mari Don Astruc, the famous leader, in the beginning of the fourteenth century, of the opposition to the rationalism of the Maimonists, in his *Minhat Kenaot*, a letter addressed to the Talmudic scholars of France and Spain, accused the rationalists of reducing the entire section of the Torah from Genesis to Exodus to nothing but allegory.

Finally, we have the Bible of the mystics, which is the product of the method of interpretation known as *Sōd*. What the Torah is, according to Jewish mysticism, is summed up in a well-known passage in the *Zohar* [14] which reads as follows: "Woe to the man who says that the Torah intends to relate to ordinary stories and everyday affairs. If that were the case, it would be possible even nowadays to compose a Torah dealing with everyday affairs, a Torah that could be of greater excellence than the one we have. Even the worldly princes would then seem to possess books of greater worth than the Torah. We could use those books as a model and compose a worldly Torah. The truth is that all the matters dealt with in the Torah are of a supernal character and contain sublime mysteries."

To the Jewish mystics, the Torah was in all literalness the very instrument wherewith God had created the universe. Hence the author [15] of the *Zohar* reasons that, since the angels in descending to the earth put on earthly garments, as otherwise they could neither stay in the world nor could the world endure them, "the Torah which created all the worlds and which sustains them," must certainly have had to put on earthly garments. "The stories of the Torah are only her outer garments, and whoever looks upon that garment as being the Torah itself, woe to that man—such a man will have no portion in the next world . . . Stupid people see only the garment, the mere narratives. Those who are wise envisage the body. But the really wise, can penetrate to the soul, the root principle of all, namely the real Torah."

We can perhaps best appreciate the perspective on life, which the Bible opened up to the Jewish mystics, if we recall that they were, with only few exceptions, not given merely to passive contemplation. They were, inherently, men of action. They believed that a knowledge of the various combinations and permutations of the words of sacred Scriptures would enable them to gain power over the forces of life. Moreover, as *Jewish* mystics, their main purpose in striving to attain such power was to be able to redeem Israel from exile. To be worthy of wielding such power, they assumed that they had no discipline themselves in all of the *mitzvot*, both ethical and ritualistic. With purposes such as these to be achieved through the study of the sacred writings, the thought-world which those writings opened up could not but be radically different from the thought-world which emerged from any of the other three methods of interpretation described above.

The diversity among the thought-worlds of the four different versions of the Bible is only half the story. The other half of the story is that there was something to these four versions of the Bible which made them one, besides the mere fact that the same text and language underlay them all. After all, these versions of the Bible cannot but be the product of human nature, as it functioned in the Jewish people. *Each version represents the moral and spiritual values which the Jewish people evolved, in response to the particular environment in which it found itself.*

The Jewish people, however, had lived for a long time in a world which is not reflected in any one of these four versions. Before any of them arose, the Jewish people had already been in existence for nearly a thousand years. That period may be roughly placed between 1600 and 600 B.C.E. It was then that the Jews produced the greater part of the writings contained in the Bible. Those writings had not yet been canonized. At that time those writings were only a kind of proto-Bible. That is the Bible which is being reconstituted by means of modern Biblical scholarship. Reflecting as it does the first thousand years of Israel's career, this proto-Bible must be included at some point in the educational curriculum. Unfortunately, in a good many instances, Biblical scholarship, especially as it was fostered in Germany, was motivated by anti-Jewish prejudice and the desire to defame the Jewish people. That fact justifies the late Solomon Schechter's quip that Higher Criticism was a form of Higher anti-Semitism. It would be a fatal mistake, however, to allow this quip to obscure the new vistas that Biblical scholarship has opened up in our understanding of the first period of Israel's history.

The proto-Bible reflects the period of spiritual gestation, when the tendencies, attitudes and habits which later became part of the Jewish consciousness were taking shape. During that period the empires of the Nile and the Euphrates were at the zenith of their power, and Israel found itself, together with numerous other peoples, competing for a place on the bridge between those empires. Tribal and natural deities, surrounded by hosts of all manner of spirits and angels and demons, then jostled one another in the imaginations of men. From a study of the proto-Bible, we begin to realize how Israel finally emerged from that medley of peoples and religions as a highly self-conscious nation, with a clear perspective and well knit life-pattern that took into account the whole of the then-known world. In a sense, that outcome was a far greater miracle than any recorded in the Bible itself.

3

THE AIMS OF BIBLE TEACHING IN OUR DAY

The main emphasis, however, when the Bible is taught nowadays must be on what it should mean to us, in view of the elements in our environment which constitute a serious challenge to Jewish life. Those elements are: modern nationalism, modern scientism and the acceptance of force as the final arbiter in human affairs. Each of these three modern developments is a menace to the existence of the Jewish people. In its struggle for survival, it has to reckon with all of them. One of the principal means at its command is the Bible. It is the duty of the Jewish teacher so to interpret the Bible as to enable the child, when he grows up, to withstand the impact of these three tendencies upon his life as a Jew in the modern world. In order that this interpretation may yield the kind of response to the present environment which will give the Jew the necessary courage and incentive to live as a Jew, and the necessary guidance for making the best use of his life, it is important to have a clear idea wherein each of the three elements menaces Jewish life.

The essence of modern nationalism is that a state is held together not by common blood or a common past, but by the present economic and political interests that grow out of the physical propinquity of its citizens. These interests demand the subordination of all trans-state interests of any group within the state to the economic and political interests of the state. This is taken to imply that, with the acceptance of civic rights, the Jews have not only renounced the hope to become a nation once again, but have also disbanded as a corporate entity. They must, accordingly, look to absorption by the majority population as their destiny.

The Jews' response to these implications of modern nationalism must necessarily be—if they are to remain Jews—that they refuse to disband as a people. The main token of that refusal is the reassertion of their historic claim to Eretz Yisrael as their national home. They are ready to back that claim with the requisite toil and sacrifice. But even those of us who cannot, or do not wish to, settle in Eretz Yisrael need it as a bond to unite us with the rest of Jewry throughout the world. We cannot forego that unity, without foregoing all that gives us human dignity, self-confidence and a purpose in life. It thus spells for us the very source of all religious values. Remove that unity and sense of Jewish peoplehood, and those values are dried up for us at the very source. No nation that claims to be democratic and to respect religious freedom should seek to undermine our peoplehood.

To be able to affirm our peoplehood in that spirit, we have to become once again Bible-conscious. To derive from the Bible moral support for our status as a people, we do not have to strain the sense of the Biblical writings, or read anything into them that is unwarranted by any of the interpretations given to them in the past. But if we want the Bible to yield us that moral support, we must abandon the approach that has been in vogue since the days of Mendelssohn, and to some extent return to the traditional approach. Thus, instead of being influenced by literary considerations, in evaluating the importance of the different books of the Bible, we should be guided by evaluations which spring from our fundamental needs.

The study of the Bible should be correlated with the two most outstanding facts about the Bible, which indicate how the Jewish people has evaluated its different parts and still does. One fact is that the Pentateuch has been the focus of attention and interpretation to an incomparably greater degree than the other books of the Bible; the other is, that the main Biblical reading at public services is always taken from the Pentateuch. These are not chance preferences. They testify to the far greater significance which the Pentateuch has for us Jews, as a means of affirming, and confirming, our peoplehood than have the other books of the Bible.

Since the basic purpose in teaching the Bible is to give the pupil an awareness of the reality of his people, it is necessary to reinstate the primacy of the Pentateuch in the Bible-study curriculum. The three aspects of the Pentateuch that should be reckoned with from the standpoint of that purpose are: the narrative, the legal and the one which stresses the significance of Eretz Yisrael. Two of the aspects, the legal and the one that has to do with Eretz Yisrael, should be utilized as a means of developing in the mind of the pupil a sense of the reality of Israel, and the narrative, a consciousness of his destiny as a member of the Jewish people.

A way must be found whereby both of these objectives—consciousness of Israel's reality and of her destiny—can be liberated from the acceptance of the narratives as historic fact, or of the laws as supernaturally revealed, and therefore as eternally binding. This liberation should be effected, while the pupil is undergoing his Jewish training. Otherwise, he is likely to repudiate the facts of Israel's reality and destiny, as soon as he discovers that the narratives are largely non-historical or fictional, and that Israel's ancient laws could not have originated as described in the Torah.

Yet neither the reality nor the destiny of the Jewish people can have any meaning, unless they are associated with Eretz Yisrael. So large does that land loom in the Torah that it is, indeed, appropriate to regard the Torah as a legal document, whereby the God of history has deeded the Land to the Jewish people. It would not at all be amiss, if the entire Torah material that bears on Eretz Yisrael were interpreted from the point of view of Israel's relation to its Land. Surely in our day, when the reclamation of Eretz Yisrael as our national home is the one purpose that spells the revival of the spirit of Israel, teaching the Torah from that point of view would knit that land with contemporary Jewish life.

The historical books of the Bible should be taught as carrying forward the main themes of the Torah, which deal with Israel's destiny. There the conditional character of Israel's hold on the Land is especially highlighted. Attention should be focused on Israel's long struggle for survival against external and internal forces of destruction. Only at the end of that struggle did Israel achieve that profound understanding of what God expected of man which rendered its religion and way of life of universal significance. The Prophetic books reveal the inner conflict. They define the main issues about which that conflict raged: idolatry, lack of confidence in the God of Israel, exploitation of the weak by the strong and self-indulgence. From the standpoint of national self-awareness, not the Prophetic books as such, but the fact of their having been canonized, and given the status akin to that of Torah, has set the standard for national self-scrutiny and self-criticism. That standard is of universal import. It will have to be adopted ultimately not only by individuals but by nations, if mankind is to survive.

A far less serious, but none the less real, menace to Jewish life than modern nationalism is modern scientism. Whereas modern nationalism threatens the Jewish people from without, the latter threatens Judaism from within. Insofar as Judaism is identified with the Jewish tradition, which assumes that God is not only the prime mover of the universe, but that He providentially wills everything that happens, it is challenged by modern scientism. For modern scientism regards all events as capable of being accounted for by the events which immediately precede them, irrespective of their significance for human life. This expresses the entire problem of religion. Without some affirmative attitude toward religion, it is impossible to teach the Bible as other than ancient literature and archeology.

It may not be possible to suggest any one affirmative idea of God that nowadays would be universally acceptable. But it is possible to indicate the difference which a genuine and active belief in God can, and frequently does, make in people's lives. It is to that difference that any instruction, which is intended to render the Bible significant in our lives, must be related. That difference expresses itself, among other things, as: holiness, humility, gratitude and faith.

The teacher's task consists, accordingly, in utilizing the Biblical content to imbue the pupil with the spirit of holiness, humility, gratitude and faith. He could not very well carry out that task efficiently, without communicating to the pupil a vivid sense of the reality of God. In what follows we shall attempt to give some examples of how these spiritual attitudes are the very soul of Biblical teaching, and how they are integrally related to what the name of God has always meant to those whose religion is more than skin deep:

(a) Holiness as a state of mind, or spiritual attitude, is awareness of being related or dedicated to that which renders life significant and saves it from frustration. Whatever, therefore, is related or dedicated to God is holy, in that it calls forth that awareness. Together with the awareness of the reality of the Jewish people, the Bible emphasizes awareness of being dedicated to God, as the state of mind which that people is expected to foster. That is the purpose given in the Torah for the entire system of ritual observances, including the Sabbath, the festivals, the sacrificial cult, the sanctuary, and the dietary laws, as well as for the entire gamut of moral laws. The commandment "Ye shall be unto me a kingdom of priests and a holy nation" [16] reflects that sense of national dedication to God which for intensity is without parallel in human history. It may not be possible to subscribe to the supernatural origin of that commandment, or to its implication that Israel alone was chosen by God to be His people. But the high degree of spiritual self-awareness, on the part of a whole people, that it should relate its entire life to God as the Power that enables it to be and do its best is an unquestionable and historic fact. That fact it was which, during the period of our Second Commonwealth, gave rise to Pharisaic Judaism, or the Judaism of tradition.

(b) The humility which has God as its point of reference, and which should be utilized to give vivid reality to the God experience is a far deeper and more inclusive character trait than is humility toward our fellow-men. Unlike the attitude of holiness which is illustrated in various situations through narrative, laws and exhortations, the humility which man must experience as part of his awareness of God is seldom the direct theme in any of the Biblical subject-matter. We learn how important is this type of humility through the repeated emphasis in the Bible on the sin of pride. That sin is illustrated in the Bible as frequently as is the virtue of holiness. The sin of pride consists in that arrogant self-sufficiency which leads man to deny his dependence on, and submission to, a higher power than himself. He who is guilty of that sinful attitude expresses it by defying all law. He plays the god, and he is a law unto himself. For a time he may pursue his evil course and achieve his vaulting ambition, but in the end his power is broken, and he is thrust from his high pedestal.

That is the principle in the light of which the great Biblical Prophets read the events in the life of their own people as well as those in the life of the great and small nations within the orbit of their experience. It is also the principle in the light of which the Torah reads the fate that befell Pharaoh, the oppressor of the Israelites. The Torah warns the Israelites themselves of that sin. In fact, the very opening story of Adam, who disobeys God, seems to point to arrogant self-sufficiency as the principal cause of all human suffering. The one book of the Bible, where religious humility, in its positive form, finds expression, is Psalms. There the *"rasha,"* the incarnation of the sin of pride, has his foil in the *"anav,"* the pious, law-abiding Israelite who is humbled by his awareness of God's transcendent majesty.

(c) Gratitude, which is the appreciation of the blessings we enjoy, has its point of reference in God. That means that we are aware of being indebted for all those blessings to the entire life process. Whatever in religion has to do with worship is intended to express and to foster the feeling of gratitude. The entire sacrificial cult, the motivating purpose of which was to convey awareness of communion with God, fostered gratitude. All songs in praise of God that are contained in the Pentateuch, the historical works and the Prophetic writings, and almost the entire collection of Psalms, are evocations of pious gratitude. Of all the states of mind which come near to experiencing vividly the reality of God, a feeling of gratitude with its overtones of serenity and dependence on a transcendent source of power is perhaps the one which most approximates that experience. Since gratitude is so closely associated with worship, everything in the Bible that has anything to do with worship, whether in the form of narrative or of legal and ethical prescription, should be carefully studied.

(d) Finally, we have the attitude of faith, which is a direct affirmation of a transcendent Power that impels and sustains man in his striving for self-fulfillment. The occasions for the exercise of faith are those in which circumstances seem to negate the existence of such a Power. When misfortune befalls us, when we suffer in our own persons or witness the sufferings of others, life tends to become meaningless, and we are apt to fall into despair. That is the time for the evocation of the courage to carry on. To the extent that we succeed in evoking such courage within ourselves, we have a direct experience of the transcendent Power which we identify as God. The outstanding example which the Bible gives of faith is the character and conduct of Abraham.

Fear and misgiving generally get the better of us, as soon as our plans go awry or our nerves are tormented by pain. The stories of the

The Future of the American Jew

Israelites in the Wilderness are intended, in the main, to dramatize what happens to people who, at the slightest encounter with trouble and difficulty, lose heart and relapse into the fear-ridden existence out of which they showed promise of emerging. Our ancestors worshipped the Golden Calf; they mutinied and demanded to be returned to Egypt and to their previous state of slavery, when they heard the intimidating report of spies; hunger and thirst rendered them oblivious of the struggle for freedom. Thus our people started its career with a lack of that confidence in God which is essential to the good life as well as to great achievement.

This lack of confidence in God haunts Israel's steps throughout the era of the First Temple. It led them to enter into entangling alliances with the neighboring nations and into political intrigues which involved them in conflict with either one or the other empire, then contending for supremacy. How the faithful leaders, the true Prophets, sought vainly to dissuade them from these fear-dictated policies is unfolded in the historical and Prophetic books of the Bible.

For the articulation of faith in God, from the standpoint of the individual, we can turn to the Psalms and Job. In the Psalms, the faith is reflected in the ability to experience God's presence, despite suffering, and to hold on to righteousness and piety, amid the mockery and taunts of the godless. In Job, we have the portrayal of faith's inner struggle that often goes on in the souls of the most trusting and loyal servants of God, when misfortunes overtake them, or when they see disaster overwhelm good people who could never have sinned so grievously as to deserve it.

It is quite evident that a person in whose character there is no place for holiness, humility, gratitude and faith is ill equipped to play his part in life as a full-fledged human being. While there is nothing in naturalism, properly understood, to warrant the negation of these values, there is nothing in naturalism to recommend them. Such is the fascination which naturalism exercises on most minds that whatever it fails to recommend is not deemed worth bothering with. This is how secondary and higher education in our day with its emphasis on that narrow interpretation of naturalism known as "scientism" is apt to produce the universe of thought in which those spiritual values have no place. It has been well said that "ours is a time bullied by science, as man never was." The imponderables which cannot be weighed or measured are denied or ignored. There is no better way of making place for them than by means of the Bible. If we use it as a medium through which to react against the prevailing world-outlook, we shall find ourselves giving the Bible an interpretation in which something of every one of the previous classic interpretations would come to life again. This is the case, because in every one of those versions of the Bible, the values of holiness, humility, gratitude and faith are part of the thought-pattern concerning God.

A third challenge to the survival of the Jewish people and Judaism is the characteristic tendency in the contemporary way of life to accept force as the final arbiter in human affairs. It may not be normal for a people to have to justify its existence by proving that it is making a contribution to the sum of human values, whether economic, ethical or artistic. But the Jewish people is for the most part a "lackland" people. Therefore, it is in the abnormal position of having to find a rationale for putting up a bitter struggle for its existence. That rationale can only be the certainty that there is something about its way of life worth struggling for. To set forth that way of life with its main implications, and to indicate wherein the alternative to it (which has gained great vogue in recent years) spells the destruction of mankind, should be the culminating purpose of instruction in the Bible.

The way of life to which we Jews are committed as a people, and the only one that gives any meaning to our struggle for existence, is summed up in the well-known verse in Zechariah: "Not by strength nor by might, but by my spirit, saith the Lord." [17] A similar summary is to be found in the less well known verse: "By strength will no man prevail." [18] The history of human civilization, of man's effort to bring his biological instincts under the control and guidance of purposes that transcend them, attests to the truth of that teaching. All peoples, insofar as they have achieved aught of *human* worth, have reckoned with, and contributed to, the power wielded by the demands of justice and lovingkindness in human relations. To that extent justice and lovingkindness play an important role in the civilizations of all peoples.

The Bible testifies to the fact that the Jewish people accorded to justice and lovingkindness, as the final arbiters of human destiny, so devout an homage as to deem them divine, and to regard them as the root of all that God, the creator of the universe, demands of man. "What doth the Lord, thy God ask of thee, but to do justice and to love kindness?" [19] By dint of this evaluation of the power of the spirit in human life as compared with that of brute force, Judaism saved Western mankind, at a most crucial point in its career, from complete moral disintegration. Incorporated into Christianity, this faith in the power of the spirit, despite its having been overlaid with a mass of irrelevant doctrine and ritual, has exercised a highly civilizing influence on the barbarian hordes that later developed into the nations of Europe.

In recent years, as a result of the inexhaustible sources of physical power opened up by modern technology, the struggle for access to that power has attained such unprecedented magnitude and bitterness as to eclipse all considerations of justice and lovingkindness. They are ceasing to receive even the lip service which was rendered them formerly. Especially in human relations which involve whole classes or peoples, the tendency is for the contending interests to flaunt their selfish purposes in all their brutal nakedness. To give this tendency the show of reason, which the human spirit cannot entirely repudiate, it is made to appear plausible with the aid of naturalism.

Having learned from Darwin that in the animal world the process of natural selection favors the strong and the cunning, Nietzsche leaped to the conclusion, which he elaborated in flaming prose, that human beings, too, must permit that process to work itself out in the life of society. His "transvaluation of values" was a denunciation of the Jewish tradition which was adopted by Christianity, as hampering the process of natural selection. He would have his Zarathustra say, "Not by spirit, but by strength and might." Karl Marx, likewise influenced by the naturalistic trends of thought, denied, at least theoretically, all intrinsic objectivity to ethical ideals, and treated them merely as reflections of the struggle for economic advantage and power.

Nietzsche's interpretation of human life gave the initial impulse to the movement that culminated in fascism and nazism. Karl Marx gave the impulse to the movement that culminated in communism. Both of these movements are hostile to the Jewish way of life. That by the same token they are also hostile to the democratic way of life points to some basic principle as common to both Judaism and democracy. That principle can be no other than the negation of brute force as the decisive factor in all relations between individuals and groups. Modern democracy arose with the recognition of justice as an ultimate imperative. It has yet a long way to go before it will be able to translate that assumption into specific economic and political policy. In the course of its struggle to achieve its goal, it has emancipated the Jews from medieval bondage. *Within the frame of democracy, we Jews are free to articulate with new clarity and vigor the very ideals most needed to strengthen it. This is our opportunity. The first and indispensable step in availing ourselves of that opportunity is to imbue the consciousness of our children with the Jewish way of life as stressed in the Bible.*

In most human relations there is generally greater power on the one side than on the other. The greater power may be due to greater physical strength, cunning, possession of instruments of power, or social position. The one who has less power in any one of these respects is at a disadvantage, because of the natural temptation which prompts the one who has more power to exploit or oppress him. To have the stronger resist that temptation, and to have him treat the weaker in such a way as not to deprive him even of the little power that he possesses, is the underlying purpose of all ethics and just law; that is *justice* or *righteousness*, which, in the parlance of our Sages was known as "within the line of law." To go further and make provision that the weak shall have this power augmented, that is *lovingkindness*. These principles run through every passage in the Bible that has either a direct or indirect bearing on the way of life that God expects a man to pursue in all his dealings and relationships with his fellow-men.

Israel's commitment to the way of life which demands the subordination of force to considerations of justice and lovingkindness became the basis of the Patriarchal stories, with their proto-history, and of the epic of Israel's redemption from Egypt. We are not reckoning here with historical fact, but with the content of the Jewish consciousness. In that consciousness, the cycle of Patriarchal stories grew out of the circumstance that the Canaanites or Amorites could not be dispossessed of their land, until the measure of sin and moral corruption was full. That the Israelites were to invade and conquer Canaan merely because they happened to be the stronger people was unthinkable. The conquest is, therefore, ascribed to the corrupt life the natives are assumed to have lived.[20]

From the vantage point of what we now know about the human mind, we may deem this rationale to justify the conquest of Canaan a very flimsy excuse for what was after all the exercise of naked force. But the very fact that this rationale gave rise to an elaborate series of Patriarchal episodes reflects a very strong feeling against sheer conquest. However unwarranted the rationale may be in itself, the conclusion that was drawn from it does much to make up for its lack of warrant. That conclusion was that the land itself was given to Israel only conditionally. The condition was that its people must not commit the sins on account of which the aborigines had been dispossessed of their land.

Yet even this commitment is rendered infinitely more binding by the epic of the redemption from Egypt. The redemption did two things for our ancestors. It formed them into a nation, and it united them to God, the Creator of the universe. That redemption is pictured in the Torah as a struggle waged by the God of Israel against Pharaoh, who plays the god, and who, taking the law in his own hand, plans to destroy a weak and helpless people. In this he is abetted by his counsellors and the entire Egyptian people. First he enslaves the Israelites and later tries to annihilate them. The God of Israel thwarts him, and brings all his plans to naught.

In the Song of the Red Sea, we have a vivid portrayal of the uneven struggle of a mighty tyrant against a helpless horde of slaves. The scales are reversed when the God of justice fights on the side of the slaves. Hence time and again the Torah reminds us of how we Jews ought to shape our lives, by reason of our having been redeemed from Egypt. Since we owe our birth as a people to events which led to the overthrow of a tyrant and an oppressor, we cannot continue as a people, unless we eliminate from our own lives all exploitation and oppression of the weak by the strong.

As background to Israel's commitment to the way of life based on *justice and lovingkindness*, the Torah describes the condition of mankind before Israel came on the scene. In Cain's murdering Abel we have the translation, into realistic terms, of what the story of Adam's disobedience is intended to convey in the language of metaphor. Cain and his descendants are pictured as building up urban civilization in what, time and again, has proved to be the pattern of exploitation, luxury and bloodshed. Then the Flood came as a sequel to such widespread corruption that God is said to have repented of having created man at all. Thus the outstanding fact in human life which, according to the Torah, renders the very worthwhileness of humanity questionable, is its tendency to commit violence. "And the earth was filled with violence. And God saw the earth and behold it was corrupt, for all flesh have corrupted their way upon the earth."

Violence is thus clearly indicated as a perversion of what should be man's way of life. That the generation after the Flood reverted to the same tendency is pointed out by means of the myth concerning the city of Babel, which figured in the minds of the ancients as the symbol of tyranny and oppression. All this, from the standpoint of the ancient world-outlook as developed in the Torah, made it necessary for God to select Abraham for the founding of a nation that would "keep the way of the Lord to do justice and righteousness." [21]

Whether the Prophets antedated or followed the Torah of tradition, there can be no question that, by the time they came on the scene, all Israel had assumed that they were covenanted to God by means of Torah, or the way of life based on justice and lovingkindness. Otherwise there would be no point to Isaiah's inveighing against Israel for having forgotten or rejected God's Torah.[22] The same is, of course, true of Jeremiah and Ezekiel.[23] The covenant between God and Israel, which was taken for granted by the Prophets and the people, consisted in Israel's obligation to conform to the Torah of God, and in God's binding Himself to maintain and protect Israel. When Israel does not live up to its obligations, it transgresses that covenant. Thus Hosea upbraids Israel "because they transgressed My covenant and rebelled against My Torah." [24]

We look in vain among the Prophetic writings for specific definitions of the ethical principles of God's Torah. Those writings should not be treated as expositions of ethics or morals, nor even as mere exhortations to ethical living. They are the passionate outcries of far-seeing divinely inspired men, who read their people's fate in the light of a newly visioned truth, namely, *that for a people to survive it must make righteousness instead of force the basis of all its actions.* So novel was that method of social prognosis that to this day very few grasp its significance or its far-reaching implications. Yet, upon its final acceptance by the generality of men depend the peace and progress of mankind.

What the Torah, or the Jewish way of life, meant to the individual Jew, in addition to what it meant to him as a member of Israel, is the theme of the numerous passages in Psalms, especially the 118th chapter. There we get an insight into what the Torah came to mean, when its text was accorded that concentration and devotion which only writings believed to have come directly from God could receive. There we get a description of the ecstatic joy which the Torah evoked from the heart of the Jew, confident as he was that it set forth the only way whereby man could achieve his destiny, and that it had come from the Author of all life and goodness. For the Jews to pass from that conception of the Torah to the one which forms the subject matter of the treatise *Abot,* where it is described as "a desirable instrument by which the world was created," [25] they had first to be reduced to a state in which they had little to look forward to in this world. Having learned to center all their hopes on the hereafter, the Torah came to be the means for securing the bliss which they associated with that hereafter.

The main purpose in teaching the Bible to our children should be to fortify their Jewish consciousness and to give it ethical and spiritual content. With that purpose in view, it is necessary to realize that the Bible itself has served, and will continue to serve, not as a static code applicable to all conditions of life, but as a dynamic guide adaptable to different climates of belief and practice. Traditional Judaism has thus evolved four different versions of the Bible. For our day there is much in all of these versions that will always be of profound interest and of vital relevance.

To render the Bible significant for our day, we have to take into account, in the first place, the proto-Bible which is being recovered through Biblical scholarship. Even more important is it to evolve an interpretation of it which will reckon with the three main sources of challenge to Jewish life and Judaism: modern nationalism, modern scientism and the transvaluation of all moral and spiritual values. These very challenges are helping us discover implied values and meanings in the Bible, which will total up to a new or fifth version of the Bible. Every word in the Bible, studied in the light of what we realize as concerning the people of Israel, the reality of God and the Jewish way of life, is giving the Bible new and inspiring meaning. To a generation raised on that kind of teaching, the question: "Why remain Jews?" would not even occur.

CHAPTER TWENTY-FOUR

HOW TO VITALIZE ADULT JEWISH STUDY

1

STUDY TO BE MOTIVATED BY NEED
OF JEWISH ORIENTATION

Our main concern in popularizing adult Jewish study should be to make it relevant and vital to present realities. We cannot create a demand for Jewish knowledge, unless we are prepared to help the Jew find some meaning in the events in which he plays a part, and to cope with the problems that beset him as a Jew. Some of us may be so conditioned as to find delight in learning anything that has to do with Jewish life, past or present, near or remote. But we should not forget that most Jews are nowadays without any cultural Jewish background. They can be roused by a harangue on anti-Semitism. But if we expect them to devote some time each week to studies that have to do with normal Jewish living and thinking, they must be convinced that those studies will help them to make the most out of their own lives as human beings; otherwise they are bound to walk out on us, no matter how much machinery of registration, credits and certificates we devise.

We shall be more likely to concern ourselves with the task of vitalizing adult Jewish studies, if we realize that they can no longer be motivated by the needs that motivated them in the past. Our purpose should not be to induce the laity to become—in Dr. Schechter's phrase—"studying engines." They who lack a sense of history assume that the indifference on the part of Jews to Jewish learning is due to the numerous distractions in present day life which the contemporary Jew, being so much weaker-willed than his ancestors, is unable to overcome. This assumption is based on a wrong diagnosis of the situation, and is bound to stand in the way of curative treatment.

The truth is that *the entire scale of values by which the Jew lived in the past has been so completely upset, as a result of his being integrated into the civic life of non-Jewish nations that it is nothing less than absurd to measure Jewish needs and desires of today by the standards of the past.* We must recall that throughout the centuries, when Jews lived a segregated life, they had to depend entirely upon their own cultural resources to avoid the danger of deteriorating into an illiterate horde, or degenerating into wandering bands like the gypsies.

469

The study of Torah gave the Jew literacy which he could not obtain elsewhere. It gave him social status in his own group, and it afforded him religious experience which gave him an outlet for self-expression.

These functions of Jewish learning have become largely irrelevant. Integration of the Jews into the general population has rendered these advantages of Torah study no longer indispensable. *The educational system of the state, and the vast chain of cultural opportunities of which the Jew either must or may avail himself, supply him with literacy, with the necessary knowledge qualifications for social status, and with occasions for such self-expression as he is capable of.* Undoubtedly, there is still enough left of the momentum which was accumulated during the centuries of segregation to impel some Jews to feel a need for Jewish study, regardless of the fact that it is no longer related to their basic needs as human beings. But it is a waning momentum, and should not be depended on to supply the motivation necessary to give permanence and assure growth to the movement for adult Jewish study.

What then shall we rely upon to furnish the incentive to the acquisition of Jewish knowledge? The more frankly and sympathetically we learn to deal with the inner conflicts which go on in the soul of every Jew, and the more eager and determined we are to utilize Jewish study as a means of helping the Jew himself to resolve them, the more likely are we to render Jewish knowledge-content relevant to the actual needs of our people. Jews are at present obsessed with doubts and questionings concerning the worthwhileness of persisting as a distinct and identifiable group. They question the truth of the facts upon which that worthwhileness has hitherto been based. They find it impossible to retain many traditional practices which have hitherto been regarded as essential to Jewish life. They are troubled on account of not being able to harmonize the traditional conception of God with the rest of their experience. This is especially the case with the men and women who are mentally awake and morally sensitive, and who exercise an influence over their fellows. These are the people whom we can ill afford to lose.

If we hope to retain the loyalty of thoughtful Jews and to stir them into participation in Jewish life, we must not treat their inner conflicts as due merely to their ignorance of Jewish history and traditions. It is due rather to their inability to orient themselves, as Jews, to the world of today. *This need for a modern orientation should be utilized as the main incentive to adult Jewish study.* The effort to overcome the ignorance of the past should constitute only the preparatory step in adult Jewish study, and only a means to the better understanding of the present. Our main objective, however, must be to train the student to think rather than merely to know or to remember, and to direct that thinking to the very difficulties he encounters as a Jew.

2

HOW TO DO OUR OWN THINKING

The fundamental purpose of Jewish study must be to stimulate the Jew's will to live as a Jew. It is known that the resolution of inner conflicts in general depends essentially not upon the psychiatrist but upon the patient himself. Likewise the resolution of inner conflicts pertaining to Jewish life depends upon our own initiative and effort. No amount of outside stimulus by itself can avail. The therapeutic treatment, in the case of any inner conflict, can at best only remove the hindrances from the sufferer's will that prevent it from coming to grips with the difficulties responsible for his affliction. But unless the will is itself roused into action, the patient is as badly off as ever. The same is true of the complexes from which the majority of thinking Jews suffer. What our men and women need is the kind of Jewish knowledge and information that will impel them to take hold of the very problems which beset them as Jews, and proceed to think and act with a view to solving them.

The chances of Jewish survival are bound to be very much reduced, if we adopt the attitude voiced by some of our leaders who object to being a problem. Our only salvation lies in having all of our people, lay and professional alike, realize not only that Jewish life is beset with problems, but that the only way to save it from destruction is by learning to grasp the true nature of those problems and to cope with them effectively.

If, therefore, we wish our endeavors in behalf of adult study to be productive of permanent results and to contribute to Jewish survival and growth, we must avoid as far as possible the oracular approach which ignores challenges, questions, and alternative solutions. We should cultivate instead the problem approach. We should take the student into our confidence, and make him aware that we are all engaged in a common search after a way of Jewish life that shall elicit from us the best we can be, and that shall enable us to bear the worst that can befall us.

The subject matter of Jewish study should be of such a character and so organized and presented as to dispel from the minds of those who engage in it the notion that they are merely going back to school, where they can make up for their failure to have obtained certain worthwhile information. This is not said in deprecation of the student attitude, or of academic atmosphere, in relation to Jewish study. This is intended only to discourage the attitude of passivity. Alert people do not expect to have information handed out in ready-made packages. After having attended certain prescribed courses, they should not entertain the feeling of having gotten through once and for all with some necessary chore. Studies pursued in that spirit will have at best the limited value of an additional ritual, which may for a time fill a void in the lives of people with something of the student in their make up. But they will leave untouched the men and the women of keen mentality, who are at present apathetic to Jewish life, and whose powers of leadership and influence must be wooed, if Jewish life is to emerge from its present abnormal state. The only way to woo them is to present the study of Jewish subject matter as an occasion for them to bring their best thought, devotion and energy to the solution of the inner problems that beset our people. Thus we shall succeed at last in having Judaism the vital concern not only of Jewish functionaries, but also of the laity. The most intelligent, high-minded and forward-looking element in Jewry will then take over its share of the responsibility for rendering Judaism livable and creative.

For the selection and presentation of Jewish subject-matter it is necessary to realize that all maladjustments in contemporary Jewish life may be classified into three categories: (1) those that arise from our uncertain status as a group, both in relation to other groups and to the individual; (2) those that are due to the lack of a clearly formulated modern Jewish way of life; and (3) those that stem from the lack of a type of worship and ritual practice that would symbolize and express a tenable conception of God.

3

TO SEE RELATION OF PAST TO PRESENT

With that awareness in mind, *our initial task should be to acquaint the student with the entire evolution of Jewish life and belief until the turning point in Jewish history, when Jews began to have civic rights, and when all those maladjustments began to manifest themselves.* One of the main purposes in giving that information should be to impress upon the student that his people was until comparatively recent times a normal people, despite its dispersion. It was a normal people, in the sense that the men and women in it regarded their affiliation with it as an asset and a privilege, and had no suppressed desires to escape from it, or to see it liquidated. The Jewish past, with its vicissitudes, with its developing beliefs and practices, with its leaders, sages and saints, should be presented, however, as something which was integrally related to a social, cultural and political setting which no longer exists.

The knowledge of the past is indispensable, for there can be no meaning to the present without it. But we must not make the mistake of investing the historical with the sanctity of the eternal. Such an attitude would only hamper us in our efforts to build a Jewish future. The sharply etched pattern of practice and faith, by which our forebears lived, stands out in sharp contrast with the amorphousness of present day Judaism. We are tempted to set up that pattern as the norm of Jewish life. That evaluation of the past will only generate in us a nostalgia which is often an escape from the urgent need to grapple with present difficulties.

The student should be guided in his study of pre-modern Jewish life so that he will discover for himself the three main factors that rendered that life centripetal in contrast with the dominant centrifugal character of present day Jewish life: 1) the nature of Jewish solidarity in the past, and the significance it had for our forebears; 2) the traditional Jewish way of life, and the reason it was regarded of supreme excellence; 3) the prevailing conception of God, and its relation to the contemporaneous world outlook.

Furthermore, if the presentation of the past is to function as a means of qualifying the student to deal more effectively with the present, it is important to emphasize the dynamic and developmental aspect of those three factors. The Jewish mind must become accustomed to the idea of their having undergone radical changes even in pre-modern times. Thanks to those changes, Jewish life was enabled to retain its centripetal character, and was prevented from disintegrating.

We are now on the threshold of a new era in Judaism.[1] These same factors will have to undergo changes in their significance and application. Due to the infinitely increased tempo of modern living as compared with that of the past, changes will now have to be made deliberately and planfully, if Jewish life is not to get entirely out of hand. This is why we have to resort to the unprecedented procedure of deliberate readjustment and change, instead of permitting the needed changes to come about haphazardly, if at all.

4

TO PARTICIPATE IN JEWISH LIFE

If the changes, however, are to result in the strengthening of the centripetal tendencies in Jewish life, they must come about through the democratic participation of an informed laity interested in the conservation and development of that life. The purpose of all adult Jewish study should not be merely to foster Jewish *literacy*, not merely to learn about Judaism and the Jewish people. It should be to afford the Jew opportunity for Jewish *experience*. This can come about nowadays only through the Jew's direct participation in the three-fold task of: (1) achieving the kind of Jewish solidarity which will overcome the centrifugal tendencies in Jewish life, and which is at the same time compatible with unhampered integration of the Jew into the body politic of the state; (2) formulating a way of life which, when put into effect, is likely to elicit the best in the Jew; and (3) developing a conception of God that shall enable the Jew to have the thrill of religious experience.

What participation in the foregoing tasks must mean, from the standpoint of the kind of subject-matter that ought to be presented in adult Jewish study courses, and of the spirit in which it ought to be approached, will now be indicated.

Studies dealing with the problem of Jewish solidarity would have to open the eyes of the Jew to the anomalous situation in which he finds himself at present, because he belongs to a group which cannot tell him in unequivocal fashion just what kind of a group it is. In contrast with the unanimity which existed among Jews and Gentiles in pre-modern times concerning the societal character of the Jews, there is at present a wide range of diversity of opinion as to what kind of a group the Jews constitute in relation to the rest of the world. In pre-modern times the Jews looked forward to the return to Eretz Yisrael as the consummation of all their yearnings. That is definitely stated in the prayer repeated daily before the morning Shema,[2]—"O bring us in peace from the four corners of the earth, and make us go upright to our land."[3] The rest of the world regarded this expectation of the Jews as an essential element of Judaism. That fact simplified the problem of the status of the Jews. They could not be anything but aliens, and as aliens they were segregated politically, socially and economically from their neighbors. But with our acceptance of civic rights and incorporation into the body politic of various nations, our status as a group has become enigmatic. The problem of our status is not merely one of finding the proper social concept, but of devising the appropriate social structure which would enable Jews to retain their corporate entity as a people, without being segregated from the rest of the population.

The need of achieving for our people new centripetal forces would become even more apparent to the student, if his attention were called to the breakdown of the uniform code of conduct based on the Torah. He should be encouraged to investigate and think through the question, whether it would be feasible to re-establish a uniform code, or whether it has become essential to resort to other means of maintaining the indivisibility of the Jewish people. It is at this point that he would have to realize the basic significance of the rehabilitation of Eretz Yisrael. The fact that Jews have virtually renounced the traditional hope of being brought back to Eretz Yisrael, through divine intervention, has given rise to the need of having that land serve as a hub to hold together the different segments of the Jewish people. There is much more involved in this way of envisaging the function of Eretz Yisrael than in accepting Zionism and subscribing to the Basle Platform. This has far-reaching implications for the conception of the Jewish people and its status in relation to other peoples.

Our conception of the Jewish people, as a whole, would naturally determine our conception of the kind of social structure we Jews must foster in the Diaspora. To grasp this problem the student should have some idea of the fundamental distinctions between the ancient and the modern nation. He should have a clear understanding of the relation of the church to the state, of the causes for their separation, and of the possibilities of their mutual adjustment. The alternative proposals that Jewish leaders have presented with regard to the status of the Jews should be fully explored from the sociological, political and ethical standpoints. The various agencies and organizations such as the synagogue, the community, the federation, the fraternal orders, should be carefully studied with a view to a recognition of their possible effectiveness as a means to Jewish survival. The purpose in all this study should be to arrive at an understanding of the kind of social structure which would give all who wish to remain Jews a sense of belonging, affording them a common platform, despite their wide diversity in outlook and mode of life, and facilitating the normal functions of Jewish group life.

5

THE APPLICATION OF JEWISH VALUES

No less necessary than arriving at a satisfactory conception of the status of collective Jewish life is it to arrive at a set of criteria that would help to define what is meant by "a good Jew." Next to helping the individual to live, the group to which he belongs should elicit from him the best of which he is capable. Throughout the past this is what the Torah did for the Jew. It set up definite standards of behavior. Conformity with its tenets and practices made one a good Jew, and the reverence in which the Torah was held made one wish to earn that title.

In the course of his Jewish studies, the Jew should nowadays be fully apprised of the causes which have rendered the Torah, in its traditional form, largely irrelevant to his needs. This knowledge would clear the ground for that process of reinterpretation which would make of Jewish tradition a means of stimulating our people to resume its quest for the good life. *It should be the purpose of adult Jewish study to train the Jew in that process of reinterpretation, so that the tradition of his people, even if not infallible, might function as a potent influence in shaping the ethical and spiritual ideals which alone can render life worth living.* The tragic experiences of our own time prove how much is at stake in reemphasizing such teachings as those concerning the fatherhood of God, the brotherhood of man, and the worth of the individual human soul. How to find in our tradition support and inspiration for those teachings, and how to translate them into an effective program of Jewish social behavior, should be one of the chief problems in adult Jewish study.

An unusual opportunity for utilizing Jewish study, as a means of raising the ethical level of life, is presented by the current social issues which hinge upon the rights and wrongs of property, of the state vs. the individual, of individual and collective uses of power, of peace and war. Abstract ethical principles, or golden rules, offer no specific guidance, when we come up against these specific issues. What we need is the cultivation of an ethical sensitivity to the principles involved in the various conflicts of interests, something of that passion for righteousness which is the eternal glory of prophetic religion. To experience that passion, we must do more than merely study and analyze the prophetic writings; we must also study and analyze the social situations—poverty, disease, the slums, unemployment, and the many other social evils, and note the extent to which they are due to selfishness, vanity, greed and stupidity, as well as to sheer inertia. It would not at all be amiss, after having acquainted the Jewish layman with a number of typical instances of Talmudic lore, which illustrate how Jewish ethical values were translated into law, to include also the study of the Constitution of the United States, and of outstanding legal decisions of the Federal Supreme Court and noteworthy ones of the lower courts, with a view to their social and ethical implications.

Finally, it should be the function of Jewish study to introduce the layman into the realm of religion. A considerable part of the prejudice Jews have against Jewish life is due to the antiquated and bizarre notions they entertain concerning traditional religion, and to their complete ignorance of religion as an integral part of normal human experience, both individual and collective. Before a modern person who has been conditioned against religion by general hearsay can come to have religious experience, he must acquire religious literacy. For instance, he ought to be made acquainted with some of the broad principles based upon the scientific discoveries concerning the way the various religions of mankind have arisen and developed.

It is especially important to emancipate the average Jew from such false notions about religion as that it is merely a matter of rites and observances, or that it is confined to supernaturalism, or that its main function is to be a sanction for ethics, and can, therefore, be dispensed with by those who think they are sufficiently ethical without it. *To have one's understanding of religion limited to the traditional view of it, and to have no knowledge of the outstanding discoveries concerning the origin and development of religion, is to be religiously illiterate.* That does not prevent one from having strong religious emotions. But emotions, that are not channeled by knowledge into rational conduct, very often become a menace to oneself and to society. Hence, if Jewish study is to reckon with the vital needs of Jewish life, it should not refrain from informing the layman of the progress that has been achieved within the last century in the understanding of religion.

Under the heading of religion should come the entire problem of what to do with the modern scientific approach to the Bible. Merely to ignore it cannot but lead to an attitude of negativity to religion as a whole. As bad, if not worse, is to take cognizance of it, and to deal with it in an artificially apologetic manner, which gives the impression that the ancients had a monopoly on truth. The *bon mot* of Schechter's to the effect that Higher Criticism (the term commonly used to designate the modern approach to the study of the Bible) was only higher anti-Semitism [4] was timely when he said it. But even then it had only limited application. When, however, it is repeated *ad nauseam*, as a reason for not availing ourselves of the light thrown by modern Biblical scholarship on the formative period of Jewish religion, it only contributes to the tendency to evade problems that refuse to be downed. If we want our people to make the Torah an integral part of their consciousness, we must be outspoken as to whether we regard it as a monolithic text of supernatural origin, or as a human document of composite authorship.

The overwhelming majority of those who take adult study courses have grown away from traditional presentation of the Bible. If that is the case, we must do two things in teaching the Bible: one from the standpoint of Jewish literacy, and the other from the standpoint of Jewish experience. From the standpoint of Jewish literacy, we should give, in popular form, those main results of Biblical scholarship which are quite indisputable. In this connection, it would be quite in place to indicate the contributions to Biblical research made by Jewish scholars, whose theories about the Bible are certainly free of any Christian or anti-Semitic bias. From the standpoint of Jewish experience, we shall have to indicate how such a scientific approach is compatible with the evaluation of the Torah as indispensable to Jewish life, and how such indispensability does not preclude our treating some of its teachings and practices as obsolete. Above all, *it will be necessary to treat the conception of God in the Torah or in the traditional interpretation of it as by no means the final form in which it must be accepted for all times, but rather as an incentive to such formulation as would guide us Jews, individually and collectively, in the living of the good life.*

In sum, if we expect adult Jewish study to avoid the Charybdis of boredom and the Scylla of short-lived faddism, it must be made relevant to the problem of overcoming the centrifugal tendencies in Jewish life which threaten to disintegrate Jewish solidarity, to vitiate the Jewish ethic and to minimize the worth of Jewish religion. It must neither pontificate nor speak with the kind of authority which treats all alternative views as either non-existent, or as unworthy of consideration, nor must it speak with the aloofness of encyclopedic scholarship, which has not the least concern whether you take or leave what it has to offer. Jewish adult study must concern itself with Jewish literacy as a means to Jewish experience. It must, above all, get as many of the Jewish laity as possible to cope personally with the problem of Jewish survival and growth, for only then will that problem receive a satisfactory solution. Such is the hope that breathes in the ancient prophecy which reads: "And all Thy children shall be taught of the Lord; and great shall be the peace of Thy children." [5]

CHAPTER TWENTY-FIVE

JUDAISM'S CONTRIBUTION TO EDUCATION FOR DEMOCRACY

Religiously and ethically, we Jews have to undergo considerable reconstruction in our organizational activities and re-education in our system of values, if we are to be in a position to contribute our share to the enhancement of American life. That, indeed, is one of the motives for such reconstruction and re-education. But to render that purpose realizable, we have to find some area within our own life and culture, where we have immediate opportunity to articulate our contribution to the life and culture of the general population. Such an opportunity is presented in the area of education.

Jews, as a people, have been supremely aware of the significance of education as a process of transmitting their group life from one generation to another. To that awareness, the Jewish people owes its unique power of survival, despite the most adverse odds. Even more remarkable, however, than the process of transmission are the values it has helped to keep alive and the spirit in which it has been carried on throughout the centuries. That miracle of Jewish survival should be an incentive to all mankind to hold on to life, in the face of overwhelming odds. What it spells, in terms of the Jewish educative process, should persuade all peoples to derive from Judaism values as inspiring as are those of ethical monotheism and the passion for righteousness. Indeed, the Jewish educative process, at least as ideally conceived in the past, points the way toward the most effective means of implementing both ethical monotheism and the passion for righteousness.

It is with that end in view that the following four sections on Judaism's contribution to education discuss the following: *First*, the aim of all education must be world improvement. Lacking that aim, all education is reduced to training in the capacity to dominate. *Secondly*, there are certain conditions which education must satisfy, if it is to enable the child, as he matures, to share in the building of a better international society. What these are is suggested by Judaism's token rite which symbolizes the educational process, namely, the Passover *Seder*. *Thirdly*, if education is to be a means of strengthening the democratic spirit of the American people, it must be so conducted as to enable the growing generation to distinguish between genuine democracy and mass tyranny, which is a spurious imitation of democracy. Judaism, reflecting the experience of the Jewish people as the historic victim of mass tyranny, can make an important contribution to that distinction. *Finally*, as a minority in whose life religion plays an all-important role, we Jews are deeply involved in the problem of church and state. It is in education, particularly, that such involvement has created highly complex problems. Since those problems, however, are shared by all religious minorities—and there is in America no religious majority group, for which we should all be grateful—any light that might be shed on them ought to be welcome. What light we Jews might supply, as a result of our having to orient ourselves to the problem of state and church, is suggested in the fourth of these sections.

1. WORLD BETTERMENT THE AIM

1

WHAT'S WRONG WITH EDUCATION IN THE DEMOCRACIES?

It is an established fact that the recent world disaster could not have happened, had not the aggressor nations systematically engaged in inculcating their young with ideals and values which culminated in the glorification of war and conquest. It is now recognized that the very survival of the human race is bound up with the educational aims which will be fostered among all nations, no less than with the political and economic frame which will finally emerge from the present melee. "The fate of this country," said a noted statesman some time ago, "and the shape of things to come depend more than ever upon education. The challenge to education is inescapable." [1]

All educational endeavors have a twofold aim: the growth of the individual and the welfare of the community. In educating a child, the purpose is to direct his growth so that he may qualify as a useful and worthy member of the community to which he belongs. He is taught beliefs, ideas and values which are intended to imbue him with a community consciousness, or an awareness of kind, in relation to the rest of his group, and with a desire to foster the common good. Thus, education may be viewed as the process by which the community or people transmits its culture from generation to generation.

Since the advent of progressive education, a different aim has come to the fore, which threatens to compete with the one of achieving a community consciousness. It is the aim of enabling the individual and society to make continuous adjustment to ever changing conditions and circumstances of life. Progressive education asks the elders to refrain from setting up their own ideals as those which the young should be expected to attain. It would have the individual child determine for himself step by step what it is that he really cares for. In that way he can be trusted to achieve his own growth and self-reliance.

But the weakness of progressive education has always been the fact that, while it encourages growth and creative self-adjustment, it offers no criteria by which we may identify them. It shuns the setting up of criteria, lest they serve as a front for the static ideals which hinder progress, and which are the cause of maladjustment in a rapidly changing world.

What have those educational aims to do with rendering life more livable? The only way to answer that question is to translate those aims into terms of power. The fact is that the purpose of all education is fundamentally to train and increase the physical and mental powers of the child, and, through him, those of the community as a whole. Any system of education that fails to render the child a competent and effective member of society is self-condemned. Competence and effectiveness constitute power. All who have anything to do with child training should, therefore, make it a point to train the child to realize that the power which he acquires through education should not be employed as a means of dominating others, but of cooperating with others for the common good. Moreover, they should inculcate in him the principle that all human beings come within the scope of cooperation.

At present, such a proposal seems entirely quixotic. There is hardly any educational system from the kindergarten up, which does not encourage mutual rivalry among the young. The competition for higher marks and prizes is used as the chief stimulus to get the young to do their best. Seldom is the inherent value of what they learn made to elicit their interest in the subject matter. It is true that officially all states and churches, and unofficially all social classes are supposed to train the pupil to share with others the power he acquires through education. But they very definitely also take care to include within the range of "others" only those who belong to their own group. The type of education that has prevailed throughout history has sought to make the pupil aware that he will be expected to contribute his talents and abilities toward the strengthening of his own group in its struggle against the rest of the world. This is the significance of the part which loyalty and patriotism have played in all educational systems.

During the interim between the recent two World Wars three nations—Italy, Germany and Japan—used their educational systems deliberately and effectively as a means of achieving enough power to threaten to bring the rest of the world under their domination. An entire generation, in those countries, was indoctrinated with the belief that all that made human life worthwhile, or all that constituted true salvation, was the sense of power over others, either directly as leaders, or indirectly through the nation of which one was a part. The average man in those countries was conditioned to use whatever power he acquired through education as a means of helping his people to demonstrate its claim to being a *Herrenvolk*, and to impose its rule on the rest of the world, even if one had to die in the attempt. The aim of education in Germany during the thirties has been properly characterized as "education for death." [2]

It was evident that nations trained on an educational system which, theoretically at least, tended to be child-centered instead of state-centered, and which was inclined to let the individual child discover for himself what was good for him, would be in no position to cope with nations which had been rendered fanatical by a systematic inculcation of lust for power. Democratic education, whether of the traditional or the progressive type, has stressed the individual, at the expense of the social, interest. The result of democratic education is that, whatever power the pupil acquires, he is very likely to utilize it for his own personal ends. Not having been trained to share it even with the rest of his own group, he uses it to gain power and advantage even over members of his own nation or church. The democracies suffer most from the vaulting ambitions of organizers, financiers, politicians and bosses of all kinds who are expert in the art of manipulating human beings as though they were puppets in a puppet show.

The common man in the democratic countries, not having been conditioned by his education to give any thought to the problem of power, to its uses and abuses, accepts as normal the uncontrolled competition among the powerful ones of his land, in their mutual rivalry to get the better of him. The very limited power at his own disposal, whether as manual laborer or as white collar worker, he sells for whatever price the market offers, either by himself, or in collaboration with others who have the same kind of limited power to offer. With whatever he gets in exchange as wages, he buys enough food, clothing and shelter for himself and his family, so as to be able to keep up his supply of power, and, with the surplus, he buys as much of the canned pleasures and excitements as he can afford.

With one generation after another brought up in ignorance of the play of human forces and of the nature, meaning, possible uses and abuses of power, it is no wonder that all the democratic nations, including our own American people, were taken aback by the fury and onset of the aggressor nations. Instead of uniting, beating them off, and rendering them harmless, the democratic nations took shelter in isolation, and, for a time, were ready to resign themselves to whatever would happen, believing that those aggressor nations were riding on the wave of the future.

What the democratic peoples then lacked, and still lack, is a clear recognition of power as that around the use of which any educational system, that is to help them live, must be built. A democratic system of education should train the young to regard all power which the individual possesses and acquires as misused, unless, it is somehow shared with all mankind. That is to be taken literally, and not merely as a pious wish. When the common man eats food, dresses in clothing, lives in houses, reads books and resorts to entertainment, he is, nowadays, brought into relation with other human beings throughout the world. Every such relationship is thus a channel of power. "It ought to be one of the most important tasks, if not the most important one, of a democratic state to familiarize its citizens from childhood with the thought of sharing the responsibility for its internal and foreign actions." These words from Bruno Walter's *Autobiography* [3] sum up the lesson he had learned from bitter experience. He confesses that he had failed to see the Nazi danger, because his education had not taught him to achieve a "happy balance between artistic and human duties."

Unless we come to realize the oneness of our world, and learn to use our powers in accordance with what such oneness calls for, we shall, each in his own way, continue to contribute to the annihilation of the human race. This is the reeducation which the democratic peoples must submit to, or perish in the impending cataclysm. It is as true today, as it was in 1937, that, as H. G. Wells put it then, at the present educational level world peace is an impossibility. If education is to be genuinely progressive, it must not be merely child-centered, nor content itself merely with combating state-centered education. Its center must be mankind and its future. *Instead of leaving it to the child to progress from self-centeredness to world-centeredness, education should stress ways and means of introducing the child to the world and give him the long-range view as early as possible, at the same time building up his individuality, and fostering in him a spirit of initiative and self-reliance.*

2

EDUCATION IN THE ART OF LIVING, THE THEME OF ABOT

This new conception of education as a means of training the young to use their natural and acquired power in a way that will bring the greatest good to the greatest number can find validation and reenforcement in the educational tradition of Judaism. It is our duty, therefore, as a people, whose destiny is bound up with the destiny of democracy to activate that tradition, both in the American and in the Jewish upbringing of our children. The philosophy which underlies that educational tradition is expressed in terms which sound alien to the modern ear. If its significance for the well-being of mankind is not to be missed, it should be translated into the language of our own thought world.

The philosophy of education has not received in the Jewish tradition that systematic attention and presentation which it did in Greek and Roman thought. Ideas about education are scattered throughout the ancient writings of our people. But the most sustained series of teachings on education is to be found in the treatise of the Mishnaic code known as *Abot*. The title by which it is generally known is "The Ethics of the Fathers." That title is misleading. That treatise is a collection of Rabbinic maxims or aphorisms which touch upon general conduct only to a limited extent. Some of the most important areas of human conduct are not even referred to. Any one who looks to this treatise for moral guidance in the continually recurrent problems which arise in our relations to one another is bound to be disappointed. The fact is that *Abot* was not intended to be such a guide. The theme of most of its sayings and maxims is primarily the study and teaching of the Torah.

Typical are such sayings as those which counsel the raising of many disciples,[4] the extension of hospitality to scholars,[5] the seeking of teachers and colleagues with whom to study.[6] The student is advised not to be shy in the presence of his teacher,[7] and the teacher is urged not to be impatient with his student.[8] Important as is the study of Torah, it should always be supplemented by the pursuit of some practical vocation.[9] Above all, it is forbidden to use the knowledge of Torah as a means of making a livelihood, or achieving power.[10]

The underlying thesis of the entire tract of *Abot* is that, if the Jew wants to achieve a share in the world to come, he should make the study of Torah the dominant interest in his life. The following quotations point clearly to that thesis: "He who acquired words of Torah has acquired for himself life in the world to come." [11] "Be diligent in the study of Torah. . . . and know before whom thou toilest, and who thy Employer is who will pay thee the reward of thy labor." [12] "If thou hast studied much Torah, much reward will be given thee; and faithful is thy Employer to pay thee the reward of thy labor; and know that the grant of the reward to the righteous will be in the time to come." [13]

These and numerous similar quotations, show clearly the main intent of *Abot*. The original folk custom of reading a chapter of *Abot* in the synagogue on every Sabbath afternoon, during the weeks between *Pesah* and *Shabuot*, and only later extended to all the Sabbaths until the beginning of the year, is in the true spirit of that little tract. It expresses the Jewish folk desire to be mentally prepared to celebrate the Shabuot festival which commemorates God's giving of the Torah to Israel. But what is the purpose to be served by the study of Torah? The answer is implied in the statement which is recited before each Sabbath reading of one of the chapters, and which says that all who are of Israel are eligible for the world to come.[14] The point is that, if Jews want to avail themselves of the great boon which God has granted them, they have to engage in the study of Torah.

Thus the main thesis of Abot *is that the study of Torah should be man's major occupation throughout his life and that, in pursuing it, he acquires a stake in the world to come.* This thesis deserves to be fully understood and adequately stressed in our day. It has implications of great significance for education as such. They are so important that we ought not to permit the antiquated form of the thesis to stand in the way of their being recognized and put into practice. To decipher them, it is necessary to find modern equivalents for the concepts of "Torah" and "the world to come."

Torah, the study of which is the theme of *Abot*, should not be thought of merely as a collection of classic religious texts. Its modern equivalent may well be the sum of all knowledge, viewed as a means to man's salvation. Hence *the study of Torah meant the education of the whole man, his intellect, his emotions and his will.* Actually all phases of human life are reckoned with in the teachings of the Torah. That those teachings are intended to help man live, in the fullest sense of the term, is plainly stated in Leviticus, where we read "which, if man do, he shall live by them." [15] All teachings, therefore, which prepare the whole man for living his life as a human being to the full, may properly come under the designation of Torah. By the same token that Jews are urged to make the study of the Torah their main occupation, *all men, non-Jews as well as Jews, should be urged to make their main aim the study of whatever will help them achieve their destiny as human beings.*

As for the concept of the world to come, a share in which was the reward and incentive of the study of Torah, that too, should be understood in the light of its pragmatic significance. It is natural for human beings to motivate and guide present action by the contemplation of some ideal future which they hope to achieve. Though the future is veiled from us, and though our days never are what yesterday we dreamed and hoped they would be, we keep on dreaming and hoping as long as we are alive. In order to live to the maximum today, we must take thought for the morrow. Not even the certainty of death should prevent us from projecting into a life beyond our own limited span of years the fulfillment of our hopes and yearnings. That is the significance of the idea of the world to come.

The form that human imagination gives to the posthumous existence in which our ideals are to be realized varies with the culture and thought pattern of the age. Whether it be the happy hunting grounds of the American Indians, the Elysian Fields of the Greeks, the messianic era of Rabbinic Judaism, the Paradise of the medieval faiths, the personal immortality believed in by so many moderns, or some version of a utopian social order for mankind here, men will always be interested in the future, and will regulate their present life by the desire to be worthy of a share in that future. Modern man, encouraged by science and the fact of evolution, can afford to picture the world to come as one in which all the preventable ills of human society, namely, disease, poverty, oppression, war and the like will be abolished. This is what the world to come means, when we translate it into the terms of our present way of thinking and feeling about life.

This enables us to grasp the significance, for modern education and modern civilization, of the traditional principle that we must occupy ourselves continually with Torah, if we wish to have a share in the world to come. Transposed into the modern key, that ancient principle might be formulated as follows: *The aim of education in a democracy should be to render human beings capable of contributing individually and collectively toward making the world a better place to live in.* Thus the study of Torah is the process of training oneself and others in the development of character through whatever thought, feeling and behavior is directed toward the building of a better and happier world for the generations to come. The adoption of this aim would revolutionize the educational systems of the democratic countries. It would render the nation brought up on such an aim not only secure against any nation that might be berserk, but cooperative with all other nations in the interests of universal justice, freedom and peace.

Democratic education will thus have to take the form of training to place our native and acquired powers at the service of world society. So far education in the democratic countries has virtually made a fetish of rugged individualism. Had the American people not been taught by the bitter experiences of economic crisis and global war to break with rugged individualism, it would in time have been shorn of its power and vitality. The only alternative to the kind of education which has brought mankind to the edge of the abyss is one in which the aim of all its efforts is to train the pupil or student to share his powers with all mankind in the interests of a better world for all mankind.

3

EDUCATION FOR WORLD CITIZENSHIP AND BETTERMENT

As Jews we should be concerned particularly with what the study of the Torah as a system of character training might contribute to a better future for mankind. We must remember that the very contents of the Torah are such, that, in imparting them to the young, we are giving them ideas that have a direct bearing on human relationships, and, secondly, that those human relationships embrace the whole of mankind, since they are always viewed as ordained by God through whose unity all mankind is rendered one.

In all specifically Jewish instruction, whether in the traditional sacred texts, in Jewish history, in the languages and literatures of the Jewish people, or in whatever else is Jewish, it is not enough to convey that information for the sake of satisfying intellectual curiosity, or bolstering Jewish pride, or perpetuating Jewish ritual, or even developing certain skills that may contribute to Jewish survival. All these achievements have their place in Jewish education as subordinate purposes. But the primary purpose must always be to qualify the Jew for such participation in the life of both the Jewish and the general community as will make for a better world. *Jewish education, that fails to extend the young Jew's spiritual perspective and to link his personal life with the life of mankind, is wasted effort.*

That explains why Jewish education must be *religious* education. Otherwise it is meaningless, especially in the Diaspora. It has to deal mainly with the promise of a better world, in the upbuilding of which all human beings must share. It is this purpose that makes Jewish education religious, and not the presumed supernatural source of the subject-matter utilized in teaching the young. The story of the exodus from Egypt, for example, may be taught with the aid of the Biblical text, together with the Rabbinic commentaries on it. As such, it is only a lesson either in language or literature; it is not part of religious education. If, on the other hand, the "secular" writings of Pinsker, Ahad Ha-Am or Brandeis are taught with a view of inspiring the student to participate in the self-emancipation of the Jewish people and of all peoples that are the victims of discrimination and oppression, they become matter for Jewish religious education.

The conception of the study of Torah as a means of character training to enable the Jew to do his share toward the making of a better world necessarily leads to another important conclusion. Not only Jewish subject-matter dealing directly with the collective experience of the Jews as a people should be utilized in the character-training of the Jew. Any subject-matter can be used for that purpose. *The concept of Jewish education should be extended to include the subjection of all educational activities to the criterion implied in the ideal of Torah study.* Jewish religious schools ought to be given an opportunity to use subject-matter taught in the public and high-schools as a base for those human and spiritual values which would relate those studies to the task of building the better world-to-be. Even the vocational training of our young ought to be supplemented with knowledge and training in all that connects the various vocations with the part they should play in the improvement of human society.

In the professional training which most people receive in the secular universities, they are given the skills necessary for their careers, without receiving any guidance as to how to use those skills in the service of life in general. Even professional or business ethics is often merely an honorific title for codes designed to protect the monopolistic interests of professional or business groups. The ancients realized clearly that knowledge was power. They therefore would not entrust knowledge to any one who had not given evidence of being trustworthy and capable of withstanding temptation. It would be folly to try to enforce such a procedure today. But there is no reason why we should not make part of the education of the adolescent and the adult the inculcation of attitudes which would lead them to use their acquired knowledge and skills for the service of mankind. Otherwise we shall go on producing what Philip Wylie in his *Generation of Vipers* refers to as that "travesty of wisdom and catastrophe of misguidance—the modern educated man."

The canvassing of all social, political and economic problems for the purpose of habituating ourselves to act in the interest of a better future for the world should formally and actively be accepted as Torah study for our day. All Jewish institutions that are concerned with influencing the quality of Jewish life should encourage the study and discussion of those problems as an expression of Jewish religion and ethics. In that way the Jew would set an example of what it means to engage continuously in the process of reeducation without which it is futile to look to a world free from war and all forms of inhumanity.

We should not infer, from the emphasis in the Jewish conception of education on the importance of aiming at world betterment, that the welfare of the individual and his own immediate interests are ignored. Though we cannot accept as ultimate wisdom the advice of Omar Khayyam to "take the cash and let the credit go," we cannot expect men to live wholly on credit and forego the ordinary currency of day-to-day satisfactions.

This, too, is a truth which our tradition recognizes. The *Mishnah* lists a number of social and spiritual activities, "the fruits of which one eats in this world, while the stock thereof remains for him in the world to come." [16] Among these activities, the study of Torah is not only included, but is regarded as equal to all others combined. Evidently the study of Torah is intended not only to provide stock for the future, but also to bear fruit in the present. The fruit is described as equal in amount to that which all those other activities are capable of producing.

If we wish to translate this statement from the language of metaphor to that of literal truth, we need but ask ourselves what we consider as the total good resulting from social and spiritual activities, to the one who engages in them, a good that is of the here and the now. The only such good which might emanate from the study of Torah, or from an all-inclusive training in the humanities, with the above suggested purpose, would be the growth and maturation of *all* our powers. An all around education which results in the growth of one's powers of intellect, of emotion and of will, of knowledge, sympathy and self-control is as rewarding, from the standpoint of this-worldly goods, as we dare hope for from anything we do.

It is not uncommon for people to improve intellectually, while emotionally and in their general behavior they are still children. Lacking self-control and being deficient in sympathetic emotion, they act on the impulse of the moment, regardless of the harm it may bring to themselves or others. The socially harmful and the self-frustrating lives, which most of the intellectual élite lead, are the fruit of our educational systems. Little thought is given in our much vaunted schools and colleges to the development of all around personality capable of exercising all the powers of mind, heart and will in the art of living together and striving to leave the world better for our having lived in it. That should have been the kind of education which the democracies of the world should have fostered.

4

THE EDUCATION THAT DEMOCRACY NEEDS

The fascist nations deliberately suppressed all tendencies to reckon with the welfare of mankind as a whole. They merely acted out, to its logical consequences, the spirit of our own educational practice. We place a premium on success and interpret success as power over others. It is evidently impossible for every one to achieve such power. But it is possible to organize the life of the nation around the ideal of world conquest. Indeed, it is very tempting to do so, because that gives every individual in the nation at least the illusion of exercising power. The young, trained in this ideal of world domination, are so certain of its attainment that they are willing to reverse Omar Khayyam's dictum and live on credit while letting the cash go. With fanatic asceticism, they readily sacrifice the normal joys to future glory, when their people shall be acknowledged masters of the world. Inevitably, however, they suffer the fate of those who live on credit without adequate cash reserve; their credit does not hold out. It is bound to be exhausted, because to compass their purpose, they cannot permit the growth of the whole man, but have to subordinate all other natural human interests to the lust of power.

The aggressor nations distorted the personality of the individual to the point of madness. The development of the intellectual powers which they encouraged, divorced from the disinterested pursuit of truth, and unchecked by human sympathy and self-control led to mental abnormality. Denying the intrinsic value of truth, they drove their profoundest thinkers to foreign shores or compelled them to rot in concentration camps. The "Fuehrer" could be surrounded only by yes-men; all others had to be purged. Raising ruthlessness and terror to a virtue, they became Ismaels of mankind; their hand was against everyone and everyone's hand was against them. As they extended their conquests, they included within their territory ever-increasing hosts of men and women who came to hate them with a bitter and implacable hatred, and were determined to wreak upon them terrible retribution at the first opportunity that presented itself. Having been trained to surrender all initiative to their leader and blindly to execute his orders, they yielded to defeatism and despair, as soon as the war machine was halted in its career of world devastation.

The sort of education implicit in the Jewish ideal of Talmud Torah would give to the democracies the one thing that they have thus far lacked, the long-range view that renders a people willing to make sacrifices for the building of a better world based on reason, righteousness and peace. At the same time, it would not require the sacrifice of those immediate satisfactions which come from the organic and harmonious development of all the essential human faculties. Recognizing that the function of the intellect must be to discover those truths about the nature of things and the nature of man that help to improve the conditions of human life, democracies would not suppress, but encourage original thought. By fostering the humane sentiments, they would enable their citizens to enjoy the fruits of free work, free play and free worship. They would give not only to the strong but also to the humble and weak a share in the present and in the future world. They would elicit from the common people loyalty and devotion rather than grudging obedience, born of fear. By stressing the need for self-control, they would instill the art of self-government, and foster the cool and disciplined courage that is not blinded by rage nor stampeded by terror.

This kind of democratic civilization can afford to base its entire economy and political policies on the maintenance of world peace. Should its existence be menaced by military aggression, it would evoke from the hearts of men an irresistible will to preserve it at all costs. Its triumph over the forces of evil would be so certain that they would not dare challenge it. American Jews can therefore make no greater and more needed contribution to American life than by fostering the ideal of Talmud Torah with all its significance and far-reaching implications. After reading a chapter from the treatise of *Abot* which elaborates that ideal, we recite the following dictum: "God wanted to vindicate Israel; therefore He gave them a copious Torah and rules of behavior." [17] We Jews would be vindicated in our own eyes and in the eyes of the rest of the world, if we utilized that ideal to further the type of reeducation which all the nations are in need of today.

2. THE EDUCATIONAL PROCESS

Some years ago the *New York Times* conducted an educational survey, with a view to finding out how much of American history college freshmen knew. Those students were supposed to have studied American history, in one form or another, for about eight years, from about ten to eighteen, yet the ignorance they displayed was appalling, and should serve as an eye-opener to the American people. It should prove how little understanding the so-called educated classes possess of the inner meaning of American life, how uninterested they are in its ideal strivings, and what distorted notions, if any, they are bound to have of democracy. Something must be radically and dangerously wrong with the kind of education which breeds such ignorance of anything beyond the routine of one's own job, or of any purpose beyond what immediately affects one's own ambitions and pleasures.

Far more disturbing, however, than the ignorance of those students, are the nature and spirit of the survey itself. Outside of one or two questions which indicated a concern on the part of those who conducted the survey in what the students knew about the underlying principles of democracy, nothing in the survey showed the least interest in the attitudes of the students toward any of the realities of American life. Those attitudes will play a decisive role, when those students come to discharge their responsibilities as citizens. The very treatment of American history, as though it consisted of a series of unrelated details, without any underlying meaning, is part of our educational negligence which explains why we are unprepared for a durable peace.

The new and better world which democracy promises will not come into being merely through legislation, indispensable as is the *right kind* of legislation. It will come only through the proper kind of education, beginning with the elementary school and ending in the university and professional school.

What constitutes the proper kind of education? The answer is to be found, of course, in the careful study of contemporaneous human needs. But there are certain human needs which are always contemporaneous, and one of them is that of transmitting the social heritage from the older to the younger generation. It is to that process which Judaism has made important contributions, thereby perpetuating its own career. It has made such a contribution, in particular through the medium of one of its institutions which was intended to be, more than anything else, a kind of model-lesson in the process of transmitting the social heritage of the Jewish people. That institution is the ritual on Passover Eve.

In the very beginning of Israel's career, the festival of Passover was transformed from a purely nature festival to a historical one, in celebration of the exodus from Egypt. Its purpose came to be not only to keep fresh the memory of that event which gave birth to Israel's nationhood, but also to initiate the young in the knowledge of what that event signified. It became a lesson in education. In ancient times it was one of the few acts which constituted the entire conscious training of the Jewish child. This educational function of the Passover festival has survived in the *Seder* ritual at the opening festive meal, a ritual which revolves around the children in the family. That fact about the *Seder* is highly significant, in that it embodies some of Judaism's principal ideas concerning education.

1

EDUCATION AS RELIGIOUS EXPERIENCE

The basic purpose of the *Seder* is to inculcate in the child a belief in God. Having been instituted in ancient times when men resorted to the tradition which recounted God's miraculous deeds, the *Seder*, in its traditional form, is an occasion for recounting the miracles whereby God led the Israelites out of Egypt. In transmitting its social heritage, the Jewish people was mainly concerned in having the child learn about God. More than that, it *sought to emphasize the importance of having all efforts which form part of the child's training culminate in the belief in God.*

Unfortunately, the first thought that comes to mind nowadays, when that kind of purpose is suggested, is that we should have the public schools include in their overburdened curriculum also the religious education of the child. That is the very thing which American democracy has been trying to avoid, by keeping the church and state separate. As a matter of fact, having educational efforts culminate in a belief in God has nothing whatever to do with any kind of organized religion. Indeed, *this business of expecting the child to get religion during the one hour which he is released from school attendance, is a travesty on genuine religious education. Education as a whole should be religious experience.*

That presupposes the kind of belief in God which means sensing that there is a Power both within and beyond man which is gradually making human beings learn to live amicably with one another. That Power impels human beings to cooperate with one another, individually and collectively, over ever widening areas, until all of humanity comes to be included within a network of mutual influence and cooperation. That Power would have human beings stop exploiting one another individually and collectively. Man has been exploiting woman, the strong has been exploiting the weak, the cunning has been exploiting the simple. This is true of tribes, and states and nations, as it is of individuals. To believe in God is to be convinced that this tendency to exploit or to make use of someone else only as a means to one's own purposes is an affront to God, the Power that calls on men to cooperate with one another on the basis of mutual respect, and, if possible, on the basis of mutual love.

In our day, this is the conception of God all education worthy of the name should strive to have the child acquire. For lack of such education the American people fought the recent war merely to survive, instead of to establish the "Four Freedoms." In our national education as Americans, the main consideration is personal success. We wish the child and the youth to acquire the power that resides in knowledge. We seldom, if ever, trouble ourselves as to how he will use that power. We leave that to the home and the church. But how can we expect the parents to educate their child in that kind of knowledge of God, when their own lives are cast in the conventional pattern, in which the average person is partly exploiter and partly exploited? All that organized religion has offered thus far has been traditional beliefs which are irrelevant, or pious platitudes which are meaningless.

The fact is that the abysmal ignorance of history displayed by our young people hardly touches the fundamental weakness of American education. It is only a symptom of a far deeper malady. The real trouble with American education is its lack of an all absorbing and inspiring purpose to motivate it. In sharp contrast with our own democratic system of education were the educational systems of the fascist states. Their system was powerfully motivated by diabolic purpose. What makes a purpose diabolic is its utilization of divine means for ends that are evil. The fascist states educated their young to cooperate in a spirit of complete self-abandon and self-surrender. Such cooperation is a divine means, but to what end did those countries employ it? So that their young should enable their nation to enslave the rest of the world. The fascists raised to a religion their exploitation of races and peoples other than their own. But we have not raised cooperation and peace to a religion. That is why individualism in our internal life, and isolationism in our international polices, still dominate the American mind.

2

EDUCATION A PARENTAL RESPONSIBILITY

A second implication of the *Seder*, which is pertinent from an educational point of view, is that the parental responsibility for the training of the child should at least be coordinate with the responsibility of the state. In the *Seder* ceremony, the father is expected to communicate to the child what he expects the child to know about his people. The instruction is, in a sense, child-centered, in that it is to be adapted to the mentality and interests of the child. According to our Sages, the Torah calls attention to four different types of children as in need of being reckoned with, when we impart to them the story and significance of the exodus from Egypt. They are the wise, the recalcitrant, the simple-minded and the inarticulate. Education, however, must not only be child-centered; it must also be home-inspired.

What bearing does that have on American needs? We surely do not want to return to the educational situation which prevailed in America a hundred years ago when the training of the young was in a sense entirely a home affair, in which the state had no part. Even if a return to a home-controlled education were desirable, it is no more feasible than a return to the horse-and-buggy mode of transportation. On the other hand, it has become quite clear by this time that, with the state monopolizing the education of the child, we are drifting dangerously near the rocks of totalitarianism on which democracy would be wrecked. Nothing is more certain to bring about the dreaded transformation of the citizen into a robot of the state, blindly conforming to the will of the dictator and his satellites, than an educational system in which the state is in full control.

The character of an educational system depends largely upon the policies by which it is governed in such matters as the extension of educational opportunity, the general pattern of the program, the relation of the school to the political structure, the social ideas and values to be fostered, the goals and purposes to be achieved, and the choices to be made affecting the future substance and pattern of society and culture. If these policies are determined by a few appointees of the state officials, the school forfeits its independence. The function of the school becomes the servile one of making the state into a modern Moloch. With nothing to check the ever increasing power of the state, and with the school surrendering all cultural and spiritual autonomy, nothing remains of the hope that organized education's role might be counted on as a force for the preservation of democracy, or the reconstruction of society. Organized education is likely to be used in America, as it has been used by the authoritarian states of Europe, mainly for the purpose of regimenting the national mind.

It is no less important to combat the educational aspect of the fascist peril which impends over democracy than the political or the economic aspect. The first step in the reconstruction of the educational system must be a concerted effort to arouse a widespread popular interest in the responsibilities and possibilities of the public school. Education must not be the monopoly of any particular group of people any more than politics. The masses must be made to realize that the schools constitute the first line of democracy's defense. This would be one way of carrying out the principle implied in the *Seder* ceremony, the principle that in the education of the child the will and the influence of the parents and the home must make themselves felt to the same degree as those of the state. To let the people have a share in the determination of educational policy is in keeping with the faith in the common man. Such faith is of the very essence of democracy.

Practically, such faith would take the form of giving the teaching profession much more responsibility than it has at present in formulating educational policy for the nation. This is nothing more than proper, for the teacher is naturally and historically the representative of the parent rather than that of the state.[1] If the teachers will assume the responsibility which their place in a democracy calls for, they can be depended on to conceive and administer the educational program in terms of the general unfolding interests of the American people. The teacher is a strategically important member of the community. The fashioners of the fascist state, aware of the teacher's influence in moulding the character of the young, made the most effective use of him in conditioning the mind of the growing generation to blind obedience to authority. If the democratic state is to survive, it must likewise recognize the importance of the teacher. But it must deal with him as a person, and not use him merely as a tool for its own ends, in which he has no say or share.

Thanks to the fact that the educational efforts of Jews throughout the centuries has been in the hands of the parents, and that the teachers of the nation acted as the representatives of the parents and not of the state or its equivalent, the Jewish people has managed to hold its own against a hostile world. This should serve as a lesson to all peoples that, in the conduct of their educational system, the teachers, who represent the parents, should be given that freedom and authority to which their expertness entitles them, and which would prevent the state from becoming the sole master of the child's future and destiny.

3

EDUCATION FOR FREEDOM

The third implication of the *Seder* ritual, which has a bearing on education, is that the most important element in any education is the training in freedom. This may be derived from the following facts: The minds of the participants in the *Seder* are focussed on the liberation of the Israelites from Egyptian bondage. The main theme of the Pesah festival is freedom. The designation for the Pesah festival is *zeman herutenu*, "the season of our freedom." All this should serve as token of the principle that *the ideal type of education is the one in which the child is trained effectively to be free, to cherish freedom and to know how to use it.*

Any system of education which succeeds in turning out well trained technicians and experts in the various callings, people stuffed with information about the things that enable them to make a living and even to win fame, but which fails to inculcate in them the love of freedom and the capacity to act as free agents is the most desirable kind of education for fascist barbarism. But it is the most dangerous kind of education for a society that tries to be civilized, and that expects to build its civilization on democratic lines.

What exactly is involved in training a child to be a free agent? It means that all who have anything to do with his education should seek to elicit from him the awareness of himself as a center of initiative. It means making him aware of the inner resources of character, goodness and moral strength that are latent in him, and stimulating him to make use of those resources. It means not only having him discover his own urge to act and to be accepted as a morally responsible person, possessing inner dignity and inalienable worth, but having him exult in this discovery, and having him explore to the utmost what he has thus discovered. The making of such persons should be the highest goal of democratic education.

To succeed in the making of such persons, democratic education should concentrate on the cultivation of the following three masteries: (1) the mastery over hungers and desires, or the so-called "primary instincts"; (2) the mastery over difficult conditions, and (3) the mastery over one's own mind. The last of these masteries can hardly be said to have been contemplated by our ancestors, to whom, like to all ancients, freedom of thought was *terra incognita*. It has to be included, however, in the reinterpretation, for our day, of the ancient ideal of freedom.

This opens up the entire problem of character training, the most important and the most difficult problem in education. One thing, however, is certain. Character education has never really been tried in the schools of democratic countries to the extent that it had in the fascist countries. The fascist governments knew very definitely the kind of character they wanted to develop in the young, and they omitted no opportunity or occasion in the entire schooling of the child to achieve their purpose. Democracy must recognize that fascism has proved superior to it in inculcating in the young the first two kinds of mastery. (1) mastery over one's instincts and (2) mastery over difficult conditions. Fascism, whether of the European or Japanese variety, deliberately aimed to make the young as hard as nails. To be sure, its primary objective was to eliminate from character all kindness and pity. But it also included in its training the power of self-control when lured by temptation or threatened by danger. There is nothing in the democratic education to compare with the methodical procedure and efficacy of the fascist education in building up this inner strength.

Democratic education, however, must not merely emulate fascist education. It must recognize that democracy is the very antithesis of fascism in the conception of the human person. Fascism with its diabolic tendency to corrupt and pervert the good, by utilizing it for evil purposes, after having succeeded in developing in the youth the power of mastering their inner impulses and outward circumstances, insisted on utilizing that very power in the service of whatever band of brigands happened to usurp the authority of the state. How did fascism manage to effect this purpose? The answer is: By suppressing the freedom of thought. Fascism cultivated the spell of imitation and suggestion as a substitute for individual and independent thought. It rendered the individual even more incapable of thinking for himself than he was ordinarily. Its purpose was to make of the nation an organized mob responsive to incitements to violence and aggression, at the bidding of the chief-gangster who succeeded in becoming the head of the state. To that end, fascism kept the individual completely hypnotized into mob-mindedness. It was aware that the least effort on his part to think for himself would break its hypnosis.

To redeem the individual from this most dangerous and destructive kind of slavery should be the chief goal of democratic education. The main task of democracy is to salvage the freedom of the mind, to recover the right of every human being to exercise the most divine power which he possesses, the power of reason. A new light dawned on mankind two centuries ago with the ushering in of the age of reason. Let not the storm clouds of class-hatred and international war, which have blacked out that light in recent years, lead us to deny its existence or its power. Mankind's only hope is in the achievement of that individual and personal freedom, that freedom of mind, which spells freedom of thought and freedom of expression, untrammeled by the tyranny of the state, or by the anonymous powers which pull the strings of the state.

If these post-war years are not to be merely a truce to be followed by an even more violent cataclysm than was the war itself, all groups of the American people should deliberately strive to establish a durable peace based on a better and warless world. That purpose calls for the political reconstruction of international relations and for the economic reconstruction of methods of production and distribution of wealth. But neither reconstruction can be of any avail without a thoroughgoing educational reconstruction. Democracy which has hitherto been thought of only in political terms must henceforth be translated into economic values and educational practice.

The underlying principles of such democratic educational practice are those which we have found implied in the *Seder* ritual. They are: (1) education must come to constitute religious experience in the life of a people; (2) the parents, teachers and educators should share with the state the responsibility for the education of the child, and have a hand in determining the policies of public education; and (3) the most important element in the education of the child, from the standpoint of democracy, is the training in freedom which essentially is the ability to emancipate oneself from the impact and pressure of mob-mindedness, and to exercise to the full the power of reason.

3. EDUCATION FOR GENUINE DEMOCRACY

1

DEMOCRACY VS. MASS TYRANNY THE MAIN ISSUE IN EDUCATION

The First World War was said to have demonstrated that it was easier to die for democracy than to define it. Nevertheless, we cannot evade the need of defining democracy, if we wish to know its implications for the education of our children.

Until recently the term "democracy" called to mind mainly the struggle against special privilege, or the tyranny of the few. All our political and educational traditions, in so far as they have to do with democracy, are directed against social power which is entrenched behind claims based on pedigree, divine right, and unjust legal sanctions, and which has sought to deprive the common man of his inalienable right to life, liberty and the pursuit of happiness.

Though special privilege, particularly in the form of monopolistic control of production, marketing and natural resources still manages to frustrate the efforts of democracy, it does not threaten its existence. The threat comes mainly from a counterfeit form of democracy. The danger to democracy lurks in mass tyranny, and takes on the form of bureaucratic rule, or state despotism. Although, in the fascist strategy, special privilege usually enters into an unholy alliance with mass tyranny, the struggle against bureaucratic rule is not merely a modified or intensified form of the struggle against special privilege. In combating the present menace to democracy, we cannot afford to rely merely on the kind of appeals to reason which were relevant when feudalism was still in force. We have to arm ourselves mentally and morally *de novo*. This makes our task doubly hard, and our responsibilities doubly onerous.

State despotism is based upon the assumption that the herd instinct in man is a better guide to social welfare than reason. It repudiates representative government and accepts government by dictators and demagogues, who are supposed to know by instinct what is good for the people. It ridicules justice, which seeks to harmonize the conflicting interests of individuals and groups, as being hypocrisy. The only justice it acknowledges is that of the mailed fist. It appeals to fear and hatred of some conjured up common enemy as a class, race, or nation. It whoops up the multitude into mass hysteria. It thrives on war and threats of war, and gives people the jitters.

No campaign against state despotism can succeed, unless we reckon with the two chief factors which have contributed to the rise of this new menace to democracy. One factor is the failure of democracy to make much headway in its struggle against special privilege, or the tyranny of plutocracy. The other factor is the phenomenal growth in the means of communication and the spread of superficial literacy. The press, the radio and compulsory education have rendered the power of the demagogue almost irresistible.

There is a Jewish legend which relates that, when King Solomon sinned, the evil spirit Ashmedai assumed the king's guise, sat upon his throne, and administered the public affairs of the land. The true king was compelled to wander about as a beggar. It was then that Solomon lamented, "Vanity of vanities, all is vanity." Democracy, too, having sinned, in not having lived up to its promise of protecting the common man's inalienable rights, is paying the penalty of being dethroned by the evil spirit of state despotism. If genuine democracy is to regain its influence and prestige, it must set right the social and economic wrongs it has permitted to continue. But, at the same time, it must do everything in its power to unmask the evil Ashmedai—state despotism—so as to prevent him from beguiling the unwary and winning their allegiance.

In the life of modern nations, education has to fill a most important role. It has to fuse disparate individuals and groups into an organic entity. It has to generate national consciousness, by having each individual in the nation so identify himself with it as to glory in its achievements, grieve over its failures, and be ready to defend it at all costs, when it is in danger. But if education is to be democratic as well as national, it must be prevented from inculcating attitudes and sentiments that make for state despotism.

To lead toward democracy, education must deliberately combat all collective hatreds, fears and megalomanias. It should seek to eradicate every form of xenophobia, from all texts, from all instruction, and from all extra-curricular activities in the schools. It should foster habits of reason and justice, by enlarging the scope of civics in the elementary schools, to include the study of democracy as a whole, of its implications in all human relationships, and of all the dangers against which it must be protected.

Granted that to live democracy is far more important than merely to talk about it. That does not mean that we can afford to minimize, as some do, the value of talking about it. State despotism has demonstrated the fatal spell of certain words in evoking the spirit of darkness. Why may not democracy demonstrate the beneficent magic of its own great words? The great words, however, that influence conduct are saved from becoming meaningless clichés only when they are part of a world outlook that actually functions in men's thinking. Unless democracy is inculcated as such a world outlook, its great slogans can easily be twisted into arguments for state despotism.

"Life and death are in the power of the tongue." [1] The life and death of democracy are in the instruments of expression, the press, the radio, the platform. *What they offer the public cannot rise higher than the source of the demand for what they have to give; that source is the education received in the schools.* There surely must be much that is wrong with our educational system, when, with the noteworthy exception of a few outstanding newspapers and radio broadcasts in this country, the greater part of what is offered to the public caters to the lower levels of mass psychology rather than to the higher. Without minimizing the importance of cultivating fine literary taste or the reading of books, it is well to remember that, for the saving of democracy, taste and judgment in the reading of the daily papers and listening to broadcasts are matters of immediate and vital concern, no less than the elementary laws of health.

2

JEWISH EDUCATION AGAINST MASS TYRANNY

All that has been said thus far applies to the general problem of education. It has, however, also a very direct bearing on religious education. Religious education, though conducted outside the general school system and merely supplementary to it, cannot run counter to the general spirit of the environment. It cannot be expected to foster democracy, once mass tyranny has actually taken over. That, however, is fortunately not yet the case, nor, let us hope, ever will be the case in our country. But if our country is to escape the curse of state despotism, all religious educational forces must take up the struggle against it.

All adherents of religion need to be reminded that religion, as such, can be made to serve the cause of mass tyranny as well as that of democracy. The cliché about Satan's quoting the Bible for his own purposes has been shown to be true times without number. A curious organization, known as the "Israel Identity Society," tried not only to prove that the British were descendants of the Lost Ten Tribes, but also that Britain alone was destined to possess colonies, "whether we desire it or not." In confirmation of this claim for Britain, one of the tracts of that society quotes the verse in Isaiah (54): "Thou shalt break forth on the right hand and on the left, and thy seed shall inherit the Gentiles and make the desolate cities to be inhabited." [2] In 1753 a bill was presented in the English Parliament proposing to grant civic rights to the Jews. This aroused such a strong opposition that a petition was presented to the King imploring him to have the bill withdrawn.[3] The reason advanced was that a people whom God Himself denounced as "laden with iniquity, a seed of evil-doers," could not be worthy of civic rights.

It would be far from the truth to say that Judaism, throughout its history, the first thousand years of which are reflected in the sacred Scriptures, has always upheld the principle of democracy, as we understand it. Judaism is a developing religious civilization, and one must expect to find in its early stages much that has become unacceptable. *To teach Judaism as an eternal and unchangeable system of doctrine and law is to prevent it from being a force for democracy.* The very notion that authority, whether of law, or of those who administer it, has its source not in the people but in some supernatural revelation, militates against democracy. If Judaism is to be a potent factor for democracy in our political and economic institutions, it will have to be presented as a way of life which reckons with man's growing needs, and which identifies as the law of God whatever helps man to make the most of, and give his best to, the life of mankind.

Judaism, educationally presented in this fashion, could play an important role in counteracting three most vicious trends of mass tyranny and state despotism: (1) xenophobia, (2) national megalomania, and (3) yielding to dictatorial authority.

To counteract xenophobia, or baseless fears of members of the "you" group, as the Chinese say, in contrast with the "we" group, Jewish education should stress the traditional teaching of the unity of mankind, and of the divinity that is in all men. Vital religion will always have to perform the educational function of helping the human being to orient himself in the universe, or to find, as it were, his spiritual latitude and longitude. It will always have to answer the question: What differentiates a human being from other living beings, and what meaning is there to the existence of different human families and peoples? The opening chapters in Genesis are meant to furnish such an orientation. Our Sages taught that the reason all mankind originated with a single pair was that no human being should be able to boast that he belonged to a higher order than any one else.[4] They inferred from the same fact that every individual human being was morally bound to insist upon his prerogatives and responsibilities as a personality.

Since we can no longer base either the unity of mankind, or the worth of the human person, upon common ancestry, it is essential to focus attention on the fact that all who have the human form possess those higher traits and possibilities which are a reflection of godhood, and which qualify them for growth and salvation. No human being, of whatever race or people, should be deprived of the opportunity to grow and to fulfill himself to the utmost. By virtue of those traits and possibilities alone, every human being is entitled to be treated justly and with lovingkindness.

These democratic inferences which were stressed by our Sages should form the basis of systematic instruction for the purpose of combating the false teachings that there are some races which are as superior to others as men are to beasts, and that just as some beasts are meant for burden and others to be destroyed, so some races are meant to slave and others to be entirely exterminated. It is essential to emphasize the ethical significance of the Biblical teaching that all races are descended from Noah, with whom God made a special covenant which is binding upon all mankind. In this covenant, according to Jewish tradition, are included the seven fundamental principles of universal justice. All who fulfill that covenant are worthy of salvation.

This conception of the unity of mankind is the main corollary of the Jewish doctrine of God's unity and uniqueness. That doctrine is not an abstract metaphysical formula intended to inform the mind about the nature of God. It is an historically evolved ethical teaching intended to direct the heart in sympathy and understanding toward the same divine principle that is in all men. In keeping with this implication of monotheism the Torah teaches, "Ye shall have one manner of law, as well for the stranger as for the homeborn; for I am the Lord your God." [5] It likewise calls upon the Jewish people to banish from its soul all hatred of the stranger. Thus we read: "And a stranger shalt thou not oppress; for you know the heart of a stranger, seeing ye were strangers in the land of Egypt." [6] Far greater even than the famous teaching, "Thou shalt love thy neighbor as thyself," [7] is the one which reads, "And if a stranger sojourn with thee in your land, ye shall not do him wrong. The stranger that sojourneth with thee shall be unto you as the homeborn among you, and thou shalt love him as thyself, for ye were strangers in the land of Egypt. I am the Lord your God." [8] As indicated above,* however, those very teachings are themselves in need of being interpreted anew, to bring them in line with the modern concept of democracy.

How is Jewish education to deal with the tendency to national megalomania? A people, like an individual, is in need of self-confidence. It needs self-confidence to be able to bear hardship, overcome danger and succeed in its undertakings. But no greater evil can befall a people than to become so inflated with self-assurance that it cannot brook criticism. A people dominated by mass tyranny bitterly resents any questioning of its actions or claims.

Jewish tradition abounds in teachings which, if mastered, could render a people immune to megalomania. The writings of the great Prophets, in particular, are models in the method of self-criticism on a national scale. Those Prophets refused to be identified with those who gave out oracles and who were part of the social and political pattern of every ancient oriental people. In our religious literature these official "seers" are known as "false prophets." Instead of pointing out evils to be corrected and dangers to be averted, they catered to the wishful

* See p. 146.

thinking of the populace and talked their contemporaries into complacent yielding to arbitrary rule and social injustice.

We get a glimpse of these official "seers," as they existed in ancient Israel, from the incident in King Ahab's court.[9] Ahab had made up his mind to attack Ramot-Gilead and he got his ally, the Judaic King Jehoshaphat, to help him. Jehoshaphat suggested that it might be advisable to obtain an oracle from a prophet of the Lord. "And the king of Israel said unto Jehoshaphat, 'There is yet one man by whom we may inquire of the Lord, Micaiah, the son of Imlah; but I hate him; for he doth not prophecy good concerning me, but evil.' " [10] This contest between the true Prophets, who grieved at the sight of their nation's rushing headlong into catastrophe, and the professional prophets who made their livelihood by telling the people only what they wanted to hear, went on for generations. The Prophet Micah sought to counteract the baleful influence of the false prophets. Likewise, the Prophet Jeremiah found it necessary to contest the optimistic oracles of many a claimant to prophecy who lulled the Jews into a false sense of security, by encouraging them in their national vanity and telling them "they were the very Temple of the Lord," [11] and therefore immune to all harm. And even later in exile, Ezekiel had to carry on the struggle against the same evil brood.

There can hardly be a more effective method of combatting demagogy, which is one of mass tyranny's chief mainstays, than by training the youth to learn to use the spirit of the true Prophets as the touchstone of true leadership. By that method, genuine religion would dissociate itself from all such dangerous tendencies of national life as evading the truth, indulging in wishful thinking and assuming that a nation can do no wrong. Religion would become a force for wholesome and constructive self-criticism, for national humility before God and God's law of justice, which cannot be violated with impunity. If democracy will cultivate faith in the God of the Prophets, mass tyranny's idolatry of the state will not long endure.

Finally, there is the danger of yielding to dictatorial authority. Traditional Jewish education possessed the means of counteracting dictatorial authority even under the aegis of supernatural revelation. Every Jew was expected to have some knowledge of the laws governing human relationships as well as those governing ritual practice. That knowledge was to consist not only of the formal rules which he was expected to obey, but also of the basic premises underlying them, and of the reasoning by which they were arrived at. In Jewish tradition this study of the law is known as *Gemara,* in contrast with *Mishnah,* which is the first post-Biblical code.

The study of the law, when pursued in the proper spirit, constituted for the Jew the highest expression of religion in action, a veritable means of experiencing the divine. When engaged in such study, the Jew felt as though he were standing at the foot of Mount Sinai and hearing anew the divine voice proclaiming what he was to do, in order that he might live the life abundant.[12] He was thus saved from falling into the habit of obeying, as Isaiah puts it, "a commandment of men learned by rote." [13] Thus, in commenting on God's saying to Moses: "And these are the ordinances which thou shalt set before them," [14] our Sages add, "Set out these ordinances before them like a well arranged table," [15] that is, let them have an intelligent understanding of the law.

Notwithstanding repeated attempts to confine the study of the law to codes or collections of categorical rules, the Jewish people insisted on cultivating the *Gemara,* or the reasoning behind the law. It is significant, for example, that Maimonides wished to spare his people the need of wading through the huge tomes of the Talmud.[16] He formulated a definite code known as *Yad Hahazakah.* The Jews paid him the compliment of accepting his code as authoritative, but they refused to discontinue the study of the reasoning upon which its conclusions were based. Thus the study of the law, motivated by the desire to understand its rationale, had the effect of discouraging all dictatorial authority in Israel. No matter how great the prestige of the rabbi who was always both administrator of justice and head of the academy, he could not silence the arguments of the poorest shoemaker or porter who knew the law. That certainly bred democracy.

The problem which we now face is: what can be done to apply the wisdom inherent in this traditional type of Jewish education to American life as it exists today? There is no occasion to make the study of the Jewish civil law part of the Jewish layman's religious training, because such law is entirely inoperative in the American environment. But there is an imperative need for the layman to develop an acquaintance with, and an interest in, American civil law. The study of the Federal Constitution and of the decisions of the higher courts along lines analogous, and in a spirit similar, to that in which our forebears studied Jewish law might well be made an essential requirement in all education.

Mere patriotic reverence of the American Constitution will not enable it to serve as dyke against the threatening tide of mass tyranny and state despotism. Not even memorizing every word of the Constitution will be of any avail. Judaism has always maintained that the written law means nothing without its interpretation, or "oral law." The interpretation of the Federal Constitution is contained in the mass of literature which records the opinions of the higher courts, both State and Federal. Selections from the vast literature of constitutional interpretation, as texts for study and discussion, could be utilized with great effect in training our youth to apply the standards of reason and justice to all human relations.

Let us hope that the time will come when such study and discussion will constitute an integral part of every high-school curriculum. In the meantime, Jewish education in this country would be very much enriched, and would become a more powerful instrument for democracy, if it were to include in its curriculum the study of American law in the spirit in which Jews were wont to study Jewish law.

It is hardly necessary to point out that of all the elements in our population, we Jews have most at stake in the struggle of democracy against mass tyranny and state despotism. There is nothing we Jews dread more than the evil slogan of mass tyranny: "One people, one state, one leader." There is nothing for which we yearn more than for the day when all men will hear the good tidings: "One humanity, one Divine Kingdom, one God."

4. THE PROBLEM OF CHURCH AND STATE IN DEMOCRATIC EDUCATION

1

THE PROBLEM STATED

The failure of the democracies, during the interim between the two world wars, to establish a smoothly functioning social and economic order paved the way for fascism. Fascism played on the feeling of disillusionment and helplessness which spread among the people of the bankrupt nations, or those bordering closely on bankruptcy, in not being able to solve their own most fundamental problems of government. It was able to persuade the masses that by surrendering all rights and responsibilities into the hands of a dictator and his henchmen, they would be relieved of a responsibility to which they were not equal.

It undertook to insure the rapid decision of issues necessitated by the accelerated tempo of our age.

In return for this self-surrender of the people and for their submitting to the most tyrannical dictatorial rule, the fascist states promised their nationals the spoils of military conquest. That reward was regarded as due them, because, in achieving world domination by dint of collective strength and discipline, they would prove their inherent superiority to the subject nations. The danger, however, to the democracies came not merely from the military aggression of the fascist states, but from the subtle attractiveness of their ideology, which seemed marvelously adapted to converting a weak and frustrated populace into an organized, proud and triumphant power. Fascism was not merely a political, but also a religious phenomenon, the birth of a new, fanatical faith which was diametrically and irreconcilably opposed to all that democratic nations had accepted as civilization and progress.

Fascism's challenge to democracy has not ended with the war. That fact is generally recognized, but there is much confusion as to how it is to be met. The feeling is growing that just as the challenge was not only political and military, so the method of meeting it calls for more than a political and military preparedness. *Faith in democracy and its possibilities for human living must be strengthened and deepened.* Democracy must be given the sanction of religion, and the system of education fostered by the democratic state must somehow take cognizance of this religious need.

If we concede that the democratic way of life is in need of religious sanctions, it follows that we have to reconsider the relations of state and church in the area of education, in which both claim an interest and a right to exercise control. Hitherto the education provided by the public schools and colleges has been mainly utilitarian. "Cultural" subjects have been taught, to be sure, but largely from the point of view of what culture can contribute to a successful career. Seldom are those subjects taught with a view to orienting the students to life as a whole, or as a discipline in the art of living together in wholesome adjustment to the fundamental realities of visible nature and of human nature. It has been tacitly assumed that the denominational churches could take care of their religious orientation and ethical adjustment. That tacit understanding is no longer satisfactory either to educators or to churchmen.

The educators recognize the need of an integrated curriculum, which would reckon with every aspect of life as it is lived in America, and with which maturing personality has to deal. Such integration is impossible, if religion has to be left out of the picture. American public schools must teach democracy, if they are to make good American citizens. But democracy is a faith; its validity is not scientifically demonstrable. It demands *a priori* acceptance of ideals which can be proved valid only by our committing ourselves to their realization. It is a scheme of salvation that implies belief in a Power that makes for salvation. If history is, as some contend, a mere resultant of blind social forces, and human consciousness a mere by-product, with no functional significance, then there is no way by which instruction in history, for example, can be made to contribute to the advancement of the democratic ideal. *Some religious faith must underlie all normative teaching, even of the so-called secular subjects.* Moreover, to entrust exclusively to denominational schools the teaching of religion exposes the American public to divisive influences that complicate, to say the least, the creation of that spiritual unity which must prevail in America, if democracy is to work.

So much for the point of view of the educator. To the religionist, the silence of the public schools on religion is, in effect, if not in intent, a deprecation of the importance of religion, at least of its importance to American life. The public schools teach loyalty to the state, for that has always been conceived as the justification of the state's interest in the school. But loyalty to the state, without loyalty to a universal God, leads directly to that apotheosis of the state which is the very essence of fascism.

It can thus be seen that education for democracy involves a problem which, far from having been solved, has grown more complicated with the years. Various attempts have been made to cope with that problem, ranging all the way from state support of denominational education to the release of an hour of public school time to be used, under church auspices, for religious education of public school children. All of these measures have been hastily conceived. They hardly scratch the surface of the problem. They are not based on a sound philosophy of religion. Without such a philosophy it is impossible to assess properly the fundamental issues involved in the relationship between church and state, as it affects the process of education.

2

RELIGIONS AS PROGRAMS FOR LIVING
AND AS ORGANIZATIONS OF POWER

To solve this problem, it is necessary to understand some elementary facts about the place of religion in human life. These facts unfortunately are not widely enough known even among otherwise well-informed educators. Only on the basis of a valid philosophy of religion is it possible to evaluate religion's role in a democracy and in a system of education for democratic living.

The first simple truth to be recognized is that religion in general has only a conceptional but not a real existence. Real existence is possible only to particular religions. The case of religion is similar to that of language. There are languages, English, French, German, etc., but language in general is only an abstract concept not a reality. Similarly, there are religions like Catholicism, Protestantism and Jewish religion, all of which are functions of definite historic movements. Religion as such is an abstraction, without specific content of its own. Perhaps at some future time, when world collaboration shall have made of all mankind an organic social community, there may be such a thing as a world religion, but until then we can only think of religion as referring to the common characteristics of the various religions of the world. *It is, therefore, impossible to teach religion without teaching some particular religious content drawn from the collective experience of some societal group, in its endeavor to orient itself to the cosmos.*

Every religion has two aspects: *a program for living* and *an organization of power*. As a program for living it sets forth what men must believe and do in order to attain salvation, or the maximum of human personality and social welfare. As an organization of power, religion uses this program of salvation to achieve social solidarity within the group, and to condition the individual for choosing those forms of conduct which make for the maximum of group collaboration. The collaboration is directed toward the personal and social objectives which further the survival of the group and of its civilization, or its way of life. Under certain conditions, a group will content itself with that use of its program which will insure the internal security and happiness of its own members, without reference to any other group. When, however, groups become involved in a tooth-and-claw struggle for power, they use their program of salvation as an instrument of expansion and domination over other groups.

Among the empires of the ancient world—Egypt, Assyria and Babylonia—military conquests betokened the victory of their gods over the gods of the conquered populations. The Prophets of Israel had great difficulty in convincing their people of the startlingly novel doctrine that their own God, YHWH, had himself decreed their defeat as a punishment for their sins,[1] and had thus asserted His sovereignty as Lord and Creator of the *whole* earth.

The Persian empire was probably the first to feel that the spread of its religion was a mission of salvation for the world, a mission that would aid the forces of Ormuzd, the god of light and goodness, to triumph over those of Ahriman, the god of darkness and evil. The Macedonian empire, which Alexander established, exercised its hold on the conquered populations, by bringing to them the theaters, gymnasia and other features of Greek culture associated with the worship of Dionysus and of the Olympian gods. Roman imperialism was not as successful in spreading Roman religion throughout the conquered area, because that religion was inadequate as a program for uniting in spirit the heterogeneous populations of the empire. The attempt to establish Emperor-worship showed, nevertheless, the endeavor to use religion as an instrument for holding together, through common worship, the scattered members of the empire. The espousal by Marcus Aurelius of the Stoic philosophy, with its scheme of salvation and its humanitarian universalism, may also have been motivated by the quest for some religious means of unifying the political structure built up by Roman conquest.

In Jewish history it is possible to trace two conflicting tendencies in the use of religion as an instrument of power, the one isolationist the other imperialist. The pre-exilic Prophets and those of the exile were isolationist. They asked only that Jewish religion should function for the communal welfare of the Jewish people itself, through the establishment of justice and peace. Under Persian influence, however, messianism arose as a dream of the domination of Judaism over the entire world. It gained strength after the success of the Maccabees. In John Hyrcanus' imposition of Judaism on the Idumeans, we see a definite attempt to utilize religion for purposes of militarist imperialism. In the work of Ezra and the Scribes and in that of their successors, the Pharisees, we see the isolationist tendency to use the Torah for organizing the internal affairs of the Jews and their social solidarity, without any effort at domination. Nevertheless, the messianic dream retained its hold, particularly, on the non-urban population, although chiefly as a hope that God's rule would assert itself over the nations. When, however, Roman imperialism became unbearable, the yearning of the Jews for emancipation from the Roman yoke availed itself of Jewish religion to organize political revolt. This was the case particularly among the *ame-ha-arez*, who were Jewish "pagans," or farmers, and the communities remote from the cultural influence of the capital. Those elements of the Jewish population were most subject to influences that had emanated from Persian dualism. They looked to the Messiah to overthrow Satan and his cohorts, which they regarded as headed by Rome, and to establish Judaism as the religion of the world.

It was, therefore, among them that the new religious movement of the disciples of Jesus to preach the message of the messianic kingdom, and the salvation that could be obtained through it for all peoples, found its original support. *Pauline Christianity was a scheme of salvation that provided a synthesis of Roman imperialism with Jewish messianism.* Evolving a doctrine of salvation that could be achieved only after death and in another world, Paul hit upon the formula which pagan Rome had sought for in vain, as a means of consolidating its empire. That formula offered the individual both personal salvation and communal fellowship. It was a formula which promised to keep its adherents united, without their coming into conflict with the authority of Rome. In their unity they constituted a "Kingdom" that was "not of this world." In time, that "Kingdom" absorbed the authority of Rome. That happened when the Emperor Constantine saw in his dream the Cross, and heard a voice proclaim, "By this sign shalt thou conquer." The Roman Church thus came to be the Roman Empire, as it was revived through Christian religion. Christian Rome's use of the religious program of salvation, as an instrument of power, proved successful in extending ancient Rome's influence over the greater part of the European continent.

The revolt of modernism against medieval religion, a revolt which embraced the Renaissance, the Reformation and the social movements that followed on their heels, can best be understood as the challenge of resurgent nationalism to the religious imperialism of Rome. The rise of nationalism was a challenge to the Catholic religion of Europe, both as a program of living and as an organization of power.

As a program of living, it challenged the other-worldly emphasis in the Church's doctrine of salvation. The Renaissance was a return to a pre-Christian evaluation of the good things of life—physical prowess, sensuous enjoyment, aesthetic creativity, intellectual curiosity. It was a secularization of the ideal of salvation. It stressed the improvement of this world rather than redemption from this world and salvation in the next. The interests of men were shifting to worldly pursuits, and men were less interested than heretofore in promises of heaven or threats of hell. Pride of intellect and independence of judgment were deemed virtues instead of vices. Skepticism and unbelief ceased eventually to be regarded as evidence of depravity, and came to be regarded as evidence of freedom from superstition and obscurantism. Much of this-worldliness came to invade the Church itself, and that evoked the reactions of the Reformation and the Counter-Reformation.

The Reformation was in some respects a return to primitive Christianity before its union with Rome. But its revolt against the authority of the Papacy was both a consequence and a cause of a growing disposition to intellectual freedom and reliance on human reason. The Counter-Reformation was an effort to purge the Church itself of modernist secularist tendencies, and was largely successful, but the Church had lost irretrievably its power to convince a great part of the Western world that its way of salvation was the only, or the best, way. For those populations which have thrown off their allegiance to the Roman Catholic Church, the hope for salvation has become more and more secularized. Even the churches themselves stress the role of religion in promoting human welfare in this world rather than in saving man *from* a world under the domination of Satan. Naturalism has taken the place of supernaturalism, and science the place of theurgy, as a result of the growing confidence of men in their own creative powers which came into play with the rise of the various national cultures of the Western world.

As an organization of power, the revolt against medieval religion led to the rise of national states. In the old feudal order, the state was the secular arm of the Church, and the feudal ruler was conceived as ruling by divine right, so long as he did not interfere with the religious prerogatives of the Church. Only the Church was authorized to define the conditions under which men could achieve salvation after death, and administer the rites requisite to salvation. When the leaders of the Reformation accepted the protection of secular rulers, the situation was often reversed; the state "established" a church as its religious arm, to promote the loyalty of the subjects to the ruler by identifying the interests of the state with those of the religious communion.

The religious wars following upon the rival claims of state-supported churches, and the confusion created by many religions coexisting in some of the states, led eventually to the idea of the separation of church and state. But coincident with this tendency, there developed changes in the conception of the state, which made it assume religious functions, though their religious nature was concealed by a secular terminology. The rise of nationalism led to the self-assertion of the urban populations against monarchic authority and aristocratic privilege. Democracy was born and sovereignty vested in the people, not in monarchs ruling by divine right. The people thus assumed responsibility for organizing social life according to their own criteria of human welfare. This, in effect, made the democratic state an instrument of salvation, a religion. The state claimed the right to inculcate, through education, the spiritual values for which it stood. It taught patriotism, the program of living necessary for the salvation of the national community. *Thus nationalism became a new religion, alongside of the traditional churches.*

3

RELIGIONS SECULARIZED AND NATIONHOOD RELIGIONIZED

The traditional policy of the separation of church and state is inadequate, because it overlooks the fact that, among modern nations, nationalism is itself a religious program of salvation, and that government utilizes this program for the organization of power. *Democracy is virtually a doctrine of national salvation, and the public schools are, to all intents, religious institutions which attempt to utilize this doctrine of national salvation, as a means of promulgating social solidarity and effective collaboration among the citizens of the nation.* The problem of church and state should, therefore, for the purpose of this discussion, be restated as the problem of the relation of the traditional historic religions to the various emergent national religions of the modern world.

When medievalism gave way to modernism, the effect on religion was twofold: (1) religion began to be secularized, and (2) nationhood began to be religionized.

Religion has become secularized in that it has come to regard the promotion of social welfare as within its scope. Though it may still cling to the doctrine that true salvation is reserved for the experience of the soul after death, nevertheless, unlike medieval religion it regards the participation of men in movements designed to promote human welfare in this world as conditioning their salvation in the next. It does not classify the world and the flesh, along with the devil, as inherently anti-God. It does not commend an ascetic withdrawal from the responsibilities of political and economic life as virtuous conduct. On the contrary, it organizes social action, exercises political pressure on legislatures, and makes the promotion of social justice and world-peace definite objectives of its program of salvation.

On the other hand, nationhood has become religionized. The function of the state is no longer limited to defending its citizens against foreign aggression, and policing their relations with one another. It is concerned with promoting the public welfare, by conditioning the individual to the acceptance and loyal support of common ideals, ideals that are conceived as having importance not merely for the nation itself, but for civilization, or mankind in general. The state thus engages in public philanthropy, public health, the promotion of science and art, public education, provision of facilities for sport and recreation and any number of other activities, which reveal its interest in the salvation of the individual, on the one hand, and in the spiritual welfare of the group, as vested with moral responsibility, on the other. Whenever its interests collide with those of other states, it is wont to justify its own way of life by referring to some universal social doctrine, which is analogous to the theological tenets maintained by the churches. It is interested in making "the world safe for democracy," or in ushering in a classless society, or in destroying pluto-democracy, so that a new moral order can be established throughout the earth.

This change from medievalism to modernism, this secularization of religion and religionizing of nationhood, have had both good and bad results. The good effected by the change is the concentration of religion on the need of improving the conditions under which we live, in order to enable men to get the most out of life. The belief that this world is damned, and that there is no hope of improving it, makes men insensitive to the evils that exist. During the Middle Ages, religion did tend to become the opium of the masses. Not only did it train the masses to resign themselves to their suffering, in itself a legitimate use of opium, but also made those who were not suffering complacent in the enjoyment of their privileges and arrogant and tyrannical in the assertion of those privileges as rights. Democratic nationalism is, therefore, significant not merely politically, but also religiously, in that it asserts the sacredness of the human soul and its dignity, as a responsible creative moral agent. It regards all men as "endowed by their Creator with . . . unalienable rights . . . among these . . . life, liberty and the pursuit of happiness." The phrase, "endowed by their Creator" was not a conventional cliché, but an expression of a profound religious evaluation of human life.

Making nationhood into a religion has also led to evil consequences. In rendering their own prestige sacred and inviolable, the nations have often sacrificed the happiness and dignity of the individual citizen. Like avowedly religious organizations of power, modern states have been intolerant of freedom of expression and jealous of loyalty to international groups. They have been guilty of regimentation and the suppression of the creative differences among men, in order to facilitate domination by those in authority. Moreover, they have used the religion of nationalism to justify domination over other nations; they have launched imperialistic wars in order to bring "civilization," that is, their own brand of civilization, to other peoples. The "law and order" effected by the religion of nationalism, in its sacrifice of the individual to interests that are presumed to be those of the nation as a corporate entity, too often has turned out to be a mirage of order in a desert of disorder. For behind this apparent order are concealed deep and bitter clashes of interest, desperate forces held momentarily in a state of equilibrium so unstable that an insignificant incident would suffice to destroy it and to bring chaos and cataclysm.

4

THE FUNCTION OF HISTORIC RELIGIONS IN THE MODERN WORLD

With nationalism tending to develop into collective megalomania, the historic religions would be derelict in their duty, if they were to ignore that menace to the human spirit, and treat it as outside their province. They alone are at present in a position to expose the selfishness that lurks behind many an appeal to national interest, and to bring under control the national passions that flare up at the slightest provocation. Only the historical religions possess the basic values by which men can learn to distinguish in nationhood the elements of blessing from those of blight, and of cooperation in behalf of a common good from that which is impelled by a common craving for dominion.

But if the historic religions are to play so important a role in the life of men and nations, they will have to include the secular interests in their programs of salvation. Without necessarily abandoning their other-worldliness, they must, nevertheless, relate salvation to the actual everyday needs of human beings, to their desires, their hopes and their fears. The *churches should not permit the term "secular" to become an antonym of "religious"; they should utilize men's secular interests for achieving religious objectives.*

As the soul functions in the life of the individual—whatever be its destiny after death—only through his bodily organs and powers, so religion can function in society only through the secular interests and institutions of men. Organized religion must, therefore, stress the relevance of its traditions to those interests and institutions. It must use its influence toward making them contribute to the sense of the supreme worth and sanctity of human life also in this world. It dare not evade issues of a political and social character. Pious platitudes, dogmatic fulminations, and metaphysical subtleties are beside the point. What people need is moral guidance and religious inspiration to help them live in peace and harmony with one another and do their share toward the betterment of society in general.

So, too, religious education must deal with present realities. It should utilize the sacred literature of religious tradition, but should not regard familiarity with sacred texts and the acquisition of religious forms as the sum and substance of religious education. Such education must aim to help the growing personality of the maturing individual to face life from day to day with wisdom and courage and find it worth living.

The bearing of all this on the problem of nationalism is that *the historical religions have to recognize that it is normal and imperative for nationhood to acquire religious significance.* It is normal, because nationality, next to physiological heredity, is the most decisive influence in a person's life. It is imperative, because any decisive influence that is under human control, as is nationhood, should be shaped as a means to salvation and should possess religious significance. American nationhood has come to possess such significance, by reason of its intimate association with democracy as a way of life. Democracy is to us Americans nothing less than a method of this-worldly salvation. As such it derives its ultimate sanction from God—the Power that makes for universal salvation. We know full well, for example, that the unalienable rights on which democracy is based cannot be validated by the actual way in which human beings behave toward one another. But we assume that "men are endowed by their Creator" with these rights. That is a decidedly religious assumption, and on such an assumption the American people builds its nationhood.

The troublesome problem of religion in the public schools could be solved very simply, if the churches would concede to the public schools the right to teach religion, the religion of democracy. The churches should realize that to instill in the child the yearning to achieve the ethical and spiritual implications of democracy and the faith that democracy is worth living for and worth dying for is to teach religion of a high order. Surely any sincere believer in God must recognize that a system of education which would inculcate in our youth that attitude toward democracy would make of the American people an instrument of divine revelation.

The Bible, whether the Old or the New Testament, together with the rites of any of the historic churches, does not constitute the only means of teaching redemptive religion. It should be possible to teach the meaning of God in human life, with the aid of American *sancta*, like the great texts, events and personalities of the American people. The schools need not teach any particular conception of God; they need merely implant in the children the conviction that there is a Power in this universe which makes for human self-realization, that every deviation from democracy is fraught with evil consequences and every achievement of true democracy is a moral gain. If our public schools did that, they would be giving a truly religious education to every child, without prejudicing the interests of any religious organization or discriminating against any one of them.

Does this then mean that there is no place for the religious denominations to educate the child in religion? Not at all. American religion, if it is true to its own avowed ideal of democracy, cannot be fascist. The fact that God manifests Himself in American life does not invalidate manifestations of His presence and His grace in the experience of other historic peoples and movements. *Loyalty to American religion does not involve disloyalty to the religious traditions of the historic churches, so long as these can be reconciled with democracy.* Since all churches in America claim to have faith in the democratic way of life, they may continue to teach their own following the religious traditions of their particular denomination. American religion, being democratic and not fascist, can be hyphenated fruitfully with any religion that is not anti-democratic and fascist. All ethical religions are, in our day, monotheistic. There can, therefore, be no inherent con-

flict between worshipping God as manifest in American life and worshipping Him as manifest in the religious traditions of the respective
denominations.

This is the true solution of the problem of religion in the public
schools. All other proposed solutions are but devices for introducing
denominational religion in public school education, in a way that
would favor the majority group at the expense of the minority. Or they
attempt to bolster up the weakness of the denominational religious
institutions, by bringing them under the aegis of the state and making
its police power available to them. In all such proposals there is great
danger to democracy and, in the long run, to religion, which must
identify itself wholeheartedly with the cause of democracy.

Finally, the historic religions should take upon themselves the task
of correcting the abuses of national religion, to which attention has
been called. They should combat the tendency of the state to achieve
social solidarity at the expense of individuality, and to engage in imperialist schemes at the expense of other nations. Historic religions
possess the advantage of being able to view life in larger perspectives
than any modern national religion. They are rooted in a more distant
past, and their membership is spread over wider areas of the earth. They
should find it easier to transcend gusts of momentary passion and narrow local prejudices. They should give their endorsement to movements which are in harmony with the great ethical tradition of mankind. They should boldly denounce those movements which betray the
interests of men as human beings, bound by a common destiny to
toil for the realization of God's Kingdom of righteousness and peace.
Thus the historic or denominational religions can help keep the religion
of nationalism on the right path.

Particularly the Christian Church, which expresses the religion of
the great majority in America, can exercise a profound influence on
the development of American religion. It has it in its own hands to
decide whether the change from medievalism to modernism shall be
a blessing or a curse to men. If it will throw the weight of its influence
on the side of democracy, by making its own program of salvation
relevant to the secular interests of men, if it will endorse and encourage
the emergence of an American religion, with democracy as its way of
salvation, if it will deliver Americanism from the temptation to fascism,
chauvinism and imperialism, then the future of both the American
religion of democracy and the traditional religion of the churches is

assured. If not, democracy is in danger, and its danger imperils all ethical religion.

The influence of Judaism is, of course, proportionately less. But that in no wise lessens the responsibility of Jews to use whatever influence they have toward the same ends. Jewish religion, no less than Christian, must utilize all its institutions—home, school, synagogues, and the whole net-work of social and cultural institutions of Jewish life—in helping its adherents and all men to achieve the good and worthful life. Jewish religion, no less than Christian, must endorse and give encouragement to all those social movements that implement the American religion of democracy, regardless of the possible danger to Jews as a minority in antagonizing those in power. It goes without saying that Judaism should hold itself especially responsible for implementing the American religion of democracy in the government of its own communal affairs.

Moreover, Jewish religion should make use of its spiritual and cultural tradition, which embraces all the generations since the beginnings of monotheistic religion and which bridges oceans and binds the continents together, as a corrective to any aberrations that American religion may be tempted to make from the path of democracy. *The American religion of democracy has room for Judaism, and Jewish religion has room for American democracy.* They serve the same God, and can serve Him in cooperation, since neither is fascist, or exclusive of the other. There can, and should, develop in this country an American Jewish religion, which is as American as it is Jewish, and as Jewish as it is American. There is no danger in such hyphenation so long as the hyphen is conceived as uniting and not dividing, so long as the relationship that it expresses is a reciprocal one.

CHAPTER TWENTY-SIX

A UNIVERSITY OF JUDAISM

1

THE PROBLEM OF JEWISH LEADERSHIP

By this time it has become clear that we must be prepared to answer the question: "What is the most immediate step which must be taken to implement the civilizational character of Judaism?" It is evident that Jewish life, its social structure, its functional organizations and its established institutions will have to undergo considerable transformation. But as a prerequisite to such transformation, and as a means of assuring the achievement of its purpose, it is necessary to concentrate on the development of a leadership that shall be as diversified in its abilities as the differentiated character of Jewish life at present calls for, and that shall focus its abilities upon getting all Jews to want and welcome one another in that profound sense which shall augment their inner security and peace of mind.

If the Jewish people is to survive its present spiritual crisis, it will have to employ consciously and deliberately the means it has hitherto employed intuitively, whenever its existence was challenged. Its principal means has always been the creation of the appropriate educational agencies to transmit its heritage from generation to generation and to foster the needed type of spiritual leadership. The crisis which has been developing in the inner life of our people, since the beginning of the Emancipation, is now coming to a head. The reservoirs of creative Jewish life in the Old World have been ruthlessly destroyed. The best of what has been salvaged of that life has found refuge in this country. If American Jewry is to emerge from the present catastrophe strengthened instead of broken, it must forthwith create the appropriate type of educational institution for those who are to minister to its needs and to foster its powers of cooperation and creativity. There they will learn to see Judaism integrally and whole, and to communicate to those to whom they minister the necessary zeal and perspective for living a normal Jewish life.

Strangely enough, it never occurred to those, who were first confronted with the task of readjusting Jewish life to the new environment created by the Emancipation, to concern themselves with the problem of the leadership which the new distribution of social functions and the new specializations would require. All that concerned them was how to train rabbis and scholars. They seemed to be blind to the realities of their new situation and to its needs. This can be seen from the plan that Abraham Geiger, the great scholar and rabbinical founder of the Reform Movement, tried to put into effect a century ago. His idea was to establish Jewish branches in the theological departments of the German universities.[1] He expected that those trained there would qualify as rabbis for the German-Jewish communities. It was only because the German universities did not choose to furnish leaders to perpetuate Jewish life that rabbinical seminaries had to be established outside the universities. Later, those who attempted to reckon with the newly arisen needs of Jewish life also recognized that most Jewish teachers of the young were not born teachers, but had to be trained. That was the furthest they went in their effort to provide our people with intelligent guidance.

2

THE KEY PERSONS IN JEWISH LIFE

If we hope to save the various institutions, organizations and agencies which are the present bearers of collective Jewish life from becoming superfluous, we must see to it that Jews shall desire to remain Jews. The achievement of this objective depends not alone upon the rabbis, the teachers, the social workers and all the other functionaries, but as much, if not more, upon those who happen to be the key persons among us. They are the opinion-moulders in Jewish life. They exercise a decisive influence upon the average Jew, every time he has to make up his mind whether to cast his lot for or against Jewish survival. By reason of their outstanding talent, character, position or possessions, they represent for the average person the embodiment and standard of what is authoritative and worthwhile. They are admired and imitated; parents point to them; children look up to them; they occupy a special place of honor in the public mind. Their advice is sought not only in the particular fields in which they have made their mark, but in all matters of vital import. The greatest educational influence for good or for ill in any community is wielded not by parents, teachers and clergy, whose function it is to mould character, but by the successful business men, financiers, politicians, organizers, executives, writers, scientists and artists.

We Jews have men and women in all of these categories. Many of them have achieved not only national but world-wide reputations. At worst, they disdain to have anything to do with the Jewish people; at best, they regard it as an anachronism which, for the good of all concerned, they think should be liquidated. Indeed, one or two more generations of such Jews, and American Jewry will be a thing of the past.

Virtually all the great Jewish entrepreneurs, executives and financiers, some of whom even contribute large sums to Jewish causes and philanthropies, are convinced that the only salvation for which Jews should strive is to be absorbed by the general population. A number of Jewish writers, poets and critics who are prominent in the world of letters recently had occasion, in a symposium conducted some time ago by the *Contemporary Jewish Record* [2] to state how little Judaism means to them. It is hardly conceivable that any young Jew who harbors the wish to achieve a literary reputation, after reading what these successful men of letters had to say about Judaism, would care to be identified with it. Jewish artists are loath to exhibit their work under Jewish auspices. When it is planned to establish a great Jewish museum, every one of the great Jewish connoisseurs either refuses, or has to be refused, the opportunity to head it, so completely estranged are almost all of them from Jewish life. Of the many famous Jewish scientists, Einstein is an illustrious exception who only proves the rule. Not even his influence has been able to counteract the self-banishment of the great Jewish scientists from Jewish life.

So alienated are these Jewish key persons from their people that, if their place is ever to be taken by key persons who would not shun Judaism, at least a lifetime of strenuous and carefully planned effort will have to be invested in the undertaking. A beginning, however must be made at once, because every day allowed to pass without some effort toward that purpose renders its achievement less feasible. Such a beginning should be made through, and with, a type of Jewish key persons who, from the Jewish point of view, are much more accessible than the type described above. What brings them within reach is the fact that they are engaged in a professional capacity in communal Jewish activities. They possess either the training or the inclination to service Jewish institutions, organizations, campaigns and funds of all kinds. They function as administrators of centers, federations, welfare funds and other forms of Jewish activity. They, too, are key persons, because they occupy a position of vantage in determining the policies of those agencies which represent the Jewish people in action.

For some inexplicable reason, it has never occurred to those of us who clamor for a more positive and intensive Judaism that these social functionaries wield a tremendous influence over our fellow-Jews, and that thus far the weight of that influence has been thrown in the scale of assimilationism. They are bound to have the ear of laymen of whom they solicit funds, when it comes to deciding how those funds should be spent. Between the rabbi to whose sermons the well-to-do contributor to Federation, or to overseas funds, listens once or twice a year—if at all—and the social service executive with whom he takes lunch frequently to discuss the specific day-to-day problems in the conduct of Jewish institutions and campaigns, it is not difficult to surmise whose opinion concerning public Jewish policies is more likely to carry weight.

What is the reason that so large a proportion of those engaged in Jewish communal service, especially among the most highly salaried ones, are negatively disposed toward Judaism? In all too many cases it is due not merely to their being Jewishly illiterate, but to some festering antagonism which they must have developed as youngsters. Some parent, or *heder* teacher, perhaps tried to beat Judaism into them, or they happened to see it practiced in some repellent fashion, devoid of any ethical or spiritual significance. So long as they remain under the shadow of such background or upbringing, they regard it almost as their mission in life, and as a humanitarian service to their fellow-Jews, to free them from the burden of Judaism. With such a dejudaizing influence as these Jewish public servants exercise on the whole network of Jewish organizations, institutions and campaigns, rabbis and teachers haven't the ghost of a chance to meet with any success in all their efforts to revitalize Judaism, hard as they may try.

In this country, there existed some time ago a professional school for Jewish social workers. It came into being because some people recognized that to be entrusted with the supervision of Jewish centers, to carry on family case work among Jews, and even to conduct Jewish philanthropic campaigns one had to know something about Jews, their background and their inner conflicts, and perhaps even believe that Judaism does not have to be scrapped. But when it came to supporting that school financially, there was only one well-to-do Jew to whom these assumptions were self-evident. He waged a one-man battle against a whole board of assimilationist Jews, who refused to subscribe to those assumptions concerning the Jewish social worker, and he lost. So the school was liquidated.

It is high time that we cease groping and fumbling in our efforts to stop the rapid atomization of American Jewish life. If we are to take seriously the problem of developing an adequate leadership for Jewry of our day, there is only one way in which that problem can be solved. We must establish a University of Judaism in which not merely rabbis and teachers, but all types of professional and lay leaders would be trained to meet the demand created by the functional differentiation of Jewish activity.

A University of Judaism is not a parochial college or university to train Jews for academic degrees, or for the general professions like law, medicine or engineering. Such colleges and universities may be needed, because of the discrimination which is practiced against Jews in many of the academies of higher learning and professional institutions. But the question whether or not we deem it advisable to establish such institutions under Jewish auspices has nothing to do with the establishment of a University of Judaism. *That school is to be a university where those who wish to serve Jewish life in a professional or lay capacity can acquire the knowledge and the techniques necessary for being most proficient in their respective services.* It is to be an institution which will send forth trained men and women who will in all phases of Jewish activity replace the empirics, the people who know the mechanics of their calling but nothing of its meaning or ideology. Such people can have little or no understanding of their opportunities and responsibilities, from the standpoint of the Jewish future.

3

THE AFFIRMATIONS OF A UNIVERSITY OF JUDAISM

The question which naturally comes to mind is: How can this university steer clear of the Scylla of denominationalism and the Charybdis of non-commitment to any affirmative philosophy of Jewish life? Either tendency would wreck it. If Jewish unity and creativity are ideologically compatible with American life, the failure to achieve them can be due only to the lack of an educational pattern that would be both affirmative and inclusive. It should be possible, however, to design the broad outlines of such an educational pattern for the training of lay and professional Jewish leadership. For such a pattern to be both non-denominational and yet definitely affirmative, it would have to be based upon the following principles:

The first principle is the primacy of scholarship. This means, that, if the knowledge of Jews and Judaism is to be employed in the service of Jewish survival and growth, it must be the result of a modern scientific approach to the historical sources of Jewish life. When over a century ago, Zunz, Frankel, Geiger and Graetz laid the foundation of Jewish scholarship, which they termed *Juedische Wissenschaft*, they deliberately departed from the traditional assumption that the kind of knowledge Jews needed was to be obtained merely through learning. Learning consists in mastering the texts as they have come down, regardless of the living or historical context in which they arose. Scholarship is the relativity theory applied to ancient sources. It insists that the true meaning of any text cannot be derived from the contemplation of the text itself apart from the social, economic, psychological and intellectual setting to which it belongs. Jewish scholarship has become the *sine qua non* of any claim to a true understanding of Judaism.

A second principle is that Judaism must be Hebraic. When Schechter fulminated against what he called a Hebrewless Judaism, pointing to the disappearance of Alexandrian Judaism as a warning of what might happen to American Judaism, he had in mind essentially the use of Hebrew in the synagogue as a medium of religious service. Since those days, as a result of the Hebraic renaissance in Eretz Yisrael and the realization that Eretz Yisrael must be counted on to become the spiritual center of world Jewry, Hebrew has come to be regarded as indispensable to the achievement of Jewish consciousness. Such a consciousness reaches far more deeply into one's soul than mere ideas or symbols ever can. A Jewish consciousness formed on a knowledge of Hebrew gives depth to the ideational and institutional content of Judaism. With the wide diversity which exists in the acceptance of the content of Judaism, Hebrew has become indispensable to that kinship of soul without which Jewish unity is unthinkable.

A third principle is that Jewish life must have plenitude. Before Jews were admitted into the body politic of the Western nations, they had only their own historic civilization to draw upon for everything that gave meaning and direction to their existence. They had no problem of how to prevent Judaism from being crowded out of their lives by the competing claims and interests of a non-Jewish civilization, such as they now depend on for their health, security and happiness. Not even in the so-called "Golden era of Medieval Spain" were Jews expected, as they are now by virtue of their civic status, to be mentally and spiritually integrated into the non-Jewish culture of the majority. A Jew nowadays must ration his very time, to say nothing of his energies and capacities, so that he may find it possible to live as a Jew as well as an American, Englishman or Frenchman. In this matter of rationing, the principle should be: *Be a Jew to the maximum degree compatible with the legitimate claims of the non-Jewish national civilization.* Being a Jew to the maximum means refraining from the tendency to reduce Judaism to the worship of solemn and sonorous generalities. There are many who propose to meet the danger of being crowded out, which Judaism faces nowadays, by rarefying Judaism into such thin doctrines concerning God and man that it would no longer occupy any space. But that proposal generally ends up in spiriting Judaism away altogether. Judaism must be lived with all the senses and not merely subscribed to by our common sense. It must be audible and tangible. Hence the maximum ritual of observance is advocated not so much because of authoritative rule, as because of the feeling that Jewish life, to have saving quality, must be abundant and not thin and ghostlike.

And finally there is a fourth principle that the American environment must not only be accepted, but accepted graciously, as capable of permanently harboring Judaism. This is addressed to the maximalists among us who contend that civilizations, cultures or religions are necessarily exclusive and jealous of one another, and will take nothing less than the whole of one's personality. Accordingly, our maximalists conclude that, under the most favorable conditions, America can only be a way station for Judaism on its return to its homeland. This philosophy of Jewish life, known as the negation of *Galut*, though seldom aired publicly, exercises a distorting influence on more of Jewish activity than we suspect.

To see the problem of building up a Jewish lay and professional leadership in the proper perspective, we must have a clear idea of the specific areas, both those in which Jews have learned, and those in which they are in need of learning, to act cooperatively. Such cooperation is an urgent desideratum not for its own sake, but for the good and happiness of the individual Jew. The object to be kept in mind in all striving after such cooperation must always be to enable the individual Jew to acquire new courage, energy and resources for living as an affirmative Jew—whether he be Orthodox, Conservative, Reform or Secularist.

4

THE EDUCATIONAL PATTERN OF
THE UNIVERSITY OF JUDAISM

The areas of Jewish life for which highly qualified leadership is essential are: religion, education, social service, art, democracy and social research.

In the University of Judaism, the rabbinic school will necessarily receive first consideration, because the rabbi is the most articulate carrier of the Jewish tradition. Our initial task would have to be to see to it that those most endowed with gifts of mind and character enter the rabbinate or devote themselves to Jewish education, whether as teachers or as administrators. These young people have to receive a much broader gauged training than they have been given hitherto. Knowledge of the Jewish past and expertness in the interpretation of the great texts of our tradition are surely basic in such training. But nowadays the rabbi and teacher have to know, in addition, much about human nature, in the individual, and in society. They must know how to resolve the inner conflicts that are part of the mentality of minority groups.

All this implies the services of far larger faculties than our rabbinical seminaries and teachers training schools have been in a position to secure. It is, indeed, questionable whether rabbis and teachers whose training, being limited to a knowledge of the past, fails to give them some expertness in the understanding and management of human affairs, are fit spiritual leaders for our day. *As a first step, it is essential for us to revise completely our notion of the scope and character of the trained Jewish leadership we should strive to develop.* Only as we learn to think in terms of a much larger perspective of the requirements for Jewish survival will we realize what it means to provide an adequate training even for the callings which have thus far engaged our attention.

The field of Jewish education is virtually fallow. We have had to confine ourselves all these years to salvaging at least the very habit of transmitting the basic content of our tradition. The odds have been so overwhelming that we have been happy to get a minimum of permanent results out of a vast expenditure of energy. We cannot, however, go on much longer at the present wasteful rate. We are soon bound to reach the point of exhaustion. Jewish educators, who have the necessary understanding of all that is involved in trying to maintain Jewish life in the American environment, and who have sufficient experience with educational techniques, will have to be encouraged and stimulated to devise some new ways of creating a demand for Jewish education. The old appeals are no longer effective. Much that is new must be provided in the supply, if we hope to revive the demand. The very conception of Judaism as a civilization should suggest a reorganization of its educational content and a rethinking of the methods of communicating it. New occasions and opportunities in the lives of our children will have to be discovered, by means of which it might be possible to circumvent the obstacles presented by their present preoccupations. It might be necessary to develop a Jewish educational system which would enable the child to absorb Jewish values and ways of living by a kind of spiritual osmosis, as well as by the direct methods of instruction. *There is urgent need for a school of Jewish education whose faculties could blaze paths in the hitherto pathless maze of Jewish educational problems and difficulties.*

In the area of social service we come upon what is at present the most dynamic and significant expression of Jewish group life. But though it is an expression of Jewish group life, it does not help to conserve it, or to give it unity and common direction. Jewish group life, as it functions at present, moves in all directions. It is largely self-cancelling and chaotic. That is due to the lack of trained leaders imbued with a faith in the possibilities of Jewish life and the value of a Jewish future. It is assumed that Jewish workers in the fields of social service and communal organization have to be efficient either in raising funds, regardless of the ballyhoo methods they employ, or in spending funds, regardless of their failure to accomplish any genuine good. Formerly, barbers practiced surgery and midwives delivered babies. There are no statistics of the premature additions which those empirics contributed to the cemetery populations. We are likewise without statistics of the numbers of our people who are alienated from Jewish life, through the ignorance and misdirected efforts of our social empirics.

In the expenditure of Jewish communal effort, whatever still remains of the Jewish sense of mutual responsibility and of the traditional tendency of Jews to care for and welcome one another comes to life again only to waste itself on some passing need, without leaving any trace behind. If communal workers had been taught to grasp the deeper meanings of the situations they deal with, whether personal or social, if they had been taught how to utilize the opportunities, which are theirs, to revive the spirit of Jewish unity and individuality as a force for social good, they would emancipate our people from the fear of being Jews, from the sense of inferiority and self-hate that gnaws at the hearts of the old and young among us. There can be no question that such communal service would have resulted in raising the ethical standards in all our human relationships, in our homes, in our shops, in our market places, and in our offices. *The personal contacts which are part of the vocational duties of the social worker place him in a position of creating a Jewish public opinion that could revive the wholesome fear of* hillul hashem—*profaning the name of God—that acted in the past as a deterrent of all forms of moral and legal violations.*

There is an urgent need for a school where young men and women with a gift for service would be taught how to bring their talents to bear upon the most neglected area of Jewish life, from the standpoint of what it might contribute to the resources and energy of Jews to live as Jews. Jewish communal life would then no longer accentuate for our youth merely the woes and burdens of being a Jew. It would evolve deep ethical and spiritual values which would enable them to see in Judaism an invaluable moral asset.

The one area in which it is still possible for Jews to achieve an awareness of kind, to learn to feel their oneness not merely through being the common target for hostility, but through a common response to values that give meaning to life, is the area of the arts. Through music, drama, poetry, dance, painting and sculpture, people of the most divergent views and modes of living can discover their common humanity and their common cultural heritage. With so many centrifugal forces playing on what still survives of the Jewish consciousness, especially with the assimilative influences exerted on that consciousness by the inexhaustible abundance of art values in the non-Jewish world, it is inevitable for our children to assume that they do not need Judaism to enrich their lives. That is all the more true of the most artistically gifted among them. With no opportunity for self-expression and creative achievement within Judaism, what is there to hold them to it? And when they make their mark in the outer world, what claim can Judaism have on their loyalty? What have they to thank Judaism for? With men and women of creative calibre completely out of touch and out of sympathy with the struggle of the Jewish people to survive, what can we expect of the average person who sees in them the culmination of what he himself would like to be? Will he see any reason for attaching significance to Judaism?

There is only one way of preventing this inevitable outcome. If we

American Jews are determined to desire and welcome one another, if, instead of being plagued, we are to be healed by our oneness and common destiny, we must cultivate the area of the arts with all the passion of the will to live. We must turn to the gifted and creative youth among us and give them the kind of basic Jewish training that will open up for them the large vistas of Jewish experience in the past and in the present, which will impel them to self-expression through whatever artistic skill nature has endowed them with and training has perfected them in. Rabbis, teachers, social workers, however able and devoted they might be to their specific callings are only trying to make bricks without straw, so long as we have not the artists to produce those values which alone can render Jewish life audibly, visibly and tangibly interesting and fascinating. Alongside, therefore, the three schools in our University of Judaism—those for rabbinics, religious education and social service— there would have to be established a school for the arts in their relation to Judaism.

In all that has thus far been said, the accent has been placed upon the need for intensifying and organizing Jewish life, to prevent it from being absorbed by the life of the environment. When that need is suggested to our people, they generally react with the apprehension that such further intensification and organization of Jewish life would be tantamount to creating a new ghetto. There is nothing that the Jew rightly dreads more than being shut, or shutting himself, into a ghetto. It is therefore essential to have within the same University of Judaism a school specially devoted to the kind of training that would dissipate all fear of ghetto-ization. There should be a School of Democracy. Such a school would be a meeting ground of representative thinkers and teachers of all faiths and trends in American life. There Jewish and non-Jewish students and Jewish and non-Jewish leaders of thought would exchange ideas and experiences in classroom and open forums. There we would learn how to retain our Jewish individuality without insulating ourselves against all communication with the rest of the world.

That kind of school would give us Jews an opportunity to put our case before the court of public opinion. The influence of such a School of Democracy might not be perceptible at first, but in the long run it would generate the kind of good-will relations among different religious, racial and cultural groups that would be deep and lasting. Such a school would enable us to mingle freely with the outer world, without any embarrassment, as Jews loyal to our heritage and faithful to the spirit of democracy.

The University of Judaism cannot content itself with schools where accumulated knowledge and experience are communicated to students preparing themselves for practical fields of endeavor. These five schools, which have thus far been sketched, depend for their effective functioning upon two additional schools, one at the top of the ladder, as it were, and another at the bottom. At the top they depend upon an institute which is to yield new knowledge and experience to be won through research. At the bottom they depend upon the acquisition of eligible youth who are in need of sufficient Jewish background to avail themselves of the specialized training in any one of the graduate schools.

The research institute is an essential part of any modern University which aims to be more than a mere assembly line for turning out academic and professional robots. Life does not stand still. There is a continuous and rapid growth of information and experience which have to be converted into the working knowledge of those engaged in the various fields of endeavor. Each one of the five schools of the University of Judaism thus far named is likely to remain static, and to fall behind in its needed adaptation to meet the changing conditions of life, unless it is in close touch with a research department in which accepted assumptions are continually being reexamined, unknown facts unearthed and newer methods studied and suggested. The ideal setup in this University of Judaism for a research institute would be one in which each of the five schools would be represented by a line of research into the particular subject matter that has a direct bearing upon the courses it gives its trainees.

At the other end of the ladder in the University of Judaism there is need for anticipating the selection of eligible young people for leadership in the various fields of Jewish endeavor. If we wait until they are through with their college courses to make up their minds about training for a Jewish career, we are likely to be too late, especially in the case of the most desirable among them. The wisest plan is to include in the setup of the University a junior college. The four years, including the last two years of high school and the first two of college, is the ideal period for giving to Jewish youth an intensive training in Jewish subject-matter and for providing them with the necessary orientation for leadership in American Jewish life, whether in a lay or a professional capacity. Even if a number of those who attend such a junior college do not pursue graduate studies in the professional schools, they are likely to constitute when they become of age, a wholesome, leavening influence within our laity which is at present without an informed and convinced leadership. Those four years of a junior college are also an ideal period, from the standpoint of the student and that of the community. For the student those are the most impressionable and decisive years in the formation of a world outlook and choice of the group affiliation. From the standpoint of the community, those years possess the advantage of giving the student the chance to share both his high-school and college education with non-Jewish students.

In short, the University of Judaism would be the new instrument which American-Jewish life must evolve in order to cope with the disruptive influences to which the modern environment with its naturalism and its nationalism is subjecting our people. This is the new way in which we can prove our fitness once again to survive on this planet as a people. Our ancestors had a word for the fitness to survive under conditions of hardship and danger. They called it miracle. We might get more meaning out of the ancient prayer which we recite every fourth Sabbath when we announce the new moon, if we recognized this fitness to survive as miracle. "He who performed miracles for our fathers," we pray, "may He redeem us in the near future and gather the homeless of our people from the four corners of the earth." This well applies to our displaced fellow-Jews who are today knocking at the gates of Eretz Yisrael. For us in America, fitness to survive as Jews will have to be demonstrated by the capacity to live as one united fellowship and communion, despite the wide diversity in religious belief and practice. For that to come about, we need the University of Judaism.

EPILOGUE

The future that awaits us American Jews is unpredictable. It depends largely upon how we shall meet the challenge of the present and avail ourselves of its opportunities. There never was a time when Jews needed to pray as fervently as they should nowadays for "strength to accept with serenity the things that cannot be changed, for courage to change what can and should be changed, and for wisdom to distinguish the one from the other." [1]

The situation in which we find ourselves at present is woefully abnormal and startlingly unprecedented. The only way to remedy it is to resort to new and unprecedented measures, measures that call for a radical reconstruction of Jewish life and thought. The fundamental premise for such a reconstruction of Jewish life is that Judaism is a religious civilization, the civilization of the Jewish people. That conception is clearly applicable to the Judaism of the past in all of the many transformations that it underwent in the course of its history. It is a conception which, if its implications are realized, can give us Jews status in the present, and enable Jewish life to survive and to flourish in the future.

We Jews are a people, one and indivisible. We are the people whose ancestors once lived in Eretz Yisrael, where they created the Jewish civilization. By their occupancy of Eretz Yisrael they gave to that area its geographic identity as a distinct country. This is what is meant by speaking of Eretz Yisrael as the Jewish national home. The historic connection of the Jewish people with Eretz Yisrael is recognized. Jewish tradition has always recognized it. But Zionism gave a new turn to that recognition. It took the first step in the restoration of status to us Jews, when it refused to depend on supernatural intervention in human affairs for the restoration of Jewish national life to its ancient homeland. It has organized us Jews to effect that restoration by our own planned activity. That is the first step in the reconstruction of Jewish life.

When, in consequence of Zionist activity, our right to re-establish our national home in Eretz Yisrael was incorporated in the San Remo treaty and accorded recognition by the League of Nations and by the United States, a further step was achieved. Implied in the Balfour Declaration, which was incorporated in the Mandate, was not merely the recognition of the right to settle in Eretz Yisrael on an autonomous basis, but also the recognition of Jewish peoplehood, of the spiritual and cultural bond of Jews the world over. Zionism is thus an essential principle of Jewish reconstruction. In a Jewish commonwealth, it is possible for Jews once again to live completely within a Jewish civilization, to lead a free and self-determined Jewish life.

But Zionism is not enough. It is clear that not all Jews will live in Eretz Yisrael. The moment, however, some of us Jews elect to remain in the Diaspora, even when we have an option of settling in the Jewish national home, we cannot consider ourselves a nation in exile as did the Jews before the Emancipation. We cannot be expected to forego our cultural identification with, or our political allegiance to, the countries in which we reside. Nor is it satisfactory for us to consider ourselves merely a sect or religious denomination.

Nevertheless, our status need not be anomalous. It has become evident that democracy is meaningless, unless it recognizes the right of religious, racial and cultural communities to pursue common interests, so long as those interests are compatible with the general welfare. We American Jews would only be exercising our constitutional rights, if we were to organize ourselves into a voluntary community in order to foster our historic culture, to promote our social welfare and to give effect to our religious and ethical ideals. We shall thus retain and strengthen the bonds that unite us wherever we live, and participate in that civilization which will flourish in Eretz Yisrael.

Such a relation between Eretz Yisrael and the Diaspora will be no anomaly in a democratic world. Moreover, it will be entirely in harmony with the fundamental characteristic of the Jewish people throughout its history. Jewish peoplehood was never identified exclusively with state or territory, although it availed itself of the state in Eretz Yisrael as an agency of its civilization. Essentially, identification with Jewish peoplehood meant participation in Jewish civilization, in the Jewish way of life, in Torah. That is precisely what it should continue to mean in the future, except that such participation would henceforth have to be hyphenated with participation in the life and culture of the nations among whom we Jews live. Jewish civilization in the Diaspora would have to function not as a competitive, but as an additive element in our life as Jews, an element added to our interest in, and devotion to, the civilization which we share with our Gentile neighbors.

The recognition of this status would enable us Jews once more to feel that we "belong," that not only our right to exist as human beings is recognized, but also our right to exist as a collective entity, as the Jewish people. We shall not feel socially isolated and unwanted, when

our Jewish identity prevents us from being accepted without reservation by Gentile society, because we shall belong to a Jewish fellowship
that is solicitous for our welfare. We shall not seek emancipation *from*
Jewish life, but the emancipation *of* Jewish life.

The Jewish community, being concerned with the well-being of
the individual Jew as well as with the survival of the group, will have
to provide the facilities that can give vital and significant form to all
those cultural and religious values of which our Torah has always been
the vehicle. To be sure, in its cultural activities, the Jewish community
will not only avoid duplicating, but will also encourage our participating in, the activities of the general community in the education of
child, adolescent and adult. Its main purpose will be to provide those
additional educational influences which we need, because we are Jews.
It will endeavor to enrich our lives with the best products of Jewish
cultural activity past and present. It will train us to meet our obligations to our people at home and abroad, and to participate in the
development of the Jewish national home in Eretz Yisrael. It will
guide us in the discharge of our duties not only as Jews, but as citizens
of our respective countries, and as men sharing responsibly in the shaping of a better social order for mankind. It will seek to raise our ethical
standards to the highest attainable level.

The very effort to link the life of the Jewish individual with that of
his people, and the life of his people with that of mankind, will inevitably lead to a renewal of religious faith. All such effort strengthens
the belief that life is not aimless and futile, not a mere play of blind and
meaningless forces, but the manifestation of spiritual purpose, the unfolding of a plan for human cooperation and brotherhood. It deepens
the faith that the spiritual insights of men are not fortuitous, but are
clues to the ultimate nature of mankind and the world, a manifestation or revelation of a universal Spirit of which the human soul is a
part.

We need not, and should not, conceive of that universal Spirit as a
sort of invisible superman characterized by the same emotional, intellectual and volitional activities as mortals. We need not, and should
not, regard God as a miracle worker. We need not, and should not,
regard Him as interested in the Jewish people more than in all others.
But we may, and we should, seek communion with God, in the sense of
endeavoring to bring the aims and purposes of our personal and communal life in harmony with these universal aims.

We should articulate, in worship, our gratitude for the powers that sustain our lives, and should express our sense of dependence on God for. the fulfillment of our legitimate needs. We must not imagine that we know the nature of God, but we must have faith that, if we earnestly strive to put ourselves at the disposal of the Spirit that makes for full, harmonious and abundant living, we help to redeem life from futility and frustration. And we must invoke God to give to the Jewish people the insight, the wisdom and the courage to play its part worthily as a cooperating member of human society, and as an agency in ushering in His Kingdom, the universal rule of freedom, justice and peace.

Such are the outlines of that reconstruction of Jewish life for which we Jews must plan and strive. It is a program difficult of achievement, but not inherently impossible. It takes full cognizance of the difficulties that confront us, but it makes no demands that are contrary to reason, inconsistent with human nature at its best, or in conflict with natural law. It provides for the continuity of Jewish life and the full utilization of the Jewish traditional heritage, but it takes full cognizance of the conditions and the needs of contemporary Jewry. It is no nostrum. To give it effect will tax our energies to the utmost and exercise the highest faculties of mind, heart and soul. But then is not that the way we are commanded to love God? Helping to regenerate the life of Israel is unquestionably an expression of the love for God.

Having to live henceforth partly in its own homeland, and partly in the Diaspora, permanently integrated with other nations, the Jewish people is bound to undergo metamorphosis. We have nothing to fear from metamorphosis. That, indeed, is how we began our career as a people. This seems to be the meaning of the story that God changed the name of "Abram" to "Abraham" [2] and of "Jacob" to "Israel." [3] There is probably an echo of an early religious metamorphosis, which took place in our pre-historic stage, in the story that at first God was known by the name of "Shaddai" and later by the four-letter name of "YHWH." [4] The metamorphosis that will give us now a new lease on life may presage that brotherhood of the nations which will mold this world of ours into the Kingdom of God.

The present condition of the Jewish people may well be compared to that of its ancestor Jacob, when, in a state of helplessness, he lay down to sleep in the wilderness at what turned out to be earth's gate to heaven. Legend has it that, as he slept, the angels ran up and down the great ladder that reached from earth to heaven to see whether there was any resemblance between the image of Jacob which was graven on God's throne and the weak and helpless Jacob who lay on the ground.

When they noted the contrast, they started to mock and deride the forlorn fugitive from Esau's wrath. But God could not bear their ridiculing Jacob, and He chased them away.[5] Thus, whenever our own doubts and despairs concerning our Jewish people seem to mock the high ideals concerning Israel which our lawgivers and our poets, our prophets and our sages have projected into their conception of God's Kingdom on earth, let us pray that God chase away those mocking and gloomy thoughts. Let us be heartened by the promise God made to Jacob: "Your descendants shall be as numerous as the dust on the ground; you shall spread abroad to the west and the east, to the north and the south, and in you and your descendants shall all the families of the earth be blessed." [6]

NOTES

PREFACE

1 N. Y. *Times Magazine Section*, Sept. 1, 1946.
2 Kaplan, Mordecai M., *Judaism as a Civilization*, Macmillan Co., N. Y., 1934.

CHAPTER ONE

1 Ezek. 37, 11.
2 *Ibid.*, 18, 2-4; 33, 10-11.
3 *Ibid.*, 33, 30-32.
4 *Ibid.*, 37, 1-14.
5 Jer. 5, 14.
6 Ezek. 6, 10.
7 *Ibid.*, 6, 9.
8 *Reform Judaism in the Large Cities*, Union of American Hebrew Congregations, 1931,
   p. 49.
9 Schweitzer, Albert, *The Decay and the Restoration of Civilization*, London, 1932, p. 48.
10 E. Solvcy, quoted by P A. Sorokin, *Contemporary Sociological Theories*, N. Y. 1928,
   p. 20.
11 Sorokin, Pitirim A. *The Crisis of Our Age*, N. Y. 1941, p. 164.
12 Philipson, David, *The Reform Movement in Judaism*, N. Y. 1931, pp. 149-150.
13 *Ibid.*, 354.
14 Kohler, K. *Jewish Theology*, N. Y. 1918, 326-7.
15 *Yearbook*, Central Conference of American Rabbis, Vol. XLVII, 1937, p. 97ff.
16 Ezek. 37, 11.
17 *Ibid.*, 37, 12.
18 Klatzkin, J. *Miklat*, Vol. I (1920), N. Y. pp. 15-24, 197-208, 369-381.
19 Kaufman, E. *Golah Venekar*, Tel-Aviv, 1930, Vol. II.
20 Rank Otto, *Will Therapy and Truth and Reality*, N. Y. 1945, p. 99.
21 Jer. 20, 1-7.
22 Ezek. Chaps. 40-48.
23 *Mishnah, Abot* IV, 16.
24 Ezek. 18, 31.

CHAPTER TWO

1 Based on the passage in *Zohar* V, 73b, which speaks of Israel, God and Torah as being
   linked together.
2 N. Y. Times, Aug. 7, 1946.
3 Baron, Salo Wittmayer, *The Jewish Community*, Phila. 1942, Vols. I-III.
4 A small parchment scroll on which are written by hand the passages in Deut. 6, 4-9, and
   Deut. 11, 13-21. The scroll is placed in a wooden or metal case and attached to the
   door post at the entrance of the house.
5 *Menorah*, a lamp or candelabra used for kindling the lights on each of the eight nights
   of the Hanukkah festival.
6 *Kiddush*, the prayer which is recited on Friday night over a cup of wine in honor of
   the Sabbath. See *Authorized Daily Prayer Book*, London, p. 122.
7 *Berit Milah*, the circumcision whereby the child is initiated into the Covenant of
   Abraham. See *Authorized Daily Prayer Book*, London, p. 304.
8 *Bar Mitzvah*, the ceremony of calling a boy to the reading from the Torah, when he
   completes his thirteenth year, to mark his reaching the age of religious duty and
   responsibility.

9 *Bat Mitzvah*, a recently established ceremony for a girl during her thirteenth year, paralleling the *Bar-Mitzvah* ceremony for a boy.

10 Brod. Max, *Jewish Frontier*, Aug. 1946.

11 Pinson, Hilda, "Jewish Music in New York, Season 1945-46," *Menorah Journal*, Winter 1947.

12 Wharton, John, *Saturday Review of Literature*, July 20, 1946.

CHAPTER THREE

1 *The Nation*, Aug. 10, 1946 (Vol. 163, No. 6).

2 *Yearbook*, Central Conference of American Rabbis, 1937, p. 94ff.

3 Deut. 6, 4.

4 Exod. 6, 7.

5 *Emmunot Ve-Deot* III, 7.

6 Janowsky, Oscar I., *The Jews and Minority Rights*, N. Y. 1933, pp. 57-62.

7 Baron, Salo Wittmayer, *Social and Religious History of Jews*, N. Y. 1937, Vol. II, pp. 226-7; Jewish Encyclopedia, *Hasidim*, Vol. VI, p. 255.

8 Ahad Ha-Am, *Al Parashat Derakim*, Berlin 1904, Vol. I, pp. 121-132.

9 *Survey Graphic*, Dec. 1946.

10 Bonsal, Stephen, *Suitors and Suppliants*, N. Y. 1946, p. 276.

11 Eugene, Rev. Brother, *Compendium of Bible and Church History*, N. Y. 1931, p. 199.

12 Moehlman, Conrad Henry, *The Christian Jewish Tragedy*, Rochester, N. Y. pp. 247-251.

CHAPTER FOUR

1 Gen. 11, 1-9.

2 Is. 66, 18.

3 Hallevi, Judah, *Kitab Al Khazari*, Part I, 115.

4 Maimonides, Moses, *Yad Ha-Hazakah*, Hilkot Melakim, VIII, 11.

5 *Shir Ha-Shirim Rabba*, I, 6; *Kohelet Rabba* I, 1.

CHAPTER FIVE

1 Lev. 19, 5.

2 Deut. 6, 5.

3 *Fortune* Vol. 33, No. 2, (Feb. 1946).

4 Plagemann, Bentz, *All for the Best*, N. Y., 1946, p. 187.

5 Van Paassen, Pierre, *Earth Could Be Fair*, N. Y., 1946, p. 128.

6 Ferm, Vergilius, *Crozier Quarterly*, Jan. 1946.

7 Pittenger, W., "Christianity is a Culture" in *Christian Century*, July 31, 1946. Morrison, Charles Clayton, "Can Protestantism Win America," *ibid.*, Vol. 63, No. 14 (April 3, 1946) and No. 27 (July 3, 1946).

8 Frank, Jerome, "Red, White and Blue Herring" in *Saturday Evening Post*, Dec. 6, 1941.

9 The Portable Thomas Wolfe, N. Y. 1946, pp. 554-5.

10 Warner, W. Lloyd and Srole, Leo, *The Social Systems of American Ethnic Groups*, Yale University Press, 1945, p. 161.

11 Zeitlin, Joseph, *The Disciples of the Wise*, N. Y. 1945, Ch. V.

12 *Sefer Torah,* a scroll of the Torah, or Pentateuch, which is placed in the Ark of the Synagogue, and out of which the weekly pericope is read on Sabbaths. The first section of the weekly pericope is read on Mondays and Thursdays.

13 *Simhat Torah* (rejoicing in the Torah), the name given to the festival immediately following the Feast of Tabernacles, because on it the weekly pericopes of the Pentateuch are concluded, and begun again.

14 *Sukkot,* Feast of Tabernacles, commemorating the journeying of the Israelites in the Wilderness.

15 *Lulav,* a palm branch together with myrtle and willow twigs held during worship on *Sukkot.*

16 Cf. Chapter XXV, Section 4 on "The Problem of Church and State in Education."

17 *Menorah Journal,* Vol. I, No. 3.

18 Fadiman, Clifton, *Sat. Rev. Lit.* Aug. 31, 1946.

19 Ps. 102, 19.

20 *Vayyikra Rabba,* XXX, 3.

CHAPTER SIX

1 Russell, Bertrand, *Education and the Good Life,* N. Y. 1936, p. 194.

2 See Article "B'nai B'rith," *Jewish Encyclopedia.*

3 *Yearbook,* Central Conference of American Rabbis, Vol. XLVII, 1937, pp. 97-100.

4 *Shabbat,* 102b.

5 *Abot,* IV, 5.

6 *Ibid.* III, 17.

7 *Bereshit Rabba,* XCVIII.

CHAPTER SEVEN

1 Ahad Ha-Am, *Al Parashat Derakim,* Berlin 1904, Vol. I, pp. 42-56.

2 *BILU,* the initial letters of the Hebrew verse: *Bet Yaakov leku venelekah,* ("O House of Jacob, come, and let us go" Is. 2, 5). This was the name adopted in 1882 by a small group of students in Russia, who gave up their professional studies to settle on the land in Palestine. Impelled to action by the pogroms of 1881, this handful of young people decided to lend their efforts to the creation of a new life for the Jewish people. They were determined to develop a new type of agricultural colony in Eretz Yisrael, and they finally succeeded in setting up Gederah, the forerunner of numerous cooperatives and colonies which now give character to the *Yishuv* (the Jewish community of Eretz Yisrael).

3 *Haggadot,* plural of *Haggadah,* the liturgy recited at the evening meal on the first and second night of the Passover.

4 *Shavuot,* Feast of Weeks, the festival in celebration of the wheat harvest. It also commemorates the giving of the Torah on Mount Sinai.

5 *Sukkot,* see Notes, Ch. V, 14.

CHAPTER EIGHT

1 Westermarck, Edward, *The Origin and Development of Moral Ideas,* London, 1912, Vol. I, p. 557.

2 *Gittin,* 61a.

[3] Exod. 12, 49; Lev. 19, 34 etc.
[4] Matthew, 10, 5.
[5] Deut. 15, 3.
[6] Lev. 19, 34.

CHAPTER NINE

[1] Goodenough, E. R. *Religious Tradition and Myth*, New Haven, 1937, p. 13.
[2] Enelow, Hyman G. *Jewish Tracts*, Cincinnati, No. 1, p. 4.
[3] See Notes, Ch. II, 1.
[4] *Ekah Rabbati, Petihata*, 2.
[5] Maimonides, *Yad Ha-Hazakah, Hilkot Teshubah* III, 11.
[6] Kohler, Kaufmann, *Jewish Theology*, N. Y. 1918, p. 7.
[7] Albo, Joseph, *Ikkarim*, Phila., 1929, Vol. I, p. 2.
[8] Maimonides, Moses, *Commentary on Mishnah, Sanhedrin*, X, 1, and Hoffman, David, *Das Buch Leviticus*, Berlin, 1905, pp. vii, and 6.
[9] Formstecher, Solomon, (1808-1889) rabbi in Offenbach, Germany, a leader of the Reform Movement, who took part in the important rabbinical conferences of the mid-nineteenth century. Author of *"Religion des Geistes,"* in which Judaism is described as a universal religion.
[10] Steinheim, Solomon L. (1789-1866), physician in Altona, Germany. Co-worker with Gabriel Riesser in the struggle for emancipation of the Jews. His chief literary work, *"Die Offenbarung nach dem Lehrbegriffe der Synagogue,"* is an attempt to ground revelation in philosophic truth.
[11] Hirsch, Samuel (1815-1889), noted Reform rabbi who served for twenty years as Chief Rabbi of Luxembourg, before coming to Congregation Keneseth Israel in Philadelphia in 1868. Author of a number of books on the philosophy of Judaism.
[12] Cohen, Hermann, (1842-1918), outstanding representative of neo-Kantian school of philosophy. Proponent of a distinctive philosophy of Judaism based on reinterpretation of the tradition in terms of the Kantian "ought." Author of many works including *"Die Religion der Vernunft aus den Quellen des Judentums."*
[13] Buber, Martin (born 1878), outstanding scholar of Hasidism, and an original thinker of the mystic school. Author of many works on Hasidism and the Bible. A strong influence in cultural Zionism; now professor of philosophy at the Hebrew University.
[14] Rosenzweig, Franz (1886-1929) distinguished philosopher. Almost on the verge of conversion, he became a devoted Jew and made an appreciable contribution to the reinterpretation on Jewish tradition. His main work is *"Stern der Erlosung."*
[15] Schweitzer, Albert, *Decay and Restoration of Civilization*, London, 1932, p. 102.
[16] Is. 42, 6.
[17] John 8, 32.

CHAPTER TEN

[1] Lev. 26, 3.
[2] Amos 4, 7.
[3] Ezek. 18, 2-4.
[4] Amos 4, 7; Malachi 3, 10; 13-19.
[5] Edman, Irwin, *The Contemporary and His Soul*, N. Y. 1931.
[6] Cf. Is. 42, 6-7.
[7] James, William, *The Varieties of Religious Experience*, N. Y. 1907, p. 464.

CHAPTER ELEVEN

[1] *Encyclical Letter on the Christian Education of Youth,* issued by Pope Pius XI, Jan. 11, 1930.
[2] Cf. Barnes, H. E., *The Twilight of Christianity,* N. Y. 1929.
[3] Durkheim, Emile, *The Elementary Forms of Religious Life,* London and N. Y., no date.
[4] Otto, Rudolf, *The Idea of the Holy,* Univ. of Oxford Press, 1923.

CHAPTER TWELVE

[1] Gen. 3, 8.
[2] *Ibid.* 18, 1-5.
[3] Deut. 34, 10.
[4] Exod. 33, 22-23.
[5] Lev. 18, 5.
[6] *Tosefta, Sanhedrin,* XIII.
[7] Maimonides, Moses, *Yad Ha-Hazakah, Hilkol Melakim* VIII, 11.
[8] Enelow, H. G. *Kawwanah: The Struggle for Inwardness in Judaism, Studies in Jewish Literature,* Berlin, 1913.
[9] *Bat Mitzvah,* a ceremony adopted, in recent years, for girls, corresponding to that of the *Bar Mitzvah.* (See Notes, Ch. II, 8.)

CHAPTER THIRTEEN

[1] Deut. 7, 7.
[2] Amos 3, 2.
[3] Exod. 19, 6.
[4] *Shir Ha-Shirim Rabba* VII, 3.
[5] *Vayyikra Rabba* XVIII, 3; *Mek.* on Exod. 20, 19; *Shabb.* 55b.
[6] *Shir Ha-Shirim Rabba* I, 2, the interpretation of I Chron. 24, 5.
[7] *Maskilim,* adherents of the movement during the 19th century among Jews of Eastern Europe to westernize Jewish life.
[8] Reformers, adherents of the movement in Germany, which arose in 1815, to denationalize and westernize Judaism. Cf. Philipson, David, *The Reform Movement in Judaism,* N. Y. 1931.
[9] Historical School, the movement to introduce changes in Jewish religious practice on the basis of inherent historical principles. It came into being when Zachariah Frankel first enunciated such principles at the Rabbinical Conference at Frankfort-on-the-Main in 1845.
[10] Kohler, Kaufmann, *Jewish Theology,* N. Y., 1918, p. 327. Joseph, Morris, *Judaism as Creed and Life,* London, 1920, p. 151.
[11] *Yebamot,* 79a.
[12] Bamberger, Bernard J., "Are the Jews a Chosen People?", *The Reconstructionist,* Vol. XI, No. 16.
[13] Exod. 32, 32.
[14] Num. 11, 29.
[15] Joseph, Morris, *op. cit.* p. 9.
[16] Is. 2, 2-4; Micah 4, 1-3.

546 Notes

17 Bamberger, Bernard J., *Ibid.*
18 *Ibid.*
19 *Ibid.*
20 Sandburg, Carl, *Lincoln*, N. Y., 1939. Vol. I, p. 570.
21 Kohler, Kaufmann, *Jewish Theology*, N. Y. 1918, p. 326; Geiger, Abraham, *Judaism and Its History*, N. Y. 1911, p. 47.
22 *Tosefta, Sanhedrin*, Ch. XIII.
23 Maimonides, *Yad Ha-Hazakah, Hilkot Melakim*, VIII, 11.
24 Adler, Felix, *An Ethical Philosophy of Life*, N. Y., London, 1927, p. 12.
25 Based on the verse in Prov. 3, 18, which is interpreted in Jewish tradition as referring to the Torah.
26 *Berakot*, 17a.
27 Calhoun, Robert Lowry, *God and the Common Life*, N. Y., London, 1935, pp. 52-72.
28 *Authorized Daily Prayer Book*, London, p. 76.
29 Bamberger, Bernard J., *op. cit.*

CHAPTER FOURTEEN

1 *Mishnah, Sanhedrin*, X, 1.
2 Jer. 12, 1; Hab. 1, 2-4; 13-14.
3 Ps. 37, 1-2; 73, 2-28.
4 Gen. 18, 25.
5 Job 9, 22.
6 *Bereshit Rabba* XLIX, 9.
7 *Authorized Daily Prayer Book*, London, p. 69.
8 Albo, Joseph, *Ikkarim*, Jewish Publication Society, Phila. 1930. Book IV, Chapters 12-14.
9 *Bereshit Rabba* IX, 8.
10 *Yebamot* 103b.
11 *Berakot* 61a.
12 Eccl. 7, 20.
13 Ben Azzai. Tal. Jer. *Nedarim* IX, 4.
14 *Yoma* 86b.
15 Job 14, 4.
16 *Yalkut Shimeoni* on Job 14, 4.

CHAPTER FIFTEEN

1 Mendelssohn, Moses, *Jerusalem in Mendelssohn's Saemmtliche Werke*, Vienna, 1838, p. 268.
2 *Authorized Daily Prayer Book*, London, 1929, pp. 89-90.
3 Schechter, Solomon, *Dogmas in Judaism, Studies in Judaism*, First Series, Jew. Pub. Society, Phila. 1938.

1. SPIRITUAL SELECTION

1 Is. 11, 7.
2 *Bereshit Rabba* I, 1.
3 Lev. 18, 5.
4 *Baba Batra* 16a.

[5] Gen. 1, 14.
[6] Eccl. 3, 19.
[7] *Ibid.*, 3, 15.
[8] *Kohelet Rabba* on Eccl. 3, 15.
[9] Zechariah 4, 6.

2. FAITH

[1] Is. 51, 1-2a.
[2] *Ibid.*, 2b.
[3] *Abot* V, 3.
[4] *Bereshit Rabba* XXXII, 3.
[5] Jer. 32, 6ff.

3. HOPE

[1] Gen. 28, 21.
[2] *Bereshit Rabba* LXX, 6.
[3] Eccl. 1, 15.
[4] *Ibid.*, 9.
[5] Prov. 6, 12.
[6] *Baba Kamma* 93a.
[7] Concluding statement of *Mishnah Makkot*.
[8] Ps. 119, 54.
[9] Maimonides, Moses, *Commentary on Mishnah Sanhedrin*, Introd. to Ch. X.
[10] *Abot*, II, 16.
[11] Ps. 18, 30.

4. HUMILITY

[1] Lev. 19, 2.
[2] Gen. 1, 26.
[3] *Shab.* 133b.
[4] Is. 14, 12-15.
[5] Ezek. 28, 2-9.
[6] Exod. 5, 2.
[7] *Ibid.*, 12, 12.
[8] I Sam. 8, 7.
[9] Cf. *Bereshit Rabba* XLI, 5.

5. INNER FREEDOM

[1] Gen. 18, 25.
[2] Job 42, 1-6.
[3] II Sam. 12, 9.
[4] I Kings 21, 19ff.
[5] Amos 6, 10-11.
[6] Is. 28, 14ff.
[7] Wells, H. G., *The Outline of History*, N. Y. 1931, p. 929.
[8] Ps. 118, 6.
[9] Num. 21, 5.
[10] Hocking, William Ernest, *Morale and Its Enemies*, Yale Press, New Haven, 1918, pp. 110-112.
[11] Prov. 4, 23.

6. PATIENCE

[1] Gen. 8, 21.
[2] Exod. 14, 3-4.
[3] Song of Songs, 2, 7.

4 *Shir Ha-Shirim Rabbah* II, 7.
5 *Sanhed.* 97b.
6 Micah, 7, 8.
7 *Shir Ha-Shirim Rabbah* VI, 10.
8 Kafka, Franz, *The Great Wall of China*, N. Y. 1946, p. 278.

7. THANKFULNESS

1 Ps. 92, 2.
2 *Mid. Teh.* LVI, 4.
3 *Mishnah Berakot* IX, 1.
4 *Menahot* 43b.
5 *Authorized Daily Prayer Book*, London, 1929, p. 51.
6 Ps. 150, 6.
7 Deut. 8, 17.
8 Ps. 36, 7.
9 *Bereshit Rabba* XXXIII, 1.
10 Gen. 32, 11.
11 Lev. 25, 23.

8. JUSTICE

1 In this section, only distributive justice is considered. What is generally termed "punitive justice" cannot be considered one of the basic values of religion, because its very nature is to a large extent problematic. The tendency of ethics is to have us dispense with legal punishment, which is a form of revenge, and to have us resort to physical penalties either as a means of restraining the offenders from committing further harm, or as a warning to potential offenders.
2 Gen. 18, 19.
3 *Baba Batra* 91b.
4 *Gittin* 6b.
5 *Bereshit Rabba* LXIII, 14.
6 *Ibid.*, IX, 8.
7 *Shabbat* 33b.
8 Eph. 5, 22.
9 Aristotle, *Politics*, Bk. I, 5.
10 Pound, Roscoe, *The Spirit of the Common Law*, Boston, 1921, p. 86.
11 Quoted from Taine's *Notes sur l'Angleterre*, by Tawney R. H. *Equality* N. Y. 1929, p. 13.
12 Tawney, R. H. *op. cit.* p. 36.
13 Nicolay, John G. and Hay, John, *Abraham Lincoln: A History*, 1890, Vol. III p. 299.
14 Quoted from Matthew Arnold's Lecture on "Equality", in Mixed Essays, ed. 1903, p. 51, by Tawney R. H. *op. cit.*, p. 12.
15 Tawney, R. H. *op. cit.*, p. 13.
16 *Ibid.*, p. 226.

9. LOVE

1 Cf. above, Ch. X.
2 Maimonides, Moses, Introd. to his Commentary on *Mishnah Seder Zeraim*.
3 Maimonides, Moses, *Guide for the Perplexed* II, 1.
4 Albo, Joseph, *Ikkarim*, Bk. III, ch. 13.
5 Deut. 4, 32.
6 *Bereshit Rabba* I, 10.
7 Lev. 19, 2.
8 Deut. 13, 5.

9 *Sotah*, 14a.
10 Deut. 4, 2.
11 Exod. 15, 2.
12 *Shabbat*, 133b.
13 Exod. 34, 7.
14 *Ibid.*, 34, 9-10.
15 Lev. 19, 18b.
16 *Ibid.*, 19, 18.
17 The Testament of the Twelve Patriarchs 18, 2.
18 Lamentations, 3, 30.
19 *Yoma*, 23a.
20 Lev. 19, 17.
21 Gen. 5, 1.
22 *Jer. Nedarim* IX, 4.
23 Hosea 11, 9.
24 Ps. 116, 11.
25 Prov. 15, 15.
26 *Baba Batra*, 145b.
27 Hersey, John, *Hiroshima*, N. Y. 1946.
28 Claessens, August, *Eugene Victor Debs*, N. Y. p. 10.
29 *Yebamot* 79a.
30 Ps. 136, 1.

CHAPTER SIXTEEN

1 *Yebamot* 79a.
2 Exod. 23, 7.
3 *Shabbat*, 55a.
4 *Yoma* 86a.
5 Lev. 19, 18.
6 *Baba Metzia* 30b.
7 *Shabbat*, 133b.
8 The ninth of the Month of Ab, a fast day in commemoration of the destruction of the First and the Second Temple.
9 *Kol Nidre*, the ritual of absolving one of vows. That ritual forms the solemn inauguration of the service of the Day of Atonement.
10 See Notes, Ch. V, 13.
11 *Purim* commemorates the day when the Jews of Persia narrowly escaped being victims of Haman's plot to exterminate them.
12 *Kinnot*, elegies recited on *Tishea Be-Ab* (Ninth of Ab) in commemoration of the destruction of the First Temple in 586 B.C.E. and of the Second Temple in 70 C.E.
13 *Hasidim*, a sect of pietists. followers of the movement inaugurated in the middle of the 18th century by R. Israel Baal Shem Tov.
14 The Ark in the front part of the Synagogue in which are deposited the Scrolls of the Torah.
15 *Bimah*, a raised reading desk either at the front or in the middle of the synagogue.
16 The curtain hung on the Ark.
17 See Notes, Ch. II, 4.
18 A decorative drawing containing appropriate religious texts hung on the east wall of the room, to indicate the direction in which to face when reciting the daily prayers.
19 See Notes, Ch. II, 6.
20 The prayer which is recited on Saturday night, to mark the conclusion of the Sabbath.
21 Pioneers, a term applied to the builders of the Jewish colonies in Eretz Yisrael.

22 Watchmen, colonists engaged in watching the farms and homes of the settlers against depredations by marauders, usually Arabs.

23 Sinclair, Jo., *Wasteland*, N. Y. 1946, pp. 222-223. Permission obtained from Harper.

24 *Piyyut*, a type of prayer in poetry or poetic prose, developed during the Middle Ages, and included in Sabbath and Festival services.

25 See Notes, Ch. II, 10.

CHAPTER SEVENTEEN

1 *Shir Ha-Shirim Rabbah*, II, 7.

2 Herzl, Theodore (1860-1904), journalist, playwright and author. Upon witnessing the famous Dreyfuss trial and the anti-Semitism it uncovered, he was aroused to seek a solution of the Jewish problem. He called the first Zionist Congress in 1897, and laid the groundwork for political Zionism.

3 Moses Nachmanides emigrated to Palestine in 1267 and settled at Acre, where he was active in spreading Jewish learning. He may be said to have inaugurated the practice of migrating to Eretz Yisrael, as an act of piety, and with a view to having one's remains interred there.

4 Founded in 1860 in Paris "for the emancipation and moral progress of the Jews everywhere." See article on "Alliance Israelite Universalle" in Jewish Encyclopedia.

5 *Hilfsverein der Deutschen Juden*, founded May 28, 1901 in Berlin. Its purposes were to centralize the efforts of German Jewry in behalf of Jewish victims of East-European and Oriental oppression, and to provide the latter with systematic political, social and cultural assistance. The *Hilfsverein* established a variety of schools in Palestine, notably the Haifa Technicum.

6 Lowdermilk, Walter C. "Palestine, Land of Promise," N. Y. 1944, p. 14.

7 Revusky, A., *Jews in Palestine*. N. Y. 1936, p. 233.

CHAPTER EIGHTEEN

1 *Shabbat*, 112b.

2 Rashi, (Solomon ben Isaac) (1040-1105) author of classic commentaries on Bible and Talmud.

3 R. Akiba ben Joseph, (50-132) Palestinian *Tanna*, described as "father of Rabbinical Judaism." He died as a martyr.

4 *Tannaim*, pl. of *Tanna*, one of the Talmudic Sages who lived before or contemporaneously with Raba Judah the Prince, the compiler of the *Mishnah* about 200 C.E.

5 *Amoraim*, pl. of Amora, one of the Talmudic Sages who lived after the generation of Judah the Prince.

6 *Berakot*, 3b.

7 Maimonides, Moses, *Commentary on Mishnah*, Introd. to Ch. X of Sanhedrin.

8 Hoffman, David, *Das Buch Leviticus*, Berlin, 1905, pp. vii, 1, 6.

9 Weiss, Isaac Hirsch, *Dor Dor V'Doreshav*, Vilna, 1904, vol. I, ch. 1.

10 Maimonides, Moses, *Guide for the Perplexed*, Bk. II, Ch. XXV.

11 *Yoma*, 28b.

12 *Ibid.*, 85b, *Sanhedrin*, 74a.

CHAPTER NINETEEN

1 Ginzberg, Louis, *Students, Scholars and Saints*, Phila. 1928, pp. 205-6.

2 Philipson, David, *The Reform Movement in Judaism*, N. Y. 1931, pp. 164-5.

Notes

551

3 A term introduced by Solomon Schechter to designate "All Israel," acting as a spiritual unit. Cf. *Seminary Addresses*, Cincinnati, 1915, pp. 22-23.

4 *Abot* I, 1.

5 Philipson, David, *op. cit.* p. 149.

6 *Mekilta* on Exod. 31, 14.

7 *Bereshit Rabba* I, 1.

8 *Eliyahu Rabbah*, 16.

9 *Gittin*, 6b.

10 Maimonides, Moses, *Yad ha-Hazakah, Hilkot Avoda Zarah*, XI.

11 See Notes, Ch. II, 7.

12 See Notes, Ch. II, 8.

13 Those authorized to slaughter animals according to ritual law.

14 Those authorized to perform circumcision.

15 *Shabbat*, 88a.

16 Hallevi Judah, *Kitab Al Khazzari*, translated by Hartwig Hirschfeld, London, 1906, Part III, p. 99.

CHAPTER TWENTY

1 As indicated by a statement like the following: "Woe to the father whose children are female" (*Kidd.* 82b), or by the benediction in the daily morning prayer to be recited by men, thanking God "who hast not made me a woman." (*Authorized Daily Prayer Book*, London, 1929, p. 6).

2 Gen. 21, 12.

3 Lev. 19, 3.

4 Prov. 1, 8.

5 *Yebamot*, 62b.

6 *Mekilta* on Exod. 19, 3.

7 Westermarck, Edward, *The Origin and Development of Moral Ideas*, London, 1912, Vol. I, p. 664ff.

8 Jud, 9, 54.

9 *Abot* I, 5.

10 *Berakot* 24a.

11 *Yoma* 66b.

12 *Authorized Daily Prayer Book*, London 1929, p. 6.

13 Westermarck, Edward, loc. cit., p. 629ff.

14 Prov. 31, 10-31.

15 Cf. Zucrow, Solomon, *Women, Slaves and the Ignorant*, Boston 1932.

16 *Kiddushin* 35a.

17 The verses from Deut. 7, 4-9 recited morning and evening daily, *Jer. Berak.*, II, 3.

18 The frontlets referred to in Deut. 7, 8; *Jer. Berak., ibid.*

19 The fringes on the corners of the garment in accordance with Num. 15, 38-9 Maimonides, *Yad, Hilkot Zizit* I, 3.

20 The ram's horn blown on the first of the Seventh month, (now celebrated as *Rosh Ha-Shanah* or New Year) in accordance with Num. 23, 24.

21 The booth for the Feast of Tabernacles, in accordance with Lev. 23, 42-3.

22 When three or four males above the age of thirteen have eaten together, they join in the "Grace after Meals." See *Authorized Daily Prayer Book*, p. 279.

23 *Noda Bi-Yehudah, Mahdura tinyana*, Sec. I.

24 *Kiddushin* 29b.

25 *Ibid.*

26 *Ibid.*
27 Maimonides, Moses, *Yad, Hilkot Torah,* I, 13.
28 *Ibid.*
29 *Sotah* 20a.
30 *Shabuot* 30a.
31 *Jer. Sotah* VI, 16.
32 *Yebamot* 117b.
33 Maimonides, Moses, *Yad, Hilkot Edut* XV, 2-3.
34 *Baba Batra* 108a, b-109a.
35 *Ketubot,* 52b; 53a-b.
36 *Mishnah Kiddushin* I, 1.
37 Exod. 21, 7-11.
38 Maimonides, Moses, *Yad, Ishut,* XXI, 7.
39 *Ibid.,* 10.
40 *Ibid.,* XIII, 11.
41 *Ibid.,* XV, 17.
42 *Ibid.,* XII, 3.
43 *Ibid.*
44 *Ibid.,* XXI, 2.
45 *Ibid.,* XXII, 5, XXIII, 4.
46 *Ibid.,* 6.
47 *Ibid., Hilkot Gerushin,* I, 1; *Mishnah, Gittin* IX, 10; *Mishneh, Le-Melek on Maim. Yad, Hilkot Gerushin* X, 21.
48 R. Gershom (960-1040) founder of Talmudic studies in France.
49 *Ketubot* 77a.
50 Epstein, Louis M., *The Jewish Marriage Contract,* 1927, p. 203.
51 The ceremony of taking off the shoe of the brother of a husband who has died childless. (Deut. 25 5-9.)
52 Maimonides, Moses, *Yad, Hilkot Yibum,* I, 16.
53 Westermarck, Edward, *The Origin and Development of Moral Ideas,* London, 1912, Vol. I, p. 653.
54 Ephesians, 5, 23ff.; I Corinthians, 11, 8ff.
55 Westermarck, Edward, *op. cit.* Vol. I, p. 663.
56 Solis-Cohen, Emily, *Woman in Jewish Law and Life,* N. Y., 1932, p. 63.
57 Deut. 17, 14-15.
58 *Sifre* on Deut. 17, 14-15.
59 Maimonides, Moses, *Yad, Hilkot Melakim* I, 5.
60 A woman whose husband has disappeared, and who cannot be remarried as long as evidence of his death is lacking.
61 *The New Palestine,* Jan. 17, 1936.
62 *Sotah,* 11b.

CHAPTER TWENTY-ONE

1 Golub, Jacob S. and Nardi, Noah, "A Study in Jewish Observance," *Reconstructionist,* Vol. XI, No. 9.
2 Philipson, David, *The Reform Movement in Judaism,* N. Y. 1931, pp. 355-6.
3 *Yearbook,* Central Conference American Rabbis, 1937, p. 97.
4 Based on Is. 10, 21.
5 An expert in Jewish traditional law.
6 Cf. Schechter, Solomon, *Some Aspects of Rabbinic Theology,* N. Y., 1909, pp. 48-169.

7 *Seder.* (order) The name given to the evening meal on the first and second nights of Passover, because it is accompanied by an elaborate ritual service.

8 The criteria of "rigorous" and "light" correspond to the punishments for violating the precepts.

9 The punishment in that case is of a severer character.

CHAPTER TWENTY-TWO

1 Smolar, Boris, *National Jewish Post*, July 5, 1946.

2 See Notes, Ch. I, 18 and 19.

3 Cf. Ch. XXV, Sec. 4. "The Problem of Church and State in Democratic Education."

4 The *Talmud* and the *Midrash* represent the Rabbinic interpretation of the Jewish tradition, as it had come down from the beginnings of Israel's career to the period of the Pharisees, during the existence of the Second Commonwealth, and the application of that tradition to contemporaneous conditions and situations.

5 Dewey, John, *Democracy and Education*, N. Y. 1917, p. 94.

6 Russell, Bertrand, *Education and the Modern World*, N. Y. 1932, p. 19.

7 Golub, Jacob S., *Israel in Canaan, In the Days of the First Temple, In the Days of the Second Temple*, published by the Union of Hebrew Congregations.

8 The plural of *Tanna*, a term generally applied to any one of the Sages quoted in the *Mishnah*, the collection of teachings edited by R. Judah the Patriarch, c. 200.

9 Jost, Isaiah Markus (1793-1860) Founder of modern Jewish historiography through his work "*Geschichte der Israeliten seit der Zeit der Makkabäer bis auf unsere Tage.*"

10 Graetz, Heinrich (1817-1891) From 1853 to 1875 Graetz worked on his monumental *Geschichte der Juden.* This was the first all-inclusive history of the Jewish people and was, therefore, a pioneering work. Author of numerous monographs on historical subjects as well as Bible exegesis.

11 Weiss, Isaac Hirsch (1815-1905) Talmudist and historian, most noted for his Hebrew work *Dor Dor Ve-Doreshav* which is a history of the Oral Law from the Bible through the *Shulhan Aruk.*

12 Plural of *Amora*, a term generally applied to the Sages quoted in the *Gemara*, which consists for the most part of the discussions of the text of the *Mishnah.*

13 Wieman, Henry M. *The Sources of Human Good*, Chicago, 1946, p. 143.

CHAPTER TWENTY-THREE

1 A Mishnaic treatise containing in the main Rabbinic teachings that deal with the significance of the study of Torah as a means to salvation. A number of ethical teachings of a general character have also been included.

2 For the meaning of the terms Tannatic and Amoraic, see Notes Ch. XXII, 8 and 12. *Midrashim* is the plural of *Midrash*, a term which is generally limited to the Rabbinic interpretation of the Sacred Scriptures.

3 *Haskallah*, a movement of enlightenment among the Jews, which started in Germany in the middle of the eighteenth century and later spread to eastern Europe. The *Haskallah* was the spiritual counterpart of the movement for the emancipation of the Jews from the disabilities imposed on them by the governments of Europe. Emerging into the broad stream of European culture, the Jews sought to adapt their own culture to that of the world around them. In Germany, this led to complete assimilation and to the modernization of the Jewish religious traditions. In eastern Europe, where the

surrounding culture was on a low plane, the *Haskallah* developed a strong nationalist trend, with the renaissance of Hebrew literature as the distinguishing feature. There, too, the process of emancipation, expected or partly achieved, together with enlightenment led, in many instances, to complete assimilation.

4 Biurists (from the Hebrew *biur*, explanation). Under the influence of Moses Mendelssohn a group of Jewish Bible exegetes attempted to develop a simple Hebrew commentary on the Bible, which would meet the needs of the Jew in the modern world. The Biurists began with a commentary on Mendelssohn's German translation of the Bible. The movement was attacked by the traditionalists, but it had a great effect in making the Bible, rather than the Talmud, central in the modernized Jewish schools, and served as an impetus to the critical study of the Bible by Jews.

5 Ahad Ha-Am, *Al Parashat Derakim*, Berlin 1913, Vol. IV, p. 145.

6 Isaacs, Nathan, "Study as a Mode of Worship," in *The Jewish Library*, edited by Leo Jung, 1928, pp. 51-72.

7 *Megillah*, 26b.

8 See Note 5 above.

9 Gen. 8, 21.

10 Exod. 29, 25; 29, 41; Lev. 2, 12; 3, 16, etc.

11 Cf. *Kiddushin* 39b for interpretation of Deut. 5, 16, and Rashi's interpretation of Lev. 18. 5.

12 Cf. *Baba Kamma* 84a for interpretation of Exod. 21, 24.

13 Cf. *Hullin* 115b for interpretation of Exod. 23, 19.

14 *Zohar* III, 152a.

15 *Ibid.*

16 Exod. 19, 6.

17 Zach. 4, 6.

18 I Sam., 2, 9.

19 Micah, 6, 8.

20 Gen., 15, 16; Lev. 18, 28; Deut. 9, 5.

21 Gen., 18, 19.

22 Is., 5, 24; Hosea, 4, 5; Amos, 2, 4.

23 Jer. 9, 12; 16, 11; Ezek. 22, 26.

24 Hosea, 8, 1.

25 *Abot* III, 14.

CHAPTER TWENTY-FOUR

1 Kaplan, Mordecai M., *Judaism as a Civilization*, N. Y. 1934, Ch. XXV.

2 The Section from Deut. 6, 4-9, the reading of which is obligatory mornings and evenings.

3 *Authorized Daily Prayer Book*, London, 1929, pp. 39-40.

4 Schechter, Solomon, *Seminary Addresses*, Cincinnati, 1915, p. 35ff.

5 Is. 54, 13.

CHAPTER TWENTY-FIVE

1. WORLD BETTERMENT THE AIM

1 Kotsching, Walter M. "Problems of Education after the War," *International Conciliation*, April 1942, No. 379, p. 243.

2 Cf. Ziemer, Gregor, *Education for Death*, London, N. Y., Toronto, 1941.

3 Walter, Bruno, *Theme and Variations*, N. Y. 1946, p. 339.

4 *Abot* I, 1.

5 *Ibid.*, I, 4.

⁶*Ibid.*, I, 6.
⁷*Ibid.*, II, 5.
⁸*Ibid.*
⁹*Ibid.*, II, 2.
¹⁰*Ibid.*, IV, 5.
¹¹*Ibid.*, II, 7.
¹²*Ibid.*, II, 12.
¹³*Ibid.*, II, 16.
¹⁴*Mishnah Sanhed* X, 1.
¹⁵Lev. 18, 5.
¹⁶*Mishnah Peah* I, 1.
¹⁷*Mishnah Makkot* III, 16.

2. The Educational Process

¹Cf. *Yearbook II, John Dewey Society*, "Educational Freedom and Democracy," p. 192ff.

3. Education for Genuine Democracy

¹Prov. 18, 21.
²Quoted by Demiashkevich, Michael, *The National Mind*, N. Y., 1938, p. 41.
³*Jewish Encyclopedia*, Article "England," Vol. V, p. 170.
⁴*Sanhedrin* 38b.
⁵Lev. 24, 22.
⁶Exod. 23, 9.
⁷Lev. 19, 18.
⁸*Ibid.*, 33-34.
⁹I Kings, 22, 5-7.
¹⁰*Ibid.*, 8.
¹¹Jer. 7, 4.
¹²*Berakot* 63b.
¹³Is. 29, 13.
¹⁴Exod. 21, 1.
¹⁵*Mekilta* on Exod. 21, 1.
¹⁶Maimonides, *Introduction to Yad Ha-Hazakah*.

4. The Problem of Church and State in Democratic Education

¹Amos 2, 4ff.

CHAPTER TWENTY-SIX

¹Geiger, Ludwig, *Abraham Geiger, Leben und Lebenswerk*, Berlin, 1910, p. 43.
²*Contemporary Jewish Record*, N. Y. Vol. VII, No. 1, Feb. 1944.

EPILOGUE

¹Based on a prayer by Admiral Thomas C. Hart, formerly of Asiatic Fleet.
²Gen. 17, 5.
³Gen. 32, 29.
⁴Gen. 6, 3.
⁵*Bereshit Rabba* LXVIII, 12.
⁶Gen. 28, 14.

INDEX

A

Aaron, 317.

Abel, 317; 466.

Abimelech, King of Shekem, 404.

Abot, as an educational tract, 485 f.; 449; concerning woman, 404.

Abraham, 231; 232; 286; 384; 403; 539; descendants of, 347; faith of, 261 f.

Absalom, 317.

Achievement, 309 f.

Adam, 267; 275.

Adler, Felix, 227; 228.

Admah, 334.

Agudaism, 228.

Agudat Yisrael, in Eretz Yisreal, 371.

Agunah, 411; 412.

Ahab, King, 287; 507.

Ahad Ha-Am, 132; 448; 450; 489.

Ahriman, 513.

Akedat Yizhak, 454.

Akiba, Rabbi, 266; 332; 374; 403.

Albo, Joseph, 329; 454.

Alenu (a prayer), 218.

Alexander, the Great, 84; 513.

Alexandrian Empire, 144 f.

All for the Best (Plagemann), 95.

Allegiance, Jewish, problem of, 67.

Alliance Israélite Universelle, 361.

Amē ha-arez, 514.

America, a cultural melting pot, 56.

American, average, his attitude toward the Jew, 95.

American life, pattern of, 344.

American-Jewish life, *see* Life (American-Jewish).

American Jewish Committee, 112.

American Jewish Congress, 112.

Americans, Christian, live in two civilizations, 97.

Americanism, 47; and Judaism, 522.

Americanization, of the Jew, 426.

Amnon, 317.

Amoraim, 444; 453.

Amos, 287.

Anglo-Saxon, 216.

Anti-Semitism, arouses interest in Jewish study, 469; awareness of, main content of Judaism with some, 44; case against, 76 f.; in democracies, 434; different reasons for combatting, 5; "higher", 456;

main accusation of, against the Jew, 19; modern vs. medieval, 17; not a passing madness, 433; not main motive for Zionism, 411; policy of governments, 363; rationale of, 19; resisting assimilation of Jews, 31; as sepsis of Gentile, 107; in Soviet Union, 7; stimulates chauvinism, 360; struggle against, 72; in U. S. A., 95.

Appreciation, 308 f.

Arabs, 126; 136.

Arama, Isaac, 454.

Aristotle, 91; impact of his thought on Judaism, 453; *Politics* of, 319.

Arnold, Matthew, 323.

Aron, 351.

Art (Jewish), 51; what is needed to evoke it, 350 f.

Art, in Jewish life, 350 f.; of living as a Jew, 117.

Artists, Jewish, 352.

Asch, Sholem, 219.

Asefat ha-Nivharim, 409.

Ashkenazim, and status of woman, 410.

Ashkenazic community, in Eretz Yisreal, 139.

Assembly of Jewish Notables (1806), 22.

Assimilation, vs. group survival, 422; of Jewish key persons, 525.

Assyria, 513.

Astruc, Abba Mari Don, 454.

Atomic energy, U. N. Commission on, 156.

Atonement, 427.

Aurelius, Marcus, 513.

Autobiography (Walter), 484.

B

Baalism, 318.

Babylon, 8.

Babylonians, 265.

Balfour Declaration, 366; an act of justice, 363; and Jewish peoplehood, 536.

Bamberger, Dr. Bernard J., 218.

Bar Mitzvah, 10; 395.

Baruch, Bernard, 156.

Basle Platform, 475.

Ben Azzai, 332; 333; 406.

Berakah, 313.

Bergson, Henri, 165.

Beruriah, wife of R. Meir, 403; 404.

557

Bet-hakenesset, 449.

Bet-hamidrash, 449.

Bible, ignorance of, 14; knowledge of, necessary for Jewish living, 187; reason for Jews' being People of the Book, 357; supernaturally revealed, 450; main motivating themes of, 451; historical books of, 458; miraculous events in, 441; prophetic books of, 458; versions of, 452 f.; new educational approach to, 447 f.; not only means of teaching religion, 520; when produced, 455; woman in, 403.

Bible study, with aid of German commentary, 448; in Diaspora, 451; effect on, of modern scientific approach, 449; in Holland and Italy of 16th century, 447; for literacy, 450; as means of recovering classic Hebrew, 448; for national self-awareness, 451; not interwoven with Rabbinic interpretation, 447; place of Pentateuch in, 457; purpose of, should be redefined, 451.

Bible, teaching of, aim of, 456 f.; referred to in *Abot,* 447.

Biblical scholarship, 455; *see* Scholarship.

Bible, translation of, into German, 447.

Bilbo, ex-Senator, of Mississippi, 158.

BILU, movement in the 1880's, 132.

Bimah, 351.

Bitahon, 307.

Biurists, 447.

B'nai B'rith, 112.

Boxer Rebellion in China, 153; 223.

Brandeis, Justice, 489.

British, administration of, in Eretz Yisrael, 371; 410; government, 366; imperialism, 312.

Britons, 221.

Brunswick Conference of 1841, 389.

Buber, Martin, 166.

Buddha, 149.

Byzantine Empire, 88.

C

Cain, 317; 466.

Canaan, 188; 465.

Cananite people, the, 146.

Cantwell vs. Connecticut, 156.

Catholic doctrine, of salvation, 247.

Catholic Church, 89; *see* Roman Catholic Church.

Catholicism, 97; 512; revival of, 165.

"Catholic Israel", 387.

Center, Jewish, 526.

Central Conference of American Rabbis (1885), 23.

Challenging mind, the, 289 f.

Chamberlain, Houston, 251.

Chaos, moral and social, 301 f.

Child, growth as salvation to, 186.

Child (Jewish), training of, 431; and Biblical account of God's doings, 185; should be taught "Jewish civics", 444.

China, Boxer rebellion in, 153; 223.

"Chosen People", *see* Election, doctrine of.

Christendom, challenge of to Jew, 30; the source of its faith, xvi.

Christian Jewish Tragedy, The (Moehlman), 78.

Christian people, the, 93.

Christianity, a civilization, 97; as collective life, 97; and doctrine of election, 213; faith of, in power of spirit, 464; Jewish heritage in, 266; principle of spiritual selection, 248; Protestant versions of, 344; and salvation, 385; spread of, 145; 152; status of woman in, 408; in U. S. A., 101.

Christianity (early), missionizing activities of, 153. Pauline, 514.

Christians, in Middle Ages, 153; attitude of, toward adherents of other faiths, 431; attitude of, toward woman in ancient times, 404.

Church, a department of state, 88; and state, seperation of, 516.

Church, the, and American religion, 521; and anti-Semitism, 77; 78; and art, 352; only instrument of salvation, 515; religious prerogatives of, 515.

Civilization, defined, 94; democratic, and world peace, 492.

Civilization (Jewish), as content of education, 44; and Jewish religion, 48.

Civilization a, right of to symbiosis, 102 f.

Civilization (historical), principle of equality in, 143.

Civilization (modern), living in two, ix; 89; 94 f.; status of woman in, 409.

Civilization (Roman), 221; 408.

Code (Jewish), divine authority of, 65; of ethical conduct and practice, 348; 349.

Code (of Maimonides), status of woman in, 406 f.

Code (Mosaic), considered divine, xv.

Cohen, Hermann, 166.

Collective Jewish mind, 379, f.

Commonwealth (First), 28; 91; 376; Second, 28; 188.

Commonwealth (Jewish), re-establishment of, in Eretz Yisrael, 37; 66; 67; 71; 124 f.; 537.

Communal (Jewish), effort, 531; service, 526.

Community councils, Jewish, 38 f.

Communism, 235; 254; 321; 322.

Community, belonging to, 129; defined, 325; spirit of, 325.

Community (Jewish), cultural activities of, 538; to include all affirmative Jews, 118; in the past, 19; principles and aims in U. S. A., 117; 537; as religio-cultural group, 71; social structure of American-Jewish life, 106 f.; synagogue no longer all inclusive of, 112; see Kenesset Yisrael.

Community organic, pattern of, 114 f.

Community organization, Jewish, 38, f.; constitutional law for, 395.

Community (Sephardic), in Eretz Yisrael, 139.

Community status, in Eretz Yisrael, 103.

Compassion (rahamim), 336.

Congregation (Jewish), see Synagogue.

"Conservative", defined, 388.

Conservative Judaism, see Judaism (Conservative).

Constantine, Emperor, 514.

Constitution (Federal), 508; 509.

Contemporary Jewish Record, 525.

Conversion to Judaism, 146.

Cooperative colonization, in Eretz Yisrael, 368.

Copernican astronomy, 250.

Copernicus, 211.

Cosmic Power, intuitive experience of, 182.

Cosmopolitanism, 90.

Cosmos, tendencies in, and salvation, 181.

Council of Vienna (1878), 366.

Counter-Reformation, 515.

Courts (higher), opinions of, 509.

Courts (English), in Eretz Yisrael, 139.

Courts (secular Jewish), in Eretz Yisrael, 410.

Creativity (cultural), 50 f.; 116.

Creeds, reinterpretation of, resented, 427.

Crisis in American-Jewish life, 3 f.

Crusades, 351.

Cynicism, 296.

D

Darwin, Charles, 247; 251.

Dat, as lex divina, 163.

David, King, 287; 317; 374; 403.

Debs, Eugene V., 338.

Declaration of Independence, 315; 321.

Defeatism, dilemma of, 297; 298.

Deity, personified, 433.

Democracies, education in, 481 f.; failure of, 509.

Democracy, and aim of education, 488; aims at world betterment, 481 f.; antithesis of fascism, 499 f.; defense of, 315; a doctrine of national salvation, 516; in England, 320; education for, 480; 491 f.; and equality, 224; an ethical way of life, viii; failure of, 321; and freedom of the mind, 500; Judaism's contribution to, 480 f.; vs. mass tyranny, 501 f.; in need of religious sanction, 510; in political institutions, 284; a process of social experimentation, 293; a quality of nationhood, 359; as a quality of social relationships, 284; in ritual observance, 398 f.; school for, 533; wrong view of, 434; in Zionist measures and undertakings, 361 f.

Democracy (American), attitude toward Catholic Church, 101; thanksgiving for, 309.

Derush, 452; 453.

Deuteronomist, his conception of Chosen People, 212.

Deutero-Isaiah, era of, 261.

Diaspora, community organization, 38; future of Jews in, 27; and future of democracy, 437; halutzim in, 370; an impetus to Eretz Yisrael, 125; Jewish art in, 355; Jewish community in, 109; Jewish education in, must be religious, 489; Jewish individuality in, 392; Jewish law in, 397; Jewish survival without religion impossible in, 46; Jews who choose to remain in, 537; nationalism (Yiddishism) in, 25; needs program of reconstruction, 141; 142; normal Jewish life in, 435; with nucleus in Eretz Yisrael, 70 f.;

secularist attitude to, 35; social structure in, 475; standard of normality for, 445; status of Jews in, 61; Zionism in, 24.

Diaspora Jewry, future of, 28; part of Gentile nations, 102; social structure of, 68; and task of Jewish teachers, 443.

Diaspora Judaism, 26; indispensable to Jewish homeland, 128 f.

Dionysos, 513.

Disillusionment, 295 f.; 300.

Diversity (religious), 50.

Divine intervention, 200.

Divorce, in Jewish law, 407.

Doctrine, of God's unity and uniqueness, 506; of hashgaha peratit, 310; of Israel's election, 247.

Dor Dor V'Doreshav, 376.

Doubts religious, 231 f.

Dreiser, Theodore, 286.

Dualism, Persian, 514.

Dubnow, Simon, 68; 70.

Durkheim, Emile, 198.

E

Earth Could Be Fair (Van Paassen), 95.

Ecclesia of Israel, 214.

Ecclesiastes, 231.

Ecclesiastics, 88 f.

Education, in the democracies, 481 f.; that democracy needs, 491 f.; Encyclical by Piux XI, on, 190; in Eretz Yisrael, 140; in England, 320; for freedom, 498 f.; for genuine democracy, 501; in Germany in the 30's, 483; implicit in Jewish ideal of Talmud Torah, 492; Judaism's contribution to, 480 f.; main issue in, 501 f.; principles of, implied in Seder ritual, 501; the problem of church and state in, 509 f.; progressive, 482 f.; religions, 504; 511; as religious experience, 494 f.; stresses the individual, 483; the theme of Abot, 485 f.; in the U. S. A., 320; for world citizenship, 488 f.

Education (American-Jewish), aim of, 429 f.; sterility of, 442.

Education (Jewish), aim of, 438 f.; the child in, 435; concept of, 489; should extend spiritual perspective, 489, failure of, to adjust aim to new needs, 440 f.; failure of, to perpetuate Judaism, 12 f.; a means of reinterpreting traditional values, 443;

pre-modern aim of, 432; present condition of, 116; program of, 40 f.; should be religious, 489; traditional type of, 443; see Education (American-Jewish).

"Education for Death", 483.

Educators (Jewish), role of, 435; number of, inadequate, 116.

Egypt, 276; 298; 489; 496; 506; 513.

Egypt, Israel's redemption from, 465; 466.

Eldad, 216.

Election (divine), 79; 343; an anachronism, 211 f.; attitude of Maskilim to, 215; attitude of reform to, 215; belief in, a source of maladjustment of Jews, 225 f.; in Christianity, 213; Deuteronomists' conception of, 212; a hindrance to Jewish peoplehood, 225 f.; inconsistent with evolutionary concept of religion, 219 f.; reinterpretation of, 214 f.; unnecessary for Jewish survival, 223 f.; vocation a valid substitute for, 228 f.

Eliab, 317.

Eliezer, Rabbi, 403; 404; 406.

Eliezer, R. ben R. Jose, the Galilean, 214.

Elijah, 287.

Emancipation Jewish, should be made complete, 79; effect on Jewish life, 16 f.; 64; 73; 75; 214; 346; 352; 435; 440; 537; status of Jews prior to, 388 f.

Emperor-worship, 513.

Empires, of Nile and Euphrates, 456.

Enelow, Rabbi Hyman G., 161.

England, 320; 396.

English Parliament, 1753, 504.

Enlightenment, 16; 248; effect of, on Jewish life, 64; 214; 291; influence of, on study of Bible, 447; spokesmen of, 244; and egalitarianism, 254; see Emancipation.

Environment, its challenge to Jewish life, 456.

Ephraim, 334.

Episcopal Church, 88.

Epstein, Louis M., 407.

Encyclical on education by Pius XI, 190.

Encyclopedia of Religion and Ethics, 315.

Equality, of groups, 147 f.; in Jewish tradition, history of, 317; as justice, 313; principle of, 143; a religious ideal, 324 f.; and social inertia, 319 f.

Equivalence, principle of, 150.

Eretz Yisrael, 8; 24; 26; 37; 38; 66; 69; 100; 117; 164; 265; 272; 313; 360; 361; 362;

364; 365; 366; 367; 369; 370; 371; 411 f.; 536; 538; achievements in, 130 f.; agricultural foundation of, 367; Arab workers in, 370; attitude of marginal Jews to, 5; and autonomy, 371; basic to revival of Israel, 134; British administration of, 371; building of, not a substitute for Jewish life elsewhere, 130; civil courts in, 138; cooperative colonization in, 368; cooperatives in, 369; cultural life in, 125; and Diaspora, 141 f.; freedom and security in, 434; halutzim (pioneers) of, 37; Hebrew renascence in, 443; home of Jewish civilization, 103; indispensable to Jewish religion in the Diaspora, 126; Jewish Commonwealth in, 37; Jewish law in, 392; Judaism as majority civilization of, 445; Judaism outside, 433; 435; Labor Socialism in, 370; law to be studied by democratic agencies in, 385; making new history, 131; marriage practices in, 139; 410; in need of a modern code, 138; new role of, 123 f.; nuclear function of, 71; rebuilding of, 10; recolonization of, in 1882, 367; renascence of Hebrew language in, 132; roster of heroes in, 131; secular Jewish courts in, 410; shortcomings of, 136 f.; significance of, in Bible, 458; significance of its rehabilitation, 475; status of Jewry in, 66; 67; 69; status of woman in, 410 f.; values emanating from, 437; Talmudic law in, 138; as theme of instruction, 444; trade unions in, 370; Turkish law in, 139; Workers' Federation in, 369; Zionist aspirations for, 125; see Education, Zionism.

Erub tabshilin, 384.
Esau, 312; 317.
Esther, 403.
Ethical Philosophy of Life, An (Adler), 227.
Ethics, 53 f.; of the group, 143; in Jewish life, 343 f.
Ethics of the Fathers (Abot), 485 f.
Ethnic consciousness, 63; 83; 84.
Europe, Jews in, 309.
Eve, 267; 275.
Evil, 197; 234 f.; 238.
Exile, Babylonian, 64; 212.
Existentialist, 286.
Experience, religion, 198.

Ezekiel, 8; 26; 28; 29; 33; 175; 275; 467; 507.

F

Fair Employment Practices Committee (FEPC), 157.
Faith, 45; 190 f.; 256 f.; 259 f.; 261 f.; 299; 315 f.; 511.
Family, 408.
Fascism, 235; 255; 321; 499 f.; 509; see nazism.
Fellowship, religio-cultural, 33.
Fichte, 168.
First Temple, 188; 462.
Five Scrolls, The, 351.
Flood, story of, 466.
Folkways and folk symbols, 86; religious, 124.
Force, arbiter in human affairs, 456.
Formstecher, Solomon, 166.
"Four Freedoms", 495.
France, Talmudic scholars of, 454.
Frankel, Zechariah, 387; 528.
Freedom, education for, 498 f.; inner, 283 f.; intellectual, 291; 500; to be Jews, 72 f.
Freedom (inner), see "Unreconciled Heart, The", 285 f.
Free-thinkers, 231.
French Revolution, 31; 360.
Future, hope for, 266; 270; of the American Jew, 536.

G

Galut, negation of, 529; Jewish education, 434.
Geiger, Abraham, 220; 524; 528.
Gemara, 453; 508.
Generation of Vipers (Wylie), 490.
Genesis, 266; 317; 332; 505.
Gentile society, and Jews, 538.
Gentiles, 383; 430; 474.
George, Henry, 364.
Ger, 146.
German Universities, and Geiger's plan, 524.
Germans, 252.
Germany, 300; education in, 483.
Gershom, Rabbenu, 139; 407.
Ghetto, 5.
God, as cosmic Power, 182; doings of, in

Bible, 185; emulation of, in Rabbinic lore, 330; existence of, 185; experiencing reality of, 192; faith in, 45; 242; 507; as helper, 171; 201; goodness and love manifestations of, 334; imitation of, 281 f.; Kingdom of, 147; 149; 202; 222; 283; 349; 360; 386; 539; love of, 149; manifest in human life, 184; manifest in moral law, 258; manifest in will to live, 172; as miracle worker, 538; name of, when profaned, 348; omnipotent, 202; promise of, to Jacob, 540; promotes righteousness, 382; saves from sin, 240; unity of, 149; 506; uniqueness of, 506; as Power making for salvation, 172; 179; 196; 334; 336; 519; as process, 183; as *Shaddai*, 539; as *YHWH*, 539.

God belief, distinct from God conception, 171; 328; implies faith in human equality, 315; meaning of, 171 f.; 495; not a *reasoned* but a *willed* faith, 182; source of, 171; 182. Soterical approach to, 180 f.

God conception, 171; 199 f.; 473; 474; fundamentalist, 192; for the child, 495; an index of, concept of salvation, 174 f.; limited to the supernatural, 192; in Torah and in tradition, 478; in true religion, 170.

Godlike, 274; 331; 336.

Goethe, J. W. von, 42.

Golden Age, 267; 268.

Golden Calf, 330; 462.

Golub, Jacob S., 442.

Good the, in Jewish life, 343 f.

Good life, the, 345.

Good-will, key to intergroup, 143 f.

Goodenough, E. R., 161.

Graetz, H., 528.

Gratitude, 461; *see* Thanksgiving.

Great Britain, 126; 221; 504.

Greece, 88; 291.

Group equality, 147 f.

Group ethics, 143 f.

Group (Jewish), individuality of, 438.

Group life, Jewish, 421 f.

Group solidarity, Jewish, 55.

Growth, 186; 438.

Guelph-Ghibelline struggle, 89.

Guiding Principles, Reform, 23.

Guinea Indians, 404.

H

Hadassah, 112.

Ha-emunah ha-yisreëlit, 163.

Haggadot, 134.

Haifa, Hebrew Technicum in, 133.

Halafta, Rabbi, 302.

Halitzah, 408.

Halukah, 361.

Halutzim (pioneers), in Eretz Yisrael, 37.

Ha-mishpat ha-shalom ha-ivri, 138.

Hannah, 403.

Hardy, Thomas, 286.

Hashgaha peratit, 310.

Hasidim, 351.

Hasidism, 309.

Haskalah, 309; 447.

Havdalah, 218; 351 f.

Hebrew, 59; 132; 164; 336; classic, 448; indispensable to Jewish unity, 528; ignorance of, 43; no Judaism without it, 133; renascence of, 443; in the synagogue, 12 f.

Hebrew Gynasium, in Tel-Aviv, 448; 450.

Hebrew Technicum in Haifa, 133.

Heder, 429.

Hegel, 168.

Heine, Heinrich, 51; **265.**

Hellenism, 47.

Heritage, Jewish, 432.

Herrenvolk, 483.

Herz, Henrietta, 409.

Herzl, Theodore, xvii; 360; 363; 364.

Hesed, 337.

Hiddur Mitzvah, 351.

High Holidays, 10; 418.

Higher Criticism, 456; 478.

Hilfsverein der deutschen Juden, 362.

Hillul ha-shem, 56; 348.

Hindus, religious philosophy of, 216.

Hirsch, Samuel, 166.

Histadrut, 369; 370.

Historical School, 93; 215; 376; 387.

Historicism, 432.

History, American, ignorance of, 493; 496.

History, Jewish, 60; 375; 444.

Hiyyah, 302.

Hocking, William, 293.

Hoffman, David, 376.

Holiness, 460.

Home (Jewish), Orthodox, 413; sanctity of, 352.

Homeland, Jewish, 128 f.; 371.
Hope, 266 f.
Hosea, Prophet, 334; 467.
Hoveve Zion movement, 123.
Hugo, Victor, 333.
Humanism, 193 f.
Humanists of the Renaissance, 216.
Humility, 274; 460.
Hyrcanus, John, 513.

I

Ibn Ezra, 454.
Ibsen, Henrik, 137; 286.
Idealism, ethical, 68.
Idumeans, 152; 513.
Ikhnaton, 285.
Illuminati, Jewish, 448; 450.
Imitation of God (Imitatio Dei), 281 f.
Imma Shalom, 403; 404.
Imperialism, American, 312; British, 221;
    religious, 221 f.; Roman, 513; 514.
India, 237.
Indians of Guinea, 404.
Indo-China, 237.
Inertia, 441.
Inequality, 323.
Inferiority, sense of, 11 f.
Institutions, Jewish, 490.
Intelligence, 196.
Intermarriage, 11; 15; 414.
Iraq, 80.
Iron Age, 267.
Irrationalism, 168.
Isaiah, 169; 260; 275.
Ishmael, 317.
Islam, 30; 93; 145; 152; 205; 385.
Isolationism, 90; 297.
Israel, 36; 214; 539; American, 421; begin-
    nings of, 28; covenant of with God, 425;
    election of, an anachronism, 211 f.; mis-
    sion of, 169; 178; reality and destiny of,
    458; redemption of, 412; role of in his-
    tory of mankind, 230; sancta of, see
    Sancta; as a nation, 360; House of, 10;
    33.
Israel Identity Society, 504.
Israelites in the wilderness, 330.

J

Jackson, Justice, 157.
Jacob, 266; 312; 317; 403; 539; 540.

Jacobi, F. H., 168.
James, William, 166; 184.
Japan, educational system of, 483.
Jeremiah, 9; 28; 29; 265; 467.
Jeroboam II, 287.
Jerusalem, 137; 427.
Jerusalem (Mendelssohn), 244.
Jesus, 79; 149; 170.
Jew, American, 94 f.; 117; 529; art of liv-
    ing as, 117; escapist, described, 353;
    "Good", the, 347 f.; maximum, 529;
    metamorphosis of, 104; modern, 11 f.;
    345; myths concerning, 19; quest of, for
    the good life, 343; secularist, 529; Se-
    phardic, 410.
Jewish Community (Kenesset Yisrael),
    409.
Jewish civics, 444.
Jewish National Fund (J.N.F.), 364; 365.
Jewish National Home, 367; 370; 536.
Jewry, assimilation of, 422; status of, in
    Eretz Yisrael, 66; 67; 69; survival of,
    422.
Jewry (American), 309; future of, 28; 33;
    536; relation to Eretz Yisrael, 128; right
    of, to function as corporate entity, 79;
    seething with activity, 9; status of, 121.
Jewry, Diaspora, xv; xvi; xvii; 394; com-
    munal status of, 389; domestic relations
    in, 393; and Eretz Yisrael, 123 f.; future
    of, 416 f.
Jewry, Polish, 69.
Jews, affirmative, 3 f.; attitude of, toward
    family, 408; civil rights of, 504; con-
    flicting attitudes of, 3 f.; 432; contact
    of, with Gentiles, 430; fellow-feeling
    among, 95; 96; German, 362; hiding
    their identity, 11 f.; of influence needed,
    115; in Levantine countries, 361; mar-
    ginal, 4 f.; 11; middle-class, 10; need a
    modern orientation, 470; need to belong,
    129; mutually responsible, 4; once linked
    together by common consciousness, 29;
    in the past, 388; Sephardic, 410; self-
    government of, 106; sex morality of, 408;
    statistics of, 98; status of, 58 f.; to do
    their own thinking, 471 f.
Jews in Palestine (Revusky), 369.
Job, 231; 232; 241; 286.
Jubilee Year, 364.
Judah Hallevi, R., 91; 399.
Judaism, 11; 12; 24; 25; 34; 35; 38; 60;

63; in America, 102; 130; 443; and Americanism, 522; contribution of, to democracy, 480 f.; conversion to, 146; in Diaspora, 38; 40; 47; in the home, 41 f.; imposed on Idumeans, 513; loyalty to, 422; meaning of, 35; and the modern Jew, 343; new era in, 474; present crisis in, 31; proselytizing activities of, 152 f.; relationship of, to Jewish religion, 162 f.; and status of woman, 409; transmission of, 441.

Judaism (Conservative), 25; 65; attitude toward Jewish law, 387; attitude of, toward ritual observance, 416; 417; and Jewish group life, 417; and principle of historic continuity, 387 f.

Judaism (Orthodox), 65; 228; 415; 417; 436; 440 f.; attitude of, to *mitzvot*, 415; attitude of, to status of woman, 409 f.; based on supernaturalism, 387; 432; belief of, in Israel's cosmic centrality, 433; and the traditional codes, 400; *see* Agudaism; Mizrachi.

Judaism (Positive Historic), (Frankel), 387.

Judaism (Reform), 22; 23; 24; 25; 31; 34; 35; 61; 64; 65; 111; 164; 238; 414; 416; 436; 440; 524; attitude of, toward legal precepts, 387; and doctrine of election, 215; and place of Israel in divine plan, 432 f.; retains ceremonials as symbols of moral principles, 413 f.; revision of, 414 f.; status of woman in, 410 f.; Zionist elements in present-day, 415.

Judaism (religio-cultural), 433.

Johanan ben Zakkai, R., 28; 29.

Jost, I. M., 444.

Judith, 403.

Justice, 313 f.; 327; 466 f.; social, Jewish stake in, 54.

K

Kaddish, 11.
Kafka, Franz, 303.
Kashrut, 414.
Kaufman, Ezekiel, 26.
Kenesset Yisrael, 409.
Kiddush, 351.
Kiddushin, 406.
Kingdom of God, see God.
Kinnot, 351.

Kinyan, 406.
Kipling, Rudyard, 312.
Klatzkin, Jacob, 26.
Knowledge (Jewish), to create a demand for, 469 f.
Koestler, Arthur, xv; xvi.
Kohler, Kaufmann, 162; 163; 220.
Koheleth, 239; 251; 267; 286.
Kol Nidre, 351.
Ku Klux Klan, 76.

L

Labor Zionists, 112.
Labor Socialism, in Eretz Yisrael, 370.
Laborite Government, 7.
Land, possession of, 87.
Landsmanschaften, 112.
Language, 84; 85; see Hebrew.
Law, interpretation of not enough, 397; meaningless without sanctions, 388; American, 509.
Law, Canon, 396; Deuteronomic, 409; Divine, 163; Germanic, pre-Christian era, 408.
Law, Jewish, attitudes of Conservative, Orthodox and Reform Judaism to, 387 f.; defunct state of, not to be accepted, 390; development of, 384; for Diaspora Jewry, 393 f.; in Eretz Yisrael, 392; Jewish life meaningless without, 389 f.; 393; for Jewish communities, 395; oral, 376; in pre-modern life, 388 f.; problem of, 387 f.; rendered defunct by Emancipation, 389; study of, 385; see Law (Jewish traditional).
Law (Jewish traditional), attitude of non-Orthodox to, 400; divorce in, 407; in Eretz Yisrael, 138; marriage in, 407; need to amend, 410 f.; status of woman in, 405 f.
Leadership, 87; 88; 89; 92.
Leadership, Jewish, 93; 116; 523 f.
League of Nations, 67; 80; 297; 363; 366; 536; Covenant of, 77.
Lecky, W. E. H., 323.
Les Miserables (Hugo), 333.
Levantine countries, Jews in, 361.
Levine, Rachel, 409.
Liberalism, of 19th century illusory, 17.
Life (American-Jewish), disintegration of, 15; 527; seething with activity, 9; must

establish a University of Judaism, 535; see Jewry, American.
Life (Jewish), aesthetic self-expression in, 350 f.; affirmative philosophy of, 527; art in, see Art, Artists; the beautiful in, 343; challenge to, 36; communal, 120; in Diaspora, 433 f.; disintegration of, 16; escaping, 11 f.; ethics in, 343; in Europe, 309; 523; home in, 352; 356; key persons in, 524 f.; maladjustment in, 472; momentum of, 28; norms needed for, 435 f.; optimism in, 391; participation in, 474; plenitude in, 528; 529; quality of, 490; reconstruction of, 539; revival of, 134; in U. S. A., 128.
Lincoln, Abraham, 321.
Literacy (Jewish), 474; 478.
Literature, Hebrew and Yiddish, 51.
Living, creatively, 117; in two civilizations, 89; 94 f.
Love, 328 f.; redemptive, 330.
Lovingkindness, (hesed), 336.
Lowdermilk, W. C., 368.
Lowell, J. R., 312.
Loyalty, 104.
Lutheran Church, 88.

M

Maccabees, 513.
Macedonian Empire, 513.
Maimonides, Moses, 91; 162; 223; 245; 269; 329; 379; 409; 441; 454; 508; creed of, 245; 441; code of, 406 f.
Maimonists, 454.
Manasseh, 317.
Mandate, for Palestine, 80; 136; 363; 366; 536.
Marcus Aurelius, 513.
Marriage, Jewish law concerning, 407; in Eretz Yisrael, 139.
Marx, Karl, 7; 255; 464.
Marxism, 255.
Maskilim, 215.
Mass tyranny, 481.
Matriarchs, 403.
Megalomania, national, 506.
Meir, Rabbi, 403; 404.
Meliorism, 298 f.
Mendelssohn, Dorothy, 409.
Mendelssohn, Moses, 244.
Meredith, George, 200.

Mesopotamia, 312.
Mesiah, 17; 100; 126; 245; 248; 268; 430; 434; 514.
Messianism, Jewish, 360; 361; 513.
Metahistory, 432.
Mexican War, 312.
Micah, 507.
Micaiah, 507.
Middle Ages, 153; 163; 270; 291; 352; 403.
Midrash, 256; 439.
Midrashic literature, 239; 447.
Mikveh Israel (Eretz Yisrael), 362.
Millennium, 302.
Milton, John, 83.
Mind, the challenging, 289 f.
Miracle, common to all religions, 199.
Miracle tales, 214; 378.
Mishnah, 404; 410; 490; 508; study of, 447.
Mission, Jewish, 62; 64; 178; 221 f.
Missionary activity, 223.
Mitzvah, 205; 351; 399; 405; 415; 425; 455; hiddur mitzvah, 351.
Mizrachi, 112; 136; 140; 410.
Modernism, 352; 447.
Moehlman, C. H., 78.
Mohammedanism, see Islam.
Mohammedans, 431.
Monarchy, 276.
Monism, political, 70.
Monotheism, 64.
Moore, G. F., 408.
Morale, 305; Jewish, 12.
Moses, v; 199; 200; 203; 216; 227; 279; 317; 330; 403; 439; 508.
Mount Sinai, see Sinai.
Murdock vs. Pennsylvania, 157.
Mount Moriah, 261.
Mystics, Bible of, 454 f.

N

Napoleon I, 22; 31; 287; 389.
Nathan, the Prophet, 287.
Nation, a, 66.
National Jewish Assembly (Asefat ha-Nivharim), 409.
Nationalism, 7; 514 f.; chauvinist, 360; democratic, xv; 73; 370; 517; modern, 18 f.; 456 f.
Nationhood, Jewish, 66.
Nationhood, religionized, 516 f.
Naturalism, xx; 18; 20; 149; 515.

Natural selection, 247; 250 f.
Nazism, 235; see Fascism.
Nebuchadnezzar, 275; 351.
Negro, 344; 405.
Neo-Orthodoxy, 23; 34; 35; 64; 414.
Neo-Thomism, 165.
New Testament, The, 77; 169; 520.
N. Y. Times, 493.
Nietzsche, 251; 252; 255; 277; 464.
Nightingale, Florence, 13.
Noah, 223.
Noahtic Laws, 223; 383.
Norms, traditional, 418.

O

Observances (Jewish), see Usages (ritual);
  Ritual observances.
O'Connell, Cardinal, 76.
Old Testament, 170; 520.
Olympian gods, 513.
Omar Khayyám, 490; 491.
O'Neill, Eugene, 286.
Optimism, 12; 391.
Orientation, Jewish need of, 414; 469 f.
Origin and Development of the Moral
  Ideas (Westermarck), 145.
Origin of Species (Darwin), 247.
Ormuzd, 513.
Orthodox Judaism, see Judaism Orthodox.
Other-worldliness, 16; see Religion (Jew-
  ish), other-worldly stage.
Otto, Rudolph, 198.

P

Pacifism, 297.
Paganism, Greek, 267; Roman, 267.
Palestine, see Eretz Yisrael.
Palestine, law of, 410.
Papacy, 515.
Parochial schools, Jewish, 13.
Passover (Pesah), 180; 424; 486; 494;
  Seder, 480; theme of, 498.
Past, the, 372 f.; 377 f.; 473.
Patience, 295 f.
Patriarchs of Israel, 199; 224; 403.
Pax Romana, 221.
Peer Gynt (Ibsen), 137.
Pentateuch, 425; study of, 447; 458.
People a, concept of, 63; significance of
  being, 82 f.

People (the Jewish), atomized, 391; its
  capacity for reconstruction, 28; for
  survival, 480; community organization
  of, 71; conception of, 475; identity of,
  435; leadership for, 92; morale of, 12;
  nationhood of, 24.
Peoplehood, sense of, 82; a living process,
  87 f.
Peoplehood (Jewish), 36; 63 f.; accepted
  by latter-day Reform, 23; affirmation of,
  457; civil code necessary for, 138; es-
  sence of, 238 f.; indispensable to Jew's
  salvation, 100; three levels of, 66 f.
Persian Empire, 513.
Personality, 63; 171; 183.
Persuasion, 88.
Peshat, 452.
Pessimism, 300.
Pharaoh, 276; 466.
Pharisees, 88; 376.
Philanthropy, 429; 526.
Philo, 454.
Philosophers Greek, 153; 176; 216.
Philosophy, Greek, 269; Hindu, 216; re-
  ligious, 167.
Pilgrim fathers, 344.
Pinsker, Lev, 489.
Pioneers, Jewish, 37.
Pittsburgh Conference of 1885, Reform,
  414.
Pittsburgh Platform (Reform), 22; 23.
Pittsburgh Platform of 1918 (Zionist), see
  Zionism.
Plagemann, Bentz, 95.
Plato, 91; 319; 453.
Platonic-Aristotelian philosophy, 180.
Playing the god, 279 f.
Poles, 69.
Politics (Aristotle), 319.
Pluralism, religious, 158; religio-cultural,
  70.
Pope Pius XI, xviii; 190.
Potter, Charles Francis, 231.
Pound, Roscoe, 319.
Power, God as, helping us overcome ob-
  stacles, 171; making for salvation, 179;
  187; 233; 304; sustaining us, 310.
Pride, sin of, 460; see Playing the god.
Primogeniture, 317.
Profanation of God's name, 348.
Program, for reconstruction of Jewish life,
  xviii f.; 34 f.

Prophets, of Israel, 26; 32; 91; 158; 199; 203; 318; 506; 507; 513.
Proselytizing activity, 153.
Protestant, doctrine, 247; statistics, 98; Sunday School, 429.
Protestantism, 101; 512.
Proto-Bible, 455; 456.
Proto-history, of Jews, 465.
Proverbs, 294; 318; 403.
Providence, 310.
Psalmist, the, 184; 292; 304; 307.
Psalms, 105.
Public opinion (Jewish), xviii.
Public schools, 510; 516.
Purim, 351.

R

Raba, 384.
Rabbinic law, 441; 425; literature, 14; 91; lore, 187; 330; maxims, 485 f.
Rabbis, in pre-modern period, 383; 403; in modern times, 11; 530; Reform, 62; 415.
Rachel, wife of R. Akiba, 403.
Rank, Otto, 27.
Rashi, 374.
Rationalism, 18th century, 168; 216; 432.
Reason, and religion, 168 f.
Recessional (Kipling), 312.
Reconstruction, a program, 34 f.
Reconstruction, in group ethics, 143 f.; of Jewish life, 539.
Reconstructionist movement, program of, xviii f.
Redefinition, of Jewish religion, 99.
Reeducation, religio-ethical, 154 f.
Reform Judaism, *see* Judaism Reform.
Reformation, Christian, 514; 515.
Reformists, Jewish, 64; 440.
Reinterpretation, of Jewish past, 379 f.; of Jewish symbols and observances, 426 f.
Religion, concept of, 219 f.; 477; 512; in contemporary Jewish life, 11; 13; 164 f.; of democracy, 520; no term for, in Rabbinics, 163; place of, in human life, 45; 173; 241; 316; and reason, 168 f.; role of, 72; 103; 172; 220; 273; 328 f.; teachers of, 149.
Religion, American, 520 f.; Christian, 522; civic, 135; cosmopolitan, 222; organized, 174; 519; Roman, 513; spiritual, 188 f.; traditional, 191; universal, 207; 222.

Religion (Jewish), basic values in, 244 f.; concept of salvation in, 203 f.; in Diaspora, 126; different stages of, 188; in Eretz Yisrael, 134; 136; faith in, 256 f.; hope in, 266 f.; humility in, 274 f.; inner freedom in, 283; and Jewish consciousness, 65; justice in, 313 f.; love in, 328; mutations in, 442; new understanding of, 161 f.; Next Stage in, Part II; 199; other-worldly stage of, 188; 205; patience in, 295 f.; a phase of Jewish civilization, 65; 162 f.; reconstruction of, 44 f.; redefinition of, 99; revitalization of, 48 f.; ritualism and symbolism in, 208 f.; spiritual selection in, 246 f.; thankfulness in, 303 f.; and universal religion, 207; what makes it Jewish, 207 f.
"Religion Exhibit" at World's Fair (1939), 166.
Religions, chief problem of, 182; function of, in modern world, 518 f.; as groping efforts of the human soul, 191; as programs for living and organizations of power, 512 f.; relation of, to one another, 150; secularized, 516; and unity of God, 149.
Remez, 452; 453; 454.
Renaissance, European, 176; 352; 514.
Renascence of Jewish life, 354.
Republic (Plato), 319.
Research, to revitalize tradition, 439; an institute for, 534.
Resurrection, 245.
Revelation, 147; 192.
Revusky, A., 369.
Righteousness, basis of people's life, 467.
Rites, *see* Ritual observances; Usage (ritual).
Ritual observances, 40; 135; 351; 356; 398 f.; 394; 413 f.; *see* Ritual, Jewish; Usage (ritual).
Roberts, Justice of U. S. Supreme Court, 156.
Roman Catholic Church, 89; 98; 99; 101; 121; 156; 515.
Roman Catholicism, challenge to, 514; revival of, 165.
Roman Empire, 145.
Rome, 88; 89; 123; 153; Christian, 514.
Rosenzweig, Franz, 166.
Rousseau, Jean Jacques, 253.
Russell, Bertrand, 110; 441.

Russia, 123; *see* Soviet Union; U.S.S.R.
Ruth, 403.

S

Saadyah, R., 66.
Sabbath, 391; 414.
Sacred Scriptures, 430.
Sadducees, 376.
Sages, of the Talmud, 92; 105; 203; 229; 239; 376; 384; 430.
St. Paul, 319; 408.
Salome, Queen, 403.
Salvation, changing conception of, 203 f.; conception of, reflected in tradition, 380; and cultural pluralism, 148; equivalent of, for child, 186; function of historic religions, 182; from God, 147; 149; 196; none outside church, 103; 515; otherworldly, 179; 204; as purpose of ritual usage, 422; this-worldly, 30; 31; 521.
Samuel bar Nahmani, Rabbi, 298.
Samuel, 276.
Sancta, 46; 418; 420; American, 520; Jewish, 179.
Sanctions, social, 400.
Sanhedrin, Napoleonic (1806), 22; 24; 61; 389.
San Remo Treaty, 536.
Sarah, 403.
Satan, 77; 305; 504; 514; 515.
Schapira, Herman, 364.
Schechter, Solomon, 245; 456; 469.
Schelling, F. W. J. von, 168.
Schlegel, F., 168.
Scholarship, Biblical, bias in, 478.
Scholarship, Jewish, 393; 528.
Schweitzer, Albert, 19; 169.
Science, 307.
Scientism, opposed to spiritual values, 462; threat of, to Jewish life, 21; 456; 459.
Second Commonwealth, 27; 28; 64; 212.
Second Temple, 443; era of, 88; 188.
Secular writings, 489.
"Secular" not an antonym of "religious", 519.
Secularism, in Jewish schools, 13.
Secularists, 64.
Seder (Passover), 424; 480; 494; 496; 498; 501.
Sefer Torah, 102; 209.
Selection, spiritual, 254 f.

Self-expression, aesthetic, 350; religious, 398.
Self-government, Jewish, 106.
Self-hate, Jewish, 15.
Selfhood, dignity of, 324.
Separation of church and state, 436.
Sex morality, Jewish, 408.
Shabuot, 486.
Shaddai, 539.
She-ar yashuv, 415.
Shema, 475.
Sherwood, Robert, 264.
Sholom Aleichem, 58.
Shotwell, James T., 77.
Shtadlan, 362.
Shulhan Aruk, 421.
Simhat Torah, 102; 351.
Sin, cardinal, 303; meaning of, to be reinterpreted, 427; original, 278.
Sinai, 214; 376; 381; 397; 403; 415; 508.
Sinclair, Jo, 353.
Slavery, in Bible, 382; in the U. S . A., 405.
Social behavior, Jewish, 476.
Social service, Jewish, 531.
Social structure, Jewish, 439; American-Jewish, 106 f.; 121.
Social workers, Jewish, 526.
Socialism, influence of, on Jews, 6 f.
Socrates, 266; 291.
Sod, 453; 454.
Sodom and Gomorrah, 232; 239.
Solidarity, Jewish, problem of, 474.
Song of the Red Sea, 466.
Song of Songs, 453.
Sorokin, Pitirim, 21.
Soviet Union, anti-Semitism outlawed in, 7; unity with rest of world Jewry proscribed in, 7; Zionism proscribed in, 7.
Soul (Personality), 171; 183.
Spain, Talmudic scholars of, 454.
Sparta, 388.
Spengler, Oswald, 251; 252.
Spinoza, Baruch, 244.
State, 517.
State despotism, 502.
Statistics, of Jews, Protestants and Catholics, 98 f.
Status, loss of, its effect on Jewish mentality, 58.
Steinberg, Jacob, 337.
Steinheim, Solomon L., 166.
Stoicism, 145; 513.

Stoics, 216; 248; 291; 454.
Study (Adult Jewish), to answer need for modern orientation, 470 f.; to help understand religion, 477; to reinterpret tradition, 476; to be relevant to present realities, 469; to raise ethical level, 477; subject matter of, 472 f.; vitalization of, 469 f.
Sukkah, 405.
Supernaturalism, 316; 432; 477.
Survival (Jewish), challenge to, 463; creative talent to be enlisted for, 33; in a democratic state, 435 f.; and doctrine of election, 225 f.; main purpose of organic community, 114; miracle of, 480; problem of, 16; 471; and ritual usage, 413; struggle for, in Bible, 459.
Susanna, 403.
Swedish settlers in Midwest, 344.
Symbolism, 208 f.; 427; see Usage (Jewish ritual).
Synagogue, failure of, 12 f.; not coextensive with community, 111 place of, in a democracy, 437.
Synagogues, Conservative, 14; Orthodox, 14; Reform, 164.
"Synagogue of Satan", 77.
Szold, Henrietta, 411.

T

Taft, William Howard, 76.
Taine, H. A., 320.
Talent, elicited by community, 118.
Talmud, 60; 302; 403; 439; 447; 508.
Talmud Torah, ideal of, 42; 349; 350; 492.
Talmud Torah schools, decline of, 13.
Tannaim, 374; 443; 444; 453.
Tawney, R. H., 323.
Teacher, Jewish, of Bible, 458; in heder, 526.
Teachers of religion, 149.
Tefillin, 405; 425.
"Temple of the Lord", 507.
Ten Commandments, The, 247.
Ten Tribes, the lost, 504.
Tertullian, 231.
Testament of the Twelve Patriarchs, 332.
Thankfulness, 303 f.; when religious, 311 f.
Thanksgiving, ritual of, 304; 306.
Theology (Jewish), needed, 417.
Theophany, Sinaitic, 224.

There Shall Be No Night (Sherwood), 264.
Thieves in the Night (Koestler), xvi.
Thirteen Principles (Maimonides), 245.
Thirty Years' War, 222.
Thoreau, Henry, 288.
Tishea BeAb, 351.
Torah, 11; 30; 36; 42; 64; 78; 107; 163; 199; 200; 210; 212; 216; 228; 244; 248; 268; 269; 274; 313; 329; 347; 348; 350; 351; 379; 391; 397; 403; 406; 414; 416; 425; 439; 441; 443; 470; 476; 486; 488; 496; 513; 537; 538; an all embracing guide, 467; compatible with scientific approach, 478; Eretz Yisrael looms large in, 458; a human document, 346; and Jewish mysticism, 454; a living tradition, 346; neither to be amended nor abrogated, 382 f.; 384; not esoteric doctrine, 439; provided moral standards, 476; reinterpretation of, 381 f.; reveals God, 187; 346; 382; represents Israel's way of life, 36; stimulus to good life, 343 f.; written and oral, 376.
Torah, scroll of, 227.
Torah, study of, 205; 345; 489; as education of the whole man, 470; elicited the best in the Jew, 476; gave the Jew literacy, 470; "for its own sake", 449; a means to salvation, 204; 449; not necessary for women, 405.
Tower of Babel, 84.
Trade Unions, in Eretz Yisrael, 370.
Tradition, 49; 129; 376; 380; 439.
Tradition (Christian), 147.
Tradition (Jewish), belongs to a different universe of thought, 438; continuity and change in, 372 f.; creation of Jewish mind, 380; historical approach to, 375 f.; in Jewish education, 442; reflects will to live, 377.
Tradition (philosophical), 319.
Treaty of Versailles, 300.
Turkey, 140.

U

U. S. S. R., 7; 70; 255; 322; 441.
United Jewish Appeals, 9.
United Nations, 80; 81.
United Nations, Commission on Atomic Energy, 156.
United States of America, 61; 70; 71; 102;

300; 366; 405; 536; education in, 320; Jewish law in, 390; religious freedom in, 396.

United States Supreme Court, 156; 477.

Unity of Mankind, 506.

University of Judaism, 523 f.; affirmations of, 527; educational pattern of, 530 f.; rabbinic school in, 530; research institute in, 534; school for the arts in, 533; school for democracy in, 533.

"Unreconciled heart, the", 285; 289.

Usage (Jewish ritual), criteria for judging importance of, 424 f.; diversity in, 421; elasticity in, 420 f.; 422; should be encouraged, 208 f.; evaluation of, 420 f.; toward a guide for, 413 f.; in home, 351; 356; in Jewish societies, 356; kashrut in, 414; 425; means to consciousness of kind, 209; 419; means to group survival, 413; 418; 422; need for new approach to, 413; 419; new forms of, 420; rationale for, 415.

Utopianism, 295 f.; 300.

V

Values (Jewish), application of, 476 f.; basic in religion, Ch. XV; traditional, 45.

Van Paassen, Pierre, 95.

Varieties of Religious Experience (James), 166.

Vatican, authority of, 101.

Vienna, Council of (1878), 366.

Vocation, and doctrine of election, 228 f.

Voelker, John D., 289.

Voltaire, 49; 95.

W

Walden (Thoreau), 288.

Walter, Bruno, 484.

Warshow, Robert S., 58.

Wasteland (Sinclair), 353.

"We feeling", 64; 82.

Weiss, Isaac Hirsch, 376; 444.

Wells, H. G., 287; 484.

Werfel, Franz, 219.

Westermarck, Edward, 145; 404.

Western world, its attitude toward Jews, 17.

What Do Jews Believe? (Enelow), 161.

White Paper (1939), the, 136.

Wieman, Henry N., 444.

Wilderness (Sinai), 376; 462.

Will, necessary for freedom, 291 f.; to life abundant, 182; to live, and religious faith, 259 f.; to live as Jews, 439; to power, 276.

Wilson, Woodrow, 76; 77; 155; 297; 365.

Witnesses of Jehovah, 156; 157.

Wolfe, Thomas, 97.

Wolfson, Harry, 104.

Woman, in ancient times, 402; 403; in the Bible, 318; 403 f.; emancipation of, 402; in Eretz Yisrael, 410 f.; Orthodoxy concerning, 409; 411; Reform concerning, 410; status of, since Emancipation, 393; 409; in Talmudic era, 403; in traditional law, 405 f.

Workers (Arab), in Eretz Yisrael, 370.

Workers (in Eretz Yisrael), courts of, 139; educational system of, 140.

Workers' Federation, in Eretz Yisrael, 369.

World betterment, the aim of democracy, 481.

World citizenship, education for, 488.

World Jewry, 121; 136; see Diaspora; Diaspora Jewry.

World outlook, pre-modern, 191.

World Parliament of Religions, 154.

World peace, 484.

World War I, 300; 365; 483; 501.

World War II, 300; 483.

World-weariness, 303.

World Zionist Organization of America, 364.

Worship, laxity in, 14; relation of to soterical God-idea, 180; study of Torah a form of, 449; what it needs, 49; 52.

Written law, see Torah.

Wylie, Philip, 490.

X

Xenophobia, 505.

Y

Yabneh, Sages of, 28; 229.

Yad Hahazakah, 508.

Yahrzeit, 11.

Yahwism, of the Prophets, 318.

YHWH, 513; 539.

Yiddish, 68; in Poland, 69; in U.S.S.R., 70.

Yiddishism (Diaspora nationalism), 25.

Yishuv, of Eretz Yisrael, 265; aspirations, 392; experiences of, 135.

Yom Kippur, 426.

You Can't Go Home Again (Wolfe), 97.

Young Men's Christian Association, 4.

Z

Zebaim, 334.

Zechariah, Prophet, 256; 463.

Zionism, 5; 9; 40; 125; 130; 354; 537; from American standpoint, 112; conditioned by European origin, 24; and democracy, 360 f.; emphasis on Eretz Yisrael, 24; has given rise to groupings, 112; of Herzl, Pinsker and Nordau, 132, lacking character, 136; a modern movement, 123; 360; has organized Jews, 536; a reconstruction of Jewish life, 359 f.; has supplied practical leaders, 93.

Zionist Congress (First, 1897), 123; 364; (Fifth, 1901), 364.

Zionist Organization of America, 112; Pittsburgh Platform of (1918), 140; 365.

Zionists (General), civil courts of, in Eretz Yisrael, 138; educational system of, in Eretz Yisrael, 140.

Zionists, Labor, 112.

Zohar, 454.

Zoroastrianism, 145.

Zunz, Leopold, 528.